Children in Sport

Children in Sport

EDITED BY:

Richard A. Magill, PhD
School of Health, Physical Education,
Recreation, and Dance
Louisiana State University, Baton Rouge

Michael J. Ash, PhD
Department of Educational Psychology
Texas A & M University

Frank L. Smoll, PhD
Department of Kinesiology
University of Washington, Seattle

HUMAN KINETICS PUBLISHERS, INC.
Champaign, Illinois

Publications Director
Richard D. Howell

Production Director
Margery Brandfon

Editorial Staff
Robert Lange

Typesetter
Sandra Meier

Text Design and Layout
Lezli Harris

Cover Design and Layout
Jack W. Davis

Photos introducing each section by Jack Phillips of Photographics, Champaign, Illinois.

Library of Congress Catalog Number: 82-82668

ISBN: 0-931250-34-X

9 8 7 6 5 4 3 2

Human Kinetics Publishers, Inc.
Box 5076
Champaign, Illinois 61820

CONTENTS

CONTRIBUTORS

THE EDITORS

Richard A. Magill is with the School of Health, Physical Education, Recreation, and Dance at Louisiana State University, Baton Rouge.

Michael J. Ash is with the Department of Educational Psychology at Texas A & M University at College Station, Texas.

Frank L. Smoll is with the Department of Kinesiology at the University of Washington in Seattle.

THE AUTHORS

Donald A. Bailey is with the College of Physical Education at the University of Saskatchewan, Canada.

Jack W. Berryman is with the Department of Physical Education at the University of Washington, Seattle.

Steven P. Chatman is with the Department of Educational Psychology at Texas A & M University at College Station, Texas.

Vincent J. DiStefano is clinical associate professor of orthopaedic surgery at the University of Pennsylvania and team physician for the Philadelphia Eagles.

Jere D. Gallagher is with the Department of Physical Education at the University of Pittsburgh.

Donna M. Gelfand is with the Department of Psychology at the University of Utah.

Susan L. Greendorfer is with the Department of Physical Education at the University of Illinois, Urbana-Champaign.

Donald P. Hartmann is with the Department of Psychology at the University of Utah.

John W. Lewko is with the Department of Physical Education at the Laurentian University at Sudbury, Ontario, Canada.

Robert M. Malina is with the Department of Anthropology and the Department of Physical Education at the University of Texas, Austin.

Rainer Martens is with the Department of Physical Education and director of the Office of Youth Sports at the University of Illinois, Urbana-Champaign.

Barry D. McPherson is with the Department of Kinesiology at the University of Waterloo, Canada.

Michael Passer is with the Department of Kinesiology at the University of Washington, Seattle.

Tara K. Scanlan is with the Department of Kinesiology at the University of California, Los Angeles.

Vern Seefeldt is director of the Youth Sports Institute at Michigan State University, East Lansing.

Thomas E. Shaffer is acting director of adolescent medicine at Columbus Children's Hospital and emeritus professor in the Department of Pediatrics at Ohio State University, Columbus.

Michael D. Smith is with the Department of Physical Education at York University in Toronto, Canada.

Ronald E. Smith is with the Department of Psychology at the University of Washington, Seattle.

Jerry R. Thomas is with the School of Health, Physical Education, Recreation, and Dance at Louisiana State University, Baton Rouge.

Katherine T. Thomas is with the Department of Physical Education at Southern University in Baton Rouge, Louisiana.

Jack H. Wilmore is with the Department of Physical Education at the University of Arizona, Tucson.

PREFACE TO THE
SECOND EDITION

Since the publication of the first edition of this book, interest in youth sports in the education and research communities has grown immensely. The number of academic courses on youth sports being offered in colleges and universities has increased, research articles dealing with youth sport issues have proliferated, youth sport conferences and symposia have been held, and centers for the scientific study of youth sports have been established. The expanded role of research in the youth scene has been particularly noticeable. And, since a primary goal of the first edition was to provide an interdisciplinary base from which further research could be developed, we believed that there was enough new material to provoke a need for updating and extending our initial efforts. The result is this second edition.

The many additions and changes in this volume reflect our intent to make it a decidedly new and relevant text as well as resource. As a text, this book is directed toward upper level undergraduate or graduate youth sport courses, or it could be used as a companion text in psychology of sport or human growth and development courses. Students from physical education, kinesiology, recreation, psychology, and many other fields who wish to achieve a better understanding of the multifaceted study of youth sports should find the information valuable. The organization and material included in this edition reflects our concern that the book be a valuable classroom tool. Consequently, we based many of the revisions on comments by instructors and students.

In addition, we maintained our primary objective, that is, to have this anthology serve as a "strong base from which much needed research will emanate." In keeping with this orientation, we not only expanded the subject matter in this edition, but we included works that provide a review of relevant research in those subject areas.

The first edition was predominantly a collection of papers from two symposia; of the original 17 papers, 10 have been kept for this edition. To that group, we have added 10 papers. Some of these were written specifically for this volume and some have been previously published elsewhere, generally in journals or conference proceedings that are difficult to procure.

In Section 1, a new paper by Vern Seefeldt extends the historical perspective by focusing on future needs in youth sports. Three papers that were part of a feature on children's athletics in the *Journal of School Health* have been added to Section 3. The first paper, by Jack H. Wilmore, is an excellent supplement to the chapters by Robert M. Malina and Donald A. Bailey in that it focuses specifically on physiological concerns of the female athlete. The other two papers by Thomas E. Shaffer and Vincent J. DiStefano are a departure from the typical works found in this book. Rather than being reviews of research literature, they provide useful guidelines for dealing with the health and injuries of young athletes.

Section 4, which concerns psychological issues, has undergone extensive revision. Two new papers, one by Michael W. Passer and the other by Ronald E. Smith and Frank L. Smoll, deal with psychological stress. This critical area of concern in youth sports has thus added a new dimension to the book.

Another new component, developmental memory factors in children's perception of sport, is dealt with by Jerry R. Thomas, Jere D. Gallagher, and Katherine T. Thomas. Their paper is a synthesis of two papers published in a monograph on youth sports in *Motor Skills: Theory Into Practice*. Finally, a new paper by Michael J. Ash and Steve P. Chatman is a useful conclusion to this section in that it reviews the key issues presented within.

Section 5, Social Processes, has two new papers, along with an updated version of a paper from the first edition. Barry D. McPherson has added important information to his excellent chapter on the social milieu of youth sports, and a paper by John H. Lewko and Susan L. Greendorfer provides an overview of the research literature on family influence and sex differences in youth sport participants. Their paper was originally published in the 1978 proceedings of the North American Society for the Psychology of Sport and Physical Activity annual conference. The last chapter in this section focuses on an issue of mounting concern in sport: violence. In a paper previously published in the *Canadian Journal of Applied Sport Sciences*, Michael D. Smith presents a scholarly view of violence as a socially based problem in ice hockey.

The study of youth sports is an exciting, multidisciplinary venture. We would like to extend our appreciation to the many individuals and organizations that have endeavored to keep this study fresh and alive, for they all are working to improve the quality of the sport experience for both youngsters and adults alike.

Richard A. Magill
Michael J. Ash
Frank L. Smoll

PREFACE TO THE
FIRST EDITION

When considering youth sport programs the immediate temptation is to plunge into a philosophic discourse on the question of their existence. Should they or should they not exist appears to be at the heart of most discussions both in the popular media as well as in scholarly journals. To avoid such a temptation is indeed a challenge, but when one realizes that approximately 20 million American youngsters between the ages of 6 and 16 are participating in organized sport programs, the temptation becomes less powerful. The obvious direction to follow seems to be one that acknowledges the existence of youth sport programs but is primarily concerned with determining how these programs affect the child and society.

Our purpose in compiling this anthology is to examine youth sport from many perspectives. We have sought to maintain an objective point of view, neither "grinding the axe" of youth sport antagonists, nor ignoring those factors that indeed seem detrimental. Viewing the involvement of children in organized sport programs from a multidisciplinary view is certainly the most appropriate way to consider such a topic, yet such an approach can be rather discouraging due to an obvious lack of substantive research in the disciplines involved. But the outlook for the future is much brighter as scholars in all fields strive to work together to study the child in organized sport.

The impetus for the development of this anthology came from two symposia which were independently developed and chaired by two of the editors. The first symposium, from which several of the papers in this volume are based, was entitled "The Child in Sport: A Symposium on

Readiness and Effects.'' Developed and chaired by Richard A. Magill, the 2-day session was sponsored by the National Association for Sport and Physical Education (NASPE), an association within the American Alliance for Health, Physical Education, and Recreation. The meeting was held in Milwaukee, in April 1976, and was organized around a multi-disciplinary theme to discuss the readiness for and effects of organized sport competition for children. The chapters in this volume by Donald A. Bailey, Robert M. Malina, Barry D. McPherson, Tara Kost Scanlan (in Section 4), Robert N. Singer, Vern Seefeldt, and Jerry R. Thomas are based on papers they presented at this symposium.

The second symposium was held at the annual meeting of the American Educational Research Association in San Francisco, also in April 1976. This symposium, entitled "The Psychological Effects of Competitive Sport for Children," was developed and chaired by Michael J. Ash. The chapters by Michael J. Ash, Brad S. Chissom, and Thomas P. Pietras resulted from presentations at that symposium.

Each of us hopes that this anthology will serve as a strong base from which much-needed research will emanate. We acknowledge, however, that research in any area is often dependent upon available funding. An obvious incentive ensuring a bright research future would be the increased support of major funding agencies. Until those agencies determine that sport is an influential factor affecting the developing child and deserves empirical investigation, the status of youth sport research will continue on its present path of seeming to raise more questions than it answers.

We hope that this anthology will satisfy a variety of needs in addition to providing a base for further research. While many theoretical issues are addressed in this volume, care has been taken to relate theory to practice. Thus, those who have a more applied or "grass roots" interest in children's sport should also find this anthology of value.

We recognize that this volume also raises more questions than it answers. However, each of the contributions does serve to shed some much-needed light on the subject of children in sport.

Richard A. Magill
Michael J. Ash
Frank L. Smoll

SECTION 1

HISTORICAL PERSPECTIVE
AND FUTURE DIRECTIONS

Sport has been an increasingly integral part of American culture and is regarded as a major social institution. Thus, it is not surprising that more and more children become involved in organized athletics each year. Under the auspices of the public schools and community agencies, youth sport programs including baseball, football, soccer, and swimming have grown to such an extent that they are changing the course of childhood.

The opening chapter in this section by Jack W. Berryman provides an historical overview of these developments. In tracing the rise of organized children's athletics, Berryman illuminates the social and cultural influences surrounding youth sports. This is particularly an informative piece for those readers who presumed youth sport to be a relatively recent phenomenon—that is, after 1939 and the formation of Little League Baseball. Also of interest are the quixotic attitude changes of professional educators toward children's athletics over the last 70 years.

Then, in chapter 2, Vern Seefeldt presents a view of the future, offering a perspective that suggests that change is imminent in youth sports programs. He identifies the four types of adult leaders who are primary agents of change and discusses the role of each leader in bringing about positive developments. Based on his analysis of the current status of youth sports, Seefeldt provides some optimistic predictions for the direction of youth sports.

CHAPTER 1

THE RISE OF HIGHLY ORGANIZED SPORTS FOR PREADOLESCENT BOYS

Jack W. Berryman

The rise of highly organized competitive sport programs[1] for boys below the age of 12 was a phenomenon of the first half of the 20th century and was indicative of the fact that sport had finally penetrated all levels of the American population. To be sure, young children played games and enjoyed a variety of sports throughout America's history, but regulated and administered sport programs by interested individuals and organizations solely for the use of small boys did not begin until after 1900. In fact, the first instances of sport teams, leagues, championships, and other examples of highly organized children's sports outside of the schools were not evident until the 1920s and early 1930s. Even then, the programs were only local affairs, usually established by communities who wanted to provide something different and special for their chil-

This is a revised and condensed version of a paper entitled "From the Cradle to the Playing Field: America's Emphasis on Highly Organized Competitive Sports for Preadolescent Boys," *Journal of Sport History*, 1975, 2, 112-131. The reader is directed to the original publication for a more detailed account of the trends and factors under discussion as well as for supporting documentation.

[1]Highly organized competitive sports have been defined as: "any athletic activity which involves a considerable amount of the leisure time of the youngster in formalized practice, which encourages extensive attendance by adult spectators, which is limited to the outstanding players, and which involves the selection of winners on a state, regional, or national basis" ("Are Highly Competitive Sports," 1952, p. 423).

dren. Little did they know that in another 10 to 15 years nationally organized and administered sports for children would be spreading throughout the country to eventually become one of the most pervasive forces in the lives of many American children.

Two separate but interrelated developments in the social and cultural milieu of American society during the early 20th century provided the most direct influence upon the rise and growth of boys' competitive sport programs. The first, of course, was the rise of sport itself in all parts of the country and the subsequent desire to participate and spectate by large numbers of the population. More specifically, though, the inclusion of sport in the school curriculum brought organized sport closer to the youth of the nation than ever before. Along with school sports came the rationale for their acceptance and promotion. This was most often provided by professional physical educators, recreation people, playground directors, and athletic coaches who were responsible for the majority of competitive sport situations during the first three decades of the 20th century.[2] But, when philosophies changed within this group during the 1930s, they dropped any sponsorship of children's sport they had previously provided and refused to condone high level competition for preadolescents. This change of outlook by professionally trained educators who were deeply involved with the early stages of sport competition for children was the first important development in conjunction with the overall rise of sport. Although it seemed to be antagonistic to the growth and development of children's sport, the alteration of philosophy would eventually lead to bigger, better, and more highly organized programs.

The second development influencing the growth of boys' competitive sport programs was that Americans began to realize the need and importance to protect and provide varied opportunities for children. Childhood became recognized as an important stage in the development of an adult, and measures were taken by concerned individuals and organizations to ensure a happy and profitable period of growing up. By means of a variety of laws and policies enacted by national, state, and community organizations, children were provided with an abundance of free time, parents took a different view of their offspring, and national programs were organized to protect the child's welfare. An entirely new branch of social welfare, called boys' work, originated in the last decade

---

[2]By the close of the 1920s, sport had become quite popular in the United States. However, with few exceptions, organized sport competition was still for the middle-aged adult population, college students, and high school students in the upper grades. Organized competitive sport had not yet developed for the elementary school aged population.

of the 19th century.[3] Boys' work groups, originally composed of all voluntary members, were organized specifically to provide wholesome leisure-time pursuits for young boys and keep them out of trouble. They began using sports and other recreational activities very early in their work and realized the importance of reaching the youthful minds and bodies of preadolescent boys. Leaders of the movement advocated the usefulness of sport for many of the same reasons that the schools turned to sport. But when the schools refused to sponsor competitive sports for the young boys, the task was left to the voluntary boys' work groups. Therefore, the linking of the overall popularity of sports and its believed values, many of which were established by school personnel in the early 20th century as well as the sport sponsorship of boys' work agencies, along with their own modifications and gradual growth, did more to promote boys' sport competition than any other factors and led directly to America's emphasis on highly organized competitive sports for preadolescent boys.

Before the 1930s, the responsibility for providing recreational activities and organized sports for small children was shared by the schools, playgrounds, and a few nationally organized youth membership agencies such as the YMCA, Boy Scouts, and Boys' Clubs. But as specific alterations of goals and purposes occurred within the physical education and recreation profession, the provision of sport competition for preadolescent boys became more and more a primary function of national voluntary boys' work agencies. Beginning in the 1930s, physical educators and professional recreation leaders denounced the overt emphasis placed on winning, the physical and emotional strain, and the attempt to organize competition into leagues for championship play which were becoming common in many children's sport programs. They also disagreed with providing competition for only the best athletes instead of allowing all children to participate. As a result, professionally trained leaders in sports and recreation retracted their support and relinquished their hold on organized competition for young children.

By allowing highly organized children's sport to leave the educational context, professional educators presented a golden opportunity to the many voluntary youth-related groups in America. These groups had no educationally imposed restrictions on their work for children and many times had the funds and support from parents and communities to provide elaborate and well-organized sport programs. The volunteer workers and members of these groups often had no educational training

---

[3]One person directly associated with the movement defined boys' work as "social engineering in the field of boyhood motivation . . . supervised leisure time education, the purpose of which is social adjustment and creative living" (Stone, Note 1, p. 28).

in child development or child psychology and operated with little or no restraints in providing the best for the children. Consequently, by giving up their support of youth sports, the school personnel could no longer enforce their rules and regulations for competition. Accordingly, the outside agencies capitalized on the child's free time from school during the evenings, weekends, and summer months, and provided numerous opportunities for competition. With very few limitations and a single goal of serving children and making them happy, boys' work groups saw no end to the sport situations they could provide.

The withdrawal of sponsorship came at a time when the values inherent to sport and its benefits to both children and society were becoming firmly established in the beliefs of most Americans. Parents, child welfare workers, and organizations established to serve youth were not easily convinced of what they believed were questionable detriments of sport competition for children. Therefore, child-related organizations, and specifically boys' work groups, stepped in to fill the void created by professional educators. The schools continued to be paramount in their sponsorship of interscholastic athletics for youth beyond the age of 12, but sport competition for preadolescent boys became the responsibility of child-oriented organizations outside of the educational framework. Their main objective was to provide wholesome character-building activities to occupy the leisure time of children in order to better enable them to make the transition from childhood to adulthood. Sport, they believed, was the one activity that was capable of providing all of the necessary conditions for this successful growth and development. Thus, it was during the 1930s, under the sponsorship of boys' work organizations outside of the educational context, that highly organized sport competition for preadolescent boys began its ascendance to present day heights.

PROFESSIONAL EDUCATORS DISCOURAGE HIGHLY COMPETITIVE SPORTS

The policy statements of the professional physical education and recreation groups as well as other leading educators from the 1930s to the 1960s illustrated their discouragement of highly competitive sports for children. A steady stream of proposals, guidelines, speeches, manuals, and periodical articles containing warnings against too much competition for elementary school children flowed from the ranks of professional educators. The statements reinforced their refusal to condone and administer such programs and were released at various times during the 30s, 40s, 50s, and 60s, when children's sport in association with boys' work groups was making rapid progress.

The first formal statements by professional physical education and recreation people declaring their concern about organized competitive sports for elementary school children came during the early 1930s. The sport programs that were already in the schools came under attack because they were not in line with educational objectives and only a few of the highly skilled students were able to compete. Later in the decade, a determined effort was made to establish official policies to eliminate all interscholastic competition for elementary age children both within and outside of the school ("Mid-West District News," 1937). The American Association for Health, Physical Education and Recreation (AAHPER) was quick in approving a resolution against highly organized sports for children at their 1938 convention in Atlanta, Georgia. Their statement, like many of the ones to follow, was based on the strenuous nature of competitive sports.

> Inasmuch as pupils below tenth grade are in the midst of the period of rapid growth, with the consequent bodily weaknesses and maladjustments, partial ossification of bones, mental and emotional stresses, physiological adjustments, and the like, be it therefore resolved that the leaders in the field of physical and health education should do all in their power to discourage interscholastic competition at this age level, because of its strenuous nature. ("Two Important Resolutions," 1938, pp. 488-489)

Before the end of the decade, the Society of State Directors of Physical and Health Educators also prepared a formal statement on the subject. Their policy statement was directed to school board members and school administrators and suggested that interscholastic athletics had no place in elementary schools. They specifically discouraged postseason games and championships, extensive travel, and "all star" teams, all of which were becoming attractive aspects of organized sport programs outside of the school (Moss & Orion, 1939).

During the 1940s, educational psychologists spoke out against the emphasis placed on competition for rewards (Duncan, 1951; Skinner, 1945) and AAHPER adopted another resolution condemning interscholastic competition for the first eight grades ("Recommendations," 1947).[4] In 1947, a Joint Statement of Policy on Interscholastic Athletics by the National Federation of High School Athletic Associations and AAHPER recommended that the competitive needs of elementary-age children be met with a balanced intramural program ("Cardinal Athletic Principles," 1947, p. 5).[5] Finally, in 1949, AAHPER and its Society of

---

[4]For a survey of common activities in elementary schools during this time see Schmidt (1944, p. 130).

[5]Also see Lowman (1947, p. 635). A large percentage of orthopedists surveyed believed interscholastic competition should be discouraged for young boys because of its strenuous nature. They were particularly critical of swimming, tackle football, wrestling, and ice hockey.

State Directors of Health, Physical Education and Recreation joined with representatives from the Department of Elementary School Principals, National Education Association, and the National Council of State Consultants in Elementary School Principals to form the Joint Committee on Athletic Competition for Children of Elementary and Junior High School Age. Their recommendations were more extensive than any of the previous statements but stayed with the same overall policy of no highly organized competitive programs (AAHPER, 1952, pp. 3-5).[6] They made an attempt to influence community agencies as well as school personnel but failed to realize that the very aspects of competitive sport they were condemning were the interesting and unique features which were attracting the young, enthusiastic, and energetic boys. Leagues, championships, tournaments, travel, spectators, and commercial sponsors were viewed by parents, community leaders, and the boys' work agencies as examples of doing a great service to the children. In addition, the young boys wanted to play on a level as close to the "big leagues" as possible and enjoyed the new form of attention provided by sport competition.

Evidence that the formal resolutions and professional policies which were passed during the 1930s and 1940s had some impact on school-sponsored programs became noticeable by the 1950s. Specifically, surveys reflected the alteration of sponsorship for children's sport programs from the schools to independent boys' work agencies. A National Recreation Association survey in 1950 of 304 departments throughout the United States indicated only 36 approved of high level competition and championship play ("Competitive Athletics," 1951). The President's Committee on Interschool Competition in the Elementary School, representing AAHPER, found that 60% of the schools surveyed in 1950 had no competition for elementary-age children. Of the 40% that did sponsor some competitive sports, none had competition below the fourth grade level (Wayman, Hager, Hartwig, Houston, LaSalle, & McNeely, 1950). The shift of support for children's programs was finally recognized and alluded to in a professional recreation journal in 1952, whereby the author successfully captured the nature of the contemporary scene.

> Although elementary schools continue to feel pressure to adopt the characteristics of the high school and college interscholastic sports program, most of the recent developments have taken place outside of the school system.
> . . . . As a result, the recent development of 'highly organized competitive athletics' for the elementary school age child has been sponsored largely by private independent groups not connected with the schools or the public recreation department. ("Are highly competitive sports," 1952, pp. 422-426)

---

[6]They believed elementary schools should only provide intramural playdays, sportsdays, and informal games.

Another survey, (Scott, 1953), indicated the attitudes of adults toward athletic competition for young children. The results illustrated one of the major reasons why highly organized programs were growing rapidly outside of the educational realm. From a group of over 1,000 respondents from seven states, which included parents, teachers, and administrators, the majority of all three groups were in favor of intensive competition. The parents were the most favorable, and within this group the fathers were overwhelmingly supportive.[7] With this type of support from parents and even some school personnel, it was evident that professional physical education and recreation groups were competing against unfavorable odds.[8]

BOYS' WORK GROUPS ASSUME LEADERSHIP

While organized sport competition at the elementary school level failed to gain support and therefore faltered after its seemingly robust beginning during the first decades of the 20th century, youth sport programs outside of the school grew rapidly in the number of total participants and in the variety of sports offered. With few exceptions, the stimuli behind these programs which arose all over the United States were parents and other interested adults associated with boys' work. Organizations identifying with the boys' work movement selected the promotion, sponsorship, and organization of competitive sports as one of the best things they could do for children. To make children happy and to give them what they wanted became one of their major objectives. They progressed by paying little or no attention to the warnings from professional educators.

The boys' work movement had its beginnings in the last decade of the 19th century and resulted from efforts of concerned adults to improve the total environment for children. Citizens of the larger cities became greatly concerned with the effects of industrialization, urbanization, and immigration and, as a result of the general child study movement, were also becoming educated to realize the basic needs of children. Welfare and reform programs were therefore instituted to improve or alleviate

---

[7]Similar results were found (Holman, Note 2) in a survey of parents having boys in Little League baseball in Fresno, California, in 1951. One hundred percent of the parents regarded the program as beneficial to their sons and repudiated the claims that competition was harmful physically, psychologically, or socially.

[8]It should be noted that parents were very concerned that their sons excelled and held their own among the peer group. Sport competition offered a unique setting where young boys could be compared and evaluated with reference to others of the same age.

such social problems as child labor, public health and sanitation, lack of wholesome play facilities, crime and delinquency, orphan and dependent children, and crowded housing. But the main factors which led adults to form programs and organizations to aid the plight of the child were the increased amount of leisure and delinquency and a growing population of underprivileged and neglected children.[9] Leaders of the boys' work movement during the late 19th century explored the ideas of organizing boys into clubs and groups to better carry on training programs. These early programs were designed to occupy leisure time in order to keep the boys out of trouble, keep them off the streets, and evangelize them. Most of them operated under the auspices of a religious education group or the social welfare program of agencies.[10] But by the beginning of the 20th century, the boys' work movement developed and achieved separate status from other welfare movements. This development represented the fact that at least a portion of American society had seen the need and value of special agencies to act as conservators and curators of child life.[11]

The use and encouragement of play, games, sports, and general recreational activities began quite early in the boys' work programs. As the emphasis moved from soul saving to one of boy guidance and concern for the "whole person" during the 1920s, organized sports became more and more popular as an acceptable method of filling leisure time hours.[12] New organizations for boys came into existence as separate enterprises. They were recreational rather than evangelical in nature, primarily because of the character-building values thought to be inherent to play, games, and sport. The concepts of clean fun as a character builder and of

---

[9]Directly related to these developments were the play movement and the child welfare movement. The combination of objectives included in each of the two distinct aspects of the overall childhood reform movement assisted the development of organized sports and additional play facilities for young children.

[10]It was realized early in boys' work that sport-related clubs and teams served as a better medium for organization than the earlier attempts at trying to reach large masses of boys at one time.

[11]Basically, the boys' work groups aided the overall society by protecting children through their dependency period, inducting children into the culture, and supplementing the family by providing for special needs and by sponsoring specific services. They were committed to a specific social obligation toward children not yet accepted by the whole society. Consequently, boys' work agencies began to provide services in education, health, and recreation, all of which they believed could be improved by organized sport programs. See Mangold (1924) and Wickenden (1960, pp. 124-147).

[12]Sport competition was believed to enhance personality adjustment and creative living in society. In addition, since boys' workers wanted to aid the transition from childhood to adulthood, they sponsored sport programs which combined association on a peer basis with adult leadership. See DeGraff (1933, p. 2) and Stone (Note 3, p. 5).

play as creative education rather than just something to keep boys out of trouble led to the formation of more playgrounds, gymnasiums, swimming pools, and outdoor athletic fields. Accordingly, civic groups, fraternal orders, and businesses joined the ranks of established boys' work organizations which already included religious bodies, philanthropic groups, national and state governments, and general child welfare groups in sponsoring and promoting sporting activities for the younger set. The primary objective of the new sponsors was to use sport as a preventive measure for juvenile delinquency.[13]

During the 20s and 30s, highly organized competitive sport programs for young boys began to be established outside the realm of the educational system by local groups representing the fundamental boys' work beliefs. As early as 1924 the Cincinnati Community Service started city baseball tournaments for boys under 13. Likewise, Milwaukee organized its "Stars of Yesterday" baseball leagues and began sponsoring a "Kid's Baseball School" in 1936. The Los Angeles *Times* conducted its Junior Pentathlon for the first time in 1928, the Southern California Tennis Association established its junior program 2 years later, and tackle football for boys under the age of 12 began in the Denver area in 1927 and in Philadelphia 3 years later. Two further developments which occurred in 1939, however, did more for the overall development of this new trend in sport than the others.

The first development was an article entitled "Life Goes to a Kid's Football Game" which appeared in *Life* magazine. It concerned the Denver Young American League and included color photographs and descriptions depicting the values of such an activity. Themes such as nationalism, courage, character, the need for similar programs in other communities, and the disgrace of "turning yellow" were discussed in the article. The second major development in 1939 was the introduction of Little League Baseball in Williamsport, Pennsylvania. Formed by Carl Stotz, a local businessman, the organization grew from a few local teams at its inception to more than 300 leagues in 11 states by 1949. Part of its success can also be linked to the publication of an article entitled "Small

---

[13]The belief that a boy busy with sports had little time to get into trouble influenced many organizations in local communities to begin sponsoring boys' competitive sports. Psychological and sociological knowledge of the time indicated that problems of delinquency originated in early childhood and not during the actual time of delinquent acts. Therefore, it was deemed important to extend the age range lower for a positive delinquency prevention program. Civic clubs such as Rotary, Lions, Kiwanis and Jaycees, fraternal orders like the Elks and Moose, and businesses such as Winchester, Curtis Publishing, General Electric, Pratt and Whitney, and John Wanamaker, all turned to sport sponsorship in the interest of protecting young children from crime and providing them with wholesome alternatives for gang life in the streets. For more information see Engle (1919), North (Note 4), Reckless and Smith (Note 5), and Shanas (Note 6).

Boy's Dream Come True" in *Saturday Evening Post* (Paxton, 1949). This article, like the *Life* article 10 years before, included beautiful colored photographs, proclaimed the values of such a program for the small boys, and emphasized the rewards reaped by communities that had already established Little League teams. The author was correct in observing that "the Little League's chief mission in life is to give a lot of pleasure to a lot of little boys. With its realistic simulation of big-league playing conditions, with its cheering crowds, it is a small boy's baseball dream come true." From this point on, the little league concept spread to almost every sport on the American scene.

Interest in providing sporting competition for young children began to spread to a variety of other youth-related agencies after the 1940s. As continued emphasis was placed on providing fun and amusement for young boys and as organizations found ulterior motives for promoting sport competition, the sponsorship of children's sports began to come from previously unexpected sources. Nationally known business firms, professional sport organizations, Olympic committees, and colleges initiated particular aspects of competitive sport sponsorship for young boys. Sponsorship came in the form of funds, facilities, manpower, advertisements, and equipment. These new sponsors joined previously established sponsors such as civic groups, churches, community councils, local merchants, and some of the older youth membership organizations. They saw a chance to assist the development of young boys but at the same time realized that boys' sport programs could help them as well. This new sidelight to sponsorship, the idea of a "two-way street" or what could be termed a form of "ludic symbiosis" in this context, differed radically from the earlier voluntary group support and added the aspects of big business and more pronounced competition to sport for young boys.

By the 1960s, highly organized sport competition for preadolescents had grown to encompass millions of American boys. Little League Baseball, Pop Warner Football, and Biddy Basketball were joined on the national level by similar developments in other sports such as Pee Wee Hockey and Little Britches Rodeo.[14] Most of these national sporting bodies had member teams and leagues throughout the United States but the youthful participants in baseball, football, basketball, and other sports did not necessarily have to belong to one of the national controlling bodies. When this occurred, local boys' sports organizations were

---

[14]Some of the other popular children's sports were Midget Lacrosse, Junior Ski Jumping, Junior Nordic Skiing, National Junior Tennis League, Junior National Standard Racing, and the Junior Special Olympics for retarded children.

oftentimes just referred to as midget leagues, the lollypop set, boys' leagues, youth leagues, junior leagues, small-fry leagues, or tiny tot leagues. The important factor, however, was that regardless of title, sponsor, or organizational structure, young boys below the age of 12 were being introduced to highly organized competitive sports in just about every community in the United States.

As indicated, radical changes occurred in the sponsorship of boys' sports programs. By the 1960s, the most prominent sponsors could be classified in six different categories: (a) private national sport bodies such as Little League Baseball; (b) youth serving organizations composed of adult members such as the Jaycees; (c) youth membership organizations composed of child membership like the YMCA; (d) youth sport development organizations such as Junior Golf; (e) quasi-commercial organizations like Ford's Punt, Pass and Kick; and, (f) an individual or community like Jim's Small Fry's or Riverdale Junior Baseball. An analysis of each of their stated objectives revealed the same idea of sport's inherent values which had existed since the turn of the century. Each sponsor claimed to support children's sport for one or more of the following reasons: physical fitness, citizenship, character, sportsmanship, leadership, fair play, good health, democratic living, and teamwork. It also was evident that a few of the sponsors took advantage of the "two-way street" concept. Boys' sports were used as training grounds for future athletes, to prevent juvenile delinquency, as proselytizing agents, to attract new members, as methods of advertisement, as means of identification and glory, and as methods for direct financial gain.

Parents, too, began to get more deeply involved with the sports of their children than ever before. Eager mothers and fathers devoted more time to sports and actually began to take part in the sports themselves. Many reasons could be given to explain this increased interest of parents, but it is believed that the increasing awareness of the athlete as a viable professional endeavor, overly competitive mothers and fathers, and the desire of "sure victory" for their children were the three major causes. Earlier in the history of children's sports, parents were content to be only spectators, but the decades of the 1950s and 60s became an era of parental entrance into competition with their child. Instances of parents constructing racers for the Soap Box Derby, fine tuning engines for youthful go-kart drivers, and engineering new gear ratios for bike racers appeared as boys' sports became more and more important to the entire family. This new emphasis placed on children's competitive sport by the family unit combined with the entrance of big business and other high pressure tactics after the early 1950s caused even the most avid sponsors to begin to take a serious look at what they had developed.

The literature after 1950 concerning highly organized competitive sports for young boys was indicative of a growing concern for the welfare of the young competitors.[15] Nationally circulated journals, magazines, and newspapers carried articles emphasizing the pros and cons of children's sport in an attempt to illustrate the current status of the ever-growing youth leagues and to present the most recent findings related to the subject. Similarly, those in favor of the highly competitive situations used the mass media to advertise the goodness and need for such programs, and even went so far as to suggest new organizations in previously unchildlike sports such as yachting, motor boating, and airplane flying. Likewise, those strongly opposed to highly organized sports attacked their obvious detriments via the printed word. The issue became increasingly visible as the debate continued, but even as late as 1970 the youth sport programs were showing no signs of decline. In fact, the decade of the 1970s has ushered in a new and eager generation of youthful competitors.

SUMMARY AND CONCLUSIONS

The rise of highly organized sport competition for preadolescent boys was an important phase of the total involvement of Americans with sport and has blossomed into a new national sporting trend. Lowering the age for entrance into competitive sport indicated the faith Americans had in it and reflected a desire to provide the young with something thought to be beneficial for their overall development. Besides illustrating the breadth and depth of the nation's involvement with sport, the guided entrance of children into sporting competition also influenced the overall growth of sport. Young children carried their interests and desires with them into adult life which were subsequently passed along to their own children. In addition, the joy, freeness, and innocence of the youthful competitors came to be seen as desirable characteristics of sport itself. These attributes were sought as highly desired traits by the adult population. The older portion of the population attached sport to the image of youth and consequently engaged in a variety of sports beyond the time when they normally would have ceased participation.

The provision of highly organized competitive sports for boys below the age of 12 and the accompanying introduction of more sporting opportunities and facilities for all young children was one of the most significant social and cultural events of recent times. It contributed an additional dimension to the age of childhood and marked the beginning

---

[15]It is interesting to note that the *Readers' Guide to Periodical Literature* did not include a topical heading for "Sports for Children" until Volume 22, (March 1959 - February 1961), p. 1564.

of a new era in American sport. An analysis of the origins of this trend, however, is also important outside of its contributions to the realm of sport because the history of developments in childhood is central to the study of overall social change and human behavior. The growth of sport for young boys illustrated a change in parental authority as well as an alteration in general child-rearing practices. The fact that sporting teams were usually organized by age or weight groupings indicated the increased sensitivity to the various stages of childhood and became an important step in the growth of child welfare. Children's sport organizations led to changes in the American family structure and, in many instances, added a new aspect to the socialization of children. In addition, the sponsorship and use of sport by boys' work agencies contributed to the belief that Americans should organize the life and activities of their children. Finally, the degree to which children's sports became organized mirrored an often-proclaimed American characteristic of being overly regimented, businesslike, and competitive.

REFERENCE NOTES

1. Stone, W.L. *What is boys' work*. New York, 1931.
2. Holman, H. *Play ball: A study of Little League baseball in operation*. Fresno, CA: Recreation Department, 1951.
3. Stone, W.L. *The place of activities in boys' work*. *Work with boys*. October 1932.
4. North, C.C. The community and social welfare. New York, 1931.
5. Reckless, W.C., & Smith, M. *Juvenile delinquency*. New York, 1932.
6. Shanas, E. *Recreation and delinquency*. Chicago Recreation Commission, 1942.

REFERENCES

AMERICAN Association for Health, Physical Education, and Recreation and Committee on Athletic Competition for Children of Elementary and Junior High School Age. *Desirable athletic competition for children*. Washington: Author, 1952.

ARE highly competitive sports desirable for juniors? Conclusions from the committee on highly organized sports and athletics for boys twelve and under, National Recreation Congress. *Recreation*, 1952, **46**, 422-426.

CARDINAL athletic principles. Washington: American Association for Health, Physical Education, and Recreation and the National Education Association, 1947.

COMPETITIVE athletics for boys under twelve—survey. *Recreation*, 1951, **45**, 489-491.

DEGRAFF, H.O. Social factors in boys' work. *Association Boys' Work Journal*, March 1933, p.2.

DUNCAN, R.O. The growth and development approach. *Journal of Health, Physical Education, and Recreation*, 1951, **22**, 36-37.

ENGLE, W.L. Supervised amusement cuts juvenile crime by 96%. *American City*, 1919, **20**, 515-517.

LIFE goes to a kid's football game. *Life*, October 9, 1939, pp. 90-93.

LOWMAN, C.L. The vulnerable age. *Journal of Health and Physical Education*, 1947, **18**, 635; 693.

MANGOLD, G.B. *Problems of child welfare*. New York: Macmillan, 1924.

MID-WEST district news. *Journal of Health and Physical Education*, 1937, **8**, 382.

MOSS, B., & Orion, W.H. The public school program in health, physical education, and recreation. *Journal of Health and Physical Education*, 1939, **10**, 435-439; 494.

PAXTON, H.T. Small boy's dream come true. *Saturday Evening Post*, May 14, 1949, pp. 26-27; 137-140.

RECOMMENDATIONS from the Seattle convention workshop. *Journal of Health and Physical Education*, 1947, **18**, 429-432; 556-557.

SCHMIDT, C.A. Elementary school physical education. *Journal of Health and Physical Education*, 1944, **15**, 130-131; 161.

SCOTT, P.M. Attitudes toward athletic competition in elementary schools. *Research Quarterly*, 1953, **24**, 352-361.

SKINNER, C.E. *Elementary educational psychology*. New York: Prentice-Hall, 1945.

TWO important resolutions. *Journal of Health and Physical Education*, 1938, **9**, 488-489.

WAYMAN, F., Hager, R., Hartwig, H., Houston, L., LaSalle, D., & McNeely, S. Report of the president's committee on interschool competition in the elementary school. *Journal of Health, Physical Education, and Recreation*, 1950, **21**, 279-280; 313-314.

WICKENDEN, E. Frontiers in voluntary welfare services. In E. Ginzberg (Ed.), *The nation's children* (Vol. 3 of *Problems and prospects*). New York: Columbia University Press, 1960.

CHAPTER 2

THE CHANGING IMAGE OF
YOUTH SPORT IN THE 1980s

Vern Seefeldt

Both supporters and detractors of youth sports have suggested that it needs a change of image. Prominent issues such as the exclusion of unskilled athletes, exploitation of children for personal and commercial gain, and the undue emphasis on winning at the expense of other values have consistently kept the proponents of youth sports on the defensive. Whether the changes are imminent, already under way, or merely wishful thinking and impossible to achieve depends upon one's point of view. The continuing popularity of organized athletics for children implies that a significant number of adults believe that the inherent benefits of sports participation outweigh their potential detrimental effects. Those who enroll their children in competitive athletic programs either agree with the operation of the program or have sufficient confidence in the sponsors to assume that the required changes will take place as soon as the conflict between tradition and new information can be resolved.

Whether the promoters of children's sports deserve the annual vote of confidence they receive from millions of parents who enroll their children in competitive athletics is an issue that has aroused considerable controversy. The media's persistent attention to youth sports has stimulated the scientific community to begin investigating the benefits and consequences of children's involvement in sports. Specialists in

This chapter was originally presented as the opening address at the Second Annual Youth Sports Forum, East Lansing, Michigan, on April 27, 1981.

sports medicine, sports psychology, sports sociology, sports physiology, and biomechanics now consider children to be legitimate subjects in their investigations (e.g., Albinson, 1976; Haubenstricker, 1976; Rarick, 1973; Seefeldt & Gould, 1980; Smith, 1979; Smoll & Smith, 1978; Thomas, 1977).

The welcome attention of scientists is destined to bring with it two important outcomes that have been missing in the turbulent history of youth sports. First, an interdisciplinary account of what happens to children as a result of their athletic participation may gradually emerge, and second, suggestions for modifying conditions that are currently not in the best interests of children may be incorporated into the rules and policies of the various sponsoring agencies. Proponents of youth sports have reason to believe that future changes in the structure and conditions under which competition takes place will be based on more abundant and valid information.

HISTORY OF YOUTH SPORTS

The children's sports programs that are supervised by adults have been immersed in controversy almost from their modest beginning on the playgrounds of New York City at the turn of the century. Berryman, in chapter 1, has chronicled the growth of sports for children from the time they emerged as an after-school recreational activity to the highly competitive, win-at-all-costs situations that resulted in their condemnation by public school educators after an existence of barely 30 years. His review reveals several important historical facts; namely, that youth sports were an outgrowth of the regular public school curriculum, that they were initiated as a diversionary activity to meet the perceived competitive needs of boys, and that they became highly competitive in a matter of years, even when they were under the auspices of public school personnel.

The withdrawal of support for competitive athletics by public school educators in the 1930s has had a lasting influence on youth sports programs. The elimination of athletic competition from many elementary school programs coincided with an increase in the number of physical education and intramural programs, and the new school-based programs emphasized the acquisition of skills for all children in lieu of specialization for a few highly skilled athletes. Withdrawal of public school sponsorship of youth sports, however, prompted a number of family-oriented agencies such as the YMCA, YWCA, and the Police Athletic League to offer competitive athletics in private facilities. These offerings became more numerous and diverse as additional agencies, created for the sole purpose of offering sports competition for children, were established.

The creation of nonschool agencies to teach sports skills to children brought about a paradox that has persisted to the present day. Schools employing personnel educated to teach motor skills and serve as coaches were offering limited opportunities for children to learn the sports of their culture, whereas nonschool agencies were spending substantially more time teaching sports skills to children, but under the direction of administrators and coaches who were generally not as well qualified to conduct the programs.

The indifference of public school personnel to the agency-sponsored sports programs that sprang up as replacements for elementary school interscholastic programs frequently led to animosity and hostility between the two groups. This unfriendly attitude prevailed throughout the 1950s and 1960s, fueled periodically by policy statements from the American Medical Association and the National Education Association, which opposed highly organized sports activities below the ninth grade. The number of programs and participants in youth sports continued to grow, however, unmindful of the unsolicited advice directed at them by physicians and educators. Ironically, children's athletics seemed to grow in direct proportion to the criticisms leveled against them.

By 1970, the opportunities for regional and national competition in children's athletics had expanded to include virtually every sport in which competition was available at the adult level. National ownership of programs also seemed to increase the intensity of competition to the point where even the agencies which proclaimed a philosophy of "everyone plays" contradicted their mottos by supporting national tournaments in which the elimination of all teams except the eventual victor was a foregone conclusion. Children also became involved in sports at younger ages. Data from the *Joint Legislative Study on Youth Sports* (1976) indicated a modal age of 8 for boys and 10 for girls as the time when competition in a specific sport began, with many children already competing at 4 or 5 years of age.

Evidence of a changing attitude about youth sports by physicians, educators, and administrators began to emerge in the 1970s. The culmination of this conciliatory position occurred at a meeting sponsored by the National Association for Sport and Physical Education in Washington, DC (Merrick, Note 1) in 1977. Two documents, *Youth Sports Guide for Coaches and Parents* (Thomas, 1977) and *Guidelines for Children's Sports* (Martens & Seefeldt, 1979), summarize the content of the historic meeting between groups that formerly opposed children's sports and representatives from the nonschool sports agencies. In essence, the two groups agreed to recognize that athletic competition for children had become an enduring part of our culture. The conditions under which healthful competition should occur were described in a "Bill of Rights for Young Athletes" (Martens & Seefeldt, 1979). A significant change in physicians' and educators' attitudes about youth sports was now a matter of record. Instead of their previous disapproval of athletic competition for children, its former antagonists now agreed to work for more desirable conditions under which competition could take place.

AGENTS OF REFORM

Changes in the image of youth sports primarily depend upon the degree to which the attitudes of its adult leaders can be modified. These modifications are initiated by the leadership at the institutions where teachers, recreation directors, sports managers, and coaches receive their formal education. This section identifies four agents primarily responsible for the education and experiences of individuals controlling youth sports in the United States. These agents include administrators and professors from institutions of higher learning, directors of recreation, administrators of single-sport agencies, and public school physical education teachers and coaches.

Administrators and Professors of Higher Education

The attitudes and values about sports competition that coaches, teachers, and recreation directors support and advance are likely to have been influenced by former instructors. To the degree that curricula reflect the importance of subject matter, as determined by faculty in departments of physical education and recreation, the management of youth sports holds a relatively low priority for those who prepare professional workers in recreation, athletics, and physical education. Few courses in these curricula are devoted specifically to the problems and proposed solutions of age group athletic competition. When the topic is included in other courses, it receives only superficial treatment. This direct or subtle omission of information about youth sports in preparing undergraduates who eventually will be responsible for guiding the athletic activities of children is an inexcusable form of negligence on the part of those in leadership positions.

In addition to providing current information about children's athletic competition, administrators and faculty members in higher education can influence the attention directed at youth sports by providing practical day-to-day experiences in planning, conducting, and evaluating sports programs, and by encouraging students to become involved in basic and field-based research with young athletes. Placing students as interns into programs with an acceptable philosophy and sound operating procedures is an irreplaceable educational experience. This model— that is, placing students into situations where they can be closely supervised as they learn their profession—is one that has been used successfully for decades. There is every indication that it would serve an equally useful purpose in the education of sports program directors and coaches.

Research pertaining to the problems in youth sports has not kept pace with its phenomenal increase in participants. Scientists who had previously concentrated on adults, however, are now attempting to learn more about the effects of athletic participation on youthful competitors.

As the intensity and duration of training programs for children increase, physiological and psychological problems similar to those observed for decades in adult competitors are likely to occur. Scientists studying children also face the additional problems of intervening variables on an immature system. Educators should apprise their students of the problems that exist and, whenever possible, enlist their assistance in conducting research that seeks basic and practical solutions.

Directors of Recreational Programs

Recreation directors are essential agents in any attempt to change the image of youth sports by virtue of their involvement with the coaches and officials who actually conduct the practices and contests. Although sports-specific agencies with regional or national affiliations conduct many programs at the local level, the vast majority of youth sports programs exist under the auspices of the local recreation department (*Joint Legislative Study*, 1976). Therefore, the philosophy and operational procedures that local recreation directors promote are likely to pervade the entire program.

Frequently, recreation directors have been accused of ignoring physical activities in their programs or acting as "activity brokers" by relinquishing their responsibility for youth sports to the first agency or service club requesting permission to sponsor the programs (Greenslit, Note 2). The criticism that recreation directors are more concerned about the number of people participating than the quality of their participation may be unfair, but it has occasionally been erected as a barrier between physical education teachers and directors of recreation programs.

Desirable changes in youth sports depend upon the acknowledgment by recreation directors that athletic competition involving children is here to stay, that it has potentially beneficial and detrimental effects, and that strong leadership within the local recreation program can increase the potential for beneficial results. Recreation directors who abdicate responsibility for youth sports programs usually generate more problems than they solve, and solving such problems becomes more difficult as time passes and habits grow into traditions.

Managers of Single-sport Agencies

Single-sport agencies are organizations that promote and sponsor competition in a specific sport for children of designated age ranges, such as Little League Baseball, Pop Warner Football, Amateur Hockey Association of the United States, and the American Youth Soccer Organization. Single-sport agencies have been instrumental in elevating children's sports to their present level of popularity, but they have also received much of the criticism for practices that some adults consider to be unacceptable for children.

Single-sport agencies receive credit for the standard rules and modifications that distinguish children's sports from those of their adult prototypes. They are also responsible for developing the concept of adult volunteer leadership that permits these programs to operate at low overhead costs to local communities. Detractors also credit single-sport agencies with a desire to maintain complete control over programs, to impose a set of inflexible playing conditions on local programs, and to extract membership fees in exchange for little more than playing rules and a tournament structure.

If single-sport agencies are to maintain their roles as leaders in the organization and promotion of sports for children, they must adjust more readily to suggestions for change from research workers, educators, and local coaches and administrators. The current inflexibility of rules and lack of local control will become increasingly intolerable to adult leaders in local programs as they become more knowledgeable through a number of emerging programs for volunteer coaches. A philosophy placing the single-sport agency in a role that facilitates the leadership of local communities in sports program management is likely to find greater acceptability in the future.

Public School Personnel

The concessions that educators have recently made to the involvement of children in athletic competition (Martens & Seefeldt, 1979) are based on the assumption that much of what is regarded as current operating procedure would change. Implicit in these changes is the role that physical education teachers, coaches, and public school administrators would have in bringing about the cooperation between public school and agency personnel. The two groups must negotiate such differences as overlap in season, eligibility of participants, frequency and intensity of competition, age when competition should begin, and the emphasis placed on the athlete's skill acquisition versus winning as the primary criterion for success.

Apparently much of the control over athletic facilities and the expertise for teaching and managing sports programs currently lies with the public schools. Consequently, it appears that they are also in a position to make the greatest contribution to the youth sports movement. The "Bill of Rights for Young Athletes" argues distinctly that this is possible without compromising the principles upon which physical education and athletic programs are based. Agency-sponsored youth sports programs can no longer be viewed as undesirable competition for physical education programs nor as "farm systems" for the athletic program. If the emphasis in agency-sponsored youth sports programs is on maximum participation and skill acquisition, there is no need to fear that overexposure and exploitation will diminish their possible contribution to the welfare of children.

PREDICTIONS FOR THE 1980s

Predictions can reflect both optimism and pessimism. The following predictions for youth sports in the 1980s are overwhelmingly optimistic. This does not imply, however, that youth sports are in a position where any change would be an improvement. The optimism is generated by the emerging information from the scientific community and the widespread desire of individuals currently involved in youth sports to provide the best experiences for children. These predictions resulted from speculation about the influence on youth sports by variables such as population migration, energy costs, structure of the family, attitudes toward handicapped persons, and childbearing practices of the various racial and ethnic groups. The following variables will be instrumental in changing the operation of youth sports programs in the 1980s.

Scientific Inquiry

The influence of science on youth sports will eclipse the importance of any other variable because of our present depressed level of knowledge about the development of children involved in intensive physical activity. Our knowledge about adults in stressful situations is relatively sophisticated because of the research that has been conducted during the past two decades. The influence of competitive stress on children has not been studied well, however; consequently, the changes that have been made in programs are based only on experience. Additional changes await the research evidence from a multidisciplinary scientific community.

Two issues are of paramount importance in athletic competition for children: (a) the influence of physical stress on biological structure and function, and (b) equality between competitors involved in the same contest. Answers to such questions as "How much physical stress is essential for optimum development and at what point does it become excessive?", "At what age should athletic competition begin?", "At what ages and in what sports can boys and girls compete on an equal basis on the same teams?", and "What are the immediate and latent consequences of certain stressful activities?" will be forthcoming in the 1980s. Leaders in youth sports must communicate their concerns to the scientific community, who must then conduct the kinds of research that will lead to practical solutions.

Certification of Volunteer Coaches

The availability of new information about children in sports will be interpreted and passed on to volunteer coaches more rapidly, for the establishment of numerous organizations which have as their purpose the education of volunteer coaches (Vogel, Note 3) will expedite the flow of materials in a form previously inaccessible to them. As managers of sports programs become aware of the information available to coaches, they will provide them with inducements for continuing their education. Minimum knowledge and competency in various subject matter areas will be identified. Credits earned by volunteer coaches will be transferable across state and regional boundaries similar to the transfer of educational credits today.

Local Ownership of Programs

As local sports managers become more knowledgeable about conducting sports programs for children, they will rely more on their own abilities to make sound decisions and depend less upon regionally or nationally based agencies for guidance. Nationally based agencies will have to restore some of the funds they currently extract from communities in order to compete with locally controlled programs. Providing educational programs for coaches, conducting research, and furnishing inducements such as insurance, certification, and newsletters are examples of how these agencies could return a portion of the membership fees to communities. Greater representation in decisions that affect local programs and increased flexibility of rules to ensure greater participation are additional concessions that nationally affiliated programs will have to make.

Shift From Public School to Municipal Athletic Programs

Loss of federal and state revenues to finance public school operations will reduce the number of sports available to elementary, middle, and high school students. When sports programs are eliminated in the public schools, the burden of providing comparable opportunities will be shifted to community recreation departments and service-oriented agencies. Of these two groups, the service-oriented agencies will be in the most advantageous position to provide temporary relief for curtailed school athletic programs because their present operating procedure already includes fundraising and fees for its participants. Until municipal recreation directors acquire the expertise needed to procure funds from extramural sources, they will face many of the same budget problems as the public schools.

Municipal recreation programs will not only receive more frequent demands for competitive programs from displaced public school athletes, but their adult clients will demand more time and space as well. Parents will have fewer children and have them at a later age, thus freeing more adults for recreational pursuits. The provision of athletic programs for women in high schools and colleges will result in more women seeking athletic experiences beyond their formal education. Increased longevity will result in two or more generations of older, healthier adults who will compete for the facilities and personnel of local recreation departments.

Greater Reliance on Volunteers

Financial constraints and the increased demand for services will cause municipal recreation departments to depend greatly upon volunteer assistance in youth sports programs. Substituting volunteer for professional staff members brings with it a series of problems, foremost of which is the need for volunteer education programs. Sports programs that depend on volunteers, however, whether they are locally controlled or offered by national sports governing bodies, will initially provide for and eventually insist on certain levels of competency for their coaches and officials.

A problem unique to having volunteers for youth sports programs is that many children are being raised in single-parent homes, most frequently by the mother (Masnick & Bane, 1980). With the exception of gymnastics, swimming, and figure skating, however, most of the youth sports coaches and officals are males (*Joint Legislative Study*, 1978). Convincing a single parent female, who also works full time, that she should devote several evenings a week plus weekends to attend coaching workshops and coach her child's athletic team may challenge the persuasive powers of any recreation director. The later age of childbearing also reduces the number of years a parent may be willing to assist as a volunteer coach, official, or administrator in a youth sports program.

Changes in Activity Patterns

The trend in adult activities for more personal autonomy and less regimentation will also be evident in children's sport. Due to a prevailing philosophy that emphasizes personal needs, the shift to local ownership and control by recreation departments will put more emphasis on personal growth and participation and less on the win-at-all-costs philosophy. Goals of sports programs will be readjusted to incorporate the qualities of social development, fun, skill acquisition, and personal fitness that historically have been a part of children's motivation for participation, but not necessarily evident in the conditions imposed on them by adults.

Sports permitting the attainment of personal goals and individual styles of play will become more popular, whereas those requiring a high degree of regimentation will decrease in popularity. Racial and ethnic preferences for specific sports will also determine the desirability of certain sports. An increase in the proportion of black and Hispanic children and a decrease in the proportion of white children suggests that soccer, baseball, and basketball will show an increase in the proportion of child participants, whereas football, ice hockey, gymnastics, and swimming will show a decrease. Due to the decreasing number of children eligible for memberships, the absolute number of youth sports competitors will stabilize and then decrease in this decade, despite attempts to make programs more accessible to them.

Integration of Mentally and Physically Handicapped Children

Despite the mandates of PL 94-142, Education for All Handicapped Children Act, and PL 93-112, Section 504 of the Rehabilitation Act, little evidence shows that special attempts have been made to incorporate handicapped persons into youth sports programs. Recent inquiries to personnel representing six nationally affiliated sports governing bodies confirmed that all of these organizations welcome handicapped persons into their competitive programs, but only one had special provisions in its rules to accommodate special handicapping conditions. One other provided incentives for enrollment to special populations.

The positive attitude of program leaders from national sports governing bodies indicates that the merger of sports programs for handicapped and able-bodied individuals is merely a matter of time. Modification of rules involving equipment, playing conditions, eligibility, and skill requirements will be forthcoming. Although the long-standing image of sports being reserved for the able-bodied will be difficult to overcome, the 1980s will result in a gradual blending of available facilities and programs until all children are accommodated.

SUMMARY

Change in youth sports programs is imminent. Plagued by controversies brought on by rapid growth and lack of a firm knowledge base, youth sports governing bodies have frequently been defensive rather than proactive in their reactions to criticism. Four categories of adult leaders have been identified as the primary agents of change in youth sports. Variables that are likely to influence the impending changes are the availability of scientific information about the effects of stressful competition on children and educational programs for volunteer coaches. Additional changes will include shifts of athletic programs from public schools to recreation departments, greater dependence upon volunteer workers to conduct the programs, and the integration of individuals with handicapping conditions into programs that have previously been reserved for able-bodied competitors.

REFERENCE NOTES

1. Merrick, R. Personal communication to members of the Youth Sports Task Force, National Association for Sport and Physical Education, American Alliance for Health, Physical Education, Recreation and Dance. Washington, DC, November 5, 1976.
2. Greenslit, J. *Youth sports programs: Whose responsibility?* Address at the Second Annual Youth Sports Forum, East Lansing, MI, 1981.
3. Vogel, P. Evaluation of current youth sports coaching programs. In V. Seefeldt (Chair), *Educational programs for volunteer youth sports coaches.* Symposium presented at the annual meeting of the Alliance for Health, Physical Education, Recreation and Dance, Houston, TX, 1982.

REFERENCES

ALBINSON, J., & Andrew, G. (Eds.). *The child in sport and physical activity.* Baltimore: University Park Press, 1976.

HAUBENSTRICKER, J. Stress hazards of competitive athletics. *Osteopathic Annals*, 1976, **5**, 16-31.

JOINT legislative study on youth sports: Phase I. East Lansing: Michigan State University, Youth Sports Institute, 1976.

JOINT legislative study on youth sports: Phase III. East Lansing: Michigan State University, Youth Sports Institute, 1978.

MARTENS, R., & Seefeldt, V. (Eds.). *Guidelines for children's sports.* Reston, VA: American Alliance for Health, Physical Education, Recreation and Dance, 1979.

MASNICK, G., & Bane, M. *The nation's families: 1960-1990.* Cambridge: MIT-Harvard Joint Center for Urban Studies, 1980.

RARICK, G.L. Competitive sports in early childhood and early adolescence. In G. Rarick (Ed.), *Physical activity, human growth and development.* New York: Academic Press, 1973.

SEEFELDT, V., & Gould, D. *Physical and psychological effects of athletic competition on children and youth.* Washington, DC: ERIC Clearinghouse on Teacher Education, 1980.

SMITH, N. (Ed.). *Sports medicine for children and youth.* Columbus, OH: Ross Laboratories, 1979.

SMOLL, F., & Smith, R. (Eds.). *Psychological perspectives in children's sports.* Washington, DC: Hemisphere, 1978.

THOMAS, J. (Ed.). *Youth sports guide for coaches and parents.* Washington, DC: American Alliance for Health, Physical Education, Recreation and Dance, 1977.

SECTION 2

READINESS FOR PARTICIPATION

Readiness to be a successful participant in youth sports is of primary importance for the development of the young athlete. Unfortunately, readiness is a word that has become clouded in the jargon of educators. This section will consider readiness specifically as it relates to the important question of what do we know and what do we need to know about when a child is ready to participate in organized youth sport programs. The chapters that follow discuss such issues as maturation and developmental patterns, readiness to learn, critical learning periods, and readiness for competition.

Vern Seefeldt, in chapter 3, considers the mechanisms of development that relate to questions about children's readiness to participate in youth sports. He first provides a concise background of the construct of readiness and then proceeds to consider the mechanisms of development. Next, he discusses children's need to develop a repertoire of motor skills, considering specificity versus generality problems and discussing the identification of the sequence of motor skill development. The direction Seefeldt offers in this chapter appears quite necessary if we are to develop guidelines for suggesting when a particular sport skill should be introduced.

A concept encountered in many discussions of readiness is that of critical learning periods. The chapter by Richard A. Magill discusses that elusive construct. He suggests that the word *optimal* be used in place of critical, thus focusing the issue on identifying when a child is optimally ready to learn a skill. Following a brief overview of how critical periods have historically been viewed in the developmental literature, Magill suggests a model of readiness that can be appropriately applied to the sport skill learning situation. In that model, maturation, past experiences, and motivations are discussed as the major components of determining optimal learning periods.

A contemporary issue in child development is that of competition. Tara Kost Scanlan discusses that issue from a readiness point of view by considering the variables involved in the antecedents of competition. Following a review of Martens' model of competition, Scanlan suggests a theoretical schema that attempts to identify the various antecedents of competitive behavior. She uses the achievement motivation literature as the basis for that schema and considers the antecedents of achievement motivation as presented by White's competence theory and Veroff's theory of achievement motivation. From that discussion, some specific antecedents of competitiveness are then established.

CHAPTER 3

THE CONCEPT OF READINESS APPLIED TO MOTOR SKILL ACQUISITION

Vern Seefeldt

The word *readiness* implies that an organism has reached a certain point in an ongoing process. In learning, this implies that an accumulation of events or experiences has taken place. We currently have no clear indications of when children are ready to learn most of the motor skills. Yet, we seem more confident about identifying the period of readiness than we are in defining the sequence of events that leads to the period of readiness. Physical education teachers are making decisions daily about the readiness of children to learn skills, but available materials indicate that most curricula are based on tradition, rather than on developmental progressions. This situation exists, I suggest, because most definitions of readiness include an overt attempt on the part of the child to perform a certain task. In other words, we depend on the performer to tell us when the state of readiness exists. If our predictive information was adequate, however, we would have at our disposal a series of readiness signs, recognizable by the teacher as the learner moves from rudimentary to mature performance levels. It is feasible that children may be biologically or mentally ready and yet not make any attempt at performing specific tasks because some of the component parts to its successful completion were missing. It seems clear that if we are to assist individuals in achieving their motor potential we must be able to (a) identify the antecedent variables that provide the state of readiness for specific tasks, and (b) recognize the immediate signs of readiness for specific skill learning situations.

The construct of readiness has undergone some changes in its interpretation during the past several decades. During the first half of the 20th century it was commonly believed that the biological maturation of children was the primary influence in their ability to perform fine and gross motor skills. However, the 1950s and 60s produced abundant evidence concerning the significant contribution that the environment makes to children's learning. An inference for readiness in learning motor skills can be drawn from Bruner's (1965) statement regarding human ability to deal with cognitive material. His chapter on *Readiness for Learning* is introduced with the statement, "We begin with the hypothesis that any subject can be taught effectively in some intellectually honest form to any child at any state of development" (p. 33). This rather recent interpretation of readiness removes the burden of prerequisite maturation from the learner. It places the responsibility for the assessment of developmental status and the provision of antecedent experiences on the teacher. Bruner's definition suggests that the child is always ready for some type of experience, but the selection and provision of the stimuli that elicit the desired responses are the responsibility of the teachers in charge of the child's activity program. The implication is that the ability to learn motor skills is no longer solely attributable to the maturational level that the learner brings to the task. Rather, it is a combination of previous experiences and a series of appropriate objectives that led to motor proficiency.

The teaching of motor skills traditionally has excluded any consideration of the learning styles that should be available to the performer. Recent attempts to identify and incorporate the hierarchy of cognitive structures into situations that involve motor skill learning are a welcome addition to the literature. Kagan's (1971) five-stage structure is vaguely reminiscent of Piaget's developmental sequence presented in 1952 which has just recently received attention in the United States. Hebb's (1949) hypothesis of how all experiences effect subsequent learning is an earlier attempt to explain the achievement of readiness to learn. He hypothesized that movements, if repeated often enough, are incorporated into cell assemblies and phase assemblies within the central nervous system. The control of similar movements in the future is thereby transferred from a series of stimuli to central processes, thus freeing the performer from the need to concentrate on numerous stimuli. As a result, attention can be focused on the important elements in complex tasks. Additional experiences add to the pool of cell and phase assemblies. This increases the possibility of transferring identical components from task to task, and the larger motor repertoire decreases the likelihood of inappropriate responses. Hebb's model suggests that experience in a variety of tasks aids the performer in (a) selecting more appropriate stimuli, (b) making finer discriminations concerning the accuracy of the response, (c) attending to a task for a longer period of time, (d) being able to depend more on transfer of elements than on learning, (e) being able to retain more of what was learned through previous experience, and (f) eliminating faulty responses from the alternatives available.

The concurrent and inseparable development of cognitive and motor processes in early life was reported by Bruner (1969) as a result of extensive research with children below 6 months of age. He noted that the ability to solve problems that require a motor response is a process that begins soon after birth. According to Bruner, the infant's initial movements are not random responses but represent the answers to hypotheses that are formed by the problems unique to early development. Out of these early movements the infant develops a hierarchy of functions that provides the basis for future learning. The reflexes and reactions that are present at birth provide the repertoire from which the infant learns to *differentiate* the actions that are effective and efficient in completing a specific task. The second mechanism, which Bruner termed *modularization*, permits the infant to partition and recombine the movements into additional patterns. *Substitution* is a means whereby one action is used in place of another, thus adding variety to the responses available. *Sequential integration* permits the selection of a variant order, in lieu of solving the same problems with a rigid sequence of movements. *Place-holding* permits the infant to carry on two motor skills while devoting alternate degrees of attention to both of them. *Internalization of action* is the ability to carry out behavior symbolically. The ability to perform complex motor operations and the transferability of these mechanisms to many motor tasks during the first 2 years of life underscore the importance of abundant stimulation in early infancy. It also illustrates the need for the concurrent study of cognitive and motor development during the periods of childhood and adolescence.

The onset of locomotion increases the opportunities for sensory stimulation available to the child. The motor repertoire is expanded when responses are made to an incessant desire for sensory stimulation. A cyclic process is initiated whereby an increase in sensory experiences contributes to the variety and frequency of motor responses. An enlarged repertoire of motor patterns provides more options to the performer while a greater proportion of successful responses contributes to a desire for additional stimulation. This cycle is self-sustaining, with the provision that the environment contains appropriate stimuli and the child has the opportunity to formulate the motor responses. On the basis of this proposed sequence, it is evident that an abundance of successful motor responses early in life is an efficient way to establish the readiness necessary for subsequent experiences.

The controversy concerning the generality versus specificity of motor skills has been answered to the satisfaction of some investigators, but in my opinion, we lack conclusive evidence that the fundamental motor skills of infancy and childhood are specific and unrelated one-to-another. The evidence most often cited in support of the specificity argument is based on correlational studies in which the data are derived, via quantitative measures, with little regard for the neurological patterns or stages of development used by the performers. Yet there is sound evidence that the substrate of the basic movements and fundamental motor skills of infancy and childhood is comprised of reflexes and reactions that are common to all human beings. The role of reflexes and reactions of future skill acquisition has been the focus of several investigations. The reports of Knott and Voss (1968) and Shambes and Campbell (1973), based on the theory of proprioceptive neuromuscular facilitation, suggest the existence of four diagonal patterns that form the basis of all movement, whether reflexive, developmental, or ontogenetic. The authors contend that once the basic diagonal patterns are perfected, all future skills are acquired through a combination or variation of these patterns in temporal-spatial relationships. Examples of other reports that trace the transition from reflexes and reactions to voluntary movement include such tasks as grasping and prehension (Twitchell, 1965), the use of the tonic neck reflex in writing (Waterland, 1967), and righting reactions in the achievement of erect posture (Milani-Comparetti & Gidoni, 1967). Milani-Comparetti's chart of the reflexes and reactions that must be suppressed or built upon for normal motor development to occur during the first year of life is an excellent example of the high level of prediction that can accompany motor function.

The orderly nature of early motor behavior has frequently led to the erroneous impression that infants and young children acquire their motor repertoire at approximately the same chronological ages. Although genetic endowment determines the boundaries within which the skills are expressed, there is a wide range in the chronological ages at which children learn basic motor skills. I would like to suggest that the classification of skill attainment by age has very little utility for teachers of movement. This is also true of the variety of scales available to assess motor performance for the purposes of compensatory or remedial motor education. These scales were developed primarily by psychologists and physicians and have basic problems in the definition of developmental patterns common to children beyond 1 year of age.

At Michigan State University, we completed a 10-year study (Note 1), one phase of which was designed to determine the manner in which children learn some of the fundamental motor skills. The pioneering work in this area was done by Gesell and his associates (1946) and in the State of Wisconsin by Wild (1938) and Hellebrandt (1961). To date we have defined developmental sequences in walking, running, hopping, jumping, skipping, throwing, catching, kicking, punting, and striking. Preliminary evidence is available in sliding, galloping, and rope jumping. The most significant information concerning this phase of the study is that almost all children display clearly definable sequences in moving from the rudimentary to the mature stages of performance in these skills.

This is true of children who function within the normal range, those who have learning disabilities, the mentally retarded and children who are blind. The evidence obtained from the motor functions of blind children, who have not had the benefit of watching others perform specific motor skills, suggests to us that the rudimentary patterns that are the basis of these skills are ingrained in the central nervous system and are expressed when appropriate biological maturation and the opportunity for practice are available.

The identification of this orderly sequence of development in various skills has provided us with practical guides concerning the readiness of children to move on to the next level of a particular skill. However, we do not yet have sufficient evidence to suggest when the introduction to specific skills should occur, nor do we know which antecedent conditions are essential or helpful in moving the child into a readiness position for the specific skills I have mentioned. It is apparent that these movements have their genesis in the reflexes and reactions displayed during the first year of life.

The concept of maturation and the use of skeletal age and body size as criteria for readiness to engage in certain activities is discussed by Malina in chapter 6. Yet, research evidence suggests that the selection and classification of performers for subsequent competition in sports and dance has been primarily a season-by-season procedure. Virtually all of the investigators in my review reported the retrospective prediction of success, often through the use of regression equations that were obtained from cross-sectional studies or computed at the termination of longitudinal studies. Few investigators attempted to predict the success of individuals in motor performance prior to their involvement in activity programs, and then conduct a longitudinal follow-up to determine the accuracy of the original predictions. We did not find a single situation in which the predictive equations were applied to other samples as a test of their validity. This is unusual, in light of the national interest that is currently focused on organized sports and dance for young children, the well-defined objectives for success that are commonly associated with these programs, and the desire on the part of most coaches and teachers to foretell the success of their clients at the earliest possible age.

The relationship between the various indicators of maturity, commonly classified under the phrase *primary and secondary sex characteristics*, is modest to high, depending on whether the individual matures early or late. As might be expected, the relationship between skeletal age and the primary and secondary sex characteristics is also in the modest to high range. Thus, if skeletal age has a high positive relationship with height, weight, breadth, and circumference measures, and with the primary and secondary sex characteristics, why is it not used more frequently as a means of predicting the readiness of children to engage in various sports?

Part of the reluctance to use skeletal age as a predictor of motor performance is attributable to its inaccessibility as a measure of maturity. The determination of skeletal age requires special competencies in its procurement and assessment that are not required when obtaining other growth data. Additional deterrents may result from a reluctance to expose children to X-irradiation except for diagnostic purposes. However, the most logical reason for its exclusion from predictive equations involving motor performance is its high positive relationship to parameters that are considerably easier to assess. If it can be demonstrated that height, weight, or other bodily dimensions account for most or all of the variance in performance attributable to physical growth, there is no need to include an estimate of biological maturity. This is precisely what research reports have indicated. Espenschade in 1940, Rarick and Oyster in 1964, and our own longitudinal data (Note 2) confirm that skeletal age adds little to the prediction of motor performance if chronological age, height, and weight are already part of the equation.

In conclusion, there is little evidence to suggest that the readiness to learn specific motor skills can be identified through chronological age, body size, or the various assessments of biological maturation. The most feasible procedure for ensuring that young performers will be ready to learn motor skills involves a task analysis of the skills to be learned, accompanied by an opportunity for the learner to acquire the requisite antecedent skills. Although the order in which children learn the sequence in fundamental motor skills is invariant, there is great variation in the rate at which they move through the sequences to maturity.

REFERENCE NOTES

1. Seefeldt, V., & Haubenstricker, J. *History and current status of the motor performance study*. Unpublished manuscript, Michigan State University, 1973.
2. Seefeldt, V., Haubenstricker, J., & Milne, C. *Skeletal age and body size as variables in motor performance*. Paper presented at the Third Symposium on Child Growth and Motor Development, University of Western Ontario, March 1976.

REFERENCES

BRUNER, J. *The process of education*. Cambridge: Harvard University Press, 1965.

BRUNER, J. Processes of growth in infancy. In A. Ambrose (Ed.), *Stimulation in early infancy*. New York: Academic Press, 1969.

ESPENSCHADE, A. Motor performance in adolescence. *Monographs of the Society for Research in Child Development*, 1940, **5**, 1-127.

GESELL, A. The ontogenesis of infant behavior. In L. Carmichael (Ed.), *Manual of child psychology*. New York: Wiley, 1946.

HEBB, D. *The organization of behavior*. New York: Wiley, 1949.

HELLEBRANDT, F., Rarick, G., Glassow, R., & Carns, M. Physiological analysis of basic motor skills. *American Journal of Physical Medicine*, 1961, **40**, 14-25.

KAGAN, J. Preschool enrichment and learning. *Interchange*, 1971, **2**, 12-22.

KNOTT, M., & Voss, D. Proprioceptive neuromuscular facilitation. New York: Harper & Row, 1968.

MILANI-COMPARETTI, A., & Gidoni, E. Routine developmental examination in normal and retarded children. *Developmental Medicine and Child Neurology*, 1967, **13**, 631-638.

PIAGET, J. *The origins of intelligence in children*. New York: International Universities Press, 1952.

RARICK, G., & Oyster, N. Physical maturity, muscular strength and motor performance of young school-age boys. *Research Quarterly*, 1964, **35**, 523-531.

SHAMBES, F., & Campbell, S. Inherent movement patterns in man. *Kinesiology*, 1973, **3**, 50-58.

TWITCHELL, T. Attitudinal reflexes. *Physical Therapy*, 1965, **45**, 411-418.

WATERLAND, J. The supportive framework for willed movement. *American Journal of Physical Medicine*, 1967, **46**, 266-278.

WILD, M. The behavior pattern of throwing and some observations concerning its course of development in children. *Research Quarterly*, 1938, **9**, 20-24.

CHAPTER 4

CRITICAL PERIODS:
RELATION TO YOUTH SPORTS

Richard A. Magill

Critical periods is a phrase often seen in behavioral science literature that is primarily concerned with human growth and development. Unfortunately, that phrase has often been misunderstood, misused, and even overused. Some of this difficulty has resulted from the lack of a consistent, interpretable definition that can be used to apply to human growth and development problems. In addition to the difficulty in establishing the definition of critical periods, some of the issues raised concern what determines the onset and duration of critical periods and whether or not it is possible to "make up" for what has not been experienced during a critical period. While these issues are primarily theoretical in nature, the practical application of the resolutions of these issues becomes apparent when the application is made to children and their involvement in sport.

The first step in developing an understanding of the meaning and implications of the concept of critical learning periods is to understand that the critical period for learning is but one of at least three types of critical periods. Each type appears to have its own meaning, means of determination, and implications. These three critical periods have been identified from different viewpoints in articles by Scott (1962) and Bronson (1965) and should be consulted for further information.

Briefly, these critical periods can be identified by their effect on (a) emotional development, (b) social development of the formation of basic social relationships, and (c) learning. The bulk of the research related to critical periods has been in the area of critical periods for social development. This research has been primarily animal research, beginning with the famous imprinting studies conducted by Lorenz in 1935. The primary orientation of this discussion will be toward a consideration of critical periods that appear to relate to learning. Because application of this discussion will follow a youth sports direction, the study of critical periods of learning appears to offer more in the way of direct application than do either of the other two types of critical periods. Although there are distinctions among the three periods, there is also a certain degree of interrelationship among the three.

McGraw (1935) is generally credited with first noticing the phenomenon of critical periods of learning in children (Scott, 1962). Her studies of Jimmy and Johnny are well-known to anyone who has studied motor development. She pointed out that for certain activities, such as walking or tricycling, early practice was no help in the child's learning. The specific finding concerning walking was later supported by Dennis and Dennis (1940) in their investigations of the Hopi Indians. McGraw further concluded that in other areas, such as roller skating, early practice was beneficial. Thus, she concluded that critical periods for learning vary from activity to activity; for each motor skill there exists an optimum period for rapid and skillful learning. Thus, before training or practice can begin or can be economically provided, McGraw (1939) stated that it is necessary to "determine, by the observation of behavior symptoms, the periods of greatest susceptibility for each type of activity" (p. 2).

DETERMINANTS OF CRITICAL PERIODS

An obvious question that arises following such a statement is what determines the critical period or "period of greatest susceptibility" for learning? McGraw (1939) seemed farily confident that the determinant of the period was primarily maturation. Her recounting of the original Jimmy and Johnny study led to the conclusion that the early practice provided for Johnny in tricycling proved ineffective because the "activity was initiated before his neuro-muscular mechanisms were ready for such a performance" (p. 3). McGraw (1945) later stated rather definitively that it is simply wasted effort to begin training before adequate neural readiness. Thus, McGraw's answer to the question of a determinant of critical periods is that *maturation* is the primary determinant.

This maturation viewpoint was merely an extension of the developmental theory established by such influential theorists as G. Stanley Hall (1921) and Arnold Gesell (1928). This approach, which can be properly labeled a "growth-readiness model" of development, proposes that certain organized patterns of growth must occur before learning can effectively contribute to development. In support of such an approach, Gesell and Thompson (1929) provided evidence from a motor skill learning study involving a pair of identical twins. At the age of 46 weeks, one twin was given special training in stair-climbing while no training was provided for the other twin. Seven weeks later, the untrained twin did not climb as well as the trained twin. However, following only 2 weeks of training, or about ⅓ of the amount given to the trained twin, the originally untrained twin surpassed her sister in performance. Gesell and Thompson (1929) concluded that better learning with less training will result when the child's maturation level is adequate for the task to be learned. Of course, a major question that must be considered here relates to what the untrained twin may have been learning during the period of no special training.

Since the time of McGraw's studies with Jimmy and Johnny, other viewpoints have been presented to explain the onset of critical periods. One of these viewpoints is expressed in the developmental theory of Piaget. According to Piaget, maturation continues to be a major contributor to development but additional consideration is given to the child's interaction with the environment and to learning. Learning, however, is given a very minor role. In regard to cognitive development, Flavell (1963) has pointed out that this model might properly be labeled an *adaptive* model.

According to this approach, progress in children's development is affected by the interaction of the children with their environment. New experiences are assimilated into existing cognitive structures which are generally determined in a sequential manner by maturation. In turn, accommodation to the demands imposed by the environment is made possible by newly acquired structures. Thus, given their developmental stage, children will perform those tasks which they are capable of performing. While closely tied to maturation, this developmental stage is not at the maturation extreme of the Gesell view. The appearance of Piaget's developmental stages may be facilitated by appropriate environmental interactions.

The primary means of arriving at these *adaptive model* conclusions has been through observational evidence. Children are presented with a task and then observed while they solve the problem. Questions are generally asked to assist in the determination of the children's understanding. Flavell's volume on Piaget's developmental psychology, published in 1963, has presented many studies supporting Piaget's model and should be consulted for further study. For purposes of this discussion, it will be sufficient to understand that maturation is still considered to be a primary determinant in development, although additional emphasis is now given to children's interaction with their environment. Learning serves only as a factor involved in adaptation, not in development.

A third model explaining developmental processes was developed by Gagné (1968, 1970). This model involves learning to a greater degree than either the *maturation* or *adaptive* models in regard to the primary determinants of the onset of critical periods of learning. Gagné has labeled this approach the *cumulative* model of learning. Briefly, Gagné

(1968) postulated that the "child progresses from one point to the next in his development . . . because he learns an ordered set of capabilities which build upon each other in progressive fashion through the processes of differentiation, recall, and transfer of learning" (p. 181). In effect, this model classifies what is to be learned into a particular type of learning, such as S-R connections, multiple discriminations, concepts, and rules. These classifications are hierarchically ordered so if something to be learned is classified as a rule, then for effective learning to occur the components of that rule must have been acquired in the categories preceding the rule level in the hierarchy.

While Gagné developed this model primarily to be representative of learning in the cognitive domain, the basic principles of the model appear applicable to learning in the motor domain. For example, a major tenet of this approach is the role of transfer of learning. Gagné (1968) stated that "any learned capability, at any stage of a learning sequence, may operate to mediate other learning which was not deliberately taught" (p. 168). In considering the stair-climbing study by Gesell and Thompson (1929), it is plausible that the untrained twin was learning subordinate skills necessary to climb the stairs. The subsequent training of that twin took less time than her sister because only the specifics of stair-climbing needed to be taught to her instead of the entire skill. Thus, maturation may not have been the primary reason for the shorter training period as Gesell and Thompson concluded, but rather the reason may have been more related to learned capabilities not specifically taught that mediated the learning of the actual task.

To summarize the three points of view discussed thus far, it will be helpful to consider these views as falling along a continuum. On one extreme of the continuum is the maturation view which contends that maturation is the primary factor involved in the determination of the onset of a critical period of learning. At that end of the continuum are the views presented by Gesell and McGraw. It should be recalled, however, that McGraw's view suggests that critical periods are highly task- or skill-specific. At the other extreme of the continuum is the cumulative model presented by Gagné. At this end, learning is seen as the primary determinant of critical periods. Near the center of the continuum, but falling on a line closer to the maturation side, is the adaptive model expressed by Piaget.

Unfortunately, no conclusive evidence exists to support any one of these approaches over any of the others. Bruner (1960), for example, began his discussion of readiness for learning from a hypothesis that would be related to the learning side on our continuum because he stated that no evidence existed to contradict his hypothesis, while considerable evidence was being collected to support it. It is also unfortunate that the learning of motor skills has only been considered by one of these theories, the maturation approach. If we are to generalize to motor skill learning from the other two theoretical postulations we may or may not run into problems.

The discussion of these three theoretical viewpoints leads us to a conclusion concerning the determination of the onset of a critical period of learning that was presented by Scott (1962). His conclusion, based on synthesized animal and human learning studies that were reported from McGraw in the mid-thirties, was a "provisional general hypothesis." The hypothesis stated that "the critical period for any specific sort of learning is that time when maximum capacities — sensory, motor, and motivational, as well as psychological ones — are first present" (p. 955). Thus, no one factor can be considered alone.

If neither maturation nor learning can be considered as the sole determinant of a critical learning period, then what should be our viewpoint concerning the critical learning period? The critical period for learning cannot be viewed as one in which the initiation of learning a skill must take place or else that skill will never be learned. Neither can it be assumed that had the skill been introduced during the critical learning period it would have been learned to a greater extent. Furthermore, even if the instruction and practice time are sufficient, the viewpoint should not be taken that any skill can be taught at any time, regardless of maturation level. The only valid position is one compatible with the whole range of research evidence. That viewpoint states that some combination of maturation and learning factors is important in the determination of the critical period. In order to understand this definition, however, those factors must be identified and their relative influences determined.

Based on this discussion, it seems feasible to consider "critical periods of learning" as "optimal readiness periods for learning." This phrase connotes the existence of periods of time in a person's life when that individual is optimally ready to learn a given skill. Seefeldt (Note 1) stated that the terms *critical periods* and *sensitive periods* can be used interchangeably. The advantage of the term *sensitive period* is the implication that learning occurs with greater efficiency at some period in life than in others. Thus, the key issue in understanding critical learning periods is the consideration of *when* a person is *ready* to learn.

Although viewing critical periods for learning from a readiness point of view may clarify some connotation problems, the problem of identifying those factors which determine this period of optimal readiness is still paramount. From the discussion thus far it should be obvious that while both maturation and prior learning are factors to be included in a readiness model, neither can be considered independently to be the determining factor of readiness to learn. What remains, then, is the question of what other factors to include in this model.

The one factor that stands out among all possible factors to add to this readiness model is motivation. No learning theorist would suggest that learning can occur without some degree of motivation being present within the organism. While that motivation may be externally induced or internally generated, its presence remains as a necessary prerequisite for learning.

Thus, the readiness model being suggested here states that the period of time during which the introduction of a skill to be learned will result in the achievement of the greatest potential for performance and/or learning is that period of time when the maturation level, prior experiences or learning, and motivation of the individual are optimum. The weighting of any one factor in determining the onset of these optimal periods will vary from task to task for the same individual, making this model both individual- and task-specific. If we consider, for example, the prior experiences portion of our model, this specificity suggests that learning to throw a baseball at a catcher is a task which child A is ready to learn. For child B of the same age, however, there are some prerequisite skills that must be acquired. Thus, the readiness of child B is to learn a subordinate skill which child A has already acquired. The same type of example could be developed for the other two parts of the readiness model.

In effect, this is what McGraw was suggesting in 1935. For Jimmy and Johnny, early training in walking was not beneficial while early training in roller skating was beneficial. Although McGraw considered maturation to be the major factor in determining when to introduce any new skill, she also noted that for certain motor skills instruction at the proper time is most beneficial. McGraw, however, only considered the acquisition of a whole skill; she did not give any consideration to the effect of instruction on efficient acquisition of certain subordinate parts of the skill.

The stair-climbing example discussed in the study by Gesell and Thompson (1929) should also be examined. They attributed poor acquisition to the introduction of the skill before the children had reached the proper degree of maturation. While this is probably quite true, the model being presented here might also be considered. Perhaps these children had not adequately learned the subordinate skills necessary for the acquisition of the skill being taught. If this were true, then it would be possible to attribute poor acquisition to maturation problems and to the other two factors in the readiness model. The children did not have the adequate prior experiences necessary to learn the skill being introduced and were probably not adequately motivated to learn them at that time. To carry this point one step futher, the later rapid acquisition of stair-climbing by the previously untrained child was probably somewhat due to an increase in maturation. However, this untrained child was permitted to explore the stairs on her own and it is possible that during that time the needed prerequisite skills were learned by the child without the benefit of the specific training provided her sibling. When the experimenters began training her to climb the stairs, the training period was minimized not only because of maturational development but also because of prior experiences and a more appropriate level of motivation to learn the skill.

At this point then, the interrelationship of maturation and prior experiences should be evident; neither can stand alone to explain the onset of optimal readiness. For certain skills such as walking there is ample evidence to show that maturation is more important as a determining factor, but for a more complex skill such as roller skating or batting both empirical and theoretical evidence points to prior experience as the more powerful determinant. The relative influence of both maturation and prior learning on the acquisition of a complex skill is a topic of much debate and worthy of investigation. For this discussion, however, it should be sufficient to indicate that for initial learning the attainment of prerequisite skills is of utmost priority.

The role of motivation in this readiness model needs further development. Motivation is herein defined as anything that acts as an energizer of performance. Just as a battery-driven toy needs a battery to operate, the human organism needs an energizer to be able to perform in a situation where learning must occur. However, unlike the battery-driven toy, that energizer does not always have to originate from within the individual. Adequate motivation to learn might exist within the individual and be very task-related or it may be induced from an outside source and be socially related (i.e., the learner may begin to learn because of outside inducements such as needs for affiliation, social approval, and esteem).

Ausubel (1968) stated that "the causal relationship between motivation and learning is typically reciprocal rather than unidirectional" (p. 365). Although he did not suggest postponing instruction when the learner is unmotivated, he did suggest the need for adequate motivation for optimal learning. He also reasoned that simply being introduced to the learning situation may be a way of arousing the necesary motivation level.

It should be clear then that when we consider the problem of determining the onset of an optimal readiness period for learning a motor skill there are at least three questions that must be considered. The first considers the physical, cognitive, and emotional maturational level of the individual; the second determines the prerequisite skills the learner is able to perform; and the third considers the motivational level of the learner. Each of these questions must be answered in relation to the skill to be learned. If deficiencies in any of these three factors are noted for the task at hand, then appropriate measures must be taken to provide compensation. This compensation may take the form of changing the task to one that involves the learning of a task which the person has the physical or mental ability to begin to acquire, the learning of a needed subordinate skill, or employing an appropriate method of motivating the learner to begin to learn the task.

APPLICATION TO YOUTH SPORTS

An obvious question remains. Since this discussion is directed toward the application of critical periods to youth sports, what does all this mean in relation to youth sports? Readiness should be an obvious consideration in any program. The activities involved in youth sports programs are specific, complex sport skills that require training to be performed well. Obviously, the better performers are the most desirable participants. Thus, the onus of responsibility rests on these programs to provide adequate training for its participants to ensure the highest degree of skilled performance possible. Involved in that training is the important component of readiness. From this perspective, then, at least four implications of the readiness model presented here can be made relative to youth sports.

First, the specific skills of any sport should be analyzed to determine the subordinate or prerequisite skills which must be effectively performed to ensure adequate performance of that sport skill. An example of this analysis in sport was provided by Singer and Dick (1974), who examined the sport of baseball and broke that sport down into its component parts. To play baseball effectively, a person must be able to throw, run, bat, and catch. Each of these skills can be further analyzed and broken down into components. For example, to be able to bat, a person must be able to hold the bat properly, time the swing properly, direct the bat at the ball properly, etc. Thus, children who cannot effectively play baseball may not be able to do so because they cannot bat effectively; they cannot bat effectively because they are unable to adequately time their swing. While this analysis could continue, these examples should be sufficient to indicate the importance of establishing competence in prerequisite abilities before training or expecting effective performance in more complex skills.

A *second* implication is that youth sports programs should encourage its participants to experience a wide variety of skills. It is deplorable, for example, to consider that a 7-year-old boy, who is large for his age and participates in organized football, is used only as a lineman. He never gets an opportunity to be a receiver, running back, quarterback, or linebacker. He is used only to serve present team needs. That same child may be an early maturer and by high school he may actually be too small to be an effective lineman. Because he has had such limited experience in handling a football at other positions, his past experiences will dictate his future lack of success in football. The same analogy could be made in other sports. The point is that for the sake of the child, he should experience a variety of different skills. The payoff may not be immediate, but it will certainly come in the future. To further support the strength of this implication, Rarick (1961) stated that the establishment of a repertoire of motor skills at an early age has a favorable influence on the attitudes that an individual takes toward his attack on new experiences.

Third, youth sports programs must be concerned about the motivation part of this model. Just as the range of early experiences influences the selection of later experiences, so does early success in the performance of motor skills. Rarick (1961) further stated that success in bodily activities increases the probability of the formation of positive attitudes toward motor skills. If children are continually confronted with activities that they are incapable of performing, it should be expected that their motivational level to continue to learn more complex skills will be quite low. Also, if the amount of early experiences is limited to very few activities, it should be expected that any drive to continue to be involved in physical activity will be quite limited. Youth sports programs have a responsibility to the individual participant that extends beyond the motivational demands of a game or a season; they must establish a desire within these participants to continue to be involved in competitive sports programs. To "turn them off" as a result of improper concern for motivational factors is a grave injustice to these youth.

Finally, an implication of the readiness model relates to the type of sports in which youth are permitted to participate. Clearly, each sport has its own unique demands on the performer. Those demands need to be compared to the maturation level, prior experience, and motivational characteristics of the age group being considered for involvement in competition. Prior experience dictates, generally, that baseball should be modified for 6-year-olds; "tee ball" appears to be an appropriate modification and has become very popular. Maturation seems to be a determining factor in the adoption of the type of football in which 6- to 12-year-olds should be involved; flag football seems to be an appropriate alternative to tackle football for this age group.

These few implications for youth sports programs are just some of many that could be developed from the readiness model presented here. Youth sports program needs are closely tied to the understanding of readiness. Those involved in the conduct of these programs have a responsibility to consider these sports programs in terms of each child's maturation status, prior skill experiences, and motivation to participate.

REFERENCE NOTE

1. Seefeldt, V. *Critical periods and programs of early intervention.* Paper presented at the national meeting of the American Alliance for Health, Physical Education and Recreation, Atlantic City, 1975.

REFERENCES

AUSUBEL, D.P. *Educational psychology: A cognitive view.* New York: Holt, Rinehart & Winston, 1968.

BRONSON, G. The hierarchical organization of the central nervous system: Implications for learning processes and critical periods in early development. *Behavioral Science*, 1965, **10**, 7-25.

BRUNER, J.D. *The process of education.* Cambridge: Harvard University Press, 1960.

DENNIS, W., & Dennis, M.G. The effect of cradling practices upon the onset of walking in Hopi children. *Journal of Genetic Psychology*, 1940, **56**, 77-86.

FLAVELL, J.H. *The developmental psychology of Jean Piaget.* Princeton: Van Nostrand, 1963.

GAGNÉ, R.M. Contributions of learning to human development. *Psychological Review*, 1968, **75**, 177-191.

GAGNÉ, R.M. *The conditions of learning* (2nd ed.). New York: Holt, Rinehart & Winston, 1970.

GESELL, A. Infancy and human growth. New York: Macmillan, 1928.

GESELL, A., & Thompson, H. Learning and growth in identical twin infants. *Genetic Psychology Monographs*, 1929, **6**, 1-124.

HALL, G.S. *Aspects of child life and education.* New York: Appleton, 1921.

MCGRAW, M.B. *Growth: A study of Johnny and Jimmy.* New York: Appleton-Century, 1935.

MCGRAW, M.B. Later development of children specifically trained during infancy: Johnny and Jimmy at school age. *Child Development*, 1939, **10**, 1-19.

MCGRAW, M.B. *The neuromuscular maturation of the human infant.* New York: Hafner, 1945.

RARICK, G.L. *Motor development during infancy and childhood* (2nd ed.). Madison, WI: College Printing and Typing, 1961.

SCOTT, J.P. Critical periods in behavioral development. *Science*, 1962, **138**, 949-958.

SINGER, R.N., & Dick, W. *Teaching physical education: A systems approach.* Boston: Houghton-Mifflin, 1974.

CHAPTER 5

ANTECEDENTS OF
COMPETITIVENESS

Tara Kost Scanlan

Competition has been a pervasive phenomenon throughout the course of human history. A moment's reflection will recall how frequently and with what magnitude competition has crept into each of our lives. Perhaps it is the pervasiveness of the phenomenon and the fact that it is an experience common to us all that has made the topic of competition a source of intrigue for numerous researchers in a variety of fields for over 40 years. Perhaps it is the fact that 20 million children are currently engaged in the competitive sport experience that has made the topic of competition a source of renewed interest and concern in recent years.

Perusal of the competition literature to date has revealed an interesting and yet not uncommon paradox. The state of the art rests with a myriad of data and a dearth of understanding. The problem appears attributable to the lack of a viable theoretical framework to order past research and guide future investigations. To overcome this problem, it is suggested that Martens' model of competition (Martens, 1975, 1976), described in some detail by Scanlan in chapter 11 be used as a basis for determining the antecedents of competitiveness. (For greater elaboration on the evaluation of various approaches to competition, see Scanlan, 1977).

This investigation was supported in part by the Biomedical Research Support Grant, UCLA, USPHS number 5-507-RR07009-11.

The author extends her thanks to Dr. Rainer Martens for his helpful suggestions and editorial comments offered during the preparation of this manuscript.

To summarize the Martens' approach, it can be stated that competition is conceptualized as a process consisting of four stages of events which integrally relate to each other. These stages are the objective competitive situation, the subjective competitive situation, the response, and the consequences. Stage one, the objective competitive situation, refers to those "real factors in the physical or social environment that are arbitrarily defined as constituting a competitive situation" (Martens, 1975, p. 69). It is operationally defined as a situation "in which the comparison of an individual's performance is made with some standard in the presence of at least one other person who is aware of the criterion for comparison and can evaluate the comparison process" (Martens, 1975, p. 71).

Stage two, the subjective competitive situation, involves the individual's perception and appraisal of the objective competitive situation. An integration of a variety of situational and intrapersonal factors affect the subjective competitive situation. An important situational factor affecting the subjective competitive situation is whether the individual voluntarily sought out the objective competitive situation or whether it was forced upon him or her. An example of forced participation would be the pressure applied by the peer group to compete. Intrapersonal factors including various motives, personality dispositions, attitudes, and abilities possessed by the individual also affect the subjective competitive situation. The subjective competitive situation is further influenced by the individual's perception of the comparison standard, his or her own response capability, whether the probable outcomes will be positive or negative, and the importance of the consequences of the comparison. Therefore, the determination of the subjective competitive situation is seen as a product of the individual's cognitive deliberation of the entire competition process, and it is during this stage that the decision of whether to approach or to avoid the objective competitive situation is made.

If the decision to approach the objective competitive situation is made, then the response stage is entered. The response can be made on the behavioral, psychological, or physiological levels and can be affected by a number of internal and external factors. Motivation, ability, and other intrapersonal factors may mediate the response. Examples of external factors affecting the response would include the weather, time, facilities, and the opponent's response.

The fourth stage of the competition process involves the consequences arising from the comparison process. The consequences can be positive, negative, or neutral, and this information is fed back to the individual for future use.

Two key terms remain to be defined. The distinction between them, although subtle, is important. The first term is *competitive behavior* which involves the manifestation of an overt, observable response. Competitive behavior can occur at two points during the competition process. First, competitive behavior is evidenced when overt action is taken to seek out the objective competitive situation. For example, if a tennis player voluntarily signs up to participate in a tennis tournament or challenges another player to a match, then he or she is evidencing competitive behavior. Second, competitive behavior is manifested in the response that an individual makes to the objective competitive situation. Therefore, if a tennis player performs vigorously while in the objective competitive situation, then he or she is also evidencing competitive behavior.

The second term is *competitiveness*. Competitiveness is a personality disposition encompassing a cluster of motives which predispose an individual to approach or avoid the objective competitive situation (Martens, 1975). Although the competitiveness variable significantly affects competitive behavior, competitiveness occurs temporally prior to actual competitive behavior. Simply stated, competitiveness is the tendency of an individual to compete or not to compete.

The focus of the ensuing discussion centers on competitiveness. The primary purpose is to determine the macroscopic antecedents of competitiveness. To place the problem in the context of the Martens' model, the antecedent variables that lead to the development of intrapersonal characteristics affecting the subjective competitive situation, and the resultant tendency to approach or to avoid the objective competitive situation are determined. Because so little specific information exists concerning the competitiveness construct, particular attention is given to the topics of achievement motivation, social comparison, and child development to determine what is already known about competitiveness from these indirect sources. A theoretical schema incorporating and ordering the relevant findings in these literatures is then developed to identify the antecedents of competitiveness.

ACHIEVEMENT MOTIVATION

The construct achievement motivation, like competitiveness, is also a personality disposition. Heckhausen (1967) broadly defines achievement motivation as the "striving to increase, or keep as high as possible, one's own capabilities in all activities in which a standard of excellence is thought to apply and where the execution of such activities can, therefore, either succeed or fail" (p. 4). Incorporated here is anything that represents comparison with a standard, including task-related, self-related, and other-related standards.

Achievement motivation, therefore, involves the predisposition or tendency to approach or to avoid achievement situations. Achievement situations are situations that involve comparison with a social or nonsocial standard in which individuals know that their performance can be evaluated by themselves and/or others. The outcome generally involves some initial uncertainty and can result in neutral, positive (success), or negative (failure) evaluation (Atkinson, 1964). The parameters just stipulated indicate that the crucial central component of achievement situations is evaluation. Consequently, achievement motivation involves the predisposition or tendency of an individual to approach or to avoid evaluation.

Competitiveness is the predisposition or tendency to approach or avoid competitive situations. The competitive situation, as defined by the objective competitive situation, also involves comparison with a social or nonsocial standard in which individuals know that their performance will be evaluated by themselves and others. The outcome generally involves some uncertainty and can result in neutral, positive, or negative evaluations. The only difference between the typical achievement situation and the objective competitive situation is that the latter specifies that someone must be in the position to evaluate the performance. This factor increases the social evaluation potential in the situation. The objective competitive situation is, therefore, a specific form of an achievement situation. Consequently, competitiveness implies a motive to achieve and to be evaluated; the achievement and evaluation are merely sought through competitive situations.

Because no specific empirical investigations have been conducted concerning competitiveness, the first step to determining the antecedents of competitiveness will be to examine the antecedents of achievement motivation. To achieve this end, a brief digression into the fundamental concepts and findings of achievement motivation is necessary to establish the characteristic differences between individuals with a strong tendency to *seek* evaluation and individuals with a strong tendency to *avoid* evaluation through achievement situations. However, only a few of the most pertinent differentiating characteristics will be discussed. (For a more detailed discussion, refer to Atkinson, 1957, 1958a, 1958b, 1964, 1974a.)

Achievement motivation theory and research have indicated that the high need achiever has a strong motive to achieve success (M_s). The M_s is a stable disposition which is characterized as "a capacity for reacting with pride in accomplishment" (Atkinson, 1964, p. 241). Further, when being evaluated through comparison with a standard, the high need achiever has a strong expectation of success rather than of failure. The behavioral tendency of an individual with a high M_s is to prefer to engage in tasks of intermediate rather than low or high difficulty. Intermediate difficulty tasks characterize the most stringent achievement situation because the probability of success is .50, and, therefore, the outcome is maximally uncertain and primarily determined by the individual's own ability. Preference for intermediate difficulty tasks indicates that the high need achiever has a strong tendency to approach achievement situations and evaluation.

The low need achiever has a strong motive to avoid failure (M_{af}). The M_{af} is a stable disposition which is characterized as "a capacity for reacting with shame and embarrassment when the outcome of the performance is failure" (Atkinson, 1964, p. 244). A strong expectancy of failure rather than success is evident and the M_{af} disposition is particularly aroused in situations where performance is to be evaluated and failure is possible. The behavioral tendency of an individual with a high M_{af} is to prefer to engage in tasks of low or high difficulty to avoid the intense evaluation characterizing intermediate difficulty tasks. Therefore, the low need achiever has a strong tendency to avoid achievement situations and evaluation.

A considerable amount of *direct* evidence has been accrued in support of the hypothesis that high M_s individuals will prefer to approach and high M_{af} individuals will prefer to avoid evaluation and tasks of intermediate difficulty (Atkinson, 1957, 1958a, 1958b; Feather, 1959; McClelland, 1958b; Weiner & Rosenbaum, 1965). *Indirect* support for the hypothesis that high M_s individuals seek evaluation and high M_{af} individuals avoid evaluation is found in another body of literature. Several studies have been conducted to illustrate the importance of the types of cues present in the situation which directly affect expectancy, incentive, and performance regardless of characteristic achievement motivation levels (Atkinson, 1958a, 1958b, 1974a, 1974b; Atkinson & Reitman, 1958; Entin, 1974; French, 1958; Smith, 1963, 1966). The findings have shown that the achievement motive is significantly aroused only if other competing motives are not present. When the motives for other goals activate expectancies, the results are often quite different. For example, French (1958) found that the achievement motive was not aroused in situations in which the affiliation motive was dominant. The achievement motive was also not aroused in situations in which extrinsic rewards were dispensed and monetary incentives activated (Atkinson, 1958a, 1958b; Atkinson & Reitman, 1958; Smith, 1966). The results from the studies cited lead to two conclusions. First, careful consideration of the situation is necessary when studying achievement motivation to ensure that the achievement motive has been appropriately aroused. Second, no behavioral differences seem to exist between M_s and M_{af} individuals in situations where cues other than achievement motivation are aroused. Hence, the critical difference between the tendencies and resultant behavior of M_s and M_{af} individuals rests with the evaluative aspects of the situation.

The first major distinction concerning competitiveness can be made on the basis of tendencies to seek or avoid evaluation. The prevailing characteristic of an individual with a strong tendency to seek evaluation is a high motive to approach success, while the prevailing characteristic of an individual with a strong tendency to avoid evaluation is a high motive to avoid failure. Consequently, it is hypothesized that the motive to achieve success is basic to high competitiveness. The motive to avoid failure will inhibit the tendency to approach the evaluation emanating from the objective competitive situation. Thus, it is hypothesized that the motive to avoid failure is basic to low competitiveness.

CRITICAL ANTECEDENTS
OF ACHIEVEMENT MOTIVATION

The role of past experience in the determination of M_s and M_{af} and their corresponding expectancies is crucial. The M_s orientation results primarily from the accrual of past experiences colored with success expectations (Heckhausen, 1967). Conversely, the M_{af} orientation results primarily from the accrual of past experiences colored with failure expectations. Explicit support indicating the critical role of past experience was offered by Feather (1965) in a study examining the relationship of success expectation to achievement motivation and test anxiety. The results indicated that individuals categorized performance situations in terms of whether past experiences in similar situations resulted in success or failure. High M_s individuals, in contrast to the high M_{af} individuals, tended to categorize the evaluative situation as one in which positive outcomes would be derived. Thus, the roles of past experiences directs us to consider a developmental approach to identifying the antecedents of the M_s and M_{af} motives. Specifically, the focus must be on early experiences because of their impact on the development and later age manifestations of M_s and M_{af} (Crandall, Preston, & Rabson, 1960; McClelland, 1958a; Moss & Kagan, 1961).

Two theoretical schemas have most effectively ordered the major findings in the developmental literature. The first is White's Competence Theory and the second is Veroff's schema of achievement motivation development. To provide a general map of the ensuing discussion, an overall conceptualization will be presented that relates the two theories and pertinent developmental findings to competitiveness. The pertinent aspects of the theories and relevant developmental literature will then be elaborated and documented.

The overall conceptual schema is illustrated in Figure 1. At the top of the figure it is seen that the ultimate goal of competence is autonomy. To achieve competence, and ultimately, autonomy, competence must be assessed. To assess competence, evaluation must be sought. The major sources of evaluation are achievement situations which can be social or nonsocial in nature. The objective competitive situation involves social evaluation and is primarily a social achievement situation. The degree to which past experiences have been positive rather than negative are greatly dependent upon early child training variables such as independence and mastery training which provide the necessary experiences or tools for successful environmental transactions.

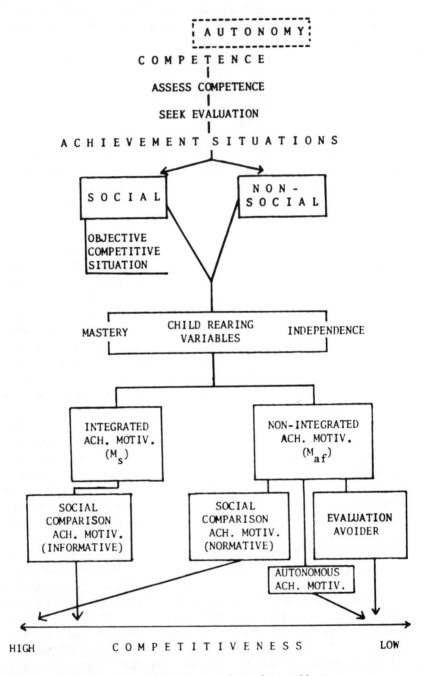

Figure 1—Theoretical framework for the antecedents of competitiveness.

The cumulation of numerous evaluations results in a success orientation and a strong tendency to approach evaluation if the results of the evaluations have generally been positive. Conversely, a failure orientation and a strong tendency to avoid evaluation result if the cumulative evaluation experiences have typically been negative. Individuals with a success orientation generally evidence high competitiveness because of the information to be gained from the social comparison process. Individuals with a failure orientation generally evidence low competitiveness. The one exception involves the very highly competitive, failure-oriented individual who seeks enhancement of self-esteem through the social comparison process. For this particular individual, the social comparison process serves a normative rather than an informative function.

White's Competence Theory

The first aspect of the conceptual schema to consider more closely is Competence Theory. The impact of Competence Theory has been felt in the developmental, achievement motivation, clinical, psychological, psychiatric, and educational literatures (Gladwin, 1967; McClelland, 1973; Moss & Kagan, 1961; Smith, 1968; Weiner & Rosenbaum, 1965; White, 1959, 1960). White, the originator of Competence Theory, defined competence as the individual's ability to carry on a series of transactions with the environment to enhance self-growth, maintenance, and flourishment. This capacity of the organism to deal effectively with the environment is evidenced by directed, selective, and persistent activity; the underlying motive to this purposive activity is termed effectance. The effectance motive is aroused by stimulus conditions which produce "difference in sameness" and the most distinct characteristic of the motive is evidenced by the individual's attempt to produce effects on the environment. The primary outcome of the motive is the satisfaction derived from feelings of efficacy. Vital concurrent learning occurs while seeking this satisfaction because mastery of a particular stimulus condition results in diminished interest and satisfaction. Therefore, new situations are sought and new transactions transpire. Each transaction provides knowledge about how to deal effectively with the environment. This knowledge causes the relatively undifferentiated effectance motive of early life to evolve into more differentiated motives in later life. The achievement motive is an example of a differentiated motive derived from the effectance motive in early life.

The development of competence is primarily dependent upon early experiences as White (1960) has ably discussed. During the anal stage, prior to the age of 2 years, the child actively explores and interacts with the environment and as a result a sense of autonomy develops. During the oral stage, an increased emphasis on motor accomplishment leading to the evolution of self-assertiveness and self-esteem occurs. The facility to locomote becomes an increasingly meaningful ability during the phallic stage. The child begins to imitate adult behavior and especially to imitate roles that depict power over the environment. For example, most young children desire to be firemen, cowboys, or policemen rather than writers. The ability to evaluate is well-developed at this stage. Consequently, when lack of ability results in failure, shame can occur. Shame is associated with a lack of competence and the result can be diminished respect and self-respect. Between 6 and 12 years of age the latency period occurs. The child's contemporaries become critical and the development of social competence becomes important. The early part of these years are generally spent learning how to function, to compromise, and to protect one's self in relation to the social world. A new spurt of independence is manifested by the individual, the peer group begins to become more important than the family, and social comparison becomes intense.

The results of the developmental process lead to the determination of a sense of competence which is the cumulative product of one's past successes and failures. The sense of competence operates as a type of set when approaching new transactions requiring the demonstration of new abilities and therefore answering the question, "Can I do it?" If past experiences have been typically successful, then the sense of competence is high and a success orientation is evidenced and reinforced. Obversely, if past experiences have typically resulted in failure, then the sense of competence is low and a failure orientation is evidenced and reinforced. The result of the gradual learning process involved in the development of competence is flexibility. This flexibility allows the individual to deal with a variety of environmental demands and increases the individual's autonomy from the environment. The importance of child rearing practices, particularly mastery and independence training, are essential to this cumulative learning process.

White (1959) contended that there is a general dynamic trend in individuals to become autonomous. The whole concept of competence revolves around the idea that humans learn to deal effectively with their environment to gain effectual autonomy from it and control over it. In short, autonomy can only be achieved through competence. But just what is autonomy? Foote and Cottrell (1955) provided a rather detailed description of the term. Autonomy was described as the clarity of an individual's own identity, the extent to which the individual operates from a stable set of intrinsic standards of personal norms, the amount of confidence and reliance on self, and the degree of self-respect maintained. In sum, autonomy is the ability to govern one's self. Operationally defined, autonomy is the "ease in giving and receiving evaluations of self and others" (Foote & Cottrell, 1955, p. 55).

To summarize Competence Theory, the ultimate goal of competence has been shown to be autonomy. Autonomy can only be achieved through the development of competence. Assessment of competence through evaluation is a necessary process for the determination of the sense of competence. The sense of competence is the gauge for determining the level of competence achieved, and therefore, how well the individual is progressing toward the ultimate goal of autonomy. The primary sources of evaluation are achievement situations because they are highly evaluative and set the stage for the question, "Can I do it?" If competence is high, then the effectance motive will be strong and will develop into more differentiated motives like achievement. A strong success orientation will be present and evaluation should be sought for the potential information to be gained. If competence is low, then the effectance motive will be weak and will develop into more differentiated motives like fear of failure. This strong failure orientation will result in evaluation being avoided because the information to be gained is often threatening to the self.

Veroff's Theory

Veroff (1969) devised a theoretical schema emphasizing the impact of past experience and defining the stages of development through which an individual passes that result in high or low achievement motivation. Using Competence Theory as a foundation for his schema, Veroff supported his theory by studies he either reviewed or conducted.

A distinction was made by Veroff between *autonomous* and *social* achievement motivation, which added clarity to the very broad and inclusive achievement motivation construct.[1] Autonomous achievement motivation was defined as the tendency to compare with one's own norms or internalized personal standards of excellence. An absolute criterion of performance can be involved but is not necessary. The self-comparison provides information as to how well the individual is progressing compared to past accomplishments and, therefore, is critical to the establishment of the sense of competence. Social approval is a possible but not a necessary result. Social achievement motivation, on the other hand, was defined as the tendency to compare with norms set by others or social comparison standards of excellence. Social achievement involves relative performance standards in that excellence in performance involves being the best in the group. Social approval often results, but not necessarily. Autonomous and social achievement motivations can operate simultaneously in the same situation but differentially vary in strength.

---

[1]The terms autonomy and autonomous achievement motivation are not to be confused. Autonomy refers to the ultimate goal of the developmental process as defined by Foote and Cottrell (1955). This definition was presented earlier. Autonomous achievement motivation is merely the term used by Veroff (1969) to define a particular stage in the development of achievement motivation.

Veroff also made an important distinction between two functions which can be served by social achievement motivation. The *informative function* provides the information necessary to accommodate one's failures and to evaluate whether personal aspirations are realistic or unrealistic in comparison with others. This function is crucial to the development of the sense of competence. The *normative function* involves social approval or disapproval from significant others as well as the world at large. Enhancement of self-esteem is often sought rather than evaluation and accurate self-assessment.

The distinction between the informative and normative functions of social comparison achievement motivation is crucial to this discussion and is supported by the findings in the social comparison literature. In his "Theory of Social Comparison," Festinger (1954) postulated that individuals possess a drive to accurately assess their abilities. To achieve this assessment, individuals compare their abilities with objective standards. In the absence of objective standards, comparisons are made with social standards. Festinger further contended that greater information about one's abilities can be derived from comparing with persons of similar rather than divergent abilities.

The evidence offered in support of Festinger's hypothesis that individuals seek to compare with others of similar abilities has received substantial support (Gruder, 1971; Hakmiller, 1966; Radloff, 1966; Singer & Shockley, 1965; Thornton & Arrowood, 1966; Wheeler, 1966; Wheeler, Shaver, Jones, Goethals, Cooper, Robinson, Gruder, & Buzine, 1969). Evidence has also been accrued which indicates that individuals do not always compare with similar others to achieve accurate self-assessments, and that the social comparison process can serve a normative as well as informative function. Greater elaboration of the findings supporting the normative function of social comparison has been provided by Singer (1966):

> People do not compare with others in order to evaluate only one ability or opinion. Implicitly, they are also evaluating their opinions of themselves. In the general case, they are evaluating their self-esteem. When a person asks 'How much X do I have?' he is also asking 'What sort of person am I for possessing that much X?' (p. 105)

Singer discussed the fact that the selected comparison person for the evaluation of X may not be the same person selected for the self-esteem issue triggered by X. Consequently, everyone will not choose an opponent of similar ability with whom to compare.

The postulation has also been made that there may be a differentiation between types of individuals and their reaction to social comparison. Specifically, Singer (1966) stated that a person with a "high stable self-image may eagerly seek out a firm evaluation of ability X with little concern for its self-image implications" (pp. 105-106). Conversely, a person with a low, unstable self-image will evidence greater concern for the self-image implications of evaluating the ability. This contention has been supported by the findings of Coopersmith's (1967) extensive study of self-esteem in which low self-esteem individuals were shown to be more readily threatened and experienced greater difficulty in coping with threat than high self-esteem individuals. Furthermore, low self-esteem individuals, in contrast to high self-esteem individuals, evidenced a lack of confidence in their ability to deal effectively with situations, and this lack of confidence increased under stress.

Thus, support for Veroff's distinction between the informative and normative functions of social comparison has been shown rather consistently. This distinction is important to the consideration of competitiveness since the objective competitive situation is a social comparison achievement situation. Specific application of the distinction will be made as Veroff's schema of the developmental stages of achievement motivation is presented and eventually applied to the antecedents of competitiveness.

Veroff (1969) traced the development of achievement motivation through three sequentially related stages. The stages of achievement motivation included autonomous competence, social comparison, and mature or integrated achievement motivation. Success at each stage is critically dependent upon the successful completion of each preceding stage. The autonomous competence stage includes the preverbal and the postverbal periods in early childhood. During the preverbal period the child participates in exploratory behaviors and begins to learn to cope with the environment. Mastery and feelings of efficacy due to attempted autonomy result. A successful preverbal period provides the critical developmental background for the future establishment of autonomous achievement goals. Once the child is able to verbalize, the evaluation of his or her own competency becomes possible. This evaluation of competence is the essential element which makes the experience an achievement. Actual autonomous achievement goals can be set, strived for, and success or failure determined. As skills take on greater clarity, autonomous competence motivation intensifies.

During the early school years, successful autonomous achievement motivation facilitates the evolution of social achievement motivation. At this stage the pressure and desire to compare socially develops. Because the social comparison process can serve both informational and normative functions, children learn about themselves and their capabilities in relation to others. They also may learn that favorable social comparison can lead to social approval from others. This stage is critical to children's assessment of their competence, autonomy, and personal standards. Therefore, failure at this stage can have deleterious effects on future adjustment and achievement behavior.

Stable patterns of achievement behavior become relatively fixed during the later childhood and adolescent ages. The specific pattern developed is directly dependent upon the degree of success or failure experienced during the earlier stages. Mature or integrated achievement motivation, that is, the integration of autonomous and social achievement motivation, can occur only after the successful completion of each earlier stage. Integration is the construct that indicates the use of the particular achievement motivation which is most appropriate to the specific situation or setting. Further, the intent of both achievement motives is to gain information about the self from the autonomous or social achievement situation. The information gained through the evaluative process is fed back into individuals to gauge the level of their competence and, therefore, their progress toward the goal of autonomy.

Veroff contended that the development of achievement does not only follow a pattern of stages, but that each stage must be able to occur at the critical age period which is determined by the child's abilities and development. For example, if the social comparison stage is entered too soon, the child may not be able to adequately cope with the evaluation from others. Conversely, if it occurs too late, no challenge would be present. This contention is not to preclude the possibility of later age learning. It merely emphasizes the most expedient and fruitful course of development. It also illustrates the difficulties involved in overcoming and rectifying a divergent course due to the accompanying failures that result and must be overcome.

Given these basic developmental patterns leading to integrated achievement motivation and competence, it follows that specific child training variables and practices are necessary components to the developmental process. At least two child training variables, mastery and independence, are necessary ingredients to the ultimate achievement of autonomy. Mastery training is closely related to competence and is concerned with the setting of demands involving successful transactions with the environment and expecting the demands to be met by the child. Independence training involves expecting the child to function with self-reliance, free from the influence of others. Thus, learning to master transactions can be viewed as the first step toward autonomy or self-governing behavior.

Although the importance of early mastery and independence training to the development of achievement motivation has been evidenced in a number of studies, disagreement exists concerning how early the training should occur (Krebs, 1958; McClelland, Atkinson, & Lowell, 1953; McClelland & Friedman, 1952; Winterbottom, 1958). For example, Winterbottom (1958) found that early mastery and independence training of 8-year-old, middle-class boys resulted in the development of strong achievement motivation. Moss and Kagan (1961) maintained that if demands were made too early or too late low achievement motivation resulted.

The lack of agreement concerning when mastery and independence training should occur is not surprising. First, individual differences have not been considered. If nothing else, we do know that children develop at variable rates with little regard to the imposition of chronological age. Recall Veroff's (1969) consideration of the criticality of entering developmental stages at the time appropriate to the child's own abilities and experiences. Second, consideration of the parental intention behind an early push to independence and achievement is an important factor (Heckhausen, 1967). To quote Heckhausen, "A massive, premature pressure for achievement on the part of the parents indicates rather a cold rejection of the child's needs which is not intended to further the child's self-reliance for its own sake" (p. 155).

Child, Storm, and Veroff (1958) and Rosen and D'Andrade (1959) found that training specific to achievement (learning to compare with standards of excellence) contributed even more to the development of achievement motivation than independence training. Perhaps these results serve merely to support the rather well-founded contention that specific transfer has stronger effects than general transfer. If so, then perhaps not only are mastery and independence training important antecedents to the development of achievement motivation, but training specific to achievement is also important. This contention should be considered only as a plausible explanation because the paucity of results in the area prohibit strong predictive statements. Much of the lack of clarity in the literature concerning specific parent-child training attitudes and practices exists because of the extremely complex and variable relationships involved. The sex of the child (Barry, Bacon, & Child, 1957; Baumrind & Black, 1967; Brown, 1966; French & Lesser, 1964; Kagan 1964; Katkovsky, Preston, & Crandall, 1964a, 1964b; Lesser, Krawitch, & Packard, 1963; Roberts & Sutton-Smith, 1969, Veroff, Wilcox, & Atkinson, 1953; Zunich, 1964), the sex of the parent (Katkovsky et al., 1964a, 1964b), the social class of the family (Berkowitz, 1964; Douvan, 1958; Rosen, 1958), and the religion of the family (Berkowitz, 1964; Cofer & Appley, 1964) are all factors contributing to the resultant maze of results.

Of these studies concerning child training attitudes and practices, the study by Rosen and D'Andrade (1959) is the most inclusive and conclusive. Typically, the other studies cited have relied heavily on ethnographic material and the questionnaire or interview methods of data acquisition. In most cases, only the maternal role in child rearing was investigated and the critical paternal role was blatantly ignored. Rosen and D'Andrade systematically observed the parent-child relations on a number of tasks which were devised to involve the parents in their son's performance on the task. The tasks were structured so that observation of the parent's behavior provided information concerning the demands parents made, the sanctions employed to enforce the demands, and the amount of independence the son was allowed. Forty family units each composed of a mother, father, and son were observed. The 40 boys were

9-11 years old and were matched by race, nationality, social class, and IQ. Two groups, high and low need achievers, were identified by use of the Thematic Apperception Test.

The results indicated the following differences between parental behaviors of high and low need achievers. Both parents of high need achievers, in contrast to low need achievers, were more competitive, more involved and interested in their son's performance, had higher aspirations for him to do well, and a higher regard for his competence at problem solving. Further, the high need achievers' parents set standards of excellence and expected above average progress toward their attainment. Findings also indicated differentiated and complementary behavior of mothers and fathers. Mothers of high need achievers were dominant, stressed achievement over self-reliance or independence, showed more involvement in the boys' activities, warmly reinforced achievement behavior, and punished inappropriate behaviors. The fathers of high need achievers stressed autonomy and allowed the boy to compete and function on his own ground, were less dominant, less pushing, and less rejecting than the mothers of high need achievers or the fathers of low need achievers. The fathers served more as important models and were not as involved as the mothers with positively and negatively reinforcing behavior. Further support to these findings was offered by Bradburn (1963), who found that strong father dominance resulted in low achievement motivation in Turkish males.

If appropriate child training and early experiences are not afforded the child, then many of the fundamental abilities and tools necessary for attaining eventual autonomy will be lacking. The stage development of achievement motivation will be hampered and integrated achievement motivation will be difficult to achieve. If failure does result during any one of the developmental stages, then an imbalance between autonomous and social achievement results and the outcome is nonintegrated achievement motivation (Veroff, 1969). Specifically, if failure occurs during the development of the autonomous competence stage, then each ensuing stage will be unsuccessful. The result is the development of a strong motive to avoid failure (M_{af}) and low competence; the consequence is evaluation avoidance.

A successful autonomous competence stage but an unsuccessful social achievement stage results in an imbalance weighted on the side of autonomous achievement. Individuals seek evaluation only through comparison with their own personalized norms or standards. The evaluative information emanating from social comparison is avoided. Consequently, individuals possess the motive to avoid failure and their competence level, although higher than the totally unsuccessful individual, is still low. Recall that autonomy was operationally defined as the "ease in giving and receiving evaluation of self and others" (Foote & Cottrell, 1955, p. 55).

If individuals are unsuccessful during the autonomous competence stage and the social achievement stage, or merely during the social achievement stage, then it is possible that social achievement situations will be vehemently sought. The lack of past success, however, results in a strong motive to avoid failure and low competence. Consequently, the informational function of the social comparison process is not sought and evaluation is avoided. Instead, individuals pursue the normative function of social comparison for the enhancement of self-esteem.

ANTECEDENTS OF COMPETITIVENESS

According to the schema presented in Figure 1, autonomy is the ultimate goal of competence and can only be achieved through the development of competence. Assessment of competence through evaluation is a necessary process for the determination of the sense of competence. The sense of competence is the gauge for determining the level of competence achieved and how well the individual is progressing toward the ultimate goal of autonomy. The primary sources of evaluation are achievement situations. Achievement situations involve comparison with a standard of excellence, outcome uncertainty, and the personal responsibility for the outcome. Consequently, evaluation is the central component of achievement situations. Achievement situations can be either social or nonsocial by nature and can serve informative and/or normative functions. The objective competitive situation is merely a form of a social achievement situation.

The degree to which evaluations result in positive rather than negative outcomes is dependent upon early child training variables including independence and mastery, as well as other experiences necessary for the successful completion of each stage of achievement motivation development. The accrual of positive evaluations results in a success orientation, the tendency to approach evaluation, high competence, and integrated achievement motivation. The accrual of negative evaluations results in a failure orientation, the tendency to avoid evaluation, low competence, and nonintegrated achievement motivation.

Recall that competitiveness is the tendency to approach or avoid competitive situations. A competitive situation is defined by the objective competitive situation as a specific type of social achievement situation. The achievement and evaluation are merely sought through competitive situations. The ensuing hypotheses are offered.

Individuals evidencing integrated achievement motivation are evaluation seekers. Therefore, the individuals are high in competitiveness because the objective competitive situation affords the opportunity to gain information from the evaluation resulting from the social comparison process. This information is crucial to the assessment of competence and the achievement of autonomy. The individuals seek an opponent of equal or slightly superior ability for accurate and realistic self-assessment. Periodically, they might select an opponent of superior ability to serve as a model for learning purposes. However, this behavior will not be frequently evidenced because realistic, precise evaluation is not possible in this situation.

If nonintegrated achievement motivation occurs as the result of failure during one of the stages of achievement motivation, then an imbalance between autonomous and social achievement motivation results. If failure occurs during the autonomous competence stage, then each ensuing stage will be unsuccessful. Consequently, these individuals develop a strong M_{af} and are evaluation avoiders. They avoid the evaluation emanating from objective competitive situations and are low in competitiveness. If forced to compete, these individuals select opponents of inferior or superior ability to lessen the evaluative component. Generally, however, an opponent of inferior ability is selected over an opponent of superior ability.

If failure occurs during the social comparison stage but the autonomous competence stage was successful, these individuals evidence high autonomous achievement motivation. The social achievement situation is avoided and low competitiveness results.

Finally, if individuals are unsuccessful during the autonomous competence stage and the social comparison stage or merely during the social comparison stage, then the normative function of the social comparison process is pursued for the enhancement of self-esteem and not evaluation. These individuals exhibit high competitiveness, perhaps even exaggerated competitiveness, but merely for normative purposes and self-esteem enhancement. The opponents selected would be of inferior ability so that victory is ensured and self-esteem protected.

CONCLUSION

In summary, the approach to competition developed by Martens has been presented and used as the basis for determining the macroscopic antecedents of competitiveness. Determining the macroscopic antecedents of competitiveness was necessary to the development of a theoretical framework that provides order to past research and guidance to future systematic investigations. Now it is possible to take the next step, which is a more microscopic investigation of the antecedents unique to competitiveness. These antecedents can only be determined through empirical investigation. In sum, the state of the art rests with a new approach, a theoretical beginning, and a myriad of empirical questions to be systematically pursued.

REFERENCES

ATKINSON, J.W. Motivational determinants of risk-taking behavior. *Psychological Review*, 1957, **64**, 359-372.

ATKINSON, J.W. Motivational determinants of risk-taking behavior. In J.W. Atkinson (Ed.), *Motives in fantasy, action, and society*. Princeton, NJ: Van Nostrand, 1958. (a)

ATKINSON, J.W. Towards experimental analysis of human motivation in terms of motives, expectancies, and incentives. In J.W. Atkinson (Ed.), *Motives in fantasy, action, and society*. Princeton, NJ: Van Nostrand, 1958. (b)

ATKINSON, J.W. *An introduction to achievement motivation*. Princeton, NJ: Van Nostrand, 1964.

ATKINSON, J.W. The mainsprings of achievement-oriented activity. In J.W. Atkinson & J.O. Raynor (Eds.), *Motivation and achievement*. Washington: V.H. Winston, 1974. (a)

ATKINSON, J.W. Strength of motivation and efficiency of performance. In J.W. Atkinson & J.O. Raynor (Eds.), *Motivation and achievement*. Washington: V.H. Winston, 1974. (b)

ATKINSON, J.W., & Reitman, W.R. Performance as a function of motive strength and expectancy of goal-attainment. In J.W. Atkinson (Ed.), *Motives in fantasy, action, and society*. Princeton, NJ: Van Nostrand, 1958.

BARRY, H., III, Bacon, M.K., & Child, I.L. A cross-cultural survey of some sex differences in socialization. *Journal of Abnormal and Social Psychology*, 1957, **55**, 327-332.

BAUMRIND, D.A., & Black, A.E. Socialization practices associated with dimensions of competence in preschool boys and girls. *Child Development*, 1967, **38**, 291-327.

BERKOWITZ, L. *The development of motives and values in the child*. New York: Basic Books, 1964.

BRADBURN, N.M. Need achievement and father dominance in Turkey. *Journal of Abnormal and Social Psychology*, 1963, **67**, 464-468.

BROWN, D.G. Sex-role development in a changing culture. In J.F. Rosenblith & W. Allinsmith (Eds.), *The causes of behavior: Readings in child development and educational psychology*. Boston: Allyn & Bacon, 1966.

CHILD, I.L., Storm, T., & Veroff, J. Achievement themes in folk tales related to socialization practice. In J.W. Atkinson (Ed.), *Motives in action, fantasy, and society*. Princeton, NJ: Van Nostrand, 1958.

COFER, C.N., & Appley, M.H. *Motivation: Theory and research*. New York: Wiley, 1964.

COOPERSMITH, S. *The antecedents of self-esteem*. San Francisco: W.H. Freeman, 1967.

CRANDALL, V.J., Preston, A., & Rabson, A. Maternal reactions and the development of independence and achievement behavior in young children. *Child Development*, 1960, **31**, 241-251.

DOUVAN, E. Social status and success strivings. In J.W. Atkinson (Ed.), *Motives in fantasy, action, and success*. Princeton, NJ: Van Nostrand, 1958.

ENTIN, E.E. Effects of achievement-oriented and affiliative cues on private and public performance. In J.W. Atkinson & J.O. Raynor (Eds.), *Motivation and achievement*. Washington: V.H. Winston, 1974.

FEATHER, N.T. Success probability and choice behavior. *Journal of Experimental Psychology*, 1959, **58**, 257-266.

FEATHER, N.T. The relationship of expectation of success to need achievement and test anxiety. *Journal of Personality and Social Psychology*, 1965, **1**, 118-127.

FESTINGER, L.A. A theory of social comparison. *Human Relations*, 1954, **7**, 117-140.

FOOTE, N.N., & Cottrell, L.S., Jr. *Identity and interpersonal competence: A new direction in family research*. Chicago: University of Chicago Press, 1955.

FRENCH, E.G. Some characteristics of achievement motivation. In J.W. Atkinson (Ed.), *Motives in fantasy, action, and society*. Princeton, NJ: Van Nostrand, 1958.

FRENCH, E.G., & Lesser, G.S. Some characteristics of the achievement motivation in women. *Journal of Abnormal and Social Psychology*, 1964, **68**, 119-128.

GLADWIN, T. Social competence and clinical practice. *Psychiatry*, 1967, **30**, 30-43.

GRUDER, C.L. Determinants of social comparison. *Journal of Experimental Social Psychology*, 1971, **7**, 473-489.

HAKMILLER, K.L. Threat as a determinant of downward comparison. *Journal of Experimental Social Psychology Supplement*, 1966, **2** (1), 32-39.

HECKHAUSEN, H. *The anatomy of achievement motivation*. New York: Academic Press, 1967.

KAGAN, J. Acquisition and significance of sex typing and sex role identity. In M.L. Hoffman & L.W. Hoffman (Eds.), *Review of child development research*. New York: Russell Sage Foundation, 1964.

KATKOVSKY, W., Preston, A., & Crandall, V.J. Parents' achievement attitudes and their behavior with their children in achievement situations. *Journal of Genetic Psychology*, 1964, **104**, 105-121. (a)

KATKOVSKY, W., Preston, A., & Crandall, V.J. Parents' attitudes toward their personal achievement and toward the achievement behaviors of their children. *Journal of Genetic Psychology*, 1964, **104**, 67-82. (b)

KREBS, A.M. Two determinants of conformity: Age of independence training and need achievement. *Journal of Abnormal and Social Psychology*, 1958, **56**, 130-131.

LESSER, G.S., Krawitz, R.N., & Packard, R. Experimental arousal of achievement motivation in adolescent girls. *Journal of Abnormal and Social Psychology*, 1963, **66**, 59-66.

MARTENS, R. *Social psychology and physical activity*. New York: Harper & Row, 1975.

MARTENS, R. Competition: In need of a theory. In D. Landers (Ed.), *Social problems in athletics*. Urbana: University of Illinois Press, 1976.

MCCLELLAND, D.C. The importance of early learning in the formation of motives. In J.W. Atkinson (Ed.), *Motives in fantasy, action, and society*. Princeton, NJ: Van Nostrand, 1958. (a)

MCCLELLAND, D.C. Risk taking in children with high and low need for achievement. In J.W. Atkinson (Ed.), *Motives in fantasy, action, and society*. Princeton, NJ: Van Nostrand, 1958. (b)

MCCLELLAND, D.C. Testing for competence rather than for "intelligence." *American Psychologist*, 1973, **28**, 1-14.

MCCLELLAND, D.C., Atkinson, J.W., & Lowell, E.L. *The achievement motive*. New York: Appleton-Century-Crofts, 1953.

MCCLELLAND, D.C., & Friedman, G.A. A cross cultural study of the relationship between child-training practices and achievement motivation appearing in folk tales. In G.E. Swanson, T.M. Newcomb, & E.L. Hartley (Eds.), *Readings in social psychology*. New York: Holt, 1952.

MOSS, H.A., & Kagan, J. Stability of achievement and recognition seeking behaviors from early childhood through adulthood. *Journal of Abnormal and Social Psychology*, 1961, **62**, 504-513.

RADLOFF, R. Social comparison and ability evaluation. *Journal of Experimental Social Psychology Supplement*, 1966, **2** (1) 6-26.

ROBERTS, J.M., & Sutton-Smith, B. Child training and game involvement. In J.W. Loy, Jr. & G.S. Kenyon (Eds.), *Sport, culture, and society*. London: MacMillan, 1969.

ROSEN, B.C. The achievement syndrome: A psychocultural dimension of social stratification. In J.W. Atkinson (Ed.), *Motives in fantasy, action and society*. Princeton, NJ: Van Nostrand, 1958.

ROSEN, B.C., & D'Andrade, R. The psychological origins of achievement motivation. *Sociometry*, 1959, **22**, 185-218.

SCANLAN, T.K. Suggested direction for competition research. *Quest*, 1977, pp. 66-75.

SINGER, J.E. Social comparison—progress and issues. *Journal of Experimental Social Psychology Supplement*, 1966, **2** (1), 103-110.

SINGER, J.E., & Shockley, V.L. Ability and affiliation. *Journal of Personality and Social Psychology*, 1965, **1**, 95-100.

SMITH, C.P. Achievement-related motivation and goal setting under different conditions. *Journal of Personality*, 1963, **31**, 124-140.

SMITH, C.P. The influence of testing conditions on need for achievement scores and their relationships to performance scores. In J.W. Atkinson & N.T. Feather (Eds.), *A theory of achievement motivation*. New York: Wiley, 1966.

SMITH, M.B. Competence and socialization. In J.A. Clausen (Ed.), *Socialization and society*. Boston: Little, Brown & Company, 1968.

THORNTON, D.A., & Arrowood, A.J. Self-evaluation, self-esteem, and locus of social comparison. *Journal of Experimental Social Psychology Supplement*, 1966, **2** (1), 40-48.

VEROFF, J. Social comparison and the development of achievement motivation. In C.P. Smith (Ed.), *Achievement-related motives in children*. New York: Russell Sage Foundation, 1969.

VEROFF, J., Wilcox, S., & Atkinson, J.W. The achievement motive in high school and college age women. *Journal of Abnormal Psychology*, 1953, **48**, 108-119.

WEINER, B., & Rosenbaum, R.M. Determinants of choice between achievement- and non-achievement-related activities. *Journal of Experimental Research in Personality*, 1965, **1**, 114-121.

WHEELER, L. Motivation as a determinant of upward comparison. *Journal of Experimental Social Psychology Supplement*, 1966, **2** (1), 27-31.

WHEELER, L., Shaver, K.G., Jones, R.A., Goethals, G.R., Cooper,

J., Robinson, J.E., Gruder, C.L., & Butzine, K.W. Factors determining choice of a comparison. *Journal of Experimental Social Psychology*, 1969, **5**, 219-232.

WHITE, R.W. Motivation reconsidered: The concept of competence. *Psychological Review*, 1959, **66**, 297-334.

WHITE, R.W. Competence and the psychosexual stages of development. In M.R. Jones (Ed.), *Nebraska Symposium on Motivation* (Vol. 8). Lincoln: University of Nebraska Press, 1960.

WINTERBOTTOM, M.R. The relationship of need for achievement to learning experiences and mastery. In J.W. Atkinson (Ed.), *Motives in fantasy, action, and society*. New York: Van Nostrand, 1958.

ZUNICH, M. Children's reactions to failure. *Journal of Genetic Psychology*, 1964, **104**, 19-24.

SECTION 3

ANATOMICAL AND
PHYSIOLOGICAL CONCERNS

There are many controversial issues pertaining to the desirability of youth sports, and one of the most frequently cited concerns is the problem of physical harm. Does participation in youth sports constitute a danger to the anatomical and physiological well-being of children and youth? Beneficial effects of physical activity on human growth and development have been well substantiated, so there is little question that physical activity is necessary for normal growth and that vigorous activity is essential for promoting optimal physical fitness. Some physicians, educators, community leaders, and parents, however, have opposed youth sports on the grounds that they may cause excessive physical stress for participants and can be potentially hazardous for youngsters. More specifically, they have expressed concern about (a) whether stresses of youth sports are sufficiently great to endanger normal growth, (b) whether sports requiring endurance have a deleterious effect on the cardiovascular system of young athletes, and (c) whether the injury risks of youth sports are worth the potential benefits of participation. The chapters which follow are directed to these concerns as well as other salient issues.

In chapter 6, Robert M. Malina presents a comprehensive survey of selected physical growth and maturity characteristics of young male and female athletes—individuals whose physical status is often compared to their nonathletic peers. In a preliminary overview, Malina summarizes the complex interrelationships among maturity status, body size, physique, and body composition in children and adolescents. This information is vital in understanding the relationships between physical growth, biological maturity and athletic performance. He then reviews the evidence on the physical growth and maturational characteristics of young athletes both within specific sports and across sports. Malina also considers the effects of participation in sports (particularly of an endurance type) on various morphological and physiological parameters such as maximal oxygen uptake, vital capacity, and heart volume.

Next, cardiovascular functioning of children and youth in sports is a major concern within the domain of exercise physiology. Donald A. Bailey, in chapter 7, approaches this topic by considering the cardiorespiratory differences between children and adults. Emphasizing that children are not simply scaled-down models of adults, Bailey cites important adult-child differences in reaction to strenuous physical exercise and training for sports. The question of whether or not functional changes resulting from training during youth persist into adult years is considered, along with an examination of problems inherent in investigating training effects in children. Bailey includes both philosophical and physiological perspectives in his discussion of factors contributing to the early identification and development of athletic potential.

The emergence of the female athlete is an interesting revolution that has occurred in youth sports. In chapter 8, Jack H. Wilmore discusses the female athlete, focusing on similarities and differences between young males and females in terms of their body build and composition, strength, cardiovascular endurance capacity, and motor skill development. This chapter, together with the preceding two chapters, provides a well-rounded view of physiological and anatomical issues as they relate to developing young athletes, both male and female.

The last two chapters of this section are written by physicians, and each presents useful guidelines on issues of concern for many youth sport participants. First, Thomas E. Shaffer in chapter 9 presents information pertaining to safeguards of athletes' health, objectives for a medical evaluation of young athletes, and a classification of sports with regard to their physical requirements. The last chapter in this section, by Vincent J. DiStefano, presents helpful guidelines for dealing with athletes' injuries. The author defines contusions, strains, and sprains and provides readers with hints for identifying these injuries. Finally, DiStefano discusses the common injuries to the knee and ankle.

CHAPTER 6

PHYSICAL GROWTH AND MATURITY CHARACTERISTICS OF YOUNG ATHLETES

Robert M. Malina

The social sanction given to childhood sports and the necessary skills for successful participation in these sports gives them awesome valence not only in the child's world, but also in the broader sociocultural complex within which the child lives. Competition is the essence of most sports and emphasis is largely placed on winning. Spectators are more numerous than players, and the winning team usually gets more support than a skillfully played match.

Interscholastic athletic competitions for boys at the high school level is an established feature of the American way of life, while most states now sponsor competitive interscholastic sports for girls at this educational level. On the other hand, interscholastic athletic competition for boys beginning at the elementary school level has increased, as has agency-sponsored athletic competition. Many communities provide some form of agency-sponsored athletic competition for both young boys and girls, often in a coeducational setting.

In addition, the frequency with which young participants compete in international sporting events is increasing. It is not uncommon to see female swimmers and gymnasts who are 12 and 13 years of age, or male swimmers and track athletes who are 15 and 16 years of age in international competitions.

Hence, a consideration of the effects of sports participation on growth and development is in order, as is an overview of the growth and maturity characteristics of youngsters successful in sports. There have been numerous discussions on the role of competitive sports in childhood and adolescence, and it is not within the scope of this review to consider the pros and cons of the situation; suffice it to note that most discussions are based on opinion rather than objective data. This report offers a survey of selected physical growth and maturity characteristics of the young athlete, most commonly between 9 and 16 years of age. Because participation in sport is concerned to a large extent with intensive physical activity in the form of training for a specific sport or event and the competition per se, the effects of regular physical activity on the growing organism also needs consideration; this topic is beyond the scope of this review, however (see Malina, 1979, 1980).

GENERAL CONSIDERATIONS:
WHO IS THE YOUNG ATHLETE?

Because young athletes are different from their age and sex peers in that they are successful in sport, we must consider whether the differences are attributable to physical training or to variability in maturation rate. The former merits serious consideration since the age range comprising childhood athletics usually encompasses the ages 9 through 16 years, and this is a period of significant biological maturity-associated variation in boys and girls (Malina, 1974, 1978; Tanner, 1962). Comparisons of athletes and nonathletes in the later teen years are complicated by the catch-up of late-maturing children, while early-maturing children have decelerated in growth or have already attained adult height. After 16 years of age, for example, the median increments in stature for boys and girls in the Fels longitudinal series were 2.8 cm and 1.1 cm, respectively. After 18 years of age, the median increments in stature for boys and girls were 0.8 cm an 0.6 cm, respectively. Weight gains after 16 and 18 years were 7.5 kg and 3.2 kg respectively in boys, and 1.6 and −0.3 kg respectively in girls (Roche & Davilla, 1975).

Young athletes are usually defined in terms of success on interscholastic or agency teams (especially football, ice hockey, baseball, basketball, and track), in national and international competitions (especially swimming, track, and gymnastics), and in selected athletic club and age-group competitions (especially swimming, gymnastics, and tennis). Young athletes are also a highly selected group, usually on the basis of size and skill. Needless to say, larger size is an advantage in a number of sports and can be a limiting factor in others. Physique might also be a limiting factor, especially at the somatotype extremes. Endomorphy tends to be negatively related to performance on a variety of motor tasks, while ectomorphy tends to be negatively related to strength. Mesomorphy generally correlates well with strength and performance. Correlations between somatotype components and performance, however, are generally low to moderate and limited in predictive utility (Malina, 1975).

One can also inquire as to relationships between physique and activity pursuits: Are individuals with certain physiques predisposed or socialized (including selection) toward certain kinds of physical activity pursuits? Astrand, Engstrom, Eriksson, Karlberg, Nylander, Saltin, and Thoren (1963), for example, studied outstanding young female swimmers who were 12 to 16 years old. They found that the girls learned how to swim, on the average, at 5.8 years of age, with a range from 2.5 to 8 years, and had begun to train before 13 years of age (earliest at 10, latest at 15 years). Further, in 28 of the 30 families represented by the swimmers, one or both parents had been a member of the same swimming club as their children or had been active in sports, whereas 29 of the girl swimmers' 38 siblings were also active in athletics. Märker's (1981) survey of East German women athletes indicated a significant number who began regular "athletic exercises" between 5.5 and 9.0 years of age, specifically in figure skating, gymnastics, and swimming. A survey of university scholarship football players (Malina, Note 1) indicated that all of them had begun playing organized football at or before the fifth grade level (about 10 years of age). Thus, the selection process for athletic ability apparently begins early in life in some sports, and familial influences appear significant. The interrelationships of these factors and genetic factors (e.g., heritability of body size and aerobic capacity) must be considered (see Bouchard & Malina, in press).

Before evaluating the growth characteristics of young athletes, the interrelationships of maturity status, body size, physique, and body composition in children must be considered. In many analyses of these relationships, early- and late-maturing children are compared. Biological maturity, however, is a continuum upon which these categories are superimposed. Early-maturing (skeletal age, age at menarche, etc.) boys and girls are generally heavier and taller age for age, and have more weight for height than their slower maturing peers. Extreme mesomorphy tends to be related to early maturation in boys, whereas endomorphy and earliness are related in girls. On the other hand, extreme ectomorphy or linearity in physique is associated with lateness in maturity in both sexes. Children advanced in maturity status have generally larger amounts of fat, muscle, and bone tissues, and a larger lean body mass, reflecting to some extent their larger body size than late-maturing children (Malina, 1974, 1975; Malina & Johnston, 1967; Malina & Rarick, 1973).

Thus, any evaluation of the relationship between maturity status and athletic performance must consider the relationships among size, build, composition, and maturity status. In their classic studies of strength and performance during adolescence, Jones (1949) and Espenschade (1940) reported positive maturity relationships for boys. Early-maturing boys are stronger age for age than their average- and late-maturing peers, with the differences between the early- and late-maturing boys being most marked between 13 and 16 years of age. These extreme differences are in part a function of the size differences between the early- and late-maturing groups. The strength differences so evident during the peak of male adolescence are considerably reduced in later adolescence with the catch-up of late maturing boys. Early-maturing girls are stronger than late maturers early in adolescence, but they do not maintain this superiority as the adolescent period approaches its termination (Jones, 1949). Motor performance of adolescent boys is also positively and significantly related to biological maturity status. Early-maturing boys generally perform better than late maturers (Ellis, Carron, & Bailey, 1975; Espenschade, 1940; Clarke, 1971). Motor performance of adolescent girls, on the other hand, is poorly related to maturity status. However, better performance levels are generally reported for later maturing girls (Beunen, de Beul, Ostyn, Renson, Simons, & van Gerven, 1978; Espenschade, 1940), and the differences between contrasting maturity groups are more apparent in later adolescence (16-18 years).

Young Male Athletes

Data considering maturity status and relationships to size, physique, and body composition in young athletes are not extensive and are limited to several sports. Much of the data are limited to height and weight, and more recently, body composition estimates. Compared to their nonathletic peers, young male athletes (approximately 9 to 16 years of age) are generally advanced in sexual and skeletal maturity, taller and heavier, more mesomorphic, and stronger. The data, however, are not entirely consistent within sports and across sports.

Combined Sports. Before looking at participants in specific sports, the early and frequently misquoted study of Rowe (1933) should be considered. Comparing growth in height and weight of junior high school athletes and nonathletes (matched on age, height, and weight) over a 2-year period from 13.75 to 15.75 years, Rowe noted that the athletes were bigger, but grew at a slower rate over the 2-year period. Since biological maturity status of the sample was not controlled, Rowe stressed that the observed differences probably reflect differential timing of the adolescent spurts: "Since the athletic group is composed of boys who have matured earlier, age considered, than the group of non-athletic boys, the athletic boy is not going to grow as much as the non-athletic boy over the period studied" (p. 115). In a similar study comparing male junior high school athetes and nonathletes, Shuck (1962) reported greater heights and weights, and "speeds of growth" (as assessed by the Wetzel Grid) among the athletes. The athletes showed no marked acceleration or retardation in height and weight growth that could be related to athletic participation. Interestingly, ninth graders participating in multiple interschool sports did not grow as well as those participating in a single sport. The reverse was true, however, at the seventh and eighth grade levels. With one exception, years of participation, total games played, and length of season apparently had no marked effect on growth in height and weight of the junior high school athletes.

Baseball. Data from the 1957 Little League World Series (Krogman, 1959) suggested that success of the young baseball players was related to their skeletal maturity status. Of the 55 finalists, 11 years to 13 years 11 months, 71% (39) had skeletal ages in advance of their chronological ages and 29% (16) had skeletal ages delayed relative to their chronological ages. To have a skeletal age within 1 year, plus or minus, one's chronological age is generally considered normal variation, comprising the broad range of "average" maturing children. Children with skeletal ages 1 or more years delayed relative to their chronological ages are "late" maturers, while those with skeletal ages 1 or more years advanced relative to their chronological ages are "early" maturers. When the Little League participants were viewed under these commonly used maturity ranges, 5 boys had delayed skeletal ages, 25 had skeletal ages in the average or normal range, and 25 had advanced skeletal ages (Krogman, 1959). In the words of Krogman (1959), "In general, the successful Little League ball player is old for his age, i.e., he is biologically advanced. This boy succeeds, it may be argued, because he is more mature, biologically more stable, and structurally and functionally more advanced" (p. 55).

Similar results were noted in a study of the pubic hair development (Crampton's 3-point scale) of 112 participants in the 1955 Little League World Series (Hale, 1956). Most of the young athletes were pubescent (37.5%) or postpubescent (45.5%). Maturity also appeared related to position and batting order: Starting pitchers, first basemen, and left fielders were generally postpubescent, and all boys who batted in the fourth position were postpubescent. In terms of height and weight, the postpubescent boys equaled the standards for 14-year-old boys. In contrast to these observations on Little League finalists, successful baseball players at the upper elementary and senior high school levels in the Medford Boys' Growth Study (Clarke, 1968, 1971, 1973) did not show significant maturity, physique, and size differences relative to nonparticipants (mean values not reported).

Basketball. Skeletal maturity, physique, and body size did not significantly differ between basketball athletes and nonparticipants from 9 through 12 years of age in the Medford study (Clarke, 1968, 1971, 1973). However, at the junior high level (12 to 15 years) height, weight, and skeletal age differed between the participants and nonparticipants. This, of course, emphasizes the variability characteristic of male adolescence and the size advantage of early-maturing boys at this time. At both the upper elementary and junior high levels (9-15 years), the basketball athletes were also significantly better in strength, the standing broad jump, and shuttle run. At the high school level (15 to 17 years), the morphological characteristic distinguishing basketball players was, as one might expect, height. Though not significant at all ages, the athletes tended to be mesomorphic. They were also consistently stronger in arm strength and faster in the shuttle run. The lack of significant skeletal maturity differences at the senior high school ages probably reflects the attainment of skeletal maturity by many youngsters as well as the catch-up of late-maturing boys.

Football. Young football athletes in the Medford Boys' Growth Study (Clarke, 1968, 1971, 1973) were significantly advanced in skeletal age, strength, the standing broad jump, and the shuttle run at all ages from 10 through 15 years compared to nonparticipating boys. They were significantly taller and heavier between 12 and 15 years, suggesting a somewhat earlier adolescent spurt. At the senior high school level, the football players were most characterized by a consistently greater strength index, which is, undoubtedly, partly a function of training procedure. Though not consistent from 15 through 17 years, the football athletes were significantly taller and more mesomorphic in some of the age group comparisons.

In a comparison of high school football and basketball players ($n = 18$) and nonathletes ($n = 20$), Novak (1966) reported significant body composition differences between the groups. The athletes and nonathletes did not differ in age (about 17 years), height, and weight; however, the athletes (combined, not separated by sport) had greater body densities, a lesser percentage of body weight as fat (7.2% compared to 14.9%), and greater musculature (estimated from creatinine excretion and corrected limb girths). The lean body mass-fatness differences between the athletes and nonathletes probably reflect training effects. It is interesting to note, though, that the body weights of both the athletes and nonathletes were approximately 10% above the standard, while the heights equaled the standard. This suggests that both groups had more weight for their height relative to the standards used. The excess weight in the nonathletes is probably associated with fatness, whereas that in the athletes is related to lean tissue.

Ice Hockey. Among 280 tournament "PeeWee" hockey players 10 to 13 years of age, Bouchard and Roy (1969) found skeletal age, on the average, slightly delayed relative to chronological age (11.7 ± 1.1 and 12.0 ± 0.4 years, respectively). When grouped by position, boys playing defense were taller, heavier, and slightly advanced skeletally (SA = 12.3 ± 1.0; CA = 12.1 $\pm$ 0.5) than goalkeepers (SA = 11.3 $\pm$ 1.0; CA = 11.9 $\pm$ 0.8) and forwards (SA = 11.5 $\pm$ 1.1; CA = 12.0 $\pm$ 0.5). Within specific age groups, however, correlations between skeletal age and game performance of forwards and defensemen (goals and assists) were low (-0.30 to $+.28$). Comparisons of the cortical bone dimensions of the second metacarpal in these young hockey players indicated absolutely larger dimensions in the defensive players, but relatively larger dimensions in the forwards after size, chronological age, and skeletal age were statistically controlled (Meleski, Malina, & Bouchard, 1981). And compared to nonathletes, the young hockey players had significantly larger cortical bone dimensions after controlling for size differences.

In a sample (n = 16) of Czechoslovak ice hockey players followed longitudinally from 12 through 15 years of age, Kotulán, Reznickova, and Placheta (1980) reported generally similar results. Compared to a sample of control subjects (n = 34), the hockey players were shorter, lighter, slightly delayed in skeletal maturity and leaner with greater $\dot{V}O_2$ max. The sample, however, was too small to compare the players by position.

Track. Track athletes in the Medford study (Clarke, 1968, 1971, 1973) did not differ from nonathletes in maturity, size, or physique at the upper elementary level (9-12 years). They were, however, significantly stronger (11-12 years) and performed better in the jump and shuttle run. At the junior high level (12-15 years), the track athletes were significantly advanced in skeletal maturity, height, strength, strength endurance, the standing broad jump, and the shuttle run compared to the nonparticipants. The track athletes were also significantly more mesomorphic and less endomorphic at 14 and 15 years of age. At the senior high school level, the track athletes and nonparticipants were not significantly different in height, but different in physique (mesomorphy), perhaps representing selection for skill in track events and perhaps the catch-up of late-maturing boys.

Among boys 11 to 18 years (n = 101) enrolled in a camp for track and field athletes, Cumming, Garand, and Borysyk (1972) reported a composite skeletal age slightly in advance of the group's chronological age (15.2 ± 1.7 years and 14.9 ± 1.3 years, respectively). Though the difference is small, it is in the direction reported earlier for track athletes at the junior high school level (Clarke, 1971). Skeletal age was a better predictor of performance in track and field tests than chronological age, but the correlations were at best moderate (partial r's controlling for height and weight ranged from .27 to .50).

Among a sample of Junior Olympic track and field athletes (18 years of age and under) Thorland, Johnson, Fagot, Tharp, and Hammer (1981) noted large size and body composition differences between throwers and those in other events. The throwers were especially larger in stature, weight, mesomorphy, lean body weight, and fatness compared to runners, hurdlers, jumpers, vaulters, and walkers. Among the latter, there were no significant body composition differences, although stature and weight varied somewhat.

Three studies which assessed the effects of endurance running training on boys between 10 and 15 years of age (Daniels & Oldridge, 1971; Ekblom, 1969a, 1969b; Eriksson, 1972) did not include measures of maturity status. The boys, nevertheless, had heights and weights at the start of training which corresponded to accepted growth standards. In

Ekblom's study, the boys (11 years old at the start of the study) who trained for 32 months ($n = 5$) showed a somewhat accelerated growth rate in weight and stature compared to Swedish standards, while the reference group ($n = 4$) did not. It is difficult to consider the accelerated growth relative to the training program, because maturity status was not controlled and the boys could have experienced all or part of their adolescent spurts (they approached 14 years of age at the termination of the program). There is, furthermore, considerable variation in the timing and intensity of the adolescent growth spurt (see Malina, 1978; Tanner, 1962). In addition, the trained boys ($n = 5$) increased in both maximal oxygen uptake (55%) and in maximal oxygen uptake per kilogram of body weight (7%) after 32 months of training. Heart volume (43%) and vital capacity (54%) also improved with training. The reference or untrained control group ($n = 4$) also improved in these functional measures after 32 months, but to a smaller extent—maximal oxygen uptake, 37%; maximal oxygen uptake per kilogram of body weight, 7%; heart volume, 36%; and vital capacity, 34%. The relative increase in maximal oxygen uptake per kilogram of body weight was identical in both the trained and untrained groups (7%).

The six boys (10-15 years of age) studied by Daniels and Oldridge (1971) trained for 22 months in endurance running. At the start of training, stature equaled the standard used, but weight was slightly below. After 22 months, stature was slightly below the standard, while body weight was considerably lower. With training maximal oxygen uptake improved (22%), but relative to body weight it remained essentially unchanged (-2%). These observations are thus in contrast to those of Ekblom (1969a, 1969b), whose trained boys showed an apparently accelerated growth rate and a relative increase in maximal oxygen uptake per kilogram of body weight. As with many studies of training effects with small samples, however, statistical significance of apparent changes is not generally reported.

Eriksson (1972, see also v. Döbeln & Eriksson, 1972) observed functional and morphological changes in 12 boys, 11 to 13 years of age, after 16 weeks of endurance training. The boys increased, on the average, 3.5 cm in height and 1.0 kg in weight over this time. However, nine of the 12 boys who had their total body potassium measured gained, on the average, only 0.5 kg in weight, but 12 grams in potassium. A 12-gram increase corresponds to a gain of about 4 kg of muscle tissue, which would indicate that the 0.5 kg gain in weight was accompanied by a loss of about 3 kg of fat during the 16 weeks of training (v. Döbeln & Eriksson, 1972). Relative to growth in height (K/H^3), the increase in potassium was 6% more than expected, while the gain in body weight (W/H^3) was about 5% less than expected. Whether these changes are the result of training or normal adolescent growth is not clear; nevertheless, the average gain of 3.5 cm in stature over 4 months would correspond to an annual gain of 10 cm, which would seem to suggest the adolescent spurt with its concomitant increase in muscularity. The trained boys also improved in maximal oxygen uptake by approximately 20%, and by 16% relative to weight and 14% relative to height squared. These relative increments are somewhat higher than those reported by Ekblom (1969a, 1969b) and clearly higher than those of Daniels and Oldridge (1971). When the maximal oxygen uptake gains with training are expressed relative to height squared in these two studies, the former boys showed a gain of 25%, while the latter had a gain of only 5% (Eriksson, 1972).

Although these studies of endurance training programs indicate some functional improvement with training, the results do not always agree, and statistical significance is not generally considered. Training programs probably varied in duration, frequency, and intensity, and in work task used. Sample sizes are characteristically small and variability is great, and the boys varied in aerobic capacity prior to the start of the training programs. For example, the six boys reported by Daniels and Oldridge (1971) had a higher average maximal oxygen uptake per kilogram of body weight (59.5) than the six of Ekblom (1969a, 1969b) (53.9) and the 12 of Eriksson (1972) (42.2) at the start of training. After training, Daniels and Oldridge's boys showed no increase relative to body weight, whereas those of Ekblom and Eriksson improved by 7% and 16%, respectively. Thus, higher max $\dot{V}O_2$ values at the start of training may explain the smaller increases with training. This is true for adults, in whom a negative relationship ($r = -.51$) between initial maximal aerobic power and induced training changes exists (Bouchard, Carrier, Boulay, Poirier, & Dulac, 1975). Note that a correlation of this moderate magnitude accounts for about 25% of the estimated variance.

Reported changes in maximal oxygen uptake with training are in part related to the phenomena of male adolescence—morphological, physiological, and endocrinological. Nevertheless, the data suggest a functional improvement with training over that expected to accompany normal growth. Relative to this suggestion for boys in endurance running programs are results of a longitudinal study of 14 active and 11 inactive boys (Mirwald, Bailey, Cameron, & Rasmussen, 1981). No significant differences in the statures of the two groups existed; however, a significantly greater $\dot{V}O_2$ max attained by age of peak velocity, a greater gain in $\dot{V}O_2$ max from the beginning of the adolescent spurt to the peak, and greater adult values were evident in the active boys. The observations suggest that adolescence is a critical period for $\dot{V}O_2$ max development, as activity before adolescence had little if any effect on $\dot{V}O_2$ max. One can thus inquire: What is normal for adolescent boys, their functional status before or after training? V. Döbeln and Eriksson (1972, p. 659) suggest it is the latter: "Living conditions of the subjects with respect to physical activity were abnormal before training . . . . The change in their body composition and physical performance reflected their normalization as a result of physical training."

Swimming. Data for young male swimmers is not as extensive as that for the preceding sports. A survey of the 28 "best young Hungarian swimmers" 8 to 15 years of age showed skeletal age to be advanced on the average by 2.6 months (s.d. 4.0 months) over chronological age (Bugyi & Kausz, 1970). Another study of 30 Hungarian swimmers (subjects were 16 males and 14 females, but the results were not analyzed by sex) had a distribution of skeletal age as follows by the authors' criteria: retarded (SA 6 months below CA)—6, average deviation 27.5 ± 12.1 months; normal (SA within ± 6 months of CA)—14; accelerated (SA 6 months in advance of CA)—10, average acceleration 14.1 ± 5.6 months (Szabo, Doka, Apor, & Somogyvari, 1972; Szabo-Wahlstab, Doka, Apor, & Somogyvari, 1973). The distribution indicated more swimmers of normal and accelerated skeletal maturity. Interestingly, the average chronological ages of the retarded and accelerated groups were 12.5 and 12.7 years respectively, while that of the normal group was 13.4 years. The accelerated maturity group, as one would expect, was heavier than the normal group, which in turn was heavier than the retarded group. The same pattern was also apparent for maximal oxygen uptake per kilogram of body weight, vital capacity, and 100 m free style swimming speed. Heart volume, however, did not differ among the three maturity groups. Although sexes were combined in this study, the results illustrate the interrelatedness of maturity, size, functional capacity, and performance in a group of young swimmers who had a training history of 5 years. A small sample ($n = 10$-11) of male swimmers under 18 years of age at the Montreal Olympic Games in 1976 were accelerated in skeletal maturity of the hand and wrist relative to reference data (Malina, Bouchard, Shoup, Demirjian, & Lariviere, in press). In addition, they were slightly taller and especially heavier than the reference data with thinner skinfolds.

Observations by Andrew, Becklake, Guleria, and Bates (1972) on young male competitive swimmers (8 to 18 years from swim clubs) over a 3-year period indicated greater body size after 12 years of age; higher lung volumes and flow rates relative to stature, especially in the older boys; higher exercise diffusion capacity; and reduced exercise cardiac output for a given $\dot{V}O_2$ compared to a reference sample of nonathletes. Similar results for young male swimmers ($n = 28$, 10 to 16 years, representing swim teams) were reported by Cunningham and Eynon (1973). The young male swimmers did not differ in height relative to the standard, but were slightly heavier. Maximal oxygen uptake and PWC_{170} were higher than those reported for nonathletic boys. Comparing 13- ($n = 11$), 14- ($n = 12$), and 15- ($n = 10$) year-old swimmers to each other and to selected reference populations, Sobolova, Seliger, Grussova, Machovcoca, & Zelenka (1971) found the athletes leaner, but not different in height and weight. The swimmers, however, had generally better functional measures, which, of course, reflected their degree of physical training. Because the maturity status of the swimmers in these studies was not considered, it is difficult to draw firm conclusions from that data relative to the contribution of physical training to the growth of young swimmers. Statements such as the following would seem to imply a relationship to the young swimmers' maturity status: "With increasing age and increasing duration of sports training, average value for height and weight approach the upper limits of normal growth even more" (Sobolova et al., 1971, p. 64). Some of the functional measures, nevertheless, obviously reflect the effects of regular, year-round training for competitive swimming. In a study of 37 age group swimmers 8 to 18 years of age, Meleski (1980) reported that the younger swimmers were taller and heavier, somewhat advanced in the development of secondary sex characteristics, and especially leaner than nonathletic reference data. At the older ages, that is, as sexual maturity is attained, the size differences were negligible, but the body composition differences persisted, apparently reflecting the training program.

In older swimmers of national caliber (mean age 17.3 ± 1.4 years) Andersen and Magel (1970, see also Magel & Andersen, 1969) reported observations similar to those noted for younger competitive swimmers. The champion swimmers ($n = 10$) were taller, heavier, and fatter (sum of three skinfolds) than nonathletic school boys of the same age. The swimmers also had larger maximal oxygen uptake, lung volumes, functional lung capacities, and pulmonary diffusing capacities.

Cycling. Studying the effects of training for bicycle racing, Berg and Bjure (1974, see also Berg, 1972) followed a small group of boys ($n = 13$, 10 to 15 years) for 3 years. The heights and weights of the boys equaled the standard, but they had a low body fat content (8%) at the start of the study. It should be noted that the boys had been training 1 to 2 years prior to the study. After 3 years of training, the boys showed only small increases in body cell mass and total body water relative to body weight and, thus, little fluctuation in relative body fatness. Maximal oxygen uptake per kilogram of body cell mass increased sharply during the first 6 months of training and remained stable thereafter. Relative to the cube of height (H^3), maximal oxygen uptake increased during the third year of training. This probably reflects the accelerated growth rate of male adolescence. Since no control group was similarly followed, Berg and Bjure (1974) commented that "it is not possible to state . . . if long-term changes observed here were actually due to training or to be expected at these different stages of puberty in all adolescent boys" (p. 189).

In a small sample ($n = 6$) of Czechoslovak cyclists followed longitudinally from 12 through 15 years of age, Kotulán et al. (1980) reported larger stature and weight, advanced skeletal maturity, extreme leanness, and greater $\dot{V}O_2$ max in the cyclists compared to 34 control subjects also followed longitudinally over the same ages. The differences were apparent in the first year of the study and persisted throughout.

Young Female Athletes

Maturity and growth observations on young female athletes are not as extensive as those for young male athletes, except for swimmers. In light of current trends, however, such data will become more available as young girls participate more in sports.

Swimming. Data for young female athletes are most available for competitive swimmers, beginning with the now classic study of girl swimmers by Astrand and his colleagues (1963). Of the 30 swimmers (11.9 to 16.4 years of age), 29 had already attained menarche, giving a mean age of 12.9 years (range 11.0 to 14.9 years). This average age is similar to Swedish reference data of the time period (Ljung, Bergsten-Brucefors, & Lindgren, 1974). In a comparison of young swimmers 10 to 12 years of age who reached the finals of a national age group competition and those who reached the semi-finals (n = 34), Bar-Or (1975) found that the finalists were somewhat more mature in the development of secondary sex characteristics (breasts and pubic hair) even though they were slightly younger chronologically (11.6 ± 0.7 compared to 11.9 ± 0.6 years). Meleski (1980), however, noted breast and pubic hair development in age group swimmers similar to that for reference data for American girls (Harlan, Harlan, & Grillo, 1980). In Meleski's sample, the mean age at menarche was 13.1 years, which is comparable to other data for swimmers (see Malina, in press). With skeletal age as the maturity indicator, young female swimmers tend to be slightly advanced for their chronological age (Bugyi & Kausz, 1970; Malina et al., in press; Szabo, 1969). The slight advancement is well within the range labeled as "average."

Growth and functional characteristics of the young female swimmers have been considered in detail by Astrand et al. (1963). As a group, the girls were taller than the Swedish standards and had normal weight for height. Examination of their school records indicated that the girls were taller than average from 7 years of age. After age 12, their heights appeared to deviate (accelerate) more from the standards than before this age. Mean deviation in height for age expressed as a fraction of the standard deviation was +0.61 ± 0.81 at the time of the study, while the mean deviation at 7 years of age was +0.37 ± 0.87. This acceleration, however, was not related to the intense swimming training. It is perhaps related to their somewhat earlier menarche: 8 girls attained menarche between 11.0 and 11.9 years, 7 girls in the 12th year, 10 girls in the 13th year, and 4 girls in the 14th year. Menarche usually follows peak velocity (Tanner, 1962), so that one might expect the girls to be somewhat taller.

Functional measures of the young swimmers were consistently above those for normal girls of corresponding body size: 11 to 15% for lung volumes except residual volume (about 1 standard deviation unit); 14% for blood volume (about 1.5 s.d. units); 19% for total hemogobin (about 4 s.d. units); 22% for heart volume (about 2.5 s.d. units); and 10% for maximal oxygen uptake relative to body weight (about 1.6 s.d. units). Within the sample of 30 girls, differences in the functional measures were related to the individual girl's "training volume" (hours/week; meters/week); that is, the girls with greater training volumes generally had greater lung volumes, heart volume, and functional capacity, and vice versa. The apparent height acceleration of the girls was not related to increased functional development relative to body size. Engstrom, Eriksson, Karlberg, Saltin, and Thoren (1971) have reported essentially identical results for lung volumes in young girl swimmers 9 through 13 years (n = 29), who were followed longitudinally for 3 years. Lung volumes increased to larger than normal after early years of training and then increased only relative to height. This latter observation would seem to relate the lung volume change to rapid height growth during adolescence. All girls in the study reached menarche between 12 and 14 years, and girls training during this period (n = 12) experienced a significantly greater increase in vital capacity relative to height than girls not in training (n = 6). The two groups of girls did not differ over this time in functional residual capacity and total lung capacity, however.

Among 40 age group swimmers 8 to 18 years of age, Meleski (1980) noted that the younger swimmers were taller and heavier than reference data; the older swimmers were lighter but did not differ in height compared to the reference data. At all ages, however, the swimmers were especially leaner. Premenarcheal and postmenarcheal swimmers had a densitometrically estimated percentage of body fat of 15.3% and 16.5%, respectively. Similar size and body composition trends were apparent in an independent sample of 38 swimmers 11 through 20 years of age (Meleski, Shoup, & Malina, in press). Similar trends are also apparent in a sample of 25 swimmers under 18 years of age at the Montreal Olympic Games in 1976 (Malina et al., in press).

Bar-Or (1975) also reported greater heights, lean body mass, vital capacity, and functional development in young female swimming finalists compared to the semi-finalists 10 to 12 years of age. Andrew et al. (1972) reported greater body size after 12 years of age, higher lung volumes, and flow rates relative to stature especially at the older ages, and reduced exercise cardiac output for a given $\dot{V}O_2$ in competitive female swimmers, 8 to 18 years of age, over a 3-year period. And, Cunningham and Eynon (1973) reported higher maximal oxygen uptakes and PWC_{170} in competitive female swimmers (n = 19, 11 to 16 years of age), although their heights and weights did not deviate from the standard. As in the case of the young boys in these studies, maturity status was not considered so that it is difficult to draw firm conclusions relative to the effects of physical training on the growth of young swimmers. Nevertheless, some of the functional improvement is obviously related to the year-round training for competitive swimming.

Track. Observations on young female track athletes are limited.

Among girls 12 to 18 years of age ($n = 158$) enrolled in a camp for track and field athletes, Cumming et al. (1972) noted a composite skeletal age slightly delayed relative to the group's chronological age (14.6 ± 1.3 and 15.0 ± 1.2 years, respectively). Skeletal age did not predict performance in track and field in these girls as well as it did for boys (see earlier discussion). After controlling for body size, skeletal age was related to performance in only four of nine track and field events (partial r's ranged from 0.009 to 0.81). These results are generally similar to those on nonathlete adolescent girls reported by Espenschade (1940). Among these girls, performance, including several track and field-related items—50 yard dash and standing broad jump—was not related to skeletal age or the age at menarche. Later maturing girls, however, tended to be the better performers.

Among a sample of Junior Olympic track and field athletes (18 years of age and under), Thorland et al. (1981) noted large size physique and composition differences between throwers and those in other events. The differences were similar to those noted earlier for males in this study. Throwers were taller, heavier, more mesomorphic and endomorphic, larger in lean body weight, and fatter than the other track athletes, who did not differ markedly from each other.

In a study of 12 girls, 8 to 13 years of age (from track clubs), who underwent 12 weeks of cross-country running, Brown, Harrower, and Deeter (1972) reported changes similar to those noted for young boys in track training. The girls showed slight height and weight gains as expected over 12 weeks of training, but improved in maximal oxygen uptake by 18.5% after 6 weeks of training and 26.2% after 12 weeks. Thus, the majority of improvement in maximal oxygen uptake occurred during the first 6 weeks of training. The maturity of these girls was not considered relative to training-associated changes. None of the girls had attained menarche prior to the start of training, although several girls over 11 years of age showed early pubertal changes. During the training program, the two oldest girls experienced menarche.

Gymnastics. Focusing on body composition changes in young female gymnasts ($n = 10$, 13 to 18 years) longitudinally over a 5-year period, Pařizkova (1963, 1973) noted fluctuations in body fatness relative to the intensity of training. Body density also showed similar variation with intensity of training. Compared to girls who did not train regularly ($n = 7$), the gymnasts had significantly less fat and more lean body mass after 5 years, even though the two groups did not differ in height and weight. These observations are thus similar to those observed in young males undergoing intensive physical training programs.

Maturity status of young female gymnasts was not considered in Pařizkova's (1963, 1973) data, but young gymnasts are generally delayed in skeletal maturity (Beunen, Claessens, & van Esser, 1981; Malina et al., in press; Novotny & Taftlova, 1971). Young gymnasts are also significantly smaller (height and weight) and leaner than reference data (Beunen et al., 1981; Malina et al., in press; Thorland et al., 1981), perhaps reflecting their delayed maturity status and/or selection for specific physique characteristics.

Retrospective Studies of Menarche in Female Athletes

Maturity status of female athletes can also be inferred from retrospective studies of athletes regarding their reported ages at menarche, or the first menstrual flow. A detailed summary of such data has recently been compiled by Malina (in press). The data suggest that, with few exceptions, menarche is attained later in athletes than in nonathletes. Swimmers are an apparent exception in that they more commonly attain menarche at an age which approximates the average for nonathletes. The data also suggest an association between delayed menarche and more advanced competitive levels.

Training and Menarche. The relationship between training before menarche and the timing of menarche is currently of considerable interest, given the conclusion of Frisch and her colleagues (1981, p. 1582) "that intense physical activity does in fact delay menarche." This conclusion, however, is based upon a small sample of 12 swimmers and 6 runners who began training before menarche. Correlation analysis indicated a relationship between training before menarche and the age of menarche. Correlation, however, indicates only a relationship between the two variables, but does not indicate a cause-effect relationship. It could well have been that the young women took up training because of their delayed maturation rather than the training causing late maturation.

If the small amount of data offered by Frisch et al. (1981) is examined more closely, one can question the representativeness of the sample. The mean age at menarche for the total sample of swimmers (13.9 years), for example, is the latest on record for contemporary swimmers (see Malina, in press). The lateness of Frisch et al.'s swimmers is due in part to two who had attained menarche at 19.1 years, and one of these had menarche induced at this age. Moreover, data on the distribution of ages at menarche in athletes from several sports rarely show menarcheal ages as late as 19 years, and this is apparent in contemporary and earlier data (Malina, in press). Thus, the normality of the two swimmers who attained menarche at 19 years of age may perhaps be questioned. It is also worth noting, perhaps, that in a report describing the critical weight hypothesis for the timing of menarche, Frisch and Revelle (1970) deleted three girls who attained menarche at weights greater than 70 kg. They were considered "clearly abnormal."

The suggested mechanism for the association between intensive training and delayed menarche is hormonal. It is suggested that intensive training and associated energy drain influences circulating levels of gonadotrophic and ovarian hormones, and this in turn delays menarche. The endocrine data offered to support this notion, however, are derived largely from studies of women, athletes and nonathletes, case studies, and extremely small samples, who have already attained menarche (see Malina, in press). The evidence indicates short-term exercise increments in hormone levels, including almost all gonadotrophic and sex steroid hormones. What is specifically relevant for premenarcheal girls is the possible cumulative effects of hormonal responses to regular training. The hormonal responses are apparently essential to meet the stress which intense physical activity imposes upon the body. Do they have an effect on the hypothalamic center which apparently triggers menarche? Such data are presently lacking.

A corrollary of the suggestion that training delays menarche is that the weight or body composition changes associated with training may function to delay menarche, that is, delay maturity of young girls by keeping them lean. This is, in turn, related to the critical weight or fatness hypothesis (Frisch, 1976) that a certain level of fatness must be attained for menarche to occur. This hypothesis has been discussed at length by many (Johnston, Roche, Schell, & Wettenhall, 1975; Malina, 1978; Trussell, 1980), with the conclusion that the data do not support the specificity of weight or fatness as the critical variable for menarche.

Training and Skeletal Maturity. Since there is a moderately high correlation between age at menarche and skeletal maturity, and a reduced variance in skeletal ages at menarche (Malina, 1978), one can inquire about the possible effects of training on skeletal maturation. The process of skeletal maturation—ossification, shape changes in epiphyseal centers and eventual union with the corresponding diaphyses—is influenced by gonadal hormones among others. Hence, if the hormonal responses to regular training influence sexual maturation, one might expect them to influence skeletal maturation, especially circumpuberally. Data for girls are not available. Two studies of Czechoslovak boys engaged in regular training (Cerny, 1969; Kotulán et al., 1980) indicate no such effects; that is, the process of skeletal maturity is not seemingly affected by regular physical training in young adolescent boys.

OVERVIEW

Young athletes of both sexes grow as well as nonathletes, i.e., the experience of athletic training and competition does not have harmful effects on the physical growth and development of the youngster. The young trained athlete is also generally leaner, that is, has a lesser percentage of body weight as fat. Young athletes, especially those in endurance-type sports, show higher functional measures, particularly maximal oxygen consumption. Maturity relationships are not consistent across sports. Male athletes more often than not tend to be advanced maturationally compared to nonathletes. These differences seem more apparent in sports or positions within sports where size is a factor. On the other hand, female athletes tend to be delayed in maturity status, except for swimmers.

Numerous opinions suggest that the larger size and/or optimal growth of the young athlete is due to training. Regular training has no effect on stature, skeletal maturity, or sexual maturity. It is a significant factor influencing the growth and integrity of specific tissues as bone, muscle, and fat, and the development and maintenance of aerobic capacity (see Malina, 1979, 1980, in press). Few studies, however, have really considered the complex interrelationships of chronological age, biological age (skeletal, menarche), and body size. For example, some data indicate that the capacity to perform near or at optimal intensity for prolonged work is related to skeletal age during growth (Beunen, et al., 1974; Bouchard, Malina, Hollmann, & Leblanc, 1976; Hebbelinck, Borms, & Clarys, 1971; Kirchhoff, Reindell, & Hauswaldt, 1958; Rous & Vank, 1970). These relationships, however, tend to be low to moderate and can be translated into common variance estimates ranging from 0 to 50%. The estimates vary with age and the nature of the physical work capacity criteria used. Some data also suggest that the relationship between skeletal age and submaximal work capacity is somewhat higher during male adolescence. Work capacity is also related to chronological age, height, and weight, however, and skeletal age, chronological age, height, and weight are themselves highly related during adolescence (Bouchard et al., 1976).

The relationships between growth, maturity, and athletic performance are indeed complex. Further, most of the data are derived from small cross-sectional samples, and the small amount of longitudinal data available is treated in a cross-sectional manner. This immediately emphasizes the need for longitudinal studies of young athletes and appropriate controls.

There is also a need for follow-up studies of young athletes, as they are related to the question of the persistence of training-associated changes. A number of changes in response to short-term training are generally not permanent and vary with the quantity of training. This is especially clear in the fluctuating levels of fatness in young gymnasts over five years (Pařizkova, 1963, 1973). Fatness varied inversely with the quantity of training. The need for continued activity is strikingly evident in a follow-up study of the young female swimmers studied by Astrand et al. (1963) (see Eriksson, Engstrom, Karlberg, Saltin, & Thoren, 1971). The 30 young swimmers were restudied 7 to 8 years after their initial examination (mean age 22.2 years) and, on the average, about 5 years after they had stopped regular swimming. The changes were marked in the functional measures relative to age and body size. In the original study, the young swimmers had maximal oxygen uptakes which were 20% higher than untrained girls; at the follow-up, this functional measure was 15% below the average for Swedish females 20 to 30 years of age. The former young swimmers' average maximal oxygen uptake per kilogram of body weight decreased by almost 29%, from 52 to 37 ml/kg/min. Total hemoglobin decreased by 13%. Their larger heart and lung volumes, on the other hand, did not change appreciably since regular training stopped. The implications of these results are obvious. Continued training is necessary to maintain the high level of functional efficiency attained during the adolescent years.

Related to the persistence of activity-related changes are "clinical" reports on young athletes in certain sports, particularly baseball, football, and tennis. Epiphyseal injuries and epiphysitis in the adolescent athlete (see, for example, Adams, 1965, 1966; Collins & Evarts, 1971; Larson, 1973; Larson & McMahan, 1966; Rogers, Jones, Davis, & Dietz, 1974; Torg, Pollack, & Sweterlitsch, 1972), though not extremely common, do represent a potential growth-influencing factor and perhaps bring about an unevenness of growth. Fortunately, most of the epiphyseal injuries which occur in young athletes are amenable to medical treatment or correction. The risk of permanent damage is, nevertheless, always present. The data reported, however, are clinical cases, and growth of the skeletal element involved is usually not considered or followed after recuperation or repair. In spite of the best medical care, epiphyseal injuries in the long bones of youngsters may give trouble with possible deformity. Further, "residual handicaps" (Larson, 1973) associated with childhood athletic injuries might influence the young athlete's subsequent activity habits in adulthood.

In summary, young athletes are comparable in growth status and progress to nonathletes. Maturity-associated variation in size and physique is a significant factor in comparing athletes and nonathletes, especially during the circumpuberal years. Data for a variety of sports have been considered, and data are more readily available for young male athletes in varied sports than they are for young female athletes. The data for young athletes are not really extensive, however, and some sports are notably omitted (e.g., wrestling and soccer). There is, thus, an obvious need for coordinated studies of young athletes across different populations.

REFERENCE NOTE

1. Malina, R.M. Familial and sport background characteristics of university football players. Unpublished survey, 1970.

REFERENCES

ADAMS, J.E. Injury to the throwing arm. *California Medicine*, 1965, **102**, 127A-132.

ADAMS, J.E. Little League shoulder. *California Medicine*, 1966, **105**, 22-25.

ANDERSON, K.L. & Magel, J.R. Physiological adaptation to a high level of habitual physical activity during adolescence. *Internationale Zeitschrift für Angewandte Physiologie Einschliesslich Arbeitsphysiologie*, 1970, **28**, 209-227.

ANDREW, G.M., Becklake, M.R., Guleria, J.S., & Bates, D.V. Heart and lung functions in swimmers and nonathletes during growth. *Journal of Applied Physiology*, 1972, **32**, 245-251.

ASTRAND, P.-O., Engstrom, L., Eriksson, B.O., Karlberg, P., Nylander, I., Saltin, B., & Throren, C. Girl swimmers. *Acta Paediatrica*, 1963. (Supplement 147)

BAR-OR, O. Predicting athletic performance. *The Physician and Sportsmedicine, 1975,* **3**, 80-85.

BERG, K. Body composition and nutrition of adolescent boys training for bicycle racing. *Nutrition and Metabolism*, 1972, **14**, 172-180.

BERG, K., & Bjure, J. Preliminary results of long-term physical training of adolescent boys with respect to body composition, maximal oxygen uptake, and lung volume. *Acta Paediatrica Belgica, 1974,* **28**, 183-190. (Supplement)

BEUNEN, G., de Beul, G., Ostyn, M., Renson, R., Simons, J., & van Gerven, D. Age of menarche and motor performance in girls aged 11 through 18. In J. Borms & M. Hebbelinck (Eds.), *Pediatric work physiology*. Basel: S. Karger, 1978.

BEUNEN, G., Claessens, A., & van Esser, M. Somatic and motor characteristics of female gymnasts. In J. Borms, M. Hebbelinck, & A. Venerando (Eds.), *The female athlete*. Basel: S. Karger, 1981.

BEUNEN, G., Ostyn, M., Renson, R., Simons, J., Swalus, P., & van Gerven, D. Skeletal maturation and physical fitness of 12 to 15 year old boys. *Acta Paediatrica Belgica*, 1974, **28**, 221-232. (Supplement)

BOUCHARD, C., Carrier, R., Boulay, M., Poirier, M.C.T., & Dulac, S. *Le développement du système de transport de l'oxygène chez les jeunes adultes*. Québec: Pélican, 1975.

BOUCHARD, C., & Malina, R.M. Genetics of physiological fitness and motor performance. *Exercise and Sport Sciences Reviews*, **11**, in press.

BOUCHARD, C., Malina, R.M., Hollmann, W., & Leblanc, C. Relationships between skeletal maturity and submaximal working capacity in boys 8 to 18 years. *Medicine and Science in Sports*, 1976, **8**, 186-190.

BOUCHARD, C., & Roy, B. L'âge osseux des jeunes participants du Tournoi International de Hockey Pee-Wee de Québec. *Mouvement*, 1969, **4**, 225-232.

BROWN, C.H., Harrower, J.R., & Deeter, M.F. The effects of cross-country running on pre-adolescent girls. *Medicine and Science in Sports*, 1972, **4**, 1-5.

BUGYI, B., & Kausz, I. Radiographic determination of the skeletal age of the young swimmers. *Journal of Sports Medicine and Physical Fitness*, 1970, **10**, 269-270.

CERNY, L. The results of an evaluation of skeletal age of boys 11-15 years old with different regimes of physical activity. In *Physical fitness assessment*. Prague: Charles University, 1969.

CLARKE, H.H. Characteristics of the young athlete: A longitudinal look. *Kinesiology review, 1968*. Washington, DC: American Association for Health, Physical Education and Recreation, 1968.

CLARKE, H.H. *Physical and motor tests in the Medford Boys' Growth Study*. Englewood Cliffs, NJ: Prentice-Hall, 1971.

CLARKE, H.H. (Ed.). Characteristics of athletes. *Physical Fitness Research Digest*, April 1973, Series 3(2).

COLLINS, H.R., & Evarts, C.M. Injuries to the adolescent athlete. *Postgraduate Medicine*, 1971, **49**, 72-78.

CUMMING, G.R., Garand, T. & Borysyk, L. Correlation of performance in track and field events with bone age. *Journal of Pediatrics*, 1972, **80**, 970-973.

CUNNINGHAM, D.A., & Eynon, R.B. The working capacity of young competitive swimmers, 10-16 years of age. *Medicine and Science in Sports*, 1973, **5**, 227-231.

DANIELS, J., & Oldridge, N. Changes in oxygen consumption of young boys during growth and running training. *Medicine and Science in Sports*, 1971, **3**, 161-165.

V.DÖBELN, W., & Eriksson, B.O. Physical training, maximal oxygen uptake and dimensions of the oxygen transporting and metabolizing organs in boys 11-13 years of age. *Acta Paediatrica Scandinavica*, 1972, **61**, 653-660.

EKBLOM, B. Effect of physical training on oxygen transport system in man. *Acta Physiologica Scandinavica*, 1969 (Supplement 328). (a)

EKBLOM, B. Effect of physical training in adolescent boys. *Journal of Applied Physiology*, 1969, **27**, 350-355. (b)

ELLIS, J.D., Carron, A.V., & Bailey, D.A. Physical performance in boys from 10 through 16 years. *Human Biology*, 1975, **47**, 263-281.

ENGSTROM, I., Eriksson, B.O., Karlberg, P., Saltin, B., & Thoren, C. Preliminary report on the development of lung volumes in young girl swimmers. *Acta Paediatrica Scandinavica*, 1971, pp. 73-76. (Supplement 217)

ERIKSSON, B.O. Physical training, oxygen supply and muscle metabolism in 11-13 year old boys. *Acta Physiologica Scandinavica*, 1972. (Supplement 384)

ERIKSSON, B.O., Engstrom, I., Karlberg, P., Saltin, B., & Thoren, C. A physiological analysis of former girl swimmers. *Acta Paediatrica Scandinavica*, 1971, pp. 68-72. (Supplement 217)

ESPENSCHADE, A. Motor performance in adolescence. *Monographs of the Society for Research in Child Development*, 1940, **5**, (serial no. 24), 1-126.

FRISCH, R.E. Fatness of girls from menarche to age 18 years, with a nomogram. *Human Biology*, 1976, **48**, 353-359.

FRISCH, R.E., Gotz-Welbergen, A.V., McArthur, J.W., Albright, T., Witschi, J., Bullen, B., Birnholz, J., Reed, R.B., & Hermann, H. Delayed menarche and amenorrhea of college athletes in relation to age of onset of training. *Journal of the American Medical Association*, 1981, **246**, 1559-1563.

FRISCH, R.E., & Revelle, R. Height and weight at menarche and a hypothesis of critical body weights and adolescent events. *Science*, 1970, **169**, 397-399.

HALE, C.J. Physiologic maturity of Little League baseball players. *Research Quarterly*, 1956, **27**, 276-284.

HARLAN, W.R., Harlan, E.A., & Grillo, G.P. Secondary sex characteristics of girls 12 to 17 years of age: The U.S. Health Examination Survey. *Journal of Pediatrics*, 1980, **96**, 1074-1078.

HEBBELINCK, M., Borms, J., & Clarys, J. La variabilité de l'âge squelettique et les corrélations avec la capacité de travail chez les garcons de 5 ième année primaire. *Kinanthropologie*, 1971, **3**, 125-135.

JOHNSTON, F.E., Roche, A.F., Schell, L.M., & Wettenhall, N.B. Critical weight at menarche: Critique of a hypothesis. *American Journal of Diseases of Children*, 1975, **129**, 19-23.

JONES, H.E. *Motor performance and growth*. Berkeley: University of California, 1949.

KIRCHHOFF, H.W., Reindell, H., & Hauswaldt, C. Untersuchungen zur beurteilung der leistungsbreite im reifungsalter. *Zeitschrift für Kinderheilkunde, 1958,* **81,** 211-238.

KOTULÁN, J., Reznickova, M., & Placheta, Z. Exercise and growth. In Z. Placheta (Ed.), *Youth and physical activity*. Brno: J.E. Purkyne University Medical Faculty, 1980.

KROGMAN, W.M. Maturation age of 55 boys in the Little League World Series, 1957. *Research Quarterly*, 1959, **30,** 54-56.

LARSON, R.L. Physical activity and the growth and development bone and joint structures. In G.L. Rarick (Ed.), *Physical activity: Human growth and development*. New York: Academic Press, 1973.

LARSON, R.L., & McMahan, R.O. The epiphyses and the childhood athlete. *Journal of the American Medical Association*, 1966, **196,** 607-612.

LJUNG, B.O., Bergsten-Brucefors, A., & Lindgren, G. The secular trend in physical growth in Sweden. *Annals of Human Biology*, 1974, **1,** 245-256.

MAGEL, J.R., & Andersen, K.L. Pulmonary diffusing capacity and cardiac output in young trained Norwegian swimmers and untrained subjects. *Medicine and Science in Sports*, 1969, **1,** 131-139.

MALINA, R.M. Adolescent changes in size, build, composition and performance. *Human Biology*, 1974, **46,** 117-131.

MALINA, R.M. Anthropometric correlates of strength and motor performance. *Exercise and Sport Sciences Reviews*, 1975, **3,** 249-274.

MALINA, R.M. Adolescent growth and maturation: selected aspects of current research. *Yearbook of Physical Anthropology*, 1978, **21,** 63-94.

MALINA, R.M. The effects of exercise on specific tissues, dimensions and functions during growth. *Studies in Physical Anthropology*, 1979, **5,** 21-52.

MALINA, R.M. Physical activity, growth, and functional capacity. In F.E. Johnston, A.F. Roche, & C. Susanne (Eds.), *Human physical growth and maturation*. New York: Plenum, 1980.

MALINA, R.M. Menarche in athletes: A synthesis and hypothesis. *Annals of Human Biology*, **9,** in press.

MALINA, R.M., Bouchard, C., Shoup, R.F., Demirjian, A., & Lariviere, G. Growth and maturity status of Montreal Olympic athletes less than 18 years of age. In J.E.L. Carter, (Ed.), *Physical structure of Olympic athletes. Part I. The Montreal Olympic Games anthropological project.* Basel: S. Karger, in press.

MALINA, R.M., & Johnston, F.E. Significance of age, sex, and maturity differences in upper arm composition. *Research Quarterly*, 1967, **38**, 219-230.

MALINA, R.M., & Rarick, G.L. Growth, physique and motor performance. In G.L. Rarick (Ed.), *Physical activity: Human growth and development.* New York: Academic Press, 1973.

MÄRKER, K. Influence of athletic training on the maturity process of girls. In J. Borms, M. Hebbelinck, & A. Venerando (Eds.), *The female athlete.* Basel: S. Karger, 1981.

MELESKI, B.W. *Growth, maturity, body composition, and selected familial characteristics of competitive swimmers 8 to 18 years of age.* Unpublished doctoral dissertation, University of Texas, Austin, 1980.

MELESKI, B.W., Malina, R.M., & Bouchard, C. Cortical bone, body size, and skeletal maturity in ice hockey players 10 to 12 years of age. *Canadian Journal of Applied Sport Sciences*, 1981, **6**, 212-217.

MELESKI, B.W., Shoup, R.F., & Malina, R.M. Size, physique and body composition of competitive female swimmers 11 through 20 years of age. *Human Biology*, **54**, in press.

MIRWALD, R.L., Bailey, D.A., Cameron, N., & Rasmussen, R.L. Longitudinal comparison of aerobic power in active and inactive boys aged 7.0 to 17.0 years. *Annals of Human Biology*, 1981, **8**, 405-414.

NOVAK, L.P. Physical activity and body composition of adolescent boys. *Journal of the American Medical Association*, 1966, **197**, 169-171.

NOVOTNY, V.V., & Taftlova, R. Biological age and sport fitness of young gymnast women. In V.V. Novotny (Ed.), *Anthropological congress dedicated to Ales Hrdlicka.* Prague: Academia Publishing House of the Czechoslovak Academy of Sciences, 1971.

PAŘIZKOVA, J. Impact of age, diet, and exercise on man's body composition. *Annals of the New York Academy of Sciences*, 1963, **110**, 661-674.

PAŘIZKOVA, J. Body composition and exercise during growth and development. In G.L. Rarick (Ed.), *Physical activity: Human growth and development.* New York: Academic Press, 1973.

ROCHE, A.F., & Davilla, G. Prepubertal and postpubertal growth. In D.B. Cheek (Ed.), *Fetal and postnatal cellular growth.* New York: Wiley, 1975.

ROGERS, L.F., Jones, S., Davis, A.R., & Dietz, G. "Clipping injury" fracture of the epiphysis in the adolescent football player: An occult lesion of the knee. *American Journal of Roentgenology, Radium Therapy and Nuclear Medicine*, 1974, **121**, 69-78.

ROUS, J., & Vank, L. Comparing calendar, somatic and skeletal age when determining working capacity of children. In M. Macek (Ed.), *Proceedings of the Second Symposium of Pediatric Group of Working Physiology*. Prague: Charles University, 1970.

ROWE, F.A. Growth comparisons of athletes and non-athletes. *Research Quarterly*, 1933, **4**, 108-116.

SHUCK, G.R. Effects of athletic competition on the growth and development of junior high school boys. *Research Quarterly*, 1962, **33**, 288-298.

SOBOLOVA, V., Seliger, V., Grussova, D., Machovcoca, J., & Zelenka, V. The influence of age and sports training in swimming on physical fitness. *Acta Paediatrica Scandinavica*, 1971, pp. 63-67. (Supplement 217)

SZABO, S. Die bedeutung und die auswirkung des biologischen lebensalters auf die wettkampfergebnisse der sportler im pubertatsalter. *Schweizerische Zeitschrift für Sportmedizin*, 1969, **17**, 47-65.

SZABO, S., Doka, J., Apor, P., & Somogyvari, K. Die beziehung swischen knochenlebensalter, funktionellen anthropometrischen daten und der aeroben kapazität. *Schweizerische Zeitschrift für Sportmedizin*, 1972, **20**, 109-115.

SZABO-WAHLSTAB, S., Doka, J., Apor, P., & Somogyvari, K. Metacarpal age, anthropometric and functional anthropometric measurements and aerobic capacity. In V. Seliger (Ed.), *Physical fitness*. Prague: Charles University, 1973.

TANNER, J.M. *Growth at adolescence*, 2nd ed. Oxford: Blackwell, 1962.

THORLAND, W.G., Johnson, G.O., Fagot, T.G., Tharp, G.D., & Hammer, R.W. Body composition and somatotype characteristics of Junior Olympic athletes. *Medicine and Science in Sports and Exercise*, 1981, **13**, 332-338.

TORG, J.S., Pollack, H., & Sweterlitsch, P. The effect of competitive pitching on the shoulders and elbows of preadolescent baseball players. *Pediatrics*, 1972, **49**, 267-272.

TRUSSELL, J. Statistical flaws in evidence for the Frisch hypothesis that fatness triggers menarche. *Human Biology*, 1980, **52**, 711-720.

CHAPTER 7

SPORT AND THE CHILD:
PHYSIOLOGICAL CONSIDERATIONS

Donald A. Bailey

It has long been recognized that the urge for physical activity in children is strong and that such activity probably constitutes one of the great needs of life during the growing years. Current activity programs for children range from unstructured free play to highly intensive competitive sports. Indeed, with the present day prestige attached to athletic success, both nationally and internationally, we are seeing vast numbers of progressively younger children entering into training and sport programs of extreme intensity and duration. What effect these programs have on the dynamics of growth of young children, and when children are ready for the rigors of intense sporting programs, are questions that warrant considerable study, but to date have received scant attention. The problem in seeking answers to these questions is complicated by the fact that consideration must be given to a multiplicity of factors such as the type of sport, the nature and frequency of the contest, the age at which the activity is started, the developmental status of the child, and the intensity and duration of training.

PERSPECTIVE

From a physiological point of view, concern has been voiced from some quarters that the stresses imposed by certain competitive sports, particularly those of an endurance nature, may make excessive demands on the cardiovascular system of children and early adolescents. There is little direct evidence, however, to back up this concern. True, there have been cases of sudden death and cardiac arrest in young athletes during or immediately following games or practices, but in most of these cases congenital factors were probably involved. The physical stress of the contest may have precipitated the event, but it is probable that the affected individual had previous damage to the cardiovascular system unrelated to physical exertion. While it is true that studies of children have shown that atherosclerotic deposits now appear to be developing in the vasculature of children at an early age (Jaffe & Manning, 1971), it is unlikely that the vascular tree would be affected enough in children to present particular problems related to heavy exertion. Thus, for this age group, Jokl's contention that exercise never caused death in a normal heart may be a helpful consideration (Jokl, 1958; Jokl & McClellan, 1971).

Similarly, there is little reason to believe that the physiological demands of sport have any deleterious effects on the physical growth of the young athlete. Numerous studies have verified that in the absence of injury, the dynamics of physical growth do not seem to be adversely affected by athletic participation. A number of recent reviews have summarized the literature related to this topic (Bailey, Malina, & Rasmussen, 1977; Rarick, 1973). Obviously, there has to be an upper limit beyond which harm could result from too much or too intensive training but what this limit is has not been determined, and as Cumming (1976) rather pessimistically states, "We do not know the 'optimal' amount of physical activity for childhood, and likely never will" (p. 75). Suffice to say, the body of a youngster is a wonderful machine with sophisticated, built-in controls and instinctive limit defining sensors that in the absence of externally created pressure functions very effectively. It is the external pressure, particularly pressure exerted by ambitious adults who belong to the "children can do anything an adult can do because they are indestructible school" that should be a cause for concern, because there are basic physiological differences between children and adults which affect performance.

CHILD-ADULT DIFFERENCES

For hundreds of years children were regarded as scaled down copies of adults. Discoveries over the past years, however, have shown that there are striking differences between children and adults. For instance, the fact that the center of gravity drops as children grow older and bigger has practical significance in the performance of some athletic skills. It may be counter-productive to teach children an adult technique before they are structurally and proportionally ready.

Similarly, it is known that there are *qualitative* differences as well. For example, children have a reduced lactacid anaerobic capacity in comparison to adults. In daily life such a difference has limited practical significance, but it may be more important in physical exercise and sports. Theoretically, children should be capable of dealing with very brief, intense exercise episodes in which primarily lactacid anaerobic metabolism is involved. However, in less intensive exercise in which the duration of work is more than 20 seconds, the energy delivery through glycolysis becomes more important. The children then should not perform as well as adults. If the duration is longer than 2 to 3 minutes, aerobic metabolism becomes responsible for most of the energy; there should be no apparent difference between children and adults. This is what theoretically should happen, but sometimes what *should* happen and what *does* happen are two different things.

Nevertheless, the theoretical expectation seems to be in close agreement with what actually occurs in swimming. Young individuals usually do better in distances lasting longer than 4 minutes, and tend to get better at the shorter distances as they get older.

The highly regarded New Zealand track coach Arthur Lydiard also seems to be in agreement with the theoretical expectation. In his book (Lydiard & Gilmour, 1967), he cautions against longer sprints as dangerous events for children. He thinks distances from 200 to 800 m are unsuitable because children run at a fast pace and, as they begin to tire, are often urged on by eager spectators. His advice is to confine young children to short sprints where they use all their reserves but won't be forced beyond them, or else to send them on a 1- to 3-mile run. Although they may get tired, their reaction will be to slow the pace or even walk, which won't harm them. A study by Eriksson and Saltin (1974) showed that the low blood and muscle lactate concentrations at maximal exercise noted in young boys had gradually increased with age until by 15.5 years the values were close to adult levels, indicating that the adult advantage in anaerobic capacity had almost disappeared at this age.

What are some other cardiorespiratory differences between children and adults that may have implications for children in sport?

1. There is a gradual increase in blood pressure throughout the entire growth period which is accompanied by a decrease in heart rate. Systolic pressure follows the developmental timetable characteristic of general growth; i.e., a rapid rise at adolescence which occurs earlier in girls than in boys, but is ultimately greater in the male.

2. The number of red blood cells (erythrocytes) and the hemoglobin in the blood increases throughout childhood and continues to rise in boys during adolescence, but ceases to rise in girls. Hemoglobin concentration is relatively lower in children than in adults, which means that the blood's O_2 binding capacity is accordingly lower.

3. Cardiac volume is clearly smaller in children than in adult males, but when expressed dimensionally on the basis of height raised to the third power, adults and children appear to be similar.

4. With regard to aerobic power, when $\dot{V}O_2$ max. is expressed per kg body weight, children have higher values than adults, ranging from 50 to 55 ml/kg/min. It should be noted, however, that young children have significantly higher values for oxygen uptake per kg body weight than older boys or adults when running at the same speed. This indicates that small children have an expensive utilization of energy per unit of time due to lower efficiency and higher stride frequency associated with their small size.

These examples are but a few of the many basic physiological differences that exist between children and adults. Astrand and Rodahl (1970) have summarized these differences by stating the following:

> It may be concluded that children are definitely handicapped compared to adults. When related to the child's dimensions, its muscular strength is low and so is its maximal oxygen uptake and other parameters of importance for oxygen transport. Furthermore the mechanical efficiency of children is often inferior to that of the adult. The introduction of dimensions in the discussion of children's performance clearly indicates that they are not mature as working machines. (p. 330)

EARLY TRAINING AND ADULT CAPACITY

Reference should also be made to a number of studies (Eriksson, Grimby, & Saltin, 1971a; Eriksson, Karlsson, & Saltin, 1971b) that have indicated that when certain physiological parameters are considered, children react differently to the stress of exercise than do adults. For example, there is some evidence that relatively more of the cardiac output during exercise is distributed to the active muscles in children than in adults.

Another child-adult difference to the stress of training has been documented by Eriksson (1972). In a training study on 11-year-old boys, he noted a pronounced increase in stroke volume after training, with the increase in boys being greater than the increase which occurs in adults. Eriksson observed that the entire increase in $\dot{V}O_2$ max. following training was the result of increased stroke volume. This distinguished boys from adult males, who show a small increase in max. a — v O_2 diff. as well as a small increase in stroke volume following training. This leads to an interesting hypothesis. A large aerobic capacity as an adult presumes a large stroke volume. If physical training is begun in prepubertal years, can a larger stroke volume be attained in adulthood than if training is initiated later in life? This hypothesis has yet to be confirmed, but the pronounced stroke volume increase in boys following training observed by Eriksson suggests that the hypothesis may be valid. Cumming (1975), in noting that considerable training is necessary to realize a significant change in stroke volume in adults, speculates that for large adult values, "some of this training may have to take place during puberty and rapid growth years" (p. 24).

In this regard, the detailed longitudinal investigation of 30 top Swedish girl swimmers studied by Astrand, Engstrom, Eriksson, Karlberg, Nylander, Saltin, and Thoren (1963) and Eriksson, Engstrom, Karlberg, Saltin, and Thoren (1971c) is of considerable interest. When first studied, the girls were 12 to 16 years old and had been training extensively for some years. Some of them trained 28 hours a week and covered a distance of 65,000 m. The findings of the study indicated that the girls who experienced the rigorous swimming training had a mean maximal oxygen uptake of 3.8 l/min as compared to 2.6 l/min in average girls of the same age. Not only was their oxygen uptake larger, but the dimensions of some components of their oxygen transporting system were also significantly larger (heart volume, lung volume, and total hemoglobin). The increased dimensions correlated well with each other as well as with maximal oxygen uptake. It was concluded that hard physical training had increased the size of the organs involved in the oxygen transport system, thereby enabling an increase in maximal oxygen uptake. There was no indication that the hard physical training had caused any damage to these girls.

Ten years after the first investigation, the same girls were reexamined (Eriksson et al., 1971c). At this time all the girls had stopped their regular training and most did not engage in any specific physical activity in their spare time. Their daily lives were filled with such activities as studying, working in their professions, doing domestic work, and working with their children. Due to the very low grade of physical activity, the girls showed a pronounced decrease in their aerobic power. The mean value for the girls' maximal oxygen uptake had decreased by 29% over the 10 years. On the other hand, the dimensions of the lungs and heart were relatively unchanged. As a consequence, there was a change in the correlation between their dimensions and the maximal oxygen uptake. The girls appeared to have retained the organic capability for high function even though their actual uptake had decreased significantly because of their markedly reduced activity level. It was concluded that the hard physical training had influenced the normal development of these girls; no deleterious effects were demonstrated. Furthermore, those organic dimensions related to the oxygen transport system may have been influenced by the training regime. In commenting on these girls, Astrand (1967) speculated,

> During adolescence there may be a second chance to improve those dimensions which are of importance for the oxygen transport system. This is an interesting problem, especially with regard to physical education in school. It may not be possible to repair later in life what is neglected during the adolescent years. (p. 760)

Thus, there is some suggestive evidence that adult functional capacity may in part be related to childhood training. Perhaps the most interesting aspect of the Swedish study, however, is the fact that the former girl swimmers were "turned off" to activity as adults. In spite of their large organic capacities due to marked reduced activity levels as adults, they were functioning at levels below average for women of the same age. When in training as children, the mean aerobic power for these girls was 20% higher than untrained girls of the same age, but as adults they had dropped to levels 15% below the mean for Swedish females of the same age. Thus, the physiological advantage gained through intensive training as a child was being wasted as an adult due to the psychological factor of having been "turned off" to activity by too intensive an early exposure. The implications of this study for people involved in children's sport is obvious.

EARLY IDENTIFICATION OF ATHLETIC POTENTIAL

On the theory that if some training is good, vast amounts must be better, we are seeing youngsters at increasingly earlier ages being subjected to intensive training regimes in the hopes of developing world champions. In some countries of the world, exceptional talent is identified at an early age and children put through intensive programs in hopes that they will eventually arrive at the top. We are not told what happens to the youngsters who don't make it.

The theory that the younger we start a child, the better the chances of becoming an adult champion deserves close scrutiny. Some studies have suggested that early success offers no promise of the same later on. Clarke (1971) found that outstanding elementary school athletes may not be outstanding in junior or senior high school and vice versa. Could it be that intensive participation and competition in the under-11 age group is not the great spawning ground it is purported to be? True, there are examples of child athletes who later set world records, but the examples are not nearly as numerous as we have been led to believe.

Swimming is often cited as an example of what can be accomplished if training is started at an early age. The youngest competitor in any sport to break a world record was Karen Muir of South Africa, who was only 12 years old when she broke the 100 m backstroke record for women. Shane Gould of Australia was 15 when she broke every freestyle record from 100 to 1500 m. On the other hand, Mark Spitz was 22 years old when he swam to seven gold medals in the 1972 Olympic games and Dawn Fraser was an unheard-of 27-year-old when she won the Olympic 100 m freestyle for the third time. In the 1976 Olympic games, the mean age of medalists in swimming was some 7.5 years younger than track medalists. Athletes seem to drop out of swimming at a much earlier age than in track. It has been said that only the very young can be convinced to spend up to 6 hours per day in the water training, hence the early prominence and early retirement.

Sweeney (1973) documents the case of a New Jersey junior high school track team called the "4:47 team." This was a junior high school team with seven boys running the mile in under 5 minutes with an average time of 4:47. Surely, here was a team that would create a dynasty in their new high school. Three years later only one member of the "4:47 team" was still participating for that school. In the ninth grade he had run 4:27.7 and as a high school senior his best time was still only 4:23. What happened? The reasons run the gamut from too much early success to not enough later on; from an overly active, highly concerned coach to a rather remote one. The point to be made from this example is that all that can safely be said about fast young runners is that they are fast young runners. Early success has only a distant relationship to future stardom.

Even granting the opposite point of view, that is, that to get a world-beater of tomorrow one must train and crown young champions at an early age (an unverified premise), and further assuming that it is possible to identify and select potential champions at an early age (a dubious assumption), the primary mandate of people working in children's sport programs should still be to respond to the long-term activity needs of all children. If athletic potential can be identified at an early age, then it is logical to assume that a lack of potential should be just as easy to identify. If this is the case, should we not devote more time to the unskilled youngsters who have no motivation or encouragement towards physical activity? Perhaps what is needed in programs for the very young is to pay less attention to the selection of athletes, and to provide more encouragement to all youngsters to take an active interest in sports, games and activities. In this way every child has a chance to realize his or her potential.

In North America a significant number of children who are late maturing and following a slower-than-average developmental timetable are denied a chance to even try to participate in sports because most competitions for youngsters and adolescents are based on chronological age. Because size is an important determinant in many activities, those youngsters who are small for their age are often discriminated against or discouraged, even though they may have potential, and may eventually be of average or even above-average adult size. Somehow we need to organize physical activity programs so that more children can experience the feeling of success that comes from someone saying "well done."

CONCLUSION

Are young children ready for sports? Perhaps the question should be rephrased. Are parents and adults ready to be involved in children's sports? At this age the burden is on the leadership; the game is for the child, not the coach. What is so wrong with the lifestyle of 8- or 9-year-olds—spontaneous, enthusiastic, innocent, and filled with excitement. The pressures of adult goals and expectations should not be laid on children. The child's future as well as the present should be considered.

From a physiological point of view the endurance capacity of the child and adolescent is more than adequate. So the question is not whether youngsters can attain or desire excellence in endurance type activities, but rather the central question is whether they should be driven to seek it.

REFERENCES

ASTRAND, P.-O. Commentary — International symposium on physical activity and cardiovascular health. *Canadian Medical Association Journal*, 1967, **96**, 760.

ASTRAND, P.-O., Engstrom, L., Eriksson, B.O., Karlberg, P., Nylander, I., Saltin, B., & Thoren, C. Girl swimmers. *Acta Paediatrica* (Uppsala), 1963, **147**, 1-75.

ASTRAND, P.-O., & Rodahl, K. *Textbook of work physiology*. New York: McGraw-Hill, 1970.

BAILEY, D.A., Malina, R.M., & Rasmussen, R.L. The influence of exercise, physical activity and athletic performance on the dynamics of human growth. In F. Falkner & J.M. Tanner (Eds.), *Human growth: A comprehensive treatise*. New York: Plenum, 1977.

CLARKE, H.H. *Physical and motor tests in the Medford boy's growth study*. Englewood Cliffs, NJ: Prentice-Hall, 1971.

CUMMING, G.R. Cardiac stroke volume: Effects of athletic training. *Journal of Sports Medicine*, 1975, **3**, 18-24.

CUMMING, G.R. Medical comment. In J.G. Albinson & G.M. Andrew (Eds.), *Child in sport and physical activity*. Baltimore: University Park Press, 1976.

ERIKSSON, B.O. Physical training, oxygen supply and muscle metabolism in 11-13 year old boys. *Acta Physiologica Scandinavica*, 1972, **384**, 1-48. (Supplement)

ERIKSSON, B.O., Grimby, G., & Saltin, B. Cardiac output and arterial blood gases during exercise in pubertal boys. *Journal of Applied Physiology*, 1971, **31**, 348-352. (a)

ERIKSSON, B.O., Karlsson, J., & Saltin, B. Muscle metabolites during exercise in 13 year old boys. *Acta Paediatrica Scandinavica*, 1971, **217**, 154-157. (Supplement) (b)

ERIKSSON, B.O., Engstrom, L., Karlberg, P., Saltin, B., & Thoren, C. A physiological analysis of former girl swimmers. *Acta Paediatrica Scandinavica*, 1971, **217**, 68-71. (c)

ERIKSSON, B.O., & Saltin, B. Muscle metabolism during exercise in boys aged 11 to 16 years compared to adults. *Acta Paediatrica Belgica*, 1974, **28**, 257-265. (Supplement)

JAFFE, D., & Manning, M. Coronary arteries in early life. *Proceedings of the 13th Annual Congress of Pediatrics*, Vienna, 1971.

JOKL, E. *The clinical physiology of physical fitness and rehabilitation.* Springfield, IL: C.C. Thomas, 1958.

JOKL, E., & McClellan, J. *Exercise and cardiac death.* Baltimore: University Park Press, 1971.

LYDIARD, A., & Gilmour, G. *Run to the top* (2nd ed.). Auckland: Minerva Ltd., 1967.

RARICK, G.L. Competitive sports in childhood and early adolescence. In G.L. Rarick (Ed.), *Physical activity: Human growth and development.* New York: Academic Press, 1973.

SWEENY, H. When interest dies. In *The young runner.* Mountain View, CA: World Publications, 1973.

CHAPTER 8

THE FEMALE ATHLETE

Jack H. Wilmore

While females have competed successfully in athletics for many years, the athletic arena has traditionally been the domain of the male. During the early 1970s, female athletics underwent a dramatic revolution. Demands were made for equality in budget, facilities, equipment, coaching, and competitive opportunities to gain a status or position in the world of athletics comparable to that enjoyed by the male. While the demands for equal opportunity were generally attended to, with moderate to major reluctance, the demand by some females that traditionally all-male sports be integrated with females was met with heated discussion and debate. Out of this controversy repeatedly surfaced the questions: Are female athletes genetically inferior to male athletes with regard to both physical and physiological characteristics? Were the sexes created equal relative to their potential athletic ability? These questions and their answers have important implications not only for the athletic world, but also for many areas of employment in which physical performance characteristics are critical. Can females perform the duties of a fireman, a police patrolman, a commercial airlines pilot, a telephone lineman, or similar occupations requiring unusual physical demands?

This article originally appeared in *The Journal of School Health*, April 1977, pp. 227-233. Copyright 1977 by the American School Health Association. Reprinted with permission.

By looking at the record books, it is apparent that the female athlete performs at a substantially lower level than her male counterpart for almost all athletic events or contests. On the basis of world records in the year 1974, the male was 11.1% faster in the 100-yard dash, jumped 19.9% higher in the high jump, ran 14.0% faster in the mile run, and swam 7.3% faster in the 400-meter freestyle swim. Do these represent true biological differences between the sexes or do these differences reflect the social and cultural restrictions that have been placed on the female during her preadolescent and adolescent development? This paper will focus on similarities and differences between males and females in those areas that directly influence athletic performance. Of primary concern will be the areas of body build and composition, strength, cardiovascular endurance capacity, and motor skill development and athletic ability.

BODY BUILD AND COMPOSITION

That the mature male and female differ with regard to body build and composition does not require scientific validation. However, even in the mature adult, the differences which presently exist between the male and female are considerably greater than they need to be. At the time full maturity is reached, the average female is 5 in. shorter than the average male, 30 to 40 lb. lighter in total weight, 40 to 50 lb. lighter in lean body weight, and considerably fatter, i.e., 25% vs. 15% relative body fat (Wilmore & Behnke, 1969, 1970). Up to the age of 13 or 14 years, however, the average female is either equal to or greater than the average male in both height and weight. This is undoubtedly due to the earlier maturation of the female (Malina & Rarick, 1973). Once full maturity is reached, the male is characterized by broader shoulders, narrower hips, and a greater chest girth relative to his total body size. With reference to absolute values, the male has a greater amount of subcutaneous fat in the abdominal and upper regions of the body, while the female carries substantially more fat in the hip and lower regions of the body. The female's hips are equal in width to the males, even though the width of other bones and areas are, on the average, 10% or greater in the male. Equal girth measurements are also found for the two sexes at the abdomen, hips, and thigh (Wilmore & Behnke, 1969, 1970). Additionally, the physique of the average female, on the basis of somatotype, tends more toward endomorphy or fatness, where the average male tends to be more linear (ectomorphy) and muscular (mesomorphy) (Malina & Rarick, 1973).

In body composition, the 18- to 22-year-old female will average between 22% and 26% relative body fat, while the male of similar age will average between 12% and 16% relative body fat (Behnke & Wilmore,

1974; Wilmore & Behnke, 1969, 1970). These differences are the result of both a lower absolute lean and a higher absolute fat weight in the female. Whether these differences are primarily biological or genetic in nature or whether environmental and cultural factors are of major importance is not clearly understood at the present time, but evidence is now available to demonstrate that each of these is important and makes a significant contribution to the total differences observed.

The higher levels of the androgen hormones in the male are undoubtedly responsible for his possessing a greater lean body weight. Similarly, the higher levels of the estrogen hormones in the female are at least partially responsible for the greater amount of fat weight in the female. The mature female has higher amounts of essential fat due to the fat in breast and other sex-specific tissue (Behnke & Wilmore, 1974). The significant question that needs to be answered relates to how much additional fat the female should be allowed to possess. At what point does this additional fat become nonessential, where athletic performance will be limited by the excess fat?

It is difficult to design a research experiment to answer these questions; however, insight into the problem is gained by observing the relative body fats of national and world class athletes whose sport, event, or activity requires speed, endurance, and mobility. Figure 1 ilustrates the relative body fat values for a large number of track and field athletes. While the values are highly variable for the group as a whole, close inspection of the data reveals that the runners were considerably leaner than those competing in the field events. Of the 78 runners evaluated, 12 had relative fat values under 10%, and 32 had values under those of the college-age male (15%). Costill, Bowers, and Kammer (1970) reported an average value of 7.5% fat for 114 male competitors at the 1968 United States Olympic marathon trial. Two of the women in Figure 1 had values of approximately 6% fat, and one of these two had initially started running because she was considered obese and wanted to use exercise in addition to diet to reduce her weight to a more normal level. She became enthused with her running program, expanded it, and became a world-record-holding long-distance runner.

While the low relative body fats for these runners may be largely the result of their inherited constitution, the previous illustation would suggest that the high-intensity endurance type of exercise engaged in by these female athletes is also a most significant factor. Training at distances of up to 100 miles or more per week requires extraordinarily high levels of caloric expenditure. Thus, it appears that the female athlete can approach the relative fat values observed in male athletes, although considerably more research will be necessary to confirm this conclusion. In addition, it would seem that the average values of relative fat for the fully mature female are considerably above what might be considered ideal. The sedentary lifestyle acquired by the average female once she reaches puberty undoubtedly accounts for these comparatively high values. Likewise, it is difficult to justify the extraordinarily high values of the few female shotputters illustrated in Figure 1. These values should not be interpreted as essential for success in this event.

Body composition of the female athlete varies considerably with the sport in which she is participating. Parizkova and Poupa (1963) reported a mean value of 9.6% relative fat for highly trained female gymnasts. Sinning and Lindberg (1972) reported a mean value of 15.5% for college-age female gymnasts. In a separate study, Sinning (1973) found female basketball players to average 20.8% relative fat, while we have found female swimmers to average 29.6% (unpublished data).

STRENGTH

It is well recognized the average male is considerably stronger than the average female. Composite strength scores from several different studies suggest that men are approximately 30% to 40% stronger than women. Even at the younger ages of 7 through 17 years, while the values are relatively close, the female is unable to exhibit the same level of strength. These results are somewhat misleading, however, for when individual values are considered for specific areas of the body, it is interesting to find that leg strength is nearly identical in the two sexes. When expressed relative to body size, leg strength is identical, and when expressed relative to lean body weight, to more accurately reflect muscle mass, the females are slightly stronger! With reference to upper body strength, however, the females' values are only 30% to 50% of the values attained by the males.

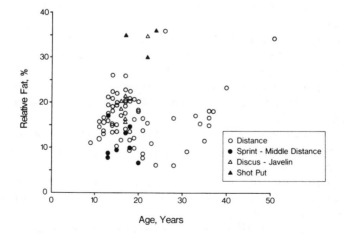

Figure 1—Body composition values of female track and field athletes.

Can females benefit from strength-training exercises? Several studies have confirmed that weight training in adolescent and college-age women can produce significant gains in strength in each of the areas trained. Brown and Wilmore (1974) reported bench press strength of 115 to 187 lb. and leg press strength of 215 to 567 lb. in seven nationally ranked female track-and-field throwing-event athletes, five of whom had just completed a 6-month intensive weight-training program. These values are considerably greater than those reported for normal, untrained males of similar age but well below values reported for male weight lifters. In a recent study, Wilmore (1974) has demonstrated that the mean strength of young, nonathletic women can be improved by as much as 30% through a 10-week weight-training program. Some of the women in this study doubled their strength in selected areas during this relatively short training period. In comparison with a group of nonathletic young men on an identical program, these women exhibited greater gains in strength, although their initial values were lower.

From this, it appears that the female has the potential to develop substantially high levels of strength, considerably higher than those normally identified in the average, typically sedentary female. Yet, while strength training does produce large increases in the female's total body strength, it does not appear to result in concomitant gains in muscle bulk. This is an important point, since most female athletes would like to increase their basic levels of strength but would be quite unwilling to strength train if they suspected they would develop excessively large, bulky muscles. The inability of the average female to gain substantial amounts of muscle with strength training is undoubtedly due to their relatively low levels of testosterone circulating in the blood, compared to the average male. Some females will notice an increased bulkiness accompanying their strength training, but it is felt that they probably have naturally high testosterone levels and probably exhibit other masculine characteristics.

Will the female ever be able to attain the same levels of strength as the male for all major regions of the body? From the similarity of the strength of the legs in the two sexes, it appears that the quality of muscle is the same, irrespective of sex. Because of the higher levels of testosterone in the male, however, he will continue to have a larger total muscle mass. If muscle mass is the major determinant of strength, the male will always have a distinct advantage. If the levels of strength one can express are independent of muscle mass, the potential for absolute strength may be similar between the sexes. Since the basic mechanisms allowing the expression of greater levels of strength have yet to be defined, it is impossible to draw any conclusions at the present time.

CARDIOVASCULAR ENDURANCE

In general, the female has a smaller stroke volume than the male for an equivalent submaximal level of work (Astrand & Rodahl, 1970). She is able to partially compensate for this by increasing her heart rate response to that level of work. This lower stroke volume is at least partially related to her smaller body size. Another important factor to the female is her lower blood hemoglobin concentration when compared to the male. Several studies have suggested that females may have values as much as 10% lower than males of the same age. With a lower maximal stroke volume and a similar maximal heart rate (which reduces the maximal cardiac output potential), in addition to lower hemoglobin levels, the oxygen carrying and delivery capacity in the female is apparently reduced considerably when compared to the male. This should result in a substantial difference in endurance capacity between the sexes, since maximal oxygen uptake ($\dot{V}O_2$ max [the best physiological index of cardiovascular endurance capacity]) should be much lower and the relationship between endurance capacity and $\dot{V}O_2$ max is very high. $\dot{V}O_2$ max values for males and females are quite similar until 10 to 15 years of age. Beyond this age, however, the female decreases rather markedly, while the male continues to improve. For the college-age male and female, this difference is quite large, with the female exhibiting a mean $\dot{V}O_2$ max between 30 and 44 ml/kg·min, while the mean value for males ranges between 45 and 53 ml/kg·min (Drinkwater, 1973; Pollock, 1973). These differences would tend to agree with, and be partially explained by, the physiological observations previously noted relative to the female's reduced maximal cardiac output and reduced hemoglobin levels. The lack of an observed difference in $\dot{V}O_2$ max at the younger ages is probably due to similarities in maximal cardiac output and hemoglobin levels up to the age of puberty, at which point these differences start to appear.

While this discussion appears to have resolved this entire area of cardiovascular endurance capacity, recent research has indicated that the female's endurance capacity at the ages beyond 10 years need not be reduced, nor be substantially below that of the male for each age. Hermanson and Anderson (1965) investigated the endurance capacity of both sedentary and athletic college-age populations and found the athletic men and women to have $\dot{V}O_2$ max values of 71 and 55 ml/kg·min, respectively, compared with values of 44 and 38 ml/kg·min, respectively, in the sedentary men and women. While the athletic men were noticeably superior, the athletic women had values 25% greater than the sedentary men.

Wilmore and Brown (1974) investigated cardiovascular endurance capacity in highly trained female endurance athletes at various ages up to and including the fourth decade of life. Eleven subjects of national and international caliber were selected from a population of female distance runners. One of these girls had won five consecutive United States and International Cross Country championships. Another held the best world time for females in the marathon, and a third held the best world time for females in the 50-mile run. The average $\dot{V}O_2$ max value for this group of women was 59.1 ml/kg·min, which is considerably higher than those values for average women or men of similar age. National-caliber male long-distance runners studied by Costill and Winrow (1970) averaged 70.3 ml/kg·min, or some 15.9% higher than these women. However, taking the three best runners from the above 11 women, they averaged 67.4 ml/kg·min, or only 4.1% lower than the average value for the 10 nationally ranked male marathon runners of almost exactly the same age.

Figure 2 demonstrates the range of values for young and older female distance runners compared to average values for the untrained male and female. It is obvious that the female has the potential to possess levels of endurance far greater than she normally demonstrates. When $\dot{V}O_2$ max is expressed relative to the athlete's lean body weight rather than body weight, the female athlete is nearly identical to the male athlete. Davies (1971) found that when the $\dot{V}O_2$ max was expressed relative to the actual active muscle mass, the differences between the sexes disappear entirely. While this may imply that men and women have the same endurance potential, Drinkwater (1973) makes the important observation that the

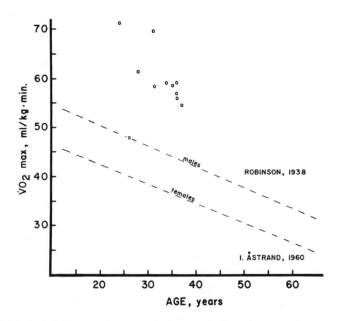

Figure 2—$\dot{V}O_2$ max values for female distance runners compared to normal untrained males and females. Normal male values obtained from S. Robinson, "Experimental Studies of Physical Fitness in Relation to Age." *Arbeitsphysiologie*, 1938, **10**, 251-323. Normal female values obtained from I. Astrand, "Aerobic Work Capacity in Men and Women with Special Reference to Age." *Acta Physiologica Scandinavica*, 1960, p. 169. (Supplement)

woman must still carry her entire body weight with her as a part of her total workload in most activities. This would undoubtedly hinder her actual performance. However, this would not be a factor in an activity such as bicycling, which should provide the female with a more equal opportunity to compete against males.

MOTOR SKILLS AND ATHLETIC ABILITY

With the exception of one activity, the softball throw for distance, boys and girls are quite similar in their performance of physical activities up to the age of 10 to 12 years. Tests of specific motor skills or general athletic ability show few differences between the sexes during this period of development. Past the age of 12, however, the male becomes considerably stronger, possesses greater muscular and cardiovascular endurance, and becomes more proficient in almost all motor skills.

It is interesting to note that, at all age levels, the female lags far behind the male in the softball throw, the female throwing only half the distance of the male, since the sexes are identical up to age 10 to 12 years for all other motor skills. In an unpublished study, Grimditch and Sockolov investigated possible reasons as to why the female does so poorly in the softball throw. Postulating this difference to be the result of insufficient practice and experience, they recruited over 200 males and females from 3 to 20 years of age to throw the softball for distance with both the dominant and nondominant arms. As they had theorized, there was absolutely no difference between the males and females for the nondominant arm up to the age of 10 to 12 years, similar to the results for other motor skill tasks. The results for the dominant arm were in agreement with what had been reported previously. Thus, the softball throw for distance results using the dominant arm appear to be biased by the previous experience and practice of the males. When the influence of experience and practice was removed by using the nondominant arm, this motor skill task was identical to each of the others.

Athletic performance differences were briefly discussed in my introduction. The female is outperformed by the male in almost all sports, events, or activities. This is quite obvious in such activities as the shotput in track and field, where high levels of upper body strength are critical to successful performance. The female uses a shot 55% lighter, and yet the world record for the female is still some 1.5 feet shorter in distance when compared to the male. In the 400-meter freestyle swimming, however, the winning time for the men in the 1924 Olympic games was 16% faster than for the women, but this difference decreased to 11.6% in the 1948 Olympics and to only 7.3% in the 1972 Olympics. The fastest female 400-meter freestyle swimmer in the early 1970s was swimming faster than the world record-holding male for the same distance in the mid-1950s.

Therefore, in this particular event, the gap between the sexes is narrowing, and there are indications that this is also true for other events and for other sports. Unfortunately, it is difficult to make valid comparisons, since the degree to which the sport, activity, or event has been emphasized is not constant, and factors such as coaching, facilities, and training techniques have differed considerably between the sexes over the years. While the performance gap appears to be closing, it is far too early to predict whether it will ever close completely for any or all sports.

MENSTRUAL AND GYNECOLOGICAL CONSIDERATIONS

One of the great concerns relative to female participation in athletics is in the area of gynecological considerations and menstruation. Do females run a high risk of damaging their reproductive organs as a result of vigorous running, jumping, or contact sports? Should females avoid exercise and competition during the flow phase of their menstrual cycle? These and many other questions were the subject of an extensive review article by Ryan (1975).

First, there appears to be a high degree of variability among females with regard to exercise and competition during the various phases of the menstrual cycle. Many females have few or no menstrual difficulties under any conditions, whether they are active or sedentary. On the other hand, a significant number of females have dysmenorrhea or other menstrual difficulties which apparently are neither helped nor aggravated by vigorous physical activity. Recently, there have been reports of a total absence of menstruation in females who train for long-distance running. This may be related to their exceptionally low total body weight and reduced levels of body fat, since several studies have reported an absence of menstruation in chronically underweight females. These female distance runners frequently train 70 to 100 miles per week, and their relative body fat typically decreases to 10% or less (Figure 1). Return of menstruation usually follows a reduction in training intensity. Similar complications have been noted in gymnasts, dancers, and figure skaters.

Physical performance seems to be best in the immediate postmenstrual period, up to the 15th day of the cycle. The number of females who perform poorly during the flow phase of the cycle is about the same as the number who experience no difference. Some have even noted an improved performance during flow, establishing records and winning world-class competition. Again, the individual variability is so great that no general rules of thumb can be given. Full participation in all types of activities should be allowed during the flow phase for those who experience no difficulties, and provisions should be made for those who do experience difficulties, so they are not forced into undesirable activity.

The potential for gynecological injuries has been a major concern in athletics for centuries. Females at one time were discouraged from participating in any activity in which there was considerable running, jumping, or bodily contact. The uterus was considered to be highly vulnerable to major injury, which could have serious consequences later in life. It is now recognized that injuries to the female genital organs are rare. Unlike the male, the female's organs are internal and in an extremely well-protected position. The breasts are in a vulnerable position, but, even here, serious injury is extremely rare, even in contact sports. Follow-up studies on former female athletes indicate that they have normal pregnancy and childbirth, and in fact may have shorter delivery times and a faster return to normal activities.

SUMMARY

From the preceding discussion, there appear to be rather substantial differences between the average female and the average male in almost all aspects of physical performance beyond the age of 10 to 12 years. Prior to this time, there are few, if any, differences between the sexes. What happens to the female once she reaches puberty? Is she physically over the hill, reaching her peak at a relatively early age, or are there other factors or circumstances that might account for her reduced physical capabilities? Recent studies on highly trained female athletes suggest that the female is not that much different from her highly trained male counterpart at ages beyond puberty. It appears that the average values used for comparative purposes beyond the age of puberty are comparing relatively active males with relatively sedentary females. Somewhere between 10 and 12 years of age, the average female substitutes the piano for climbing in the tree and sewing for chasing the boys down the street. It is well known that once one assumes a sedentary lifestyle, the basic physiological components of general fitness deteriorate; that is, strength, muscular endurance, and cardiovascular endurance are lost and body fat tends to accumulate. Similar trends can be noted for the male by the time he reaches 30 to 35 years of age, which corresponds to a reduction in his activity patterns. So, what appears to be dramatic biological differences between the sexes may be, in fact, more related to cultural and social restrictions placed on the female as she attains puberty. Further research into this intriguing area is certainly needed.

With regard to the female athlete, there appears to be little difference between her and her male counterpart in strength, endurance, and body composition. Strength of the lower extremities, when related to body weight and lean body weight, is similar between the sexes, although the male maintains a distinct superiority in upper body strength. Strength training, formerly condemned as a mode of training for women because of its supposed masculinizing effects, is now recognized as valuable in developing the strength component, which is usually the weakest link in the physiological profile of the female athlete.

Endurance capacity in the highly trained female distance runner approximates values obtained in the highly trained male distance runner when the values are expressed relative to lean body weight and, for the better female runners, are relatively close when expressed relative to body weight. Although the female is far below the male in lean body weight, the highly trained female distance runner has a relative body fat similar to the male distance runner.

Because of these similarities, and because their needs are basically the same, there is little reason to advocate different training or conditioning programs on the basis of sex.

REFERENCES

ASTRAND, I. Aerobic work capacity in men and women with special reference to age. *Acta Physiologica Scandinavica*, 1960, p. 169. (Supplement)

ASTRAND, P.-O., & Rodahl, K. *Textbook of work physiology*. New York: McGraw-Hill, 1970.

BEHNKE, A.R., & Wilmore, J.H. *Evaluation and regulation of body build and composition*. Englewood Cliffs, NJ: Prentice-Hall, 1974.

BROWN, C.H., & Wilmore, J.H. The effects of maximal resistance training on the strength and body composition of women athletes. *Medicine and Science in Sports*, 1974, **6**, 174-177.

COSTILL, D.L., Bowers, R., & Kammer, W.F. Skinfold estimates of body fat among marathon runners. *Medicine and Science in Sports*, 1970, **2**, 93-95.

COSTILL, D.L., & Winrow, E. Maximal oxygen uptake among marathon runners. *Archives of Physical Medicine and Rehabilitation*, 1970, **51**, 317-320.

DAVIES, C.T.M. Body composition in children: A reference standard for maximum aerobic power output on a stationary bicycle ergometer. *Acta Paediatrica Scandinavica*, 1971, **217**. (Supplement)

DRINKWATER, B.L. Physiological responses of women to exercise. In J.H. Wilmore (Ed.), *Exercise and sport sciences reviews* (Vol. 1). New York: Academic Press, 1973.

HERMANSON, L., & Anderson, K.L. Aerobic work capacity in young Norwegian men and women. *Journal of Applied Physiology*, 1965, **20**, 425-431.

MALINA, R.M., & Rarick, G.L. Growth, physique, and motor performance. In G.L. Rarick (Ed.), *Physical activity: Human growth and development*. New York: Academic Press, 1973.

PARIZKOVA, J., & Poupa, D. Some metabolic consequences of adaptation to muscular work. *British Journal of Nutrition*, 1963, **17**, 341-345.

POLLOCK, M.L. The quantification of endurance training programs. In J.H. Wilmore (Ed.), *Exercise and sport sciences reviews* (Vol. 1). New York: Academic Press, 1973.

ROBINSON, S. Experimental studies of physical fitness in relation to age. *Arbeitsphysiologie*, 1938, 10, 251-323.

RYAN, A.J. The female athlete: Gynecological considerations. *Journal of Health, Physical Education, and Recreation*, 1975, **46**, 40-44.

SINNING, W.E. Body composition, cardiovascular function, and rule changes in women's basketball. *Research Quarterly*, 1973, **44**, 313-321.

SINNING, W.E., & Linberg, G.D. Physical characteristics of college age women gymnastics. *Research Quarterly*, 1972, **43**, 226-234.

WILMORE, J.H. Alterations in strength, body composition, and anthropometric measurements consequent to a 10-week weight training program. *Medicine and Science in Sports*, 1974, **6**, 133-138.

WILMORE, J.H., & Behnke, A.R. An Anthropometric estimation of body density and lean body weight in young men. *Journal of Applied Physiology*, 1969, **27**, 25-31.

WILMORE, J.H., & Behnke, A.R. An anthropometric estimation of body density and lean body weight in young women. *American Journal of Clinical Nutrition*, 1970, **23**, 267-274.

WILMORE, J.H., & Brown, C.H. Physiological profiles of women distance runners. *Medicine and Science in Sports*, 1974, **6**, 178-181.

CHAPTER 9

THE YOUNG ATHLETE

Thomas E. Shaffer

Fifty years ago, the school-age boy or girl had few choices in selecting an athletic activity. For the boys, the only options were football in the autumn, basketball in the winter, and baseball or track and field in spring. Girls had even more limited opportunities. There might be chances for them to play field hockey in the fall, basketball in the winter (under rules we consider antiquated now), and nothing to look forward to in the spring. Many young people made their own games on the playground or in the backyard, either with recognizable rules and regulations or those they themselves improvised.

The situation in scholastic sports is very much different now compared to those "good old days" and continues to change dramatically from year to year. Records published by the National Federation of State High School Associations (1972, 1974) show that in junior and senior high schools in the United States in 1971 there were 26 different officially recognized interscholastic competitive sports for boys, in which there were 3.6 million participants. Every one of these sports could not be found in each state, of course. For example, there were only 10 officially recognized interscholastic sports for boys in Ohio in 1971. In 1974, the

This article originally appeared in *The Journal of School Health*, April 1977, pp. 222-226. Copyright 1977 by the American School Health Association. Reprinted with permission.

National Federation reported that the number of scholastic competitive sports for boys had increased to 32, with 4 million participants (the variety of sports activities in Ohio had increased from 10 to 13). The 30% increase in kinds of sports activities and 9% increase in male participants showed us some interesting new projects, including competitive archery, crew, pentathlon, table tennis, and weight lifting. Certainly, this list would be appealing to many students who had interests and talents different from those of boys primarily interested in the traditional football, baseball, and basketball.

The most unexpected change has been in sports for girls. National Federation statistics show that, in 1971, in the entire United States, one could find only 14 different interscholastic sports available to girls, and only 287,000 girls participating. Within 3 years, the number of sports listed as officially recognized in at least one or more states had increased from 14 to 25, and participants in girls' interscholastic sports had risen in that period to 1.3 million, a 350% increase in young female athletes. Sports newly appearing on the scene for girls during this short span included archery, badminton, baseball, fencing, ice hockey, lacrosse, riflery, and table tennis—an exciting choice for any girls who enjoy physical activity. When, in 1967, Muriel Grossfeld, an Olympic gymnast, said, "A dozen years ago I knew every girl gymnast in the country; now there must be 10,000," she was only vaguely anticipating the changes that in 1974 would produce 61,000 scholastic girl gymnasts in just the high schools of this country.

Notable as the increase in opportunities to participate has been, the rising popularity of newcomers on the interscholastic sports scene has been even more surprising. Boys show more interest in cross country, wrestling, swimming, tennis, and ice hockey each year, while basketball, track, volleyball, tennis, and cross country have blossomed as popular sports for girls. Just for the record, though, the old favorites are still at the top of the list—for the present, at least. Basketball is number one for boys, followed by track and baseball, while basketball, volleyball, and track and field events still attract the largest number of female athletes.

The facts I have given to you are indicative of a trend to a broad spectrum in organized athletics for boys and girls and are a change and a challenge for those who are responsible for the planning and administration of physical education and athletics.

Years ago, when organized athletics were limited to a few sports, when league championships were rare, and bowl contests were unheard of, one thing stood out—boys and girls played games to have fun (Michener, 1976). Competition was a kind of recreation and, if the rules had to be stretched a bit or improvised, it was still fun. As schools assumed more responsibility for supervising organized athletics, the atmosphere surrounding competitive sports slowly began to change, with the advent of coaches, interschool competition, and intensified community interest.

Since the 1950s, pressures, at a low key initially, have been more and more evident and there has been less and less fun in the games. There are some indications, however, that high school students are at least beginning to resist the pressure on being a specialist in one sport and the emphasis on being the champion. In one state, some 2,000 high school students indicated in a poll that 86% rated fun and enjoyment as their major objective for participating, and elsewhere, the majority of high school athletes were critical of pressures brought on them by their coaches and parents. It seems likely that the many options in sports available to young people in the 1970s may be due to subtle efforts by students to escape from traditional team sports and initiate the kinds that are more informal, involve one-on-one competition rather than highly organized teamwork, and more importantly and most fortunately, will carry over to later life as games adults can play for fun and recreation.

A survey of the total US population of attitudes toward involvement was done recently by the Neilsen rating organization, which also rates nationwide radio and television programs. The most popular sports in number of participants in rank order were swimming, bicycling, fishing, camping, bowling, table tennis, pool, boating, softball, and ice skating. A study by a national magazine a few months ago revealed that the two fastest growing sports among teen-age boys are skiing and tennis, but camping and bicycling are the most popular. The classic interscholastic sports all showed a decline during a 2-year period.

Many physicians and educators have violently opposed organized sports for young people on grounds that they are overemphasized, potentially hazardous, promote improper values to children and parents about winning, and bring about harmful physical and emotional stress for the participants. These arguments have not had any significant effect on the course of events. Organized sports for youths continue to thrive in schools and in community-sponsored programs. It is inevitable that young people will play, will compete, and many will become members of organized teams and leagues, whether there is vigorous sponsorship from the schools or other agencies.

Proponents of organized sports argue that sedentary habits of living in our society today threaten the fitness of our youths and that it has become necessary to make opportunities for participation in vigorous physical activities, but always with the essential ingredients of competent leadership, supervision, and proper precautions for safety and health. A policy statement by the American Association for Health, Physical Education and Recreation (1963) began with the following preamble: "We believe that participation in athletics should be included in the educational experiences offered to all students in the schools and colleges of the United States." I would have suggested underlining "educational experiences" as a reminder that every program for young people should give priority to this factor.

My comments about the scope of the athletic program in our schools and the number of participants do not take into account the millions of boys and girls in so-called agency-sponsored or community programs. In view of the involvement of so many youths in athletics, it is clearly necessary for professionals in the health fields to take some responsibility for declaring policies and standards that will make participation healthy and safe (Shaffer, 1973). Infectious diseases did not diminish simply because physicians believed they were bad for children, but they did yield to medical research and public health regulations which controlled them. There are many other situations today in our society, including prevalence of accidents, effects of smoking, and improper use of drugs, which will not go away until we have research and plausible controls for their solution. The potential health hazards of sports are in this same category. Understanding, research, reasonable policies, and some regulation will be more effective than rejection and the hope that they will disappear.

SAFEGUARDS FOR AN ATHLETE'S HEALTH

Every young athlete, boy or girl, of any age, has the right to expect certain safeguards for health—a kind of "bill of rights." The elements of a sensible program for athletes are five in number, each relating to a distinct aspect of sports. Those who have responsibility for the health of athletes should consider each of them as being singularly important to a comprehensive program. The well-planned health program for athletes must include policies and procedures to provide:
1. Proper conditioning.
2. Intelligent coaching.
3. The best possible equipment and facilities.
4. Capable officiating.
5. Competent medical care.
There is a shared responsibility in accomplishing these safeguards. Standards and policies to prevent injury and illness and to provide medical care are primarily within the medical field. Proper conditioning to attain physical fitness for strenuous activity is accomplished by cooperation between physicians and coaches. Procurement and maintenance of proper equipment are a responsibility of the coach or athletic trainer, while the basic responsibility for furnishing satisfactory coaching, officiating, and physical facilities rests with the athletic department and the school administration. However, this does not mean that the school physician, the team physician, and the school nurse should shun their responsibility in seeing that every one of these five safeguards for the health of young athletes is given proper consideration.

QUALIFICATIONS FOR PARTICIPATION

There must be assurance from a physician that a young athlete is physically qualified for participating in a specific sport before conditioning procedures are started, which also means before participation in practice or games is permitted (AMA, 1976).

The medical examination of athletes should go beyond the limits of simply assuring parents and coaches that the young person has a sound body. There are three cardinal objectives in the medical evaluation of young athletes:

1. Are growth and development equal to that of other participants?

2. Is this boy or girl physically qualified for the particular sport under consideration? If there is a health problem, can prompt treatment be arranged to correct it?

3. If some restrictions are necessary, are there *any* sports for this individual at the same academic level which would be appropriate?

Children and adolescents like to be involved with their peers in almost any kind of activity, and this is especially true about those who enjoy games and sports. Thus, it is especially important that quick decisions about restrictions or exclusion from sports be avoided until every option for each child has been thoroughly considered (Gallagher, 1956).

The level of physical maturity varies greatly among adolescents of similar age (Figure 1). Estimation of physiological development is as important in health appraisal as is the clinical examination of physical or emotional health. There is a close relationship between the stage of adolescent development and the individual's strength, endurance, coordination, agility, and nutritional needs (Tanner, 1962). Such an evaluation can easily be accomplished during health appraisal by observing the degree of sexual development (Figure 2) and, in girls, ascertaining the time of menarche. Matching of candidates is very important for safety and

Figure 1—Boys in the same eighth-grade physical education class.

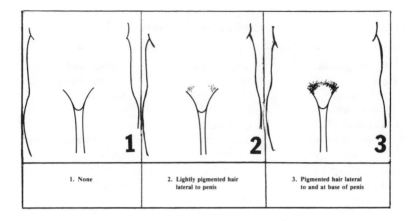

1. None

2. Lightly pigmented hair lateral to penis

3. Pigmented hair lateral to and at base of penis

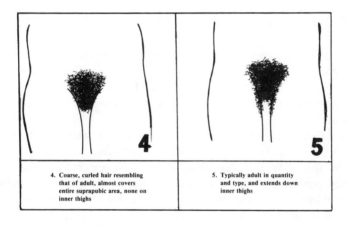

4. Coarse, curled hair resembling that of adult, almost covers entire suprapubic area, none on inner thighs

5. Typically adult in quantity and type, and extends down inner thighs

Figure 2—Stages of pubic hair development in adolescence (male or female).

achievement in strenuous sports, and the degree of physical maturation is as significant in this regard as is height, weight, and age, because of its relationship to the special requirements of superior physique. In addition, the need for special attention to nutrition, rest, and avoidance of fatigue is clearly indicated for the adolescent who is in the early stages of maturation, for it is at this stage of maturation that the sharp and relatively brief acceleration of physical growth occurs.

CLASSIFICATION OF ATHLETIC ACTIVITIES

It is desirable to classify sports into groups according to physical requirements so that as many young people may participate as possible (Table 1). Sports can be classified as *strenuous* involving *contact*, *strenuous*

Table 1
Classification of Sports

Strenuous	Strenuous (Cont.)	Moderately Strenuous
Contact	Noncontact	Baseball (limited contact)
Ice hockey	Cross country	Badminton
Wrestling	Fencing	Golf
Football	Gymnastics	
Lacrosse (boys)	Swimming	**Nonstrenuous**
	Swimming	Archery
Limited Contact	Tennis	Bowling
Basketball	Track and field	Riflery
Soccer	Skiing	
Volleyball		
Lacrosse (girls)		
Field hockey (girls)		

with *limited body contact*, *strenuous* with *no collision and body contact*, *moderately strenuous*, and, finally, *nonstrenuous*. This last group includes activities in which even an individual with some physical disability could participate, if he or she is helped by encouragement and special planning.

When there is a wide variety of sports available, with varying requirements of physical capability, it should be possible to recommend some kind of sports activity for almost every young person, regardless of physical condition. A medical examination of candidates for athletics must not be the occasion for simply sorting the "fit" from the "unfit" and sending only the "perfect physical specimens" into the sports program. Those making decisions about health qualifications for sports participants must be cognizant of the total variety of sports in the athletic program and also be familiar with the physical requirements for participation in each of them. If there really are valid reasons for restrictions from physical activity of any kind, they should always be clearly explained to the boy or girl, with enough time for planning to follow through with diagnostic evaluation and treatment for the individual who must stand aside. It is quite natural in the preseason rush and excitement about organizing a team and looking forward to playing for those in charge to focus attention on the competitors, while forgetting those who were not approved but need special attention for diagnosis and treatment of physical or emotional problems.

The ideal athletic program for adolescents would be sufficiently broad and varied to include all boys and girls who wish to participate in some appropriate physical activity—even those who must have limited medical sanction.

REFERENCES

AMERICAN Association for Health, Physical Education, and Recreation. *Athletics in education: Platform statement*. Washington, DC: National Education Association, 1963.

AMERICAN Medical Association. *Medical evaluation of the athlete: A guide*. Chicago: Author, 1976.

GALLAGHER, J.R. Rest and restriction: Their conflict with an adolescent's development. *American Journal of Public Health*, 1956, **46**, 1424-1428.

MICHENER, J.A. *Sports in America*. New York: Random House, 1976.

NATIONAL Federation of State High School Associations. *Official handbook, 1972-73*. Elgin, IL: Author, 1972.

NATIONAL Federation of State High School Associations. *Official handbook*, 1974-75. Elgin, IL: Author, 1974.

SHAFFER, T.E. The adolescent athlete. *Pediatric Clinic North America*, 1973, **20**, 837-849.

TANNER, J.M. *Growth at adolescence* (2nd ed.). Oxford: Blackwell Scientific Publishers, 1962.

CHAPTER 10

ATHLETIC INJURIES

Vincent J. DiStefano

The major factor in the management of athletic injuries is the earliest possible determination of the type and extent of injury. Athletics are unique in this respect, because in few other instances in life do we find physicians or paramedical personnel in attendance who actually anticipate an injury, often witnessing it and then ministering to the victim within seconds of trauma.

Athletes as patients are unique in that they are young, otherwise healthy, individuals in their physical prime, strongly motivated, with generally average to above average intelligence. Furthermore, the results of treatment must be consistent with a high level of physical performance, since, if the athletes are to return, there can be no significant detriment to the quality of their participation following therapy. This charges the treating physician with the responsibility of rendering a diagnosis quickly and accurately and instituting treatment without delay. For instance, the practice of "hiding" an acutely injured knee in a plaster cast until the optimal time for repair has passed is to be strongly condemned.

Injury may be defined as a disruption of normal tissue continuity, either microscopic or macroscopic, and suggests the infinite gradations

This article originally appeared in *The Journal of School Health*, April 1977, pp. 234-237. Copyright 1977 by the American School Health Association. Reprinted with permission.

of injury possible which gain clinical expression in degrees of immediate or delayed pain, degrees of swelling, degrees of response to local treatment, and degrees of healing per unit time. Such a basic definition requires that the physician be familiar with the anatomy of the traumatized area to visualize in his or her mind's eye the actual tissues involved, render an opinion on the functional significance of the injury, and extrapolate from these factors the course of treatment, response, and prognosis. The most common athletic injuries encountered fall into the categories of contusion, strain, and sprain.

CONTUSION

Contusion by definition is a bruise and involves the skin and underlying tissues. The injury not infrequently results in bleeding or hematoma formation in the subcutaneous tissues and muscle, resulting in local swelling, tenderness, and induration. The involved muscles become secondarily spastic and inelastic, causing diminished motion at the joints they are responsible for moving.

"Charley horse" is a term frequently heard in athletic circles. It describes a contusion of the thigh, more specifically, elements of the quadriceps musculature. Because of injury, the muscle is unable to elongate or reciprocally relax with hamstring contraction and, as a consequence, knee flexion may be limited. Myositis ossificans is an infrequent but troublesome complication of a "charley horse," which results from either ossification of a subperiosteal hematoma or the formation of a plaque of bone within the muscle mass. A contusion causing a periosteal or intramuscular hematoma is the inciting cause. Suspicion is first aroused when a contusion fails to undergo a normal resolution within a week or so. The area of the thigh becomes warm and tender, and a mass of varying consistency is often palpable. Often, a dark red serous fluid can be aspirated at this stage. As the mass undergoes maturation into bone, local symptoms subside, but the patient is unable to fully flex the knee because the involved muscle has lost elasticity and is unable to elongate. A carefully supervised program of physical therapy to restore mobility is advised at this stage, but the best treatment is prevention by prompt attention to the initial injury.

The "hip pointer" is a particularly painful kind of contusion affecting the bone of the iliac crest and usually involving the aponeurotic attachments of the abdominal and hip musculature (Figure 1). The physical findings include acute local tenderness with eventual ecchymosis and pain associated with activities involving contraction of the abdominal muscles and flexion of the trunk to the opposite side.

The initial treatment of most contusions over the first 48 hours involves rest and the local application of cold and compression to diminish

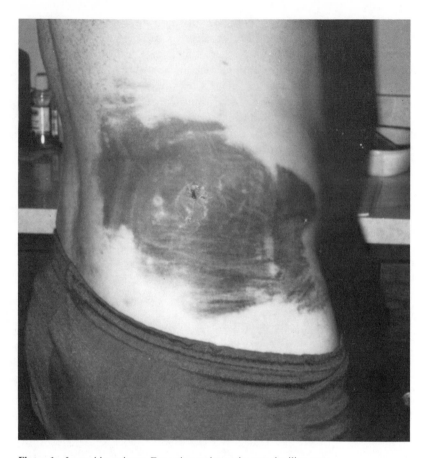

Figure 1—Large hip pointer. Extensive ecchymosis over the iliac crest.

bleeding, swelling, and pain. Beyond this time, various modalities of heat may be useful in promoting healing and dispersal of excessive products of inflammation and relief of stiffness. Protection from re-injury by proper padding is a consideration on the athlete's return to the playing field. This basic treatment may, at times, be supplemented by the local injection of an anesthetic agent, such as Xylocaine, combined with hyaluronidase (Wydase) to disperse the products of injury and, optionally, a corticosteroid to effect a state of quiescence in the inflammatory process.

Occasionally, if dispersal does not take place, encystment, or the development of a fibrous-retaining sac around the hematoma, may occur and result in a semisoft, fluctuant mass at the site of injury, which may wax and wane in size depending on activity, recurrent trauma, and treatment. The most effective treatment consists of aspiration of the serous

fluid, coupled with instillation of corticosteroid derivative, compressive wrapping, protective padding, and some modification of physical activity. Surgical excision of the fibrous sac is rarely necessary.

STRAIN

Strain, often referred to as a "pull," is defined as an injury to any portion of the musculotendinous unit and thus may involve the musculoperiosteal origin, the substance of the muscle itself, the musculotendinous junction, the tendinous portion, or tendo-osseous insertion.

Common representative samples of these variations include:

1. *Musculoperiosteal Junction—Adductor or "groin pull"; avulsion, ischial tuberosity.* "Groin Pull"—Muscular strain in the groin is quite common and may involve the hip flexors or adductors in this area. The patient complains of local pain aggravated by stretching and active contraction of these muscles. Initial treatment is, for the most part, symptomatic.

Avulsion of the Ischial Tuberosity—"Hurdler's injury" results from a sudden, forceful strain of the hamstring group, as a result of hip flexion with the knee extended. The presence of local symptoms over the ischial tuberosity, aggravated by passive hip flexion with the knee extended in conjunction with a typical x-ray appearance, confirms the diagnosis. Surgery in the form of excision or replacement of the avulsed fragment is sometimes necessary. Recovery is usually delayed.

2. *Muscle—Rectus femoris strain; hamstring strain.* Quadriceps and hamstring "pulls" are among the chief causes of time lost on any athletic team. Local pain with stretching and activity is the chief complaint. The most common cause of a chronic strain is inadequate rehabilitation of the original injury. The principal components of muscle function (elasticity, strength, and endurance) must be restored by stretching and progressive resistive exercises before the athlete is returned to play.

3. *Musculotendinous Junction.* Strain of the medial head of the gastrocnemius muscle at the musculotendinous junction has been labeled as "tennis leg" because of its reported frequency in that group of athletes. It is a result of a single, violent stress. From a diagnostic standpoint, it may be confused with such entities as phlebitis, plantaris tendon rupture, or rupture of a small blood vessel.

4. *Tendon—Achilles tendinitis, rupture; infrapatellar tendon—"jumper's knee."* Achilles Tendinitis, Rupture—One examiner has measured forces on the order of 2,000 lb. in the Achilles tendon during periods of rapid running, so it is not surprising to learn that Achilles tendon problems are fairly common in the athlete. The injury takes the form of acute strain or chronic overload and not infrequently provokes a tenovaginitis

of the tendon sheath, producing local pain during activity. The main ingredient in the treatment program is rest and, when properly handled, a full recovery from these injuries can be expected. A small percentage will fail to heal, however, and the area of injury will actually increase in size and ultimately gain expression as a complete rupture of the Achilles tendon. The explanation appears related to the combined effects of inadequate initial treatment, peculiarities of the tendon vasculature, regressive changes in the local blood supply coincident with age and, perhaps, the deleterious effects of locally injected corticosteroid. The actual rupture most often occurs as the individual is pushing off on the balls of the foot, as in the start of a sprint, and produces a factitious sensation of being struck with a stone, racquet, etc. The limp and diffuse swelling and ecchymosis that follow may lead to the incorrect diagnosis of ankle sprain. Palpable defect in the tendon (Figure 2) and a positive Thompson test (Figure 3)—failure of plantar flexion of the foot to occur with compression of the gastrosoleus—are pathognomonic of complete rupture and, in most instances, direct a surgical approach to the problem.

Infrapatellar Tendinitis—"Jumper's knee." Patellar tendinitis and "jumper's knee" are common synonyms used to describe tendinitis of the patellar tendon. It most commonly occurs in basketball players and track athletes whose activities involve rapid deceleration and jumping and is characterized by local pain and tenderness, usually at the origin of the patellar tendon just beneath the inferior pole of the patella. Not infrequently, it is confused with an internal derangement of the knee. The pathomechanics are the same as those occurring in Achilles tendinitis,

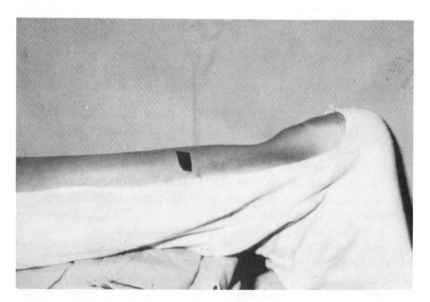

Figure 2—Visible defect at the site of Achilles tendon rupture.

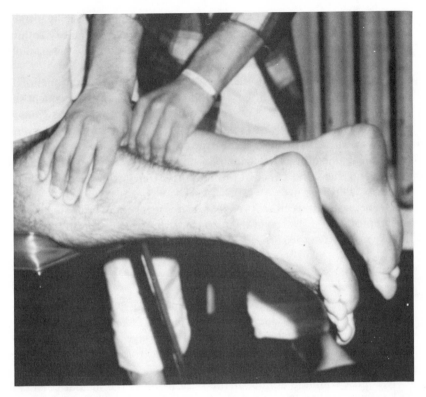

Figure 3—Positive Thompson test in a patient with complete Achilles tendon rupture (background). Calf compression causes plantar flexion of the foot on the normal side (foreground).

and the ultimate complication is complete rupture of the tendon from the patella, a rare occurrence. In the early stages, the area of involvement in the tendon is small and usually responds to rest, although, occasionally, debridement is required to effect a cure.

   5. *Tendo-osseous Insertion—Quadriceps tendinitis, rupture.* The pathology of quadriceps tendinitis is identical to lesions of the patellar and Achilles tendon. Pain and tenderness are present about the superior pole of the patella.

SPRAIN

A "sprain" is defined as an injury to some part of a ligament and may be classified on the basis of severity as first, second, or third degree.

   A first degree sprain implies minor stretching or tearing, with minimal break in continuity of the structure. It is not particularly disabling, responds to symptomatic treatment, and has a good prognosis.

A second-degree sprain results in partial discontinuity of the ligament, with adequate normal tissue remaining to ensure a satisfactory result, providing the structure is protected from re-injury during the healing process.

In a third-degree sprain, there is complete rupture and functional discontinuity, with instability of the joint. No portion of the ligament remains intact, nor do the ruptured ends remain approximated. Consequently, optimal healing is unlikely to ensue without surgical intervention. A special kind of third-degree sprain is a "sprain-fracture" caused when the ligament pulls a fragment of bone loose from one of its attachments. The true significance of this injury is often lost in the casual diagnosis of "chip fracture."

In general, then, treatment for first-degree injury may be characterized as symptomatic; for second-degree injury, protective; for third-degree injury, restorative (or surgical).

KNEE

Despite the fact that the knee joint is the most massive joint in the body, it is particularly vulnerable because it supports 90% of the individual's body weight. It is situated at the ends of the longest bones in the body, which act as levers in the transmission of great forces to the soft tissues of the joint.

The most common sprain of the knee involves the medial collateral ligament (Figure 4). The outer, or superficial, portion of this ligament in the adult extends obliquely downward from the adductor tubercle of the femur a distance of approximately 10 cm. It is reinforced by a deeper, shorter portion, at times referred to as the medial capsular ligament. This structure is usually injured when a blow is delivered to the outer aspect of the knee with the foot planted. The main symptom of an incomplete first- or second-degree injury is pain over the medial aspect of the joint. Such incomplete injuries may be more symptomatic than the completely ruptured ligament, which is usually benumbed immediately afterward and gains expression as instability or a sense of "the knee opening up" as the athlete attempts to walk. Careful palpation along the entire course of the ligament usually outlines the area of involvement, and the degree of instability may be determined by stress testing. Such an injury is usually not accompanied by a large bloody effusion, a finding that should always arouse suspicion of a more serious injury to the interior of the joint.

ANKLE

Most ankle sprains involve the lateral ligaments, particularly the anterior talofibular ligament. This is partly due to the fact that the fibular or

sport psychology to the moral development of children. The number of stated goals of children's athletics that are related to broader moral behaviors which society expects of its citizens illustrates the importance of this issue. Also, Martens shows coaches, through several specific recommendations, how they can help athletes develop appropriate moral standards.

The issue of how children remember and interpret their experiences in sport is discussed by Jerry R. Thomas, Jere D. Gallagher, and Katherine T. Thomas in chapter 16. First, the authors introduce the issue of children's causal attributions in sports settings and the relationship of these attributions to intrinsic and extrinsic motivation for participation in sports. Focusing on winning and losing as well as motivation, the authors provide a model of children's information processing to show that children do not handle information in the same way as adults. The authors then consider concerns such as how the consistency of winning and losing and receiving rewards affects children's perception of their sports experience, and they relate these concerns to their model. Finally, the authors direct their attention to parents, coaches, and educators by providing them with some direct, practical application of the preceding discussion.

Michael J. Ash and Steven P. Chatman, in the final chapter of this section, provide an overview and organization of current psychological issues in youth sports. The emphasis here is on describing the "interconnections and structure" of research dealing with these issues. In so doing, the authors focus on four major areas of research: the effects of competition on children, the role of "others" in the sport experience, an analysis of the characteristics of children who participate in sports, and therapeutic interventions in the competitive experience. In each of the discussion of these concerns and in the discussion that follows, the authors identify promising directions for youth sport research.

CHAPTER 11

SOCIAL EVALUATION: A KEY DEVELOPMENTAL ELEMENT IN THE COMPETITION PROCESS

Tara Kost Scanlan

Currently, a classic paradox exists in the area of competition. The need to understand the complex relationship between competition and psychosocial development is great, yet the pertinent literature is meager. What is a viable approach to systematically attack such a complex problem with so little available data? A necessary first step is to gain a clear understanding of the competition process typically encountered by children and to identify the key elements of the process. Once these elements have been determined, the developmental literature can be examined with the appropriate focus to establish and empirically test theoretical links between competition and relevant developmental processes. Only then can the effects of competition on psychological and social development be determined.

This discussion is concerned with understanding the competition process that occurs in the naturalistic competitive situation which is the realistic competitive arena typically encountered by children participating in competitive youth sports. Of primary interest are children between the ages of 4 and 12. The focus is to examine *social evaluation* as one key element in the competition process because it is the most central and pervasive element. Also discussed is whether social evaluation is actually perceived by children and, if so, whether the evaluative information is actively sought. Potential theoretical links to relevant developmental processes are provided. Finally, to clearly delimit this discussion it should be mentioned that although the competition process is carefully examined, the judgmental issue of whether competition is good or bad is not addressed.

IDENTIFICATION OF A BASIC APPROACH

To understand the complex competition process, it is necessary to determine what basic approach to use as a viable starting point and to define important terms. Two major approaches to the study of competition are the traditional reward approach and a more recent formulation by Martens (1975, 1976). The reward approach defines competition as a situation in which rewards are distributed unequally among participants based on their performance in an activity (Church, 1968). The many problems with the reward approach that have limited its scientific viability have been enumerated extensively by Martens (1975, 1976) and will be reviewed only briefly. The major limitation is that the competitive situation defined on a reward basis cannot be clearly operationalized. It is difficult to achieve "consensus on the criteria for the distribution of rewards, on the subjective value of the rewards, and on the goal to be achieved" (Martens, 1975, p. 70). It is quite possible that the goals strived for and the rewards sought might be entirely different for each competitor involved in the competition. Therefore, use of the reward definition forces the experimenter to make the critical assumptions and inferences about the individual's perceptions, responses, and response consequences regarding the competitive situation.

The more recent approach to the study of competition conceptualized by Martens (1975, 1976) has overcome the major deficiencies of the reward definition and provides a more workable alternative for scientific inquiry; it will be used to provide the underlying framework for the ensuing discussion. Martens provides clear operational definitions and makes no assumptions regarding how the individual perceives the competitive situation, the response made to it, or the consequences of the response. Instead, these factors have been divided into stages to be examined systematically.

Martens (1975) has conceptualized competition as a process consisting of four interrelated stages which filter through the individual. The stages include the objective competitive situation, subjective competitive situation, response, and consequences.

The *objective competitive situation* refers to those "real factors in the physical or social environment that are arbitrarily defined as constituting a competitive situation" (Martens, 1975, p. 69). The objective competitive situation (OCS) is based on social evaluation rather than reward and is defined as a situation

in which the comparison of an individual's performance is made with some standard in the presence of at least one other person who is aware of the criterion for comparison and can evaluate the comparison process. (p. 71)

The comparison standard can be an individual's past performance level, an idealized performance level, or another individual's performance.

The second stage of the competition process is the *subjective competitive situation* (SCS) and involves how the individual perceives, appraises, and accepts the OCS. The SCS is very important because it is the manner in which the individual perceives reality, and therefore, it is from this base that the individual operates. The resultant *response* emitted in stage three is a direct function of the SCS. Responses can be made on a psychological, physiological, or behavioral level. Possible responses include the decision to compete or to avoid competition, attempts to modify the objective competitive situation, and overt competitive behavior.

The fourth stage of the competition process involves the *consequences* arising from the comparison process which can be perceived as positive, negative, or neutral. The perceived consequences provide important information which updates the subjective competitive situation and affects future competitive responses.

Beginning with this framework, which identifies social evaluation as a key component of the competition process, it is now possible to detail the social evaluation potential in the naturalistic objective competitive situation encountered by children engaged in competitive youth sports. The subjective competitive situation and response stages will be examined to determine if children perceive the social evaluation potential in the OCS and, if it is perceived, how children then respond in terms of information-seeking and self-protective behavior. The consequences of the competition process will be discussed in terms of implications for psychosocial development. Figure 1 provides a schematic overview of the ensuing discussion.

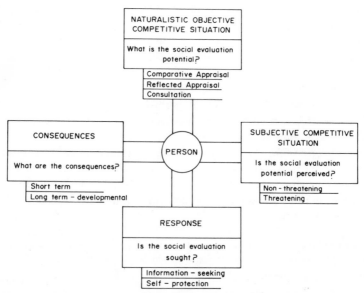

Figure 1—The role of social evaluation in the sport competition process.

SOCIAL EVALUATION POTENTIAL IN THE
NATURALISTIC OBJECTIVE COMPETITIVE SITUATION (OCS)

The naturalistic OCS typically encountered by children encompasses considerable social evaluation potential. Social evaluation is the appraisal of one's ability based on information received from other persons (Jones & Gerard, 1967). Children have been found to be active information seekers who derive information from both social and nonsocial sources with most of their information coming from social sources (Jones & Gerard, 1967; White, 1959, 1960). The developing child has little past experience to draw upon and, consequently, is very dependent on others for information about reality and the adequacy of his or her abilities for dealing with this reality (Jones & Gerard, 1967). As depicted in Figure 1, the typical OCS includes at least three separate social evaluation processes of ability, including comparative appraisal, reflected appraisal, and consultation.

The Comparative Appraisal Process

Comparative appraisal is the process of comparing with others to determine one's own relative standing on some ability (Jones & Gerard, 1967). Comparative appraisal occurs in the OCS when the comparison standard is another individual's performance rather than a past or idealized performance standard. The developmental findings clearly indicate that this comparative appraisal process becomes very important to children at approximately 4 to 5 years of age and intensifies through the elementary school years (Masters, 1972; Veroff, 1969; White, 1960). The following developmental progression indicates why this seems to occur.

Very young children do not compare or compete with others (Greenberg, 1932, 1952; Masters, 1972; Veroff, 1969; White, 1960). Instead, their time is spent autonomously accruing information about their own personal abilities. This is accomplished through exploration, solitary play, mastery attempts, and striving to attain autonomous achievement goals (Cook & Stingle, 1974; Veroff, 1969; White, 1959, 1960). Eventually, however, personal or absolute ability has to be placed into a larger relative framework through comparative appraisal to achieve an accurate, meaningful, and complete assessment of ability. Developmentally, the child appears to be ready to engage in this process around 4 or 5 years of age when the first signs of comparative and competitive behavior are evidenced (Cook & Stingle, 1974; Greenberg, 1932, 1952; Leuba, 1933; Masters, 1972; Veroff, 1969). Further, there is an increase in comparative and competitive behavior with age throughout the elementary school period with the greatest intensity occurring around grades four, five, and six (Cook & Stingle, 1974; Kagan & Madsen, 1972; McClintock & Nuttin, 1969; Nelson, 1970; Nelson & Kagan, 1972;

Veroff, 1969). It is during this important age period that many children are engaged in competitive youth sport activities and in this arena that much of the comparative appraisal occurs. Further, the focus of the appraisal is motor ability. To excel motorically is one of the most prized and esteemed abilities of children, particularly boys, of this age level. Therefore, the comparative appraisal process involves a central ability, making the outcomes potentially very important.

The Reflected Appraisal Process

Reflected appraisal is the second social evaluation process that can occur in the OCS. This is the process by which the child "derives an impression of his position on some attribute through the behavior of another person toward him" (Jones & Gerard, 1967, p. 321). Children can obtain extensive information about their motor ability by carefully attending to the overt or covert cues emitted by another person who is in the position to evaluate their ability. Both comparative and reflected appraisal are similar in that evaluative ability information is derived from a social source. But the two processes differ in the following ways. First, in comparative appraisal, children evaluate their relative ability by comparing with another person's ability, but do not make any reference to the other person's direct behavior toward them (Jones & Gerard, 1967). Reflected appraisal involves the evaluation being "mediated by the behavior of the other person toward the person himself" (Jones & Gerard, 1967, p. 324). Second, comparative appraisal involves evaluation through comparison with social standards, but reflected appraisal includes comparison with either social or objective standards. For example, a coach might unintentionally transmit reflected appraisal cues to a child after the child has won or lost a wrestling match where the comparison standard was social, or after the child has caught or missed a fly ball where the comparison standard was objective and not social.

A considerable amount of reflected appraisal exists in the OCS. First, most competitive situations are quite public so there are numerous persons from which to extract cues including coaches, parents, teammates, opponents, and spectators. Second, evaluation from "significant others" is more important and creates a greater impression on children than evaluation from persons of lesser status (Jones & Gerard, 1967). Third, numerous evaluative cues may be unintentionally emitted but obvious to the child as exemplified by parental cues of pride and approval after a touchdown, and embarrassment and disapproval after a fumble. Other examples include the nonverbal indicants of elation by coaches, teammates, and supporting fans when a player of superior ability steps up to bat with the bases loaded or the chagrin of these same individuals when an inferior player is placed in a similar situation. These latter examples also illustrate how reflected appraisal frequently represents an evaluation that is based on many observations rather than on a one time occurrence. This only tends to increase the potency of reflected appraisal. Fourth, evaluative cues in the OCS are often very overtly manifested. Spectators often cheer or jeer, teammates frequently offer praise or reproof, and opponents sometimes congratulate or ridicule.

The Consultation Process

Consultation, the third social evaluation process, involves children directly asking another person for an ability appraisal or directly receiving an evaluation without explicitly requesting one (Jones & Gerard, 1967). Again, this evaluation is usually received from significant others. For example, parents are often very concerned about their child's motor ability and consequently have much to say about his or her performance. It is the coach's job to evaluate ability, and players receive extensive information during practices that indicates their strengths, weaknesses, progress, and areas requiring improvement. Frequently coaches must make overt evaluations that indicate their appraisal of a player's ability compared to other players; this provides important information for the comparative appraisal process. Selecting a team, choosing who starts and who substitutes, and picking all-star candidates are all examples of evaluations coaches must make.

In sum, the OCS encompasses extensive potential social evaluation through the processes of comparative appraisal, reflected appraisal, and direct consultation. Much information is available from which to establish rather accurate, complete, and stable ability assessments. Participation in the competition process occurs during the age period when the social evaluation process is particularly intense and important. Furthermore, motor ability, the specific ability being appraised, is of central importance. Therefore, it is contended that the social evaluation potential in the OCS is quite high.

THE SUBJECTIVE COMPETITIVE SITUATION (SCS)

The subjective competitive situation is the individual's perception of the objective competitive situation and it must be examined to determine if social evaluation is actually perceived by the competitors (see Figure 1). It must be determined whether social evaluation is a real and an important factor to the competition process.

The SCS is very difficult to assess because it is a cognitive variable, and inference is required. One indicant used to assess the social evaluation potential in the SCS has been the perception of threat to self evidenced by state anxiety. Potential threat to self generally increases when social evaluation potential is maximized, when success and failure are clearly defined, and when negative outcomes and evaluation can be incurred. This perceived threat can induce psychological stress as manifested by state anxiety. State anxiety is defined by Spielberger (1966) as "subjective consciously perceived feelings of apprehension and tension, accompanied by or associated with activation or arousal of the autonomic nervous system" (p. 17). State anxiety is a "right now" reaction to the immediate situation and can be assessed by physiological measures of autonomic arousal, by observation, and by psychological inventories. Two of the best psychological inventories currently available are Spielberger's State Anxiety Inventory (SAI) and his version of the scale for children (SAIC). Research with these scales has consistently shown that state anxiety increases under conditions of psychological stress (Hodges, 1968; Kieffer & Tennyson, 1973; McAdoo, 1970; Spielberger, 1973; Spielberger, Gorsuch, & Lushene, 1969). The SAI or SAIC have been used in most of the studies that have examined the SCS. The few studies that provide some insight into the SCS and the perception of threat are reviewed in the next two sections.

Empirical Evidence from Laboratory Studies

A laboratory study was conducted by the author to assess threat in the SCS and to determine intrapersonal and situational factors that induce it (Scanlan, 1975, 1977). Specifically, the effects of competitive trait anxiety (A-trait) and success-failure on state anxiety (A-state) manifested prior to and after a highly socially evaluative competition were investigated. This experiment is discussed briefly because it is one of the few studies conducted for the particular purpose of assessing perceived threat resulting from high social evaluation potential in the OCS.

Competitive A-trait, assessed by the Sport Competition Anxiety Test (SCAT), is a very important intrapersonal factor related to perceived threat. It is a "relatively stable personality disposition that describes a person's tendency to perceive competitive situations as threatening or non-threatening" and to respond with varying A-state levels (Martens & Gill, 1976, p. 699). Findings in the general anxiety literature have shown consistently that high A-trait individuals exhibit greater A-state than low A-trait individuals when in psychologically stressful situations (Hodges, 1968; Hodges & Durham, 1972; Lamb, 1972; Sarason, 1960, 1968). Therefore, it was hypothesized in this study that high competitive A-trait children would evidence higher A-state than low competitive A-trait children when facing a stressful competitive situation.

The degree of success or failure experienced during competition is an important situational determinant of perceived threat to self. Individuals achieving success should be less threatened by the information about their ability, should expect greater positive evaluation from others, and should be more confident in their ability to effect positive outcomes in similar future encounters than individuals incurring failure. Individuals incurring moderate-success outcomes receive little definitive evaluative information and should approximate precompetitive perceptions. Results from the general anxiety literature have indicated consistently that A-state decreases with success and increases with failure (Hodges & Durham, 1972; Ishiguro, 1965; McAdoo, 1970). Therefore, it was hypothesized that children experiencing success during competition would evidence a significant decrease in A-state, children experiencing moderate-success would evidence no change, and children experiencing failure would evidence a significant increase in A-state after competition outcomes were received.

The experimental design was a Competitive A-trait × Success-Failure (2 × 3) factorial. The two levels of the first factor were high and low competitive A-trait. The Sport Competition Anxiety Test (SCAT) was administered to 306 boys between 10 and 12 years of age several weeks prior to the experimental phase of the study. The 41 high competitive A-trait boys and the 42 low competitive A-trait boys representing the respective upper and lower quartiles on SCAT were selected as participants. The three levels of success-failure were induced by manipulating the win percentage. The success group won 80% (W_{80}), the moderate-success group won 50% (W_{50}), and the failure group won only 20% (W_{20}) of the 20 contests. Both high and low A-trait subjects were randomly assigned to success-failure conditions.

A-state was assessed by Spielberger's State Anxiety Inventory for Children (SAIC) at four different time periods. An initial basal measure was taken after a lengthy rest period. Assessments were also made just prior to competition, after competition, and after a final debriefing session.

The findings indicated that competitive A-trait and success-failure are important factors of the perception of threat and provided support for the two hypotheses. Competitive A-trait was found to be a significant predictor of precompetitive A-state with high competitive A-trait individuals indicating greater A-state than low competitive A-trait individuals when anticipating the pending competition. The findings also indicated that significantly higher A-state or perceived threat is elicited after failure than after success.

These findings were replicated in an experiment conducted by Martens and Gill (1976) that used similar procedures and the identical task. This study also included a midcompetition assessment of A-state which was made after 10 of the 20 competition trials were completed. The greatest difference between the anxiety groups was evidenced during this midcompetition period with high competitive A-trait children indicating even greater A-state than during the precompetition period. It seems that at midcompetition, the competition is pressing and apparent, but the outcome is still uncertain and, therefore, maximally threatening to those who characteristically perceive competition as threatening.

The results of these experiments indicate that the subjective competitive situation is more threatening for high competitive A-trait individuals when anticipating a socially evaluative competition or during competition when the outcome is still uncertain and negative evaluation can still be incurred. Further, success or failure experiences significantly influence threat perception. Threat in the subjective competitive situation significantly increases with failure experiences and decreases with success experiences. The evidence indicates that the social evaluation potential in the SCS is actually perceived.

Empirical Evidence from Field Studies

The findings from three experiments conducted in the field setting provide external validity for the previous laboratory results and add further insight into the perception of threat in the subjective competitive situation. Scanlan and Passer (1977) tested the same two hypotheses assessed in the laboratory experiments of Martens and Gill (1976) and Scanlan (1977). Subjects were 11- and 12-year-old boys participating in youth soccer. Preseason assessments of competitive A-trait and basal A-state (SAIC) were taken. Pre- and postgame A-state were assessed at the eighth game of the season. The results supported previous findings that competitive A-trait was positively related to pregame A-state or perceived threat. Further, losing players evidenced greater postgame state anxiety than winning players.

Klavora (1975) examined the A-state manifested by high and low A-trait junior and senior high school boys prior to noncompetitive and competitive situations. A-trait and A-state were assessed by Spielberger's State-Trait Anxiety Inventory. A-trait is a construct similar to competitive A-trait but is less specific to the competitive situation (Spielberger, 1966).

Practice sessions represented the low stress, noncompetitive situation in Klavora's experiment. Regular season and play-off games depicted the high stress, evaluative competitive situation. A-state assessments were made approximately ½ hour prior to practices and games. The findings showed that both high and low A-trait subjects manifested significantly greater A-state in the competitive situation than noncompetitive situations. Again, high A-trait players evidenced greater A-state across all conditions than low A-trait players.

A-state also increases significantly when the focus of a competitive game centers on an individual player executing a skill. Hanson (1967) used telemetry to monitor the heart rates of Little League players prior to participating in warm-up activities and while at bat. The mean heart beats increased from 110 prior to warm up to 166 while at bat when social evaluation is most intense.

In sum, the findings of the five experiments that have been reviewed provide insight into threat in the subjective competitive situation. Extensive social evaluation potential existed in the objective competitive situation of each experiment. Further, competitive A-trait and general A-trait were found to be two intrapersonal factors that affect the amount of threat perceived when anticipating participation in a highly evaluative objective competitive situation or midway through the competition when outcome uncertainty is still maximal. Success-failure and being the focus of attention during skill execution were found to be two situational factors important to threat perception. How the subjective competitive situation is responded to in terms of seeking the available ability information and subsequent evaluation is examined next.

RESPONSE

It has been shown that children are very aware of the social evaluation potential in the objective competitive situation and can be threatened by it. Referring again to Figure 1, the next question of interest is to determine how children respond to this social evaluation. Do they actively seek the information about their ability that emanates from the evaluation, or do they avoid this evaluative ability information, when possible, to protect themselves? These questions need to be answered to further determine how important and pervasive this socially evaluative information is.

A question of particular relevance to this discussion is to determine how children under different levels of perceived threat structure the competitive situation if they are given the opportunity to do so through selecting their own future opponent. Is the situation structured to maximize or minimize information about their ability? Festinger's social comparison theory provides some insight into the issue.

Festinger (1954) developed a theory of social comparison based on the premise that human beings are motivated to seek evaluative information about their abilities and, in the absence of objective standards, seek comparative appraisal. Further, comparison is made with similar-ability others to maximize information gain. The usual paradigm used to assess this hypothesis has been structured in the following way. Subjects are told that their score, representing performance on a positively or negatively valued attribute, has fallen at the median of a list of rank-ordered scores. Subjects are then asked which score in the ranked list they would like to see. Typically, if the extreme scores have been established and the trait is positive, subjects choose to see the score of a similar or slightly superior other in the rank order (Gruder, 1971; Hakmiller, 1966; Radloff, 1966; Singer & Shockley, 1965). This consistent finding indicates support for Festinger's information-seeking hypothesis.

However, several findings have indicated that when threat to self exists in social evaluation situations, self-protective behavior occurs. Further, such behavior increases as the probability of incurring threatening ability information increases. Findings indicate that individuals reduce the probability of receiving this threatening information by comparing with individuals of lesser relative ability, and thereby assuring successful comparative appraisal (Dreyer, 1954; Friend & Gilbert, 1973; Hakmiller, 1966).

The following hypotheses can be derived from the social comparison findings. First, successful, unthreatened subjects structure the situation to maximize information gain by selecting opponents of equal or slightly greater relative ability. Conversely, unsuccessful, threatened subjects minimize information gain by selecting opponents of lesser relative ability. In this way, they protect themselves from incurring further threatening negative comparative and reflected appraisal.

Scanlan (1977) tested these two hypotheses in the competition experiment presented earlier. Opponent preference questions were administered during the postcompetition period immediately after postcompetition A-state was assessed. The results supported the first hypothesis but not the second. Children in all three success-failure groups indicated a strong preference for opponents who were equal to them in ability. These findings indicate that children engage in maximum information seeking behavior during competition regardless of the level of threat perceived by them.

CONSEQUENCES

The final stage of the competition process involves the short- and long-term consequences which may be positive, negative, or neutral (see Figure 1). Whenever social evaluation of ability occurs, positive or negative consequences can result during any given competition. The child might receive successful comparative appraisal information and positive evaluation from significant others. Conversely, unsuccessful comparative appraisal and negative social evaluation might be incurred. However, the consequences of any *one isolated* competitive experience probably have minimal effects on psychosocial development. The important point is that many children engage in intense competition over extended periods of time with similar consequences being repeated over and over again. It is this repetition that makes developmental considerations relevant. It is through this repetition that the potential accrual of primarily successful or primarily failure experiences can result. It is also through this repetition that success or failure experiences might somewhat balance out leading to relatively neutral long term consequences.

The second important point is that the consequences of the competition process must be kept within the perspective of the total socialization process. The extensive evaluative information available in the objective competitive situation can result in children establishing an accurate assessment of an ability that is very important to them. Whether or not this information, be it positive or negative, results in perceived favorable, neutral, or adverse consequences is probably dependent upon the manner in which significant others evaluate and interpret the information and what perspective they provide. For example, children who continually receive negative comparative appraisal but gain support and guidance from their parents and coaches might benefit considerably from the competitive experience. The potential negative consequences might be neutralized. The children might learn to accept their limitations and capabilities, they might learn to set and to strive for realistic goals, and they might learn to cope with success and failure. The potential negative impact of the consequences might further be reduced if the children can demonstrate other abilities, function competently in other evaluative settings, and receive positive evaluation from significant others.

In sum, the competition process must be placed within the larger socialization process to be adequately investigated. Although competition is an important process, it cannot be isolated from the child's greater social context. The role of significant others and competence in other situations must be considered as they influence the positive, negative, or neutral long-term consequences of competition.

With social evaluation and resulting positive, negative, or neutral consequences as the focus, the developmental literature can now be examined to establish links between the competition process and various developmental processes. Findings indicate that the development of several attributes is centrally influenced by the cumulative positive or negative consequences of evaluation. Some of these attributes include self-esteem, A-trait, competence, and achievement motivation (Coopersmith, 1967; Heckhausen, 1967; Scanlan, Chapter 5 in this volume; Smith, 1969; Veroff, 1969; White, 1959); others need to be determined. Empirically testing the effects of competition on the development of these attributes is a starting place. Veroff (1969), for example, has indicated that a successful social comparison stage must be achieved for mature, integrated achievement motivation to be developed. How, then, does continual positive or negative comparative, reflected, and consultation appraisal from significant others, during an extended competitive experience, influence the achievement motivation development of the highly sports-oriented child?

REFERENCES

CHURCH, R.M. Applications of behavior theory to social psychology: Imitation and competition. In E.C. Simmel, R.H. Hoppe, & G.A. Milton (Eds.), *Social facilitation and imitative behavior*. Boston: Allyn & Bacon, 1968.

COOK, H., & Stingle, S. Cooperative behavior in children. *Psychological Bulletin*, 1974, **81**, 918-933.

COOPERSMITH, S. *The antecedents of self-esteem*. San Francisco: W.H. Freeman, 1967.

DREYER, H.S. Aspiration behavior as influenced by expectation and group comparison. *Human Relations*, 1954, **7**, 175-190.

FESTINGER, L.A. A theory of social comparison processes. *Human Relations*, 1954, **7**, 117-140.

FRIEND, R.M., & Gilbert, J. Threat and fear of negative evaluation as determinants of locus of social comparison. *Journal of Personality*, 1973, **41**, 328-340.

GREENBERG, P.J. Competition in children: An experimental study. *American Journal of Psychology*, 1932, **44**, 221-248.

GREENBERG, P.J. The growth of competitiveness during childhood. In R.G. Kuhlen & G.G. Thompson (Eds.), *Psychological studies of human development*. New York: Appleton-Century-Crofts, 1952.

GRUDER, C.L. Determinants of social comparison. *Journal of Experimental Social Psychology*, 1971, **7**, 473-489.

HAKMILLER, K.L. Threat as a determinant of downward comparison. *Journal of Experimental Social Psychology Supplement*, 1966, **2**(1), 32-39.

HANSON, D.L. Cardiac responses to participation in Little League competition as determined by telemetry. *Research Quarterly*, 1967, **38**, 384-388.

HECKHAUSEN, H. *The anatomy of achievement motivation*. New York: Academic Press, 1967.

HODGES, W.F. Effects of ego threat and threat of pain on state anxiety. *Journal of Personality and Social Psychology*, 1968, **8**, 364-372.

HODGES, W.F., & Durham, R.L. Anxiety, ability and digit span performance. *Journal of Personality and Social Psychology*, 1972, **24**, 401-406.

ISHIGURO, S. Motivational instructions and GSR on memory, especially as related to manifest anxiety. *Psychological Reports*, 1965, **16**, 786.

JONES, E.E., & Gerard, H.B. *Foundations of social psychology*. New York: Wiley, 1967.

KAGAN, S., & Madsen, M.C. Rivalry in Anglo-American and Mexican children of two ages. *Journal of Personality and Social Psychology*, 1972, **24**, 214-220.

KIEFFER, L.F., & Tennyson, R.D. Effects of concurrent negative feedback on performance of two motor tasks. *Journal of Motor Behavior*, 1973, **5**, 241-248.

KLAVORA, P. Emotional arousal in athletics: New considerations. Mouvement. *Proceedings of the Seventh Canadian Psycho-Motor Learning and Sport Psychology Symposium*. October 1975, pp. 279-287.

LAMB, D.H. Speech anxiety: Towards a theoretical conceptualization and preliminary scale development. *Speech Monographs*, 1972, **39**, 62-67.

LEUBA, C. An experimental study of rivalry in children. *Journal of Comparative Psychology*, 1933, **16**, 367-378.

MARTENS, R. *Social psychology and physical activity*. New York: Harper & Row, 1975.

MARTENS, R. Competition: In need of a theory. In D.M. Landers (Ed.), *Social problems in athletics*. Urbana, IL: University of Illinois Press, 1976.

MARTENS, R., & Gill, D. State anxiety among successful and unsuccessful competitors who differ in competitive trait anxiety. *Research Quarterly*, 1976, **47**, 698-708.

MASTERS, J.C. Social comparison by young children. In W.W. Hartup (Ed.), *The young child*. Washington, DC: National Association for Education of Young Children, 1972.

MCADOO, W.G., Jr. *The effects of success, mild failure, and strong failure feedback on A-State for subjects who differ in A-Trait*. Unpublished doctoral dissertation, Florida State University, 1970.

MCCLINTOCK, C., & Nuttin, J. Development of competitive game behavior in children across two cultures. *Journal of Experimental Social Psychology*, 1969, **5**, 203-218.

NELSON, L.L. *The development of cooperation and competition in children from ages five to ten years old: Effects of sex, situational determinants, and prior experiences*. Unpublished doctoral dissertation, University of California, Los Angeles, 1970.

NELSON, L.L., & Kagan, S. The star-spangled scramble. *Psychology Today*, 1972, **6**, 53.

RADLOFF, R. Social comparison and ability evaluation. *Journal of Experimental Social Psychology Supplement*, 1966, **2**(1), 6-26.

SARASON, I.G. Empirical findings and theoretical problems in the use of anxiety scales. *Psychological Bulletin*, 1960, **57**, 403-415.

SARASON, I.G. Verbal learning, modeling, and juvenile delinquency. *American Psychologist*, 1968, **23**, 254-266.

SCANLAN, T.K. *The effects of competition trait anxiety and success-failure on the perception of threat in a competitive situation.* Unpublished doctoral dissertation, University of Illinois, Urbana-Champaign, 1975.

SCANLAN, T.K. The effects of success-failure on the perception of threat in a competitive situation. *Research Quarterly*, 1977, **48**, 144-153.

SCANLAN, T.K., & Passer, M.W. The effects of competition trait anxiety and game win-loss on perceived threat in a natural competitive setting. In D.M. Landers & R.W. Christina (Eds.), *Psychology of motor behavior and sport* (Vol. II). Champaign, IL: Human Kinetics, 1977.

SINGER, J.E., & Shockley, V.L. Ability and affiliation. *Journal of Personality and Social Psychology*, 1965, **1**, 95-100.

SMITH, C.P. The origin and expression of achievement-related motives in children. In C.P. Smith (Ed.), *Achievement-related motives in children*. New York: Russell Sage Foundation, 1969.

SPIELBERGER, C.D. (Ed.). *Anxiety and behavior.* New York: Academic Press, 1966.

SPIELBERGER, C.D. *Preliminary test manual for the state-trait anxiety inventory for children* ("How I Feel Questionnaire"). Palo Alto, CA: Consulting Psychologists Press, 1973.

SPIELBERGER, C.D., Gorsuch, R.L., & Lushene, R.E. *The State-Trait Anxiety Inventory (STAIC) test manual for form X*. Tallahassee, FL: Author, 1969.

VEROFF, J. Social comparison and the development of achievement motivation. In C.P. Smith (Ed.), *Achievement-related motives in children*. New York: Russell Sage Foundation, 1969.

WHITE, R.W. Motivation reconsidered: The concept of competence. *Psychological Review*, 1959, **66**, 297-334.

WHITE, R.W. Competence and the psychosexual stages of development. In M.R. Jones (Ed.), *Nebraska symposium on motivation* (Vol. 8). Lincoln: University of Nebraska Press, 1960.

CHAPTER 12

PSYCHOLOGICAL STRESS
IN YOUTH SPORTS

Michael W. Passer

Whether participation in highly organized sports engenders unhealthy or excessive levels of psychological stress in children has been the subject of long-standing debate. Physical educators and recreation leaders first voiced reservations about children's ability to cope with the psychological pressures of intense athletic competition nearly 50 years ago (Berryman, 1975; also see chapter 1 in this volume). Today, psychologists, sociologists, and educators continue to express concern about stress in children's sports (Brower, 1979; Ogilvie, 1979; Staniford, 1976). In fact, a recent survey of youth sport researchers and practitioners indicates that competitive stress is considered one of the most important psychological issues confronting that field (Gould, Note 1).

The prominence attached to the topic of stress in the youth sport literature is not surprising. The tremendous expansion of nonschool sport programs for children during the past decade has sparked a commensurate interest in understanding their psychological effects and has led to a heightened awareness of athletic competition as an important social and developmental process (see chapter 11 by Scanlan in this volume; Smoll & Smith, 1978). Concurrently, popular and scientific interest in stress has been stimulated by mounting evidence of its potential-

The author was supported during the preparation of this chapter by a grant from the Graduate School Research Fund, University of Washington.

ly deleterious effects on physical and mental health, social adjustment, and performance (Johnson & Sarason, 1979; Neufeld & Mothersill, 1980), and by indications that the effects of stress on children and adolescents may parallel those experienced by adults (Johnson & McCutcheon, 1980). Thus, with more children competing in athletics than ever before and with competition beginning at progressively younger ages, there is a growing need to examine the extent, determinants, and consequences of psychological stress among youth sport participants.

THE STRESS PROCESS

Numerous models and definitions of psychological stress have been proposed (e.g., Lazarus, 1966; Martens, 1977; McGrath, 1976; Sarason, 1980; Smith, 1980) and important differences exist between them. Nevertheless, some recurrent themes appear and a basic attempt at integration can be made. The stress process is viewed in this chapter as having four stages (see Figure 1), and begins when the individual is confronted with a situation (stimulus) that presents some type of demand, constraint, or opportunity (McGrath, 1976; Sarason, 1980). The term "demand" will be used in a broad sense to encompass these conditions, all of which imply the need for some type of action or adjustment. The label "situation" does not refer exclusively to the immediate, external situation, however. As Smith (1980) has noted, internal stimuli such as thoughts, images, and memories also may initiate the stress process.

The person's appraisal or interpretation of the situation represents the second stage of the stress process. The nature of the demand, its importance, and the available personal resources (e.g., skill, time, motivation, money) will be evaluated. An important construct that several investigators (Lazarus, 1966; Martens, 1977; Spielberger, 1972) introduce at this stage of the process is *threat*, which Lazarus (1966) defines as "the

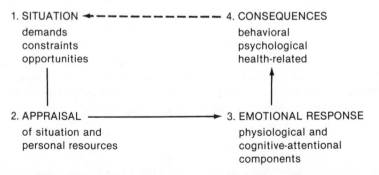

Figure 1—The stress process.

condition of the person when confronted with a stimulus that he appraises as endangering important values and goals" (p. 28). Psychological stress indicates situations judged by the individual as threatening in some way. The perception of threat often occurs because the individual considers it important to meet the situational demand but either appraises personal resources to be inadequate ("I can't do it") or is uncertain whether those resources are adequate ("I don't know if I can . . . I'm not sure"). At times, however, threat can occur because the situation does not demand enough from the person (McGrath, 1976; Martens, 1977). For example, a competent worker may perceive the continual assignment of easy or trivial tasks as threatening because it constrains the possibility of demonstrating superior ability to the boss and hinders chances of promotion.

Emotional response represents the next stage of the stress process. Unpleasant emotional states such as anxiety, anger, and guilt constitute a major class of stress responses (Lazarus, 1966; Smith, 1980) and are viewed in this model as having physiological and cognitive-attentional components. The manner in which a situation is appraised has a significant influence on each of these components. That is, the perception of threat may trigger not only a physiological response, but also self-preoccupational thoughts that divert the individual's attention from task-relevant cues. For example, the individual may worry about the possibility of failure, dwell on anticipated negative evaluation, or become mired in thoughts of personal helplessness (Sarason, 1980). The emotion that is experienced will depend upon the interaction of these two components and the specific appraisal processes that elicited them. Some investigators propose that the intensity of the emotion will be determined primarily by the level of physiological arousal, whereas the label attached to the emotion (e.g., anxiety, anger) will be governed by cognitions about the situation (Geen, 1980; Schachter, 1964; Zillmann, 1972). Thus, taking a test or competing in sports may produce an arousal response in most children, but those who perceive the situation as nonthreatening may respond with feelings of excitement while others who perceive threat may have feelings of anxiety and fear.[1]

The fourth stage of the stress process focuses on the behavioral, psychological, and health-related consequences of emotional response.

---

[1]Although appraisal processes are portrayed in this model as occurring prior to physiological arousal, it should be noted that both factors can be simultaneously elicited by situational cues (Zillman, 1972), and in some cases, perceived physiological activation may actually initiate appraisal processes (e.g., "I wonder why I'm feeling aroused."). In the latter regard, it has been suggested that unexplained arousal is perceived as aversive, and thus, the presence of such arousal not only may lead to a search for its cause, but also may bias that search in favor of a congruent aversive label (Maslach, 1979). Regardless of the temporal sequence, however, it is proposed that emotional *labeling* will be mediated by appraisal processes.

Behavioral consequences in youth sports would include players' performance, whether they continue to participate or drop out, and their interactions with coaches, teammates, and parents. Psychological consequences would include players' subsequent attitudes and feelings of satisfaction about their sport experience. We might also examine whether stress has any acute or chronic effects on players' physical health, such as increasing their susceptibility to illness or injury. Finally, these personal consequences can modify the situation that initiated the stress process. For example, poor performance may cause the coach to change the demands placed on a player (e.g., demotion to a substitute role or less central position). Dropping out of competition also would alter the situation for the child by, in effect, eliminating it.

Given this model we may now ask how the term "stress" should be defined. Does stress represent the characteristics of the situation causing a negative emotional state or does it actually constitute that emotional state? Is stress an intervening variable, namely, the appraisal of threat? An examination of the literature indicates that stress has been defined in each of these ways. The approach adopted here, however, roughly corresponds to that of several investigators (Lazarus, 1966; Martens, 1977; McGrath, 1976) who view stress not as any one of these components but as the situation-person interaction. That is, stress connotes an unpleasant or aversive emotional state that is a result of situational demands appraised as threatening.

The model outlined above provides a useful framework for the examination of stress in youth sports. First, the major situational demands in youth sports, and players' appraisal of these demands and their resources, will be discussed. Second, research on players' emotional responses to athletic competition will be reviewed. Third, the consequences of stress for the young athlete will be addressed. The chapter will conclude with a brief discussion of methods for reducing players' stress.

THE YOUTH SPORT SETTING: DEMANDS AND APPRAISAL

Participation in youth sports can be stressful because players are confronted with numerous demands that are appraised as important but that may not be fulfilled. The fundamental demands of athletic competition are the same as those inherent in all competitive activities: (a) some type of performance must occur, that is, an ability or attribute must be demonstrated, (b) this performance must be compared with some standard such as the performance of others or the person's past performance, and (c) at least one person must be present, other than the performer, who can evaluate the comparison process (Martens, 1975). The significance of these demands to youth sport participants is clear. First, sports involve the demonstration of athletic ability, which is a highly valued attribute among children and adolescents (Buchanan, Blanken-baker, & Cotten, 1976; Coleman, 1961). Second, the opportunity for ability comparison is important because it is a major means by which children acquire information about themselves. As Scanlan notes in chapter 11, social comparison becomes important to children around the ages of 4 to 5 and takes on increasing significance during the elementary school years, a time when many children compete in organized non-school sports. Third, children in youth sports are extensively evaluated by adults and peers. This evaluation is readily transmitted by numerous verbal and nonverbal cues (e.g., praise and criticism, facial expressions, designation as a starter or substitute) and is important because it conveys substantial amounts of information to children about their ability (see chapter 11 in this volume).

Obviously, the youth sport setting involves many demands other than those concerning the demonstration, comparison, and evaluation of athletic ability. For example, such attributes as leadership, sportsman-ship, intelligence, and likeability also may be the focus of evaluation, and feedback about these characteristics can be quite stress-inducing. Studies examining the participation motivation of young athletes provide additional insight on the nature and appraisal of situational demands. Although opportunities for success and achievement are consistently perceived as important reasons for participating, other motives emerge as well: affiliation, skill learning and improvement, and a desire for physical fitness, to name a few (Alderman & Wood, 1976; Gill, Gross, & Huddleston, Note 2; Gould, Feltz, Weiss, & Petlichkoff, Note 3). Thus, children who view sports as a setting in which to make friends may be stressed if they experience rejection by their teammates. Analogously, stress can occur when players are strongly motivated by the opportunity for skill acquisition but find themselves playing for a coach who is a poor teacher or who places inadequate emphasis on skill instruc-tion.

Thus far, this section has focused on situational demands and how they are appraised. Some direct information also exists about youth sport participants' appraisals of their capacity to meet these demands. For example, children differ considerably in athletic ability and it ap-pears that players establish fairly accurate perceptions of their skill level (Passer & Scanlan, Note 4). Players also differ in their general and game-specific expectancies of personal and team performance: While some players express a high certainty of success, others are uncertain about performance outcomes (Scanlan & Passer, 1979a, 1981; Passer, Note 5). Further, the structure of most athletic contests is such that certain situa-tional demands (e.g., winning) cannot be satisfied by all children at all times. If we recall Lazarus' definition of threat (i.e., the perception that important values and goals are endangered), it is clear that the youth sport setting will, at times, be perceived by some children as threatening.

EMOTIONAL RESPONSES TO COMPETITION

A variety of unpleasant or aversive emotional states can serve as indicants of stress. Examination of the youth sport literature, however, reveals that discussions and research on stress have focused primarily on children's state anxiety reactions to competition. State anxiety represents a transitory response to a particular situation and is defined as "subjective consciously perceived feelings of apprehension and tension, accompanied by or associated with activation or arousal of the autonomic nervous system" (Spielberger, 1966, p. 17). Like other emotions, state anxiety can be assessed in several ways: Perhaps the most common technique in youth sport research is the administration of self-report measures, such as the State Anxiety Inventory (Spielberger, Gorsuch, & Lushene, 1970), that ask respondents to indicate how "nervous," "jittery," "worried," "calm," and so on they feel at a particular point in time. Physiological recordings represent a second method of assessing state anxiety. Included in this category would be measures of cardiovascular responses (e.g., heart rate, blood pressure, skin temperature) and electrodermal activity (e.g., skin conductance level, conductance response frequency). A third technique used to assess state anxiety is the observation of overt behaviors such as trembling, pacing, avoidance and escape, and alterations in eating and sleeping patterns. Research examining these types of behavioral responses will be discussed in the section on the consequences of stress. For the moment we will focus on investigations that have assessed the cognitive and physiological components of children's emotional responses to sport competition.

Between-Sport Comparisons

Agency-sponsored youth programs exist in a wide variety of sports and this diversity creates an obvious problem in attempting to draw general conclusions about the stressfulness of athletic competition for children. Fortunately, some research has been conducted to determine whether certain types of sports are more stress-inducing than others. The best example is a study by Simon and Martens (1979), which examined the precompetition state anxiety of 468 9- to 14-year-old boys who were drawn from one of the following youth sports: baseball, basketball, football, ice hockey, gymnastics, swimming, and wrestling. State anxiety was assessed by the Competitive State Anxiety Inventory (Martens, Burton, Rivkin, & Simon, 1980), which is a shortened, sport-specific form of Spielberger et al.'s (1970) State Anxiety Inventory. This test was administered to players within 10 minutes (and usually within 2 or 3 minutes) before the start of competition.[2]

---

[2] A baseline (resting) measure of state anxiety also was taken from each player in a nonevaluative situation. This measure was then used as a control factor (i.e., covariate) in the between-sport analyses.

The findings indicated that participants in individual sports generally had higher state anxiety prior to competition than players in team sports. Specifically, wrestling and gymnastics were the two most anxiety-inducing sports and elicited significantly higher anxiety than football, hockey, and baseball, which were the least stressful activities. A general comparison of contact (wrestling, football, hockey) versus noncontact (gymnastics, swimming, baseball, basketball) sports revealed no overall difference between the two groups. Thus, Simon and Martens' (1979) study suggests that one important dimension of athletic competition influencing children's stress is whether the sport represents an individual or team activity.

Additional data on this issue are provided by Griffin (1972), who examined the precompetition state anxiety of female athletes from four individual sports (gymnastics, swimming, tennis, track and field) and four team sports (basketball, field hockey, softball, and volleyball). The 682 participating athletes were drawn from three age groups—12 to 13, 16 to 17, and 19 years and older—and were administered the State Anxiety Inventory within 1 hour prior to competition. Unfortunately, it is not clear how many of the athletes participated in school-sponsored as opposed to agency-sponsored sports (it is likely that most, if not all, did). Nor were the findings presented separately by age group.[3] With these cautions in mind, the results indicated a significant difference in state anxiety as a function of sport. Gymnasts had the highest precompetitive state anxiety followed (in rank order) by participants in track and field, swimming, tennis, football, volleyball, basketball, and field hockey. Thus, Griffin's results are consistent with those of Simon and Martens (1979) in revealing that individual sports, which maximize the social evaluation potential of competition, generally elicit higher levels of pre-event anxiety than team sports.

Situational Determinants of Stress During Competition

Competitive circumstances vary in the amount of stress that they induce. As the studies cited in the preceding section indicate, the nature of the sport (i.e., individual versus team) is itself a determinant of how much stress children experience prior to competing. Other investigations have examined how players' stress during competition is affected by specific situational factors that accompany or occur within a particular match. For example, Lowe and McGrath (Note 6) examined the effects of situation criticality and game criticality on the stress of 60 boys, 10 to 12 years of age, throughout an entire 18-game season of Little League Baseball.

---

[3]The lack of an age breakdown for the results is particularly unfortunate because a significant age × sport interaction was found.

Situation criticality represented the importance of the immediate situation within a game and took into account the difference in score between the two teams, the inning of play, the number of outs in the inning, and the number and location of any base-runners. Game criticality represented the importance of the game itself and was a function of the ranking of the two teams within the league, the difference in their won-lost percentage, and the remaining number of games in the season. Stress was assessed by two physiological measures, pulse rate and respiration rate. Because of practical constraints, these recordings were taken each time a player was in the dugout, waiting to go to the on-deck circle (i.e., the player was two turns from coming to bat). As predicted, higher pulse and respiration rates were found under conditions of either greater situation or game criticality.[4] Although the average magnitude of physiological change across conditions was not great (e.g., about 8 to 11 heart beats per minute mean difference between situations of lower versus higher criticality), the fact that response variation occurred when players were still in the dugout is noteworthy. Overall, game criticality seemed to have a greater effect on players' arousal than did situation criticality, which led Lowe and McGrath to suggest that the importance of the total situation (i.e., the game) may be a greater determinant of arousal than specific events within the situation.

Hanson (1967) conducted another study examining within-game variation in children's stress. The subjects were 10 boys between the ages of 9 and 12 who participated in Little League Baseball. Each player was observed for a single game during which his heart rate was monitored by telemetry. Recordings were taken when the player was at bat, standing on base after a hit, sitting in the dugout after making an out, standing in the field, and sitting and standing at rest before and after the game. The most striking finding was the magnitude of response shown when players came to bat. As compared to an average pregame resting heart rate (while standing) of 110 beats per minute (bpm), the average rate when batting was 166 bpm. In comparison, the average heart rate for players while in the field was 128 bpm. Substantial variation was found within and between players. The highest heart rate recorded while at bat was 204 bpm; the lowest was 145 bpm. There is a parallel between these results and those obtained by Lowe and McGrath (1971). Although Hanson did not measure situation criticality per se, batting is clearly one of the most important and evaluation-laden activities in baseball and it is not surprising that players responded to this situational demand with elevated

---

[4]A positive relation between game criticality and pregame arousal also was obtained. Lowe and McGrath used a behavioral index of stress, the amount of physical activity emitted by the player while in the on-deck circle (i.e., one turn from coming to bat), which did not increase significantly as a function of either greater situation or game criticality.

arousal. There also is an interesting anomoly in Hanson's findings. Based on players' physiological responses, Hanson concluded that the emotional stress of being at bat was high, but short-lived. After the game, however, most players reported that they did not feel particularly nervous while batting. One interpretation of this apparent inconsistency between players' self-reports and their physiological responses is that they refused to acknowledge that they were feeling anxious (Brower, 1979). Another possibility is that players were not feeling especially nervous and their arousal while at bat primarily reflected some other emotional state (e.g., excitement, feeling psyched-up).[5]

Although the studies by Hanson (1967) and Lowe and McGrath (Note 6) provide information about players' physiological reactions to various game conditions, there is a lack of research directly examining the cognitive component of players' emotional responses during ongoing competition. Practical constraints in the field setting of youth sports make it difficult to administer self-report inventories to players during a contest; this difficulty is accentuated when measurements must be taken on multiple occasions within a single match or game. Several laboratory experiments, however, have been able to use self-report measures to assess children's stress during competition at motor-skill tasks. Specifically, these experiments indicate that children's midcompetition state anxiety, as measured by Spielberger's (1973) State Anxiety Inventory for Children, is significantly influenced by the performance outcomes they have experienced up to that point of the match: Children who find themselves trailing their opponents (i.e., children who are losing the early trials of a multitrial contest) become more anxious than those who find themselves ahead (Gill & Martens, 1977; Martens & Gill, 1976).

In sum, these field and laboratory studies suggest that the criticality of the game, the importance of the situation within the game, the specific activity in which the player is engaging (e.g., batting, fielding), and whether one is ahead of or behind the opposition are situational factors that can influence children's stress during competition. Of course, there may be many other situational determinants of players' stress while they

---

[5]The problem here is that physiological measures do not provide information about the cognitive (phenomenological) component of emotional responses such as anxiety. If psychological stress is regarded as a process pertaining to negative emotional states (as it is in this chapter) rather than general emotionality (i.e., arousal), conclusions about stress based solely upon physiological recordings must be made with caution. There are additional problems with using physiological measures to index stress or specific emotional states such as anxiety, and self-report and behavioral measures have their share of imperfections as well. Moreover, research consistently indicates that the correlations between self-report, physiological, and behavioral indices of anxiety are poor. For a more thorough discussion of measurement issues about stress and anxiety, see Borkovec, Weerts, and Bernstein (1977), Holroyd & Appel (1980), Landers (1980), and Singer (1980).

compete. Among these factors might be the position that they play, the size of the crowd, and the behavior of the coach, parents, and other spectators.

Success, Failure, and Postcompetition Stress

Winning and performing well may not be the only goals that youth sport participants value, but there is little doubt that these achievement goals are viewed as important (see Passer, 1981). We would expect, then, and research has consistently shown, that success-failure outcomes exert a strong effect on children's postcompetition stress. Two studies by Scanlan and Passer (1978b, 1979b) illustrate this point. In the first study 191 boys, 11 and 12 years of age, were administered Spielberger's (1973) State Anxiety Inventory for Children 30 minutes before and immediately after a youth soccer game. A baseline (preseason) measure also was taken. The second study, which was conducted a year later, involved 176 10- to 12-year-old girls and employed the same procedure. The findings from the two studies were virtually identical, with losing players having substantially higher postgame anxiety than winning players. Game win-loss accounted for 40% of the variance in boys' and 55% of the variance in girls' postgame anxiety. Further, a direct comparison of players' pre- and postgame scores indicated that losers were more anxious after the game than before the game, whereas winners evidenced a decrease in pre- to postgame anxiety.

In their study of male players, Scanlan and Passer (1978b) were also able to examine the relationship between game closeness and postcompetition anxiety. Based on the pattern of scoring and the final margin of victory or defeat, games were classified as being very close (1 goal margin), close (2 goal margin), and not close (3 goal margin). The closeness of the game did not influence the postgame anxiety of winners, suggesting that a victory by any margin was sufficient to minimize stress after competition. Game closeness, however, did affect losers' anxiety: Players who lost a very close game had higher postgame anxiety than players who lost either a moderately close game or a game that was not close (the latter two groups did not differ). Scanlan and Passer speculated that losers of very close games may have entertained hopes of a victory or tie right up to the end of the game, and thus, the experience of failure would have been especially acute during the postgame period.

The fact that several games happened to end in a tie afforded Scanlan and Passer the additional opportunity of examining the effects of this outcome on players' postgame anxiety. Data from three games in the girls' study indicated that tying players were significantly more anxious after the game than before the game, although the increase was not as large as that evidenced by losers (Scanlan & Passer, 1979b). The results from one tie game in the boys' study revealed that under some circumstances (e.g., playing a bitter rival and relinquishing the lead within the final minute of play), a tie can be just as anxiety-inducing as a loss (Passer & Scanlan, 1980). Overall, the findings from both studies suggested that a tie is perceived as an aversive outcome.[6]

Laboratory research in which competition outcomes at motor skill tasks are experimentally manipulated provides further evidence about the effects of success-failure on stress. The findings consistently reveal that children who lose or compete unsuccessfully demonstrate higher postcompetition anxiety (assessed by self-report measures) than children who win or compete successfully (Corbin & Nix, 1979; Gill & Martens, 1977; Martens & Gill, 1976; Scanlan, 1977). Finally, a questionnaire survey of 8- to 15-year-old boys playing Little and Middle League Baseball provides some information about players' typical feelings after failure (Skubic, 1956). Only 7% of the 95 respondents indicated that they were not disappointed when their team lost, and 80% reported that they felt very bad when they played a poor game. In sum, it is clear that success-failure is a major situational determinant of children's postcompetition stress.

Intrapersonal Factors Related to Competitive Stress

The amount of stress experienced in a particular sport setting will often vary considerably from one child to another. Some children, for example, may feel very anxious before the start of a game or during competition while others feel calm and relaxed. This raises an important issue, namely, whether any intrapersonal factors account for these individual differences and help predict children's stress reactions to specific competitive situations.

Martens (1977) has proposed that competitive trait anxiety is an important mediator of stress responses to athletic competition. Competitive trait anxiety reflects a person's general tendency to perceive competitive situations as threatening and is assessed by the Sport Competition Anxiety Test (Martens, 1977). As compared to state anxiety, which is a transitory emotional response to an immediate and specific situation, competitive trait anxiety represents a more stable disposition that is thought to develop as a function of "the accumulated consequences of participation in the competitive process" (Martens, 1977, p. 32). Presumably, individuals with high competitive trait anxiety have experienced more failure and negative social evaluation in past competitive situations than have persons with low competitive trait anxiety (Scanlan & Passer, 1978a).

---

[6]Losers, as opposed to winners, also rated the quality of their own and their team's performance as lower, were less satisfied with that performance, and reported having less fun playing the game. In general, the responses of tying players fell in between those of losers and winners (Passer & Scanlan, 1980).

Several investigators (Gill & Martens, 1977; Martens & Gill, 1976; Scanlan & Passer, 1978b, 1979b) have assessed children's competitive trait anxiety a few weeks or months prior to a specific athletic or motor skill contest and examined how well this disposition could predict state anxiety responses to that match. Overall, the results form an interesting pattern. Before competition starts, high competitive trait anxious children show greater state anxiety than low competitive trait anxious children. During competition a similar but slightly weaker relationship is obtained, and it appears that competitive trait anxiety and ongoing success-failure outcomes have an equally strong influence on players' midcompetition state anxiety. The relationship between competitive trait anxiety and state anxiety is weakest (and often nonexistent) after the game or match is over; at that time, state anxiety is strongly determined by the final success-failure outcome. In sum, research indicates that competitive trait anxiety is a significant mediator of children's pre- and midcompetition state anxiety. Moreover, neither coaches nor general trait anxiety scales predict athletes' pregame state anxiety as well as competitive trait anxiety (Martens, 1977; Martens, Rivkin, & Burton, 1980; Martens & Simon, 1976), though these findings have yet to be replicated in the nonschool youth sport setting.

Several other intrapersonal factors influence children's precompetition stress. Using regression analysis, Scanlan and Passer (1978b, 1979b) found that youth soccer players who were more state anxious before the game had not only higher competitive trait anxiety, but also lower self-esteem and lower expectancies about how well they and their team would play in the game. None of these factors, however, was related to players' postgame state anxiety (which, again, was largely determined by the game outcome). It appears, then, that precompetition stress is significantly influenced by intrapersonal factors that reflect children's perceived response capabilities in meeting upcoming performance demands; postcompetition stress is primarily determined by situational factors that provide feedback to children about the adequacy of their actual response to those demands (Scanlan & Passer, 1978b, 1979b).

Current evidence suggests that the intrapersonal factors of gender, athletic ability, and age are not related to players' competitive stress in specific game situations. In comparing the results of their boys' and girls' field studies, Scanlan and Passer (1978b, 1979b) found that the state anxiety responses of the two sexes were remarkably similar both before and after competition. Laboratory experiments also reveal that gender is unrelated to children's pre- and postcompetition state anxiety (Gill & Martens, 1977; Martens & Gill, 1976). With regard to ability, it might be expected that players with less skill would find competition to be more threatening and anxiety-inducing. Scanlan and Passer (1978b, 1979b), however, found no relationship between youth soccer players' ability (as rated by coaches) and pre- or postgame state anxiety. One explanation for these findings might be that while ability does have some influence on how well a child expects to play (Scanlan & Passer, 1979a, 1981), other factors such as intended effort may be more important. Second, it is possible that players with more ability simply have more demands placed on them by others, perceive that more is being demanded of them, or demand more of themselves (i.e., set a higher standard of comparison by which they judge success). Third, the potential for individual social evaluation is reduced in sports that are highly interactive and involve continuous performance, such as soccer. It would be interesting to see if the absence of a direct relationship between ability and competitive stress holds true in individual sports or in team sports that involve sequential, isolated individual performance (e.g., baseball).[7] In terms of age, Lowe and McGrath (Note 6) found that two physiological measures of stress (heart and respiration rate) generally did not differentiate between players of different ages, although a behavioral index of stress (physical activity in the on-deck circle) did, with younger players being more active. The age range in this study was rather narrow (10- through 12-year-olds) and research using a broader age distribution is clearly needed.

Stress in Youth Sports Versus Other Achievement Activities

Although situational and intrapersonal determinants of stress *within* the youth sport setting have been reviewed, the question of whether children find athletic competition more stressful than other evaluative or achievement activities has not yet been addressed. The most complete information on this topic is provided by Simon and Martens (1979), who compared the precompetition state anxiety experienced by 468 boys in the youth sport setting (discussed earlier) with the anxiety experienced by 281 other boys just prior to their participation in one of the following events: an interclass physical education softball game, a school test, a band group competition, and a band solo competition (see Figure 2). Overall, team sports were no more anxiety-inducing than a PE softball game, school test, or band group competition. Individual sports, on the other hand, generally elicited more anxiety than a softball game or school test but did not differ significantly from band group competition. All sports were *less* anxiety-inducing than band solo competition. The fact that band solo competition proved to be the most stressful of the 11 activities (followed by wrestling and gymnastics) further attests to the greater

---

[7]Scanlan and Passer (1978b, 1979b) found that the teams' ability, as measured by their overall win-loss record and whether they had previously beaten their current opponent, also failed to directly predict players' pregame anxiety. These team success-failure factors, however, did influence players' team performance expectancies which in turn were related to pregame state anxiety.

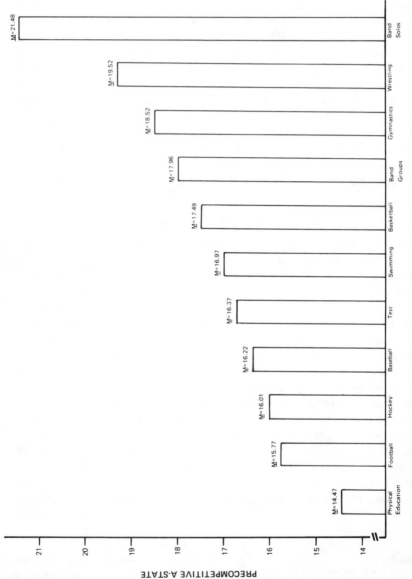

Figure 2—Children's precompetitive state anxiety in 11 sport and nonsport evaluative activities (scale range is 10 to 30). From J. Simon and R. Martens, *Journal of Sport Psychology*, 1979, **1**, 160-169. Reprinted with permission.

stress-inducing potential of individual as opposed to group or team events. This is somewhat ironic because the popular media and youth sport critics typically focus on team sports when discussing or illustrating the stressful nature of athletic competition.

Additional evidence about stress in youth sports versus other activities is provided by Skubic (1955), who assessed the galvanic skin response (GSR) of 9- to 15-year-old boys when they competed in youth league baseball games and physical education class softball games. For both of these activities, Skubic took GSR measurements immediately before, immediately after, and 1½ hours after competition. The findings revealed no significant differences at any age level between players' GSR scores prior to competing in league games as opposed to PE class softball. Few significant differences were found when league versus physical education comparisons were made for each age group immediately after and 1½ hours after competition, respectively; when differences occurred, as often as not it was softball competition that elicited greater arousal. Skubic concluded that, overall, players did not differ in the degree to which they were emotionally stimulated by competition in youth league games as opposed to physical education class games. She noted, however, that this conclusion must be viewed with caution because it was not possible to discern the exact nature of the emotions players experienced. Thus, players may have been equally aroused before competition in the two activities, but the accompanying cognitions (e.g., fear, worry, thrill) may have been different. Nevertheless, Skubic's data are consistent with those of Simon and Martens (1979) in suggesting that the degree of children's emotional reactivity to youth sport competition is similar to that experienced when participating in other achievement or competitive activities.

CONSEQUENCES OF STRESS

Youth sport research has primarily focused on three consequences of competitive stress: disruption of players' daily routines, avoidance (i.e., dropping out or not participating), and performance effects. Two studies, for example, have assessed whether involvement in sports affects players' eating or sleeping patterns. In Skubic's (1956) survey of Little and Middle League Baseball players, 11% of the respondents stated that losing a game diminished their appetite and 60% reported occasional or frequent sleep disruption the night before or after competition. The sources of sleep loss, unfortunately, were not examined.

The State of Michigan Youth Sports Study (1978) provides more definitive data regarding sleep disruption. Of 1,118 male and female youth sport participants sampled from around the state, 21% indicated that there were times when they did not receive enough sleep because of their involvement in sports. Of the players experiencing sleep loss, 46% rated worrying about performance as a contributing factor and 25% indicated that being upset after losing was a cause. Other sources of sleep disruption, however, were not directly related to competitive stress: These included the time of day at which games and practices were scheduled (46%), being too excited about winning (38%), and travel time (29%). (Of course, sleep disruption may itself make some players feel psychologically stressed regardless of the initial cause.) Another interesting finding was that a representative sample of children engaging in recreational activities other than youth sports (e.g., music, drama, clubs) reported an even higher incidence (36%) of sleep loss, and for these children, the two most prominent causes were the time of day at which the activity was scheduled (67%) and concern about performing well (50%). Thus, it appears that athletic competition affects children's sleeping patterns no more than other activities, and when loss of sleep occurs, competitive stress is only one among several causes.

Perhaps one of the most important issues on the effects of stress in youth sports is whether it causes participants to drop out of competition. A related concern is whether nonparticipants avoid sports because of various fears and worries. Based on interviews of 8- and 9-year-olds, Orlick and Botterill (1977) noted that most children who shy away from involvement in sports do so because of fear of failure or stress resulting from the disapproval of others. These authors also stated that, in most cases, negative experiences that cause children to drop out are related to an overconcern with perfection. In a recent study of 10- to 17-year-olds conducted by Pierce (1980), 26% of 106 agency sport participants drawn from basketball, swimming, and gymnastics reported that certain worries (e.g., about performance or evaluation from others) bothered them so much that they might not play in the future. Similarly, 26% of 80 sport drop outs (from agency and school sports) and 32% of 89 nonparticipants stated that various worries might inhibit them from future participation. McPherson, Marteniuk, Clark, and Tihanyi (cited in McPherson, chapter 18 of this volume) in a study of over 1,000 Canadian agegroup swimmers, found that too much pressure, conflict with coaches, and insufficient success were among the reasons swimmers reported for why their friends dropped out of competition.

Research also indicates that many of the reasons children give for discontinuing or avoiding sport involvement appear to have little to do with competitive stress. For example, sport drop outs and nonparticipants in Pierce's (1980) study indicated that involvement in other activities, a simple loss or absence of interest in sports, and the belief that sports were too time-consuming represented the major reasons for their current lack of involvement in athletics. (Once again, it could be argued that the time needed for games, travel, and practice is a potentially stressful demand, but I am not aware of any data that indicate how many children actually feel stressed by such time requirements.) The safest conclusion that can be drawn from current research is that some children experience, or anticipate experiencing, a sufficient amount of competitive stress to contribute to cessation or avoidance of sport involvement. As McPherson (chapter 18) notes, much more information is needed about why children drop out, because we should not assume that the causes are constant across age, sex, or type of sport.

It is widely recognized that stress can have significant effects on motor skill and athletic performance. This issue has received frequent empirical attention from sport psychologists and others, yet debate still occurs over the nature of the stress-performance relationship, the underlying mechanisms that mediate this relationship, and the methodological adequacy of existing research (see Landers, 1980; Martens, 1974). Drawing conclusions about the effects of competitive stress on children's athletic performance is further complicated by the fact that only one study (Lowe & McGrath, Note 6) has directly examined this relationship in the youth sport setting, and questions about the interpretation of the data (i.e., as supporting a positive linear function) have been raised (Martens, 1974). Some interesting data are provided by Pierce (1980), who found that 31% of agency sport participants and 50% of sport drop outs reported various worries prevented them from playing their best. Overall, worries about making mistakes and not playing well were the most common sources of perceived performance impairment, followed by fears about what one's teammates and coach would think or say. This study did not, however, ask players to rate how frequently these worries affected their performance. Nor are the data based on actual observations of performance, and it would be interesting to determine how well players' self-perceptions of performance impairment correspond with behavioral assessments. Nevertheless, Pierce's findings are important and indicate that a significant number of children feel they experience enough stress to adversely affect their performance.

Although youth sport research has focused on negative consequences of stress, this should not imply that stress always has detrimental effects. At times, stress may have no consequences beyond the immediate unpleasantness associated with the person's emotional state. Pierce (1980) noted, for example, that many players in his study did not feel that their worries were sufficient to cause performance impairment or to inhibit their future involvement in sports. Further, although losing is stressful, it does not appear to cause appetite or sleep disruption for the vast majority of participants. Stress can also have short- and long-term consequences that are favorable for the individual. For example, certain amounts of stress can facilitate athletic and motor-skill performance. Exposure to stressful events may also help a person deal more effectively with such situations in the future provided, as Sarason (1980) noted, the individual has learned effective coping responses. These comments are not meant to suggest that making a person feel stressed is the only, best, or even a desirable way to facilitate performance; nor do they imply that stress in youth sports will be beneficial for children. Rather, these remarks merely call attention to an extremely complex question, namely, whether stress necessarily has undesirable consequences (for more discussion, see Martens, 1978).

FURTHER ISSUES

Two important issues have not been addressed and only brief attention can be given to them here. The first is whether youth sports are *too* stressful for children. Several investigations reviewed in this chapter have used self-report or physiological measures to assess players' stress before, during, or after competition. These studies provide needed information about the types of situations that create the most stress and the types of children for whom competitive stress will be greatest; they do not, unfortunately, reveal whether that stress is excessive. As Martens (1978) has noted, there are no absolute standards by which to judge how great an anxiety test score or physiological response must be to indicate that a child is too psychologically stressed. Moreover, children who experience the same "operational" level of stress (e.g., anxiety score or heart rate) may differ not only in how aversive they perceive that stress to be, but also in their behavioral responses (e.g., some may exhibit performance impairment while others show facilitation).

If we turn to studies examining the consequences of competitive stress, the issue is equally complicated. How many children have to drop out, experience sleep loss, or undergo performance impairment because of sport-related anxieties in order for youth sports to be considered too stressful? How chronic or severe do stress effects have to be in order to constitute a "problem" for a given child? Although the amount of stress that children encounter in youth sports may be comparable to that found in other achievement activities (Simon & Martens, 1979; Skubic, 1955; State of Michigan, 1978), we might ask if those activities also engender too much stress. In sum, there is no simple answer to the question of whether youth sports are too stressful.

Several investigators (Martens, 1978; Seefeldt & Gould, 1980) recently have suggested that the problem of competitive stress in youth sports has been overemphasized by critics. The present review supports this conclusion, at least to the extent that critics portray youth sports as an atypically stressful achievement activity or contend that the majority of players suffer deleterious effects from competitive stress. Athletic competition has the potential to be quite stressful, however, and these investigators note that stress is a problem for some players in some situations. Again, research reviewed in this chapter suggests that competitive stress has adverse consequences for a number of youth sport participants, and in that sense, the issue of stress in youth sports cannot be emphasized enough. These considerations bring us to another question, namely, how stress in youth sports can be minimized.

Efforts aimed at reducing psychological stress in youth sports are discussed in detail in chapter 13 by Smith and Smoll, and I will simply note that such methods fall into two general categories. The most frequent approach is to modify the competitive setting to which children are exposed. On an organizational level policies can be implemented to minimize situational demands that many players find stressful. For example, to reduce the emphasis on winning and concomitant stresses involving fear of failure and fear of evaluation, some programs do not keep game scores, league standings, or individual performance statistics. Obviously, such leagues may be attractive to some children (and parents) but not to others. The competitive situation can also be modified by providing coaches with training that assists them in relating more effectively to their players. Smith, Smoll, and Curtis' (1979) program of Coach Effectiveness Training and Martens' (1981) American Coaching Effectiveness Program illustrate this approach. Players' stress should be minimized to the extent that coaches establish a supportive rather than punitive environment.

Psychological intervention at the level of the individual athlete represents the second general method of reducing players' competitive stress. In certain cases, young athletes have sought psychiatric counseling because of performance deterioration or other problems caused in part by sport-related stress (e.g., Ogilvie, 1979). Other interventions have been used to provide youngsters with various stress-coping skills. Smith's (1980) program of Stress Management Training, for example, attempts to reduce players' stress by teaching them to (a) alter irrational beliefs that cause the competitive situation to be appraised as threatening, (b) use muscular relaxation to lower physiological arousal, and (c) replace self-preoccupational thoughts with internal statements that are task-oriented. Clinical evidence indicates that counseling and stress-management programs can be very beneficial to some players. These interventions, however, typically do not alter the stress-inducing characteristics of the competitive situation. If the general goal of educators, youth sport personnel, parents, and others is to minimize psychological stress associated with athletic competition, by far the most efficacious approach is to make the youth sport setting as nonthreatening as possible.

CONCLUSION

Athletic competition presents children with numerous demands that are important to them. The potential for stress exists in youth sports because players may doubt or feel uncertain about their capability to meet these demands or may receive feedback that, in fact, these demands have not been met. Current research suggests that children's competitive stress is related to several situational and intrapersonal factors including the type of sport being played, the criticality of the game and specific situation within the game, success-failure outcomes, performance expectancies, competitive trait anxiety, and self-esteem. It appears that, for a minority of youth sport participants, competitive stress has adverse consequences such as loss of sleep, performance impairment, and cessation of sport involvement. The precise number of children thus affected and the frequency and duration of these problems cannot be specified at this time. Evidence suggests, however, that youth sports are no more stressful than other evaluative activities in which children participate. Further, the frequency of stress-related problems found among youth sport participants does not appear to be greater than that found among children engaged in other recreational activities.

Whether these findings are viewed in their entirety as cause for optimism or pessimism (or both) about the state of youth sports is a matter of personal judgment. What is clear, though, is that the amount of research on psychological stress in youth sports is relatively small despite the recent growth of empirical work in this area. Many of the conclusions drawn in this chapter are based upon only one or two studies and there are other important issues on which no or only indirect data exist (see Passer, 1981). This does not deny that advances in our knowledge about children's competitive stress have been made; it merely indicates that the major challenge for researchers and others interested in youth sports still lies ahead.

REFERENCE NOTES

1. Gould, D. *Sport psychology in the 1980's: Status, direction and challenge in youth sports research.* Paper presented at the annual meeting of the North American Society for the Psychology of Sport and Physical Activity, Asilomar, CA, June 1981.
2. Gill, D.L., Gross, J.B., & Huddleston, S. *Motivation in youth sports.* Paper presented at the annual meeting of the North American Society for the Psychology of Sport and Physical Activity, Boulder, CO, May 1980.
3. Gould, D., Feltz, D., Weiss, M., & Petlichkoff, L. *Participation motives in competitive youth swimmers.* Paper presented at the Fifth World Congress of Sport Psychology, Ottawa, August 1981.
4. Passer, M.W., & Scanlan, T.K. *A sociometric analysis of popularity and leadership status among players on youth soccer teams.* Paper presented at the annual meeting of the North American Society for

the Psychology of Sport and Physical Activity, Boulder, CO, May 1980.
5. Passer, M.W. *Toward determining the antecedents of competitive trait anxiety.* Paper presented at the annual meeting of the North American Society for the Psychology of Sport and Physical Activity, Asilomar, CA, June 1981.
6. Lowe, R., & McGrath, J.E. *Stress, arousal, and performance: Some findings calling for a new theory.* Project report, AF 1161-67, AFOSR, 1971.

REFERENCES

ALDERMAN, R.B., & Wood, N.L. An analysis of incentive motivation in young Canadian athletes. *Canadian Journal of Applied Sport Sciences*, 1976, **1**, 169-176.

BERRYMAN, J.W. From the cradle to the playing field: America's emphasis on highly organized competitive sports for preadolescent boys. *Journal of Sport History*, 1975, **2**, 112-131.

BORKOVEC, T.D., Weerts, T.C., & Bernstein, D.A. Assessment of anxiety. In A.R. Ciminero, K.S. Calhoun, & H.E. Adams (Eds.), *Handbook of behavioral assessment.* New York: Wiley, 1977.

BROWER, J.J. The professionalization of organized youth sport: Social psychological impacts and outcomes. *Annals of the American Academy of Political and Social Science*, 1979, **445**, 39-46.

BUCHANAN, H.T., Blankenbaker, J., & Cotten, D. Academic and athletic ability as popularity factors in elementary school children. *Research Quarterly*, 1976, **47**, 320-325.

COLEMAN, J.S. Athletics in high school. *Annals of the American Academy of Political and Social Science*, 1961, **338**, 33-43.

CORBIN, C.B., & Nix, C. Sex-typing of physical activities and success predictions of children before and after cross-sex competition. *Journal of Sport Psychology*, 1979, **1**, 43-52.

GEEN, R.G. Test anxiety and cue utilization. In I.G. Sarason (Ed.), *Test anxiety: Theory, research, and applications.* Hillsdale, NJ: Lawrence Erlbaum Associates, 1980.

GILL, D.L., & Martens, R. The role of task type and success-failure in group competition. *International Journal of Sport Psychology*, 1977, **8**, 160-177.

GRIFFIN, M.R. An analysis of state and trait anxiety experienced in sports competition at different age levels. *Foil*, 1972 (Spring), pp. 58-64.

HANSON, D.L. Cardiac response to participation in Little League baseball competition as determined by telemetry. *Research Quarterly*, 1967, **38**, 384-388.

HOLROYD, K.A., & Appel, M.A. Test anxiety and physiological responding. In I.G. Sarason (Ed.), *Test anxiety: Theory, research, and applications*. Hillsdale, NJ: Lawrence Erlbaum Associates, 1980.

JOHNSON, J.H., & McCutcheon, S. Assessing life stress in older children and adolescents: Preliminary findings with the Life Events Checklist. In I.G. Sarason & C.D. Spielberger (Eds.), *Stress and anxiety* (Vol. 7). Washington: Hemisphere, 1980.

JOHNSON, J.H., & Sarason, I.G. Recent developments in research on life stress. In V. Hamilton & D.M. Warburton (Eds.), *Human stress and cognition: An information processing approach*. London: Wiley, 1979.

LANDERS, D.M. The arousal-performance relationship revisited. *Research Quarterly for Exercise and Sport*, 1980, **51**, 77-90.

LAZARUS, R.S. *Psychological stress and the coping process*. New York: McGraw-Hill, 1966.

MARTENS, R. Arousal and motor performance. In J. Wilmore (Ed.), *Exercise and sport sciences reviews* (Vol. 2). New York: Academic Press, 1974.

MARTENS, R. *Social psychology and physical activity*. New York: Harper & Row, 1975.

MARTENS, R. *Sport Competition Anxiety Test*. Champaign, IL: Human Kinetics, 1977.

MARTENS, R. *Joy and sadness in children's sports*. Champaign, IL: Human Kinetics, 1978.

MARTENS, R. American Coaching Effectiveness Program. *Sportsline*, 1981, **3**(4), 2-3.

MARTENS, R., Burton, D., Rivkin, F., & Simon, J. Reliability and validity of the Competitive State Anxiety Inventory (CSAI). In C.H. Nadeau, W.R. Halliwell, K.M. Newell, & G.C. Roberts (Eds.), *Psychology of motor behavior and sport—1979*. Champaign, IL: Human Kinetics, 1980.

MARTENS, R., & Gill, D.L. State anxiety among successful and unsuccessful competitors who differ in competitive trait anxiety. *Research Quarterly*, 1976, **47**, 698-708.

MARTENS, R., Rivkin, F., & Burton, D. Who predicts anxiety better: Coaches or athletes? In C.H. Nadeau, W.R. Halliwell, K.M. Newell, &

G.C. Roberts (Eds.), *Psychology of motor behavior and sport—1979.* Champaign, IL: Human Kinetics, 1980.

MARTENS, R., & Simon, J.A. Comparison of three predictors of state anxiety in competitive situations. *Research Quarterly*, 1976, **47**, 381-387.

MASLACH,C. Negative emotional biasing of unexplained arousal. *Journal of Personality and Social Psychology*, 1979, **37**, 953-969.

MCGRATH, J.E. Stress and behavior in organizations. In M.D. Dunnette (Ed.), *Handbook of industrial and organizational psychology.* Chicago: Rand McNally, 1976.

NEUFELD, R.W.J., & Mothersill, K.J. Stress as an irritant of psychopathology. In I.G. Sarason & C.D. Spielberger (Eds.), *Stress and anxiety* (Vol. 7). Washington: Hemisphere, 1980.

OGILVIE, B. The child athlete: Psychological implications of participation in sport. *Annals of the American Academy of Political and Social Science*, 1979, **445**, 47-58.

ORLICK, T., & Botterill, C. *Every kid can win.* Chicago: Nelson-Hall, 1977.

PASSER, M.W. Children in sport: Participation motives and psychological stress. *Quest*, 1981, **33**, 231-244.

PASSER, M.W., & Scanlan, T.K. The impact of game outcome on the postcompetition affect and performance evaluations of young athletes. In C.H. Nadeau, W.R. Halliwell, K.M. Newell, & G.C. Roberts (Eds.), *Psychology of motor behavior and sport—1979.* Champaign, IL: Human Kinetics, 1980.

PIERCE, W.J. *Psychological perspectives of youth sport participants and nonparticipants.* Unpublished doctoral dissertation, Virginia Polytechnic Institute and State University, 1980.

SARASON, I.G. Life stress, self-preoccupation, and social supports. In I.G. Sarason & C.D. Spielberger (Eds.), *Stress and anxiety* (Vol. 7). Washington: Hemisphere, 1980.

SCANLAN, T.K. The effects of success-failure on the perception of threat in a competitive situation. *Research Quarterly*, 1977, **48**, 144-153.

SCANLAN, T.K., & Passer, M.W. Anxiety-inducing factors in competitive youth sports. In F.L. Smoll & R.E. Smith (Eds.), *Psychological perspectives in youth sports.* Washington: Hemisphere, 1978. (a)

SCANLAN, T.K., & Passer, M.W. Factors related to competitive stress among male youth sport participants. *Medicine and Science in Sports*, 1978, **10**, 103-108. (b)

SCANLAN, T.K., & Passer, M.W. Factors influencing the competitive performance expectancies of young female athletes. *Journal of Sport Psychology*, 1979, **1**, 212-220. (a)

SCANLAN, T.K., & Passer, M.W. Sources of competitive stress in young female athletes. *Journal of Sport Psychology*, 1979, **1**, 151-159. (b)

SCANLAN, T.K., & Passer, M.W. Determinants of competitive expectancies of young male athletes. *Journal of Personality*, 1981, **49**, 60-74.

SCHACHTER, S. The interaction of cognitive and physiological determinants of emotional state. In L. Berkowitz (Ed.), *Advances in experimental social psychology* (Vol. 1). New York: Academic Press, 1964.

SEEFELDT, V., & Gould, D. *Physical and psychological effects of athletic competition on children and youth*. East Lansing, MI: Michigan State University, 1980. (ERIC Document Reproduction Service No. ED 180 997)

SIMON, J.A., & Martens, R. Children's anxiety in sport and nonsport evaluative activities. *Journal of Sport Psychology*, 1979, **1**, 160-169.

SINGER, J.E. Traditions of stress research: Integrative comments. In I.G. Sarason & C.D. Spielberger (Eds.), *Stress and anxiety* (Vol. 7). Washington: Hemisphere, 1980.

SKUBIC, E. Emotional responses of boys to Little League and Middle League competitive baseball. *Research Quarterly*, 1955, **26**, 342-352.

SKUBIC, E. Studies of Little League and Middle League Baseball. *Research Quarterly*, 1956, **27**, 97-110.

SMITH, R.E. Development of an integrated coping response through cognitive-affective stress management training. In I.G. Sarason & C.D. Spielberger (Eds.), *Stress and anxiety* (Vol. 7). Washington: Hemisphere, 1980.

SMITH, R.E., Smoll, F.L., & Curtis, B. Coach effectiveness training: A cognitive-behavioral approach to enhancing relationship skills in youth sport coaches. *Journal of Sport Psychology*, 1979, **1**, 59-75.

SMOLL, F.L., & Smith, R.E. (Eds.). *Psychological perspectives in youth sports*. Washington: Hemisphere, 1978.

SPIELBERGER, C.D. Theory and research on anxiety. In C.D. Spielberger (Ed.), *Anxiety and behavior*. New York: Academic Press, 1966.

SPIELBERGER, C.D. Anxiety as an emotional state. In C.D. Spielberger (Ed.), *Anxiety: Current trends in theory and research*. New York: Academic Press, 1972.

SPIELBERGER, C.D. *Preliminary test manual for the State-Trait Anxiety Inventory for Children*. Palo Alto, CA: Consulting Psychologists Press, 1973.

SPIELBERGER, L.D., Gorsuch, R.L., & Lushene, R.E. *Manual for the State-Trait Anxiety Inventory*. Palo Alto, CA: Consulting Psychologists, 1970.

STANIFORD, D.J. Cross-cultural reflections: Competition and the young child. *Physical Educator*, 1976, **33**, 143-145.

STATE of Michigan. *Joint legislative study on youth sports programs: Phase II, agency sponsored sports*. East Lansing, MI: Author, 1978.

ZILLMANN, D. The role of excitation in aggressive behavior. *Proceedings of the Seventeenth International Congress of Applied Psychology*, 1971. Brussels: Editest, 1972.

CHAPTER 13

PSYCHOLOGICAL STRESS: A CONCEPTUAL MODEL AND SOME INTERVENTION STRATEGIES IN YOUTH SPORTS

Ronald E. Smith and Frank L. Smoll

As organized sports for children have become more highly structured and as adults have often shaped them to reflect a win-oriented professional sport model, a vigorous debate has arisen over the desirability of such programs for developing children. Critics have frequently charged that extreme performance pressures are sometimes being placed on children before the youngsters are developmentally prepared to cope with them (Brower, 1978; Fisk, 1977; Michener, 1975; Roberts, 1975; Sayre, 1975; Shah & Morris, 1978; Underwood, 1975). Perhaps because of the widespread belief that the competitive setting is a highly stressful one for many children, the question of exactly how stressful sports are, especially in comparison with other activities, has begun to receive increasing empirical attention. Both physiological and self-report measures of stress have been obtained from children before and during sport events to evaluate the extent to which stress responses occur. As the preceding chapter by Passer indicates, stress in youth sports may not be as widespread or intense as is sometimes assumed. The results of existing research appear to suggest that for children in general, sport participation is not exceedingly stressful, especially in comparison with other activities involving performance evaluation.

But it is equally clear that the sport setting is capable of producing high levels of stress for certain children (Martens, 1977; Scanlan & Passer, 1978, 1979). Instead of finding athletic competition to be an enjoyable and challenging activity, such children undoubtedly experience it as threatening and anxiety-producing. One unfortunate response to such threat can be avoidance of the anxiety-arousing situation. In one study, for example, 75% of a sample of 8- and 9-year-old sport nonparticipants indicated that they would like to compete, but were fearful of performing poorly or of failing to make a team (Orlick & Botterill, 1975).

Aside from detracting from the enjoyment of sport, stress can have negative effects on performance, foster the potential development of psychosomatic disorders, and increase the risk of injury. A growing research literature is demonstrating relationships between high levels of life stress and physical illness in children (e.g., Coddington, 1975). The unfortunate effects of severe competitive pressures are all too frequently seen in young athletes who develop stress-related dermatological and gastrointestinal problems. Not surprisingly, such disorders appear to occur with highest incidence in sports requiring extreme time, training, and competitive commitments from participants, such as competitive figure skating. But they can occur in any sports setting that proves extremely stressful to the child athlete.

The potential sources of stress in the lives of children are many and varied. Studies of high school and college athletes indicate that the stress produced by life changes requiring readjustment is related to an increased incidence of sport-related injuries (Bramwell, Masuda, Wagner, & Holmes, 1975; Coddington & Troxell, 1980; Seese & Passer, Note 1). Family problems, difficulties with peers, achievement-related challenges, changes in residence, new developmental and relationship demands, and other experiences are all capable of generating stress. But the amount of stress the child experiences is a joint function of the demands of the situation and the coping skills possessed by the child. Such skills are, in turn, developed by dealing successfully with challenging situations. It might therefore be argued that one of the potential virtues of competitive sport situations is that they provide a setting in which effective coping skills can be acquired and used to deal more adaptively not only with competitive stress, but with other stressful life events as well. Moreover, the developmental period spanned by youth sport programs would appear to be an ideal time for the acquisition of stress coping skills.

It is our position that given appropriate adult guidance, the youth sport setting can be one which fosters the psychological growth of the child. We also believe that the sport psychologist can play an influential role in helping coaches and parents to facilitate this process (Smith & Smoll, 1978). Our present discussion will focus on a conceptual model of stress and its implications for stress reduction, and will describe several promising intervention strategies designed to reduce psychological stress in youth sports.

A CONCEPTUAL MODEL OF STRESS

The term "stress" is typically used in two different, but related ways. First, we use the term to refer to situations which tax the physical and/or psychological capabilities of the individual. The term "stressor" is also used to refer to these external situational demands. Second, the term is used to refer to the emotional response of the individual to situational demands. Clearly, these two referents for the term are not synonymous, because individuals may vary widely in terms of how "stressful" they find the same objective situation to be. In our discussion of ways of reducing stress in children's sports, we shall therefore be concerned with measures designed to reduce situational stress as well as with ways to help individuals develop more effective coping skills.

The conceptual model which has been influential in guiding our research and intervention programs is derived from the contributions of a number of theorists, including Arnold (1967), Ellis (1962), R. Lazarus (1966), and Schachter (1966). The model (see Figure 1) emphasizes relationships between the situation, the individual's cognitive appraisal of the situation and his or her ability to cope with it, physiological arousal responses, and behavioral responses to the situation. Each of these components is, in turn, influenced by the child's motivational and personality characteristics.

The stimuli constituting the stress-eliciting situation may be either external or internal in origin. Ordinarily we think of emotional responses as being stimulated by an external situation, but internal stimuli in the form of memories or images may also be part of the stimulus complex to which the child responds. In the youth sport setting, many aspects of the external situation may be stressful, including the behaviors of coaches, teammates, opponents, and parents, closeness of the score, nature of the task demands on the child, adequacy of performance to this point, and so on. Memories of similar past situations and anticipations of future consequences may interact with the current external situation to affect its psychological meaning and its effects on the child.

Typically, people view their emotions as being directly triggered by certain situations. But in most cases, situations exert their effect on emo-

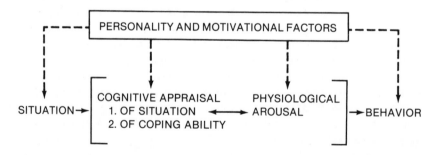

Figure 1—A conceptual model of stress showing hypothesized relationships between situational, cognitive, physiological, and behavioral components. Motivational and personality factors are assumed to affect all of the basic components of the model.

tionality through the intervening influence of thought. Their cognitive appraisal of the situation creates the psychological reality to which people respond, and the nature and intensity of emotional responses are a function of what individuals tell themselves about the situation and about their ability to cope with it. R. Lazarus (1975) uses the terms "primary" and "secondary" appraisal to refer, respectively, to subjective judgments about the nature and meaning of the situation and to judgments about one's own ability to cope successfully with it. Stress is likely to occur when children perceive the task requirements to be too demanding for their response capabilities and when this imbalance or its consequences (e.g., others' disapproval) is perceived as catastrophic or indicative of low self-worth.

The third component, physiological arousal, is elicited by cognitive appraisal processes and, in turn, provides feedback about the intensity of the emotion being experienced. Arousal feedback contributes to the ongoing process of appraisal and reappraisal. An athlete who becomes aware of increasing arousal may appraise the situation as more threatening than one who experiences low arousal in a potentially stressful situation.

The fourth component of the model consists of the behaviors that occur in response to the situation. These include task-oriented, social, and coping behaviors.

The four components discussed so far are each affected by individual differences in personality and motivation. Personality and motivational variables create predispositions to seek out certain situations and to think, perceive, and respond in certain ways. Thus, the nature and intensity of instrumental responses to the situation are in part a reflection of the child's personality and motivation. Conversely, the child's habitual ways of behaving and the kinds of goals and incentives that are sought help to determine the nature of the situations the child experiences. Some children, for example, have a positive achievement motive to excel, whereas others are motivated primarily by a negative fear of failure. Some strive for the positive incentive of approval from parents, coaches, and peers, whereas others are primarily motivated to avoid any sign of disapproval from significant others. Those children who are motivated by positive incentives tend to experience less anxiety in the sport situation than do those who are striving to avoid disapproval or failure. The latter are likely to appraise competitive sport situations as more threatening and therefore to experience more stress and anxiety in them. Likewise, children who have low self-esteem and low personal performance expectancies have been found to be subject to competitive stress reactions (Scanlan & Passer, 1978, 1979). Finally, both intensity of motivation and certain personality variables are known to be related to measures of emotional arousal and lability (Eysenck, 1967).

APPROACHES TO STRESS REDUCTION

The conceptual model just presented suggests a number of points at which intervention strategies might be employed to reduce stress in children's sports. Perhaps the most time-consuming and intensive intervention would be required at the level of motivation and personality. Although intensive counseling and psychotherapeutic intervention might be indicated in some cases of extreme disturbance, this level of direct professional intervention clearly cannot be considered a practical, necessary, or economically justifiable answer to solving stress-related problems in children's sports. Some economical and appropriate measures, however, can ultimately affect motivation and personality.

At the situational level, changes in certain features of the athletic environment may dramatically alter its capacity to generate stress. For example, coaches and parents can be instructed in ways to reduce the contributions they make to the stress in organized youth sports. A more unfortunate example of situational change has occurred when youth leagues have deemed it necessary to ban parents from attending games in order to reduce the stress placed on children and officials (Martens, 1978).

Another approach to change at the situational level involves modification of the sport itself. For example, the height of the basketball goal could be lowered for elementary school children (Henry, 1979). This decreases performance demands on growing children, thereby increasing their chances of success and enjoyment. Similarly, the organization and administration of a sports program can be the focus of environmental change aimed at eliminating potential sources of stress. For example, it is well known that children differ greatly in their physical and psychological maturity. Diverse programs should therefore be offered to provide for varied levels of skill as well as degrees of competitive intensity. Youngsters can then select the level at which they prefer to participate. Other methods of matching children to the appropriate level of competition can serve to combat stress associated with inequity of competition and risk of injury. Specifically, homogeneous grouping procedures include (a) keeping the age range as narrow as possible (i.e., leagues for 9-10-year olds and 11-12-year olds, rather than 9-12-year olds), (b) using measures of height and weight in conjunction with chronological age for grouping purposes, and (c) using sport skills tests to group children (Martens & Seefeldt, 1979).

Environmental change can also be produced by changes in the behavioral component. Clearly, behavior is influenced by the environment, but the opposite is also the case (Bandura, 1981). Thus, acquisition of various types of skills by the child athlete may significantly alter the environment. Training which increases sport skills can make athletic demands easier to cope with, and interpersonal skills can help athletes to develop a more benign interpersonal environment with teammates and coaches.

Yet another point at which stress can be reduced is at the level of physiological arousal. Arousal-reduction skills such as muscular relaxation or meditation can help children to control physiological arousal. Children as young as 4 years of age can readily learn voluntary relaxation skills (Siegel & Peterson, 1980; Smith, 1980) that provide them with a highly generalizable means of counteracting physiological arousal.

Finally, intervention can be directed at modifying the cognitive appraisal processes which, in actuality, generate physiological stress responses. This is, in many respects, the key component in the model, because most of the interventions directed at other components ultimately are mediated by or exert their effects on the appraisal processes. Worrying and dwelling on the "horribleness" of failure or disapproval dominates the thought patterns of many high-stress child and adult athletes. Conversely, athletes described as "mentally tough" seem to be able to think and direct their attention in ways that facilitate performance and keep arousal within manageable limits.

In the discussion to follow, we will focus on the "athletic triangle" consisting of coach, parent, and child athlete. First, we will describe some guidelines and procedures we have found useful in working with coaches and parents to reduce situational stress and to enhance the athletic situation for children. Then we will describe a stress management training program that has been applied to child athletes to help them acquire cognitive and physiological coping skills.

COACH EFFECTIVENESS TRAINING

It goes without saying that coaches occupy a central and critical role in the youth sport setting. The nature of the relationship between coach and player is widely acknowledged as a primary determinant of the ways in which children are ultimately affected by their participation in organized athletic programs (Martens, 1978; Seefeldt & Gould, 1980; Smith, Smoll, Hunt, Curtis, & Coppel, 1979; Smoll, Smith, & Curtis, 1977). Moreover, their influence can extend into other areas of the child's life as well. During a developmental period in which children are seeking varying degrees of independence from parental influence, the child's relationship with the youth coach can become a highly significant and influential one. The manner in which coaches structure the athletic situation, the goal priorities they establish explicitly and implicitly, and the ways in which they relate to their players can markedly influence how children appraise the situation and the amount of stress they experience. It follows, then, that measures designed to assist coaches in creating a less stressful and more enjoyable athletic atmosphere can have a significant positive impact on youth sport programs.

Most nonscholastic youth sport programs .are staffed by volunteer coaches. Such adults frequently are well versed in the technical aspects of the sport, but they rarely have had any formal training in creating a positive psychological environment for their players. Through the mass media, these coaches are often exposed to role models who coach at the college or professional level; they may come to emulate behaviors and a "winning is everything" philosophy that are highly inappropriate in relating to youngsters in a recreational and skills development context. The vast majority of youth coaches are committed to providing a positive experience for their players (Martens & Gould, 1979; Smith, Smoll, & Curtis, 1978), however, and our experience has shown that coaches are responsive to attempts to provide them with information and behavioral guidelines. The opportunity therefore exists for sport psychologists and other concerned professionals to make a valuable contribution by providing consultation to coaches.

A research program carried out at the University of Washington constitutes one attempt to formulate research-derived behavioral guidelines for coaches and to develop a training program that can be disseminated to volunteer coaches. The 7-year project had two major phases: First, research was carried out to establish empirical relationships between specific coaching behaviors and children's attitudes toward their coach, teammates, and themselves. Phase I was guided by an information-processing model of coach-player relationships (Smoll, Smith, Curtis, & Hunt, 1978). A major assumption of this model is that coaching behaviors do not directly affect children's reactions to them. Their impact is instead affected by the child's perceptions, evaluations, and recall of the behaviors. In a sense, the youngsters serve as a filter whose psychological processes mediate between the coaches' behaviors and the attitudes and reactions which they ultimately evoke. This assumption is schematically presented in the following simplified diagram:

	Players'	Players'
Coach	Perception	Evaluative
Behaviors	and Recall	Reactions

Following this model, if we wish to understand how coaching behaviors affect players' reactions, we need to take into account the mediating processes that occur in the player. More specifically, we need to be able to measure the actual coaching behaviors, the players' perceptions and recall of these behaviors, and their attitudes in response to what the coach does. This is the approach that we took in Phase I.

To measure coaching behaviors, a behavioral assessment system was devised to permit the direct observation and recording of coaches' behaviors. Using a 12-category coding system known as the Coaching Behavior

Assessment System, trained observers recorded the behaviors of coaches (Smith, Smoll, & Hunt, 1977). To establish relationships between coaching behaviors and player variables, 51 male Little League Baseball coaches were observed during a total of 202 complete games. A behavioral profile was established for each coach based on an average of 1,122 of his behaviors. At the conclusion of the season, 542 players ranging in age from 8 to 15 years were interviewed individually in their homes to obtain measures of their perception and recall of their coaches' behaviors and of their personal reactions to the coach, teammates, and other aspects of their athletic experience. Thus, in Phase I, we attempted to determine what coaches were doing, what the children thought the coaches had done, and how the children felt about their experience and about themselves. On the basis of statistical relationships between observed coaching behaviors, players' perceptions and recall of such behaviors, and player attitudes (Smith, Smoll, & Curtis, 1978), a series of behavioral guidelines were developed.

Our guidelines are designed to assist coaches in relating more effectively to child athletes. The series of coaching "dos and don'ts" are based primarily on (a) a conception of success or "winning" as consisting of giving maximum effort (Smoll & Smith, 1981), and (b) a positive approach to social influence that involves the use of reinforcement and encouragement while discouraging the use of punishment and criticism (Smoll & Smith, 1979; Smoll et al., 1977).

An important goal of our guidelines is to increase the desire of young athletes to learn and to give maximum effort while reducing their fear of failure. The fear of failure component of athletic stress is assumed to arise because the athlete has in the past been punished for failing to achieve a desired outcome. Such punishment may come from coaches, parents, and other children, or it may be self-administered by athletes themselves when they fail to measure up to their own internalized performance standards. But if coaches demand of their athletes only that they give their best, and if they reinforce effort rather than focusing only on outcome, players can learn to set similar standards for themselves. As far as winning is concerned, if athletes are well trained, give maximum effort, and have a positive motivation to achieve rather than performance-disrupting fears of failing, winning will take care of itself within the limits of their abilities. And young athletes are more likely to develop their athletic potential in an enjoyable rather than in a stressful sport environment.

In Phase II of our research project, we attempted to modify coaching behaviors and evaluated the success of the intervention program. Thirty-one Little League Baseball coaches were randomly assigned to an experimental (training) group or to a no-treatment control group. The experimental group coaches were exposed to a preseason training program designed to assist them in relating more effectively to children. The intervention program was conceptualized within a cognitive-behavioral framework (cf. Bandura, 1977). Behavioral guidelines were presented both verbally and in written materials given to the coaches. The verbal presentation was supplemented with actual demonstrations of how to behave in desirable ways (i.e., modeling). In addition to the information-modeling portion of the training program, behavioral feedback and self-monitoring procedures were employed to increase the coaches' self-awareness and to encourage compliance with the coaching guidelines. A comprehensive discussion of principles and techniques used to implement psychologically oriented coach training programs is presented elsewhere (Smoll & Smith, 1980).

The effects of the experimental training program were measured by essentially repeating the Phase I procedures. Behavioral profiles were developed by observing experimental and control coaches during four complete games. At the end of the season, a total of 325 players were interviewed to obtain player data. The experimental and control coaches were then compared on all of the behavioral and player measures.

The results of the study were quite encouraging. On both behavioral measures and in players' perceptions of their coaches' behaviors, the trained coaches differed from the controls in a manner consistent with the behavioral guidelines. They gave more reinforcement and encouragement and were less punitive than the controls. The behavioral differences were reflected in their players' attitudes as well, despite the fact that the average won-lost records were quite similar. Trained coaches were better liked and rated as better teachers of baseball skills, and players on their teams liked one another more. Perhaps most importantly, children who played for the trained coaches exhibited a significant increase in general self-esteem as compared with scores obtained a year earlier; control group children did not. Finally, children low in self-esteem showed the greatest differences in players' attitudes toward trained as opposed to control coaches. This was also encouraging, because it is low self-esteem children who probably most need a positive athletic experience. Such children apparently respond very favorably to coaches who adopt the guidelines, and they exhibit an increase in their feelings of self-worth (Smith, Smoll, & Curtis, 1979).

The results of our research thus indicate that coaches can be trained to relate more effectively to child athletes and to create a more enjoyable and less stressful athletic environment for their players. The training program, which we call Coach Effectiveness Training, began with Little League Baseball, but it is now being offered for other sports as well. Workshops have been presented to soccer, football, basketball, bowling, swimming, wrestling, and hockey coaches. Coaches in youth organizations, such as the Boys'/Girls' Clubs, the YMCA, the United States Soccer Federation, and the Catholic Youth Organization, are participating in Coach Effectiveness Training.

INTERVENTION WITH PARENTS

Although coaches have the most direct contact with children within the sport environment, parents also play an important role. Specifically, the literature on sport socialization of children confirms that parents are instrumental in determining children's sport involvement (see chapters 18 and 19 in this volume). Moreover, in spite of relatively sparse research on parents, the negative impact which they can have on child athletes is all too obvious. Some parents assume an extremely active role in their children's sport participation, and in some instances, their influence constitutes an important source of stress (Passer, Note 2; Pierce & Stratton, Note 3).

It is generally believed that parents can strongly affect the quality of their children's experience in sports. Because of this, there have been several attempts in the popular literature to guide and educate parents about their responsibilities toward their children's sport participation (e.g., Ferrell, Glashagel, & Johnson, 1978; Martens, 1980; Rosen, 1967; Thomas, 1977; Vandeweghe, 1979). There has been no attempt, however, to systematically develop and assess the effects of an educational program for parents to help them facilitate their children's personal growth through athletics.

By establishing contact with parents, sport psychologists may serve an important educational function. A key to reducing parent-produced stress in youth sports is to impress upon parents that youth programs are for *children* and that children are not miniature adults. Parents need to acknowledge the right of each child to develop his or her potential as an athlete in an atmosphere which emphasizes participation, personal growth, and fun.

The conception of success or "winning" as giving maximum effort is as relevant to parents as it is to coaches. Indeed, it may be more important for parents to grasp its implications, because they can apply it to many areas of the child's life in addition to athletics. Likewise, the basic principles contained in the "positive approach" to social influence apply equally to parents. By encouraging youngsters to do as well as they are currently able, by rewarding effort as well as outcome, and by avoiding use of criticism and punishment when the child fails, parents can foster the development of positive motivation to achieve and prevent the development of fear of failure.

In our Coach Effectiveness Training workshops, we encourage coaches to organize a preseason meeting with parents to discuss the goals of youth sports and the conception of "winning" they will promote. The coaches emphasize to parents that by placing excessive pressure on children, they can detract from the potential that youth sport participation can have for enjoyment, personal growth, and skill development. They also discuss the "positive approach" to coaching they will be using and encourage the parents to reinforce it in their interaction with the child. Finally, they discuss desirable and undesirable behavior by spectators at games in an attempt to create a "positive" atmosphere and to eliminate spectator-produced stress on the children.

DEVELOPING COPING SKILLS IN CHILD ATHLETES

Intervention at the coach and parental level is designed to reduce potential sources of environmental stress. The third point in the athletic triangle that may be the focus of intervention is the child athlete. Given that the amount of stress the child experiences is a joint function of the intensity of environmental stressors and the way the child appraises and copes with them, it follows that actively assisting the child in developing coping skills can increase his or her ability to deal effectively with athletic stress. Moreover, developing a range of highly generalizable coping skills should enhance children's ability to handle stress not only in the athletic situation but also in other areas of their lives.

The emergence during the past decade of training programs in behavioral and emotional self-control has been a significant development. A wide range of skills have been successfully acquired in such programs, including stress management coping behaviors. Although most stress management programs have been applied to adults, recent attempts to train child athletes in coping skills have yielded promising results (Smith, 1980). Work with child athletes would appear to have promise on several counts. First of all, childhood seems to be an excellent time to acquire adaptive coping responses because of the stormy adolescent period soon to come. Moreover, children have not generally developed maladaptive coping strategies that are deeply ingrained, as is often the case with adults. Finally, child athletes are required to cope with situations of competitive stress on a regular and predictable basis. They therefore have many opportunities to practice and strengthen their coping skills in situations that are unlikely to be so stressful that they exceed the children's coping ability.

The training program that follows is directed at the cognitive appraisal and physiological arousal components of the conceptual model described earlier. The program provides for the learning and rehearsal of physical relaxation skills and of self-statements and self-instructions that are designed to reduce or prevent stress. For descriptive purposes the stress-management training (SMT) program can be divided into three major phases: (a) conceptualization and pretraining assessment phase, (b) skill acquisition, and (c) skill rehearsal. An overview of the program is presented in Table 1.

In the initial phase, children are introduced to a simplified version of the conceptual model of stress. The relationships between situations, thoughts, and feelings are described. The purpose of the conceptualiza-

Table 1
Steps Through Which the Cognitive-Affective Stress
Management Training Program Proceeds

Step 1.   Orientation and relaxation training. The nature of emotion and stress is discussed as is the nature of coping with stress. Training is begun in deep muscular relaxation, which serves as a physical coping response.

Step 2.   Continuation of relaxation training and discussion of the role of mental processes in coping with stress.

Step 3.   Practice in the use of relaxation to control emotional responses induced during the session through imagining of stressful situations. Development of mental coping responses.

Step 4.   Practice in using relaxation and stress-reducing mental statements to control emotional reactions induced through imagination.

Step 5.   Continued practice in use of coping mechanisms with emphasis on development of the end product of the program: the "integrated coping response."

Step 6.   Training in the use of a meditation technique having stress-reducing properties.

tion phase is to help the children to understand the nature of their stress responses and to provide a rationale for the training program. As Meichenbaum (1977) has emphasized, the initial conceptualization of the problem is of crucial importance in obtaining commitment to a training program. It is suggested that the basic difference between high- and low-stress athletes is that the latter have been fortunate in having previous life experiences that enabled them to learn the kinds of coping skills to be taught in the program. Following a description of the program, the children begin to explore with the trainer their particular stress reactions (i.e., the specific situations in which they occur, the nature of their thoughts and feelings, the ways in which they try to cope, etc.).

The goal of the second, or skill acquisition, phase is the development of an "integrated coping response" having relaxation and cognitive elements. This phase involves (a) the learning of voluntary muscular relaxation skills, and (b) an analysis of thought processes and the replacement of stress-eliciting ideas and self-statements with specific cognitions designed to reduce stress.

Training in voluntary relaxation begins immediately, using a variant of Jacobson's (1938) progressive muscle relaxation technique. Individual muscle groups are tensed, slowly relaxed halfway, and then slowly relaxed completely. This procedure is designed to enhance discrimination of slight changes in muscle tension as well as the ability to quickly and deeply relax the muscles. The written training exercises are presented elsewhere (Smith, Sarason, & Sarason, 1978, pp. 258-260). As training proceeds, increasingly larger groups of muscles are combined until the body is being voluntarily relaxed as a unit. The role of deep breathing in facilitating relaxation is also stressed. Deane (1964) has shown experimentally that respiration amplitude and frequency can affect heart rate as well as subjective feelings of anxiety. The children are taught to breathe slowly and deeply and to emit the mental command "Relax" while they exhale and voluntarily relax their muscles. The command is thus repeatedly paired with the relaxation that occurs with exhalation, so that with time, the mental command becomes an eliciting cue for inducing relaxation, as well as an important component of the integrated coping response that will eventually be learned. Once mastered, the relaxation response is a highly effective means of reducing or preventing stress responses because it is incompatible with physiological arousal.

Training in cognitive coping skills is carried out concurrently with relaxation training. With the aid of the trainer, the child is assisted in developing a series of mental self-statements which can be used to adaptively appraise the situation, to challenge and repudiate self-defeating thoughts which elicit stress, or to give self-instructions which direct attention and enhance performance. Two related procedures, cognitive restructuring (Goldfried & Davison, 1976; A. Lazarus, 1972) and self-instructional training (Meichenbaum, 1977), are used. In cognitive restructuring, dysfunctional stress-producing ideas (e.g., "It would be awful if I failed or if someone disapproved of me") are rationally analyzed, challenged, and replaced with self-statements that are both rationally sound and likely to reduce or prevent a stress response (e.g., "All I can do is give 100 percent. No one can do more"). The same philosophy of "success"—striving and giving maximum effort—that is stressed in working with coaches and parents is emphasized in helping children to develop a way of appraising athletic achievement that is less likely to generate stress than the belief, "If I don't win, I'm a worthless failure."

In self-instructional training, the focus is on helping children develop and use specific task-relevant self-commands that can be employed in relevant situations. Examples of such commands are "Don't get shook up. Just think about what you have to do." "Pay attention to what's happening. Don't get distracted." "Take a deep breath and relax." For many children who are not psychologically minded enough to profit from extensive cognitive restructuring, self-instructional training proves to be far more helpful. But in most instances, both approaches are used in the development of cognitive coping skills.

Stress coping skills are no different than any other kind of skill. In order to be most effective, they must be rehearsed and practiced under conditions that approximate the "real life" situations in which they will eventually be employed. A skill rehearsal phase is therefore an integral part of the stress management program. To enable them to rehearse coping skills, children are asked to imagine as vividly as possible stressful situations such as getting ready to shoot a crucial free throw or having just made a critical error. They are then asked to focus on the feeling that the imagined situation elicits, and the trainer suggests that as the feeling is focused upon, it becomes increasingly stronger. When a state of arousal is produced in this way, the child is asked to "turn it off" with a relaxation coping skill. Then, self-statements alone are used. Finally, the two types of coping responses are combined into an "integrated coping response" which ties both into the breathing cycle. As children inhale, they emit a stress-reducing self-statement. At the peak of exhalation, they mentally say the word "So," and as they slowly exhale, they instruct themselves to "Relax" and deepen muscular relaxation. Thus, both classes of coping responses are integrated into the breathing cycle in a manner that enables children to employ them repeatedly within stressful situations.

The stress management training program ends with training in Benson's (1976) meditation technique. The meditation technique cannot ordinarily be used in stressful athletic situations, but it is a useful generalized tension-reduction technique.

The goal of stress management training is *not* to completely eliminate emotional arousal. Some degree of arousal facilitates athletic performance. Rather, the goal of the training is to give children greater control over emotional responses so they can reduce or prevent high and aversive levels of arousal that interfere with performance and enjoyment.

Some degree of stress is endemic to the competitive sport situation. It is as much a part of sport as is striving for victory. But unnecessary sources of stress can also be produced by coaches, parents, and by unrealistic beliefs and attitudes on the part of athletes themselves. These unnecessary stresses detract from the potential of organized sport to provide children with enjoyment and personal growth. This paper has outlined three areas in which intervention can be carried out. Sport psychologists and other concerned professionals are exhibiting a growing interest in helping youth sport programs to enhance the welfare of children, and most programs stand ready to welcome our assistance. We hope that in the coming years, research, combined with soundly conceived intervention strategies, will expand the scope of our contributions.

REFERENCE NOTES

1. Seese, M.D., & Passer, M.W. *Life stress and athletic injury.* Paper presented at the annual meeting of the North American Society for the Psychology of Sport and Physical Activity, Monterey, CA, June 1981.

2. Passer, M.W. *Toward determining the antecedents of competitive trait anxiety*. Paper presented at the annual meeting of the North American Society for the Psychology of Sport and Physical Activity, Monterey, CA, June 1981.
3. Pierce, W.J., & Stratton, R.K. *Perceived sources of stress in youth sport participants*. Paper presented at the annual meeting of the North American Society for the Psychology of Sport and Physical Activity, Boulder, CO, May 1980.

REFERENCES

ARNOLD, M.B. Stress and emotion. In M.H. Appley & R. Trumbull (Eds.), *Psychological stress*. New York: Appleton-Century-Crofts, 1967.

BANDURA, A. *Social learning theory*. Englewood Cliffs, NJ: Prentice-Hall, 1977.

BANDURA, A. In search of pure unidirectional determinants. *Behavior Therapy*, 1981, **12**, 30-40.

BENSON, H. *The relaxation response*. New York: Avon, 1976.

BRAMWELL, S.T., Masuda, M., Wagner, N.N., & Holmes, T.H. Psychological factors in athletic injuries. *Journal of Human Stress*, 1975, **1**, 6-20.

BROWER, J.J. Little league baseballism: Adult dominance in a 'child's game.' In R. Martens (Ed.), *Joy and sadness in children's sports*. Champaign, IL: Human Kinetics, 1978.

CODDINGTON, R.D. The significance of life events as etiologic factors in the diseases of children, II: A study of a normal population. *Journal of Psychosomatic Research*, 1975, **16**, 205-213.

CODDINGTON, R.D., & Troxell, J.R. The effect of emotional factors on football injury rates—A pilot study. *Journal of Human Stress*, 1980, **6**, 3-5.

DEANE, G. Human heart rate responses during experimentally induced anxiety. A follow-up with controlled respiration. *Journal of Experimental Psychology*, 1964, **67**, 193-195.

ELLIS, A. *Reason and emotion in psychotherapy*. New York: Lyle Stuart, 1962.

EYSENCK, H.J. *The biological basis of personality*. Springfield, IL: Charles C. Thomas, 1967.

FERRELL, J., Glashagel, J., & Johnson, M. *A family approach to youth sports*. La Grange, IL: Youth Sports Press, 1978.

FISK, M.C. Danger: Children at play. *Woman's Day*, October 18, 1977, pp. 38, 40, 42.

GOLDFRIED, M.R., & Davison, G. *Clinical behavior therapy.* New York: Holt, Rinehart & Winston, 1976.

HENRY, G.M. Should the basket be lowered for young participants? *Journal of Physical Education and Recreation*, 1979, **50**, 66-67.

JACOBSON, E. *Progressive relaxation.* Chicago: University of Chicago Press, 1938.

LAZARUS, A. *Behavior therapy and beyond.* New York: McGraw-Hill, 1972.

LAZARUS, R.S. *Psychological stress and the coping process.* New York: McGraw-Hill, 1966.

LAZARUS, R.S. The self-regulation of emotions. In L. Levi (Ed.), *Emotions: Their parameters and measurement.* New York: Raven Press, 1975.

MARTENS, R. *Sport Competition Anxiety Test.* Champaign, IL: Human Kinetics, 1977.

MARTENS, R. *Joy and sadness in children's sports.* Champaign, IL: Human Kinetics, 1978.

MARTENS, R. *Parent guide to kids wrestling.* Champaign, IL: Human Kinetics, 1980.

MARTENS, R., & Gould, D. Why do adults volunteer to coach children's sports? In G.C. Roberts & K.M. Newell (Eds.), *Psychology of motor behavior and sport—1978.* Champaign, IL: Human Kinetics, 1979.

MARTENS, R., & Seefeldt, V. *Guidelines for children's sports.* Washington, DC: American Alliance for Health, Physical Education, Recreation and Dance, 1979.

MEICHENBAUM, D. *Cognitive-behavior modification.* New York: Plenum, 1977.

MICHENER, J.A. The jungle world of juvenile sports. *Reader's Digest*, December 1975, pp. 109-112.

ORLICK, T., & Botterill, C. *Every kid can win.* Chicago: Nelson-Hall, 1975.

ROBERTS, R. Strike out little league. *Newsweek*, July 21, 1975, p. 11.

ROSEN, A. *Baseball and your boy.* New York: Funk & Wagnalls, 1967.

SAYRE, B.M. The need to ban competitive sports involving preadolescent children. *Pediatrics*, 1975, **55**, 564.

SCANLAN, T.K., & Passer, M.W. Factors related to competitive stress among male youth sports participants. *Medicine and Science in Sports*, 1978, **10**, 103-108.

SCANLAN, T.K., & Passer, M.W. Sources of competitive stress in young female athletes. *Journal of Sport Psychology*, 1979, **1**, 151-159.

SCHACHTER, S. The interaction of cognitive and physiological determinants of emotional state. In C. Spielberger (Ed.), *Anxiety and behavior*. New York: Academic Press, 1966.

SEEFELDT, V., & Gould, D. *Physical and psychological effects of athletic competition on children and youth*. Washington, DC: ERIC Clearinghouse on Teacher Education, 1980.

SHAH, D.K., & Morris, H. Peewee football. *Newsweek*, December 4, 1978, pp. 129, 131.

SIEGEL, L.J., & Peterson, L. Stress reduction in young dental patients through coping skills and sensory information. *Journal of Consulting and Clinical Psychology*, 1980, **48**, 785-787.

SMITH, R.E. Development of an integrated coping response through cognitive affective stress management training. In I.G. Sarason & C.D. Spielberger (Eds.), *Stress and anxiety* (Vol. 7). Washington, DC: Hemisphere, 1980.

SMITH, R.E., Sarason, I.G., & Sarason, B.R. *Psychology: The frontiers of behavior*. New York: Harper & Row, 1978.

SMITH, R.E., & Smoll, F.L. Sport and the child: Conceptual and research perspectives. In F.L. Smoll & R.E. Smith (Eds.), *Psychological perspectives in youth sports*. Washington, DC: Hemisphere, 1978.

SMITH, R.E., Smoll, F.L., & Curtis, B. Coaching behaviors in Little League Baseball. In F.L. Smoll & R.E. Smith (Eds.), *Psychological perspectives in youth sports*. Washington, DC: Hemisphere, 1978.

SMITH, R.E., Smoll, F.L., & Curtis, B. Coach effectiveness training: A cognitive-behavioral approach to enhancing relationship skills in youth sport coaches. *Journal of Sport Psychology*, 1979, **1**, 59-75.

SMITH, R.E., Smoll, F.L., & Hunt, E. A system for the behavioral assessment of athletic coaches. *Research Quarterly*, 1977, **48**, 401-407.

SMITH, R.E., Smoll, F.L., Hunt, E., Curtis, B., & Coppel, D.B. Psychology and the Bad News Bears. In G.C. Roberts & K.M. Newell (Eds.), *Psychology of motor behavior and sport—1978*. Champaign, IL: Human Kinetics, 1979.

SMOLL, F.L., & Smith, R.E. *Improving relationship skills in youth sport coaches*. East Lansing, MI: Michigan Institute for the Study of Youth Sports, 1979.

SMOLL, F.L., & Smith, R.E. Psychologically-oriented coach training programs: Design, implementation, and assessment. In C.H. Nadeau, W.R. Halliwell, K.M. Newell, & G.C. Roberts (Eds.), *Psychology of motor behavior and sport—1979*. Champaign, IL: Human Kinetics, 1980.

SMOLL, F.L., & Smith, R.E. Developing a healthy philosophy of winning in youth sports. In *A winning philosophy for youth sports programs*. East Lansing, MI: Michigan Institute for the Study of Youth Sports, 1981.

SMOLL, F.L., Smith, R.E., & Curtis, B. Coaching roles and relationships. In J.R. Thomas (Ed.), *Youth sports guide for coaches and parents*. Washington, DC: American Alliance for Health, Physical Education, and Recreation, 1977.

SMOLL, F.L., Smith, R.E., Curtis, B., & Hunt, E. Toward a mediational model of coach-player relationships. *Research Quarterly*, 1978, **49**, 528-541.

THOMAS, J.R. (Ed.). *Youth sports guide for coaches and parents*. Washington, DC: American Alliance for Health, Physical Education, and Recreation, 1977.

UNDERWOOD, J. Taking the fun out of a game. *Sports Illustrated*, November 17, 1975, pp. 86-98.

VANDEWEGHE, E. *Growing with sport: A parents guide to the child athlete*. Englewood Cliffs, NJ: Prentice-Hall, 1979.

CHAPTER 14

SOME DETRIMENTAL EFFECTS OF COMPETITIVE SPORTS ON CHILDREN'S BEHAVIOR

Donna M. Gelfand and Donald P. Hartmann

Our interest in studying the possible deleterious effects of competition was originally stimulated by Leonard Berkowitz's (1962) writing on the topic. Berkowitz has portrayed competition as a stressful interaction in which both the eventual winner and the eventual loser are aroused and uncertain about the outcome. The repeated thwarting experienced by all participants during competition is a frustrating experience that should promote interpersonal aggression and hostility, in Berkowitz's view. Although the frustration should be greater for the loser, the winner also undergoes threat of defeat and anxiety about the outcome. Thus, either failure or success in competition should heighten aggression. If this theory is correct, then athletic contests should promote participants' aggression, rather than reduce aggression as various catharsis theories would predict (Lorenz, 1966; Miller, Moyer, & Patrick, 1956). Because these two opposing theoretical views have such contradictory implications for the use of athletic competition in controlling children's hyperaggressive behavior, it is important to establish which theory is the more veridical. We shall hold in abeyance for a time a third position, that of Albert Bandura (1969, 1973) regarding the arousing, but not necessarily aggression-producing, effects of competition.

This article originally appeared in T.T. Craig (Ed.), *The Humanistic and Mental Aspects of Sports, Exercise, and Recreation.* Chicago: American Medical Association, 1976. Copyright 1976 by the American Medical Association. Reprinted with permission.

CATHARSIS OR FRUSTRATION-AGGRESSION
THROUGH COMPETITION

As a first attempt to pit the frustration-aggression position against the catharsis formulation of competition, Nelson, Gelfand, and Hartmann (1969) conducted a laboratory analogue experiment with 5- and 6-year-old children. Pairs of children first observed either an aggressive or a nonaggressive adult who served as a model. The aggressive model assaulted a large inflated plastic doll in relatively novel ways such as smashing it with a mallet. In contrast, the nonaggressive adult model joined the children in playing with clay. Then each child either won or lost in competition with a peer, or did not compete. Two competitive games developed by Gelfand (1962) were used: a hand-strength measure and a bowling accuracy task. Although the outcomes seemed to be skill-determined, they were actually experimentally determined in advance. (We hasten to add that at the conclusion of the participation, the losers were given credible success experiences to counteract any negative emotional reactions they may have had to defeat.)

Now, if Berkowitz's modified frustration-aggression theory is correct, the competition should increase the children's aggressive behavior during a subsequent free play period. But if competition has a cathartic effect, children's subsequent play should become less aggressive. Our results clearly supported the view that competition promotes aggression, even above the heightened aggression ordinarily caused by exposure to an aggressive model.

In a second experiment Christy, Gelfand, and Hartmann (1971) posed the question of whether competition invariably promotes aggression or whether competition effects are determined by the type of behavioral models available. The frustration-aggression formulation would predict an aggressive outcome of competition. An alternate view, Bandura's (1969) social learning position, holds that competition has emotional arousing properties that will intensify whatever response pattern is dominant in the subject's response repertoire. The response repertoire is determined by the person's past social learning experiences, including observation of parental and other models. The repertoire is also determined by various past response consequences the person has experienced, in the form of positive reinforcement or punishment for particular behaviors. In Bandura's opinion, only when aggression has been learned as a dominant response will frustration-induced aggression occur.

Our experiment introduced highly-active but nonaggressive models, as well as the customary aggressive models. Because the results of the first experiment revealed that boys were more affected than girls by the competitive games, only 6- and 7-year-old boys served as subjects in the second study. We will return later to the topic of sex differences in reactions to competition. The results of our second study clearly supported Bandura's formulation regarding the effects of arousal in intensifying the prepotent response. The boys responded to the competition with increased imitation of whatever model they had witnessed. Those who had seen the highly active model became more active, but not more aggressive. Those who had seen the aggressive model became even more aggressive after competition. But they did not become more physically active in nonaggressive ways. Apparently adult models, whatever their behavior, play a major role in determining the nature of boys' responses to frustration induced by competition. If these effects hold in naturally occurring competitive games and sports, they could provide moderately good news for parents and teachers. The provision of appropriate social models could counteract any untoward behavioral effects of interpersonal competition.

To determine the generalizability of our laboratory findings, we must examine the field research literature. If the laboratory analogue is to be meaningful, then field observational studies and naturalistic field experiments must yield supporting results. First, let us examine the question of whether naturally occurring competition in games does heighten participants' aggression. The results of a number of field studies support this contention. In two observational studies, Harold Rausch and his colleagues (Rausch, 1965; Rausch, Dittmann, & Taylor, 1959) have observed increases in boys' unfriendly behavior during competitive games. In one study (Rausch, 1965) a group of normal American 10- to 12-year-old boys were observed in their natural environment. Overall, 89% of their interactions were friendly. But when they were engaged in competitive games, 42% of their acts were unfriendly. In contrast, only 5% of their acts were unfriendly at mealtimes. Moreover, in game situations, friendly behavior was less likely to be reciprocated in kind. In 31% of the instances studied, friendly acts in games led to unfriendly responses from the other boys. But at mealtimes, friendly acts led to unfriendly responses only 4% of the time. Apparently, as Rausch (1965) concluded, "The situation sets a tone influencing the likelihood that certain acts will occur" (p. 491). And competitive game situations make unfriendy behavior highly probable.

It appears that wars can be started, as well as won, on the playing fields at Eton. The classic studies by Sherif and Sherif and their colleagues (Sherif, Harvey, White, Hood, & Sherif, 1961; Sherif & Sherif, 1953) on group cohesivenes, intergroup conflict, and aggression employed athletic contests and other frustrating situations. In one experiment boys at a summer camp who were initially friendly with each other were placed on two opposing teams in a series of softball, soccer, tug-of-war, and other athletic competitions. Strong within-group loyalties and excessive intergroup rivalries appeared among the former friends. The losers engaged in various rationalizations and perceptual distortions to account for their defeats by the better-organized winning team. In tug-of-war, the consistent losers attributed the other team's success to lucky breaks such as a favorable footing location, and to sabotage of the rope and other forms of cheating. The adult counselors were careful not to provide the boys with any type of model for the acceptance of either success or defeat.

Other research (Herbert, Gelfand, & Hartmann, 1969; Thelen, 1969) has indicated that children's comments about their own failure in games are powerfully influenced by verbal models provided by adults. If the adult model engages in self-criticism or self-blame, the child observers will do so also when they in turn encounter failure. In the situation devised by Sherif and Sherif, the boys had only their uninstructed peers as models. And these peer models engaged in self-serving rationalizations and ill-founded accusations against their opponents.

Although the morale of the consistently victorious team was high, the losers turned upon each other. The boy whom the losing team had selected as their leader blamed and ridiculed the low status members of his own group for their team's losses. In a different study of boys' athletic teams, Pepitone and Kleiner (1957) found a similar group disintegrative effect of expectation of defeat. These latter investigators found that the higher the threat of loss of status for a team, the less the within-group cohesiveness as measured by members' choices of companions. In marked contrast to the reactions of the defeated team in the Sherifs' study, though, Pepitone and Kleiner found increased cooperation and sharing among the teams who lost and who were led to believe that they would continue to lose. Social learning theory would predict that other factors being held equal, differential modeling cues, perhaps provided by the team leaders, might well account for these contrasting reactions to losing.

Berkowitz (1970) has suggested a mechanism that could explain the decreased helpfulness, scapegoating, and increased aggression of competitors, particularly toward potential or actual rivals. Berkowitz postulates that any situation that increases self-concern will decrease concern for others. Thus, any threat to status, any evaluation or other stress that heightens concern over oneself and one's own performance could reduce prosocial behavior directed toward others. Athletic performance is considered of paramount importance in determining boys' peer group status (Campbell, 1964; Clarke & Clarke, 1961; Stein & Smithells, 1969; Tuddenham, 1951). Therefore, athletic competitions should be most likely to arouse boys' self-concern. Because loss in athletic competitions does not typically threaten girls to the same degree, they are both less involved in and less affected by such contests.

In their recent extensive review of sex differences in behavior, Maccoby and Jacklin (1974) commented on the male's greater interest in competitive sports. Our own research has revealed that boys were more affected by participation in simulated athletic competitions than were girls. It is noteworthy also that in the field experiments on competition, boys have almost invariably served as subjects and sports contests were used to induce competition. In other types of competitions such as in the frequently studied Prisoner's Dilemma game, females may equal or even surpass males in competitiveness (Maccoby & Jacklin, 1974). As Maccoby and Jacklin have concluded, the tendency for boys to be more competitive than girls is highly subject to situational and cultural variations. It may very well be that recent trends toward increased participation of women and girls in organized sports will reduce the sex differences in interests and involvement that have existed in the past (Sutton-Smith & Rosenberg, 1961).

BEHAVIORAL MODELS

Let us return now to the matter of the types of behavioral models typically presented to the children who participate in athletic competition. Who are the models and are they likely to increase or decrease the children's antisocial aggression? Parents are likely to attend their children's games, and they are notoriously likely to dispute rulings by the officials and to place a ludicrously high value on their offspring's winning (Moore, 1966).

No one in the stands is shouting to encourage the players to have sympathy, concern, and compassion for their opponents, or even advising them to be good sports. And high school basketball and football games all too frequently become the occasion for all-out war between the opposing schools, especially if they are traditional rivals (Turner, 1970). Fist-fights predictably break out among the spectators. Presumably, the participants of such brawls have never heard of Lorenz's (1966) theory regarding the moderating effects of athletic competition on spectators' aggression. Even the professional athletes who serve as exemplary models for many children may present inappropriate behavior for emulation. Sports broadcasts frequently highlight flagrant rule violations, unnecessary roughness, and fist-fights and disputes among athletes. And broadcasters may comment on these unsportsmanlike behaviors in approving or admiring ways. These lessons are not lost on child viewers.

We have seen that the excitement of competition and the aggressive modeling displays frequent in children's athletic contests can produce increases in the children's undesirable aggressive responses. Fortunately, these aggression-enhancing factors can be reduced or even eliminated by making some changes in children's organized athletics. Specifically, we would offer the following recommendations:

1. De-emphasize the most competitive aspects of children's sports as was recommended by Moore (1966). Ensure that each player has the opportunity to play in each game, shorten seasons and give recognition for

participation, effort, or improvement rather than for winning. Hill and Korchendorfer (1969) recommend no trophies, medals, or awards for sport victories for children. These tokens of victory also make defeat more visible and increase children's motivation to cheat or violate rules in order to avoid defeat.

2. Emphasize for both parents and children the noncompetitive aspects of sports, including skill acquisition and recreation.

3. Apprise parents of the dangers of excessive emphasis on winning, and work with them to try to promote more prosocial modeling. And this means more than the form letter warning parents that they will be ejected from games in which they use profanity or strike either a coach or an official. Certainly more could be done to help parents better perform their socializing role as regards athletic competition.

4. Involve league members in cooperative activities toward superordinate goals. The research summarized by Sherif (1966) indicates that involvement in superordinate goals, such as repairing the league's playing field, reduces conflict and hostility between rival teams.

5. Be alert and responsive to serious rule violations and other instances of unsportsmanlike behavior. The German research by Volkamer (1971) suggests that conditions likely to heighten serious rule violations include a close, low-scoring contest, being on a losing team and playing an away-from-home game. If aggressive and other unsportsmanlike contact is not likely to be detected, it will often produce a competitive advantage, effectively reward the perpetrator, and provide antisocial models for all participants. Thus, coaches must be vigilant to cheating and other rule violations by child members of their own teams.

6. Intensify the aversive consequences of serious rule infractions by professional and other well-publicized athletes, since these persons are important role models for children. Thus, playing privileges should be revoked for meaningful periods of time, so both the player and his team make a considerable sacrifice. Furthermore, discourage sports commentators and newscasters from highlighting and commenting approvingly on dirty tactics and fighting among athletes.

7. And finally, encourage kids to take up other types of sports such as golf, tennis, swimming, and skiing that they can use in later years and that don't typically produce such combative reactions among parents and other spectators.

So long as sports victories bring recognition, status, and tangible benefits, it will be difficult to discourage cheating, scapegoating, enmity among rivals, and heightened self-concern. But the recognition of these problems will help us to detect and counteract them should they arise.

REFERENCES

BANDURA, A. *Principles of behavior modification.* New York: Holt, Rinehart & Winston, 1969.

BANDURA, A. *Aggression: A social learning analysis*. Englewood Cliffs, NJ: Prentice-Hall, 1973.

BERKOWITZ, L. *Aggression: A social psychological analysis*. New York: McGraw-Hill, 1962.

BERKOWITZ, L. The self, selfishness, and altruism. In B. Maculay & L. Berkowitz (Eds.), *Altruism and helping behavior*. New York: Academic Press, 1970.

CAMPBELL, J.D. Peer relations in childhood. In M.L. Hoffman & L.W. Hoffman (Eds.), *Review of child development research* (Vol. 1). New York: Russell Sage Foundation, 1964.

CHRISTY, P.R., Gelfand, D.M., & Hartmann, D.P. Effects of competition-induced frustration on two classes of modeled behavior. *Developmental Psychology*, 1971, **5**, 104-111.

CLARKE, H.H., & Clarke, D.H. Social status and mental health of boys as related to their maturity, structural, and strength characteristics. *Research Quarterly*, 1961, **32**, 326-334.

GELFAND, D.M. The influence of self-esteem on rate of verbal conditioning and social matching behavior. *Journal of Abnormal and Social Psychology*, 1962, **65**, 259-265.

HERBERT, E.W., Gelfand, D.M., & Hartmann, D.P. Imitation and self-esteem as determinants of self-critical behavior. *Child Development*, 1969, **40**, 421-430.

HILL, J.P., & Kochendorfer, R.A. Knowledge of peer success and risk of detection as determinants of cheating. *Developmental Psychology*, 1969, **1**, 231-238.

LORENZ, K. *On aggression*. New York: Harcourt, Brace & World, 1966.

MACCOBY, E.E., & Jacklin, C.N. *The psychology of sex differences*. Stanford, CA: Stanford University Press, 1974.

MILLER, F.A., Moyer, J.H., & Patrick, R.B. *Planning student activities*. Englewood Cliffs, NJ: Prentice Hall, 1956.

MOORE, R.A. *Sports and mental health*. Springfield, IL: Thomas, 1966.

NELSON, J.D., Gelfand, D.M., & Hartmann, D.P. Children's aggression following competition and exposure to aggressive models. *Child Development*, 1969, **40**, 1085-1097.

PEPITONE, A., & Kleiner, R. The effect of threat and frustration on group cohesiveness. *Journal of Abnormal and Social Psychology*, 1957, **54**, 192-199.

RAUSCH, H.L. Interaction sequences. *Journal of Personality and Social Psychology*, 1965, 2, 487-499.

RAUSCH, H.L., Dittman, A.T., & Taylor, T.J. Person, setting, and change in social interaction. *Human Relations*, 1959, **12**, 361-379.

SHERIF, M. *In common predicament*. New York: Houghton-Mifflin, 1966.

SHERIF, M., Harvey, O.J., White, B.J., Hood, W.R., & Sherif, C.W. *Intergroup conflict and cooperation: The robbers cave experiment*. Norman: University of Oklahoma Press, 1961.

SHERIF, M., & Sherif, C.W. *Groups in harmony and tension*. New York: Harper, 1953.

STEIN, A.H., & Smithells, J. Age and sex differences in children's sex-role standards about achievement. *Developmental Psychology*, 1969, **1**, 252-259.

SUTTON-SMITH, B., & Rosenberg, B.G. Sixty years of historical change in the game preferences of American children. *The Journal of American Folklore*, 1961, **74**, 17-46.

THELEN, M.H. Modeling of verbal reactions to failure. *Developmental Psychology*, 1969, **1**, 297.

TUDDENHAM, R.D. Studies in reputation: III. Correlates of popularity among elementary school children. *Journal of Educational Psychology*, 1951, **42**, 257-276.

TURNER, E.T. The effects of viewing college football, basketball and wrestling on the elicited aggressive responses of male spectators. *Medicine and Science in Sport*, 1970, **2**, 100-105.

VOLKAMER, M. Zur aggressivitat in Konkurrenz-orientierten zozialen system. *Sportweissenschaft*, 1971, **1**, 68-76.

CHAPTER 15

KID SPORTS: A DEN OF INIQUITY OR LAND OF PROMISE

Rainer Martens

Should Johnny play ball?
Little leagues: good or bad?
How good are organized sports for your child?
These are some of the headlines bannered by journalists writing about youth sports. Katherine Bryn (1974) writing in *Science Digest* queried her readers with the title, "Does kids' competition really make better adults?" and answered with the subtitle, "Playing to win has dangerously eclipsed playing for fun at the youngest levels of organized sports thanks to parents who failed to fulfill their own dreams of grandeur on the playing field." The subtitle of an article by June Robbins (1969) in *McCalls* boldly states, "An angry and sorrowful mother tells why it is that the only kids who still play baseball as it should be played are Charlie Brown and his pals."

"Don't knock Little League" is the title of Bob Feller's (1956) article in *Collier's* and Fran Tarkenton's (1970) essay is captioned, "Don't Let Your Son Play Smallfry Football." One article warns, "Leave your little leaguer alone" while another states, "Parent leadership is essential in kid sports." And the flood of contradictory prose goes on and on by journalists who are self-appointed instant experts in sport psychology. If

This article originally appeared in the *Proceedings of the Annual Convention of the National College of Physical Education Association for Men*, 1976, pp. 102-112. Copyright 1976 by NCPEAM. Reprinted with permission.

these journalists have not alarmed parents about youth sports, they at least have confused them.

Parents naturally are concerned about the well being of their children in sports—and in sports such as "pee wee" football and midget hockey physical injury is a legitimate worry. But parents today are even more concerned about the psychological well being of their children when participating in sports.

According to journalists, in increasing numbers kids are turned off, burned out, and hung up after participating in sports. They tell us that impressionable kids are learning by example how to swear, cheat, and fight. In spite of the criticisms, parents do see a great deal of good in youth sports. And youth sports programs continue to flourish, with boys and girls alike participating in greater numbers than ever. Youth sports create a dilemma for concerned parents: They want their kids to participate, but they are uncertain as to whether youth sports create sinners or saints.

After the All-American Soap Box Derby winner of 1973 was disqualified for cheating, the prosecuting attorney lamented, "It's like seeing apple pie, motherhood, and the American flag grinding to a halt." In growing numbers, concerned adults are wondering whether sport is helping or hindering in the moral development of America's youth.

Asking whether sport creates sinners or saints, however, is asking a moot question. The obvious answer is that youth sports programs can facilitate moral development when conducted correctly and also can facilitate the development of immoral or amoral behavior when conducted incorrectly. The more pregnant question is: What experiences in youth sports enhance moral development and what experiences contribute to immoral development? I will seek to answer this question, at least in part, from existing knowledge in social, developmental, and sport psychology.

My objective in this paper is to suggest how psychological research can be applied by youth sports coaches in helping to develop moral standards among young athletes. In the sections to follow, I first consider the three progressive phases of moral development. Next, I discuss several social learning principles that may be used by coaches to facilitate the child's development of moral standards. And finally, I suggest a perspective for youth sports programs—a perspective that creates an environment where not only moral development is likely to be nurtured, but the total development of the child is enhanced.

Before proceeding, a brief digression about research and researchers will help you understand my frame of reference in this paper. So often we researchers unwittingly communicate in the negative. We describe at great length our experimental masterpieces, only to commit our results to death with a thousand qualifications. We take pride in being capable of uncovering the unreliability and invalidity of the extant literature. We spew forth with computer-like speed reams of questions that we are unable to answer, leaving our audiences dazed and bored—but mostly bored.

In the following section, I will discuss not the thousand qualifications nor the reams of questions, but rather what we know. Research in psychology has taught us much about how to raise kids to enhance their moral and social development. Moreover, I am astounded by how often the research findings lead to conclusions that appear obvious; that is, they correspond with my notion of common sense. I hope you find this to be true as well; to the extent you do, it increases the validity of these observations. While practitioners rely extensively on their own experiences as a source of knowledge, researchers sometimes neglect or demise this source. In the study of moral development, having been a child once is an important source of knowledge.

MORAL DEVELOPMENT

In 1908 William McDougall wrote "the fundamental problem of social psychology is the moralization of the individual by the society." Through the process of moralization all the major phases of social development arise and are resolved by one means or another. Moral development is the development of the conscience or superego. Children's consciences are developed from experiences with their environment, providing them with opportunities to internalize society's standards. Successful moralization of children eliminates the necessity for constant surveillance and threats of punishment by society. Moral behavior within a sport context is called sportsmanship.

Psychologist Lawrence Kohlberg (1969) demonstrated that children may move through three distinct phases of moral development. Each phase emerges out of and subsumes its predecessor and is more cognitively complex than the one before it. *Premoral hedonism* is the first phase of moral development; children behave simply to avoid punishment. "You scratch my back and I'll scratch yours" expresses children's conception of morality in this phase. From premoral hedonism, children's consciences develop into a phase where their moral behavior is guided by what they believe others will approve of and by an increasing concern for external rules and sanctions. This phase is known as the *conformity phase*. In the final phase of moral development, individuals place greater reliance on internal moral principles. Persons enter what is known as the *internalization phase* of moral development when they have learned that external rules which lead to absolute judgments must be tempered by internal moral principles. It is a morality based on the need for harmony between persons rather than inflexible conformity to rules (Sutton-Smith, 1973).

Socialization Through Sport

Philosophers, psychologists, and physical educators have eulogized play, games, and sports as a means not only for developing morality in children but socializing them to many facets of society. According to these academicians, games may act as a buffer, permitting children to learn the realities of life without sustaining the total impact of negative consequences. But play is not "play" to kids; play is serious business. Through the eyes of a young boy, failure to learn to ride a bicycle is just as serious as his father's failure in business.

Play may be a source of self-discovery, a means for learning new social roles, a medium for parent and child to communicate. Games and sports may permit a child an opportunity to learn how to cheat in the process of learning the meaning of fair play. But just as play, games, and sport have the capacity for positive socialization, they also may breed deceit, hatred, and violence. Thus, it is not the game, the play, or the sport that automatically determines the worth of these activities for the child; it is the nature of the experiences within these activities. It is the interactions with parents, teammates, and coaches that determine if sports help children develop morally or immorally. Now on to some examples of how reinforcement principles and modeling can be used by coaches to make sport an experience that enhances moral development.

Reinforcing Moral Behavior

Through popular psychology it is easy to obtain the impression that the application of reinforcement principles in modifying behavior is straightforward. We simply reward moral behavior and punish immoral behavior. But the use of reinforcement principles with humans is not as easy as Skinnerians have led us to believe because people are not pigeons or rats (at least not most of them)!

Bad Billy. Seven-year-old Billy, a goalie with the Buffalo Bombers of the midget hockey league, becomes entangled with teammates and opponents in a skirmish around his net. Billy is hit and dazed, but is uncertain by whom or what. In his anger, Billy retaliates by punching the nearest opponent in the nose with a solid right. The referee throws Billy out of the game and his coach punishes him by sitting him out of the next game. As a result, Billy may hesitate to hit an opponent again in a similar situation to avoid punishment, but he may not understand why he should not. If, on the other hand, the coach explains that it is wrong to hurt people, Billy may also hesitate to hit other children when he is off the ice.

The point in this example is that the things coaches say to children are of particular importance to the internalization of moral standards because they help form thoughts that children associate with rewards and punishments. When coaches tell children why they are being punished, the coaches may provide the children with a general rule that helps them control their own behavior in a variety of situations.

Let's look again at Billy's act of aggression. This time the referee and Billy's coach overlook his violence. The presence of these adults and their failure to intervene when Billy behaved immorally may indicate to him that his fighting is not really bad after all. That is, the failure to punish immoral behavior may reinforce that behavior. Moreover, Billy observes that the older players and the pros, with whom he identifies so closely, engage in much more violence than he, and yet they often go unpunished. But Billy's parents have always punished him before for fighting. Billy begins to wonder if it is wrong to fight only when Mom and Dad are watching. Billy's confusion is no surprise because he observes inconsistencies in the punishment of aggressive behavior. The more inconsistent adults are in rewarding and punishing Billy's moral and immoral behavior, the more difficult it is for him to attain the higher stages of moral development.

Understanding the Golden Rule. In the hockey game, Billy retaliated because he was hurt. He was unconcerned whether the other players intended to hurt him or if the hurt was accidental. Children younger than 7 or 8 years of age seldom show concern for the intent of the act. With cognitive development, occurring in part from maturation but more through learning experiences, children become aware of other persons' intentions by developing the ability to place themselves into the role of the other person. Role-taking, which normally develops in the 8-12 year age span, is an essential skill for the development of morality. The Golden Rule, "do unto others as you would have them do unto you," has no significance to children unless they can take the role of others.

Youth sports provide valuable opportunities to develop the role-taking ability. Sport is a social situation and the role-taking ability can only develop in a social context. The more social experiences and interactions, i.e., the more opportunity for social learning, the greater the role-taking opportunities available to children. Role-taking is very susceptible to reinforcement and modeling influences (Sutton-Smith, 1973). Coaches, parents, and other involved adults have unique opportunities through sport to develop children's role-taking capacity. Coaches especially can do much to teach their aspiring paladins to look beyond the act and understand the intent of the actor. In brief, through sport coaches with empathy strive to teach their players empathy.

Undermining moral development. Another hazard in the use of rewards and punishments is that extrinsic rewards may undermine the development of intrinsic motives (Greene & Lepper, 1974). Too often in youth sports children's intrinsic interest in a sport is decreased by inducing them to engage in that sport as an explicit means to some extrinsic goal, such as a trophy, a trip, or a state championship. When these extrinsic rewards for playing are removed, children may lose all intrinsic motivation to participate in the sport. In some cases, this may generalize from a specific sport to sports in general.

Using extrinsic rewards to undermine intrinsic motivations was put to clever use in the following story.

[An] old man lived alone on a street where boys played noisily every afternoon. One day the din became too much, and he called the boys into his house. He told them he liked to listen to them play, but his hearing was failing and he could no longer hear their games. He asked them to come around each day and play noisily in front of his house. If they did, he would give them each a quarter. The youngsters raced back the following day and made a tremendous racket in front of the house. The old man paid them, and asked them to return the next day. Again they made noise, and again the old man paid them for it. But this time he gave each boy only 20 cents, explaining that he was running out of money. On the following day, they got only 15 cents each. Furthermore, the old man told them, he would have to reduce the fee to five cents on the 4th day. The boys became angry, and told the old man they would not be back. It was not worth the effort, they said, to make noise for only five cents a day. (Casady, 1974)

Analogously, the stringent extrinsic control of moral behavior will not foster the development of internalized moral standards. For those who function as socialization agents for our children, including youth sports mentors, an ever-present danger prevails that extrinsic rewards and punishments may undermine the internalization of moral standards. As one witty youngster said to his strict father, "Must your conscience be my guide?" If children's consciences are to develop fully, if moral standards are to become internalized, as children mature rewards and punishments must slowly be withdrawn and replaced with increasingly complex reasoning to help them form rules of behavior. When individuals have internalized the moral standards of society, they will forgo external rewards and punishments to behave in socially acceptable ways, even in private.

Psychological Punishment. Parents inevitably must decide how they will punish their children. Among the most significant findings in the child development field is the discovery that children punished psychologically, using love-withdrawal or approval-withdrawal and reasoning, develop stronger consciences and are more susceptible to guilt feelings than children punished physically (Berkowitz, 1964). Children disciplined mostly by corporal punishment tend to display substantially more overt hostility.

Later research (see Hoffman, 1970) has shown that love-withdrawal is not as critical a factor in shaping the conscience as the reasoning given to the child for the withdrawal of love. As we observed before, reasoning with children encourages them to take the role of others and it helps children internalize moral standards by providing them with thoughts that they associate with rewards and punishments. If the reasoning with a child is overly complex, however, it may be of little value because it will not be understood. What is important in the moral development of children is that they have experience with moral judgments more advanced than their own, but not so advanced that they cannot understand them. Children in the premoral phase will not understand the use of advanced reasoning, helpful for internalizing moral standards, but instead will learn more from teammates and adults who talk in conformity terms. Corporal punishment, on the other hand, inhibits internalizing moral standards because it engenders hostility, modifies behavior only because of fear, and often leads to rebellion.

A parent's or coach's threat to use psychological punishment obviously will not be overly upsetting to children who have no love for their parents or respect and admiration for their coach. Coaches' threats to withdraw their approval become effective reinforcers only when children are concerned with what the coach thinks; children must have respect for their coach. It is not a coincidence that adults who are unable to obtain respect from children are the same persons who rely most on corporal punishment to control children's behavior. Obviously they must!

Pygmalion and Sport. My final observation about the use of rewards and punishments for moral development concerns the powerful effects that expectations can have on the behavior of young people. Popularized recently as the Pygmalion effect, but more aptly described as the self-fulfilling prophecy, social psychological research has shown that kids sometimes become what we prophesy for them. If a coach has the expectation that some children will not be good athletes or that they are immoral (and irrevocably so), the children may sense their coach's expectation and act to fulfill it.

Rosenthal (1973) reports that coaches' expectations may influence children's learning of skills and moral standards through one or more of four factors. Coaches may create a warmer social-emotional mood around their "special" athletes; they may give more feedback to these athletes about their performance and behavior; they may teach more material to these athletes; and they may give their special athletes more opportunities to participate and question events.

I suspect as kids we all have been in situations where we sensed that others felt we were inferior. Kids with self-confidence usually confront such expectations as a challenge to be proven wrong. Kids lacking self-confidence, however, may simply accept their lot and behave to fulfill their coaches' negative expectations. The process, of course, may function in reverse. Coaches' positive expectations may help motivate kids to achieve what they otherwise thought could not be attained. What coaches must remember is that expectations can reinforce both positive and negative behavior and that these expectations are communicated not only knowingly but often unknowingly.

Modeling

Kids learn moral behavior not only by being rewarded and punished, but by observing other people behave morally and immorally (Bandura, 1969). Learning by observing is pervasive in children. They imitate mom and dad in their games, mimic their siblings and peers in play, and model themselves after their sport heroes. But kids do not instinctively imitate everyone in their environment. Children are likely to imitate those who command resources or have access to desirable goals. Coaches who control children's participation in sports and games often command an important resource or goal for the children. Thus, it is no surprise that kids often imitate their coach.

Kids may not only imitate specific behaviors of their coach, but may strive to become exactly like him or her. Known as *identification*, this complete imitation of an emulated person has a profound influence on the development of children's self-concepts. To the extent children perceive that their attributes match those with whom they identify and that the culture regards these as good, they develop a positive self-concept.

Superficialness. Children show less development of strong moral standards when they grow up with adults who reinforce only the surface appearance of their behavior. Adults who serve as models for kids can create, by overly assertive and domineering behavior, the attitude that an immoral act is only immoral when it is detected and punished (see Aronfreed, 1969). Coaches in particular may easily give the impression that cheating is not really wrong unless it is detected, and then only to the extent that it hurts the chances of winning. When coaches promote immoral behavior to attain victory, youngsters may conclude that "the-end-justifies-the-means" attitude is a proper code of morality.

Child development research shows that working class adults, more so than middle class adults, give greater attention to the surface appearance of their children's actions (Berkowitz, 1964). Working class adults seek to develop in their children obedience, whereas middle class adults strive more to have their children develop appropriate internal standards so that they will regulate their own moral behavior. That is, working class adults more often are satisfied to have their children reach the conformity stage of moral development, but middle class adults strive for the internalization phase. Could it be then that youth sports are even more important in helping kids from working class families attain the internalization phase of moral development?

Adult Aggression. It is not surprising that social psychological research discovered that kids physically punished for aggression later behave more aggressively than kids who are psychologically punished (Bandura, 1969; Hoffman, 1970). Adults who physically punish kids for aggressive behavior provide a model for that very behavior. Moreover, coaches who display hostility toward the officials and contempt for the other teams' coaches and players may wittingly or unwittingly reinforce their behavior as appropriate.

For example, after a heated debate with the umpires an emotional coach returns to his young players and announces, "You have to show those umps who's the boss; you can't let them push you around. They better start calling them right, or I'll really give it to 'em!" And if the next close call favors the vociferous coach's team, he may proudly declare it was his intimidation that led to the favorable call. Pliant kids, particularly those who identify with the coach, may conclude that intimidation is an appropriate success strategy.

Fortunately, intimidating behavior of this type does not always get coaches what they want. When kids see that a coach's negative behavior is unproductive, or better yet psychologically punished, their observations are likely to be a didactic experience. If children are made cognizant that an adult's immoral behavior is inappropriate and undesirable, it will help them form appropriate moral standards.

Hypocrisy. One of the difficulties in working with kids is that we want them to be better than we are ourselves. Too often we preach one thing and practice something else, or one day we do one thing and the next day we do the opposite; or one parent says one thing and the other does the opposite. This is exemplified by the mother who always said to her son when he hit his brother, "Hands are to love with, not to hit with." And a few weeks later the boy's father bought him boxing gloves for Christmas!

These inconsistencies must be resolved by children if they are to form a stable conscience. Do they do as we say, or as we do? Does our preaching or our practice have a greater influence on our children's moral behavior? Recent evidence showed, for example, that when generosity was modeled by adults, kids increased their own generosity, but exhortations to be generous did not prompt increased generosity (Bryan, 1969). More importantly, hypocrisy did not affect the children's generosity; that is, kids were as generous when observing a generous model who preached avarice or stinginess as those who practiced and preached generosity. If we dare to generalize from these findings, our conclusion must be that actions *speak louder than words*.

This is to the chagrin of American religious, educational, and sport institutions who have had great faith in the value of precepts in moral education. Reciting such precepts as "love thy neighbor as thy self" or "honesty is the best policy" or "cheaters never win" has little to do with the moral development of our children (Berkowitz, 1964). Instead, if we want our kids to mature morally, the bellwethers of sport must be paragons of virtue.

PUTTING IT INTO PERSPECTIVE

Although brief and oversimplified, I have discussed a few social learning principles that may help young athletes enjoy and benefit from their experience in sports. But implementing these principles, as well as knowledge from other sport sciences, into positive coaching behaviors is impeded because (a) the lack of an effective delivery system for communicating what is known to adults working with young athletes, and (b) inadequate means for motivating these adults to use this knowledge when coaching. The latter problem is particularly vexing. So often we know what is right for our kids, but we do something less than what is best. We know that screaming derogatory remarks at children when they make a mistake does not help them, but in the midst of the contest we sometimes forget. We repress children's needs for ours. We lose our perspective. But these problems are surmountable—we can develop an effective delivery system and we can help coaches maintain their perspective. Let's consider next some facets of youth sports that the critics say are not in perspective.

Competitive Stress

Undeniably, there is at times an overemphasis on winning in youth sports, but no one knows for certain the magnitude of the problem. Among the major criticisms of the winning-is-everything philosophy is that it places too much stress on kids. Critics impute that the resultant fear of failure leads to competitive stress equivalent in some cases to the stress manifested by soldiers in combat. When the fear of failure outweighs the fear of detection, immoral behavior such as cheating is more likely to occur unless the child has a well-developed conscience. Consequently, it would be helpful to know precisely how much stress kids can handle for each of the three phases of moral development.

You should not be surprised to learn that sport psychologists are unable to provide simple and accurate prescriptions for the proper dosage of competitive stress. Although desirable, sport psychologists cannot prescribe for Johnny, who is in the hedonistic phase of moral development, three units of competitive stress mixed with 50 cc of self-confidence; or for Mark, who is in the advanced stage of the conformity phase, seven units of competitive stress and 100 cc of achievement motivation. The inability to provide simple prescriptions have led some coaches to conclude that sport psychologists have nothing to offer. But simple answers to complex behavioral problems do not exist, and those with illusions that they do should discard them.

To understand the proper dosage of competitive stress, we need to examine further the complexities of competitive stress. First we must consider whether the stress to excel in youth sports is unilaterally detrimental or are there occasions when this stress may be beneficial. Some experts tell us that we should seek to eliminate all sources of stress for our children or at least keep them to a minimum; kids will have enough stress in adult life and they do not need to be burdened with it as children. These same experts tell us that youth sports are entirely too stressful; they should be eliminated and children should be encouraged to participate only in unstructured play.

Other experts believe kids must learn the harsh realities of the world and coping with stress is one of these realities. Learning the hard knocks of life as a youngster will prepare the child better for a successful adult life. These experts usually promote "miniaturized" big league sports programs; they encourage extremely competitive, highly organized programs because they build character.

Stress research and common sense suggest a position between these extremes. We can, no doubt, overstress our kids: We can burn them out, damage their self-concept, and retard their moral development. On the other hand, kids raised in sterile environments, who have little opportunity to learn to cope with stress, have significantly greater problems in adjusting to adult life. Children need opportunities to learn to cope with increasing degrees of stress. This was a widely accepted belief of our grandparents as stated in the maxim, "As the rainbow needs both rain and sun, virtue needs both the bitter and the sweet to shine clearly."[1]

Youth sports provide many opportunities for learning to cope with moderate stressors, but they are equally amenable to placing too much stress on children. The key to whether youth sports are opportunities for learning to cope or jungles where a high degree of coping is essential to survive, is dependent upon the objectives emphasized by parents, coaches, and sport organizers. When the predominant emphasis is toward children's physical and psychological development and not just on winning, the chances increase that competitive stress will be in perspective.

More on Winning

To discuss the issue of winning further we need to consider what the objectives are of youth sports in our society. Minimally, we want youth sports to be fun without having negative consequences on children's development. Optimally, they are to be fun while contributing to the physical, psychological, and social development of children. Most adults involved in youth sports will tell you that winning is not the important goal, but their behavior sometimes defies their words.

---

[1]In the Crown Prince's Book of Stories and Mottoes for Children written in 1780.

Critics of youth sports are the first to point out that all too often these developmental objectives conflict with adults' desire to win. Competing to win, however, is not necessarily a negative goal; striving to achieve can foster personal growth, in fact it may be that moral development is nurtured more when moral decisions come into conflict with winning. Walter Kroll (Note 1), in an impressive paper on sportsmanship, made this point vividly. He writes:

> Perhaps we need to inspect the notion that noteworthy acts of sportsmanship seem always to involve sacrifices of success strategy in favor of a decision guided by moral criteria. Success is not easily relinquished when it is so highly esteemed, but the conduct prescribed by a code of moral behavior can—and often does—compel the individual to forego the rewards of success. . . .Unless winning is important, putting success in jeopardy in favor of conduct compatible with a moral code fails to qualify as a noteworthy event. Such a proposition really needs to be considered by those harsh and outspoken critics of athletics who lambast the emphasis upon winning, who urge that cooperation replace competition. (p. 22)

Competition as a process of striving for a valued goal is unjustifiably maligned by critics intending to say something else. Competition is not a den of iniquity nor is cooperation utopia. Competition and cooperation are not antithetical, but complementary. What the critics intend to say when they attack competition and extoll the virtues of cooperation is that winning is *overemphasized* and the cooperative emphasis will bring winning back into balance.

The crux of the problem then is knowing when winning is overemphasized. Actually, it is not as difficult as it may appear to detect the win-at-all-cost philosophy. We can with some accuracy infer coaches' motives by observing their behaviors. When coaches play injured youngsters, when they leave players sitting on the bench the entire season, and when they routinize practice so that it becomes a complete bore, overemphasis is indicated. When in the frantic race to be first, the developmental objectives blur into the background, winning is out-of-bounds.

Socialization is Imperfect

We recognize of course that no social institution is perfect and youth sports programs are no exceptions. Obviously, youth sports have their virtues—kids do have fun, they do learn lifetime leisure skills, and they do develop physically and psychologically. Not every child, though, experiences all of these good things. There are abuses in, and misuses of, youth sports. But youth sports programs do not stand alone in their failure to realize their full socialization potential; religious and educational institutions have also failed to significantly affect children's moral development.

Given that social institutions are imperfect, those adults leading youth sports must strive to maximize the positive outcomes and minimize the negative outcomes of these programs. I have discussed some social learning principles that increase the likelihood of helping kids develop morally and socially through participation in youth sports. In some cases, coaches will be faced with a difficult choice in implementing these principles; they may have to choose between an action that increases their chances of winning the game but potentially having adverse effects on the psychological development of the child, and losing the game but potentially facilitating the child's moral development. It often is easier to take the action that leads to the immediate and more visible goal of winning. It takes perspective to act in ways that favor children's physical, psychological, and social development at the possible expense of victory.

CONCLUSION

Youth sports are not inherently evil nor are they inherently good—they are what we make them. Youth sports are more likely to build character when coaches with character have some knowledge of social learning principles and apply them. Coaches cannot permit themselves to repress their players' needs in order to satisfy their own need to win. A moderate degree of competitive stress, created by an environment where winning is prized and losing is not scorned, is more likely to be helpful than harmful in the moral development of children.

To enhance the probability that youth sport participation will help the psychological and social development of our children they need an environment that is warm and friendly, where adult behavior is firm but consistent, and where opportunities are ample to make decisions within their cognitive capacity. How the environment we create can influence our kids is succinctly expressed in these words:

If a child lives with criticism, he learns to condemn.
If a child lives with hostility, he learns to fight.
If a child lives with fear, he learns to be apprehensive.
If a child lives with encouragement, he learns to be confident.
If a child lives with praise he learns to be appreciative.
If a child lives with approval, he learns to like himself.
If a child lives with recognition, he learns to have a goal.
If a child lives with honesty, he learns what trust is.[2]

---

[2]Abridged from a "Great Cities Project Report" which was reprinted in the *Baltimore Bulletin of Education*, 1965-66, **42** (3).

REFERENCE NOTE

1. Kroll, W. *Psychology of sportsmanship.* Paper presented at the Sport Psychology meeting, National Association for Sport and Physical Education (NASPE), American Association for Health, Physical Education and Recreation, Atlantic City, NJ, March 1975.

REFERENCES

ARONFREED, J. The concept of internalization. In D.A. Goslin (Ed.), *Handbook of socialization: Theory and research.* Chicago: Rand McNally, 1969.

BANDURA, A. Social-learning theory of identifactory processes. In D.A. Goslin (Ed.), *Handbook of socialization: Theory and research.* Chicago: Rand McNally, 1969.

BERKOWITZ, L. *The development of motives and values in the child.* New York: Basic Books, 1964.

BRYAN, J.H. How adults teach hypocrisy. *Psychology Today,* December 1969, pp. 50-52; 65.

BRYN, K. Does kids' competition really make better adults? *Science Digest,* November 1974, pp. 38-44.

CASADY, M. The tricky business of giving rewards. *Psychology Today,* September 1974, p. 52.

FELLER, B., with Lebovitz, H. Don't knock little leagues. *Colliers,* August 3, 1956, pp. 78-81.

GREENE, D., & Lepper, M.R. Intrinsic motivation: How to turn play into work. *Psychology Today,* September 1974, pp. 49-54.

HOFFMAN, M. Moral development. In P.H. Mussen (Ed.), *Carmichael's manual of child psychology* (3rd ed., Vol. 2). New York: Wiley, 1970.

KOHLBERG, L. Stage and sequence: The cognitive-developmental approach to socialization. In D.A. Goslin (Ed.), *Handbook of socialization: Theory and research.* Chicago: Rand McNally, 1969.

ROBBINS, J. The case against little league mothers. *McCalls,* July 1969, pp. 55; 130.

ROSENTHAL, R. The Pygmalion effect lives. *Psychology Today,* September 1973, pp. 56-63.

SUTTON-SMITH, B. *Child psychology*. New York: Appleton-Century-Crofts, 1973.

TARKENTON, F. Don't let your son play smallfry football. *Ladies' Home Journal*, October 1970, pp. 146-147.

CHAPTER 16

DEVELOPMENTAL MEMORY FACTORS IN CHILDREN'S PERCEPTION OF SPORT

Jerry R. Thomas, Jere D. Gallagher,
and Katherine T. Thomas

An estimated 20 million children now participate in sport in the US. Although the immediate exercise benefits that children obtain from their sport experience is certainly valuable, even more important is how children perceive their sport experience, because perception is ultimately the major determinant of continued participation in sport and regular exercise.

What do we really know about how children remember and interpret their experience in sport? Do kids perceive the events and outcomes of sport contests in the same way as adults? Research evidence suggests two important factors about kids in sports: First, although much of the sport experience is positive, coaches and parents may be inadvertently structuring experiences that contribute to children "dropping out" of sport; second, the literature shows that, compared to older children and adults, young children do not process all available information in many situations, and this affects their perception of events. In this paper we will discuss children's perception of the events that occur to them and others. This perception of events may differ within and between age levels and may not be congruent with the actual facts.

This paper is a compilation of two papers which appeared in Morris, A. (Ed.), *Motor Development: Theory into Practice* (Monograph #3). New Town, CN: Motor Skills: Theory into Practice, 1981. The papers are "Introduction: Children's Processing of Information in Physical Activity and Sport" by J.R. Thomas, K.T. Thomas, and J.D. Gallagher and "How Do Children Perceive the Sport Experience" by J.R. Thomas and J.D. Gallagher.

Given an obvious cause for a behavior, both children and adults will attribute their behavior to this cause. In fact, four rather common causes of behavior (ability, effort, task difficulty, and luck) are used as the basis for attribution theory (Heider, 1958; Kelley, 1967, 1972). Comments of players and coaches following a victory or defeat often show this attributional process:

- "Our team is really loaded with talent this year" (ability).
- "The girls really played hard" (effort).
- "The other team just had too many skilled players" (task difficulty).
- "Gee, every bounce went against us" (luck).

Considerable evidence supports the view that children and adults use factors such as those just listed to make decisions about engaging in competitive situations as well as in explaining the outcomes of these situations. That is, when confronted with sport competition, children assess the situation as they perceive it, evaluate their ability, the difficulty of the task, and how much effort is needed, compare with past experiences, and then decide whether to attempt the particular task or not. If they decide to attempt the task, they then demonstrate the most appropriate behavior for that task. The child then evaluates the outcome (or is helped to do so) and ascribes the results to some combination of ability, effort, task difficulty, and luck. This information is then stored in memory for use in similar future circumstances. When ascriptions threaten our self-esteem, we employ an ego-defensive mechanism referred to as "self-enhancing" behavior (Feather & Simon, 1971; Wortman, Costanzo, & Witt, 1973). In an athletic situation, then, a player on a losing team has a tendency to think that the other performers on the team did not give their best effort during the game, but that he or she gave a lot of effort (Roberts, 1975).

Also, children in sport often wonder if they are in control of their own lives. Although parents and coaches try to lead children to greater independence through sport, we find that most of children's experiences in sport are controlled by adults. Although we believe that sports participation can be positive, we are also concerned, because if the results of a survey in Michigan (Seefeldt, 1976) can be generalized to the entire country, a great number of children drop out of sport (percentages vary by sport) between the ages of 12 and 17. Although the problems of children's attributions and general lack of control over their sport experience are not solely responsible for this dropout rate, they can be important factors.

Children should be and are intrinsically motivated to participate in sport. The enthusiasm of young children in sport is obvious; however, this enthusiasm sometimes wanes as they grow older. Do adults contribute to this loss of intrinsic motivation by the way they organize and conduct children's sport experience? We suspect that many of the following situations (and others) decrease rather than increase intrinsic motivation for sport and regular exercise.

1. How does an audience affect the interest and motivation of a poorly skilled player?

2. Is the self-image of poorly skilled players affected when the coach only allows them to play when the game is clearly won/lost?

3. Do all the awards in sport increase the motivation of players? Does this depend upon their skill level and/or age?

4. Will players who are "cut" from teams continue to have positive motivation?

In the review that follows, we attempt to focus on two aspects of children's sport experience—winning and losing, and motivation—for considerable evidence exists on these two factors and their influence on children. First we will discuss how children differ from adults in how they process information. We will also discuss how this fact must influence their perception of events and should be considered by coaches, parents, and other educators.

HOW CHILDREN PROCESS INFORMATION
IN PHYSICAL ACTIVITY AND SPORT

The change in people's motor behavior can be attributed to three sources: external information, that is, situational demands and feedback from the sports performance environment; internal feedback, proprioceptive information resulting from the specific skilled performance; and internal information that has been retained in memory from previous performances or similar situations. The ability of a person's memory system to use all of the sources of information to reinforce and/or change perceptions, decisions, and behavior is referred to as cognitive or information processing. Thus, the use of the memory system not only affects our own perception and performance in sport and physical activity but also influences how we perceive others' behavior and the causes of this behavior.

Children are not "miniature adults," but instead are in the process of developing physically. We sometimes forget that this is true of their emotional and cognitive development. The fact that adults process verbal and motor information more efficiently than children has been supported by numerous studies (Chi, 1976; Drucker & Hagen, 1969; Eimas, 1969; Farnham-Diggory, 1972; Gallagher, 1980; Gallagher & Thomas, 1980; Hagen, 1972; Thomas, 1980; Thomas, Mitchell, & Solomon, 1979; Winther & Thomas, 1981). With increased age, children can cognitively process more information within the same time limits, or process the same information in a shorter time frame (Chi, 1976). Clearly then, shortening or lengthening the processing time will affect motor performance, particularly in younger children (Gallagher & Thomas, 1980).

This decrement and the type of information children process can be observed in sport. For example, a young boy playing tee ball will see the ball bouncing in his direction, chase it, catch it, and then think, "Now what?" He must pause to determine where to throw or perhaps run with the ball and then plan and execute the actual movement. There are three separate operations all of which demand time and processing in this example. A more experienced, older child will begin to get into position as soon as the ball is hit. The catch and throw will occur without any delay, almost as if it is one movement, one operation. In the first case, the child has attended to three separate acts, each cueing the next. In the second case, the situation has cued a response which included the acquisition of the ball, the choice of where to throw the ball, and the throw. What, then, causes the memory process of young children to be less efficient or to respond more slowly to their demands?

Several aspects of movement information need processing, including extent (distance), location, angle, acceleration, and velocity (speed). Children often are not aware of these parameters and their role in motor performance. Children can, when cued to do so, use these components of a task to improve their performance, however. For example, children can learn to define the point in an overarm throw where acceleration occurs to produce a short throw or a long throw.

We propose that several processes used in the memory system are much less efficient in younger children. Figure 1 presents a model of memory designed to reflect the developmental nature of learning and performance. Several characteristics of this model are related to memory development. Information is fed into this system from the various sensory registers (vision, audition, kinesthesis, etc.), and these registers are not related to development after very early childhood.

The three aspects of the model most related to development are short-

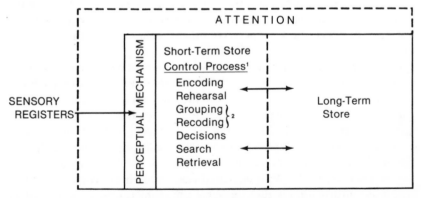

¹Control processes develop with aging
²Grouping and Recoding, when combined, is organization

Figure 1—Information processing model with developmental implication.

term store (STS), long-term store (LTS), and attention. STS is used to evaluate incoming information from the sensory registers, search LTS for data on related past experiences, rehearse relevant information, make decisions, initiate actions, and monitor these actions as they are performed. The ability to use these many effortful processes (encoding, rehearsal, grouping, recoding, decision making, search and retrieval) in STS develops throughout childhood and into adolescence. Younger children do not use some of these processes and they use others in very inefficient ways, resulting in slower and less effective information processing. Thus, the result is poorer motor performance and learning.

Two studies (Winther & Thomas, 1981; Gallagher & Thomas, Note 1) demonstrate that manipulating either rehearsal strategies or labels (one form of encoding) for movement positions can enhance younger children's motor performance and depress that of older children and adults. These two studies support the production-mediation deficiency hypothesis (Flavell, 1971) reported in the developmental memory literature. This hypothesis indicates that children may or may not be capable of producing a desired cognitive strategy at a given age; however, just because they may produce the strategy does not mean they will necessarily employ it (mediation deficiency). A 5-year-old child can rehearse (does not have a production deficiency) when cued to do so; however, the child will not spontaneously produce a rehearsal strategy (does have a mediation deficiency). Generally, spontaneous rehearsal does not begin until about 7 years of age. Between 7 and 11 years, a considerable increase occurs in the use and quality of rehearsal strategies. The child of 11 or 12 uses a strategy similar to that of an adult.

The young child typically rehearses the same item over and over, whereas an adult will rehearse several items in combination. Because the adult strategy improves performance, teaching this strategy to children should result in improved skill acquisition; for example, practicing fielding and throwing to a base rather than repetitively catching and throwing in isolation.

Labeling is viewed as rehearsal for children under 5 years of age. With these children, and to some extent with adults, relevant labels will enhance memory for an item. Therefore, recall with a label is greater than with no label or with an irrelevant label. A labeling strategy could be applied to the glove position for a ground ball—"fingers on the ground"—or for a fly ball—"fingers to the sky."

Another important memory process which develops throughout childhood is organization of memory (a combination of grouping and recoding). The placing together of independent units of incoming information as one unit is called grouping. For instance, adults will typically group a series of random numbers into groups of three for rehearsal and storage in LTS. A young child will rehearse and store each number independently. Even though memory span (sometimes used to measure

STS capacity) may appear greater for adults, children's poorer performance is caused by inefficient use of the memory process of grouping and not by a deficit in memory capacity. Evidence indicates that remembering a series of movements is affected in the same way (Gallagher & Thomas, Note 2).

Incoming stimuli can be manipulated to faciliate learning in young children by breaking movement sequences into logical units that can be rehearsed together. Using the previous example, a coach might cue a certain strategy by reminding players that when the batter comes up, they should "throw all the balls to first." Players would then have rehearsed the angle and catch-throw sequence together.

The second aspect of organization is recoding. Recoding involves searching LTS for two or more independently stored pieces of information which logically could be put together. The two pieces of information are combined (recoded) in STS and re-entered into LTS. When needed they will require less space in STS because they have become one unit instead of two. Grouping and recoding are two ways to reduce the demand for working space in STS.

Recoding could take two well-learned movements such as catching and running, combine them and create a new skill—the pass reception in football—or it could take a concept or perception of an event and transform that information into something new. For example, combining the current outcome of a contest with past contest outcomes involves recoding.

For greatest efficiency, the demand for space in STS must be reduced because this working space is limited. LTS is believed to be unlimited. Motor skill learning involves continually practicing a particular movement until it becomes increasingly automatic and requires no thought. Thus, the performance of the skill requires less working space in STS (recoding is occurring). Because STS has a limited capacity, reducing the demands for controlling a particular movement (or movement series) frees working space for other cognitive aspects of skillful performance. When the pass reception, which is a recoded run and catch, has become automatic, it can be combined with other football skills to comprise more interesting, difficult, and well-rehearsed sequences.

Figure 2 provides a hypothesized view of how rehearsal and organization develop in STS relative to motor performance. A series of studies by Gallagher (1980) provides empirical support for this developmental trend. This figure indicates that rehearsal strategies begin to be used spontaneously at about age 7, with a rapid increase in both frequency and quality of rehearsal between ages 7 and 11. Organization in memory lags considerably behind rehearsal in its use, however. The test of utility for a strategy is whether it will transfer to similar situations. By 11 years of age rehearsal strategies transfer, but organization of memory may not.

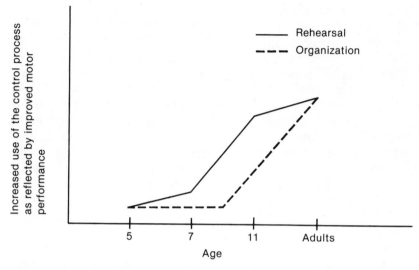

Figure 2—Age related changes in use of control processes.

We should remember this information about strategy development when teaching children. Younger children (4-6 years) must be cued to rehearse, but children between the ages of 7 and 11 will use a rehearsal strategy spontaneously with increasing sophistication and transfer. Organization of memory (to reduce STS demands) begins to occur at about age 7, but children frequently need to be cued to do so. At approximately 10 or 11 years, the use of this strategy increases considerably.

Also, as the developmental memory literature supports, the other memory processes (speed of encoding, decision making, and search and retrieval) increase across the childhood years. Specific developmental patterns in relation to motor performance and learning have not yet been identified, however.

The data base in LTS is the second aspect of this developmental model (Chi, 1976; Thomas, 1980). Although LTS is viewed as unlimited in capacity, the data base of young children is not nearly as extensive or well-developed as it is in adults. This results in less information with which to compare incoming stimuli, as well as fewer units to recode. In fact, one might hypothesize that recoding as a process develops later in childhood because there is a limited data base in LTS from which to recode. Apparently this developmental deficit of information in LTS is partially responsible for the poorer motor performance and learning of younger children. In addition, fewer sport experiences in LTS affect the perception of future sport contest. This should be kept in mind when sports performance demands recoding. Coaches and teachers need to be aware of the typical content of LTS and to systematically attempt to expand and use it.

Attention is particularly interesting as a memory process. Sometimes attention is used very specifically in order to select the pertinent aspects from the sensory register (Hoving, Spence, Robb, & Schulte, 1978). At other times, attention has assumed a much more pervasive part in memory function, which might cause it to be classified a control process (Hagen & Stanovich, 1977). Note that our model supports this more general view of attention. Its placement suggests two things: First, attention can be directed to any aspect of memory from selecting important features of a sensory display, to rehearsal in STS, to search and retrieval of LTS; and second, the amount of attention is limited. If simultaneous demands within or between components of memory exceed the available attention, performance will deteriorate. Of course, this perspective is not originally ours (e.g., see Kahneman, 1973).

Attention is also developmental, that is, children learn to control it more effectively with age (for a theoretical explanation, see Ross, 1976; for applied sports examples, see Stratton, 1978). This fact, in combination with recoding of movement information, reduces attentional demands in STS with increased age. Thus, increased amounts of attention can be directed to different needs in the memory system. For instance, when learning to play softball, people often first direct their attention to the specific skills and then toward the strategy (from individual catching and throwing skills to specific game situations).

In summary, the processing model we propose is not particularly unique, but it does combine nicely with developmental changes in memory and their effects upon age-related changes in both the perception and performance of sports skills. In this paper, almost every consideration involves cognitive processing of sport information. The literature suggests that age differences affect winning or losing and motivation; thus, decisions about these concerns should be related to the development of the memory system.

OUTCOMES OF SPORT CONTESTS

Children who consistently face losing situations have different causal ascriptions for current outcomes, future expectations, and continued task persistence than those consistently experiencing winning situations (Daughdrill, 1978; Iso-Ahola, 1977; Roberts, 1975). Daughdrill (1978) and Roberts (1975) found that participants use a self-serving strategy when causally attributing outcomes to themselves, but adopt a logical information-processing approach when attributing outcomes to teams. Iso-Ahola (1977) found that players used the standard of team performance as the criterion for self-perceived behavior.

Players in consistently losing situations believed they were low in ability, exerted less effort, faced a more complex task, and considered luck to be an important factor. Conversely, consistently winning teams that lost did not differ much from the winning teams that won except their team attributions consisted of a decreased effort on the part of team members with a strong effort of the individual (Daughdrill, 1978). Additionally, the consistent winners that lost attributed the outcome to bad luck and increased task difficulty.

Consistently experiencing winning or losing affects children's perception of future outcomes. Obviously, consistently winning teams, no matter what the current outcome, expect to win in the future. A consistently winning team that loses ascribes performance to unstable factors (bad luck, increased task difficulty) and expects to experience future success. Consistently losing teams that currently win attribute winning to unstable factors (good luck, increased effort); they do not expect to win in the future but instead expect to experience failure.

Ascriptions for consistent winners and losers may produce behavioral characteristics of high or low achievement-oriented behavior. Repeated failure is related to low-achievement behavior which elicits a desire to terminate participation, whereas continued success is related to high-achievement behavior and the desire to continue participation and try harder (Scanlan, chapter 11 of this volume). She proposes that children who continually receive negative comparative appraisal but receive support and guidance from significant others, such as their parents and coach, might benefit considerably from the competitive experience. With support, these children might learn to accept their limitations and capabilities and learn to function realistically, thus developing the ability to set and strive for realistic goals as well as cope with success and failure.

Differences in Males and Females

Until recently, differences between young males and females in their ascription of winning and losing in sport had not been studied. Daughdrill (1978) determined that with increasing age females attributed successful outcomes to external causes, whereas males attributed successful outcomes to internal causes and unsuccessful outcomes to external causes. With increasing age the female players attributed winning more to luck while exerting less effort, with the opposite holding true for the males. Consequently, with increased age, females attributed successful outcomes more to external factors (luck) and considered themselves as exerting less effort (internal factor). This finding was apparently due to societal pressure for sex role development (Fontaine, Note 2).

Effects of Aging

Roberts' (1975) and Iso-Ahola's (1977) subjects were not divided into age groups for analysis purposes. Daughdrill (1978), however, who used 8-,

10-, and 12-year-old subjects, noted a trend in her data, although she was unable to render conclusive support for age differences in attributing winning and losing. Regardless of past experiences and outcome, the younger players were more confident that they would win the next game played. She found, however, that as the children grew older, a consistent past outcome (winning or losing) increasingly biased their future expectations—losers expected to lose while winners expected to win. These data support the notion that young children do not use all available information; they ignore past experiences and consider only current outcome. Older children consider all the information they have and attach more importance to consistent past experiences.

In summary, children must selectively attend to task-appropriate cues, recall past experiences, evaluate expected outcomes in relation to actual outcomes, and make attributions about future expectations. Consistent winners tend to attribute winning to internal factors (increased ability and effort), causing heightened task persistence, whereas consistent losers attribute losing to internal factors (decreased ability and effort) which may increase the tendency to drop out of sport.

The data from one research study (Daughdrill, 1978) support the existence of differences between males and females. Females attribute winning more to external causes and males to internal causes, although this difference may be due to cultural pressure on the females. Additionally, Daughdrill (1978) investigated attributional processes from a developmental perspective. Some support was provided for the idea that younger children failed to use all the task-relevant information in determining future expectations. Sport psychologists need to perform more research on this processing deficits hypothesis (Chi, 1976; Thomas, 1980) with regard to attributional processes in sport.

REWARDS IN SPORT

The "overjustification" hypothesis is an explanation of how external rewards may undermine intrinsic motivation in performance situations (Greene & Lepper, 1974; Lepper & Greene, 1975; Lepper, Greene, & Nisbett, 1973). This effect has been found in cognitive activities (Karnoil & Ross, 1975; Ross, 1975), naturalistic play activities (Greene & Lepper, 1974; Lepper & Greene, 1975; Lepper et al., 1973), puzzles (Deci, 1971, 1972), and physical skills (Halliwell, 1976; Thomas & Tennant, 1978). Also, Ryan (Note 4) has found that older scholarship athletes in college viewed their athletic participation as being less enjoyable than their nonscholarship counterparts, demonstrating that this effect carries over to college athletics.

Giving rewards to athletes, however, can provide them with information about their skills or abilities if the rewards are awarded according to the quality of performance (Lepper & Greene, 1975; Ross, 1975; Thomas & Tennant, 1978). This results in an increase in performance and motivation. Rewards not contingent to performance, which reduce intrinsic motivation and act as a bribe, might cause athletes to feel a loss in control over themselves and their situation, whereas rewards solely contingent upon performance provide feedback about that performance.

Studies in self-perception and other perception have noted a discrepancy in the age at which rewards undermine intrinsic motivation. Halliwell (1976) suggested a developmental continuum ranging from information about oneself in a naturalistic setting (self-perception), which would be the least complex to process, to ascription of other people's behavior (other perception) from an audiotape, which would be the most difficult to process. Because youth sports mainly involve the children's perception of their own behavior in a naturalistic setting, we will consider only this aspect.

Greene and Lepper (1974), Lepper et al. (1973), and Lepper and Greene (1975) found that in a naturalistic play setting, 5-year-old children's motivation was undermined by extrinsic rewards. Thomas and Tennant (1978), using a physical skill, found that rewards for 5-year olds increased the time at target activity. Differences in explanation were due to several viable methodological differences. Regardless of the age at which undermining occurs (Halliwell, 1976; Karnoli & Ross, 1976), increasing age results in greater amounts of discounting in noncontingent reward situations (for self-perception, see Thomas & Tennant, 1978; for other perception, Halliwell, 1976; Karnoli & Ross, 1976). By age 7, no differences in motivation can be found between the control and reward groups. By age 9, however, all children view the noncontingent reward as a bribe to participate in the task, seriously undermining their persistence in a free choice situation.

These findings concur with developmental information-processing theory. Younger children are unable to remember the necessary information for the rewards to be perceived as a bribe. Because the use of control strategies increases with age, however, older children become able to process such information. They then perceive noncontingent rewards as bribes to participate. Because the reward becomes their reason for participating, their intrinsic motivation is reduced.

CONSEQUENCES FOR PARENTS, COACHES, AND EDUCATORS

Children must not be treated as miniature adults, regardless of the type of behavior (cognitive, affective, or psychomotor). They process the events in their world differently and thus have different perceptions of the causes of these events.

The outcome of an individual game has a limited influence on young children's perception. Outcomes that become consistent, however, do influence both current attributions and children's future expectancy, especially older children's. This effect is most disturbing when children are placed on teams that lose consistently, for these children then grow to view themselves as low in ability and expect to lose in the future. They also seem to adopt the self-protecting mechanism of giving less effort during future contests, saying "I really didn't try very hard, so it's not so bad to lose." Taken together, these factors decrease children's enjoyment of the sport situation and increase the likelihood that they will cease to participate. Of course, if the Daughdrill (1978) study is correct, this effect is even more pronounced for girls. The effects of consistently losing seem to increase with age.

What can we do? Aren't games either won or lost? How do we control this? Several alternatives have been suggested elsewhere (Thomas, 1978). The most pertinent factor to recognize, however, is that "game outcome" is not the most important consideration in children's sport. Coaches and parents must help children to focus instead on a self-directed, effort-ability question; that is, "Did I try my best and do better than I have previously?" This kind of focus puts children in control of their own performance, for the question is an internal one.

Participants in individual sports (i.e., swimming, track and field, gymnastics) can easily focus on their past performance. Coaches could conduct a meet in which the individual and team score is based on a comparison of an athlete with the average of some previous number of his/her own performances. For instance, a girl's swimming performance in the 50 m free style could be compared to her average time in this event in the past three swim meets. She could then score points for her team depending on whether she swam faster or not. Although this is not the only acceptable form of comparison and scoring, comparison with others does not have to be the only valued measure.

Another consideration in age group sports (individual, dual, team) that affects contest outcome is team composition. We see very little long-term value in the traditional method of keeping all children on the same team. Some system to rotate children among teams during the season does not affect individual contest outcome, but does solve the problems associated with consistent winning and losing—which is the factor that seriously alters attributional patterns.

This raises the whole issue of league, city, state, and national champions. Why is it important to establish who won such championships? Perhaps the more relevant question might be, "To whom is it important?" To children? We doubt it. More likely, it is parents and coaches. The question then becomes, "Shall we cause the problems children develop from consistently losing so parents and coaches can determine who's number one?"

The second important consideration in the literature presented dealt with rewards. Nearly everyone we know in children's sports believes that rewards have assumed too much importance. The literature supports the fact that rewards not based upon the quality of the child's performance undermine intrinsic motivation. Although rewards based on the quality of the child's performance increase motivation, many of the so-called performance-based rewards in sport are available to only the outstanding performer. Surely average players on a team recognize that they have no chance to obtain the "most valuable player" award. So for practical purposes, it seems unlikely that this type of award will increase intrinsic motivation for most children.

We believe the problem becomes particularly acute in individual sports like swimming and gymnastics, where a child may earn several hundred medals and trophies over a 2- to 3-year period. The value of so many awards to anyone is questionable.

We do not know where to set the limits on awards. Certainly, they should be reduced considerably (particularly in individual sports) and they should carry special meaning when given. The best example we know is the banana award (Thomas, 1978). In this instance, the coach wrote the title of the award and the boy's name on the side of a banana. He called the boy up in front of his peers and parents and presented the banana. Then he had the boy peel and eat the banana right on the spot. The moral is: Because success in sport is like a banana, you have to earn it fresh every day. If you try to keep what you had, it goes rotten.

Sport is neither inherently good or bad. The people who conduct sport make it a positive or negative experience for children. We believe all the people involved in children's sport want to help kids. We also believe they inadvertently do some things that reduce children's enjoyment and enthusiasm. By raising and confronting important questions, by reviewing theory and research on these questions, and by suggesting some alterations in practice for those controlling sport, perhaps we can make kids' sport a more positive experience for its participants.

REFERENCE NOTES

1. Gallagher, J.D., & Thomas, J.R. *Rehearsal effects on developmental differences in movement reproduction*. Paper presented at NASPSPA, Boulder, CO, May 1980.
2. Gallagher, J.D., & Thomas, J.R. *Adult-child differences in movement reproduction: Effects of kinesthetic sensory store and organization of memory*. Paper presented at AAHPERD, Detroit, MI, April 1980.
3. Fontaine, C.M. *Attributions and self-evaluation in women*. Paper presented at the annual meeting of the Midwestern Psychological Association, Chicago, IL, May 1977.
4. Ryan, E.D. *Attribution, intrinsic motivation, and athletics*. Paper

presented at NAPECW-NCPEAM joint meeting, Orlando, FL, January 6-9, 1977.

REFERENCES

CHI, M. Short-term memory limitations in children: Capacity or processing deficits. *Memory and Cognition*, 1976, **4**, 559-572.

DAUGHDRILL, K.C. *A developmental study of causal attributions and future expectations in children's athletics*. Unpublished master's thesis, Louisiana State University, 1978.

DECI, E.L. Effects of externally mediated rewards and intrinsic motivation. *Journal of Personality and Social Psychology*, 1971, **18**, 105-115.

DECI, E.L. Intrinsic motivation, extrinsic reinforcement, and inequity. *Journal of Personality and Social Psychology*, 1972, **22**, 113-120.

DRUCKER, J., & Hagen, J. Developmental trends in the processing of task-relevant and task-irrelevant information. *Child Development*, 1969, **40**, 371-382.

EIMAS, P. Multiple cue discrimination learning in children. *Psychological Record*, 1969, **19**, 417-424.

FARNHAM-DIGGORY, S. The development of equivalent systems. In S. Farnham-Diggory (Ed.), *Information processing in children*. New York: Academic Press, 1972.

FEATHER, N.T., & Simon, J.G. Attribution of responsibility and violence of outcome in relation to initial confidence and success and failure of self and other. *Journal of Personality and Social Psychology*, 1971, **18**, 173-188.

FLAVELL, J.H. What is memory development the development of? *Human Development*, 1971, **14**, 225-286.

GALLAGHER, J.D. *Adult-child motor performance differences: A developmental perspective of control processing deficits*. Unpublished doctoral dissertation, Louisiana State University, Baton Rouge, 1980.

GALLAGHER, J.D., & Thomas, J.R. Effects of varying post-KR intervals upon children's motor performance. *Journal of Motor Behavior*, 1980, **12**, 41-46.

GREENE, D., & Lepper, M.R. Effects of extrinsic rewards on children's subsequent intrinsic interest. *Child Development*, 1974, **45**, 1141-1145.

HAGEN, J. Strategies for remembering. In S. Farnham-Diggory (Ed.), *Information processing in children*. New York: Academic Press, 1972.

HAGEN, J.W., & Stanovich, K.B. Memory: Strategies of acquisition. In R.V. Kail & J.W. Hagen (Eds.), *Perspectives on the development of memory and cognition*. Hillsdale, NJ: Erlbaum, 1977.

HALLIWELL, W. *The influence of cognitive development and alternative media upon causal attributions in social perception*. Unpublished doctoral dissertation, Florida State University, 1976.

HEIDER, F. *The psychology of interpersonal relations*. New York: Wiley, 1958.

HOVING, K.L., Spence, T., Robb, K.Y., & Schulte, D. Developmental changes in visual information processing. In P.A. Ornstein (Ed.), *Memory development in children*. Hillsdale, NJ: Erlbaum, 1978.

ISO-AHOLA, S.E. Immediate attributional effects of success and failure in the field: Testing some laboratory hypotheses. *European Journal of Social Psychology*, 1977, **7**, 275-296.

KAHNEMAN, D. *Attention and effort*. Englewood Cliffs, NJ: Prentice-Hall, 1973.

KARNOIL, R., & Ross, M. The development of causal inferences in social perception. *Journal of Personality and Social Psychology*, 1976, **34**, 455-464.

KELLEY, H.H. Attribution theory in social psychology. In D. Levine (Ed.), *Nebraska symposium on motivation* (Vol. 15). Lincoln, NE: University of Nebraska Press, 1967.

KELLEY, H.H. Causal schemata and the attribution process. In E.E. Jones, D.E. Kanouse, H.H. Kenney, R.E. Nisbett, S. Valins, & B. Weiner (Eds.), *Attribution: Perceiving the causes of behavior*. New York: General Learning Press, 1972.

LEPPER, M.R., & Greene, D. Turning play into work: Effects of adult surveillance and extrinsic rewards on children's intrinsic motivation. *Journal of Personality and Social Psychology*, 1975, **31**, 479-486.

LEPPER, M.R., Greene, D., & Nisbett, R.E. Undermining children's interest with extrinsic rewards: A test of the "overjustification" hypothesis. *Journal of Personality and Social Psychology*, 1973, **28**, 120-137.

ROBERTS, G.C. Win-loss causal attributions of Little League players. *Mouvement: Proceedings of the Seventh Canadian Psycho-motor Learning and Sport Psychology Symposium*, Quebec City, October 1975, pp. 315-322.

ROSS, A. *Psychological aspects of learning disabilities and reading disorders*. New York: McGraw-Hill, 1976.

ROSS, M. Salience of reward and intrinsic motivation. *Journal of Personality and Social Psychology*, 1975, **32**, 245-254.

SEEFELDT, V. *Joint legislative study on youth sports programs: Agency sponsored sports phase I*. State of Michigan, November 1976.

STRATTON, R.K. Information processing deficits in children's motor performance: Implications for instruction. *Motor Skills: Theory into Practice*, 1978, **3**, 49-55.

THOMAS, J.R. Is winning essential to the success of youth sports contests? *Journal of Physical Education and Recreation*, March 1978, **49**, 42-43.

THOMAS, J.R. Acquisition of motor skills: Information processing differences between children and adults. *Research Quarterly for Exercise and Sport*, 1980, **51**, 158-173.

THOMAS, J.R., Mitchell, B., & Solmon, M.A. Precision knowledge of results and motor performance: Relationship to age. *Research Quarterly*, 1979, **50**, 687-698.

THOMAS, J.R., & Tennant, L.K. Effects of rewards on changes in children's motivation for an athletic task. In F. Smoll & R.E. Smith's (Eds.), *Psychological perspectives in youth sports*. New York: Hemisphere, 1978.

WINTHER, K.T., & Thomas, J.R. Developmental differences in children's labeling of movement. *Journal of Motor Behavior*, 1981, **13**, 77-90.

WORTMAN, C.B., Costanzo, P.R., & Witt, T.R. Effect of anticipated performance on the attributions of causality to self and others. *Journal of Personality and Social Psychology*, 1973, **27**, 372-381.

CHAPTER 17

AN ANALYSIS OF PSYCHOLOGICAL RESEARCH AND THEORY IN YOUTH SPORTS: QUESTIONS AND NEW DIRECTIONS

Michael J. Ash and Steven P. Chatman

Psychosocial research and theory on youth sports has grown, not only in absolute size, that is, in the number of articles per year in scholarly journals, but in quality (Ash, 1978). The field has evolved from a "let's see what effect sport competition has on children" approach to a much more integrated analysis of an important, but not consuming, aspect of children's lives.

In this paper, we will try to provide an overview and organization of the current psychological issues in youth sports and to raise some critical questions or issues that face the field in the next decade or so. We do not intend to review the literature in the field; rather, we seek to describe the interconnections and structure of psychological research on youth sports.

Our "gestalt" of youth sport research finds four major areas of activity: (a) concern for the effects of sport participation on children, (b) the role of others—coaches, parents, and peers—in the sport participation process, (c) analyses of the characteristics of the children who participate, and (d) construction and trial of a variety of training or therapeutic interventions in the competitive situation. In the remainder of the paper, we will detail important aspects of each of these areas of research and theory, as well as identify promising new directions.

EFFECTS OF COMPETITION

The granddaddy of youth sport concerns—the effects of competition on children—is still a driving force in the research on children's sport. A careful cataloging of possible harmful effects of competition continues (see chapter 14 by Gelfand & Hartman). But more importantly, researchers are making real progress ferreting out the crucial elements of the competitive situation (see chapter 11 by Scanlan, chapter 12 by Passer, and chapter 13 by Smith & Smoll). All three of these papers exemplify the kind of theoretically based thinking that is required for progress to occur in this area of research.

Investigators are also comparing the amount of stress produced by competitive sports with other "real life" competitive situations in children's lives (Martens, 1980; Seefeldt & Gould, 1980; Simon & Martens, 1979). For far too long, researchers were preoccupied with comparing competitors with noncompetitors, as if the noncompeting group served as an adequate control. Fortunately, more recent research (Simon & Martens, 1979) has begun to take advantage of the naturally occurring situations in competition that children face. We need more of such work.

THE ROLE OF SIGNIFICANT OTHERS
IN YOUTH SPORT

Coaches, peers, parents, and siblings are an important aspect of youth sport. As Tara Scanlan points out in chapter 11, social comparison is an important variable in understanding the nature of the competitive situation. Of course, researchers have been interested in the impact of coaches and parents on the child's sport experience, but more and more investigators are taking a close look at the role that peers and siblings play as well. To the extent that these researchers operate from a theoretical model (see chapter 11 as an example), their work will have more impact and generalizability.

An additional area of research in the area of significant others that remains to be explored is the prospect of an a priori screening of potential youth sport coaches. Certainly, the work of Smith and Smoll (presented in chapter 13) provides the potential for data that could serve as predictors of appropriate coaching style. To our knowledge no one has attempted to provide such data in a systematic manner, but this information could prove very interesting and perhaps useful.

CHARACTERISTICS OF PARTICIPANTS

Research examining the psychological characteristics of youth sport participants has been the mainstay of research on children's athletics, for researchers have always exhibited strong interest in this area. Ash (1978), in a review of such research, has detailed the variety of studies of characteristics like self-concept, causal attributions, personality factors, locus of control, social desirability, motivational needs, attitudes toward competition and sports, and more.

Two crucial elements are still missing from such a description. First, we still do not have an adequate discussion of sex differences or similarities in the child athlete. Even though investigators have called for such research (Ash, 1978), only a few studies have appeared (Bird & Williams, 1980). With the increase of both sex-isolated female sports and sex-integrated children's athletics, this information is needed to fully understand the characteristics of the male or female child competitor.

Secondly, research on the characteristics of children in sport has been uniformly nomothetic in nature. In order to flesh out our knowledge in this area, we need some well-designed idiographic studies that examine, in detail, the characteristics of a single athlete. As in other areas of psychology, group characteristics and individual characteristics provide their own unique perspective of phenomena.

For example, the gifted athlete, the prodigy of individual sports, deserves individual analysis. Ice skaters, gymnasts, swimmers, and so on often begin practice at very young ages and spend countless hours striving to reach national and international stature. To these children, sport is a way of life, and their development is significantly influenced and significantly different from the average child's. What is the influence of competition on these children?

Another factor relating to the psychological characteristics of developmental changes is children's ability to perceive and interpret their experiences in sport. Of course, much attention has been given to the patterns of physical development, but what of age-related changes in thinking, remembering, and other information-processing factors? Thomas, Gallagher, and Thomas in chapter 16 have made a start, but much more remains to be done.

TRAINING EFFECTS

One of the newer and most exciting entries into research on youth sports is the notion that when a certain situation exists, for example, anxiety in the presence of stress, a training regimen (sometimes called therapy) can be used to intervene to change the young athlete's psychological characteristics. Smith and Smoll in chapter 13 have made a giant stride in this direction.

In related attempts, some investigators are beginning to work with parents (Ferrell, Glashagel, & Johnson, 1978), whereas others (see chapter 13 by Smith & Smoll) have focused on modifying the behaviors of coaches to facilitate a positive and harmonious youth sport environment. These interventions may contribute a great deal to our knowledge of the youth sport experience.

Similarly, Smoll and Smith and their co-workers (Smith, Smoll, & Curtis, 1979; Smoll & Smith, 1979) have provided some important insights into the relationship between coaches and the child athletes. Their educational/therapeutic model is an impressive beginning in what we hope is an emerging area of research interest.

QUESTIONS AND NEW DIRECTIONS

In this section, we hope to stimulate the reader to think beyond what the field has done to what could be done. The following discussion is designed to facilitate active questioning of some of the psychometric and psychological issues in youth sports.

Anxiety

Anxiety is a highly abstract concept. Major psychological theories and personality theories have conceptualized anxiety in the following ways. Psychoanalytic theories focus on the failure of ego to express unacceptable libidinal impulses in a manner consistent with conscious perception of reality. Learning theories focus on classically conditioned associations with aversive stimuli. Phenomenological/existential theories view anxiety as a reaction to perceived basic threat to self.

We propose that anxiety in competition results from a disparity between perceived task demands and individuals' perception of their ability to meet those demands (see chapters 11 and 12). Anxiety is real and yet it resides within the individual and thus must be inferred. Efforts to infer the existence of anxiety can be divided into three areas: self-report measures, physiological response, and behavioral effects.

Self-report measures of anxiety like the Manifest Anxiety Scale (Taylor, 1953), Spielberger's State Anxiety Inventory for Children (Spielberger, 1973), and the Competitive State Anxiety Inventory (Martens, 1980) attempt to operationalize anxiety as a quantity without defining a point at which one can say that an individual is anxious. All A-State or A-Trait measures merely reflect relative assessment; they do not define a point at which anxiety is detrimental. If experimental group means are significantly less than control groups' means, so what? Without inferring that self-reports are worthless constructs (Ericsson & Simon, 1980), it should be recognized that no number exists which differentiates unacceptable from acceptable levels of anxiety. That remains a value-laden construct in child sports research. Secondly, defining anxiety as a number can easily lead to a definitional circle without adding valuable information like ability to perform or to learn. Current criticism of the construct "intelligence" as measured by intelligence tests can serve to illustrate the dangers of self-reliance in definition.

Attempts to correlate anxiety as measured by self-report questionnaires often produce substantial correlations (Ruebush, 1963; Sarason,
Davidson, Lighthall, Waite, & Ruebush, 1960). When substantiation is
sought with response modes other than questionnaires (physiological
arousal and avoidance behavior), correlations are low or negligible.
Generally, measures of autonomic arousal tend to be unrelated to self-
report inventory measures (Katkin, 1965; Martin, 1961). When physiologic measures of heart beat while at bat (mdn = 163 beats/minute) exceed median level heart rates under "fielding conditions" by 36
beats/minute, it could be inferred that batting has high anxiety potential;
most subjects, however, reported that they did not get unduly nervous at
bat. Either children illustrate adult-like ignorance of their physiological
states, or because anxiety is largely a cognitive labeling process (Lazarus
& Averill, 1972), batting is not a particularly aversive experience and
would not tend to be avoided.

Behavioral effects proposed to evidence anxiety (sleeplessness,
enuresis, fatigue, loss of appetite, etc.) often fail to recognize normal fre-
quencies of those behaviors. The Berkeley Guidance Study (MacFarlane,
Allen, & Honzik, 1954) examined 46 problems under four categories—
biological functioning and control, motor manifestations, social standards, and personality patterns (e.g., shyness)—in 86 "normal" children
from 21 months of age to 14 years. One third or more of the children exhibited behavioral problems at various age levels. This study and the
Buffalo Study (Lapouse & Monk, 1958) illustrate the high levels of
behaviors believed indicative of anxiety within normal children. Certainly, a normal child cannot be defined as one who has no problems
(Clarizio, 1976). Attempts to measure behavioral effects of anxiety obviously run the risk of collecting data reflecting normal developmental
occurrence levels of such behaviors.

Either very low levels of anxiety or high levels of anxiety inhibit the acquisition of new behaviors, for learning and performance are integrally
tied with anxiety levels (the Yerkes-Dodson Law). The same is true in
sports competition. To attempt control of anxiety levels would be a much
simpler process if optimal levels were not idiosyncratic. An individual's
heightened anxiety, as measured by physiologic response or anxiety-state
inventories, may be a realistic and highly adaptive response within sports
competition. A child at bat may fear the social ramifications of striking
out or the child may fear being hit by the ball. We must avoid inferring
both the existence of anxiety and the cause of anxiety. The perception of
anxiety is a cognitive determination and as such is individual.

Although the efforts of Smoll and Smith (1979) significantly affected
the enjoyment and social communication of experimental subjects, the
win/loss records were equivalent. If we assume that the anxiety level of
control subjects was too high, why didn't experimental subjects outper-
form controls? The efforts of Smith and Smoll are to be lauded; the

strength of outcomes is not diminished by the equivalence of records. But if the Yerkes-Dodson Law is applicable, why did the experimental subjects' performance exceed control subjects? Further, will humanistic efforts have any effect on societal practices if performance is not enhanced? The problem of microlevel efforts within more pervasive images of sports will be the topic of the next section.

A learning theory approach to anxiety and stress in youth sports is at times contradictory. An avoidance behavior formed through association of a stimulus and an aversive experience is very difficult to extinguish. How important are isolated traumatic events? Any neutral stimuli directly or vicariously associated with aversive events or outcomes will come to elicit anxiety on their own. Aversively conditioned emotional reactions may generalize to new stimuli through semantic or physical similarity. Participation in youth sports would seem to increase the likelihood of a traumatic experience and subsequent emotional problems.

Conversely, and still within the predictions of learning theory, continued sports participation should increase the likelihood of adaptive anxiety coping skills. Organized sports is the repetitive presentation of situations which may be stressful within a controlled environment. The acquisition of coping skills should be facilitated by continued participation. Theoretically, these learned coping skills will generalize to other anxiety-producing situations. Should sports participation be viewed as potentially too emotionally harmful or as a tremendous opportunity for learning? It may appear that the learning approach offers conflicting predictions. On one hand, participation maximizes the opportunity to learn effective coping skills. On the other hand, participation increases the probability of rare, traumatic experiences.

Inconsistent Messages

Pregame stress is related to at least four factors: the perceived importance of the game, the competitive trait anxiety of the child as measured by self-report, level of expectancy, and level of self-esteem. During competition, anxiety is heightened in trailing players and in close contests. At the conclusion of competition, one variable tends to obliterate all differences. That variable is win/loss. Winners consistently experience reduced anxiety and losers consistently experience heightened anxiety. Tying increases anxiety in all players but not to levels produced by loss.

The impressive training effort presented in chapter 13 by Smith and Smoll illustrates that a multifaceted effort to reduce stress by teaching that winning should be defined as maximal effort can be successful in increasing measured enjoyment and self-esteem. The actual impact of this new definition cannot be assessed due to Smith and Smoll's design characteristics. Obviously, the improvement of enjoyment and self-esteem is a worthwhile effort, but the issue is whether or not extensive training efforts to alter participant's definitions are realistic in a society that expounds the virtues of achievement and winning.

Rewards, both societal and monetary, are awarded to those who win, not to those who "tried hard." The macro structures of society (work ethic, achievement orientation) fundamentally oppose any definition of winning other than as beating another. It is not a sport if both teams can win. When societal ideals oppose individual efforts, can we realistically expect individual efforts to have anything but a limited impact? There comes a point in children's competitive experience when they will not be encouraged to simply try hard. They will only be allowed to play if they are best. Isn't that the true message we as a society convey?

Imagine young children, the product of developmental interaction, who have formed accurate perceptions of the importance of competition as covertly and overtly stated by the social models within their families, in their communities, and through national media (see chapter 20 by Smith). These children will logically desire to win. Given a choice, they will even choose those opponents who will provide them with competition levels that maximize the unpredictability of outcome. These children seek many things through competition; one thing they probably do not seek is a coach who is unconcerned with the quantitative outcome. A coach or a situation that deemphasizes the win/loss nature of competition runs the risk of being more aversive than the actual competition. Even if these children continue to participate, their self-concepts could be diminished. If they perceive the deemphasis of winning as a reflection on their ability to win, such children will find it difficult to form an adequate sense of self.

SOCIAL CLASS DIFFERENCES

Sport is often heralded as the great equalizer. It is supposed to be a milieu which all may enter regardless of race or socioeconomic condition. In many instances, this has been true. Often it is not. Beyond the fact that perhaps too many minority children view sports as a ticket to fame and glory, does children's social class have any effect on their participation in sports? Being properly outfitted for any sport can be costly. Even tennis shoes are a status item. Getting to and from practice or games may require transportation that is not available. To what extent do economic factors influence a child's participation in sports?

Life-long benefits of sports competition for even successful high school or college players who fail to maximize academic possibilities due to complex psychosocial factors or simply a lack of time are indeed questionable. The chance that sports participation will alter social class is small. We must be aware of differing messages to differing classes and to differing perceptions by differing classes. These issues need to be scrutinized.

CONCLUSION

Although the field of research into child sport competition has grown dramatically in the last decade, many questions remain. We have presented only a few of the many psychological concerns that need to be addressed. What is the impact of a uniform on sports competition? How are neighborhood, self-organized sports like organized sports? How do they differ? Is competition a natural growth of children's search for themselves or is it indigenous to certain societal constructs? Answers to these and other important questions remain to be found.

REFERENCES

ASH, M.J. The role of research in children's competitive athletics. In R.A. Magill, M.J. Ash, & F.L. Smoll, (Eds.), *Children in sport: A contemporary anthology* (1st ed.). Champaign, IL: Human Kinetics, 1978.

BIRD, A., & Williams, J.M. A developmental-attributional analysis of sex role stereotypes for sport performance. *Developmental Psychology*, 1980, **16**(4), 319-322.

CLARIZIO, H.F. Normality: A developmental perspective. In H.F. Clarizio & G.F. McCoy (Eds.), *Behavioral disorders in children* (2nd ed.). New York: Thomas Crowell, 1976.

ERICSSON, K.A., & Simon, H.A. Verbal reports as data. *Psychological Review*, 1980, **87**(3), 215-251.

FERRELL, J., Glashagel, J., & Johnson, M. *A family approach to youth sports*. La Grange, IL: Youth Sports Press, 1978.

KATKIN, E.S. Relationship between manifest anxiety and two indices of autonomic response to stress. *Journal of Personality and Social Psychology*, 1965, **2**, 324-333.

LAPOUSE, R., & Monk, M. An epidemiologic study of behavior characteristics in children. *American Journal of Public Health*, 1958, **48**, 1134-1144.

LAZARUS, R.S., & Averill, J.R. Emotion and cognition: With special reference to anxiety. In C.D. Spielberger (Ed.), *Anxiety: Current trends in theory and research* (Vol. 2). New York: Academic Press, 1972.

MACFARLANE, J., Allen, L., & Honzik, M. *A developmental study of the behavior problems of normal children between twenty-one months and fourteen years*. Berkeley: University of California Press, 1954.

MARTENS, R. Reliability and validity of the Competitive State Anxiety Inventory. In C.H. Nadeau, W.R. Halliwell, K.M. Newell, & G.C. Roberts (Eds.), *Psychology of motor behavior and sport—1979*. Champaign, IL: Human Kinetics, 1980.

MARTIN, B. The assessment of anxiety by physiological behavioral measures. *Psychological Bulletin*, 1961, **58**, 234-255.

RUEBUSH, B.E. Anxiety. In H.A. Stevenson et al. (Ed.), *Child psychology. The sixty-second yearbook of the National Society for the Study of Education*. Chicago: University of Chicago Press, 1963.

SARASON, S.B., Davidson, K.S., Lighthall, F.F., Waite, R.R., & Ruebush, B.E. *Anxiety in elementary school children*. New York: Wiley, 1960.

SEEFELDT, V., & Gould, D. *Physical and psychological effects of athletic competition on children and youth*. Washington, DC: ERIC Clearinghouse on Teacher Education, 1980.

SIMON, J.A., & Martens, R. Children's anxiety in sport and nonsport evaluation activities. *Journal of Sport Psychology*, 1979, **1**, 160-169.

SMITH, R.E., Smoll, F.L., & Curtis, B. Coach effectiveness training: A cognitive-behavioral approach to enhancing relationship skills in youth sport coaches. *Journal of Sport Psychology*, 1979, **1**, 59-75.

SMOLL, F.L., & Smith, R.E. *Improving relationship skills in youth sport coaches*. East Lansing, MI: Michigan Institute for the Study of Youth Sports, 1979.

SPIELBERGER, C.D. *Preliminary test manual for the State-Trait Anxiety Inventory for Children*. Palo Alto, CA: Consulting Psychologists Press, 1973.

TAYLOR, J. A personality scale of manifest anxiety. *Journal of Abnormal and Social Psychology*, 1953, **48**, 285-290.

SECTION 4

PSYCHOLOGICAL
ISSUES

North American society has traditionally believed that sport participation makes an important contribution to the character and psychological make-up of the competitor. With the recent growth of youth sport programs, however, many parents, educators, and other interested parties have become increasingly concerned about the psychosocial effects of children's sports. In response to this concern, psychologists and physical educators have joined forces to determine the positive and negative effects of participation in youth sports. This section reflects this new coalition, and the chapters within focus on the relationship between participation in youth sports and the psychological variables of aggression, anxiety, competition, self-concept, and morality. They also raise some intriguing questions facing the emerging field of children's sport psychology.

To begin this section, Tara Kost Scanlan discusses the effects of competition on the psychological development of the child by considering social evaluation in the competitive process. Using a four-stage model of the competitive process, Scanlan investigates social evaluation as a key element in this process and as a source of ability appraisal information as it may be perceived and sought by a child.

The next two chapters by Michael Passer and by Ronald Smith and Frank Smoll address two important questions about children's sport participation: Are children's sports too psychologically stressful, and what can be done to alleviate undue amounts of stress in competitive situations? In chapter 12, Michael W. Passer describes stress as a process involving situational demands, appraisal processes, aversive emotional responses and consequences; he then reviews research pertaining to children's stress in sports within this framework. Passer first discusses the demands inherent in the athletic setting and children's appraisal of this setting. Next, he presents empirical findings on the cognitive and physiological components of children's emotional responses to competition, paying particular attention to identifying the situational and intrapersonal determinants of children's pre-, mid-, and postcompetition stress. Finally, Passer examines the behavioral consequences of competitive stress, including loss of sleep, sport avoidance, and performance impairment. To conclude the chapter, Passer briefly discusses the controversial issue of whether sports are too stressful for children, and he offers some basic recommendations for minimizing competitive stress.

In a sequel to the Passer chapter, Ronald E. Smith and Frank L. Smoll present a conceptual model of stress and its implications for stress reduction in children's sports. The model emphasizes relationships between the situation, cognitive appraisal processes, physiological arousal, and behavioral responses to the situation. After describing their model, Smith and Smoll consider a number of points at which intervention strategies might be employed. They then offer readers guidelines and procedures that have proven effective in working with coaches and parents to reduce situational stress and enhance the quality of the athletic environment for children. Last, Smith and Smoll describe their management program, which has been used to help child athletes acquire cognitive and physiological coping skills.

In chapter 14, Donna M. Gelfand and Donald P. Hartmann discuss the detrimental effects of children's involvement in organized sport on their psychological development. These two investigators have been primarily concerned with a possible relationship between sport participation and cognitive deficits and interpersonal difficulties, and they report the results of their research examining children's competition and observational learning. It may be that children's participation in sports, particularly at an early age, prematurely terminates their exploratory and fantasy play. Moreover, the age and sex segregation that is typical of youth sports seems to minimize a child's normal involvement in informal mixed-sex games. This represents a marked change in what has been described as the *normal* course of interpersonal development. Gelfand and Hartmann's research suggests that the competitive behavior of participants may increase in aggressiveness and self-concern and produce rule violations and other behaviors of questionable morality. If such results continue to be supported, those individuals who conduct youth sport programs need to become acutely aware of the possibility of these detrimental effects.

Chapter 15 by Rainer Martens applies psychological research, particularly related to socialization and moral behavior, to the youth sports context. Specifically, he relates findings from social, developmental, and

SECTION 5

SOCIAL PROCESSES

The social processes involved in organized sports for children and youth are complex and elusive. In this section, two major areas of these social processes, the social milieu and the dynamics of groups, are considered. Chapter 18 by Barry D. McPherson considers the influence of the social milieu on the child in sport. He discusses the factors influencing the socialization process, why children choose the sports they do, and the role of significant others in regard to children's involvement in sport. He also considers such specific issues as social mobility, adult domination, aggression, and the dropout in sport.

In chapter 19, John Lewko and Susan L. Greendorfer review the research literature dealing with family influences and sex differences in children's sport socialization. From their review, they generate hypotheses centered on clarifying the role of parents in the sport socialization process and addressing the area of perceived appropriateness of sport activities. The authors offer eight hypotheses that researchers will find to be readily testable and therefore useful guidelines for research related to children's sport socialization processes.

An issue of increasing concern in youth sports is the role of violence in sport. In chapter 20, the last chapter of the book, Michael D. Smith describes violence in ice hockey and establishes that the main sources of hockey violence are socially based. He identifies the prominent sources of this violence, including the hockey system; the mass media with its portrayal of the professional game; and significant others, such as parents, coaches, and teammates, who influence participants. Smith's disturbing look at one of the world's most popular sports provides some beneficial insights into issues related to violence in all sports for all ages of participants.

CHAPTER 18

THE CHILD IN COMPETITIVE SPORT: INFLUENCE OF THE SOCIAL MILIEU

Barry D. McPherson

In recent years there has been an increasing interest[1] and concern about the involvement of children in competitive sport by journalists and scholars who have focused on the immediate problems and long-range consequences for the child involved in highly competitive sport programs. To date, the psychological well being of the child-athlete (Skubic, 1955; Hale, Note 1); the moral development of the child (Martens, chapter 15 in this volume); personality and attitudes (Bird, 1979; Brown, 1970; Purdy, 1980; Seymour, 1956; Mantel & Vander Velden, Note 2); sportsmanship (Kroll, Note 3); skill development (Rarick, 1973); growth and development patterns (Malina & Rarick, 1973); the causal attributions for success and failure in sport (Bird & Williams, 1980; Bukowski & Moore, 1980; Iso-Ahola, 1979; Scanlan & Passer, 1980); and, such sport-related trauma as the little league elbow and the importance of safe, well-fitting equipment have been studied. However, little attention has been devoted to the social processes and past experiences in a variety of social systems which influence whether, and at what stage in life, a child ever becomes involved in sport, and whether the individual receives the opportunity to realize his/her inherent potential to achieve at a high level of competition. That is, whereas psychological and physiological

---

[1] A search in August, 1981 of the SIRLS file at the University of Waterloo generated a print-out containing 723 citations pertaining to the child or adolescent and sport.

processes may account for involvement and performance in sport at a given point in time, the sociological processes and parameters function early in life and continue to be influential over a longer period of time. For example, whereas the biological sciences may be able to explain physical and structural differences between those who are involved in sport and those who are not, between those who are successful and those who are not, between male and female athletes, and between those of different racial origins, they cannot explain why two children with apparently similar structural characteristics become involved in different sports or why one doesn't become involved in sport. Similarly, they cannot explain why individuals from one country are more involved or successful in a particular sport than those from another country with a similar population and geographical features or why one region of the country produces more elite athletes than another region (cf. Rooney, 1974). That is, much of the variation in involvement and subsequent success in sport is accounted for by the social milieu in which one is socialized as a child. Heredity and hard physical work alone will not account for involvement and success in sport. Rather, ascribed social categories and cultural and ethnic values, norms, and ideology which are found in a variety of micro and macro social systems must be considered in any attempt to explain children's involvement in competitive sport, and the resulting social problems which accrue in contemporary North American sport.

Therefore, the purpose of this chapter is to: (a) outline the social structure of the child's sport milieu; (b) outline the factors in the social milieu influencing the child to become involved in sport; (c) identify and discuss social problems inherent in the child's sport milieu, especially where adults intrude and dominate; and, (d) present some future research directions for those interested in studying this multidisciplinary phenomenon from a sociological perspective.

THE SOCIAL STRUCTURE OF THE SPORT MILIEU

Involvement in sport, as in all other forms of social behavior, is often determined by the social structure of the environment in which the social action occurs. Thus, in order to better understand the child in a competitive sport environment, it must be recognized that sport is but one of many systems in which the child interacts. Figure 1 illustrates the various social systems to which a child may be exposed. Within each of these systems a set of values and social norms determines the attitudes and behavioral patterns that may be exhibited, the positive sanctions which reward normative behavior, and the negative sanctions which discourage behavior that may deviate from that which is considered socially acceptable. Figure 2 illustrates some socially acceptable and deviant role-relationships which are possible within a sport system.

fluence of significant others varies over time. Of interest is the fact that approximately 75% of the respondents reported that they were secondarily involved via the mass media (i.e., television, radio, and newspapers) prior to their participation in the sport.

In summary, it appears that college athletes receive a stimulus to compete from involved peers and from a home environment which considers sport to be an important facet of life. This latter finding is supported by Pudelkiewicz (1970), who reported that a positive evaluation of sport by Polish parents gives rise to sport interests among the children. Similarly, Orlick (1973) and Snyder and Spreitzer (1973) found a positive relationship between parents' interests in sport and the respondent's sport involvement, for both sexes and all three dimensions of sport involvement (behavioral, affective, and cognitive). Most recently, Watson (Note 6) noted that children perceive their parents as being an important reference group for sport involvement. He also found that families with children involved in community sport programs share a more intensive involvement in the community and place a higher value on the participation of their children in community activities. Family support may be even more essential for female athletes as noted by Malumphy (1970), who reported that the family was a major factor in college women continuing to compete. Furthermore, the influence of the mother may be more important for some sports than for others. The study reported by Kenyon and McPherson (1973) indicated that mothers were more influential in arousing interest and providing reinforcement for tennis players than for hockey players. A study by Hall (1976; Note 7) of 552 Canadian and 576 British women between the ages of 18 and 30 revealed that attitudes and behavior dispositions were unimportant determinants of female sport involvement compared to past experiences and present situational factors.

The professional athlete is also an important significant other, especially for young males. In the study reported by Kenyon and McPherson (1973), almost all respondents reported they had an "idol," and since a Canadian sample was utilized, it is not surprising that most of the idols listed by both the hockey and tennis players were outstanding professional hockey players. Furthermore, as the tennis respondents reached college age and began to specialize in that sport, a highly ranked tennis player often replaced the hockey idol. For the hockey players there was a positive relationship, which increased with age, between the position played by the respondent and that played by the idol.

In a related study by Kenyon and Grogg (cited in Kenyon & McPherson, 1973), 87 intercollegiate athletes in a variety of sports at the University of Wisconsin were interviewed. The social situation in which interest in a specific sport was first generated varied by sport. For example, interest in baseball was initiated about equally in the home and the school; for fencing and crew, the school was most important; for football and hockey, the home and neighborhood; for swimming, the home and club or recreational agency; for tennis, the school and club or recreational agency, and for track, the home and the school. The data also suggested "opportunity set" differences. For example, the athlete's place of residence during high school varied among sports in that none of the hockey players, swimmers, or tennis players grew up in the open country or on a farm, indicating that certain facilities and a motivational climate necessary for learning and perfecting certain sport roles are not readily available in rural areas.

Vaz (1972), in a study of the culture of young hockey players, found that certain criteria were essential for initiation into the role of professional hockey player. He reported that aggressive fighting behavior is normative institutionalized conduct, and as such is an essential facet in socializing future professional hockey players. This behavior, because it is institutionalized, becomes an integral part of the role obligation of young hockey players and is learned by subsequent novices via formal and informal socialization. A similar, but more detailed analysis of professional hockey has been provided by Faulkner (1975).

In one of the first attempts to utilize path analysis in the study of sport phenomena, Kenyon (1970) examined the factors influencing college students to become involved in sport at two stages in the life cycle: high school and college. An examination of the path coefficients indicates that a male who has a high level of sport aptitude, who lives in a large community which has adequate facilities and instructors (i.e., a good opportunity set), and who receives encouragement from significant others from within and outside the school will have a greater chance of being socialized into a primary sport role.

In summary, it appears that college athletes and Olympic aspirants become interested and involved in sport by age 8 or 9; they participate, usually with a great deal of success, in a number of sports before they begin to specialize in one sport; and they receive positive sanctions to become involved and to compete from a number of significant others, of which the family, peer group, and coaches appear to be the most influential.

EFFECTS OF BEING INVOLVED IN THE SPORT MILIEU

Having become socialized into competitive sport roles,[3] children find themselves in a social milieu which has the potential to enhance or inhibit their personal growth. In this section, some social problems inherent in children's sport and the issue of socialization *via* sport are discussed.

---

[3]Ralbovsky (1974b, p. 3) indicated that in 1973 there were approximately 9 million males and a few thousand females between the ages of 9 and 19 involved in some form of organized sport.

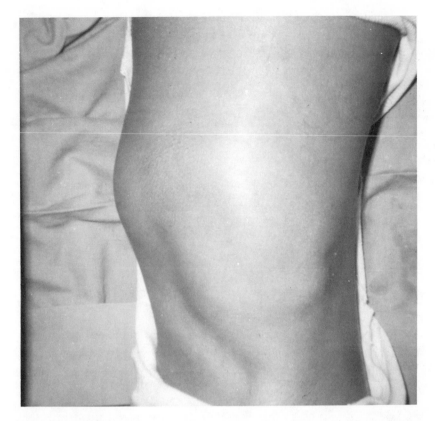

Figure 4—Swelling over medial aspect of the knee at the site of rupture of the proximal portion of the medial collateral ligament.

lateral malleolus extends distally to the subtalar joint and forms an effective bulwark against eversion force, while the medial malleolus is more proximally situated and acts as a fulcrum for the talus to rotate over. The history is that of an acute inversion force with "turning-over on the ankle" accompanied by pain over the anterolateral aspect of the joint. With the more severe sprains, local then diffuse swelling and ecchymosis ensue. Stress testing under local or general anesthesia and arthrography are valuable diagnostic adjuncts in determining the degree of injury. In general, treatment of nonsurgical injuries consists of an initial period of ice and compression followed by supportive strapping and ambulation within the limits of comfort. The degree of weight-bearing and the need of a crutch or cane during ambulation are determined on an individual basis: local symptoms and patient tolerance permitting, there is no contraindication to full weight-bearing on the injured extremity. Continuous supportive strapping is advised in moderate sprains for a minimum of 4 weeks and during practices and games thereafter.

Although social problems involving children such as delinquency, poverty, and drug addiction have been identified and studied, it is only in recent years that conditions inherent in the sport milieu have become intolerable and classified as a social problem. Most of this attention has consisted of anecdotal accounts by journalists (e.g., Ralbovsky, 1974a, 1974b), field observations (e.g., Voigt, 1974), or conceptual analyses of a particular sport (e.g., McPherson, Note 8). Little concrete evidence is presently available to assist us in understanding the inherent problems, even though we know they exist. For example, the following headlines, while isolated and perhaps atypical, do suggest that there is a problem in children's sport that must be faced and solved. Furthermore, these situations must be eliminated because the more frequently they appear in the popular press, the more likely government officials, educators, and taxpayers will question whether funds should be allocated for new stadia and minor sport organizations. The headlines included:

Bloodshed, Brutality: That's Hockey
Emphasis on Muscle
Referee Files Charge Against Fan
Parents, Pressure and the [Hockey] Puck
Unhealthy Climate in Minor Hockey
Should Johnny Play Ball?
Little League: Good or Bad?
It's Fun for Adults, Heartbreak for Kids
Ban Parents from Sport Events
Taking the Fun Out of a Game
Don't Let Your Son Play Smallfry Football
Kid Sports: A Den of Iniquity or Land of Promise
Little League Filled with 'Little' Adults
Manager Assaults Umpire with Bat

Although the following topics have been discussed frequently by journalists and scholars, thereby creating an increased awareness of the problems, there is little understanding as to how or why the problems develop or how they can be controlled or eliminated.

Social Mobility and Unrealistic Career Aspirations

For years a common theme has been that sport provides an avenue for upward social mobility. Unfortunately, because of methodological and conceptual weaknesses there is little empirical support for this hypothesis. For example, the absence of longitudinal studies or studies using subjects matched on education or original socioeconomic status of parents have made it impossible to determine whether mobility occurred because of sport success or because a particular cohort improved their socioeconomic status through social change. Although studies (Gruneau, 1972; Loy, 1969) have indicated that athletes in certain sports come from lower class backgrounds, receive a college education, and subsequently achieve success in high level amateur or professional sport, few studies have shown to what social status athletes rise 10 to 15 years after their college or professional career is completed. One exception is the journalistic field report by Ralbovsky (1974a) of a world championship Little League team 20 years later. Of the players on that team, none have become a major league star or a senator as was predicted the year they became champions. Weinberg and Arond (1952) suggested that most professional boxers experience rapid social descent once their success begins to decline, while Roy (1974) found that despite having a successful career as a player, few Francophones occupy managerial positions in the National Hockey League. As Gruneau (1975) notes:

> Mobility through sport for both the lowest classes and status groups may in fact stop at the comfortable level of middle class athlete. In this sense, the structure of rewards is not so much a ladder on which individuals may continue to climb but rather a tree wherein a specified limb spells the absolute extent of upward travel. (p. 167)

Closely related to the question of mobility is the effect that participation in sport has on school grades and career aspirations. While studies involving most sports have found that athletes are not inferior students when compared with nonathletes, the samples have usually involved college athletes and have considered the athlete's grades at one point in time. One exception was a study by King and Angi (1968) of Ontario Hockey Association players in grades 9 and 12. In grade 9 the grades of the hockey players were similar to the non-hockey-playing students. By grade 12, however, their grades were significantly lower than the non-hockey players and many had dropped out of school. Thus, future research is needed in this area to determine the effect that competitive sport programs have on the educational pursuits of 7- to 15-year-old youngsters. Furthermore, child athletes must be informed about the realistic chances of achieving a career in professional sport. For example, there are approximately 400,000 boys playing organized minor hockey in Canada, but there are only 300-500 positions available in the major and minor professional leagues. Thus, the chance of making a team in professional hockey is not high. Because similar ratios hold for other professional sports, coaches and parents should not provide excessive encouragement to aspire exclusively in this type of career. Instead, young children should be encouraged to achieve in both the educational and the sport domain. As Conacher (1971) noted, "with an education, sport will always be a thing of choice, rather than a necessity" (p. 20).

Adult Domination

For a variety of reasons, adults organize and ultimately dominate the child's sport milieu. Although strong empirical evidence is lacking, some of the hypothesized reasons for this adult control include:

1. Faced with an otherwise unexciting life-style, they hope to receive gratification and prestige in the sport milieu (cf. Bend, Note 9) by becoming emotionally involved in children's play.

2. They are involved to vicariously experience success that is unavailable to them in the adult world (Sherif & Rattray, 1976).

3. As parents, they get involved to facilitate the attainment of career aspirations they may hold for their child in either college, professional, or elite amateur sport.

4. Many parents become involved to protect their own child from some of the practices and values that may be forced on the child by coaches who have a "win-at-all-costs" philosophy.

As a result of this adult control, which was not present years ago (cf. Brower, 1979; Coakley, 1979; Devereux, 1976), the levels of aspiration and the degree of commitment and involvement held by the child-athlete are frequently unrealistic as reflected in the norms and goals which they are forced to adhere to and strive for (e.g., win at all costs, play with pain, only a winner can be proud, etc.). For example, Brower (Note 10) found that what appears to be fun and games were really for the pleasure and benefit of adults. He reported that the boys were like pawns in a chess game where the adults call the shots and the kids get in line and do what they are told. What appears to be fun for adults is often heartbreak for some of the boys. He indicated that while many boys who take part in playground leagues do not have the skill and muscular coordination that is needed, coaches and managers continue to demand these qualities because they are looking at the game from an adult orientation and they expect kids to perform at the skill level of young men. Thus, they scream at the kids and criticize them harshly, acting in the manner they think coaches are expected to act. For many of the boys, this takes the fun out of playing. Brower noted that another problem found in little league sport, specifically baseball, is that the executives of the league make a real effort to attract players from outside the natural area of their playground (cf. Boigt, 1974, p. 13). When these efforts are successful, the teams become more successful. Brower found that some leagues had players who came 7 or 8 miles to practice and play games. He commented that if sport was really just for the boys, the organizers wouldn't be trying to recruit players from outside the territory. However, because they want to win, they must have a league which is well supplied with excellent players and adequate teams. Brower concluded that he has seen boys playing unorganized baseball without adult supervision and noted that spontaneity and fun were present—something he did not see when adults were in charge.

Further evidence for some of the problems introduced by adults when they become involved in children's competitive sport can be found in David Q. Voigt's (1974) personal autobiography of his involvement as a Little League manager. Recruiting was one problem Voigt described:

Thanks to a new league ruling that changed to our advantage the month of a boy's age eligibility. It was a ruling Fred and I helped to push through . . . . Given this diplomatic coup, I planned to . . . lure one of the star players from the Updyke Boy's League into our camp. If this new strategy worked we had a darned good shot at the championship. (p. 13)

Parents as fans are also seen as problems:

The Union fans . . . screamed their frustrated Nixonian expletives. . . . Confronting [the opposing coach] I shoved my face close to his and shouted, "What the hell kind of sportsmanship is this? Why are you booing my ballplayer? He's only 12 years old. Call off your dogs!" (pp. 51-52)

A study by Larson, Spreitzer, and Snyder (1975) also reported that the role of the parent is of central significance in a youth sport program because they are a special kind of participant who often dress like the players (by buying team jackets) to enhance their sense of identification with the team. Based on responses to 61 of 200 mailed questionnaires, they found a disparity between the ideal and actual goals of the youth hockey program as perceived by the parents.

Devereux (1976) suggested that highly organized little league sport extinguishes the spontaneous culture of free play and games which, in the past, was a characteristic of most societies, including our own. As a result, children are having less fun and are being deprived of some of their most valuable learning experiences. Based on an observational study of the behavior of 3,600 children as they left elementary school in a variety of neighborhoods, Devereux (1976) found little evidence of spontaneous play, especially that involving traditional games. This contrasts with previous generations who had knowledge of games, the motivation to play, and the ability to organize and pace their own activities without adult stimulation or supervision. Thus, it appears that there should be a greater tendency to let the children select and establish their own levels of aspiration and the mechanism of attaining the desired end.

In recent years there have been some attempts to change the structure of minor sport in order to reduce the pressure on the participants and to reduce the level of ego-involvement on the part of coaches and parents. For example, some communities operate unstructured leagues where no standings or individual records are kept and there are no play-offs. Although these leagues have had to replace some coaches who couldn't accept the change and operate within this structure, the players seem to have accepted the system. Other areas have initiated instructional programs for 7- to 10-year-olds and eliminated the organized games and leagues in order that each player will have more time in which to learn the skills of the game. These innovative programs pose a great challenge to the "instructor-coach" to provide interesting and educational sessions each week.

Thus, we must realize that many of the problems in minor sport arise because of the organizational structure established by adults who initially have honest intentions to provide the best opportunity for children to play a sport, but at some point in time the end (i.e., winning, success, their own prestige) becomes more important than the means, and the child is forgotten as the league becomes more structured and, in many cases, more restrictive to the individual players. This not only increases the pressure on the participants but also leads to rules where the rights of young players are denied. Fortunately, the opposition to these practices by intruding adults is beginning to appear (Kaplan, 1976) and educators and government officials are instituting voluntary or mandatory training and certification programs for minor league coaches and officials. For example, the Canadian Amateur Hockey Association operates a 5-level certification program for coaches and a similar program for referees. In Ontario, the Ministry of Culture and Recreation offers the Ontario Coaching Development Program for coaches in all sports. At the present time these training programs are optional, although mandatory certification to a certain level is being discussed or has already been implemented in a number of sports. Furthermore, the Ontario government sponsored an investigation and inquiry into violence in amateur hockey (McMurtry, 1974), the outcome of which was the formation of the Ontario Hockey Council to monitor and promote the development of amateur hockey in all regions of the province. This Council published and distributed 300,000 copies of a booklet entitled *You and Your Child in Hockey*[4] in an attempt to subtly influence the behavior and expectations of parents about their child's involvement in this particular sport. Other developments in Canada include the production of two films: *Call Me Coach*, by the Canadian Amateur Hockey Association and *Hockey Is . . .* , a film stressing the development of skill rather than aggression and violence in hockey by the Ontario Hockey Council. Both of these are designed to provide guidelines for changing attitudes and learning appropriate behavior in the child's sport milieu.

Socially Induced Aggression

The occurrence of aggression appears to be socially induced and learned via the socialization process (Bandura & Walters, 1963; Berkowitz, 1962). Through exposure to significant others (role models) and reference groups, an individual observes aggressive behavior or is explicitly taught to be aggressive in certain situations. For example, Smith (1971) suggests that within some sporting social systems there are:

---

[4]This booklet was written for the Ontario Hockey Council by B. McPherson and M. Smith and can be obtained from the Ontario Government Bookstore, 880 Bay Street, Toronto, Ontario, M7A 1N8.

values which legitimize aggression, norms which provide rules for the conduct of aggression, and mechanisms by which individuals are mobilized into aggressive roles. The techniques of violence may be socially learned, legitimized, and reinforced by various types of reference groups. (p. 25)

Vaz (1972) also suggests that physically aggressive behavior is normative, institutionalized behavior that is learned during the formal and informal socialization process of young hockey players. In a participant observation study of boys 8 to 20 engaged in minor league hockey, Vaz found that many of the attitudes and values common to minor league hockey fit into the general value system of the lower socioeconomic strata. He noted that physical aggression, especially fighting, is normative, institutionalized behavior learned via socialization and is part of the role expectations of the player. As a result, under certain conditions a failure to fight is negatively sanctioned by coaches, players, and spectators (parents). In fact, Vaz observed that illegal tactics are both encouraged and taught; rough play and physically aggressive performance are strongly encouraged, and sometimes players are taught the techniques of fighting (Vaz, 1972, p. 230). He further noted that at the midget level the criteria for evaluation changes and coaches begin to teach and emphasize "playing the man," and "taking the opponent out of the play." Vaz and Thomas (1974) further found that 68% of the 15- to 16-year-olds (versus 26% of the 7- to 9-year-olds) reported that one of the most important qualities that the coach seeks is "being aggressive at all times."

Smith (1980, Note 11), Pooley (1979, 1980), and Faulkner (1975) have also studied aggression in youth sport. Faulkner, in a case study of a minor league professional team, found that players consider violent behavior (e.g., fighting) to be a personal and occupational resource to be used in achieving and maintaining mastery over opponents, and for attaining positive evaluations from their work peers. These are the role models which children imitate!

How can aggressive behavior in children's sport be eliminated, or at least controlled? First, role models exhibiting violent forms of behavior should be eliminated as much as possible so that children will have few opportunities to imitate and will therefore be less likely to learn these deviant patterns of behavior. This requires legislation in the form of severe negative sanctions. Other ways to reduce violent behavior include changing the behavioral norms which coaches require their players to meet, and understanding players so that when signs of frustration appear the player can be removed from potentially aggressive situations. Finally, coaches should stop emphasizing the importance of aggression and violence in order to win games. While this is difficult for one individual to accomplish by himself, sport associations must arrive at a common philosophy as to how the game should be played with respect to the amount of aggression or violence they are willing to tolerate in their particular social milieu. This requires a meeting between coaches, officials, parents, and players. Such change will never occur unless all individuals involved in the sport are in agreement. This is especially important when individuals are attempting to change a behavioral pattern that already exists. If the change is to be successful then it must be uniform and involve consistent reinforcement from all significant others (e.g., coaches, parents, and officials) to whom the child is exposed.

Declining Involvement in Sport

In recent years a major concern has been the drop-out rate from organized youth sport programs (cf. McPherson, Guppy, & McKay, 1976). Although many of the children have been forced to leave by a coach when they were "cut," an increasing number are making a personal decision that organized sport is no longer enjoyable because of the size of the playing areas, the length of the games, the amount of physical contact or violence, and the minimal amount of activity, especially for those who are substitutes (cf. Devereux, 1976; Orlick, 1973). In order to overcome some of these limitations, Sherif (1976) argues that there should be an emphasis on the degree of success rather than on the zero-sum, "win-lose" value structure which presently exists, while Loy (1973) advocates that a satisfaction orientation (winning is not the major purpose of sport) should be instilled in contemporary sport organizations.

In a field study, Orlick and Botterill (1975) interviewed 60 athletic dropouts who had been a member of a competitive team at one time in either cross-country skiing, hockey, soccer, baseball, basketball, or swimming. They found that 67% dropped out of sport for reasons related to the emphasis on competition, 31% left due to the development of other interests, and 2% quit because of injuries. A further analysis of the responses enabled the authors to categorize the main reasons for becoming uninvolved. For those who quit because of the competitive emphasis, 50% blamed the program (e.g., too serious, too much emphasis on winning, experienced a sense of failure) while 17% cited the coach as the main reason (e.g., they criticize too much, they are not fair to everyone, they never let me play). Similar reasons are cited in Ralbovsky (1974b). For those who reported conflict of interest as major reason, 21% dropped out because sport conflicted with other interests (e.g., social life, school, job), while 10% indicated that they had developed a greater interest in other sports.

With respect to this latter point, Guppy (1974) found that there were shifts in the degree and type of involvement and in the social system (e.g., from school to community) where sport takes place. Moreover, he noted that parents and coaches should be aware that a child may cease to be involved at one level, but may continue to be involved at another level. Finally, Guppy suggests that there may be unique sport differences in the drop-out rates and in the reasons for becoming uninvolved.

It was also found by Orlick (1973) that the reasons for quitting differed by age. For example, at high school age, 60% dropped out because of the competitive emphasis and 39% dropped out because of a conflict of interest, whereas at the elementary school level *all* children stopped participating because of the competitive emphasis in the program. Specific reasons frequently given by elementary school students included lack of playing time (40%) and the experience did not prove to be successful or rewarding (60%). As Orlick (1973) noted, these experiences "led to feelings of unworthiness, unacceptance and unfun, which in turn lead to a rejection of sport as a viable alternative" (p. 13).

Finally, in a recent survey of over 1,000 active age group swimmers in Ontario (McPherson, Marteniuk, Clark, & Tihanyi, Note 12), 69% of the active swimmers reported that one or more of their friends had stopped swimming competitively in the last year. Of those who quit, 24% did not become involved in another competitive sport, but more seriously, 33% did not choose to participate in a sport at the noncompetitive recreational level. Among the reasons cited for their friends quitting swimming were too much pressure, they were not progressing, it wasn't fun anymore, they were not winning, too time consuming, conflict with the coach, too much emphasis on training, and too expensive. Furthermore, the swimmers were asked why so few age group champions became successful senior swimmers. The responses revealed that they became bored, started competitive swimming too early and encountered too much stress, poor coaching, and lack of motivation. Among the remedies suggested to retain these early champions were placing less pressure on the young swimmers, starting competition later, including more stroke work, and introducing more fun into workouts.

In summary, it is clear that children are dropping out of organized sport programs for a variety of reasons. If these reasons are related to conflict of interests, then this may be of little concern to coaches except with respect to how they can make their program more interesting. However, if the reason for the dropout emanates from the values inherent in the sport and from the behavior on the part of coaches or parents, changes must take place. As this section has indicated, many children do not enjoy the overemphasis on competition and are very sensitive to the way in which the coach relates to them as human beings. Finally, coaches must realize that the reason for dropping out varies by age, sex, and perhaps sport. Therefore, future research should be directed toward understanding why children are dropping out of specific sports at certain points in time. That is, we must determine whether the reasons for declining involvement are general across all sports, or whether some reasons are more prevalent in certain sports. Sport organizations must study those who drop out at all ages, especially those between 8 and 14 years of age, to determine why sport is no longer a satisfying leisure pursuit. A similar study would also be worthwhile to determine why adults volunteer as coaches, and why, since there is often a very high turnover rate among little league coaches, they cease to be involved. Some preliminary attempts to study the role of coach have been initiated by Albinson (1973), Sage (1975), and McPherson (Note 8).

SOCIALIZATION VIA SPORT

Although not a social problem in itself, socialization via sport is problematic in two respects. First, there is little empirical evidence that the process operates at all, and second, if it does, it may result in the learning of socially unacceptable or deviant behavior and may lead to role conflict, especially for females as they try to resolve sex-role identification.

The variety of socialization outcomes that have been predicted to result from participation in sport and physical activity include the development of individual traits and skills (personality, integration, creativity, need achievements, independence, self-esteem, emotional dispositions, character, citizenship, etc.), learning *about* the environment, and learning to *interact with* the environment (e.g., survival of the fittest). Because it is beyond the scope of this paper to review this literature, the reader is referred to Kenyon (1968), McPherson (1972; 1981a), Stevenson (1975), and Staniford (1978), who concluded that little empirical evidence exists to substantiate the many claims that have been made for the contribution of sport, physical education, and physical activity, and to Loy and Ingham (1973) who concluded that:

> Socialization via play, games and sport is a complex process having both manifest and latent functions, and involving functional and dysfunctional, intended and unintended consequences. Since research on the topic is limited, one must regard with caution many present empirical findings and most tentative, theoretical interpretations of these findings.

Sex-Role Identification

One process in which socialization via games and sport seems to have some influence is sex-role identification. In North American society, males have traditionally been expected to be aggressive, independent, and competitive while females are expected to behave in a passive and supportive manner. These expectations are particularly evident in the social world of play, games, and sport. As in society at large, then, stereotyped assumptions are made regarding how males and females should conduct themselves in various social systems. In the North American culture, participation in sport has been positively associated with the male sex role and negatively associated with the female sex role. In fact, research by Lewis (1972a, 1972b) indicates that social influences may affect the child's play activities before he or she is 1 year old. Lewis found that parents allowed boys freedom to explore the play environment, to display aggressive behavior, and to engage in vigorous activities with toys. Thus, it would appear that parents are influential in maintaining cultural expectations with respect to how children should play. In the game stage, these expectations are reinforced when parents assign toys and clothing to their children on the basis of sex differences. In this way children engage in what Stone (1962) termed "anticipatory socialization," whereby the child plays roles which he or she is likely to enact later in life.

The girl who wishes to participate in competitive sport is often discouraged from doing so by parents and peers. A multitude of conventional wisdoms are presented to convince the aspiring female athlete that sport participation is unladylike, masculine, and physiologically harmful. Thus, the girl who decides to play the athletic role finds that she experiences role conflict and is then faced with the dilemma as to whether she should behave according to what is expected of her in the ascribed sex role (whatever that may be in her local community) or whether she should follow her interests and strive to achieve and learn new roles such as that of the athlete. In this situation they are in a double-bind; they have to worry not only about failure but also the reaction of others if they are successful (Harris, Note 13). This role conflict may be resolved in a number of ways. *First*, they may engage in instrumental acts to modify the external ecology such as attempting to prove their femininity in dress or action (e.g., verbal reactions to the "sex" tests at the Olympic Games); by separating the conflicting roles in time and space so that they do not compete in school sport, but only in the community so that they are known as a "female" at school; or, by playing the two roles in a Jekyl and Hyde routine whereby they are highly competitive while playing sport roles and then refuse to discuss sport while playing other social roles. The *second* way to resolve the conflict is to attempt to change the beliefs of others and convince them that the "athlete" role is compatible with the "female" role; or they may try to change their own beliefs by arguing that others do not have the right to hold expectations about them, or they may refuse to accept the female stereotype and follow an alternative life-style. The *third* way to resolve the role conflict is the most serious and yet the most common as females reach the adolescent years. That is, they drop out of sport as a participant. In summary, socialization via sport contributes to the normative socially induced sex-role identification process. More specifically, children are prepared for the roles which society expects them to enact later in life by being involved or uninvolved in sport.

Achievement Values

Involvement in competitive sport may also lead to the acquisition or strengthening of achievement values which are highly valued in the success-oriented North American culture (Maloney & Petrie, 1972; Webb, 1969). On the other hand, however, these achievement values may be learned prior to involvement in sport and may be necessary prerequisites for success. For example, studies by Guppy (1974), Maloney and Petrie (1972), and Mantel and Vander Velden (Note 2) have suggested that those involved in competitive sport programs possess higher achievement values than those in less competitive intramural programs. Thus, the evidence to date is inconclusive, and two competing explanations may be offered to account for differences in achievement values at different levels of competition. First, individuals may be socialized into these values while participating at a certain competitive level, or second, individuals may be selected into, or place themselves into, different levels because of the fit between their personal achievement values and the perceived values in a given sport milieu.

Socialization as a Dysfunctional Process

While many have considered children's sport to be a functional process, Spencer (1896) believed that games and sports were essentially useless for society. Soule (1966) noted that many consider the frivolity of games to be damaging since adult life requires the performance of many serious and unpleasant duties, whereas play and games overemphasize pleasure-seeking pursuits. Similarly, Aries (1962) stated that tennis, bowling, and the like are essentially quasicriminal activities, no less serious in their deleterious social effects than drunkenness or prostitution. Bend (Note 9) identified a number of dysfunctional effects of sport including the intrusion of adult expectations on the play of children, an overinvolvement in one activity rather than involvement in a number of leisure pursuits, pressure from parents to participate and achieve, and, the emergence of deviant normative patterns such as the "win at all costs" philosophy and unethical practices by coaches and athletes. Some passages by Voigt (1974) provide observational data that competitive sport programs contribute little to the socialization process or may in fact be detrimental to the individual:

A player berating his own team mate underscores the seamy side of little league baseball. I personally felt the ugly emotion of hate, a surge of uncontrollable rage tempting me to lash out at my players and my gloating rivals . . . .

It is this kind of emotional reaction that is so often cited in the charges against the character-building claims of little league baseball . . . .

I now confess that my Brockton team experience affords no evidence that any of these character-building virtues gets into my players. (pp. 40-41)

As for sportsmanship, it was lacking from the start . . . . The plumbers suffered the most, being treated by the regulars as incompetents, which says little for baseball's claim for inculcating brotherhood or community solidarity. (p. 41)

Nor did parents set examples . . . parents of rivals constantly hassled us . . . at home, our supporters returned rivals the same kind of treatment. That our parents gave a bit less . . . owed simply to . . . our big leads and heavy hitting . . . . If there is a point in all of this, I think it demonstrates the fact that in baseball, sportsmanship and good character go mostly to the winners and regular players and only slightly to benchwarmers.

I conclude that little league baseball is no shaper of lofty values or ethics. Rather it merely provides one setting for the playing out of norms and values already embedded in our culture. (p. 42)

To summarize, to date there is little empirical support for the many beliefs and hypotheses concerning the positive or negative role of competitive sport in the general socialization process.

FUTURE RESEARCH DIRECTIONS

As noted throughout this chapter, there is an urgent need for empirical evidence for the many claims and hypotheses concerning children's involvement in sport, especially with respect to the outcomes or effects of their involvement in competitive sport. We really do not know very much about how or why children get socialized into competitive programs, why they continue to be involved, or how and why they become desocialized (i.e., withdraw). Furthermore, as educators, researchers, and parents, we must recognize that many of the more serious problems in children's sport lie outside the educational setting, and therefore more efforts should be directed toward understanding this social milieu. More specifically, there is an urgent need for greater understanding of the interpersonal dynamics within the "Little League Triangle"—namely, the coach-parent-child triad.

Methodologically, national rather than local isolated studies must be initiated. If this is not possible, then there should be replication of studies in a variety of communities, both within a society and cross-nationally in order to control for historical and environmental effects. To date, most evidence is anecdotal and therefore greater efforts should be directed toward initiating field studies employing such methods as interviews, questionnaires, and both obtrusive and unobtrusive participant observation. Further efforts should also strive to include both sexes, and control for social class, age, and level of competition. Finally, the initiation of longitudinal studies employing twins might eliminate some of the problems inherent in the retrospective type of research which has been most common to date.

POSTSCRIPT-AUGUST 1981

Since the publication of the first edition of this book in 1978, interest in social phenomena related to youth sport has continued to grow. This is illustrated by the establishment of at least three centers for the study and advancement of youth sport, including:

- The Institute for the Study of Youth Sports at Michigan State University, which publishes *Spotlight on Youth Sports,*

- The Office of Youth Sports in the Department of Physical Education at the University of Illinois, Champaign, which publishes *Sportsline,*

- The North American Youth Sport Institute in Kernersville, North Carolina, which publishes *Sport Scene,*

by the completion of at least two major studies of youth sport systems, including:

- *The Joint Legislative Study on Youth Sport Programs in the State of Michigan, 1978* (V. Seefeldt, Project Director), Department of Physical Education, Michigan State University, East Lansing.

- *Minor Hockey in Ontario: Toward A Positive Learning Environment for Children in the 1980s* by Barry D. McPherson (Toronto: Province of Ontario Bookstore, 880 Bay Street, 1980),

by the publication of numerous books, manuals, and pamphlets for use by volunteer leaders, including:

- the newsletters cited above

- Martens, R., and Seefeldt, V., *Guidelines for Children's Sports.* Washington, DC: AAHPER, 1979.

- National Task Force on Children's Play. *Fair Play Codes for Children in Sport.* Ottawa, Canada: Canadian Council on Children and Youth, 1979.

- Thomas, J. (Ed.). *Youth Sports Guide for Coaches and Parents.* Washington, DC: AAHPER and Manulife, 1977.

- Smoll, F., and Smith, R. *Improving Relationship Skills in Youth Sport Coaches.* East Lansing, MI: Institute for the Study of Youth Sports, 1979.

by an increase in the number of publications and the number of undergraduate and graduate courses which focus on youth sport. In particular, recent studies on youth sport have focused on such topics as the creation of unique team cultures among youth teams (Fine, 1979), the process and problems of socialization into sport for young girls (Duquin, 1981; Greendorfer, 1979; Lever, 1978), the social control of little league baseball players (Kleinman & Fine, 1979), policy-oriented research in youth sport (McPherson, 1981b), and the impact of competition on youth (Roberts, 1980; Scanlan & Passer, 1978, 1979a, 1979b). Perhaps what is most surprising is that few studies have asked children what they do or do not like about organized sport, and what changes, if any, they would like to see in their sport world. Hopefully, future research will focus on all social actors in the children's sport milieu, including the central participant, the child.

REFERENCE NOTES

1. Hale, C.J. *Athletic competition for young children.* Paper presented at the Conference on Sport and Social Deviancy, Brockport, NY, December 1971.
2. Mantel, R., & Vander Veldon, L. *The relationship between the professionalization of attitudes toward play by preadolescent boys and participation in organized sport.* Paper presented at the Third International Symposium on the Sociology of Sport, Waterloo, Ontario, August 1971.
3. Kroll, W. *Psychology of sportsmanship.* Paper presented at the American Alliance for Health, Physical Education, and Recreation National Convention, Atlantic City, NJ, March 1975.
4. Marple, D.P. *An analysis of the discrimination against the French Canadians in ice hockey.* Paper presented at the meeting of the Canadian Sociology and Anthropology Association, Toronto, August 1974.
5. Gould, D., & Landers, D. *Dangerous sport participation: A replication of Nisbett's birth order findings.* Paper presented at the annual meeting of the North American Society for the Psychology of Sport and Physical Activity, Houston, March 1972.
6. Watson, G.G. *The meaning of parental influence and intrinsic reward in children's sport: A case of little athletics.* Paper presented at the Conference on Sport, Society, and Personality, Bundoora, Victoria, Australia, May 1975.
7. Hall, M.A. *Women and physical recreation: A causal analysis.* Paper presented at the Women and Sport Symposium, University of Birmingham, Birmingham, England, September 1973.
8. McPherson, B.D. *The social milieu of minor hockey in Canada: A review and analysis.* Unpublished manuscript prepared for the Canadian Amateur Hockey Association Technical Development Committee, 1974.
9. Bend, E. *Some potential dysfunctional effects of sport upon socialization.* Paper presented at the Third International Symposium on the Sociology of Sport, Waterloo, Ontario, August 1971.
10. Brower, J. *Little leagues mostly for parents.* Unpublished manuscript, California State University at Fullerton, 1973.
11. Smith, M.D. *Parents, peers, and coaches sanctions for assaultive behavior in hockey.* Paper presented at Olympic Congress, Munich, Germany, August 1972.

12. McPherson, B.D., Marteniuk, R., Clark, W., & Tihanyi, J. *An analysis of the system of age group swimming in Ontario.* Final Research Report submitted to the Canadian Amateur Swimming Association (Ontario Section), 559 Jarvis St., Toronto, Ontario, July 31, 1977.

13. Harris, D.V. *The social self and competitive self of the female athlete.* Paper presented at the Third International Symposium on the Sociology of Sport, Waterloo, Ontario, August 1971.

REFERENCES

ALBINSON, J.A. Professional attitudes of volunteer coaches toward playing the game. *International Review of Sport Sociology*, 1973, **9**, 77-86.

ARIES, P. *Centuries of childhood.* New York: Vintage Books, 1962.

BANDURA, A. Social learning theory of identificatory process. In D.A. Goslin (Ed.), *Handbook of socialization theory and research.* Chicago: McNally, 1969.

BANDURA, A., & Walters, R.H. *Social learning and personality developments.* New York: Rinehart & Winston, 1963.

BERKOWITZ, L. *Aggression: A social psychological analysis.* New York: McGraw-Hill, 1962.

BIRD, E. Multivariate personality analysis of two children's hockey teams. *Perceptual and Motor Skills,* 1979, **48**, 967-973.

BIRD, A.M., & Williams, J. A developmental-attributional analysis of sex role stereotypes for sport performance. *Developmental Psychology,* 1980, **16**, 319-322.

BOILEAU, R., Landry, F., & Trempe, Y. Les Canadiens-Francais et les grand jeux internationaux. In R.S. Gruneau & J.G. Albinson (Eds.), *Canadian sport: Sociological perspectives.* Don Mills, Ontario: Addison-Wesley (Canada Ltd.) 1976.

BRIM, O.G., & Wheeler, S. (Eds.), *Socialization after childhood.* New York: Wiley, 1966.

BROWER, J. The professionalization of organized youth sport: Social psychological impacts and outcomes. *Annals of the American Academy of Political and Social Science,* 1979, **445**, 39-46.

BROWN, R.C. The relationship between physical performance and personality in elementary school children. In G.S. Kenyon & T.M. Grogg (Eds.), *Contemporary psychology of sport.* Chicago: Athletic Institute, 1970.

BUKOWSKI, W., & Moore, D. Winners and losers attributions for success and failure in a series of athletic events. *Journal of Sport Psychology,* 1980, **2**, 195-210.

CLAUSEN, J.W. (Ed.), *Socialization and society.* Boston: Little, Brown & Co., 1968.

COAKLEY, J. Play group versus organized competitive team: A comparison. In S.D. Eitzen (Ed.), *Sport in contemporary society: An anthology.* New York: St. Martin's Press, 1979.

COAKLEY, J. Play, games and sport: Developmental implications for young people. *Journal of Sport Behavior,* 1980, **3**, 99-118.

CONACHER, B. *Hockey in Canada: The way it is.* Richmond Hill, Ontario: Gateway Press, 1971.

DEVEREUX, E.C. Back yard versus Little League baseball: The impoverishment of children's games. In D. Landers (Ed.), *Social problems in athletics.* Urbana: University of Illinois Press, 1976.

DUQUIN, M. Reflections on sexual segregation in youth sports. *The Physical Educator,* 1981, **3**, 65-70.

EGGLESTON, J. Secondary schools and Oxbridge blues. *British Journal of Sociology,* 1965, **16**, 232-242.

EITZEN, D.S., & Sanford, D.C. The segregation of Blacks by playing position in football: Accident or design? *Social Science Quarterly,* 1975, **55**, 948-959.

FAULKNER, R.R. Coming of age in organizations: The comparative study and career contingencies of musicians and hockey players. In D.W. Ball & J.W. Loy (Eds.), *Sport and social order.* Reading, MA: Addison-Wesley, 1975.

FINE, G. Small groups and culture creation: The idioculture of Little League Baseball teams. *American Sociological Review,* 1979, **44**, 733-745.

GOSLIN, D. (Ed.), *Handbook of socialization theory and research.* Chicago: Rand McNally, 1969.

GREENDORFER, S. Differences in childhood socialization influences of women involved in sport and women not involved in sport. In M. Krotee (Ed.), *The dimensions of sport sociology.* West Point, NY: Leisure Press, 1979.

GRUNEAU, R. *A socioeconomic analysis of the competitors of the 1971 Canada Winter Games.* Unpublished master's thesis, University of Calgary, 1972.

GRUNEAU, R. Sport, social differentiation and social equality. In D.W. Ball & J.W. Loy (Eds.), *Sport and social order.* Reading, MA: Addison-Wesley, 1975.

GUPPY, N. *The effect of selected socialization practices on the sport achievement orientations of male and female adolescents.* Unpublished master's thesis, University of Waterloo, 1974.

HALL, M.A. Sport and physical activity in the lives of Canadian women. In R. Gruneau & J. Albinson (Eds.), *Canadian sport: Sociological perspectives.* Don Mills, Ontario: Addison-Wesley (Canada Ltd.), 1976.

ISO-AHOLA, S. Sex-role stereotypes and causal attributions for success and failure in motor performance. *Research Quarterly,* 1979, **50**, 630-640.

KAPLAN, J. A wintry heritage. *Sports Illustrated.* February 9, 1976, pp. 35-36.

KEMPER, R.D. Reference groups, socialization and achievement. *American Sociological Review,* 1968, **33**, 31-45.

KENYON, G.S. Sociological considerations. *Journal of Health, Physical Education and Recreation,* 1968, **39**, 31-33.

KENYON, G.S. The use of path analysis in sport sociology with special reference to involvement socialization. *International Review of Sport Sociology,* 1970, **5**, 191-203.

KENYON, G.S., & McPherson, B.D. Becoming involved in physical activity and sport: A process of socialization. In G.L. Rarick (Ed.), *Physical activity: Human growth and development.* New York: Academic Press, 1973.

KENYON, G.S., & McPherson, B.D. An approach to the study of sport socialization. *International Review of Sport Sociology,* 1974, **9**, 127-138.

KING, A.L., & Angi, C.E. The hockey playing student. *Canadian Association for Health, Physical Education and Recreation Journal,* 1968, **34**, 25-28.

KLEINMAN, S., & Fine, G. Rhetorics and action in moral organizations: Social control of little leaguers and ministry students. *Urban Life,* 1979, **8**, 275-294.

KNOPP, T.B. Environmental determinants of recreation behavior. *Journal of Leisure Research,* 1972, **4**, 129-138.

LANDERS, D. The effects of ordinal position and sibling's sex on males' sport participation. In A.W. Taylor (Ed.), *Training: Scientific basis and application.* Springfield, IL: Charles C. Thomas, 1972.

LARSON, D.L., Spreitzer, E., & Snyder, E. Youth hockey programs: A sociological perspective. *Sport Sociology Bulletin,* 1975, **4,** 55-63.

LEVER, J. Sex differences in the complexity of children's play and games. *American Sociological Review,* 1978, **43,** 471-483.

LEWIS, M. Culture and gender roles: There's no unisex in the nursery. *Psychology Today,* May 1972, pp. 54-57. (a)

LEWIS, M. Sex differences in play behavior of the very young. *Journal of Health, Physical Education and Recreation,* 1972, **43,** 38-39. (b)

LOY, J.W. The study of sport and social mobility. In G.S. Kenyon (Ed.), *Aspects of contemporary sport sociology.* Chicago: Athletic Institute, 1969.

LOY, J.W. Social origins and occupational mobility patterns of a selected sample of American athletes. *International Review of Sport Sociology,* 1972, **7,** 5-26.

LOY, J.W., & Ingham, A. Play, games, and sport in the psychosocial development of children and youth. In G.L. Rarick (Ed.), *Physical activity: Human growth and development.* New York: Academic Press, 1973.

LOY, J.W., & McElvogue, J.F. Racial segregation in American sport. *International Review of Sport Sociology,* 1970, **5,** 5-24.

LUESCHEN, G. Social stratification and social mobility among young sportsmen. In J.W. Loy & G.S. Kenyon (Eds.), *Sport, culture and society,* Toronto: MacMillan, 1969.

MALINA, R.M., & Rarick, G.L. Growth, physique and motor performance. In G.L. Rarick (Ed.), *Physical activity: Human growth and development.* New York: Academic Press, 1973.

MALONEY, T.R., & Petrie, B. Professionalization of attitude toward play among Canadian school pupils as a function of sex, grade and athletic participation. *Journal of Leisure Research,* 1972, **4,** 184-195.

MALUMPHY, T.M. The college woman athlete—Questions and tentative answers. *Quest,* 1970, **14,** 18-27.

McMURTRY, W.R. *Investigation and inquiry into violence in amateur hockey.* Toronto: Ministry of Community and Social Services, 1974.

McPHERSON, B.D. *Socialization into the role of sport consumer: The construction and testing of a theory and causal model.* Unpublished doctoral dissertation. University of Wisconsin, 1972.

McPHERSON, B.D. Consumer role socialization: A within-system model. *Sportwissenschaft,* 1976, **6,** 144-154. (a)

McPHERSON, B.D. Socialization into the role of sport consumer: A theory and causal model. *The Canadian Review of Sociology and Anthropology,* 1976, **13,** 165-177. (b)

McPHERSON, B.D., Guppy, L.N., & McKay, J.P. The social structure of the game and sport milieu. In J.G. Albinson & G.M. Andrew (Eds.) *Child in sport and physical activity.* Baltimore: University Park Press, 1976.

McPHERSON, B.D. Socialization into and through sport involvement. In G. Lueschen & G. Sage (Eds.), *Handbook of social science and sport.* Champaign, IL: Stipes, 1981. (a)

McPHERSON, B.D. Collaborative policy-oriented research in youth sport: Purpose and method, trials and tribulations, problems and prospects. *Proceedings of the North American Society for the Sociology of Sport.* Champaign, IL: Human Kinetics, 1981. (b)

NISBETT, R.E. Birth order and participation in dangerous sports. *Journal of Personality and Social Psychology,* 1968, **8,** 351-353.

ORLICK, T.D. Children's sports: A revolution is coming. *Canadian Association for Health, Physical Education and Recreation Journal,* 1973, **39,** 12-14.

ORLICK, T., & Botterill, C. *Every kid can win.* Chicago: Nelson-Hall, 1975.

PASCAL, A.H., & Rapping, L.A. The economics of racial discrimination in organized baseball. In A.H. Pascal (Ed.), *Racial discrimination in economic life,* Lexington, MA: D.C. Heath, 1972.

POOLEY, J. An alternative model to reduce competitiveness in sports for youth: The case of soccer. *Review of Sport and Leisure,* 1979, **4,** 65-88.

POOLEY, J. Player violence in sport: Consequences for youth. In P. Klavora & K. Wipper (Eds.), *Psychological and sociological factors in sport.* Toronto: University of Toronto Press, 1980.

PUDELKIEWICZ, E. Sociological problems of sport in housing estates. *International Review of Sport Sociology,* 1970, **5,** 73-103.

PURDY, D. Youth sports participants: The relationship among self-esteem, competition anxiety and competitiveness. *Review of Sport and Leisure,* 1980, **5,** 115-136.

RALBOVSKY, M. *Destiny's darlings.* New York: Hawthorne, 1974. (a)

RALBOVSKY, M. *Lords of the locker room.* New York: Peter H. Wyden, 1974. (b)

RARICK, G.L. Competitive sport in childhood and early adolescence. In G.L. Rarick (Ed.), *Physical activity: Human growth and development*. New York: Academic Press, 1973.

ROBERTS, G. Children in competition: A theoretical perspective and recommendations for practice. *Motor Skills: Theory Into Practice*, 1980, **4**, 37-50.

ROETHLISBERGER, F.A. *Socialization of the elite gymnast*. Unpublished master's thesis, University of Wisconsin, 1970.

ROONEY, J. *The geography of American sport*. Reading, MA: Addison-Wesley, 1974.

ROY, G. *The relationship between centrality and mobility: The case of National Hockey League*. Unpublished master's thesis, University of Waterloo, 1974.

SAGE, G.J. An occupational analysis of the college coach. In D.W. Ball & J.W. Loy (Eds.), *Sport and social order*. Reading, MA: Addison-Wesley, 1975.

SARBIN, R., & Allen, D. Role theory. In G. Lindzey & E. Aronson (Eds.), *Handbook of social psychology* (Vol. 1). Reading, MA: Addison-Wesley, 1968.

SCANLAN, T., & Passer, M. Factors related to competitive stress among male youth sport participants. *Medicine and Science in Sports*, 1978, **10**, 103-108.

SCANLAN, T., & Passer, M. Sources of competitive stress in young female athletes. *Journal of Sport Psychology*, 1979, **1**, 151-159. (a)

SCANLAN, T., & Passer, M. Factors influencing the competitive performance expectancies of young female athletes. *Journal of Sport Psychology*, 1979, **1**, 212-220. (b)

SCANLAN, T., & Passer, M. The attributional responses of young female athletes after winning, tying, and losing. *Research Quarterly*, 1980, **51**, 675-684.

SCULLY, G.W. Discrimination: The case of baseball. In R.G. Noll (Ed.), *Government and the sports business*. Washington: Brookings Institution, 1974.

SEWELL, W.H. Some recent developments in socialization theory and research. *The Annals of the American Academy of Political Science*, 1963, **349**, 163-181.

SEYMOUR, E.W. Comparative study of certain behavior characteristics of participants and non-participants in Little League Baseball. *Research Quarterly*, 1956, **27**, 338-346.

SHERIF, C. The social context of competition. In D. Landers (Ed.), *Social problems in athletics*. Urbana, IL: University of Illinois Press, 1976.

SHERIF, C.W., & Rattray, G. Psychosocial development and activity in middle childhood: 5-12 years. In J.G. Albinson & G.M. Andrew (Eds.), *Child in sport and physical activity*. Baltimore: University Park Press, 1976.

SKUBIC, E. Emotional responses of boys to Little League and Middle League competitive baseball. *Research Quarterly*, 1955, **26**, 342-352.

SMITH, M.D. Aggression in sport: Toward a role approach. *Canadian Association for Health, Physical Education and Recreation Journal*, 1971, **37**, 22-25.

SMITH, M.D. Interpersonal violence in sport: The influence of parents. In P. Klavora & K. Wipper (Eds.), *Psychological and sociological factors in sport*. Toronto: University of Toronto Press, 1980.

SNYDER, E.E., & Spreitzer, F. Family influence and involvement in sports. *Research Quarterly*, 1973, **44**, 249-255.

SOFRANKO, A.J., & Nolan, M.F. Early-life experiences and adult sport participation. *Journal of Leisure Research*, 1972, **4**, 6-18.

SOULE, G.H. *Time for living*. New York: Viking Press, 1966.

SPENCER, H. *The principles of psychology*. New York: Appleton, 1896.

STANIFORD, D. *Play and physical activity in early childhood socialization* (CAHPER Sociology of Sport Monograph Series). Vanier City, Canada: CAHPER, 1978.

STEVENSON, C.L. Socialization effects of participation in sport: A critical review of the research. *Research Quarterly*, 1975, **46**, 287-301.

STONE, G. Appearance and the self. In A. Rose (Ed.), *Human behavior and social process*. Boston: Houghton-Mifflin, 1962.

VAZ, E. The culture of young hockey players: Some initial observations. In A.W. Taylor (Ed.), *Training: Scientific basis and application*. Springfield, IL: Charles C. Thomas, 1972.

VAZ, E., & Thomas, D. What price victory: An analysis of minor hockey players attitudes towards winning. *International Review of Sport Sociology*, 1974, **9**, 33-53.

VOIGT, D.Q. *A little league journal*. Bowling Green, OH: Bowling Green University Press, 1974.

WEBB, H. Professionalization of attitudes towards play among adolescents. In G.S. Kenyon (Ed.), *Aspects of contemporary sport sociology*. Chicago: Athletic Institute, 1969.

WEINBERG, S.K., & Arond, H. The occupational culture of the boxer. *American Journal of Sociology*, 1952, **57**, 460-469.

WOELFEL, J., & Haller, A.O. Significant others, the self-reflexive act and the attitude formation process. *American Sociological Review*, 1971, **36**, 74-87.

YETMAN, N.R., & Eitzen, D.S. Black Americans in sports: Unequal opportunity for equal ability. *Civil Rights Digest*, 1972, **5**, 21-34.

ZIGLER, E., & Child, I.L. Socialization. In G. Lindzey & E. Aronson (Eds.), *A handbook of social psychology* (Vol. 3). Reading, MA: Addison-Wesley, 1969.

CHAPTER 19

FAMILY INFLUENCE AND SEX DIFFERENCES IN CHILDREN'S SOCIALIZATION INTO SPORT: A REVIEW

John H. Lewko and Susan L. Greendorfer

Recent federal legislation in the form of Title IX has focused attention on the area of physical education and sport at all age levels. Discrimination on the basis of sex is now illegal, and educational institutions must provide equal opportunity for girls and women to participate in sport programs. One critical factor in meeting the challenge of more equitable experiences is an understanding of the underlying determinants of children's sport involvement. Without such insights it will be difficult to redress the fundamental reasons for the current predicament.

Despite recent concern for children in sport, the social processes which influence their participation in sports activities have been virtually ignored (Albinson & Andrew, 1976; McPherson, Note 1). Considerable attention has been directed to questions of socialization and sport involvement, but most of the research has focused on the adult population and, in particular, highly trained participants (Kenyon & McPherson, 1973, 1974). What little research does exist on children focuses on boys in competitive sport programs or on children who have dropped out of such programs (Orlick & Botterill, 1975). Sherif and Rattray (1976) stated, "Psychologists and social scientists in fact know comparatively little about children's physical activity and sports" (p. 98).

Central to the problem of sex discrimination in sport is understanding the way individuals are socialized into sex roles and, in particular, sport

From Landers, D.M., and Christina, R.W. (Eds.), *Psychology of Motor Behavior and Sport*, 1977, pp. 434-447. Copyright 1977 by Human Kinetics. Reprinted with permission.

roles. As Mussen (1969) has indicated, "It is a banal truth that the individual's sex role is the most salient of his many social roles. No other social role directs more of his overt behavior, emotional reactions, cognitive functioning, covert attitudes and general psychological and social adjustment" (p. 707). The family, peers, teachers, and members of the community have been identified as critical elements in children's evolving perceptions of their sex/sport roles. The extent to which such key individuals influence a child toward a sex-linked concept of sport participation should be of primary concern in understanding the process of socialization and sport involvement. The purpose of this paper is to review the extant literature pertaining to sex differences and children's socialization into sport, propose some areas for future research, and generate testable hypotheses which can further clarify the sport-socialization process.

SEX DIFFERENCES AND SOCIALIZATION

Before discussing the literature on sex differences and sport-role socialization, it is enlightening to consider some information that is divergent from the traditional stereotypes of male and female. The stereotyped male is an individual who is self-reliant, achievement oriented, in control of his feelings and slow to express them, and who has a concern for rule conformity. The stereotyped female, on the other hand, is nurturant, obedient, and responsible. She is emotionally expressive and oriented toward close interpersonal relationships. Fortunately, a recent comprehensive review of literature on sex differences necessitates modification of the assumptions underlying our sex stereotypes.

Maccoby and Jacklin (1974) found the following beliefs about sex differences unsubstantiated: girls are more "social" than boys; girls are more "suggestible" than boys; girls have lower self-esteem; girls are better at role learning and simple repetitive tasks and boys at tasks that require higher-level cognitive processing and the attendant inhibitions of previously learned responses; boys are more analytic; girls are more affected by heredity and boys by environment; girls lack achievement motivation; girls are auditory and boys visual. On the other hand, several sex differences were reasonably well-established: girls have greater verbal ability and peripheral vision than boys; boys excel in visual-spatial ability; boys excel in mathematical ability; males are more aggressive. In addition, those areas left open to further investigation due to lack of evidence or ambiguous findings included tactile sensitivity, fear, timidity, and anxiety, activity level; competitiveness; dominance; compliance; nurturance and "maternal" behavior. It is obvious that our vague stereotypes of males and females are either unfounded or much more complex than initially anticipated.

Physical activity and sport were not major areas of concern in the Maccoby and Jacklin (1974) review. The primary reason for this is the paucity of research in the area which may reflect a lack of interest on the part of researchers concerning sex difference and sport. Second, even when the basic research concern would have been directly relevant or exemplified by a sports context the connection was not made. In order to address the issue of socialization and sport involvement, existing literature will be discussed under the following headings: sex differences in play behavior; behavior of significant others; perception of sex roles; and the sport-role socialization of children.

SEX DIFFERENCES IN PLAY BEHAVIOR

It has been well established that early sex-role socialization results in behaviors which are clearly differentiated. The separation that is first observed in infancy becomes quite stable by the preschool years (Maccoby & Jacklin, 1974; Mischel, 1970). Differential treatment of infants has been reported, with baby girls being touched, handled, and talked to more until by 13 months of age they reciprocate by touching and talking to their mothers more than baby boys (Goldberg & Lewis, 1969; Kagan & Lewis, 1965). Goldberg and Lewis (1969) suggested that such differential treatment resulted in distinctive play behavior for the two sexes. Girls were more dependent, showed less exploratory behavior, and their play reflected a more quiet style. Boy infants, on the other hand, played with toys requiring gross-motor activity, were more vigorous, and tended to bang their toys (Goldberg & Lewis, 1969; Lewis, 1972a).

In an observational study of toddlers, Fagot (1974) reported that boys played with blocks and manipulated objects significantly more than girls, while the girls asked for help, played with dolls, danced, and dressed up significantly more than boys. Furthermore, it has been reported that nursery school girls spent more time in activities involving sitting at a table and fine-motor manipulation while boys preferred activities that required gross-motor movements (Clark, Wyon, & Richards, 1969), and that boys spent more time with novel toys than did girls (Rabinowitz, Moely, Finkel, & Clinton, 1975).

By the preschool years, clear sex differences are reported in children's preferences for toys. Boys tend to play with toy trucks, guns, and toy tractors while girls sew, string beads, and play at housekeeping (Maccoby & Jacklin, 1974; Sears, Rau, & Alpert, 1965). These differences are very strong, and boys are more likely to avoid sex-inappropriate toys than are girls (Hartup, Moore, & Sager, 1963). It appears that different sets of play behaviors begin to evolve for males and females at very early ages and primarily under the direction of parents and caretakers.

These different sets of play behaviors seem to be a function of social learning—more specifically, a function of child-rearing practices which indicate that boys and girls receive differential treatment by parents according to activities. Although some of the early investigations in child development found little support for the notion that infant boys and girls receive any significant differential treatment by either or both parents (Barry, Bacon, & Child, 1957; Sears, Maccoby, & Levin, 1957), such findings have been recently challenged. Several researchers have presented evidence to the contrary (Kagan & Lewis, 1965; Lewis, 1972a, 1972b). Observational studies by Goldberg and Lewis (1969) have revealed that there are sex differences in the way a mother treats a child by the age of 6 months, particularly in the sphere of exploratory behavior. A mother is more likely to pick up an infant daughter and thus restrict the range and area over which the daughter may explore. Similarly, Lewis (1972a, 1972b) found that parents allowed boys more freedom to display aggressive behavior and to engage in more vigorous activities with toys.

Additional evidence further supports the notion that differential expectations from parents exist, based on the sex of their children (Aberle & Naegele, 1952; Hartley, 1959; Rothbart & Maccoby, 1966). Inkeles (1968) reported that boys are trained to attain different objectives than are girls. Relative to game or sport experience, Stoll, Inbar, and Fennessey (Note 2) found that sports participation is related to the expression of achievement values for males but not for females. Tasch's (1952) data demonstrated that fathers instill certain types of motor abilities in sons in contrast to other types of abilities instilled in daughters. Specifically, fathers wrestle more with sons and are more apt to teach them gross-motor skills. Such findings suggest that sex-typed notions are incorporated into child-rearing practices and may also be related to the stereotypic notion that females are more fragile than males.

Sex differences in play behavior of children have been found by several investigators. Lewis (1972a, 1972b) found sex differences in play behavior at 1 year of age quite reminiscent of sex-role differences found in older children and adults. In a study of play choices Sutton-Smith, Rosenberg, and Morgan (1963) demonstrated the existence of sex preferences at 8- and 9-years of age. They also discovered that from puberty onwards playing games was a masculine phenomenon in American culture. In a study of play choices over a period of time, Sutton-Smith and Rosenberg (1961) found that the sexes have become increasingly similar in game preference over the last 60 years, and that the increasing similarity in game preferences was primarily due to shifts in female preference. This phenomenon of a wider choice of games by prepubertal girls has also been demonstated by Brown (1958) and Ward (1968). Zoble (1973) considered such findings to be a consequence of a more generally prescribed sex role for females prior to puberty, hence a wide range of play choices. Zoble believes that such choices would narrow after puberty when society offers a more definite stereotyped female sex role.

Relative to social and ecological organization of children's play behavior, one of the more pervasive findings is that boys prefer outdoor play significantly more than girls (Erickson, 1951; Fagot & Littman, 1975; Harper & Sands, 1975; Lever, 1976). In a study involving children ages 10 and 11 years, Lever (1976) found that 40% of the girls were outdoors for less than ¼ of their playing time compared to 15% of the boys. In addition, Long and Henderson (1973) reported that boys ages 9 to 11 spent more time in free play while girls the same age spent more time in organized activities and chores.

In a similar study, Saegert and Hart (1977) found that spatial ranges of activities differed significantly according to sex—a more liberal definition of range allowed for boys than girls. For example, there was a significant tendency for boys to play farther away from home than their age-matched female counterparts. A study by Hart (1976) indicated a gradual increase in these boy-girl differences with age.

Lever's (1976) research concerned with structural and organizational factors related to children's play revealed several important differences between boys' and girls' activities. First of all, girls were restricted in body movement because they played indoors. In addition Lever found that boys tended to play in large, age-heterogeneous groups while girls played in smaller groups. Furthermore, distinct differences in the nature of boys' and girls' games were found. Boys played competitive games more often than girls; more of their games were competitively structured (54% compared to 30%), even when team sports were eliminated from consideration. Perhaps related to this phenomenon is the fact that boys' games are of longer duration and the ceiling of skill is higher. Thus, the type of game adopted by boys can be played in "more simple" versions or with less skill at younger ages and become more challenging with age as higher levels of skill and strategy are incorporated into such games (i.e., baseball and basketball). In contrast, the type of games adopted by girls (i.e., jump rope and tag) seem to be less structured and less challenging with increasing age because the ceiling of skill was achieved at an earlier age.

In summary, sex differences in the play behavior of children can be found early in life and in a variety of activities. While boys learn at a very early age which activities are sex inappropriate, and hence, are to be avoided, girls are permitted a wide range of play activities and choice throughout childhood. By the age of puberty, however, game and sport participation are a male phenomenon. Differences in types of games, the nature of games, and the values emphasized in play activities may all be a result of parents incorporating sex-stereotypic notions into child-rearing practices. Several investigations strongly suggest that this is the case. Therefore, the role of significant others and their influence on play, games, and sport need to be considered.

THE BEHAVIOR OF SIGNIFICANT OTHERS

Parents have been identified as major socialization agents, especially during the preschool years. As such, they would be expected to be the primary shapers of a child's perceptions of and preference for different types of games and play activities. It was reported earlier (Goldberg & Lewis, 1969) that sex-role socialization begins from the moment of birth with differential treatment of male and female infants. Although much attention has been directed to the mother as the primary socializing agent, evidence now suggests that the father is perhaps an even more critical figure.

Absence of the father during the first 5 years of a male child's life has been associated with preadolescents who were significantly less aggressive, had more feminine preferences, and avoided competitive games (Biller, 1969, 1970; Stanrock, 1970). This effect might be explained by the findings that fathers differentiate on sex roles more strictly and encourage stronger sex typing than do mothers (Block, 1973; Goodenough, 1957). Fathers have been reported to show more positive reactions when their boy chooses "boyish" activities than when their girl chooses "feminine" activities (Fling & Manosevitz, 1972; Lansky, 1967). However, a daughter's choice of sex-appropriate toys was positively related to her father's encouragement (Fling & Manosevitz, 1972). Sears, Rau, and Alpert (1965) found a significant relationship between the femininity of nursery school girls and their fathers' views on girls' participation in feminine activities. Similarly, Mussen and Rutherford (1963) reported that fathers of highly feminine girls offered their daughters more encouragement in sex-appropriate activities than did fathers of unfeminine girls. As Block (1973) has stated "The father appears to be a more crucial agent in directing and channeling the sex-typing of the child, both male and female, than has been supposed" (p. 517).

Identification of the father as a crucial figure in the socialization process does not discount the effect of the mother or of both parents together. It has been reported that both parents elicit gross-motor behavior more from their sons than daughters (Lewis, 1972b; Moss, 1967; Tasch, 1952; Yarrow, Rubenstein, & Pederson, Note 3). Parents also react more strongly to male selection of inappropriate (feminine) activity than a girl's selection of a masculine activity (Lansky, 1967), and both parents chose more sex-appropriate activities for their sons than for their daughters (Fling & Manosevitz, 1972). Hartup, Moore, and Sager (1963) have suggested that in general there is more social pressure against inappropriate sex typing for boys than for girls.

Although the peer group has been identified as a major force in socialization, very little information is available regarding its contribution to differential sex-role development or, more specifically, sport-role development (McCandless, 1969). Because the peer group is primarily same-sexed for both male and female children, sex typing logically proceeds along the lines of reinforcing sex-appropriate notions and discounting sex-inappropriate behaviors, many of which have been initiated by the parents. This notion is supported in a recent study by Siman (1977), who suggested that the peer group "acts as a filter for parent norms, where the parent standards of individual group members are compared against an average for parents of group members and reacted to by the individual adolescent on the basis of this comparative appraisal" (p. 272). This peer-group screening probably operates in children's circles as well. In regard to children's sport involvement, the previous sex typing of activities by parents would be compared within the peer group. As the above-cited evidence suggests, such sex typing is generally rigid in the mind of both males and females in terms of play and games, and there should be very little discrepancy. Hence, the sex-typed behavior is generally reinforced by a child's peer group resulting in perpetuation of differential sport participation by males and females.

In summary, the available data suggest that although both parents contribute to the socialization of their children, the father is perhaps the most crucial significant other for both male and female children. Therefore, the father should be the most influential figure in the sport socialization process. In addition, the peer group appears to function as a frame of reference for comparing parental definitions of expected child behavior. As such, one would expect the peer group to exhibit differential reactions to involvement in sport activities which had been previously defined by parents as sex appropriate or sex inappropriate.

PERCEPTION OF SEX ROLES

By the time children reach the age of 6 years, they are able to distinguish male and female roles and identify themselves accordingly (Maccoby & Jacklin, 1974). There is evidence to suggest that sport as a role is also differentiated for the sexes and embraced primarily by males. When elementary-school-aged children ranked a list of desirable school behaviors, girls identified "to be nice" and "to be smart" as the most important, while boys identified "to be good in sports" and "to be a leader" as the most important (Caplan & Kinsbourne, 1974). In a similar vein, Wiggins (1973), investigating self-perceptions and academic aspirations of ninth graders, reported that males perceived themselves as more science and sports-oriented than did females, while the females viewed themselves as more teacher-oriented and more competent in the area of interpersonal relations. Stein, Pohly, and Mueller (1971) also reported that children defined active sports as more masculine than feminine, and masculine games appeared to have more prestige value among children (Lynn, 1959; Rosenberg & Sutton-Smith, 1960). When children in grades 4 through 6 were asked what was the most important attribute for popularity, the boys indicated sports while the girls reported grades (Buchanan, Blankenbaker, & Cotten, 1976). Thus, there were clear indications of considerable sex typing in physical activity and sport. It is therefore not surprising to find differences in sport participation on the basis of sex.

Perhaps the most relevant information regarding sport participation per se is provided by a study currently being sponsored by the State of Michigan (1977). Although the figures are somewhat confounded by failure to control for the number of sports any one subject could report, it is possible to make some sex comparisons within the most popular sports. The most popular sport for males was baseball, with one out of three children participating to some degree. The most popular sport for girls was softball, with one out of five indicating participation. Of more interest, perhaps, is a comparison of the number of males and females who completed a season of either baseball or softball. Whereas 1 in 4 males completed the season, only 1 in 10 females did so. This suggests that although a large number of females are involved in agency-sponsored sports, their persistence in the activity is much less than that of their male counterparts. A second finding of interest was the trend for the participation across age, similar for both males and females. For most of the sports there was a progressive increase in participation up to ages 11, 12, or 13, at which time there was a general but progressive decline through age 17.

One of the key factors in children's participation in an activity appears to be their perception of the sex appropriateness of the activity as defined by their parents (Fling & Manosevitz, 1972; Hartup, Moore, & Sager, 1963; Lansky, 1967; Mussen & Rutherford, 1963). Such perceptions would contribute to defining sport as more a male role than a female role. Although few studies are available which explore the possible effect of such perceptions on sport participation, one study by Montemayor (1974) has demonstrated the potential strength of this influence. In the Montemayor (1974) investigation, children in grades 1 and 2 played with a new game which was labeled as either sex appropriate, neutral, or sex inappropriate. The author reported a significant interaction on performance between the sex of the child and the sex-typing of the game. Males performed slightly better when the game was labeled sex appropriate and the girls' performance in that condition was significantly better than in either the neutral or sex-inappropriate condition.

Because sport participation appears to be perceived as more appropriate for males than for females, it is important to further examine the process by which various activities come to be so defined. Particularly because labeling of an activity appears to influence a child's performance, it is important to explore the extent to which traditional sport activities are perceived as appropriate for the sexes and whether these perceptions might also influence a child's willingness to learn and participate in a sport activity. In addition, it is important to understand which attributes of the person and which characteristics of the activity result in significant others identifying certain activities as more or less appropriate for each sex. Without such information, it is difficult to determine the validity of these definitions and, if invalid, to determine how both parental and child sport-role stereotypes can be modified.

CHILDREN'S SOCIALIZATION INTO SPORT

Very little research has been concerned with the general process by which children are socialized into sport and, more specifically, any systematic differences based on sex. One example, however, was a study by Watson (1975), who investigated male and female participants ages 9 through 12 involved in the Little Athletics program in Australia. He reported that boys identified more strongly with their fathers and girls with their mothers. Girls were also reported to identify more with their coach but less with their peers, while the reverse was found for boys. This suggests that for the boys the father and peers were important socializing agents and for the girls the mother and the coach.

Orlick (Note 4) also identified the parents as instrumental in their children's participation in organized sports. He reported that sons who actively participated in sports usually had parents who were themselves active participants. It was suggested that the parents were acting as role models for the child and that the family reinforced the son's participation in sport activities. Orlick did not consider the importance of parents and family for female participants. However, Snyder and Spreitzer (1976) have reported a positive relationship between parental interest, coaches' encouragement, and the sport participation of high-school-aged females. Similarly, Greendorfer (1974, Note 5) has indicated that a sport-oriented family environment in which parents actually participate in sport appears to be a significant factor in female sport involvement.

Somewhat contrary to the previous findings are data reported by Seagoe (1970) which suggest that the school is the major factor in determining a child's play patterns, particularly in discouraging individual play and promoting competitive team play. The school seemed to emphasize cooperative play more for girls and team play more for boys. As Seagoe (1970) has stated, "The school clearly leads the home and other social agents in fostering socialization in play, particularly beyond the age of eight" (p. 142).

In contrast to the paucity of research available on children's sport socialization, several investigators have studied male Olympic and intercollegiate athletes, utilizing a social learning paradigm as a general framework to identify which social systems contribute to sport-role learning (Kenyon, 1970; McPherson, 1972; Roethlisberger, 1970; Kenyon, Note 6; McPherson, Note 7). These investigations demonstrated that the school is the most influential setting in which male sport socialization takes place. Moreover, data reveal that although peers, coaches, and family are the most influential social systems, such influence may be differential over time, may be sport specific, and may vary according to ethnic or racial background. Unlike the pattern found in males, research on female athletes demonstates that the school is not an important setting (Greendorfer, 1977, Note 5; Lewko & Greendorfer, Note 8). Rather, the school seems to reinforce behavior patterns learned elsewhere. Female athletes appear to be influenced by peers throughout their life cycle, while the role of the family may be significant only during childhood (Greendorfer, 1974).

Despite these differences in the sport-socialization process between the sexes, several patterns reveal striking similarities. For example, male and female athletes begin to participate while quite young (usually around the ages of 6 to 8), tend to come from middle class or above backgrounds, receive positive sanctions or rewards for participation, and are encouraged by a variety of significant others to participate in sport.

From the limited research available it appears that male and female children are socialized differently in terms of sport participation, with parents the primary source of such socialization. However, the dynamics of this process have not been fully explored creating a void in our understanding of the sport-socialization process. Insight into the way that sex types are instilled in early sport socialization could shed some light on the differential participation of boys and girls, thereby providing a basis for promoting greater involvement of both sexes in physical activity and sport. To this end, the following specific hypotheses are stated, based on the previous literature review:

1. The family rather than schools and peers is the most influential social system on children's sport socialization.

2. Parents are more influential than siblings in socializing children into sport.

3. The father is the most relevant significant other in the sport-socialization process, regardless of sex of the child.

4. The school is a more influential social system for boys than for girls.

5. Fathers are the most significant others in typing sport activities as sex appropriate or inappropriate for both boys and girls.

6. Perceived sex appropriateness of a sport activity influences active involvement of both sexes, with females affected more negatively than males.

7. Boys have more rigid perceptions of the sex appropriateness of sport activities than girls do.

8. Sport activities are valued more highly by boys than by girls.

REFERENCE NOTES

1. McPherson, B.D. *The child in competitive sport: Influence of the social milieu.* Paper presented at a symposium on the Child in Competitive Sport: Readiness and Effects, Milwaukee, WI, 1976.
2. Stoll, C., Inbar, M., & Fennessey, J. *Socialization and games: An exploratory study of sex differences* (Report No. 30). Baltimore: The Center for the Study of Social Organization of Schools, The Johns Hopkins University, 1968.
3. Yarrow, L.J., Rubenstein, J.L., & Pedersen, F.A. *Dimensions of early stimulation: Differential effects on infant development.* Paper presented at the meeting of the Society for Research in Child Development, 1971.
4. Orlick, T.D. *Family sports environment and early sports participation.* Paper presented at a meeting of the Fourth Canadian Psychomotor Learning and Sports Psychology Symposium, University of Waterloo, Waterloo, Ontario, 1972.
5. Greendorfer, S.L. *A social learning approach to female sport involvement.* Paper presented at the meeting of the American Psychological Association, Washington, DC, September 1976.
6. Kenyon, G.S. *Explaining sport involvement.* Paper presented at the meeting of the Eastern Association of Physical Education for College Women, Lake Placid, NY, October 1969.
7. McPherson, B.D. *Psychosocial factors accounting for learning the role of tennis and hockey player.* Unpublished study, University of Wisconsin, 1968.
8. Lewko, J., & Greendorfer, S.L. *Family influence and sex differences in children's socialization into sport.* Unpublished study, University of Illinois, 1977.

REFERENCES

ABERLE, D.F., & Naegele, K. Middle-class fathers' occupational role and attitudes toward children. *American Journal of Orthopsychiatry*, 1952, **22**, 366-378.

ALBINSON, J.G., & Andrew, G.M. (Eds.). *Child in sport and physical activity.* Baltimore: University Park Press, 1976.

BARRY, H., III, Bacon, M.K., & Child, I.I. A cross-cultural survey of some sex differences in socialization. *Journal of Abnormal and Social Psychology*, 1957, **55**, 327-332.

BILLER, H.B. Father absence, maternal encouragement, and sex role development in kindergarten-age boys. *Child Development*, 1969, **40**, 539-546.

BILLER, H.B. Father absence and the personality development of the male child. *Developmental Psychology*, 1970, **2**, 181-201.

BLOCK, J.H. Conceptions of sex role: Some cross-cultural and longitudinal perspectives. *American Psychologist*, 1973, **28**, 512-526.

BROWN, D. Sex-role development in a changing culture. *Psychological Bulletin*, 1958, **55**, 232-242.

BUCHANAN, H.T., Blankenbaker, J., & Cotten, D. Academic and athletic ability as popularity factors in elementary school children. *Research Quarterly*, 1976, **47**, 320-325.

-CAPLAN, P.J., & Kinsbourne, M. Sex differences in response to school failure. *Journal of Learning Disabilities*, 1974, **7**, 232-235.

CLARK, A.H., Wyon, S.M., & Richards, M.P. Free-play in nursery school children. *Journal of Child Psychology and Psychiatry and Allied Disciplines*, 1969, **10**, 205-216.

ERIKSON, E.J. Sex differences in the play configurations of preadolescents. *American Journal of Orthopsychiatry*, 1951, **21**, 667-692.

_ FAGOT, F.I. Sex differences in toddlers' behavior and parental reaction. *Developmental Psychology*, 1974, **10**, 554-558.

FAGOT, F.I., & Littman, I. Stability of sex role and play interests from preschool to elementary school. *Journal of Psychology*, 1975, **89**, 285-292.

FLING, S., & Manosevitz, M. Sex typing in nursery school children's play interests. *Developmental Psychology*, 1972, **7**, 146-152.

GOLDBERG, S., & Lewis, M. Play behavior in the year-old infant: Early sex differences. *Child Development*, 1969, **40**, 21-31.

GOODENOUGH, E.W. Interest in persons as an aspect of sex difference in the early years. *Genetic Psychology Monographs*, 1957, **55**, 287-323.

-GREENDORFER, S.L. *The nature of female socialization into sport: A study of selected college women's sport participation.* Unpublished doctoral dissertation, University of Wisconsin, 1974.

GREENDORFER, S.L. Role of socializing agents in female sport involvement. *Research Quarterly*, 1977, **48**, 304-310.

HARPER, L.W., & Sands, K.M. Preschool children's use of space: Sex differences in outdoor play. *Developmental Psychology*, 1975, **11**, 119.

HART, R. *The child's landscape in a New England town.* Unpublished doctoral dissertation, Clark University, Worcester, MA, 1976.

HARTLEY, R. Children's concepts of male and female roles. *Merrill-Palmer Quarterly*, 1959, **6**, 83-91.

HARTUP, W.W., Moore, S.G., & Sager, G. Avoidance of inappropriate sex typing by young children. *Journal of Consulting Psychology*, 1963, **27**, 467-473.

INKELES, A. Society, social structure and child socialization. In J.A. Clausen (Ed.), *Socialization and society*. Boston: Little, Brown, & Co., 1968.

KAGAN, J., & Lewis, M. Studies of attention in the human infant. *Merrill-Palmer Quarterly*, 1965, **11**, 95-127.

KENYON, G.S. The use of path analysis in sport sociology with special reference to involvement socialization. *International Review of Sport Sociology*, 1970, **5**, 191-203.

KENYON, G.S., & McPherson, B.D. Becoming involved in physical activity and sport: A process of socialization. In G.L. Rarick (Ed.), *Physical activity: Human growth and development*. New York: Academic Press, 1973.

KENYON, G.S., & McPherson, B.D. An approach to the study of sport socialization. *International Review of Sport Sociology*, 1974, **9**, 127-138.

LANSKY, L.M. The family structure also affects the model: Sex-role attitudes in parents of preschool children. *Merrill-Palmer Quarterly*, 1967, **13**, 139-150.

LEVER, J. Sex differences in the games children play. *Social Problems*, 1976, **23**, 478-487.

LEWIS, M. Culture and gender roles: There is no unisex in the nursery. *Psychology Today*, May 1972, pp. 54-57. (a)

LEWIS, M. State as an infant-environment interaction: An analysis of mother-infant behavior as a function of sex. *Merrill-Palmer Quarterly*, 1972, **18**, 95-121. (b)

LONG, B.H., & Henderson, E.H. Children's use of time: Some personal and social correlates. *Elementary School Journal*, 1973, **73**, 193-199.

LYNN, D.B. A note on sex differences in the development of masculine and feminine identification. *Psychological Review*, 1959, **66**, 126-135.

MACCOBY, E.E., & Jacklin, C.N. *Psychology of sex differences*. Palo Alto, CA: Stanford University Press, 1974.

MCCANDLESS, B.R. Childhood socialization. In D.A. Goslin (Ed.), *Handbook of socialization theory and research*. Chicago: Rand McNally, 1969.

MCPHERSON, B.D. *Socialization into the role of sport consumer: The construction and testing of a theory and causal model.* Unpublished doctoral dissertation, University of Wisconsin, 1972.

MISCHEL, W. Sex-typing and socialization. In P.H. Mussen (Ed.), *Carmichael's manual of child psychology* (Vol. 2, 3rd ed.). New York: Wiley, 1970.

MONTEMAYOR, R. Children's performance in a game and their attraction to it as a function of sex-typed labels. *Child Development*, 1974, **45**, 152-156.

MOSS, H.A. Sex, age, and state as determinants of mother-infant interaction. *Merrill-Palmer Quarterly*, 1967, **13**, 19-36.

MUSSEN, P.H. Early sex role development. In D.A. Goslin (Ed.), *Handbook of socialization theory and research.* Chicago: Rand McNally, 1969.

MUSSEN, P.H., & Rutherford, E. Parent-child relations and parental personality in relation to young children's sex-role preferences. *Child Development*, 1963, **34**, 589-607.

ORLICK, T., & Botterill, C. *Every kid can win.* Chicago: Nelson-Hall, 1975.

RABINOWITZ, F.M., Moely, B.D., Finkel, N., & Clinton, S. The effects of toy novelty and social interaction on the exploratory behavior of preschool children. *Child Development*, 1975, **46**, 286-289.

ROETHLISBERGER, A. *Socialization into the role of gymnast.* Unpublished master's thesis, University of Wisconsin, 1970.

ROSENBERG, B.G., & Sutton-Smith, B. A revised conception of masculine-feminine differences in play activities. *Journal of Genetic Psychology*, 1960, **96**, 165-170.

ROTHBART, M., & Maccoby, E.E. Parent's differential reactions to sons and daughters. *Journal of Personality and Social Psychology*, 1966, **4**, 237-243.

SAEGERT, S., & Hart, R. The development of environmental competence in girls and boys. *TAASP Newsletter*, 1977, **3**, 8-13.

SEAGOE, M.V. An instrument for the analysis of children's play as an index of degree of socialization. *Journal of School Psychology*, 1970, **8**, 139-144.

SEARS, R.R., Maccoby, E.E., & Levin, H. *Patterns of child rearing.* Evanston, IL: Row, Peterson, 1957.

SEARS, R.R., Rau, L., & Alpert, R. *Identification and child rearing.* Stanford, CA: Stanford University Press, 1965.

SHERIF, C.W., & Rattray, G.D. Psychological development and activity in middle childhood. In J.G. Albinson & G.M. Andrew (Eds.), *Child in sport and physical activity.* Baltimore: University Park Press, 1976.

SIMAN, M.L. Application of a new model of peer group influence to naturally existing adolescent friendship groups. *Child Development,* 1977, **48**, 270-274.

SNYDER, E.E., & Spreitzer, E. Correlates of sport participation among adolescent girls. *Research Quarterly,* 1976, **47**, 804-809.

STANROCK, J.W. Parental absence, sex-typing and identification. *Developmental Psychology,* 1970, **2**, 265-272.

STATE of Michigan. Joint legislative study on youth sports programs. East Lansing, MI: State of Michigan, 1977.

STEIN, A.H., Pohly, S., & Mueller, E. The influence of masculine, feminine and neutral tasks on children's achievement behavior, expectancies of success, and attainment values. *Child Development,* 1971, **42**, 195-208.

SUTTON-SMITH, B., & Rosenberg, B.G. Sixty years of historical change in game preferences of American children. *Journal of American Folklore,* 1961, **74**, 17-46.

SUTTON-SMITH, B., Rosenberg, B.G., & Morgan, E.E. The development of sex differences in play choices during pre-adolescence. *Child Development,* 1963, **34**, 119-126.

TASCH, R.G. The role of the father in the family. *Journal of Experimental Education,* 1952, **20**, 319-361.

WARD, W.D. Variance of sex-role preference among boys and girls. *Psychological Reports,* 1968, **23**, 467-470.

WATSON, G.G. Sex role socialization and the competitive process in Little Athletics. *The Australian Journal of Health, Physical Education and Recreation,* 1975, **70**, 10-21.

WIGGINS, R.G. Differences in self-perceptions of ninth grade boys and girls. *Adolescence,* 1973, **8**, 491-496.

ZOBLE, J. Femininity and achievement in sports. In D.V. Harris (Ed.), *Women and sport: A national research conference* (HPER series, No. 2). University Park: Pennsylvania State University, 1973.

CHAPTER 20

SOCIAL DETERMINANTS OF VIOLENCE IN HOCKEY: A REVIEW

Michael D. Smith

I don't see any violence in two players dropping their gloves and letting a little steam escape. I think that's a lot better than spearing somebody. I think it's an escape valve because you know yourself pressure builds up and there's no way to release it and if fighting is not allowed then another violent act will occur (NHL player, circa 1977).

Surely this is hockey's most durable folk theory: that the speed and body contact—the very nature of the game—causes an accumulation of aggressive impulses (usually described as "frustration") which must be released, if not one way, then another, and that prohibiting fist-fighting would result in more vicious and dangerous illegal use of the stick. The majority of professional and amateur players appears to believe this; so do their fans (Smith, 1979a). The 1,256-page transcript of the McMurtry (Note 1) inquiry into violence in Ontario amateur hockey is packed with this kind of testimony for the "defense."

But this "theory" is based more on faith than on fact. Regarding the notion, first, that violence (defined in this paper as any physical assault proscribed by the official rules) is an inevitable by-product of the game: Large team and individual differences in amounts of violence are evident at all levels of hockey. If violence were inherent in hockey, surely

This article is a slightly modified version of one that originally appeared in the *Canadian Journal of Applied Sport Sciences*, 1979, **4**(1), 76-82. Copyright 1979 by the Journal of Applied Sport Sciences. Reprinted with permission.

violence would be more evenly distributed throughout it, in Canada and elsewhere. Would one argue that the notorious Birmingham Bulls of the World Hockey Association get more penalties than other teams because they get more frustrated? Or that the Bulls are somehow compelled to respond to frustration with aggression, while other teams are not? Shaky logic, at best. Hockey may well have its frustrating moments (what sport does not?), but as researchers have repeatedly shown, human beings may or may not respond to frustration with aggression. Like most behavior, responses to frustration are shaped by culture and learning. "Frustration" seems more an excuse for, than a cause of, violent behavior in hockey.

The safety-valve corollary, that fisticuffs provide a relatively safe outlet for aggression, is based on the notion of catharsis. The weight of scientific evidence, however, is against the catharsis hypothesis. Behaving aggressively, or watching others behave aggressively, tends to lead to more, not less, aggression (Goranson, 1976, Note 2). Putting a stop to fist fighting may indeed lead to an increase in illegal stick work, as hockey insiders claim, but not for the reason implied: that those aggressive feelings just have to come out; rather, at most levels of the sport players learn that violence, by fist *or* stick, pays, in one way or another. As long as violence pays more than it costs, it will continue.

To answer the questions of how violence pays and how players learn that it pays, the *real* determinants of hockey violence must be examined. Research indicates these lie in (a) the social organization of the hockey "system," (b) the ways in which the communications media portray the professional game, and (c) the attitudes of players' reference others, especially parents, coaches, and teammates.

THE SOCIAL ORGANIZATION OF HOCKEY

Canadian boys typically enter organized hockey around age 7. The ablest are quickly funnelled into highly competitive "select" leagues and begin a training at the end of which, around 16, those who have remained emerge, as Vaz (1976) puts it, a "tough fighting unit prepared for violence whose primary objective is to win hockey games" (p. 212). Fighting and other illegal forms of assault (though not hard body contact) tend to be discouraged among younger boys, but around 13 to 14 years of age the criteria for player evaluation begin to change, for it is then that potential for junior professional and professional hockey is thought to reveal itself. By Midget age (i.e., 15) coaches are looking for players who can mete out, and withstand, illegal physical coercion; indeed, some youngsters this age are upwardly mobile primarily because they are good fighters (Smith, 1979c).

These are qualities appreciated by North America's roughly 50 professional teams, which depend upon professionalized minor hockey for a steady output of talent and to whose ranks most of the best players aspire. Because motivation is strong to advance to higher level minor teams, then to junior professional (or American college, now professional hockey's second ranking source of supply), and then to the big leagues, and because the number of these teams progressively diminishes, competition for positions is fierce. The structure of the system compels aspirants to conform increasingly to prevailing occupational standards, which include the necessity of employing at least a minimum amount of what might be called "force-threat" (Goode, 1975).

The influence of the professional game is weaker in house leagues, but it is still present. Decades of mass media consumption have helped stamp the professional imprint more or less on all Canadian hockey.

MASS MEDIA PORTRAYALS OF PROFESSIONAL HOCKEY

Consumption of professional hockey, via newspapers and television, in particular, is voracious. Fifty-three percent of minor and junior professional performers in Toronto, and 39% of their nonplaying peers, read about hockey in the newspapers daily. Almost 70% of these players and 60% of the nonplayers watch televised professional hockey at least once a week (Smith, 1978a). It may be that hockey players are attracted to violent sports in general. A study prepared for the Royal Commission on Violence in the Communications Industry reports that 152 hockey-playing children and youths watched more aggressive sports on television than did youngsters participating in, in this case, baseball (McCabe & Moriarty, 1975). Two other Royal Commission studies found that newspaper, television, and radio sports news in Ontario did not report undue amounts of violence (Gordon & Ibson, 1975; Gordon & Siner, 1975), but this research was conducted at the end of May when little or no hockey is played, and neither study addressed itself to the tone of that violence which was presented.

The proportion of media-mediated hockey violence that could be said to have a pro-violence slant is not known, but unquestionably the media not infrequently convey the idea that fighting and the like is acceptable, even desirable, behavior.[1] Indicators of media acceptance include attention-grabbing newspaper pictures of fights, radio and television reminiscences about famous brawls of the past, and newspaper and magazine articles overtly or covertly glorifying tough guys. Regarding

---

[1]Comiskey, Bryant, and Zillmann (1977) demonstrate, in a laboratory study, that sportscasters' commentary stressing rough play (in a hockey videotape) (a) increases the perceived entertainment value of the action for viewers and (b) makes "normal" play appear rough.

the celebrated Gordie Howe, for instance, on the occasion of his 50th birthday:

> It's not as if he plays some Caspar Milquetoast game, shying from the corners, relying on speed and finesse. He is of the generation that disdains the now accepted protection of helmets and he never was one to skate from a fight. After he was nearly killed from a check into the boards by Ted Kennedy of Toronto Maple Leafs—a skull operation saved his life—he returned as one who knows it is better to give than to receive, that retribution is best administered quickly and decisively. With Lou Fontinato of New York Rangers he participated in what many regard as the greatest hockey fight in the history of the NHL. Fontinato was the terror of the league then, intimidating everyone, pulverizing even the mighty Rocket Richard, but Howe destroyed him in that fight. He broke his nose, splattered Fontinato's blood over his face and jersey, and Fontinato never was as terrifying again. (O'Malley, p. 40, 1977)

The net result of this sort of coverage is, at least, to condone violence, at most, to glorify it.

Do young players actually learn from professionals how to commit acts of assault? Research suggests that conditions for learning hockey violence via television, for example, are almost ideal (see Goranson, 1975, pp. 4-5). In a study of 83 high school players, those who perceived their favorite NHL performers (and most had favorites) as rough and tough received more assaultive penalties in a season's play than those who chose less violent models (Smith, 1974; also see Russell, Note 3). More specifically, in a sample survey of 604 Toronto minor and junior professional players, which will be referred to frequently in the following pages,[2] the interviewees were asked if they had "ever learned how to hit another player illegally in any way from watching pro hockey?" Fifty-six percent responded "yes," then gave detailed descriptions of what they had learned, summaries of which are shown in Table 1.

When asked how many times during the season they had actually used one or more of these tactics, 60% said "at least once or twice." Official game records verified players' responses; those who claimed they performed these acts received significantly more major and minor penalties than those who said they did not.

It would be misleading, however, to point to professional hockey, with its media cheerleaders, as the sole source of violence in youth hockey, for a climate of violence approval permeates the latter environment. The extent to which this is so is considered next.

REFERENCE OTHERS' INFLUENCE

Reference others, in general, are persons and groups who help orient the individual in some way in a course of action or in attitude. Normative

---

[2]Unless otherwise indicated, the remainder of the data presented in the paper are based on this research; these data are either unpublished or in Smith (1978a, 1979a, 1979b, 1979c).

Table 1
Examples of Illegal Hitting Learned from
Watching Professional Hockey

I learned spearing and butt-ending.

You sort of go on your side like turning a corner and trip him with a skate.

Charging. You skate towards another guy who doesn't have the puck and knock him down. Or coming up from behind and knocking him down.

Sneaky elbows, little choppy slashes Bobby Clarke style.

Hitting at weak points with the stick, say at the back of the legs.

Coming up from behind and using your stick to hit the back of his skates and trip him.

Butt-end, spearing, slashing, high sticking, elbow in the head.

Put the elbow just a bit up and get him in the gut with your stick.

Along the boards, if a player is coming along you angle him off by starting with your shoulder then bring up your elbow.

The way you "bug" in front of the net.

Clipping. Taking the guy's feet out by sliding underneath.

Sticking the stick between their legs. Tripping as they go into the boards.

I've seen it and use it: when you check a guy, elbow him. If you get in a corner you can hook or spear him without getting caught.

Giving him a shot in the face as he's coming up to you. The ref can't see the butt-ends.

How to trip properly.

Like Gordie Howe, butt-ends when the ref isn't looking.

others, in particular, provide the individual with a guide to action by advocating norms of conduct, usually through some expression of approval or disapproval. Research indicates that parents, coaches, and teammates are especially significant for young hockey players in this regard and that players' perceptions of these others' approval or disapproval of violence affect players' behavior.

Parents

One of the obligations of parents is to transmit to their son(s) male standards of behavior, some of which promote physical aggression. This aspect of the male role may be most salient in lower socioeconomic environments (e.g., Dietz, 1978) but cuts to some degree across class lines (Baker & Ball, 1969). Parents communicate their attitudes regarding violence directly and indirecty, by word, gesture, and deed, often in the name of child-rearing.

To what extent do parents of amateur hockey players approve of violence? Table 2 presents the responses of 604 randomly selected players (age 12 to 21, at the house-league, select, Junior B, and Junior A levels) to questions about their parents' and others' approval of fighting. The boys were asked if they thought these others would approve of a minor hockey player punching another player in four situations: (a) if ridiculed, (b) if threatened, (c) if shoved, (d) if punched by the other player. Table 2 shows variations in players' responses to these items, by age and level of competition. Only the percentages of players who thought their reference others would approve in *at least three* of the situations—the high approvers—are reported (Smith, 1979c).

Mothers, followed by fathers, clearly are least approving of hockey fighting. Overall, only 4% of the former and 16% of the latter were seen as high approvers. But approval increases sharply with age and level of competition; though only 3% of 12-13-year olds saw their fathers as high approvers, 41% of 18-21-year olds viewed their fathers as such. In short, a significant number of older boys, particularly those in select leagues, perceive considerable approval for fighting from their fathers. The data are not shown here, but fathers' socioeconomic status and educational attainment are only weakly related to fathers' violence approval.

To understand parents' perspectives, it helps to grasp the intensity of most parents' emotional involvement in their progeny's hockey, especially in the case of younger boys in highly competitive leagues. First, most parents are avid watchers. Sixty-one percent of the above fathers attended their sons' games at least once a week; 75% attended at least two

Table 2
Players' Perceptions of Their Reference Others' Approval of Hockey Fighting (in percent)

	Mothers' Approval	Fathers' Approval	Coaches' Approval	Teammates' Approval
Age				
12-13	3	3	9	54
14-15	3	9	11	61
16-17	5	22	25	70
18-21	7	41	52	78
Level of Competition				
House-league	0	6	8	59
Select	8	29	36	71

or three times a month. Nineteen percent watched practices at least once a week and 27% at least two or three times a month.

Qualitative data help convey the nature of parents' involvement. Typically families arrive at the arena anywhere from 1 hour to ½ hour before a game, and while the players dress, parents stand in the lobby talking, usually about hockey. Some wear team insignia (jackets, scarves, hats, buttons). During the game most sit together, distinctly apart from opposing parents. As the action unfolds on the ice, in the stands bodies strain, faces contort, people jump to their feet. Organized cheering and spontaneous bursts of applause are frequent. Immersion in the game is total and attuned principally to the performance of one's son. Booing and catcalls are directed sometimes at opposing players, frequently at referees. Occasionally groups of rival parents engage in unfriendly verbal exchanges; fights are not unknown. The more important and exciting the game, the greater the likelihood of this sort of (mis)behavior.[3]

Hitting, or "taking the body," usually elicits shouts of approval; this is regarded as a sign of "desire" and of "character." A conversation between two fathers at a Minor Peewee (age 11) game went like this: "Stick checks, never body checks," exclaimed the first, disgustedly. Then, yelling, "Take the body, for Chrissakes!" Father two: "Boy, little Ian isn't afraid to hit." Verbal promptings for legal hitting often extend to the encouragement of semilegal acts, and sometimes to fighting and more extreme behaviors.

Fisticuffs also appear to be character-building in the eyes of some parents who see hockey as a training ground for later life. One father, an official in a minor hockey organization, put it this way: "It's a violent society, eh? This is a tough society we're in. I put my own kid in hockey so he would learn to take his lumps." He said he saw "nothing wrong with taking off the gloves" and that "the day they turn hockey into a namby pamby game for sissies is the day I get out." Consider this arena lobby scene after an Atom (10-year-olds) game which featured a multiplayer semifight (real fights start about age 12 and increase with age in frequency and ferocity): Two of the combatants approach a group of parents; the father of one says, smiling, "Looks like we've got a couple of scrappers." Following is a dialogue tape-recorded at a party for Bantam parents.

Parent one (father): "There's nothing wrong with a good fist fight in hockey as long as everyone drops their gloves and sticks first. Having skates on is the great equalizer anyway. No one is really going to get hurt during a hockey fight. If the referees see

---

[3]See Russell and Drewry (1976) and Smith (1978b) for data on relationships between hockey players and spectators in general.

that one guy is killing another guy they'll step in and break it up fast enough."
Parent two (mother): "I agree. The fights seem to do some good. The boys get it out
of their systems and they usually end up playing better hockey in the long run."
Parent three (father): "I think if the boys had dropped their gloves earlier in the
game the other night that number 5 wouldn't have gone after Joey with his stick."
Parent four (father): "That's the sad part now. Kids today don't know how to get
the gloves off and get the fists up. Everyone is hitting everyone else with their sticks.
I think fighting with the fist is a good way to toughen a boy up. He's got to learn to
take his lumps as well as give them out. The problem is that everyone in hockey is
too sneaky now. They hit you when you're not expecting it. I haven't seen a good
fist fighter in two years in this league."

Can it be demonstrated empirically that parents' attitudes regarding
fighting and the like are related to their children's attitudes and
behavior? Yes. Fathers' sanctions for a variety of illegal, aggressive acts
have been statistically related to their sons' attitudes regarding the same
acts (Clark et al., 1978); and fathers' approval of fighting has been
statistically related to the number of fights their sons are in over a
season's play (Smith, 1979c). The more violence approval, the more
violence.

Coaches

To what extent do coaches approve of violence? Almost all of 83 high
school players stated their coaches would approve (most of them strongly) of "hard but legal bodychecking" (Smith, 1975); over half of approximately 2,000 boys who filled out questionnaires for Vaz and Thomas
(1974; also see Clark et al., 1978; Vaz, 1976) reported their coaches
regularly "emphasized playing rough and being aggressive." This is not
surprising; body contact is a legitimate part of the game. What of *illegal*
assaults? Table 2 reveals that minor hockey players see coaches as somewhat more approving of fighting than fathers; still, only 16% of all
coaches come under the high approval heading. But this figure obscures
age and house-league/select differences. Over 50% of 18-21-year olds
and 36% of select-leaguers see their coaches as high approvers.

Field data suggest that coaches, like fathers, encourage physically aggressive play, including fighting and other illegal acts sometimes, both
for what it symbolizes (character) and for its utility in winning hockey
games. Since their careers (or at least their self-images) in most professionalized minor hockey depend to some degree on producing winning
teams, coaches tend to choose players on the basis of size and toughness,
among other attributes.[4] Almost from the start, big kids who can handle

[4]For data on amateur coaches' motives for, and attitudes about, coaching, and their background characteristics, see Albinson (1976) and McPherson (Note 4, Note 5).

heavy going are selected over smaller, less aggressive, though sometimes more skilled performers. By 13 or 14, a boy's willingness and ability to hit are highly important in determining his upward mobility, as this pregame "pep talk" suggests:

> I hope you guys realize if you don't start playing better hockey you've probably reached the end of the line at this level. From here on things are a lot tougher. I was talking to Metcalfe (the Midget coach) and he said that right now he figures there are only two guys on this club who can make it in Midget. He saw the way you guys were pushed around by Nats the other night and said there was no way that kind of stuff goes in Midget. You realize that there are only four guys from that club moving up next year and probably a couple of guys will get cut. So at most there are only likely to be six openings, and that's not counting anyone he recruits. You can see that if you hope to move on next year, you've got to start showing some hustle. Teams have just been walking by our defense all year without being touched. We've gotta start knocking them on their cans. Guys know they don't have to keep their heads up when they come into our end.

Legal hitting almost always leads to the penalty-getting kind of hitting, for the line between the two is often fine. Coaches do not approve of penalties per se, of course, but accept a certain number as a consequence of spirited, aggressive play and ever present "frustration." Then there is the "good penalty." "You should have tripped him," said a house-league coach to a wide-eyed boy, 8. "*Never* let a guy go around you." The majority of minor hockey coaches also expect players to retaliate to flagrant fouls; a few tolerate, even nurture, "goons," or "animals," as young as 14 in some professionalized minor leagues. In Junior B and A ranks, this is standard practice. The adolescent bully is certainly not a recent phenomenon, but his sponsorship by adults on the scale evident in youth hockey may be somewhat unique.

Many minor leagues also have their so-called "crazies," a small but obtrusive minority of coaches who habitually lose their poise in stressful situations. To illustrate: As the buzzer sounded to end a penalty-filled Peewee game, one boy appeared to spear another in the stomach. The coaches began shouting at one another as the teams left the ice. Coach A: "What the hell's the matter with you guys. You beat us five-nothing and now you want to take one of our players out for the season." Coach B: "Ah, shut up and go home you goddam crybaby." Coaches and players filed together down a corridor toward the dressing rooms. Coach A said to the player who was speared: "You have my permission to go and punch the shit out of that son-of-a-bitch," indicating the other player. The first player threw down his stick and gloves, charged his opponent, and began pummeling him from behind. Surprised, the latter went down, his assailant on top, punching. Coach B attempted to pull him off. Coach A pushed coach B. A short, shoving match ensued which was broken up by bystanders.

Professional coaches appear to have much the same attitudes about violence as their amateur counterparts. The professional coach, of course, must concern himself above all with producing a winning team and filling seats. To do this, certain player types are required, among them tough, combative "grinders" who can win the physical battles for the puck and who can fight if necessary. Also needed is at least one "policeman," "enforcer," "hit man," "cement head," or "designated fighter" (these roles are not exactly the same). Professional coaches, and players, accept this as a fact of hockey life. But coaches, NHL players say, do not expect everybody to be a fighter, or even to be highly physically aggressive, if it is not their "nature" (and if they compensate with other valuable skills). There are minimum requirements, however: You must help teammates in trouble; you cannot let opponents' attempts at intimidation affect your performance (cf. Faulkner, 1974; Smith, 1979c; Vaz, 1977, 1978).

Coaches' sanctions have an impact on performers' conduct at all levels of hockey. Vaz and Thomas (1974) report statistically significant associations in all age divisions between coaches' emphasis on "playing rough and being aggressive" and players' approval of taking out opposing players "any way you can." Smith (1979c) has shown that the more coaches approve of fighting the more players fight, and the more major penalties they receive (also see Clark et al., 1978).

Players

The importance of peers in understanding violence in fighting gangs, "subcultures of violence," and in a variety of sporting and nonsporting occupations is a constant theme in sociological literature. Getting and keeping colleagues' respect is what counts; toughness, willingness to scrap—these are what earn respect.

For hockey players, this ethos begins to emerge around age 12, when some leagues become rough indeed. Youngsters begin to evaluate one another's gameness. Reputations are being forged. By 14, most boys are well versed in the informal norms that regulate the use of violence. Deviants, "chickens," suffer varying degrees of contempt, depending on how well they compensate for lack of heart with other attributes. At 16, some players are veteran brawlers; others have developed extensive repertoires of dirty tricks. Tough talk—the hockey violence argot—is *de rigueur*.

Players' perceptions of their teammates' approval of fighting are shown in Table 2. In every row, the data indicate that a majority of performers saw their teammates as highly approving. Not shown are players' own attitudes regarding fighting; these in fact are significantly less supportive of violence than those imputed to teammates, though more supportive of violence than coaches' attitudes. Private sentiment is one thing; performance in the presence of peers is another. As players get older, however, and increasingly socialized into the occupational culture, attitudes toward violence tend to come into line. Also, as the less pro-violent get older, they quit hockey at increasingly faster rates than the more pro-violent, some altogether, others going from select to house-league. In other words, socialization and selection processes operate jointly to produce relative homogeneity in the way performers feel about violence (cf. Russell, 1974).

Youngsters learn early what is required to get ahead. The statements shown in Table 3 were presented to Smith's 604 interviewees, who were asked if they agreed or disagreed that the statements applied in their leagues. Table 3 reveals that agreement was widespread and increased sharply with age; furthermore, house-leaguers, who made up 54% of the total sample, reduce the percentages in the Peewee through Juvenile divisions.

Perhaps of greater interest is whether players would *prefer* less fighting and other sorts of illegal rough play. The above were asked: "Would you like to see more, about the same, or less fist-fighting in your games?" Forty-five percent said "less." When asked, "Would you like to see more, about the same, or less illegal stick work in your games?", 82% said "less" (also see McCabe and Moriarty, 1975). How many boys quit

Table 3
Players' Agreement With Statements Regarding the
Utility of Violence (in percent)

	Minor Midget through Juvenile (N = 169)	PeeWee through Bantam (N = 313)	Junior B and Junior A (N = 122)
If you want to get personal recognition in hockey it helps to play rough. People in hockey look for this.	52	70	88
Roughing up the other team might mean getting a few penalties, but in the long run it often helps you win.	51	64	74
Most people in hockey don't respect a player who will not fight when he is picked on.	31	42	59
To be successful, most hockey teams need at least one or two tough guys who are always ready to fight.	43	57	84

hockey because of violence? This question has yet to be adequately answered, but more than a few, one would suspect.

Interviews with 60 NHL players indicate that the large majority views much of what we have called violence as merely part of the job. They use the word "violence" for only the most potentially, or actually, injurious acts, usually involving the stick. Fist-fights are not big deals because no one gets hurt, they say. Even "goons," or designated fighters, seem to be tolerated, if not always highly esteemed. Asked how they felt about someone like Dave Schultz, at one time professional hockey's preeminent pugilist, most of the professionals responded like this one:

> I've got nothing against Schultz because he's trying to make a living and it's not his fault that he's there in Philadelphia. That's the type of player they wanted there and he's that type of guy so they put him in there and he's going to do the job. If they're paying you eighty or a hundred thousand a year, or whatever, it's pretty hard to turn that down.

Only ultraviolence is "violence" in the world of big league hockey. A veteran goalie explained:

> Let me tell you what violence is. Violence is when the guy is standing there and he gives you a spear, OK, and you don't think anything of it, but you just hammer him over the head with a stick and down he goes. He's unconscious for five minutes. That might be violence. What do you get? You get a five minute penalty. I know, because it happened to me. A guy came up and speared me. Standing in the goal crease, he speared me. I just upped and hammered him over the head with my goal stick.

Stick work of this sort is generally feared and hated by players but occurs nonetheless. When lesser assaults are tolerated and encouraged, more serious ones inevitably follow, albeit much less frequently because of their greater costs (see Cullen & Cullen, 1975).

The NHL players were asked how they and their teammates react to someone who refuses to fight when challenged. About half were unequivocal: "I'd rather see a guy fight and lose than turn his cheek and not fight at all, and I think a lot of the players are like that. You pretty well realize that you have to fight, otherwise the guys look down on you." The nonfighter threatens group cohesiveness. "You get a couple of guys trying to beat you up, you know he's not going to be there to help you out. That's a big thing. You don't look at these guys with much respect really." The other half stated that fighting per se is not required, but a player at least has to be willing to grapple with a man in a melee to prevent ganging-up, and has to be tough enough to withstand opponents' coercive tactics. These are also coaches' requirements and they apply as well in minor professional hockey (Faulkner, 1974).

As for those whose role is to start fights, the professionals talk about two main types. Both are supposed to (a) protect weaker teammates, (b) lift their team by drubbing an opponent, and (c) intimidate opposing players, stars especially. But they go about their tasks differently. The "cement head," or "goon," does not adhere to the "rules" of fighting and is thus feared and disliked for his unpredictability and potential to injure, though more so by opponents than teammates who stand to benefit by the havoc he wreaks. The "honest" policeman can be divided into two subtypes. Both basically adhere to the rules of fighting; both are respected, even admired. The first looks for fights—anyone, anytime—never avoiding a potentially faster gun. The second fights infrequently, but his menacing reputation acts as a deterrent on those who might think of challenging him, or one of his teammates.

Hockey players approve of violence, it seems, to the extent that its use brings respect (expressive violence) and works as a game tactic (instrumental violence), individually and collectively (see McCarthy & Kelly, 1978). Analytically separate, these two uses merge empirically, each reinforcing the other, and although instrumental violence becomes increasingly salient as players learn the occupational culture, expressive violence remains important. Even when counterproductive in terms of winning, players—grown men—cling to rituals of fighting left behind by most males in the schoolyard.

CONCLUSION

Research indicates that the main sources of hockey violence are social. The organization of the "system," the ways in which the professional game is portrayed in the mass media, the attitudes of players' reference others—all contribute to a social environment in which users of violence perceive that its rewards, by and large, outweigh its costs. It follows that reversing the reward/cost ratio would lead to less violence, assuming this is desirable. Sporadic efforts in this direction have been made, most of them aimed at punishing offenders. Is increasingly heavy-handed disciplinary action the answer (e.g., Rapport Néron, Note 6)? Alternatively, could a scheme be devised whereby "good" behavior is *in fact* rewarded more than "bad" (e.g., Vaz, 1979)? This sort of question is more easily asked than answered, but a solid foundation of research now makes informed attempts at the latter at least possible.

REFERENCE NOTES

1. McMurtry, W.R. *Investigation and inquiry into violence in amateur hockey*. Report to the Honourable René Brunelle, Ontario Minister of Community and Social Services. Toronto: Ontario Government Bookstore, 1974.

2. Goranson, R.E. *Sports violence and the catharsis hypothesis.* Paper presented at the Canadian Society for Psychomotor Learning and Sport Psychology Conference: Symposium on Violence, Toronto, November 1978.
3. Russell, G.W. *Hero selection by Canadian ice hockey players: Skill or aggression?* Paper presented at the Third Biennial Meeting of the International Society for Research on Aggression, Washington, September 1978.
4. McPherson, B.D. *Career patterns of a voluntary role: The minor hockey coach.* Paper presented at the Canadian Sociological and Anthropological Association Annual Meetings, Toronto, August 1974.
5. McPherson, B.D. *The social milieu of minor hockey in Canada: A review and analysis.* Paper prepared for the Technical Advisory Committee of the Canadian Amateur Hockey Association, 1974.
6. Rapport Néron. *Rapport du comité d'étude sur la violence au hockey.* Editeur officiel du Quebec, 1283 Ouest Boulevard Charest, Quebec, 1978.

REFERENCES

ALBINSON, J.G. The "professional orientation" of the amateur hockey coach. In R.S. Gruneau & J.G. Albinson (Eds.), *Canadian sport: Sociological perspectives.* Don Mills: Addison-Wesley, 1976.

BAKER, R., & Ball, S.J. *Violence and the media.* Washington, DC: United States Government Printing Office, 1969.

CLARK, W.J., Vaz, E., Vetere, V., & Ward, T.A. Illegal aggression in minor hockey: A causal model. In F. Landry & W. Orban (Eds.), *Ice hockey: Research, development and new concepts.* Miami: Symposium Specialists, 1978.

COMISKEY, P., Bryant, J., & Zillmann, D. Commentary as a substitute for action. *Journal of Communication,* 1977, **27**(2), 150-153.

CULLEN, J.B., & Cullen, Jr., F.T. The structural and contextual conditions of group norm violation: Some implications from the game of ice hockey. *International Review of Sport Sociology,* 1975, **2**(10), 69-78.

DIETZ, M.L. The violent subculture: The genesis of violence. In M.A. Beyer Gammon (Ed.), *Violence in Canada.* Toronto: Methuen, 1978.

FAULKNER, R.R. On respect and retribution: Toward an ethnography of violence. *Sociological Symposium,* 1973, **9**, 17-36.

FAULKNER, R.R. Making violence by doing work: Selves, situations, and the world of professional hockey. *Sociology of Work and Occupations,* 1974, **1**, 288-312.

GOODE, W.J. Force and violence in the family. In S.K. Steinmetz & M.A. Straus (Eds.), *Violence in the family*. New York: Dodd Mead, 1975.

GORANSON, R.E. Television violence effects: Issues and evidence. In *Report of the Royal Commission on Violence in the Communications Industry* (Vol. 5). Toronto: Ministry of Government Services, 1975.

GORDON, D.R., & Ibson, L. Content analysis of the news media: Radio. In *Report of the Royal Commission on Violence in the Communications Industry* (Vol. 3). Toronto: Ministry of Government Services, 1975.

GORDON, D.R., & Siner, B. Content analysis of the news media: Newspapers and television. In *Report of the Royal Commission on Violence in the Communications Industry* (Vol. 5). Toronto: Ministry of Government Services, 1975.

MCCABE, A., & Moriarty, D. Studies of television and youth sports. In *Report of the Royal Commission on Violence in the Communications Industry* (Vol. 5). Toronto: Ministry of Government Services, 1976.

MCCARTHY, J., & Kelly, B. Aggressive behaviour and its effects on performance over time in ice hockey athletes: An archival study. *The International Journal of Sport Psychology*, 1978, **9**(2), 90-96.

O'MALLEY, M. Some day they'll retire Gordie Howe's sweater—If, of course, he takes it off. *McLeans*, December 20, 1977, **4**, 40.

RUSSELL, G.W. Machiavellianism, locus of control, aggression, performance and precautionary behaviour in ice hockey. *Human Relations*, 1974, **27**(9), 825-837.

RUSSELL, G.W., & Drewry, B.R. Crowd size and competitive aspects of aggression in ice hockey: An archival study. *Human Relations*, 1976, **29**(8), 723-735.

SMITH, M.D. Significant others' influence on the assaultive behaviour of young hockey players. *International Review of Sport Sociology*, 1974, **3-4**(9), 45-56.

SMITH, M.D. The legitimation of violence: Hockey players' perceptions of their reference groups' sanctions for assault. *The Canadian Review of Sociology and Anthropology*, 1975, **12** (March), 72-80.

SMITH, M.D. From professional to youth hockey violence: The role of the mass media. In M.A. Beyer Gammon (Ed.), *Violence in Canada.* Toronto: Methuen, 1978. (a)[5]

SMITH, M.D. Precipitants of crowd outbursts. *Sociological Inquiry,* 1978, **48**(2), 121-131. (b)

SMITH, M.D. Hockey violence. *Canadian Dimension,* 1979, **13**(6), 42-45. (a)[6]

SMITH, M.D. Hockey violence: A test of the violent subculture thesis. *Social Problems,* 1979, **27**(2), 235-247. (b)

SMITH, M.D. Towards an explanation of hockey violence: A reference-other approach. *The Canadian Journal of Sociology,* 1979, **4**(2), 105-124. (c)

VAZ, E.W. The culture of young hockey players: Some initial observations. In A. Yiannakis, T.D. McIntyre, M.J. Melnick, & D.P. Hart (Eds.), *Sport sociology: Contemporary themes.* Dubuque, IA: 1976.

VAZ, E.W. Institutionalized rule violation and control in professional hockey: Perspectives and control systems. *The Canadian Association for Health, Physical Education and Recreation Journal,* 1977, **3**(3), 6 ff.

VAZ, E.W. Institutionalized rule violation and control in organized Minor League hockey. *The Canadian Journal of Applied Sport Sciences,* 1979, **4**, 1.

VAZ, E.W., & Thomas, D. What price victory? An analysis of minor hockey league players' attitudes towards winning. *International Review of Sport Sociology,* 1974, **2**(9), 33-53.

---

[5]A longer version of this article appears in F.L. Smoll and R.E. Smith (Eds.), *Psychological Perspectives in Youth Sports,* Washington: Hemisphere, 1978, under the title "Social Learning of Violence in Minor Hockey."

[6]This article also appears in W.F. Straub (Ed.), *Sport Psychology: An Analysis of Athlete Behavior,* Ithaca, New York, under the title "Hockey Violence: Interring Some Myths."

Dance as a Theatre Art

SOURCE READINGS IN DANCE HISTORY FROM 1581 TO THE PRESENT

EDITED WITH COMMENTARY BY

Selma Jeanne Cohen

DODD, MEAD & COMPANY
New York · 1974

PREFACE

The idea for this anthology came from dance-book editor Nancy Reynolds, who thought to ask some teachers of dance history what kind of book they wanted for their classes. At the same time, I was struggling with the problem of making materials available for my students in survey courses at Connecticut College and the New York University School of the Arts, where my alternatives were either utter frustration or astronomical Xeroxing bills. The library might have a single copy of an important work; many of the most valuable books were out of print or had never been translated into English; wonderful articles lay hidden away in old periodicals. Despite entreaties, I did not want to produce still another one-volume overview, skimming the evolution of dance from the caveman to the present and cheating the student who had a right to learn from original texts. The answer had to be an anthology of primary sources.

Because I planned these readings to serve a single, introductory course, I limited their scope severely. And rather than presenting the student with a multitude of tidbits, I chose fewer but more substantial pieces, believing that intensive study yields greater understanding, which can then be applied to whatever other texts the reader wishes to pursue. The introductions provide continuity as well as historical background for the various periods; the bibliography suggests possibilities for further exploration.

I am particularly indebted to Miss Reynolds, who waited so patiently for me to complete this work and never ceased to believe in its importance. I am grateful to Edwin Binney 3rd, Mary-Jean Cowell, Angelika Gerbes, Leonore Loft, Patricia McAndrew, and Julia Sutton for providing heretofore unpublished English translations. I made extensive use of the Dance Collection of The New York Public Library and want to thank its curator, Genevieve Oswald, and her staff, especially Barbara Palfy, for their constant support. For help in locating materials I am grateful to Jack Anderson, Mary Clarke, George Dorris, Gladys Laskey, and John Wiley. Dorine Waszkiewicz typed the introductions from my barely legible drafts. John E. Mueller, The University of Rochester; Christena L. Schlundt, University of California, Riverside; and Shirley Wynne, the

Ohio State University, read the manuscript and made valuable suggestions for its improvement.

Most of all I want to thank those of my students who have gone on to
develop their own courses in dance history, creating a constituency that
did not exist when I started.

SELMA JEANNE COHEN

CONTENTS

Introduction

THE EVOLUTION
OF THEATRE DANCE

We cannot know precisely when man began to dance, but we may surmise that it was sometime in the dawn of prehistory.

In nearly all surviving tribal cultures we find dances that are not merely spontaneous outbursts of feeling—jumps of joy or stamps of anger—but patterned, rhythmical sequences, performed in a special place and designed to make a particular impression on the spectators. Most often the place is just a clearing in the grass, and the spectators are the gods whom the dancer beseeches to make the rain fall, the crops grow, the tribe increase. From these rituals, with no stage and no human audience, how did theatrical dance evolve?

We can see one instance of the development with some clarity. The most widely accepted view of the origin of the Greek theatre traces it to the Dithyramb, a song and dance performance that was part of the spring festival of Dionysus. At first the celebration was wild and improvised, but in time it began to conform to the more set structure of ritual, using composed songs and dances. In 508 B.C. a contest in the Dithyramb was inaugurated. Groups entering the competition were trained by a *choregus* (the root of our word "choreographer") and performed in the *orchestra,* the circular dancing space of the open-air theatre. Now with an audience at hand and a prize to be won, the dances became increasingly more elaborate and virtuosic. Meanwhile, a form of spoken drama was developing at the Dionysian festival; and it too had its singer-dancers, in this case forming a chorus who reacted to and commented on the action with symbolic, stylized gestures known as *cheironomia*.

The performers at the Dionysian ceremonies were amateurs, considered to be servants of the gods. But Greece also had its professional dancers, slaves who entertained at dinner parties, where they juggled with hoops and turned somersaults, but also enacted brief mimetic scenes depicting stories of the gods. Thus the professionals incorporated both the virtuosity of the later Dithyramb and the expressive gestures of the dramatic chorus.

The professional dance developed in Rome, whose pantomime entertainments are said to have originated in 22 B.C. with two great artists named Pylades and Bathyllus. Both were expert in portraying entire tragedies or myths in solo performance. Aided by appropriate music and by a variety of costumes and masks, the dancer depicted in succession all the various characters involved in the story. The mimes enhanced their mute characterizations with brilliant turns, twists, bends, and springs; but the display of physical skills was not the primary aim of the art. According to Lucian of Samosata, who wrote in the second century A.D. "it is the dancer's profession to show forth human character and passion in all their variety; to depict love and anger, frenzy and grief each in its due measure . . . there is meaning in his movements; every gesture has its significance; and therein lies his chief excellence."

Thus, nearly twenty centuries ago all the elements of standard theatre dance were present: a performer equipped with movement skills; a role to be played; a stage to play on; music, costume, and décor to enhance the spectacle; an audience to respond to it. The relative importance of these elements was subject to discussion for centuries to come. Through the ages the answers have differed, depending on a number of changing, interacting factors that have influenced the constantly evolving nature of the art.

First there is the taste of an era, its climate of ideas, the scale of values set by a particular society that incline it, in one period, to admire formal structure; in another, to care more for spontaneous expression. Tastes swerve from stylization to realism, from virtuosity to drama, from escapism to contemporary protest. Trends are incited or accelerated by social, political, economic conditions—as is true of all the other arts.

Many of these arts also influence the development of dance. The tempos and rhythms of music, the size and weight of costumes, the style of décor, the shape of the stage, the nature of lighting equipment —the state of all of these at any particular time determines a great deal of what a choreographer can and cannot do. He may find ingenious ways of coping with the limitations imposed on him by composers or designers; or he may rebel against them, instigating important reforms. Theatre dance is a collaborative art and all the participants, of necessity, affect one another.

An especially significant factor for dance is the technical skill of the performers. Unlike the actor, whose physical potential has remained virtually unchanged, the dancer has constantly extended the scope of his capacities,—striving to master movements that are higher, faster, more elaborate than any seen before. To help him, his training has been lengthened and intensified, becoming more scientific in its molding of strength, flexibility, and coordination. Each age has enriched the dance vocabulary, providing greater resources for the next generation of choreographers.

Lastly, there is the most mysterious but possibly most potent factor of all—the individual creator. Partly because of his time, partly in spite of it, the figure of genius rises suddenly to change the course of dance, lifting it into unsuspected heights of artistry.

In a single volume we cannot consider all these factors in detail. Nor can we stop to examine more than a few manifestations of the creative vitality of dance, and these limited to the theatre of the Western world since the Renaissance. Regretfully, we are omitting not only the theatre dance of the East, but also such forms as folk dance, mime, musical comedy, and film—not because they lack significance but because their inclusion would have eliminated the possibility of any in-depth study.

From the sixteenth century, when this anthology begins, we can trace the development of theatrical dancing, virtually without a break, down to the present. While contemporary forms began to evolve well before our starting point of 1581, the publication of a considerable body of accessible materials, enabling us to study the interaction of technical accomplishments and choreographic ideas, stems from this date. Of the many documents that might have been chosen, we have made selections from only three categories: technical manuals; statements of theory; librettos or discussions of particular productions. The bibliographies will lead the student to some of the other vast resources that await his perusal.

History shows the dancer his heritage, his place in a line of distinguished, artistic ancestors. It is a legacy to instill a sense of pride—and responsibility. For those of us who love to watch dance, a study of history broadens our perspective by enlarging our range of experience. Our personal knowledge of dancing is largely limited by the time and place in which we live, and we tend to attach value to what we know, to what is comfortable because it is easily understood. The vicarious experience obtained from a knowledge of history shows us that different forms are not invalid simply because they are unlike our own. Such knowledge increases our tolerance by expanding our capacities to perceive values in the unfamiliar. At the same time, history makes us discriminating: we learn to recognize forces of outworn convention and deterioration, to distinguish the fashionable novelty from the genuine innovation. History teaches us not only tolerance but a critical attitude.

Within the past forty years theatrical dancing has attained an unprecedented popularity. Within this time, the United States has witnessed a great renaissance in classical ballet and the establishment of an idiom called "modern dance." We have seen a surge of interest in dance as drama followed by a swing back to concern with dance as pure movement, succeeded by a counterswing toward symbolic action. We have seen brilliant developments in stage design and have seen dance move away from stages into museums and city streets. We have seen dance adjust to the use of slide projections, films, and tape recorders. Now, with changes occurring so rapidly, may be the time to refresh ourselves with a knowledge of the past in preparation for a fresh evaluation of the present.

Section One

THE COURT BALLET

The pantomime theatre, popular throughout the Roman Empire in the early years of the Christian era, was thoroughly disliked by the Church fathers, who told their congregations that since devils had stage plays in hell that was reason enough not to have them on earth. Players, however, apparently continued to perform extensively at least through the fifth century, when the religious diatribes against them finally lessened. We have evidence too of traveling entertainers, including dancers, who amused the gentry of the manor houses throughout the Middle Ages.

Quite apart from the professionals, the people continued to dance. Much as the Church authorities wanted to stop pagan rituals, they found the traditions almost impossible to uproot, though they did succeed in stripping them of their original magical significance. In accordance with a pattern that we will see recurring, the pastimes of the folk were taken up by the nobility, dignified and elaborated however to serve the social functions of courtly life.

The fertility rites of the pagan spring were usually accompanied by mimetic enactments of death and rebirth by costumed and often masked performers who believed themselves possessed by the spirits they were made to resemble. Deprived of their mystical purpose, such rituals became social diversions. In fifteenth-century England, noble maskers paraded through the streets, entering houses to play a game of dice in silence. In Italy, bands of maskers roamed through towns on May Day, New Year, and Carnival, singing and dancing and playing practical jokes on the bystanders.

Meanwhile, specifically Christian spectacles were developing. Italian *edifizi* (pagents) bore masked performers through the streets, where they enacted Biblical episodes in dumb show. From *nuvole* (clouds), their wooden frames and wires hidden by cloth sprinkled with stars, the actors descended to the playing platform to tell their story.

As the Renaissance brought renewed interest in classical antiquity, the devices of both the secular masquerade and the religious processional were used to portray mythological subjects. In the lavish *trionfi* (triumphant parades) of Lorenzo de' Medici maskers were carried on elaborately designed floats, while verses were circulated among the onlookers to explain the symbolic significance of the characters represented. As the procession filed past the throne of state, each float in turn would pause as the maskers descended to declaim verses, sing, and dance. At the end, performers from all the floats joined in a grand dance.

As individual Italian dukedoms began to vie with one another for power and prestige, similar lavish entertainments were provided at court banquets. One of the most elaborate was given by the Duke of Milan in 1489, when the serving of roast lamb was heralded by a portrayal of the legend of Jason and the Golden Fleece; the course of wild boar was introduced by Atalanta, while the fruits were accompanied by the appearance of Pomona. Attendants to the main characters danced appropriate measures during each of the episodes.

In the early sixteenth century these dances are first referred to as *balletti*, meaning simply a figured dance, a composition characterized by the arrangement of the performers in sequences of changing floor patterns. Though each dance had a theme, it was related to the others only by the mythological nature of its content. No more cohesion than this was attempted.

Basically the *balletti* were staged, or semistaged, versions of the social dances of the day, some of them originating in the protocol of court etiquette, others stemming from the rough and hearty pleasures of the peasants but refined by contact with the prevailing, decorous restraint of the style of the nobility. Some treatises concerning these dances have come down to us from the mid-fifteenth century, though they are not as clear and precise as one might wish them to be. From those by Guglielmo Ebreo, Antonio Cornazano, and Giovanni Ambrosio we learn that the dances were divided into two major groups: the *bassa danza*, considered the queen of them all, was slow, solemn, and dignified, the feet being kept always close to the floor; the *ballo* was a livelier type in which the feet were raised. The basic movements, which included stately walking but also gracious swayings of the body and gentle turns, were combined in a variety of sequences to form individual dances, each being given some fanciful title by the master who composed it. The directions stipulate how many performers are involved and whether they are arranged in couples or in a line.

By the late sixteenth and early seventeenth centuries the texts have become much more precise. From Italy we have two by Fabritio Caroso and one by Cesare Negri; but the most accessible is *Orchésographie* by the French canon Jehan Tabourot, writing under the pseudonym of Thoinot Arbeau. Published in 1588, *Orchésographie* provides the first specific definitions of the proper placing of the dancer's feet at the beginning of steps, the basis of what have become the five positions of classical ballet. Only three are named, however, and they are not identified by numbers but by descriptive names: *pieds joints, pieds largis, pieds obliques*. Illustrations show the feet pointing outward away from the body—not so much as to require any special flexibility but enough to give an impression of elegance. Here is the beginning of the balletic turnout. The rudiments of many steps are here also, though often under different names: Arbeau's *entretaille* is like our *coupé*; his *capriole* is like our *entrechat*.

While all these manuals were intended as guides for social dancing, their directions are relevant to the history of theatre dance, for at this time "ballets" were not performed by professionals but by members of the court, for the entertainment of their peers. Although the choreographers were professionals, they were employed primarily to teach ballroom dancing to the nobility and were well aware of the limited capacities of their student-performers. Therefore, when a performance was required, they obliged by arranging simple steps in intricate patterns that made them interesting to observe. Encumbered by heavy, fashionable apparel and trained only to the extent of proper social proficiency, the dancers hardly provided inspiring material for technically exciting choreography. Besides, the ballets were performed, not on raised stages, but in the central space of large halls with the audience seated above the floor in galleries that extended around three sides of the dancing area. The wise masters reasoned out that the way to dazzle was not with steps, which the performers could not do expertly and the audience could not see well, but with floor patterns—complex geometrical shapes that formed, dissolved, and reformed to display a tantalizing variety of designs. Precision and memory, lightness and grace, an elegant ease of execution, were admired. Arbeau urged his pupil to observe virtue and decorum, to keep his head and body erect, to have his hose well secured and his shoes clean.

As folk customs had been refined into courtly diversions, so now it was time for the social dances of the Renaissance to nourish the burgeoning form that was to become the dance of the theatre. Artistic innovation was not the motivating force, however. When Catherine de' Medici of France commissioned her musicians and designers in 1573 to produce a lavish entertainment of song and dance, her purpose was political. It was a matter of diplomacy—a gesture to impress the Polish ambassadors who had arrived to negotiate a royal marriage—which brought about the event of the *Ballet des Polonais*, an elaborate figured dance performed by sixteen ladies of the court representing the sixteen provinces of France. The invited audience commended the dancers for their "interlacings and confusings, encounters and arrests, in which not one lady ever failed to turn in her place nor in her rank, so well that every one was amazed by such confusion and such disorder never ceasing from a superior order."

France's next major dance venture, also politically motivated, came in 1581. This is commonly called the "first ballet," though the accuracy of the designation depends largely on the definitions used. Although Balthasar de Beaujoyeulx, the choreographer of the *Ballet Comique*, claimed the idea of combining dancing, music, and poetry, the concept had been formulated some time before when Jean Antoine de Baïf had founded an academy to attempt the revival of the chorus of Greek tragedy with its synthesis of theatrical elements. Baïf, however, did not carry out his ideas in any actual productions; Beaujoyeulx did. Further, breaking with the tradition of combining unrelated interludes of music and dance, he used recitation, song, and movement to convey a single story line, the triumph of virtue, represented by Jupiter, over evil, personified by the goddess Circe. This dramatic coherence marks the historic significance of the *Ballet Comique*, but it was the lavishness of its production that made it famous throughout Europe. Here the *edifizi* and *nuvole* of the Italian *trionfi*, the rich costumes, the complex figures of the dance combined to stir the emulation of all who saw them. The dramatic line that we find of such significance was of lesser moment to the audience of the *Ballet Comique*.

Beaujoyeulx's work was a tremendous success, but nothing like it was produced again; it was just too expensive. In place of the patiently skilled interweaving of plot, music, and dance, succeeding choreographers resorted to a simpler form, one more easily contrived and less costly to execute. The following years saw the creation of a genre that became known as *ballets mascarades*—sequences of episodes loosely connected by a thread of plot. Replacing the grand mythological subjects were slighter scenes built on topics and characters drawn from everyday life, more amusing than ennobling. Generally each episode was introduced by a spoken verse or song which was followed by a dance, called an *entrée*. Then for a time there was a return to narrative, but this was soon dropped for the *ballet à entrées*, a series of thematically related dances, serious and comic, concluding with a grand figured dance in which all the characters appeared together. It is this form that is described by M. de Saint-Hubert.

Elsewhere in Europe French models were eagerly copied and often staged by French ballet masters. Some of the most lavish were presented in Sweden, where the philosopher Descartes wrote a libretto for one at the request of Queen Christina. Holland and Italy also had their share of elaborate productions. The Italians were especially intrigued with a form derived from the elaborate floor patterns of the ballet combined with the ideas of courtly tournaments. Using classical plots, songs, and décors, choreographers staged spectacles for riders on horseback. The steeds were trained to execute elaborate figures, all in strict time to the accompanying music.

England evolved its own form of the *ballet de cour*, the masque, a unique form merging elements borrowed from the masquerade of the Italians and the figured dances of the French. The masque was a production involving dialogue, song, music, and dance, terminating in "revels" in which the masked performers invited the audience to join them in social dancing. All these components were present also in the *Ballet Comique*, but in the hands of poet Ben Jonson and architect Inigo Jones the emphasis was altered; the masque had more elements of drama than of dance. It was in France that classical ballet really developed.

The most famous dancer of the mid-seventeenth century was Louis XIV; garbed as Apollo, the Sun-King, he dominated the ballet of France, which dominated the ballet of Europe. Though the general public was now sometimes admitted to performances and occasional professionals appeared in some of the *entrées*, the ballet was primarily a vehicle for the nobility. Louis chose the finest talent to compose for him: Isaac de Benserade wrote verses for his ballets; Jean-Baptiste Lully composed their music; in 1661, Molière contributed the first of his brilliant comedies, with dance interludes cleverly linked to the text. That same year, a group of dancing masters obtained permission from the king to establish the Académie Royale de Danse. Though most of their meetings were held at a local tavern and consisted of little more than theoretical discussions, they had formed a professional organization. When Louis stopped dancing in 1670, possibly because of his increasing corpulence, ballet was on its way to becoming a professional art.

Fabritio Caroso (c. 1530–1605)
RULES AND DIRECTIONS FOR DANCING THE "PASSO E MEZO"

Translated from the Italian and edited with notes by Julia Sutton

Caroso was a prominent Italian dancing master. His published work provides us with an extensive vocabulary of contemporary steps and with instructions for performing more than 100 dances.

    Caroso's manual was intended for ballroom dancing, but evidence indicates that the staged dances of the time followed much the same rules, though giving more attention to the showier steps. In both cases, the performers were members of the court. While the author provides directions for a substantial number of slow group dances, his descriptions also include a variety of livelier dances, such as the **Passo e Mezo***; and though he obviously advocates grace and elegance of execution, his frequent urgings to the dancer to "show off" indicate the potential of this social style for evolving into theatrical forms.*

Of the Reverences [*Riverenze*], and First of the Grave[1] Reverence
Rule II

The grave reverence is made by keeping the body and legs quite straight, with half the left foot ahead of the right, and four inches away from it, noting that the toes of both feet have to be quite straight. Now because in most of the *Balletti*[2] there are eight perfect beats of music, which equal sixteen ordinary beats, one must know that in the first four beats one begins and ends the entire reverence; and in the last

---

SOURCE: From *Il Ballarino* (Venice, 1581).

    [1] Grave simply means slow; its precise metric value is defined for each rule. Other terms referring to metric length are:
    Beat (*battuta*): semibreve, or one half note.
    Ordinary beat (*battuta ordinaria*): minim, or one quarter note.
    Perfect beat (*battuta perfetta*): normally, a beat with a triple subdivision, but Caroso is not entirely clear on this point. Most frequently he equates this with a semibreve, regardless of how it is subdivided. The music is usually marked off with a bar line for every semibreve.
    [2] A *Balletto* is a generic dance type of the sixteenth century, consisting of choreography for one couple, though the term is applied to other groupings as well. Most commonly there is a series of dance variations to two sections of music in contrasting meter (usually a slow duple followed by a more rapid triple meter), each section being repeated as often as necessary. Usually the basic musical material of all sections is the same.

four, the two continences, as will be described in the appropriate place. In the first beat, one stands facing [the lady] with the left foot forward, as I have said, and with one's face turned toward that of the lady (and not as others do, who continue to face toward the surrounding onlookers; for if they do this, they seem to despise the lady with whom they are dancing); for she must ever be revered and honored with all [due] affection.

During the second [beat] one has to pull the left foot back in a straight line, so that its toe is level with the right heel, keeping it [the left] flat on the ground, and without raising the heel at all. In pulling the foot back, be sure to bend the head and body somewhat, accompanying this action with all the grace one possesses, and keeping both knees quite straight. During the third one must bend the legs together with the body, gracefully separating the knees a little. During the fourth and last one must raise oneself, returning the left foot to the right, at the same time raising the body and the head.

I had you begin the reverence with the left foot because one shows reverence to someone close to one's heart; and also because the strength and stability of one's body is in the right foot, which must not be moved first when making a reverence or when dancing. Note also that every action or movement at the beginning of the dance must always be done with the left foot. . . .

Of the Two Continences [*Continenze*], the Grave and the Minim
Rule V

The first continence [which is called] grave, must be begun in this way: having completed the grave reverence, which is begun and ended during four perfect beats of music, and with the left foot, the man must move toward the left four inches, joining the right foot to the left; or else he can do it more gracefully by drawing the heel of the right foot toward the arch of the left. And in moving this way he must lower his body a little, raising it then as gracefully as he can, as I said in the rule for the grave reverence. And one must strut[3] a little toward that side on which one is doing [the continence]; this effect is usually achieved by raising the hip a little toward that side on which one is completing the continence. And do not do as others do, who neglect to show off and to bend and raise themselves, standing still with feet together, a way which is very awkward and dry, even though it is done in time and accurately; therefore it should be avoided.

[3] Italian *pavoneggiandosi*; literally, "peacocking oneself."

The second continence, which is called minim, must be divided into half the time of that above, and done in two beats for each continence; and it must be done with all the actions and movements I explained above. [4]

Of the Grave Pointed [*Puntate Grave*]
Rule VI

The grave pointed [step] is . . . done in two beats. Move the left foot during the first, thrusting it so far forward as to pass the toe of the [right] foot a little, and having it four or five inches laterally apart from the same foot, strutting all the time; then stop a little, as if to pause. Then, in the middle of the second beat, one moves the right foot, joining it to the left, bending the body a little and raising it gracefully. . . .

Of How to Learn to do the Grave Steps [*Passi Gravi*] in *Balletti*
Rule VII

The grave steps in *Balletti* are all done in one beat, moving the left foot and thrusting it forward, as I just said of the grave pointed step; then moving the right foot past [the left], one will do the same as he has done with the left. And all [movements must be done] with grace and beauty, accompanying them a little with the body and strutting. Be sure to keep the toes of the feet straight and the knees quite straight.

Of the Quick Steps [*Passi Presti*] in *Cascardas* [5]
Rule VIII

The quick steps in *Cascardas* are done as above, except that while those are done in one beat of music, these [are done] in half [a beat] and quickly.

Of the Ordinary Sequence [*Seguito Ordinario*]
Rule XII

The ordinary sequence is done . . . in three steps, and in four ordinary beats, though to tell the truth, during the last beat one holds his body still the entire time. And it is done in this way: one begins on the first beat with the left foot, thrusting it on the toe so far forward that its heel is level with the toe of the right and about two inches away from it. Then, raising the right on the second beat, it also must be thrust forward on the toe and as far away from the left as the left

[4] This continence equals two minims, or one semibreve.
[5] A rapid couple dance in triple meter.

was before. Then, during the third beat, the left is thrust forward in the same way, but ending with both feet flat on the ground, precisely as one should stand when facing [one's partner] in the reverence. Now this is the way one must hold oneself, as has been said, during the time of the fourth beat. Then, at the beginning of the fifth beat, one has to continue on, thrusting the right foot forward according to the rule given for the left. Note that in each sequence one must strut a little with one's body.

Of the Half-Double Sequence [*Seguito Semidoppio*]
Rule XIII

One does this sequence in the time of four ordinary beats, beginning with the left foot. In the first two beats one takes two steps [see Rule VIII] and in the other two beats [one does] a broken sequence [see Rule XVI], beginning also with the left foot, and accompanying each step and sequence with that grace and beauty which these movements deserve.

Of the Broken Sequence [*Seguito Spezzato*]
Rule XVI

One does this broken sequence in two ordinary beats in this way. First (standing with feet together), on the first beat one must thrust the left foot half a palm[6] forward and two inches away from the right, keeping [i.e., placing] it quite flat on the ground. Then, at the beginning of the second beat, one must move the right foot, first raising the heel, and one must place its toe near the heel of the left foot. Now at the same time, as one touches the ground with the toe of the right, one must raise both heels a little, simultaneously with the body; then, at the end of the beat, one must lower the heel of the left simultaneously with the body. After this, at the beginning of the third beat, one must move forward with the right in the same way as was done with the left. And this sequence is called broken because one does two of the aforesaid in the time of an ordinary sequence by breaking it.

Of the Way to do the Grave Leaning Jump [*Trabuchetto Grave*]
Rule XXIIII

The grave leaning jump is done this way: standing with feet together, one must spread the left foot to the side by means of a small jump, about one palm away from the right; and at the moment that the left touches the ground, one must raise the right, bringing it within about

6 A palm is a unit of measurement based on the breadth of the hand.

two inches of the left (which is lightly on its toe), keeping both legs quite straight, but not touching the ground with the right foot. Then, returning the right foot to its original place, one must repeat with the left what was done with the right. Note that one must strut a little with each leaning jump and do it with bodily agility and dexterity. . . . The time of each of these leaning jumps is one perfect beat of music.

Of the Way to do the Ordinary Flourish [*Fioretto Ordinario*]
Rule XXVI

The ordinary flourish must be done by raising the left foot and thrusting it so far ahead of the right that the left heel is two inches from the toe of the right, but one inch to the side and raised two inches, with the knees quite straight. At the same time elevate the body somewhat by doing a little jump [see Rule XLIII], placing the right on its toe so far forward that the end of the heel is near the toe of the left and about two inches away from it. Then, raising the left foot, one must put it [down] in place of the right, which must be raised as was the left at the beginning of this flourish; and one must follow the same order as with the left. Others, when they finish the ordinary flourish (raising the left foot and putting it in place of the right after raising that foot forward a little, as I have said), bring it together [flat] with the right, ending it this way. Now even though this procedure seems good, I like the first much better. For the body is rendered more graceful by stepping nimbly on the toes than by placing the feet flat on the ground. The time of each of these flourishes is one minim beat.

About the Five Steps [*Cinque Passi*] of the Galliard[7]
Rule XXX

. . . . First one does a limping hop [see Rule XXXIX] with the right foot on the ground, raising the left forward. Then, dropping [the left], one raises the right backward; and placing its toe to the heel of the left, one immediately lifts the left, which will [then] be put down in the place where it was before [while] again lifting the right foot forward. Then dropping it [the right] and drawing it back, one does the cadence [see Rule LIII], adding grace to it by separating the knees a little, and ending with the right behind. . . . Note that the legs must always be kept quite straight, with the toes down and the arms down, but showing

---

[7] The Galliard was the showy, vigorous dance of the sixteenth century. Its basic step pattern was known everywhere: in France as the *cinq pas*, in Italy as the *cinque passi*, in England as the *five steps* or *sinkapace*. Caroso's version is a simple one. Innumerable variations exist in the manuals of the period, many of them involving double *tours en l'air*, *entrechats*, and *pirouettes*.

off occasionally with the right [arm] because it would look ugly if it were always held straight. Do not move the fingers, and carry your body erect and your head high.

Of the Limping Hop [*Zoppetto*]
Rule XXXIX

The limping hop is done (beginning with feet together, or otherwise, according to the circumstances which can occur in the Galliard), by raising both feet [at once], the first a little above the ground and the other passing forward. One does as many of them as will be required by the variations and they will be done this way, keeping one of the feet raised forward or keeping it similarly raised to the side. These movements have taken the name of limping hop because one keeps one foot forward, raising the other by hopping, exactly as if one were to limp.

Of the Foot Under [*Sottopiede*]
Rule XLI

One does the foot under always to the side in this way: first one does one leaning jump to the left with the left foot. Then, in putting the left down, one lifts the right back, putting it down in the place where the left was and raising the left in the air. And with it [the left] one goes on to do more of them. Thus the name foot under is derived from this movement of placing one foot where the other was.

Of the Little Jumps with Feet Together [*Balzetti à Piedi Pari*]
Rule XLIII

These little jumps are done by standing with feet together (one inch apart), lifting both feet above the ground about two inches, and landing with them at the same time a little distance away from where they were, keeping them together in the same way. One jumps this way with little jumps, now to the left, now to the right, according to circumstances, and one does as many as the variations require. . . .

Of the Knot [*Groppo*]
Rule XLIIII

This is done by beginning with the body and feet in the same position as when one prepares to do the reverence. First, one does a leaning jump to the left with the left foot. Then, at the same time as one lands on the left, one crosses the right behind. With this one does another

From *Il Ballarino*

To help his readers understand the starting position of the *Passo e Mezo*, Caroso wisely provided an illustration. At this point the gentleman has removed his hat according to the rules that insure his making this action graceful and attractive, and he is shown performing the third beat of the reverence. The disparity of the costumes clearly shows that the man could enjoy far more freedom of movement than could his lady.

leaning jump to the right, crossing the left behind the right. Then one does another leaning jump to the left with the left, crossing the right behind it. With this [right] foot one does a foot under (putting it in place of the left, which must be raised), keeping the left foot raised forward a little. And drawing back that [foot] and thrusting the right forward, one does the cadence, and thus one ends this knot. Now from this crossing over of the feet in a knotlike way, this name has been derived.

Of the Toe and Heel [*Punta e Calcagno*]
Rule L

This is done by taking one limping hop on the ground with the right and at the same time putting the toe of the left on the ground four inches from the right. Then do another limping hop again with the right, putting the heel of the left on the ground and holding its toe up four or five inches from the ground. Finally, putting the left down flat as in the limping hop, one begins [again] doing the toe and heel in the same order with the right. . . .

Of the Cadence [*Cadenza*] in the Galliard
Rule LIII

First one raises the left foot forward; and pulling oneself backward, and simultaneously lifting oneself up a little, one lands with both feet on the ground; that is, with the left in back and the right in front. And from this way of landing with both feet at the same time, this movement has taken the name of cadence.

Step and a Half [*Passo e Mezo*][8]
Author Unknown
With Variations and a New Promenade by the Author of this Book
In Honor of the Most Illustrious and Excellent Signora, The Duchess of Monte Lione

This *Passo e Mezo* is begun with the couple facing each other without holding hands, as appears in the illustration, doing the grave reverence and two continences facing each other. Then, promenading together in a circle to the left, they will do two grave steps and an ordinary sequence, beginning with the left. They will continue by doing one grave step with the right and two quick steps, one with the left and the other with the right, and one grave leaning jump with the left.

---

[8] The *Passo e Mezo* may be related to the Pavane, the slow processional dance of the period. With Caroso it is an extremely sophisticated and showy dance whose introduction alone shows traces of the basic Pavane. Musically, the *Passo e Mezo* is based on either of two repeated bass patterns (*bassi ostinati*), known as the *passamezzo antico* and *passomezzo moderno*; and many sets of virtuosic variations for instruments on these basses were written at this time. Caroso's choreography is equally virtuosic; the original gives six variations for each partner, plus two variations for the couple. We have chosen one variation for each. This dance is in duple meter.

Dropping the right foot (which will have been raised), they will do a little jump with feet together to the right. Having finished this promenade, they will repeat it once again.

The Gentleman's First Variation
and the Lady's Promenade

When they have finished doing these first two promenades together, the gentleman will begin his first variation by raising his left foot a little in the air, and making a quick reverence[9] with it. Then, with the same foot, he will do a limping hop in the air, and one step with the right as in the Galliard, and a cadence with the same foot behind, immediately [following this] with a knot to the left and two quick reverences with the left. Then he will continue with a leaning jump to the left, one foot under to the right, [then] a toe and heel, first with the right and then with the left, with one leaning jump, one foot under to the left, a quick reverence, [and] a Galliard cadence with the left behind. Then he will do one limping hop with the left in the air, a step of the Galliard with the right forward, and conclude in time with the music with a cadence with feet together.

At the same time as the gentleman is doing his first variation, the lady will promenade, doing two grave steps and one ordinary sequence to the left, beginning them with the left foot. Then, turning to the right, she will do one grave step with the right and two quick steps, one with the left and the other with the right, followed by one grave leaning jump to the left. Then, putting the right foot down (which will have been raised), she will gracefully do one little jump with feet together to the right.

The Lady's First Variation
and the Gentleman's Promenade

The lady will begin her first variation by doing two broken sequences sideways forward, plus three grave leaning jumps, beginning with the left foot. She will then repeat the same once more in the opposite direction, being careful to do the last leaning jump with feet together. At the same time as the lady is doing her variation, the gentleman will do two grave steps and a half-double sequence, beginning with the left foot; then, turning to the right, he will do one quick step with the right and three flourishes turning to the left, with a Galliard cadence with the right foot behind. Then he will do two steps of the Galliard and a cadence with feet together. . . .

[9] The quick reverence is not described in the rules.

Balthasar de Beaujoyeulx
BALLET COMIQUE DE LA REINE
Translated from the French by Mary-Jean Cowell

Baltazarini di Belgiojoso, wise to the ways of political promotion, took a French name when he left Italy for Paris around 1555 as a member of a band of violinists. He became court valet to Catherine de' Medici and as such was responsible for the royal entertainments.

In the "first ballet," dancing was only one of several important elements: instrumental music, songs, spoken verses, costumes, and scenic effects all received attention. In fact, the author of this libretto devotes far more space to the texts of the speeches and songs and to descriptions of the decorations than he does to the dances. After all, most of his readers knew the steps from their own experience in court ballrooms, where rules like Caroso's prevailed. The Ballet Comique *was first of all a grand spectacle designed to enhance the glory of France. Since the audience consisted exclusively of invited dignitaries, the publication of the libretto provided a means of extending recognition of the national image.*

To the Reader

In as much, dear Reader, as the title of this book is unprecedented, the word "Comic" having never been applied to a Ballet, nor has any Ballet been published previous to this one, I ask you not to find my usage peculiar.

As for the Ballet, it is a modern invention or is, at least, a revival from such distant antiquity that it may be called modern; being, in truth, no more than the geometrical groupings of people dancing together, accompanied by the varied harmony of several instruments. I confess to you that, merely presented in print, the recitation of a simple Comedy would have had much novelty but little beauty; nor would such an offering be distinguished or worthy of so noble a Queen who desired to present something magnificent and splendid.

Therefore, I bethought myself that to combine the two would be in no way improper: to diversify the music with poetry; to interlace the poetry with music; and most often to intermingle the two, even as the ancients never recited poetry without music and Orpheus played only with verse.

SOURCE: From *Balet Comique de la Royne* (Paris, 1582).

I have, nevertheless, given the first title and honor to the dance, and the second to the story, which I designated "Comic" more for its beautiful, tranquil, and happy conclusion than for the nature of its characters, who are almost all gods and goddesses or other heroic personages.

Thus I enlivened the ballet and made it speak, and made the Comedy sing and play; and, adding some unusual and elaborate décor and embellishments, I may say that I satisfied the eye, the ear, and the intellect with one well-proportioned creation.

I entreat you not to judge this work harshly because of its title or novelty; for my invention, being principally composed of two elements, could not be designated a Ballet without slighting the Comedy clearly evident in the scenes and acts; nor could it be called a Comedy without prejudice to the Ballet which ornaments, enlivens, and completes with harmonious movements the beautiful meaning of the comedy.

Having amply explained my intentions, I ask your indulgence of my title and hope you will find the work pleasing, since I, for my part, wished to satisfy you.

[The libretto begins with an explanation of the author's commission to create the ballet: the Queen Louise had requested him to contribute to the festivities planned for the marriage of her sister, Mlle. de Vaudemont, to the Duke of Joyeuse. The queen approved the design Beaujoyeulx brought her, bidding him to execute it promptly. Since he felt he could not take the responsibility for all the parts of the work, the queen assigned the poetry to Lord de la Chesnaye, the music to Lord de Beaulieu, and the painting to Master Jacques Patin.

Beaujoyeulx then describes the arrangements he directed to be made in the Bourbon hall. At one end he had constructed a low dais to serve for the seating of the king, the queen, the princes and princesses. On each side of the dais were places for the ambassadors and for ladies of the court. Others sat on the two galleries that stood around the walls of the hall. To the King's right was a grove for Pan and the dryad nymphs. Directly opposite was a gilded vault, called the "golden," where the music was performed. On the ceiling between the grove and the vault was an immense cloud from which Mercury and Jupiter would descend.

In the center of the hall at the end opposite the king was Circe's garden and behind it, the wall of a castle. On either side of the garden was an arched trellis with imitation leaves and grapes, and through these trellises passed the interlude musicians and the mobile sets that presented themselves to the king. Circe, played by Mlle. de Sainte-Même, was to sit at the portal of the castle, dressed in a golden

From the *Ballet Comique*

The reader looks over the shoulder of the King as the Fugitive Gentleman delivers his complaint against Circe. Also to be seen are Pan's grove (right), the golden vault (left), and Circe's castle and garden (background center). The highest ranking members of the court are seated by the King; other invited guests fill the galleries along the side walls.

robe with many jewels and holding a golden rod. One hundred white wax candles shed their radiance on the garden, while further light shone from the "infinite" number of torches at the top of and all around the hall.

On Sunday, the fifteenth of October, some 900 renowned and notable persons took their places in the hall.]

At the tenth hour of the evening, silence being imposed, the sound of hautboys, cornetts, sackbuts, and other soft instruments issued from behind the castle. This music having ended, lord de la Roche (a gentleman in the service of the Queen mother, handsomely attired in silver cloth, his garments covered with jewels and pearls of great value) ran out of Circe's garden to the middle of the room where he stopped short and looked back, terrified, at the garden to see if the enchantress Circe were pursuing him. And having seen that no one was running after him, he drew from his pocket a gold-trimmed handkerchief with which he wiped his brow, as if he perspired from fatigue or fear. Then, being somewhat reassured and having caught his breath, he walked slowly toward the King. And after a deep bow to his Majesty, he began in a confident manner and in language expressing sage eloquence, to speak as follows.

THE FUGITIVE GENTLEMAN'S SPEECH TO THE KING

Always some fatal evil intervenes
In that which gracious Heaven is disposed
To send to mortals, and the man too much
Desirous of good, by hope deceives himself.
    I wished first to announce the tidings that
The season of iron, cruel and inhumane,
Was changing to a better age, and the Gods
Holding, with Saturn, the world in their grasp,
Came to live as intimates of men in France,
Forever gracing her with peace and wealth.
But whom did I encounter on the way?
Oh, Gods, turn evil back upon its wicked chief!
    This was not a woman: none who breathes
Has so much beauty or such great wrath . . .
No sooner had I seen her, e'en as soon,
My life and liberty were well nigh ravaged.
She, for her pleasure having some concern,
Came toward me, speaking to me thus:
    ["]Halt, Cavalier, fear nothing and approach,
And if your heart is neither wood nor stone,

Yield without struggle, yield to the laws
Of this winged archer, God of all-pervasive power,
To whom (perhaps) you would make vain resistance.
Because he holds Gods subject to his power,
I feel now the sharp touch of his darts,
And, vanquished by your eyes, surrender to you.
I would not, with my wand, form you as beast,
You have some destiny which makes me love you,
Come, possess my riches, use my wealth,
And like myself, be served by these goddesses.["]
   I followed, for there is no stronger bond
Than the conception of pleasure and of wealth,
Dwelling there I was happy (if he who yields
To pleasure's rule may so be called)
When an evil Destiny, a Fate severe,
Poisoned with hate and jealousy the heart
Of Circe, who in a moment bewitched me,
Struck me on the chest with her golden wand
Transformed my body into that of a Lion,
And shut me in a park among her herds.
But some occasion softened the sorceress,
Who made me regain my earlier form.
Wary of the jurisdiction of her
Cruel laws (who dares trust spells too often?)
I made my escape while she, agitated
By suspicion, which makes her distrust
Her arts, mounted to the top of a tower
Where she goes to spy on the nymphs from afar,
In order to charm them with cunning magic
And keep them from seeing this King who calls them
To a temple in France, with the other Gods
The golden age brings back from the skies.
   More than a cruel Serpent, one whose spine
The fleeing shepherd breaks with a staff,
Her eye is inflamed, and fear which combats
Her dubious hope beats in her breast.
   To this King, who has assumed the Gods' defense,
I come swiftly to disclose the action,
And to entreat his aid against this Circe.
   Will you not, great King, help so many Gods?
You will, Henry, more valiant than Hercules
Or he who killed the murderous Chimera,
And for so many mortals and Gods held fast

In the Fairy's bonds, you will be divine,
And posterity, which will build you temples,
Will crown your temples with verdant laurel.

His speech completed, he knelt on one knee near the King, as if placing himself under his protection. Then Circe came out of her garden, holding her golden wand raised high; she rushed to the center of the room turning her gaze to all sides to spy out the gentleman who had escaped from her prison. And failing to detect him, having lifted her eyes to the cloud suspended above, she began with a sorrowful voice and a grace few damsels could imitate and none surpass, to lament in the following manner.

CIRCE'S LAMENT, HAVING LOST A GENTLEMAN

I pursue in vain, with no hope
Of ever seeing him again in my power.
Ah, Circe, what have you done?
You should never re-form as human
One you once deprived of reason.
Alas, Circe, little cunning and sly,
Who comes to be wary through her error!
This fugitive, fearless, will go his way,
Everywhere spreading your shame, to your detriment.
Vain, the spells you cast upon your captives,
Vain, your magic murmurs which transform,
For you are mutable, and cruelty
And pity each have a half of you.
Foolish, thrice foolish Circe, senseless and
Believing one restored to native form
Would love you still, and be deceived by pleasures
When he could exercise his reason.
Expel this mercy which renders you fickle.
Kindness becomes ill deed when detrimental.
Follow your natural self: your ways are wrath
And cruelty; leave good to another.
Come, come, cast off such feeble courage
And arm your heart with serpents and with ire
That none struck by your wand may later vaunt
Himself that he escaped your bondage.

As soon as Circe had vented her anger in this complaint, she returned to her garden with the countenance of a most irritated woman. She sallied from the hall, leaving the spectators astonished by the two acts they had seen, as much by the fugitive gentleman as by the furious Circe.

But when silence was established, there came from one of the trellises three Mermaids and a Triton with their tails, fashioned of burnished gold and silver scales, with barbels and fins of burnished gold, tucked up in their arms. Their bodies and locks were entwined with golden threads, hanging down to the waist; and all carried golden mirrors in their hands. Thus attired, they entered the hall singing the following song, each stanza of which was answered by an ensemble in the golden vault, singing unaccompanied.

THE MERMAIDS' SONG

MERMAIDS: Hoary father ocean,
                Father of the Gods,
                Shall we leave the waves
                At the summons of this Triton?

GOLDEN VAULT: Go, daughters of Achelaus,
                Follow Triton, who calls you,
                Blend your voices with his horn
                In endless praise of a noble king.

MERMAIDS: The goddess Thetis
                Emerges from the sea,
                With the attendance of
                The chorus of Nereid sisters.

GOLDEN VAULT: Go, daughters of Achelaus, etc.

MERMAIDS: Jupiter is not alone above,
                The sea lodges a thousand Gods,
                But one king only reigns in France,
                Henry, great King of the French. . . .

Having made a full circuit of the hall, these marine creatures retired near the trellis, where they encountered a fountain which one could truly say was the most beautiful in superb design and artifice and the most magnificent in embellishment that had ever been seen. . . .

[Beaujoyeulx then describes the fountain, which contained three basins adorned with sculptures of dolphins, mermaids, and tritons made of burnished gold and silver. Scented water flowed from the topmost basin into the third and largest basin, which had twelve golden pulpits on its rim. In these sat the queen and eleven other royal ladies representing naiads, dressed in silver cloth and wearing many precious

From the *Ballet Comique*

Beaujoyeulx' fountain, lighted by one hundred white wax candles, had its highest basin supported by the burnished tails of three dolphins. From spouts at the top of the pyramid, water fell down to the feet of twelve Naiads seated on the lowest basin. The choreographer says nothing of the Naiads' dancing, but is eager to note that their attire was esteemed the richest and most stately ever seen in a masquerade.

stones. The mermaids joined this company. Then, to music and singing, the fountain moved toward the king, made a turn in front of
him, and slowly withdrew, leaving the hall empty.]

Once behind the castle, the Naiads climbed down from their fountain,
and immediately ten violinists entered the hall through the two trellises,
five from one side and as many from the other, dressed in white satin
trimmed with gold tinsel, beplumed and adorned with egret feathers;
and in this apparel they began to play the first entry of the Ballet.
Following these violinists, the twelve pages entered the room through
the same trellises, six from one side and six from the other; and the
pages being in place, the twelve nymphs quickly appeared after them,
also entering six by one trellis and six by the other; who were no sooner
spied by the violinists than they changed their tune in order to commence
the second part of the entry of the Ballet, in which these nymphs came
dancing up to their majesties the King and the Queen his mother, in
this fashion. During the first passage of the entry, there were six, all
in a line across the room, and three in front in a quite large triangle,
the Queen being its foremost point, and three behind in like manner.
Then, in accord with variations in the music, they also revolved, winding
backwards around each other, sometimes in one fashion, sometimes
in another, and then returned to their original position. Having arrived
close to the King, they went on continuously with the part of this Ballet
composed of twelve Geometric figures, all different the one from the
other; and at the last passage, the violins played a very lively tune
called "The Little Bell."

Circe, still hidden in her garden by the closing of the curtain, had
no sooner heard the sound of the little bell than she emerged in a
rage, holding in her right hand her golden wand raised high. She came
the full length of the hall to the nymphs (arranged in the form of a
crescent facing their majesties), touching them one after another with
her golden wand, which light touch suddenly rendered them immobile
like statues. She did likewise to the violinists, who could no longer
sing nor play, thus remaining without any movement whatsoever. And
afterward, she returned to her garden, with a bold and gleeful countenance like that of a Captain who has won a glorious victory in some
perilous and difficult enterprise of his own. Thus she could rightly vaunt
herself, having brought low such an intrepid grandeur of courage as
that of the nymphs.

When Circe, therefore, had retired to her garden in such glory, from
the top of the ceiling of the room and above the cloud, one heard a
great clap of thunder which rumbled and murmured for some time;
which having ceased, the cloud described above suddenly began to

descend little by little, wherein was borne and enveloped Mercury, messenger of the God Jupiter, by whom he was sent to earth to break the spells of the fairy Circe and to deliver the Naiads from her enchantment with the juice of the Moly root. Mercury was attired just as the poets describe him: in Spanish carnation satin, laboriously laced with gold, with gilded boots having wings at his heels to signify the fleetness of his course; his head also covered with a small cap winged on both sides and gilded all over; his mantle being of violet gold cloth; and bearing in his hand the caduceus with which of old in the service of Jupiter he lulled Argus to sleep. This God while descending sang the verses inserted below most pleasingly, being represented by lord du Pont, an attendant of the King having many honorable accomplishments.

MERCURY'S SONG

    I, common messenger of all the gods,
Winged of heel, flitting, nimble, swift. . . .
Bear the Moly root of excellence
To cure the mind disarmed of reason, which,
Forsaking virtue, was beguiled by pleasure. . . .
    This Circe has eyes shameless in desire,
Mistrusted at first glance by everyone,
And the lure of Cupid is no more swift.
But pleasure past is odious to her,
The men she renders self-oblivious,
Losing their reason with their human form.
    She knows how to subdue nymphs with her art,
But she cannot transform them into beasts,
For of their nature, Gods are immutable.
Yet by the Gods she makes herself revered,
Striking them with her wand, making them
Stay, charmed of foot, more stable than a rock.
    I wish the art to disclose her fantasies,
I have distilled in water the Moly root,
And would undo her craft with my stronger art.
I know how much power and strength she has,
But great peril pleases the victor, after
Honored by the name of a powerful foe.

    While Mercury was still in the air some two feet above the nymphs, having ended his song, he scattered the Moly root potion, which he had in a golden vial, over the heads of the nymphs, and cast it with such industry that it also splashed on the violinists, who were no sooner sprinkled by this water than they suddenly began to play again, the nymphs also beginning to dance and to continue their Ballet as before their enchantment. However Circe, thinking that Mercury did her great wrong and injury by usurping her art, resolved to make him feel what she knew how to do and what power she had over him and even over the strength of his caduceus.

For this purpose she again came out of her garden and, almost in a frenzy, rushed to the center of the room. Passing through the lovely troop of dancers, as she had done before, she touched them a second time, likewise the violinists, returning them to the state from which Mercury had delivered them; and retiring four steps backward, she began to speak as follows:

CIRCE

Man is never content with his lot, but yearns
Continually for greater happiness. . . .

All human action proceeds from appetite,
Where one is incited or led by pleasure.
Of rest and labor, pleasure is the guide,
Presiding o'er the movements of the will:
The action pleasing and commonly practiced
Serves as rule of life and law for everyone. . . .

I will imprison this foolish Mercury
Who comes presumptuously with craft and courage
To aid the nymphs, also promising himself
To have some power against my golden wand,
And to dissolve my spells with a root which one day
Served Ulysses as a medicine against
My poisons; but it was Pallas guarding
Ulysses, not he, who hindered my success.
Of the gods this Minerva alone I fear,
Only she preserves mankind from my arts.

Having completed her speech, Circe drew near to Mercury, who was still enveloped by the cloud, and raising her golden wand, struck him: who no sooner had felt the blow than, abandoning his caduceus, he stood enchanted, and thus the cloud bore him immobile to earth. Then taking him by the hand, Circe led him to her garden, the nymphs following prettily in line two by two, with no other movement than that which seemed to be given them by the power of Circe's spell. Once inside her garden, the nymphs disappeared instantly, so that no one was able to perceive what had become of them. Immediately the curtain which covered Circe's garden dropped, clearly revealing the beauty of this delightful garden, which sparkled with a thousand kinds of flames and lights. Moreover, one saw Circe in front of her castle door, seated in majesty with the evidence of her victory: at her feet Mercury lay on his back, unable to move in any way without the permission of the enchantress. After the opening of the curtain, a large stag emerged from the garden and passed in front of Circe, followed by a dog, and the dog by an elephant, the elephant by a lion, the lion by a tiger, the tiger by a hog, and the hog by other beasts—men thus transformed by her sorcery and the power of her enchantments.

The preceding act being finished, the second interlude began to enter from the other trellis. . . .

[After further songs and discourse, Pallas entered in a car drawn by a serpent. She called on Jupiter, who descended on a cloud. As all the divinities assaulted Circe's palace, Jupiter struck the enchantress with a thunderbolt and led her captive before the King.]

Then the violinists began to play the entrance of the grand Ballet, composed of fifteen passages, arranged in such a manner that at the end of each passage all faced toward the King; having arrived before his majesty, they danced the grand Ballet of forty passages or Geometric figures. These were exact and considered in their diameter, sometimes square, now round, and with many and diverse forms, and as often triangular, accompanied by some square and other small figures. Which figures being no sooner traced out by the twelve Naiads, dressed in white (as was said) than the four Dryads dressed in green came to break them; so that the one ending, the other immediately began. In the middle of this Ballet a chain was formed, composed of four interlacings different from each other, such that to see them one would have said this was a battle array, so well was the order kept, and so dexterously each endeavored to observe her rank and cadence; so that everyone believed that Archimedes could not have better understood Geometric proportions than these princesses and ladies employing them in this Ballet. And in order that one might recognize how many different airs it was necessary to use, some austere, others gay, some in triple time, others for a step smooth and slow, I wished to show them also, as you see below, so as to have nothing lacking and imperfect in the relation of all that took place.

[Ballet Music]

This Ballet completed, the Naiads and Dryads made a deep reverence to his majesty; and the Queen, approaching the King her lord, took him by the hand and made him a present of a large gold medallion, having thereon a Dolphin swimming in the sea, which all took for a certain omen of he [the heir] that God will give to them for the prosperity of this kingdom.

Following the Queen's example, all the princesses, dames, and ladies, according to their rank and degree, took the princes, lords, and gentlemen who pleased them; and to each one, they made their golden present, with their emblems, all nautical things, in as much as they represented the nymphs of the seas, as you see below. . . .

[Beaujoyeulx then enumerates the gifts bestowed by each lady.]

In this order and rank, they led out the princes to dance the grand Ball; and this ended, they began branles and other dances customary at great feasts and celebrations. These being finished, their majesties the King and Queens withdrew, the night being already well advanced; seeing that this Comedy Ballet lasted from ten o'clock in the evening until three hours and a half after midnight, without such length boring or displeasing the spectators, each one being so greatly satisfied; seeing most especially such a noble, excellent, dignified, and sovereign lady so much honoring her subjects as to humble herself to take part in the pastimes created to delight her, and to present herself in public; so that all recognized that our Kings and Queens, since they reign over a liberal people, also treat them liberally, and with all kindliness, freedom, candor, and courtesy.

Saint–Hubert
HOW TO COMPOSE SUCCESSFUL BALLETS
Translated from the French by Andrée Bergens

Unfortunately we know nothing of the life of M. de Saint-Hubert beyond what he tells us in this little book.

Marie-Françoise Christout has remarked on Saint-Hubert's "common sense and clarity of mind." Indeed, he packs a great deal of sound instruction into this very brief treatise (only the last section, concerned with the role of the stage manager, is omitted here), telling us a great deal about the structure and values of the ballet à entrées. *He makes no claim to particular originality and, from what we know of contemporary librettos, rather reflects the taste*

SOURCE: From *La Manière de composer et faire réussir les ballets* (Paris, 1641).

of his time. An interesting advance over the previous century is revealed, how-ever, in Saint-Hubert's remark that he likes to see people dance according to the characters they represent, even though he later admits that the dancers should be given only such steps as they can perform with what they have to carry, since the audience identifies them by their properties. The next century will carry the concept of expressive movement much further.

I did not intend to have this little discourse published for I was afraid of wronging my profession, and if one of my friends had not tried to make me believe (which is true) that dancing is one of the three activities of nobility, it would never have appeared. Everyone knows that, for a young nobleman to be polished, he must learn how to ride, to fence, and to dance. The first skill increases his dexterity, the second his courage, the last his grace and disposition. Each of these exercises being useful at an appropriate time, one can say that they are of equal value, since Mars is no less the god of war when resting on Venus' bosom than when thundering in the midst of battles.

And even kings, princes, and noblemen enjoy this divertissement; it must be praiseworthy and, this being so, I decided to express my opinion, which will be shared by those who approve of it; as to the others, who do things which are not worthwhile, they will do as they like. I will accordingly say that there are two kinds of ballets, the serious and the grotesque which, when well made, can be equally successful.

A great ballet, which we call a royal ballet usually includes thirty *entrées.*

A fine ballet contains at least twenty *entrées.* And a small ballet, from ten to twelve. Not that it is necessary to comply with this rule but rather with the subject that requires the number to be either increased or decreased.

Since *mascarades* do not usually tell a story, no rule can be applied. The *mascarade* is improvised by people who disguise themselves with no specific purpose in mind and just follow their fancy. It is just a pretext for wearing imaginative costumes, and the participants sing tunes and dance steps of their own choice, most frequently ordinary dances but with the ladies who are present.

In order to produce a fine ballet, six things are necessary: subject, airs, dancing, costumes, machines, and organization, concerning all of which I shall give my opinion.

Of Subjects

I shall start with the subject, upon which all the rest depends and to which everything must be subordinated. The most important requirement for making a successful ballet is finding a good subject, which is the most difficult thing.

I find many perfect musicians for the airs, excellent dancers for the *entrées*, good designers for the costumes, extremely skillful craftsmen for the machines, but very few people are able to deal with a good subject and follow its necessary progression.

To be fine, it must be new and it also must be well developed so that none of the *entrées* will be irrelevant; each must be pertinent. If there is a mixture of the serious and the grotesque, two grotesque *entrées* should not appear in succession; if they can be harmoniously mixed in with the serious, they will be much more diverting, and the audience will be more inclined to admire the former and laugh at the latter.

When I say that it is necessary to make a ballet that has not yet been seen, I mean only the main part of the subject, for, as far as the *entrées* are concerned, it is impossible to make more than a few that have not been seen. For example, if during the development of the story there is a need for noblemen, Turks, or young ladies, one should not hesitate to use such characters simply because they already have appeared in several ballets. They are no longer the ones belonging to those previous subjects but integral parts of yours, which is completely different from the others, and you use them because they belong here and not because you saw them before.

If you can find *entrées* and costumes that have not yet been seen, this will enrich your ballet and make your inventiveness more admirable. So look for a fine new subject of your own devising, since it is the trend nowadays. And may Ovid's *Metamorphoses* no longer be danced as in former times.

This reminds me of a gentleman I know who once asked my opinion concerning an idea he had of presenting Homer's *Iliad* in ballet form. I told him frankly that it would be a play rather than a ballet, that the ceilings of the halls were too low for the masts of the Greek vessels, that the horses of Hector's chariot, if frightened, might injure people, and that the burning of Troy would scare the ladies.

Entrées should be organized in such a way that the number of dancers appearing in each will be different; that two using the same number will not be too close together; and that *entrées* with just one or two protagonists will be kept at a minimum. Those with three, four, five, six, seven, and eight dancers are the most attractive and make possible the most beautiful figures; it is true that those with seven and eight are rarely used because they would require too many dancers except for a finale or in great ballets which require brilliance, or when they are necessary to indicate the conclusion of a ballet. I strongly advocate writing out the story of the ballet, either in prose or in verse, so that it can be passed out to the audience before the performance to let them enjoy it more by knowing what it is about.

Of Airs

It would be well for the airs not to be written before the subject is perfectly set and the *entrées* carefully planned so that they will be appropriate and will follow what the dancers are to do and represent, and the musician will be much more successful in this way than by composing many airs which can only with difficulty be adjusted to the *entrées* and the subject afterwards.

Of Dancing

One must fit the dancing and the steps to the airs and the *entrées* so that a vine-grower or a water-carrier will not dance as a knight or a magician. I would like to see people dance according to the characters they represent and sometimes there are *entrées* where perfect dancing is not necessary. I remember that in the first ballet in which I had the honor of performing in the presence of His Majesty, I impersonated a student and I constantly danced out of step and against the beat. Everyone believed I was doing it on purpose and my *entrée* was very much appreciated. It is possible to have many types of individuals dance in ballets, even lame persons, who in certain things can be as successful as others. It is not that good dancers would not be even more successful, but there are some *entrées* where it is a waste to use them; they should be kept for fine dancing and the best steps, for the beauty of a ballet requires that there be some good dancers and *entrées* perfectly danced.

I cannot stand short steps and capers against the beat so commonly used by men who take ladies' or other women's parts. Instead of modest dancing, they do two or three serious steps, then start skipping about in a wild and crazy way. I have seen others representing limping or maimed people who, after coming on stage with crutches, dance a little, then throw away their canes and crutches, and caper about as if ballet could miraculously cure the halt and lame.

It is necessary that *entrées* conclude as they began, since what is shown at the end is what was shown at the beginning (unless it is a metamorphosis). I think it is not right for people to arrive in one way and leave in another as most of our dancers customarily do when they impersonate soldiers, villagers, or porters. The soldiers arrive with swords and shields, the villagers with baskets, and the porters with hooks. This is fine, but as soon as they have danced one figure in this attire, they throw swords, baskets, and hooks into the hall in order

The characters in the court ballet were identified more clearly by what they wore than by what they danced. For *Ballet des Fêtes de Bacchus*, performed in 1651, here are designs for the Marquis de Pify-Genlis as Autumn, with headdress of sheaves of wheat and overflowing cornucopia (left), and the Marquis de Villequier as the River of Forgetfulness, strewn with poppies (right).

to be more at ease in their dancing, and one can no longer recognize what they were, which is very bad. They should have signs on their backs to identify them, like those used by painters who, when they have made a poor picture, write the name of an animal so badly represented that it could not be recognized if they had not done so.

Ballet being a silent play, costumes and actions must enable the spectators to recognize what is represented, and the choreographer must create steps and figures that permit the dancers to perform with what they have to carry; everything will be much better thus. He also must be sure to have an uneven number of figures instead of an even one, and he will keep in mind that comical *entrées* with grotesque costumes ought to be short, for sometimes what seems excellent at first because it is ridiculous becomes boring before long, like good tales that make the wise laugh only once.

As to the serious *entrées*, well danced and with handsome costumes, they must be made to last even longer; if they include five or six figures, airs and steps must be varied to avoid boredom.

It is also very important to take time to study steps and *entrées*. Improvised things are never successful; two weeks are not too much for a great ballet, one week for a small one; and for every three or four *entrées* there must be a dancing master to create the steps and rehearse with singing accompaniment when they will later be accompanied by violins. There is always something that has to be redone; I know very well that those who are used to dancing ballets can learn a step or an *entrée* in a day, but if they dance it well with two days' practice, they will dance even better with four and much better still with eight. Time allows people to see their faults and to correct them, both in dancing and other necessary things. This is not possible when things are done in a hurry.

Of Costumes

Ballet costumes can never be too handsome provided they are made according to the subject. To this end, they must be carefully designed since tailors and headdress-makers follow very exactly the sketches they are given. It is very important that the dancers be dressed in accordance with the characters they represent. One may object that if a cook were to be clothed according to his trade, he would have to be given a greasy outfit and towels, which would nauseate the company; but I would answer by saying that he can be dressed in a more embellished way and one can give him, instead of a greasy towel, one of white taffeta or gauze. It would be ridiculous to see a vine-grower wearing embroidered clothes and a nobleman coarse cotton. One should seek not so much lavishness as fitness, since a buckram or a frieze costume, well related to the subject, will be finer and better than an inappropriate silk one. It is not by spending more but by carefully observing a ballet's organization that one will make it more pleasant.

I have created ballets in which gold-and-silver-bedecked costumes cost no more than a crown apiece, and this is easy to believe since for five pennies I would bespangle it in such a way as to make it appear as impressive by candlelight as a richer one. This device is perfectly satisfactory for those whom I want to delight at little expense. Everything I have said about costumes applies to headdresses, especially the importance of having the costumes of those who represent the same thing look alike, without any difference.

Of Machines

As to machines, they bring a great embellishment to ballets and add to their brilliance when they are beautiful, skillfully maneuvered, and made to fit appropriately into the story. One can give an idea of how to build them only when the subject is perfect and one knows what they are to represent. It is up to the author of the subject or to the organizer to look for good craftsmen to build them and to put them in the hands of people who know how to move them at the right time.

Section Two

DANCE FOR THE EYE
AND THE HEART:
THE EIGHTEENTH CENTURY

In 1682 Claude Ménestrier published a treatise titled *des Ballets anciens et modernes*. Looking back to the standard format of the *ballet de cour*, he agreed with Saint-Hubert that a good subject was most important and also agreed that a dancer's character was established by means of costumes, symbols, and masks as well as by appropriate movements. But going further than his predecessor, Ménestrier asserted that the motions of the body were capable of depicting inner feelings that could be made known in no other way. He distinguished "*danse simple*," which merely observed musical cadences, from "ballet," which was an imitation, in Aristotle's sense, of the actions and passions of man. Alas, he sighed, dancers would rather do pretty steps than represent something—thus setting the problem for the coming century.

When he retired from performing in 1670, Louis XIV had established a school for the training of dancers and therefore the following year, when the Paris Opéra opened, its directors knew where to turn for a corps de ballet. At first all the dancers were men, but as early as 1681 a Mlle. Lafontaine appeared on the Opéra stage. Her ballet master was Charles-Louis Beauchamps who, we are told, got ideas for choreographic patterns by watching pigeons as they scurried after the corn he threw them. He was succeeded by Louis Pécour, and soon other dancers are being mentioned—Marie-Thérèse Subligny, Jean Balon, Louis Dupré.

In 1700 Raoul Feuillet published his *Chorégraphie*, describing a system of dance notation that conveniently tells us a good deal about the technique of the time. All five positions are now properly numbered. Many of the steps notated by Feuillet sound familiar to us—*coupé, pirouette, entrechat, sissonne*. In most instances their execution was somewhat different from ours, but the basic shape of the movement was sufficiently similar that we can recognize the foundation of our present forms.

Most important was the increasing emphasis on the turnout, which now had the feet placed to form a right angle. Since the introduction of the proscenium arch in the mid-seventeenth century, dancers had been performing on a stage with an audience seated in front of them. The floor patterns which had been so dazzling to spectators placed above and around three sides of a ballroom were no longer visible. Very visible, however, were the designs made by the individual dancer. Light jumps became more frequent and were ornamented with small beats; varieties of *pirouettes* appeared. By increasing his turnout, the dancer found such movements easier to perform; his legs moved more freely in the hip sockets and his base of support was more stable.

There was still comparatively little distinction between the steps of the ballroom and those of the stage, both aiming for the qualities admired in the most typical of eighteenth-century dances, the minuet. Nobility, precision, grace, and lightness were the attributes of the accomplished dancer. Rameau's *The Dancing Master* (1725) illustrates the five turned-out positions, but they are demonstrated by a gentleman in full courtly regalia, ready to embark on a minuet.

As dancing masters perfected their teaching methods and professional dancers acquired greater skills, the gulf between social and theatre dance widened. Decorum remained the standard, but for the stage the norm was somewhat relaxed. Soame Jenyns marked the distinction in his *The Art of Dancing* (1729):

'Tis not a nimble Bound or Caper high
That can pretend to please a curious Eye;
Good judges no such Tumblers Tricks regard,
Or think them beautiful because they're hard;
Yet in Stage-dancing, *if performed with Skill
Such active Feats our Eyes with Wonder fill.* . . .

Soon after the Restoration (1660) French dancers began appearing in England, most often in dances inserted between the acts of a play or in afterpieces to a dramatic offering. Their formal, elegant manoeuvres were brightened by dazzling bits of virtuosity that made them the delight of London. Native dancers often appeared on the same bills, but usually in what we would now call character dances, with titles like "The Highland Lilt" and "The Dutch Skipper." Nevertheless, it was the Englishman Josias Priest who choreographed the distinguished ballets in the operas of Henry Purcell, beginning with *Dido and Aeneas* (c. 1689).

Another choreographer, John Weaver, commended Priest for his ability to represent "all manner of passions," but he derided the visiting Balon for showing nothing more than "modulated motion." In his *Essay Towards an History of Dancing* (1712) Weaver asserted that with a genuine performer

the Spectator will not only be pleas'd and diverted with the Beauty of the Performance *and Symmetry of the* Movements; *but will also be instructed by the* Positions, Steps *and* Attitudes, *so as to be able to judge of the* Design *of the Performer. And without the help of an Interpreter, a Spectator shall at a distance, by the lively Representation of a just Character, be capable of understanding the* Subject *of the Story represented, and able to distinguish the several* Passions, Manners, *or* Actions, *as of* Love, Anger, *or the Like.*

This sounds like Ménestrier, with the important difference that Weaver makes no mention of the aids to characterization afforded by costumes, masks, and verses. Indeed, he felt them unnecessary, believing that bodily movement by itself was sufficient to make the dramatic points. Significantly Weaver's favorite ballerina—the first produced by England—was the lovely Hester Santlow, who later became a distinguished actress.

Unfortunately, the few pantomimes that Weaver produced in accordance, he believed, with the principles of the ancient Greeks, were not nearly so successful with the public as the virtuosity of the inexpressive French dancers or the rollicking Harlequinades of his rival John Rich, who diverted his audiences by being hatched from an egg and turning into a flower.

Across the channel, the vogue for virtuosity accelerated. Probably a number of women wanted to emulate the jumps of the men, but they were weighted down with farthingales or panniers. Marie Camargo, who made her Paris Opéra debut in 1726, is credited with shortening the ballerina's skirt by several inches to gain freedom and visibility for her *entrechat quatre.* Since she was the first woman on the Parisian stage to manage this jump, enhanced by a quick beating together of the feet, she had reason to want her ankles to show. She may also have been the first to dance in heelless slippers, another innovation explainable by the desire for elevation, which is facilitated when the starting position is a solid *plié* with the heels firmly planted on the floor.

While Camargo was famous for her brilliant style, her rival Marie Sallé was known as a dancer-actress. Sallé was not happy in Paris and danced frequently in London, which appreciated her dramatic abilities. Her costume reforms were even more extreme than Camargo's, but she made them for purposes of characterization rather than display. In *Pygmalion*, which she danced in 1734, she discarded not only the conventional skirt but even her corset, wearing a simple muslin robe draped like that of a Greek statue. Sallé was the first woman choreographer of note, and *Pygmalion* was her own composition. A contemporary critic, Louis de Cahusac, remarked that one could read in Sallé's movements a whole range of emotions.

But among dancers Sallé was an exception, and she had no immediate followers. Succeeding ballerinas, like Anna Heinel, the first woman to do double *pirouettes*, concentrated on virtuosity. In this area the ballerinas had strong competition, for in the second half of the eighteenth century the male dancers were supreme. Outstanding among them were Gaetan and Auguste Vestris, the father and son who dominated the Paris Opéra. Both were vain, Auguste claiming that there were only three great men in Europe—Voltaire, the King of Prussia, and himself; Gaetan admitted Auguste's superiority, but attributed it to the advantage of his having so great a father.

Fortunately, they were not rivals for roles, since the Opéra maintained strict categories. Gaetan was a *danseur noble*, tall and stately in bearing, suited to the serious and heroic ballets. Of medium height, Auguste played lighter roles in the *demi-caractère* class. The third rank was that of *danseur comique*, who played humorous roles exclusively; there was no crossing of the lines. Rigidly, the Opéra designated which steps were to be allotted to which category. Whether the characters were courtiers or gods, they danced in the same majestic manner; when they were Turks or American Indians, as in *Les Indes Gallants* of 1735, the costumes rather than the movement style remained their chief mode of identification.

Outside of Paris, however, some choreographers were working to promote the cause of the *ballet d'action*. In Vienna Franz Hilverding staged mimed versions of the great tragedies; his student, Gasparo Angiolini, was especially concerned with dramatic gestures that were closely related to musical rhythms and phrases, and he numbered Gluck among his collaborators.

The best known of the dramatic choreographers was Jean Georges Noverre, who not only created many ballets but also wrote about his artistic convictions with proselytizing zeal. While his contemporaries at the Paris Opéra were devising nothing but pretty combinations of steps to exhibit the fancy new *pirouettes* and *entrechats*, Noverre insisted that ballet should represent action, character, and feeling. He was more vehement than Weaver in his proclamations. The art, he complained, in his *Letters* of 1760, "has remained in its infancy only because its effects have been limited, like those of fireworks designed simply to gratify the eyes; although this art shares with the best plays the advantage of inspiring, moving, and captivating the spectator by the charm of its interest and illusion. No one has suspected its power of speaking to the heart." Noverre's ballets, with their finely wrought dramatic structure and well-developed characterizations, won him the admiration of the great English actor David Garrick. The nymphs and gods of Noverre, unlike those of Beaujoyeulx, who conceived them as symbols of good or evil, were individuals; even when composing for the corps de ballet, Noverre wanted expressive movement to replace the formal symmetry that then dominated the stage of the Opéra.

Still, Noverre was a man of his time. When he said that dance should be an imitation of nature, he was quick to qualify that he meant "beautiful" nature. His characters were nymphs and shepherds, goddesses and epic heroes; the plots were filled with noble passions and sentiments of grandeur. His pupil, Jean Dauberval, shared his master's beliefs but felt the influence of the ideas that were rapidly changing European society. He was the first ballet choreographer to treat peasants as real people, and though *La Fille Mal Gardée* hardly presented a realistic view of folk life, its ambitious mother, willful daughter, rich fiancé, and simple suitor were likeable and believable.

Dauberval's student Salvatore Viganò, whom Stendhal compared to Shakespeare, carried the idea of dramatic movement still further. Though his early works provided opportunities for set dances, his later ballets made fewer concessions. In 1819 his last production, *The Titans*, told its epic story of greed and violence in unrelieved stretches of rhythmic pantomime.

Ménestrier had remarked that dancers would rather do pretty steps than represent something. Now that their technical skills were approaching new heights, it was unlikely that they would consent for long to appear in ballets that offered no occasions for them to display their virtuosity. A solution was at hand—but it arrived with another era.

Gottfried Taubert (c.1673–17?)
THE MINUET
Translated from the German by Angelika Gerbes

Born around 1673, Taubert lived in Saxony, spending eleven years at the University of Leipzig. In 1702 he moved to Danzig, where he had an apparent monopoly on the teaching of dance and decorum. He returned to Leipzig in 1714.

Taubert's description of the minuet, agreeing in many respects with the French manuals, is clearer than most contemporary accounts and is especially interesting for the extent of the embellishments it specifies. The details he gives should be viewed in the context of the period style, which is so well described by Shirley Wynne in "Complaisance, An Eighteenth-Century Cool" (Dance Scope *[Fall, 1970]):*

SOURCE: From *Der Rechtschaffener Tantzmeister* (Leipzig, 1717).

To move impulsively, explosively, or exuberantly was a breach of etiquette. . . . Ball dances and ballets, the lines of separation between them being still very indistinct in the earlier period, conformed entirely to these social codes. The chief action features of these dances can be described as vertical (no elevation implied), narrow, and slender, with a general gathering in toward the vertical axis; the torso remained still, with a firm upright tension, while the head tilted and turned, and the shoulders shifted slightly in an épaulement limited in ladies during the turn of the century by the shoulder bands of the corset. The forearms, wrists and fingers, the lower legs and feet were highly decorative. They performed fluttering embroideries on the periphery of a controlled and tranquil center.

Dance—*Révérence*, social—gentleman

1. Both knees bend gently and not very far. In rising, one steps a little back with the right leg (that is: with the right leg *coupiret*[1] to the back). Others, not without reason, pull the right foot up against the left one during the knee bend either in front, to the side, or also in back as it is customary in the *coupé*. Others, before the bend, beat several times with the extended right leg against the front of the extended left leg. Still others beat in front and back, and only then *coupiren* with it to the back or side and brush back with the left. . . . In straightening up [after the bow[2]] the right foot, with the heel released from the ground, is at the same time pulled high onto the half-toe and held there quietly for a moment.

(This is the first cadence or dance measure. . . .)

Then 2. Both knees bend again. In rising, the right foot high on point is brushed forward toward the left side. Then with bent knees step on the heel, and balance the body over the right leg. In rising, the left one is placed against the right one. On the toes of the right foot make a quarter turn to the right to come to rest facing the partner, who has swung to her left. (During the turn for purposes of grace one can beat with the left foot several times in back, or also once in front and back. This is the other cadence.)

Finally, 3. Once again both knees bend. In rising one steps with the left one away upwards [up the hall] on a straight side line, so that one can see heel next to heel but with the space of a foot between them. Then, in the third cadence, the other back-*révérence*, which is performed toward the lady, is brushed back with the right foot. . . .

[1] *Coupiret*, also *coupiren* or *coupire* depending on the usage, consists of the French *coupé* with a German ending. The term describes the cutting action of the leg as it is brought from fourth position back through first position to fourth position front.

[2] Of the bow, Taubert says, "the body gently and slowly bends deeper and deeper from the hips . . . letting the arms hang naturally in front."

Dance—*Révérence*, social—lady

Like the gentleman, the lady makes a double *révérence* both before and after the dance. In both instances she performs the ordinary back *révérence*. . . . [3] One *révérence* is toward the spectators and the other one toward her partner. With the exception of the *battement* of the feet all that her partner does on the right leg the lady performs on her left and vice versa. . . .

Pas ordinaire or common step in dancing

The *pas ordinaire* or ordinary straight steps which in dancing are executed without bending have their name from the ordinary steps in walking. They are performed as in walking, except that instead of occurring on the whole foot they are executed on the toes.

Each of these steps be it forward, backward, or sideward can be divided into two parts. The first part contains three considerations. While standing firmly and straight on one leg:

1. the heel of the other foot is lifted off the ground with a slightly bent knee.
2. The whole foot is raised, and
3. is brought bent and close over the ground up to the heel of the other foot.

The second part has four considerations. Namely: the foot which was brought to the side of the other one

1. from there is extended close to the ground a good shoe's length (according to the person's stature) either to the front, back, or side (depending into which direction one is dancing).
2. There, well turned-out and neatly closed, it is set down on the toes.
3. The body is brought onto it firmly and in good balance.
4. The other foot, as has already been mentioned in the first part, is made to follow bent, and is firmly pulled close either in front, back, or to the side (depending upon the direction in which one has made the stiff step). . . .

Demi-coupé

Part I

1. The left leg having been set forward and with the body resting on it, one bends both knees well out to both sides, but not too deeply.
2. During the bending the right foot advances close to the ground up to and next to the heel of the left. (The point may thereby not rise

[3] Her bow is like the man's but she replaces the forward bend of the torso with a bending of the knees.

up. The body must remain steadily in a perpendicular line.) And that is the *plié*.

Part II

1. One rises and extends both knees again, and
2. during the extending, places the right foot forward without brushing. And this is the *pas élevé*.

In short: a half *coupé* is when one bends with both knees at the same time, and in rising places the back foot down in front. . . .

Coupé

Part I

After having placed the body weight over the left leg, which is located not too far in front of the right leg, and at the same time having lifted the heel of the right foot (which is in back) off the ground,

1. one bends both knees at the same time, and
2. while the bending continues, advances the right leg forward until it is next to the left one. (This is the *plié*.)

Part II

1. One *coupiret* and finishes by bringing the right leg off the ground and bent to the front.
2. Then one rises somewhat more strongly than in the *demi-coupé*. (This is the *pas élevé*.)

Part III

1. In rising one brings the left foot to the heel of the right one, and
2. from there brushes it forward on the point. (This is the *pas glissé*.)

Here it is to be noted that like the *demi-coupé* the whole *coupé*

1. can be performed on the left as well as the right leg as well as
2. forward, backward, and sideward to the left and right,
3. that the other step is not always a brush but very frequently can be a *pas ordinaire*. . . .

Tems de Courante or *Pas grave*—forward

Part I

1. Resting on the left leg, both knees are bent and well turned out.
2. In bending, the ankle bone of the right foot is brought close up against the back of the left one. (Some bring the right heel next to the left heel during the bending. And this is the *plié*.)

Part II

1. During the rising the right foot goes side right. Then with the heel

it is brought around the left heel to the front of the ankle [of the left]. This is the *élevé*.

2. From there it is brushed stiffly and high on the point straight forward. This is the *pas glissé*. . . .

Port de Bras of the *Pas de Menuet*

1. In the upbeat or last quarter note of the previous cadence while resting on the left leg but both knees bending, the arms are brought at the same time from both sides (or only one if one is leading the lady by the hand)
2. slightly bent and with cupped hands and finger ends more inward toward each other and [facing] behind one instead of away from each other sideward or forward,
3. gently fall together in front, but not all too exactly.
4. One carries them like this in the cadence (i.e., during the downbeat) and rising of the first *coupé*
5. for the duration of three quarter notes during the first two steps with the right and left leg, of which either both or only the right one is bent, and the other one executed straight.
6. With the elbows still slightly bent and the hands related,
7. very slowly and gradually they move apart from each other directly to both sides, but not all too far from the body.
8. One extends and rotates them during the extending, which coincides with the second ¾ measure, for the duration of two quarter notes stiffly under the shoulders so that the cupped hands for the most part face forward.
9. Once again they are prepared for the lowering in front which occurs on the fourth step and last quarter [note] of the measure.

And all this must be considered not only for each main *pas* in the Minuet, but also in all low chamber dances which consist of *pas de Menuet*, no matter what their names or figures.

High *Port de Bras*

1. Whenever the first foot [right] executes a *pas*, then (from the shoulders to the elbows both arms held nearly at the same height) at the same time the left arm, attractively bent at the hand and elbow, is carried upward to a point where the fingers are level with the ear or at least with the shoulder. The right arm is gently extended and lowered a little.
2. When the left foot performs a *pas* or movement unit, then the right arm must follow along in the above described manner, and the left arm is extended and lowered.

Pas de Menuet à deux mouvements—forward

1. If the left foot is in front not far from the right, one bends both knees gently outward (whereby the right one lifts slightly off the ground and goes to the side of the left one, so that the left supports the weight). One rises, and during the rise lifts the right foot forward. (The left one follows close to the ground to the side of the right, so that both legs close with straight knees. Consequently the weight is supported by the right leg, because the left foot which was brought up against the right may not make contact with the floor with the ball of the foot. Instead it must be well turned out and extended downward.)
2. One places the left foot (from the side) stiff and well stretched forward on the point;
3. also the right one, and brings the body weight unnoticed onto it.
4. With the weight on the right, one bends both legs. (During the bending one draws the ankle of the left foot up against the back of the right ankle, or also to the side with the heel against the right heel.) Then one rises and during this rise places the left foot (well stretched outward . . .) forward on the point and brings the body weight perpendicularly onto it.

In continuing the dancing one bends again on the left leg right away. During the bending the right heel is brought next to the left one. Thereby the next *pas* has started with this *plié*, with which some persons always conclude the Minuet *pas* for the sake of the connection [continuity]. . . .

[Like all the other basic steps, the *pas de menuet* was also done backwards and to either side. Taubert describes the execution of the step in each direction in detail.]

[Taubert here begins to describe the sequence of the performance of the Minuet.]

. . . After completing two *révérences*, as they have been described in the discussion of the dance *révérences*, one takes the lady by her left hand with the right hand and leads her through a side *pas* and a forward *pas* straight up the hall, and with two side *pas* around one half to the left coming to rest in the center of the floor facing each other, he facing down and she facing up the hall. Letting go of hands, both dance directly back and away from each other with a *pas en fleuret*. . . .

Then both perform the main figure "Z" with two side *pas* to the left, two forward *pas* for the diagonal, and two side *pas* to the right. . . . The hat, which until now has been carried in the left hand, is replaced after the gentleman has passed the lady once.

From P. Rameau, *Le Maître à danser*

In the eighteenth century the King's grand ball was conducted with the strictest social decorum. The correct order of procedure stipulated that the King and Queen dance the first minuet. When His Majesty had returned to his throne (as shown in the illustration), the Queen could lead out a gentleman of her choice or could let the prince next in rank select a lady. Only one couple danced at a time.

Further, after having danced the main figure two, three, or at the most four times, they take right hands and execute one side *pas* to the left, a *contretems* straight forward, two forward *pas* in a circle, and two *pas fleuret* directly behind themselves. . . .

Immediately thereafter they take left hands and both execute a side *pas* to the right, a *contretems* forward, two forward *pas* in a circle, a *fleuret* to the right, and two *pas de Bourrée* to the left and right. . . .

Then they either dance the main figure again once or twice and then take both hands, or take hands immediately after the presentation of the left hand. This happens with a side *pas* to the left, a *contretems* straight forward (for the lady, instead of the *contretems*, we have always prescribed two *pas graves*), and three forward *pas* to the right in a circle. (Here it is to be noted that the gentleman coming downward from up the hall must describe one and one half circles in three main *pas* and therefore in the last main *pas* must turn one quarter with each of the last three steps. The lady, however, moving up from down the hall, describes only one complete circle.) Together they move to their starting place, he with a back *pas* and she with a forward *pas*, and having arrived there finish as they began with a double *révérence*. . . .

[Variations used in the Minuet]

Chassé battu or *de Gigue en tournant*—whole circle

. . . After having made the *plié* in the upbeat, the right foot chases the left foot from its place with a gentle leap, so that it comes to be in the air over the buckle of the right. In this position one makes a complete turn to the left, steps forward with the crossed over left foot, and also with the chasing right, but well outward a little to side right. In the upbeat one takes the preparation for the other *chassé*, which is executed in the same way to the right on the left foot, during the other ¾ measure.

If one wishes to precede this with a half *pirouette* with the right foot behind the left, then the left chases the right around the other half of the circle to the right. . . . But if one wishes to turn the half *pirouette* with the right in front over the left, then the *chassé battu* is completed around to the left by the right foot. . . .

It is even more pleasing if one makes a complete *pirouette* with the right over the left foot as follows: At first, having made a *plié* during the upbeat, during the first two quarter notes the right foot is thrown over the front of the left foot, and a complete turn is made on the toes with both knees straight while rising up. Then, in the third quarter while turning [the body] a little toward the left, the left foot is placed down well outward and the preparation for the *gigue chassé* is taken on it. This *pirouette* and *chassé* together take up the same amount of time as a main *pas de Menuet*, and they can be repeated.

One can also make this whole *pirouette* twice in a row to the left. And after that one can also perform the *chassé* with a complete turn twice in a row, the first one to the left and the other to the right. If there is occasion to frolic a little longer, one can also add a *pas de sissonne* with the right and left leg springing around to the right. . . .

Pas de sissonne

. . . In short: One springs either forward or backward [landing with the legs] bent and crossed so that the feet are well turned out and close together and the knees are well bent outward. The legs are closed so that the calves touch each other. In this elevation one can occasionally turn one quarter or one half. Then one springs again into the air on one leg [going from two supports to one] and at the same time again extends one foot sideward.

This crossed air step can occur on the left or right leg, as well as in front or in back of the other leg. Also, after the crossed springing sometimes the stepping foot and sometimes the other foot is lifted to the side. . . .

Straight *capriole*—from one leg onto the other

A very attractive *capriole*, used in the Minuet either in moving forward or backward across the dance floor or while standing still, is one in which one springs from one leg to the other several times in a row. Each time one makes in the air either quick little beats with both legs extended next to each other while suspended, landing with the springing foot earlier than the other one, or one beats two or three times from the side with the leg on which one lands. In that case the calves are not brought in contact with each other. One can also spring from one leg to the other so that in the air the back foot always beats over the front one.

This springing from one leg onto the other can be repeated four or eight times in the Minuet, that is, repeated four times in each dance measure. As in the main *pas de Menuet*, each time the first elevation requires two quarter notes and the second one only one quarter, the third again two, and the fourth only one quarter note of the measure. . . .

The best place for variations is at the end of the main figure in turning about. Not only has one room to turn here, especially if one prepares for it in time, but one also has the lady in line of vision and can therefore see exactly when she turns so that at all times one can continue forth with her and not confuse her with prolonged variations. . . .

In short: a well-prepared dancer must not tie himself down in the Minuet. Instead, he should mingle in this place and that place these steps, and another time those steps, but always attractively and fitting correctly into the cadence.

John Weaver (1673–1760)
THE LOVES OF MARS
AND VENUS

Born in Shrewsbury, Weaver probably taught there before coming to London in 1702. We have only a few records of him as a performer, but he left us three librettos of his "dramatick entertainments of dancing" along with several major historical and theoretical works on the art. Though he apparently attracted a small, loyal following, there is no evidence that his innovations caused any great theatrical excitement; perhaps he lacked the aggressiveness of Noverre, who later proposed similar reforms, or perhaps the time was not yet ripe. Sometime after 1733 Weaver returned, contentedly it would seem, to teaching in Shrewsbury, where he was remembered as "a little dapper cheerful man."

The libretto for **The Loves of Mars and Venus** *shows that the verses and songs of the* **Ballet Comique** *have vanished and that the dancers no longer need to carry badges of identification. Now the choreographer could create individual portraits in movement—if he so wished. At this time John Weaver was practically unique in wishing to do so.*

Preface

I know it will be expected that I should give the Reader some Account of the Nature of this kind of Entertainment in Dancing, which I have here attempted to revive from the Ancients, in Imitation of their Pantomimes: I call it an Attempt, or Essay, because this is the first Trial of this Nature that has been made since the Reign of Trajan, as far as I have been able to trace it; Pliny, in his Panegyrick to that Emperor, being the last Author of the Ancients that takes any Notice of 'em:

SOURCE: *The Loves of Mars and Venus; A Dramatick Entertainment of Dancing, Attempted in Imitation of the Pantomimes of the Ancient Greeks and Romans* (London, 1717).

Therefore I am in hopes the Town will judge favourably of this Performance; and I have the more reason to depend upon their Candour on this Account, because that I have not been able to get all my Dancers equal to the Design; not but that I must acknowledge my Obligations to all the Performers for their obliging Willingness, and being ready to perform, as far as they were capable of entring into a Design so entirely novel and foreign to their present Manner of Dancing.

It will be necessary that I let my Reader know, that these Mimes and Pantomimes were Dancers that represented a Story or Fable in Motion and Measure: They were Imitators of all things, as the Name of Pantomime imports, and perform'd all by Gesture and the Action of the Hands, Fingers, Legs and Feet, without making use of the Tongue. The Face or Countenance had a large Share in this Performance, and they imitated the Manners, Passions, and Affections, by the numerous Variety of Gesticulations. And it is evident from the Writers of those Times, that they pursued the Rules of the Drama in their mute Performances, by confining each Representation to a certain Action, with a just Observation of the Manners and Passions, which that Action naturally produced. No Body can deny, but that their Performances were surprizing, and that the Difficulty of doing it appear'd almost beyond Conception; yet the Testimonies of those who saw these Things done, are too strong to suffer us to doubt of the Matter of Fact. Indeed the Force and Beauty of graceful Motion, and handsome Gesture, were so little understood amongst us some few Years ago, that it seem'd still more incredible: And I am satisfied, that the agreeable Appearance some of our best Players make upon the Stage at this Time, is as much owing to the Justness of their Action, as any other Qualification whatsoever.

In short, this is an Art or Science imitative and demonstrative, and not to be attain'd without Difficulty and Application: And a Master who would manage this Art skilfully, ought to be endued with a good Fancy, and sound Judgment, actively apt and industrious in observing Mens Natures, and assimilating their Manners, and imitating all things with Gesture; for Nature assign'd each Motion of the Mind its proper Gesticulation and Countenance, as well as Tone; whereby it is significantly and decently express'd: And indeed Decency of Expression doth so depend on this Art, that the Grammarians observe, Decency is properly spoken of Gesture.

Tho' I have endeavour'd to enter into the Characters, I represent, and describe their Manners and Passions by proper Actions and Gesture suitable to the Fable: Yet I must confess it may be objected, that I have in this Entertainment too much inclin'd to the Modern Dancing; but when the Spectator shall consider the Greatness of such a Design, and could he be apprized of the Difficulties attending such an Undertaking, with the Necessity of having both Dancers and Spectators instructed by degrees, with the Rules and Expressions of Gesticulation, I hope they will readily excuse my not sticking so very close to the Pantomime, especially since this Performance was design'd only as an Attempt to encourage others more capable of bringing it to its ancient Perfection.

Those who would know more of the Pantomimes, may look into the Essay towards the History of Dancing.

Drama

MARS,—The God of War, the Son of Juno. The Ancient Latins gave him the Title of Salisubsubus, from Dancing and Leaping; he intrigued with Venus, was discover'd in his Amour by Vulcan, and taken by him in a Net. Danc'd by Mr. Dupré, Senior.

VULCAN,—Son of Jupiter and Juno; for his Deformity Jupiter threw him down from Heaven; he fell on the Isle of Lemmos, and broke his Leg in the Fall; he kept a Forge there, and work'd for the Gods; he was Husband to Venus. Danc'd by Mr. Weaver.

VENUS,—The Goddess of Love and Beauty, was Daughter of Jupiter and Dione; she was Wife to Vulcan, and Mistress to Mars. Danc'd by Mrs. Santlow.

AGLAIA, THALIA, EUPHROSYNE, were the 3 Graces, constant Attendants on Venus/ Mrs. Bicknall, Mrs. Younger, Mrs. Willis.

THE FOUR FOLLOWERS OF MARS/ Danc'd by Mr. Prince, Mr. Bovall, Mr. Wade, Mr. Birkhead.

FOUR CYCLOPS. They were Workmen to Vulcan.

THREE MORE CYCLOPS.

GALLUS, Attendant on Mars.

ONE OF THE HOURS attending on Venus.

CUPID.

JUPITER, JUNO, APOLLO, DIANA, NEPTUNE, THETIS/ Gods and Goddesses.

SCENE I. A CAMP

The Entertainment opens with a Martial Overture; at the Conclusion of which four Followers, or Attendants of Mars, arm'd with Sword, and Target, enter and Dance a Pyrrhic to a March; then follows a Warlike Prelude which introduces Mars attended by Gallus carrying his Sword and Buckler; he performs his Entry, and then joyns in Pyrrhic Mood with his Followers; wherein he appears engaged sometimes with two at a time, and sometimes with all four: At last he clears the Stage; which finishes the Entry, and first Scene. . . .

The manner of the Performance of the Pyrrhic Dance seems to have consisted chiefly in the nimble turning of the Body, the shifting, and avoiding the Stroke of the Enemy; and therefore, this was one of the Exercises in which young Soldiers were train'd; and was in such Esteem in Thessaly that they stil'd their Princes, and Generals, Leaders of the Dance. The Nature then of this Dance being warlike; and as we have shewn, made use of by the Ancients for the Discipline and Marshalling their Soldiers, I thought it the most proper for the introducing the Character of Mars. . . .

SCENE II

After a Simphony of Flutes, etc., the Scene opens and discovers Venus in her Dressing-Room at her Toilet, attended by the Graces, who are employ'd in dressing her. Cupid lies at her Feet, and one of the Hours waits by. Venus rises, and dances a Passacaile: The Graces joyn her in the same Movement, as does also the Hour. The Dance being ended, the Tune changes to a wild rough Air. Venus, Graces, etc., seem in Surprize; and at the Approach of Vulcan, the Graces, and Cupid run off.

Enter to Venus, Vulcan: They perform a Dance together; in which Vulcan expresses his Admiration; Jealousie; Anger; and Despite; And Venus shows Neglect; Coquetry; Contempt; and Disdain.

This last Dance being altogether of the Pantomimic kind; it is necessary that the Spectator should know some of the most particular Gestures made use of therein; and what Passions, or Affections, they discover; represent; or express.

Admiration. Admiration is discover'd by the raising up of the right Hand, the Palm turn'd upwards, the Fingers clos'd; and in one Motion the Wrist turn'd round and Fingers spread; the Body reclining, and Eyes fix'd on the Object; but when it rises to

Astonishment. Both hands are thrown up towards the Skies; the Eyes also lifted up, and the Body cast backwards.

Jealousy. Jealousy will appear by the Arms suspended, or a particular pointing the middle Finger to the Eye; by an irresolute movement throughout the Scene, and a Thoughtfulness of Countenance.

Upbraiding. The Arms thrown forwards; the Palm of the Hands turn'd outward; the Fingers open, and the Elbows turn'd inward to the Breast; shew Upbraiding and Despite.

Anger. The left Hand struck suddenly with the right; and sometimes against the Breast; denotes Anger.

Threats. Threatening is express'd by raising the Hand, and shaking the bended Fist; knitting the Brow; biting the Nails, and catching back the Breath.

Power. The Arm, with impetuous Agitation, directed forwards to the Person, with an awful Look, implies Authority.

Impatience. Impatience is seen by the smiting of the Thigh, or Breast with the Hand.

Indignation. When it rises to Anguish, and Indignation, it is express'd by applying the Hand passionately to the Forehead; or by stepping back the right foot, leaning the Body quite backward, the Arms extended, Palms clos'd, and Hands thrown quite back; the Head cast back, and Eyes fix'd upwards.

These are some of the Actions made use of by Vulcan; those by Venus are as follows:—

Coquetry. Coquetry will be seen in the affected Airs, given her self throughout the whole Dance.

Neglect. Neglect will appear in the scornful turning the Neck; the flirting outward the back of the right hand, with a Turn of the Wrist.

Contempt. Contempt is express'd by scornful Smiles; forbidding Looks; tossing of the Head; filliping of the Fingers; and avoiding the Object.

Distaste. The left Hand thrust forth with the Palm turn'd backward; the left Shoulder rais'd, and the Head bearing towards the Right, denotes an Abhorrence, and Distaste.

Detestation. When both the turn'd-out Palms are so bent to the left Side, and the Head still more projected from the Object; it becomes a more passionate Form of Detestation, as being a redoubled Action.

SCENE III

With this last Action Venus quits the Stage in order to meet Mars; Vulcan remains, and moving up the Stage strikes at the Scene which opens to Vulcan's Shop, where the Cyclops are discover'd at Work; some at the Forge; some at the Anvil; some Hammering; and some Fileing; while Cupid is pointing his Arrows at the Grindlestone. Jupiter's Thunder; Mars's Armour; Neptune's Trident; Pallas's Spear, etc., are all laid on the Floor. A rough Consort of Musick is heard while they are at Work, adapted to the particular Sounds of the Shop; after which four of the Cyclops advance, and perform their Entry; with whom Vulcan joyns; and in the Dance, delivers Wire to the Cyclops to form a Net; and turns them in, to their Work, and the Scene shuts.

To exalt, or lift up the stretch'd-out Hand, expresses some notable Exploit in Hand.

SCENE IV—A GARDEN

A Prelude of Trumpets, Hautbois, Violins and Flutes alternate; to which
   Mars with his Followers enter on one Side; and Venus, with Graces,
   etc., on the other. Mars and Venus meet and embrace; Gallantry,
   Respect; Ardent Love; and Adoration; appear in the Actions of Mars:
   An affected Bashfulness; reciprocal Love; and wishing Looks, in Venus;
   they sit on a Couch, while the four Followers of Mars begin the Entry;
   to whom the Graces joyn; and Afterwards Mars and Venus: At which
   time Cupid steals away the Arms of Mars and his Followers.

This Performance is alternate, as representing Love and War: It is
somewhat in Imitation of a Dancing among the Ancients, in which
the Lacedemonian Youth delighted much, as being equally inclin'd to
Love, and Arms; one singular Beauty in this sort of Dance, is; that
Strength, and Softness, reciprocally, and alternately are seen in their
full Power: when in the same Representation; and at the same time;
the Fire; Robustness; and Strength of the Warrior is seen, mixt with
the Softness, and Delicacy of Love; Boldness, and Vigour, in one, and
a coy, and complying Reluctance, in the other.
   As to the Gestures made use of in this Scene; they are so obvious,
relating only to Gallantry, and Love; that they need no Explanation.
   The Dance concludes, with every Man carrying off his Woman.

SCENE V

Vulcan is discover'd leaning in a thoughtful Posture on his Anvil; the
   Cyclops appear working the Net; they joyn it together; Vulcan dances.
   The Cyclops having finish'd, bring it forward, and shew it Vulcan,
   he approves of it, and they carry it off, etc.

Pleas'd at some Contrivance. To rub the Palms of the Hands together,
after the manner as those who take Pains to heat their Hands; is an
Expression of being pleas'd at some Thought of Deceit.

SCENE VI

A soft Symphony of Flutes, to which the Scene draws and discovers
   Mars and Venus sitting on a Couch; Gallus sleeping; and Cupid play-
   ing; etc. Mars and Venus express by their Gesticulations, equal Love,
   and Satisfaction; and a pleas'd Tenderness which supposes past
   Embraces. Vulcan and Cyclops enter; the Net falls over Mars, and
   Venus, who seem slumbering, and being catch'd, appear in the utmost
   Confusion. An insulting Performance by Vulcan and the Cyclops.
   After which enter Jupiter, Apollo, Neptune, Juno, Diana and Thetis.
   Vulcan shows them his Prisoners. Shame; Confusion; Grief; and Sub-

mission, are discover'd in the Actions of Venus; Audacity, Vexation; Restlessness; and a kind of unwilling Resignation; in those of Mars. The Actions of Vulcan are of Rejoicing; Insulting; and Derision. Neptune intercedes with Vulcan for them. Vulcan at length condescends; and forgives them; and they are releas'd. Mars, with the rest of the Gods, and Goddesses, dance a Grand Dance, which concludes the Entertainment.

Triumphing. To shake the Hand open, rais'd above our Head, is an exulting Expression of Triumph, Etc.

Entreaty. The stretching out the Hands downward toward the Knees, is an Action of Entreaty, and suing for Mercy.

Grief. Grief is express'd by hanging down the Head; wringing the Hands; and striking the Breast.

Resignation. To hold out both the Hands joyn'd together, is a natural Expression of Submission and Resignation.

Forgiveness. To extend and offer out the Right Hand, is a Gesture of Pitty, and Intention of Forgiveness.

Shame. The covering the Face with the Hand, is a Sign of Shame.

Reconciliation. To shake the given Hand, or embrace the Body, is an Expression of Friendship, Reconciliation, and the like.

FINIS

Jean Georges Noverre (1727–1810)
TWO LETTERS ON DANCING
Translated by Cyril W. Beaumont

Trained at the Paris Opéra, Noverre longed to be ballet master there, a goal he achieved in 1776 only to leave a few years later, embittered by jealousies and intrigues. Previously he had served the courts of Stuttgart and Vienna, where he taught the young Marie Antoinette. Noverre's first visit to London was nearly disastrous due to the outbreak of hostilities between England and France, but his later engagements there met with great success. Acclaimed by many of his contemporaries as a genius whose works were unsurpassed for taste and imagination, Noverre excited less enthusiasm for his backstage behavior, being

SOURCE: II and IV from *Letters on Dancing and Ballets* (London: Beaumont, 1951)

recalled as "a passionate little fellow" who "swore and tore behind the scenes."

The temperament is amply evident in the famous Lettres sur la danse et les ballets, *which was first published in Stuttgart in 1760 and went through several editions in the author's lifetime. Here he inveighs against prevailing customs of costume design; the use of masks that hid the potentially expressive features of the dancers; the composition of dances to suit the personality and skills of the performer rather than the dramatic needs of the role. Unlike Weaver, Noverre attracted disciples, who carried on his concepts of the* ballet d'action *in spite of the cool indifference of the Paris Opéra.*

Letter II

I cannot refrain, Sir, from expressing my disapproval of those *maîtres de ballet* who have the ridiculous obstinacy to insist that the members of the *corps de ballet* shall take them as a model and regulate their movements, gestures and attitudes accordingly. May not such a singular claim prevent the development of the executants' natural graces and stifle their innate powers of expression?

This principle appears to me the more dangerous in that it is rare to meet with *maîtres de ballet* capable of real feeling; so few of them are excellent actors competent to depict in gesture the thoughts they wish to express. It is so difficult, I say, to meet with a modern Bathyllus or Pylades, that I cannot avoid condemning all those who, from self-conceit, have the pretension to imitate them. If their powers of emotion be weak, their powers of expression will be likewise; their gestures will be feeble, their features characterless, and their attitudes devoid of passion. Surely, to induce the *figurants* to copy so mediocre a model is to lead them astray? Is not a production marred when it is awkwardly executed? Moreover, is it possible to lay down fixed rules for pantomimic action? Are not gestures the offspring of feeling and the faithful interpreters of every mood?

In these circumstances, a careful *maître de ballet* should act like the majority of poets who, having neither the talent nor the natural gifts necessary to declamation, have their works recited and rely entirely on the intelligence of the actors for their interpretation. They are present, you will say, at the rehearsals. I agree, but less to lay down precepts than to offer advice. "This scene appears to me feeble; in another, your delivery is weak; this incident is not acted with sufficient fire, and the picture which results from that situation leaves something to be desired": that is how the poet speaks. The *maître de ballet*, for his part, must continually rehearse a mimed scene until the performers have arrived

JASON ET MEDEE   BALLET TRAGIQUE.

In a scene from Noverre's *Jason and Medea*, as performed in London in 1781, the dancers are (left to right) Giovanna Baccelli, Gaëtan Vestris, and Madame Simonet. Noverre based many of his ballets on the plots of such classical Greek tragedies. The histrionic gestures, which seem exaggerated to us, are similar to those depicted in contemporary prints of actors and probably show the influence of the style of David Garrick.

at that moment of expression innate in mankind, a precious moment which is revealed with both strength and truth when it is the outcome of feeling.

A well-composed ballet is a living picture of the passions, manners, customs, ceremonies and customs of all nations of the globe, consequently, it must be expressive in all its details and speak to the soul through the eyes; if it be devoid of expression, of striking pictures, of strong situations, it becomes a cold and dreary spectacle. This form of art will not admit of mediocrity; like the art of painting, it exacts a perfection the more difficult to acquire in that it is dependent on the faithful imitation of nature, and it is by no means easy, if not almost impossible, to seize on that kind of seductive truth which, masking illusion from the spectator, transports him in a moment to the spot where the action has taken place and fills him with the same thoughts that he would experience were he to witness in reality the incident which art has presented to him in counterfeit. What accuracy is required to avoid passing above, or falling below, the model it is desired to copy! To over-refine a model is as dangerous as to disfigure it: these two faults are equally opposed to truth; the one transcends nature, the other degrades it.

Ballets, being representations, should unite the various parts of the drama. Themes expressed in dancing are, for the most part, devoid of sense, and offer a confused medley of scenes as ill-connected as they are ill-ordered; however, in general, it is imperative to submit to certain principles. The subject of every ballet must have its introduction, plot and climax. The success of this type of entertainment depends partly on the careful choice of subjects and their arrangement. . . .

Diana and Acteon, Diana and Endymion, Apollo and Daphne, Tito and Aurora, Acis and Galatea, as well as all other themes of this nature, cannot provide the plot for a *ballet d'action* without the inspiration of truly poetic genius. Telemachus, in the Isle of Calypso, offers a wider field and would provide the theme for a very fine ballet, always presuming the composer had the skill to omit everything of no value to a painter, to introduce Mentor at the right moment, and to remove him the instant his presence became superfluous.

If the licence that is taken daily in theatrical productions cannot be stretched so far as to make Mentor dance in the ballet of Telemachus, then it is a more than sufficient reason that the composer should not employ this character save with the greatest caution. If he do not dance he is foreign to the ballet, besides, his powers of expression, being deprived of the graces which dancing affords to gestures and attitudes, would make him appear less animated, less passionate, and consequently of less interest. A genius may break ordinary rules and advance by new paths when they lead to the perfection of his art. . . .

Mentor, in a ballet, can and ought to dance. This will offend against neither truth nor probability, provided that the composer has the skill to devise for him a manner of dancing and expression consonant with his character, age and employment. I believe, Sir, that I would hazard the adventure, and that I should avoid the greater of two evils, that sense of tedium which should never be experienced by the spectator. . . .

Undoubtedly, one of the essential points in a ballet is variety; the incidents and pictures which result from it should succeed each other with rapidity; if the action do not move quickly, if the scenes drag, if enthusiasm be not communicated everywhere equally; indeed, if the ballet do not constantly increase in interest and attraction in proportion to the development of the theme; the plan is ill-conceived, ill-ordered; it sins against the laws of the theatre, and the representation has no other effect on the spectator than that of the boredom induced by it. . . .

Every complicated and long-drawn-out ballet which does not explain to me, simply and clearly, the action which it represents, the plot of which I cannot follow without constant reference to the programme—every ballet of which I do not understand the plan, which does not afford me an introduction, plot and climax—will be no more, in my opinion, than a simple entertainment based on dancing, more or less well executed. It will move me but little, since it will be expressionless and devoid of action and interest.

But the dancing of our time is beautiful, it will be said, able to captivate and please, even when it does not possess the feeling and wit with which you wish it to be embellished. I will admit that the mechanical execution of that art has been brought to a degree of perfection which leaves nothing to be desired; I will even add that it often has grace and nobility; but these represent only a portion of the qualities which it should possess.

Steps, the ease and brilliancy of their combination, equilibrium, stability, speed, lightness, precision, the opposition of the arms with the legs—these form what I term the mechanism of the dance. When all these movements are not directed by genius, and when feeling and expression do not contribute their powers sufficiently to affect and interest me, I admire the skill of the human machine, I render justice to its strength and ease of movement, but it leaves me unmoved, it does not affect me or cause me any more sensation than this arrangement of the following words: *Fait . . . pas . . . le . . . la . . . honte . . . non . . . crime . . . et . . . l'échafaud.* But when these words are ordered by a poet they compose this beautiful line spoken by the Comte d'Essex:—

Le crime fait la honte, et non pas l'échafaud. [1]

It may be concluded from this comparison that dancing is possessed of all the advantages of a beautiful language, yet it is not sufficient to know the alphabet alone. But when a man of genius arranges the letters to form words and connects the words to form sentences, it will cease to be dumb; it will speak with both strength and energy; and then ballets will share with the best plays the merit of affecting and moving, and of making tears flow, and, in their less serious styles, of being able to amuse, captivate and please. And dancing, embellished

---

[1] The crime causes the shame and not the scaffold. A celebrated passage from Act 4, Scene 3 of the *Comte d'Essex* (1678) by the playwright Thomas Corneille (1625–1709). The phrase is imitated from Tertullian—*martyrem fecit causa, non poena.*

with feeling and guided by talent, will at last receive that praise and applause which all Europe accords to poetry and painting, and the glorious rewards with which they are honoured.

Letter IV

. . . Painting and dancing have this advantage over the other arts, that they are of every country, of all nations; that their language is universally understood, and that they achieve the same impression everywhere.

If our art, imperfect as it is, seduce and captivate the spectator: if dancing stripped of the charm of expression sometimes occasion us trouble and emotion, and throw our thoughts into a pleasing disorder; what power and domination might it not achieve over us if its movements were directed by brains and its pictures painted with feeling? There is no doubt that ballets will rival painting in attraction when the executants display less of the automaton and the composers are better trained.

A fine picture is but the image of nature; a finished ballet is nature herself, embellished with every ornament of the art. If a painted canvas convey to me a sense of illusion, if I am carried away by the skill of the delineator, if I am moved by the sight of a picture, if my captivated thoughts are affected in a lively manner by this enchantment, if the colours and brush of the skilful artist react on my senses so as to reveal to me nature, to endow her with speech so that I fancy I hear and answer her, how shall my feelings be wrought upon, what shall I become, and what will be my sensations, at the sight of a representation still more veracious and rendered by the histrionic abilities of my fellow-creatures? What dominion will not living and varied pictures possess over my imagination? Nothing interests man so much as humanity itself. Yes, Sir, it is shameful that dancing should renounce the empire it might assert over the mind and only endeavour to please the sight. A beautiful ballet is, up to the present, a thing seen only in the imagination; like the Phoenix it is never found.

It is a vain hope to re-model the dance, so long as we continue to be slaves to the old methods and ancient traditions of the *Opéra*. At our theatres we see only feeble copies of the copies that have preceded them; let us not practise steps only, let us study the passions. In training ourselves to feel them, the difficulty of expressing them will vanish, then the features will receive their impressions from the sentiments within, they will give force to exterior movements and paint in lines of fire the disorder of the senses and the tumult which reigns in the breast.

Dancing needs only a fine model, a man of genius, and ballets will change their character. Let this restorer of the true dance appear, this reformer of bad taste and of the vicious customs that have impoverished the art; but he must appear in the capital. If he would persuade, let him open the eyes of our young dancers and say to them:—"Children of Terpsichore, renounce *cabrioles, entrechats* and over-complicated steps; abandon grimaces to study sentiments, artless graces and expression; study how to make your gestures noble, never forget that it is the life-blood of dancing; put judgment and sense into your *pas de deux*; let will-power order their course and good taste preside over all situations; away with those lifeless masks but feeble copies of nature; they hide your features, they stifle, so to speak, your emotions and thus deprive you of your most important means of expression; take off those enormous wigs and those gigantic head-dresses which destroy the true proportions of the head with the body; discard the use of those stiff and cumbersome hoops which detract from the beauties of execution, which disfigure the elegance of your attitudes and mar the beauties of contour which the bust should exhibit in its different positions.

"Renounce that slavish routine which keeps your art in its infancy; examine everything relative to the development of your talents; be original; form a style for yourselves based on your private studies; if you must copy, imitate nature, it is a noble model and never misleads those who follow it.

"As for you young men who aspire to be *maîtres de ballet* and think that to achieve success it is sufficient to have danced a couple of years under a man of talent, you must begin by acquiring some of this quality yourselves. Devoid of enthusiasm, wit, imagination, taste and know-ledge, would you dare set up as painters? You wish for an historical theme and know nothing of history! You fly to poets and are unac-quainted with their works! Apply yourselves to the study of them so that your ballets will be complete poems. Learn the difficult art of selec-tion. Never undertake great enterprises without first making a careful plan; commit your thoughts to paper; read them a hundred times over; divide your drama into scenes; let each one be interesting and lead in proper sequence, without hindrance or superfluities, to a well-planned climax; carefully eschew all tedious incidents, they hold up the action and spoil its effect. Remember that *tableaux* and groups provide the most delightful moments in a ballet.

"Make your *corps de ballet* dance, but, when it does so, let each member of it express an emotion or contribute to form a picture; let them mime while dancing so that the sentiments with which they are imbued may cause their appearance to be changed at every moment. If their gestures and features be constantly in harmony with their feelings, they will be expressive accordingly and give life to the representation. Never go to a rehearsal with a head stuffed with new figures and devoid of sense. Acquire all the knowledge you can of the matter you have in hand. Your imagination, filled with the picture you wish to represent, will provide you with the proper figures, steps and gestures. Then your compositions will glow with fire and strength, they cannot but be true to nature if you are full of your subject. Bring love as well as enthusiasm to your art. To be successful in theatrical representations, the heart must be touched, the soul moved and the imagination inflamed.

Section Three

THE INVASION OF THE AIR: THE ROMANTIC ERA

The era of the romantic ballet was one of the greatest that theatrical dance has ever known. It resulted from a marvelous simultaneity of developments: of ideas, technical progress, mechanical inventions, and—inevitably—the appearance of persons of genius who could mold the disparate elements into a single artistic entity.

In the last years of the eighteenth century the Paris Opéra, under the despotic direction of Pierre Gardel, stubbornly perpetuated ballets based on the old Greek myths that no longer had much appeal for the general audience. In spite of a few ventures into patriotic propaganda just after the French Revolution, choreography remained dignified, calculated, cold. The popularity of Jean Dauberval's *La Fille Mal Gardée* should have warned Gardel that tastes were changing. So should the success in London of Charles Didelot's *Flore et Zéphire* in 1796. Though still of classical derivation, the plot of this ballet was treated much like a pretty romance whose protagonists merely happened to be gods. Most important in the ballet was Didelot's use of flying, the dancers' aerial travels made possible by invisible wires attached to their waists. Audiences were equally enchanted by other Didelot ballets that employed picturesque settings—Scotland was used in one, Poland in another—for here was a new kind of subject matter for ballet. But Didelot did not combine the themes of ethereal creatures and exotic lands. That was yet to come.

In Paris, while the Opéra remained stuffy, the popular stages did not. The boulevard theatres, as they were known, catered to a less elite audience—the rising middle class—which liked exciting action, a bit of mystery, and a touch of bourgeois sentiment. From these boulevard houses came melodramas of Jocko, a Brazilian ape; of the Incas of Peru; of Captain Cook in Tahiti—all later made into successful ballets. The noble savage—untutored, spontaneous in action, motivated by feeling rather than decorum—was replacing the classical hero.

At the 1830 premiere of Victor Hugo's *Hernani*, which extolled the image of the passionate social outlaw, Théophile Gautier appeared wearing flowing hair to his shoulders and a brilliant rose-colored waistcoat. He became a symbol of the romantic revolution.

The new themes demanded a new style of dancing—freer, lighter, more versatile. And at this very time the dancer's technique had advanced to a point where such a style was possible. In Carlo Blasis' *Code of Terpsichore* (1820) we see the legs rotated to a full 180 degree turnout. The ballet class had become codified into a progressive set of exercises, starting with simple, controlled movements, then building up to the most complex and vigorous leaps and turns. Such scientific training stimulated the rapid progress of technical mastery. New strength produced a new style, *ballonée*, as opposed to the earlier *terre à terre* manner.

Women were discovering their special technical innovation. Probably it evolved gradually, for we have no record of anyone suddenly exclaiming, "Look, she's dancing on the tips of her toes!" But she was. At first it was very likely a momentary pose, then a few fleeting steps, and then a few more. In time the ballerina learned to reinforce the tips of her slippers with darning to provide a touch of support (the blocked toe shoe came much later), and her new-found strength provoked fresh experiments. There was the fascination of a protracted balance in *arabesque*, the back leg extended waist high; there was the *bourrée*, rapid little running steps on the *pointes*. But more than the creation of individual steps, the technique eventually engendered a wholly new way of moving.

Our first evidence of *pointe* work comes from engravings that date before 1820 and that show women hovering somewhat awkwardly on their narrow supports. But it took another decade for the technique to find its true function. Then Marie Taglioni—painfully thin, round-shouldered, with arms too long for her body—nurtured her capacities for speed and lightness so that the audience had no time to notice her defects. In 1831 her teacher and father, Filippo, presented her in Paris in the opera *Robert le Diable*, in which she led a group of dead nuns in an eerie scene of supernatural spirits. But the success of this work was only the harbinger of her first really great triumph, which came the following year in *La Sylphide*.

In this ballet the themes of romanticism—the ethereal and the exotic—were combined and enhanced by the technical innovations of the past decade. The sylphide is the ideal but unattainable woman who lures the Scotsman James away from his peasant sweetheart and off into the misty highlands, where he seeks in vain to tame her evasive flights. The essence of a dream, the sylphide skims over the stage on her delicate *pointes*; unlike earthly creatures she seems unconstrained by the laws of gravity. In *La Sylphide* a technical achievement had acquired a dramatic motivation.

Helping the illusion considerably were the varied effects of illumination now possible because of the introduction of gas lighting. Even more recent was the practice of lowering the curtain between the acts of a play or ballet so that the audience did not see the mechanics of scene changing. Now too the lights in the auditorium were lowered while the spectacle was on, and new rules banished boisterous members of the audience from sitting on the stage to watch the performance. Music had become less formal, more descriptive and evocative. And there was the novel costume devised for the ballerina—a fitted bodice topping a buoyant skirt of white gauze. The sylphide indeed seemed to float on waves of mist and moonlight, an apparition of loveliness, untouchable and all the more desirable for being unreal.

Parisian women dressed their hair "à la Sylphide" and "taglioniser" became a verb. Later London and St. Petersburg were equally enchanted with this and other ballets that Filippo Taglioni created for his daughter. A Russian critic wrote that "it is impossible to describe the suggestion she conveyed of aerial flight, the fluttering of wings, the soaring in the air, alighting on flowers and gliding over the mirror-like surface of a river. . . ."

But it was Paris that set the fashions. At the Opéra, Director Louis Véron inaugurated the star system and, in 1834 when his success with Taglioni had been generally acknowledged, he cleverly turned his attention to promoting a rival, arousing even greater interest—and box-office receipts—by stirring up a popular controversy. Gautier characterized Taglioni as a Christian dancer, Fanny Elssler as a pagan; and he found the virginal grace of the former less to his taste than the sensuous passion of the latter. Though Elssler was also admired for her elegance, grace, and lightness, the Viennese ballerina excelled in those earthy dances of other lands that had become so popular as a foil to the flights of the sylphide. In particular, Gautier delighted in Elssler's Cachuca:

Now she darts forward; the castanets begin their sonorous chatter. With her hand she seems to shake down great clusters of rhythm. How she twists, how she bends! What fire! What voluptuousness! What precision! Her swooning arms toss about her drooping head, her body curves backwards, her white shoulders almost graze the ground.

No wonder that when she danced in Washington Congress had to adjourn for lack of a quorum! In Transcendental Boston, Margaret Fuller exclaimed, "This is poetry." But Ralph Waldo Emerson replied, "No, it is religion."

The romantic ballet that is still most widely performed today was inspired by a ballerina who combined the ethereal qualities of Taglioni with the dramatic powers of Elssler. Gautier conceived the scenario of *Giselle* (1841) as a vehicle for Carlotta Grisi. Early in the ballet she was an innocent peasant girl; later, having died for the love of a count in rustic disguise, she reappeared as a spirit, forgiving but elusive. In the first part she was said to be "nature and artlessness personified"; in the second she exhibited "lightness . . . a chaste and refined seductiveness." Adolphe Adam's music, with its extensive use of leitmotifs associated with dramatic episodes, set a high standard. Though the choreography was officially credited to the Paris Opéra ballet master Jean Coralli, it was generally known that Grisi's husband, Jules Perrot, had composed most of her dances. Having started his career in the boulevard theatres, Perrot was adept at inventing expressive movement, as he was to prove in later works that acknowledged his authorship.

Perrot was almost unique in this period for being recognized as a great male performer. On the whole, this was a time of eclipse for the male dancer. With the development of *pointe* work and the emergence of the sylphide character, attention was focused on the ballerina. Innovations in theme, in technique, costume, all centered on her. The concept was epitomized in 1845 when Benjamin Lumley, director of Her Majesty's Theatre in London, gathered together four outstanding ballerinas to perform a *pas de quatre* especially choreographed for them by Perrot. Joining Taglioni and Grisi were the fleet-footed Italian Fanny Cerrito and the poetic Dane Lucile Grahn.

It was Grahn who created the title role in the Danish version of *La Sylphide* (1836), choreographed by Auguste Bournonville. Apart from this one production, Bournonville generally domesticated the romantic themes of the period into cozy romances, ending with happy village weddings that were celebrated with brilliantly theatricalized folk dances. The majority of his ballets were simple love stories, full of the *joie de vivre* that critic Svend Kragh-Jacobsen has noted as the special distinction of the Danish style. Bournonville's choreography reflected the qualities he attributed to himself: "I danced with virility, my spirit and my energy have created the same impression in every theatre. I brought joy to the audience, and before they admired me they had to like me."

At this same time Italy was turning to melodrama: kidnapped princesses, swashbuckling outlaws, chaste heroines, valiant lovers, and cruel villains were rampant on stages from Milan to Naples. Since the plots were extraordinarily complicated, a distinctive system of double casting was employed: *ballerini per le parte* mimed the action with stylized, rhythmical gestures; *ballerini* performed the dances that were inserted wherever the plot could be made to justify an entertainment or a celebration. The arrangement, similar to the recitative-aria division of opera, seemed to satisfy both the adherents of the *ballet d'action* and the devotees of virtuosity; actually, it obliterated the touchstone of expressive movement that marked the peak of the romantic ballet.

Meanwhile, the romantic style had found its way to America. In the United States, ballet had gotten off to a slow start. Prior to the War of Independence, Puritan morality had inhibited the development of any kind of theatre, for playhouses were referred to as "schools of seduction" and "resorts of the licentious"; even in 1784 entertainments were cautiously advertised as "lectures." The first native American dancer was John Durang, whose specialty was the hornpipe. Largely self-taught, he was soon outshone by foreign, classically trained performers who began to arrive in the early 1790's as refugees from the French Revolution. Most prominent among them was the notable rope-dancer, acrobat, actor, singer, and choreographer Alexandre Placide. For some time Durang appeared with the Placide company, whose repertory included "heroic pantomimes" on historical themes as well as "dancing ballets" of pastoral romances. While some patriotic spectacles commemorated the 4th of July and the birthday of George Washington, the basis of the repertory consisted of adaptations of ballets that the new Americans remembered from their European performances.

In 1837, as the romantic ballet was flourishing abroad, two young girls made a joint debut in Philadelphia. Mary Ann Lee was to enjoy a brief but important career. After a period of study in Paris, where she learned several of the currently popular ballets, she returned to the United States, becoming the first American to dance *Giselle*. When she performed the famous role a Boston critic reported the "loud and continued plaudits at the grace and agility of the beautiful heroine," and added that "her salient qualifications evinced a truthfulness of action that conveyed as plainly almost as in language the feelings and passions of the character." The other debutante, Augusta Maywood, left the United States in 1839, never to return. In the course of a brilliant career, Maywood danced throughout Europe, enjoying particular success in the course of twelve years spent in Italy, where she was called "the queen of the air." Rather ironically, one of her triumphs was in a ballet based on an American novel; *I Bianchi ed i Negri* was Giuseppe Rota's version of *Uncle Tom's Cabin*.

From 1840 to 1842 Elssler toured America. Since ballets with large casts obliged her to assemble additional performers in each city where she appeared, a number of Americans had the opportunity of dancing with her. Probably the most important of these was George Washington Smith. In the remarkable years that followed his tours with Elssler, Smith supported a number of other visiting European ballerinas, partnered Mary Ann Lee in *Giselle*, choreographed for companies of Spanish dancers, and staged a number of ballets from the romantic repertory. He was the first outstanding male classical dancer of American origin.

By around 1850 the romantic ballet had run its course in both Europe and America. The fashion for sylphs had faded, leaving ballerinas with *pointe* work and male dancers with nothing much to do. Men's roles were commonly assumed by women, a matter that seemed satisfactory enough to the audience, for one critic remarked of a *travesti* performer that she "dances as much like a man as can be desired"—meaning not too much.

Tastes turned to spectacle. *The Black Crook,* premiered in New York in 1866, established a vogue for extravaganzas. The Italian ballerinas Marie Bonfanti and Rita Sangalli were deemed "exceedingly graceful"; but observers were most impressed by the production's "startling transformations," "elegant scenes," "brilliant effects," "lavish richness," and "barbaric splendor." Fairies floated on silver couches; chariots descended from clouds. With constant revivals, *The Black Crook* ran for some forty years.

European ballet moved in similar directions. A single work has survived from this time: *Coppélia*, choreographed in 1870 in Paris by Arthur Saint-Léon. The hero was danced in *travesti*, but the mischievous heroine delighted audiences by pretending to be a doll come to life, and Delibes' music enhanced the entire work. In the period since the demise of the romantic ballet, only two potential ballerinas had appeared: Emma Livry, a protégée of the aging Taglioni, and Giuseppina Bozzachi, who created the leading role in *Coppélia* at the age of seventeen. Both died tragically young. Ballet in Western Europe went into a state of decline. Now it was Russia's turn.

G. Léopold Adice
AN ACCOUNT OF THE PRINCIPLES OF OUR TRADITIONS
Translated from the French by Leonore Loft

After more than a decade of performing at the Paris Opéra, Adice taught the male dancers there from 1848 to 1863. He was then the instructor for the elementary boys' class until his retirement in 1867.

We have no records prior to the nineteenth century of the structure of a ballet class, but the lesson described by Blasis in Code of Terpsichore *(1820) was probably the culmination of a form that had been evolving for some time. The development of intensive training was certainly accelerated by the needs of the romantic choreographers, who required dancers with strength and control to realize their characterizations. The class described by Adice is aimed at nurturing energy and endurance; the emphasis is on sustained movement, what Blasis called* grands temps *and we now call* adagio. *The dancers acquired precision by the daily execution of set exercises. Blasis says they should be done "with the hand resting on something firm"; Adice names the support—it is a* barre. *Writing in a period of decadence, he urges a return to the high standards of the romantic ballet. If this is the class that Filippo Taglioni gave to his daughter Marie, we can appreciate the story that she fainted when it was over.*

After I have extolled traditional dance and disapproved of the new methods with such vigor, both young students and advanced dancers, always desirous of improvement, would without doubt like to know exactly what these traditions are . . . A description given by Blasis of the daily exercises used in his time . . . provides details on the first dance exercises the students had to execute in their classes. . . .

"The student first practices *pliés* in all positions, then both *grands* and *petits battements, ronds de jambe sur terre,* and *en l'air,* followed by *petits battements sur le cou-de-pied.* He must then go on to *temps de courante simples* and *composés* [with any kind of elaboration], *coupés* in first position, then in second position, and then *composés.* He will then do *attitudes, grands ronds de jambe,* and *temps de chaconne,* and finally *grands fouettés de face* [*flic-flac*] and *en tournant, quarts de tour, pas de bourrée,* and several combinations using various kinds of *pirouettes.*

SOURCE: From *Théorie de la gymnastique de la danse théâtrale* (Paris, 1859).

"These exercises serve to form a good dancer and to give him the means to succeed."

Let us remember these final words, for we shall need to cite them frequently as we continue.

"The lesson ends with *pirouettes, temps terre à terre,* and *temps de vigueur.*"

Such was the lesson that we executed each morning without fail, and often, in order to hasten our progress, we would repeat parts of it alone during the day when we had returned home.

Now we are going to complete what M. Blasis has given us. We shall describe this lesson in detail. . . .

"The student first practices *pliés.* . . .

What is indicated here is all our basic elementary exercises at the *barre*, for in those days, whatever the level or strength of the dancer, he never allowed himself to begin work in the center without having first spent a half hour at the *barre*. This was not done as it is today, by simply extending the legs in some isolated exercise, which may have

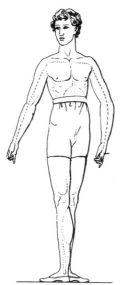

From Carlo Blasis, *Code of Terpsichore*

Here Blasis illustrates the correct manner of standing in third and fourth positions as well as the proper height and form of a *grand battement* in second position and in fourth (facing page). Although third position is seldom used any more and contemporary choreographers expect extensions considerably higher than the hip level shown here, the degree of turnout and the placement of the body demanded by Blasis would be perfectly satisfactory in today's ballet classroom.

some use though it is done without care and as if it were of little consequence, but rather by making an integral sequence of all the exercises that we are about to describe, still in keeping with the text of M. Blasis.

"Practice *pliés* in all positions." The five principal positions. In first, in second, in third with the right leg in front, repeat placing the same leg in back; in fourth with the right leg in front and once again placing the same leg in back; in fifth with the right leg in front and then with the same leg in back. Six *pliés* in each position, three slow and three sharp, or accelerated. There are forty-eight *pliés* altogether.

One then went on to the *grands battements*. These were done in the following manner: *grand battement* in fourth position front with the right leg; repeat with the left leg. *Grand battement* in second [closing in] front with the right leg; repeat with the left. *Grand battement* in fourth position back with the right leg; repeat with the left leg. *Grand battement* in second [closing in] back with the right leg; the same with the left. Sixteen for each leg [in each position]; in all, there are one hundred and twenty-eight.

Then follow the *petits battements*, which are *petits battements glissés par terre* from the third position *élémentaire* [with the whole foot on the floor] to the second position *dérivée* [*pointe tendue*]. Thus: *petits battements glissés* in front with the right leg; repeat with the left leg. *Petits battements glissés* in back with the right leg; repeat with the left leg. Twenty-four for each leg [in each direction]; ninety-six in total.

Then *ronds de jambe sur terre*. These include *petits ronds de jambe arrondis par terre* without leaving the floor, passing through first position *élémentaire* each time. Thus, *petits ronds de jambe arrondis par terre en dehors* with the right leg; repeat with the left leg. *Petits ronds de jambe arrondis par terre en dedans* with the right leg; the same with the left. Thirty-two for each leg [in each direction]; in all, one hundred and twenty-eight.

And *en l'air*. These are the same *petits ronds de jambe* that are done in demi-second position [extended only halfway to the side], always with the lower part of the leg curved and the knee firmly turned out. Thus, *petits ronds de jambe* in demi-second position *en dehors* with the right leg; repeat with the left. *Petits ronds de jambe* in demi-second position *en dedans* with the right leg; repeat with the left. In all, one hundred and twenty-eight.

After this, *petits battements sur le cou-de-pied*, etc. Here Blasis has once again failed to indicate slow and rapid steps. Let us first describe the slow ones. These slow *petits battements sur le cou-de-pied* are those that all students know and execute by placing the leg in demi-second position while simultaneously bringing [the lower part of] the same leg in and extending it in a straight line, bringing the foot to the inner [front or back] ankle once and once to the outer [side] ankle, without changing the position of the knee. Thus, slow *petits battements sur le cou-de-pied* with the right leg; repeat with the left leg; thirty-two for each leg; sixty-four altogether. Rapid *petits battements sur le cou-de-pied* with the right leg; repeat with the left leg. Sixty for each leg; in all, one hundred and twenty. A total of six hundred and forty-eight gymnastic movements before going on to the lesson in the center!!. . . .

Now all this difficult work, which frightens you, was merely a preliminary exercise. After the work at the *barre*, the dancers moved to the center of the floor to repeat exactly the same exercises without holding on before proceeding to the *aplombs* [exercises of balance]; and this, as has already been said, was done every day and even twice a day. M. Blasis can testify to this.

Now we come to the lesson done in the center of the floor. Once again we shall take the text of M. Blasis while adding commentaries as we go along. The *temps de courant*, *simples* and *composés*. This is an exercise now given only to young beginners to practice; artists have rejected it, feeling that it has little importance to their training and improvement. There are even those who are literally ignorant of the sequence, which is composed of *pliés* in third and in second *élémentaire*, with rounded movements of the arms *en dehors* and *en dedans;* first simple, which means with only one movement of the arm, and then *composé*, which indicates a doubling of this same movement with both arms moving in opposite directions. This was done four times *en descendant* [downstage; that is, forwards] and four times *en montant* [upstage, backwards] simple, and the same thing *composé*, so that this same sequence was repeated sixteen times, with thirty-two *pliés*, serving as a prelude to the lesson in the center—after the exercises described above, of course. These sequences were meant to prepare the arms, the body, and above all the hips, the knees, and the insteps, for the *temps d'aplomb* that were to follow. . . .

Then they did *demi-coupés* in first, in second, and *composés*. This study is at present completely ignored in all classes. It is done with preparation in third position *élémentaire, dégagé* to second *dérivée*, return and *coupé* right to first *élémentaire.* While in *demi-plié, coupé* right in front to fourth *dérivée*, placing the heel *par terre* in line for *coupé* and *dégagé* with the other leg in *grande seconde*, lowering it and placing it in second *dérivée*, and begin the sequence once again in order to work out the opposite leg. The same thing is done *en montant;* however, after having completed *coupé* from second *dérivée* to first *élémentaire* and *demi-plié*, one continues with *dégagé* to fourth *dérivée* in back, placing the heel in line for *coupé* and *dégagé* with the other leg in *grande seconde*, lowering it once again to second *dérivée*. One then begins the sequence once again from the opposite side. The word *"composé"* merely indicates that when the same sequence is done again it is done in double time, and when the leg is in *grande seconde* one is slowly turning on *demi-pointe* in a *tour d'aplomb en dehors*. Similarly, *en montant*, this is done with a *demi-tour, grand rond de jambe*, and *tour d'aplomb en dedans*. Then beginning once again and immediately afterwards, doubling the same sequence *en descendant* and *en montant*, with a *grand rond de jambe* and *double tour d'aplomb en dehors* and *en dedans*. Four times *en descendant* and four times *en montant*. In all, there are thirty-two *coupés*.

Then came the *attitudes*. These were not done, as they are now, with simple poses and easy transitions of short duration, but rather as in the preceding sequence, with a long, integrated series involving a preparation of *demi-coupés* in third, one of *relevés* in fourth, and *jetée allongée*. Four *en descendant* and four *en montant en face*, with the preparation of *demi-coupé*. The same number is done *en descendant* and *en montant*, with the preparation of *relevé* in fourth and *jetée allongée;* repeat *en tournant;* one turn, again with two turns. In all, there are thirty-two *attitudes*.

Then follow the *grands fouettés de face* and *en tournant*, not in ornamental poses, as students say now, or in detached steps, but once again by an extended sequence of twelve *en face* and the same number *en tournant*, beginning with one for each leg, two and then three *en face*, and similarly with one, two and three turns after having done them *en face*. In sum, there are twenty-four *fouettés*.

Then the class continued with *temps de chaconne*, or *fouettés ballottés*; not two *en face* and two *en tournant*, as children do, but by connecting twenty-four *posés*, beginning very slowly and accelerating progressively into the *enchaînement sauté*, all in one breath and without interruption. In all, forty *fouettés ballottés*.

Then they proceeded to the quarter turns, not interrupted by resting after each half-sequence, but done all together; first *en face* and then *en tournant*, both *en dehors* and *en dedans*, eight *en face*, eight turns *en dehors* by quarter turns, four by half turns and two with one turn. Exactly the same number is done *en tournant en dedans*. There are thirty-six in total.

Several combinations using various different kinds of *pirouettes* followed. These combinations were preparations for *pirouettes* in *grande seconde en face*, beginning with one, two, and three for each leg. This has been eliminated from modern teaching, as have preparations for *pirouettes en face d'attitude*, done in a similar way, with one, two, and three for each leg. Finally they did preparations for *pirouettes sur le cou-de-pied*, not in an isolated and interrupted manner as they are done today, when by chance—once or twice a month—someone really wants to practice them; but each day, on a regular basis and without fail, in studies of sequences of one, two, and three for each leg *en face* and *d'aplomb en tournant*. Altogether, there were forty-eight preparations for *pirouettes en face* before going on to the prolonged execution *en tournant*. . . .

There are other studies in *pirouettes*, which Blasis has forgotten. . . . These were *pirouettes* in *grande seconde* and *pirouettes serrées sur le cou-de-pied*, in *grande seconde serrée en attitude*, in *grande seconde liée* with *arabesque*, and *pirouettes, renversées, simples,* and *composés*, each in a series of three, six, or even more, depending upon the inclinations of the dancer. And to finish off the session, the class attacked the *temps terre à terre* and the *temps de vigueur*. The latter were sequences of *entrechats sous le corps* [without traveling], of *ronds de jambe, brisés*, of *entrechats à cinq*, of *fouettés sautés*, of *sissonnes*. These were designated by the name of *entrée de ronds de jambe, entrée de fouettés*, etc., and from them each dancer chose the one that seemed fitting to his inclinations. He gave particular attention to the task of perfecting it in order thus to create for himself a kind of dance and execution of it that were uniquely his. Unfortunately, there is not even a question of such a thing occurring today when all trained dancers, both men and women, resemble one another in their imperfection and the monotony of their execution.

Such was the lesson of the past—this is what is called tradition. In keeping with it, we fulfilled these exercises religiously each day, without change or variation.

In this description we have advisedly itemized the *adages*, which make up the part that has been most neglected by modern teaching, even though it is the most useful in furthering the progress of young students and in perfecting dancers. . . .

As for exhaustion, we admit it was enormous; but as a result it produced talent, which is never the fruit of today's lessons, which have been made more gentle and are aimed at the level of the lazy among our coquettes and pusillanimous women.

August Bournonville (1805–1879)
LA SYLPHIDE.
A ROMANTIC BALLET
IN TWO ACTS

Translated from the Danish by Patricia N. McAndrew

Born in Copenhagen to a French father and a Swedish mother, Bournonville was a loyal Dane all of his life. He studied under Auguste Vestris in Paris and could have won fame throughout Europe as a performer, but chose instead to develop the artistry of the Royal Danish Ballet, which he served almost without interruption for forty-seven years.

Bournonville had seen Taglioni's Sylphide *in Paris. Taking the original libretto of Charles Nourrit, he commissioned a new score from Herman Løvenskjold and created his own choreography. Though the Sylphide was his protégée Lucile Grahn, he considerably strengthened the role of James, making him more important than he had been in the French version, for thanks to Bournonville's remarkable teaching methods, Danish male dancers maintained their status even during the romantic period. The Danish* Sylphide *was an immediate success and has been kept consistently in the repertory, the roles being passed down from one generation to the next; this is the version most often seen today. Erik Bruhn, the great contemporary interpreter of James,*

SOURCE: Libretto (Copenhagen, 1836). Theatre History Museum, Copenhagen.

has aptly characterized the lasting validity of the role; "All he wants to catch is a dream which exists only in his head and which nobody else can see. He is a true escapist. . . . He believes only in this dream and it is sad that he could never grasp reality."

The Characters

THE SYLPHIDE.
ANNA, a tenant farmer's widow.
JAMES, her son.
EFFY, her niece, James's bride.
GURN, a peasant lad.
MADGE, a fortune-teller.
Scottish Peasant Folk. Sylphides and Witches.

The scene is laid in Scotland.

Act One

A spacious room in a farmhouse. In the background, a door and a staircase leading to the sleeping chamber. To the right, a window. To the left, a high fireplace. Dawn.

James is asleep in a large armchair. A feminine being in airy raiment and with transparent wings is kneeling at his feet. Her arm is resting on the seat of the chair. With her hand beneath her chin, she fixes her loving gaze on the sleeping youth. She expresses the joy she feels in being near the one she loves. She hovers round him and flutters her wings in order to cool the air he breathes.

James slumbers restlessly. In his dreams he follows every one of the airy creature's movements and when, carried away with tenderness, she approaches him and lightly kisses his brow, he suddenly wakens, reaches out to grasp the lovely image and pursues it about the room as far as the fireplace, into which the Sylphide vanishes.

Beside himself at the sight of this vision, which has already enchanted him several times in dreams but now stood alive before his eyes, James awakens and questions the farmhands, who are sleeping in the same room. Confused and sleepy, they do not know what he is saying and do not understand his questions. He rushes out the door in order to see whether the Sylphide might still be outside; but he does not notice that in his haste he has run into Gurn, who has already been out hunting. Gurn and the farmhands regard one another with astonishment, but when James immediately returns to overwhelm them with questions about the airy figure who knelt by his couch, kissed his brow, fluttered about the room, and flew up through the chimney, their wonder dis-

Photo, Fred Fehl

La Sylphide was the first ballet to crystallize the concept of romanticism by setting a supernatural heroine among earthly peasants and by dooming the mortal who tries to possess her ethereal perfection. Constant surveillance by the Royal Danish Ballet has preserved much of Bournonville's choreography. Here Carla Fracci attends the dreaming Erik Bruhn in the American Ballet Theatre production of 1968.

solves into laughter and they strive to convince James that the whole thing has been a dream.

James comes to himself again and remembers that this very day he is to be betrothed to his cousin, the amiable Effy. Vexed, Gurn leaves him, bemoaning the injustice he must suffer because of the superiority that Effy bestows upon this daydreamer.

James sends the farmhands away to prepare everything for the celebration and quickly finishes dressing in order to please his lovely bride. But as he draws closer to the fireplace, he falls ever deeper in thought. Effy is brought in by her aunt. Her first glance is directed at James, who takes no notice of her. Gurn, on the other hand, is immediately at her service. He begs her not to reject the spoils of the hunt and gives her a bouquet of fresh wild flowers. Effy rather absent-mindedly accepts his compliment and goes over to the thoughtful James in order to ask him what he is brooding about, whether he is distressed, and why. He begs her to forgive him for being so distracted and assures her that he is really very happy, especially today, when he shall be united to the one he loves and will live for eternally. Tender and happy, Effy gives him her hand to kiss. Gurn also tries to take one of her hands, but she quickly withdraws it. James threateningly steps between her and Gurn, who, ashamed and distraught, goes away in order to hide the tears he can no longer hold back. His sorrow is further augmented by seeing Anna unite the young couple who, kneeling, receive her blessing.

Some young girls, friends of Effy, come to congratulate the loving

The original costume design for Bournonville, in a water color by Christian Bruun, shows James confident and oblivious of Madge, who crouches by the fireplace, plotting his destruction. The virile Bournonville established a tradition of strong male dancing in Denmark where it was preserved long after the ballerinas reigned supreme on the other stages of western Europe.

couple. They bring presents for the bride; a plaid, a scarf, a wreath, a veil, a bouquet; in short, everything that can delight her. Gurn begs them to put in a good word for him but they make fun of him and offer him their love amid laughter and teasing. Weeping, he tears himself loose and goes over to sit down in a corner.

Effy thanks and embraces her childhood playmates while James once more becomes lost in thought. He approaches the fireplace—but what does he see! A loathsome figure! Old Madge, the fortune-teller, who has stolen in among the young girls. "What are you doing here?" "I am warming myself by the fire!" "Get away from here, witch! Your presence is an evil omen." James is about to drive her away but the girls plead for her. Gurn bids her be seated and offers her a glass of spirits, which she greedily swallows.

Madge knows hidden things and the girls cannot resist their desire to know what lies in store for them. They surround the witch and hold out their hands in order to have her predict their fortunes. To one she promises happiness in marriage, while she tells the other she will never be wed. This one is but a child and gets no prediction at all, but another has her fate whispered in her ear, and walks away blushing. Finally, Effy asks if she will be happy in marriage? "Yes!" is the answer. "Does my bridegroom love me sincerely?" "No!" James begs her not to believe this hateful old woman. Gurn also gets the desire to question Madge. "AH!" she says, "this man loves you with his heart and you will soon come to regret the fact that you have spurned his love." James now becomes furious, seizes the fortune-teller, and hurls her to the door. Gurn quotes her statement and makes yet another effort to hinder the wedding he detests so much, but everyone laughs him to scorn and calms James by reassuring him that they do not believe at all in the prophecy.

Anna and the young girls follow Effy to her room to array her in festive dress. Gurn goes sadly away, looking back at Effy all the while. James wishes to accompany his beloved but the girls hold him back and Effy blows him a parting kiss. James is delighted with this amiable bride but the memory of the Sylphide soon returns to his soul. He cannot account for the nature of this being. Perhaps she is his good angel, a powerful fairy who watches over his destiny! With this, as if by a gust of wind, the casement opens. The Sylphide is seated in the corner, melancholy and hiding her face in her hands.

James bids her approach, and she glides down from the wall. He asks the cause of her grief, but she refuses to answer. When he continues to demand her confidence she finally confesses that his union with Effy constitutes her misfortune; from the first moment she saw him her fate was joined to his and this hearth is her favorite place of refuge.

She hovers about him, visibly and invisibly, night and day, follows him on the hunt, among the wild mountains, watches over his sleep, wards off the evil spirits from his bed, and sends him gentle dreams. James has listened to her with mounting agitation. He is touched by the Sylphide's love, but does not dare to return it. Effy has received his vow: his heart belongs to her alone. The Sylphide rushes desperately away. She has nothing to hope for, only death to desire. James calls her back. He cannot hide his confusion; he does not understand what magic is controlling him; but despite his love for Effy he is enraptured by the Sylphide.

She expresses the liveliest joy, regains her airy lilt, and hovers about the youth as she flutters her transparent wings. She tries to use his agitated state of mind in order to lure him away with her, but he shudders at the thought of deserting Effy, tears himself loose from the Sylphide, and spurns her. But the Sylphide has wrapped herself in Effy's plaid, and when he turns around he finds her at his feet, reminding him of the beloved object. James is intoxicated at this sight. He raises the Sylphide, presses her to his heart, and enthusiastically kisses her.

Gurn, who has witnessed part of the foregoing scene, hastens to acquaint Effy with everything that has happened, but when James hears a noise he hides the Sylphide in the armchair and covers her with the plaid. Gurn has summoned Effy and her friends in order to take the unfaithful bridegroom by surprise. At first, they see nothing at all. However suspicion soon falls on the covered armchair. James is bewildered; Effy turns pale with jealousy and, together with Gurn, lifts the plaid aside. The Sylphide has vanished. The girls laugh. Effy becomes angry at Gurn, who stands ashamed and startled.

All of the villagers arrive to celebrate the betrothal of James and Effy. The old folk sit down at table while the young ones enjoy merry dancing. James is so distracted that he forgets to ask his bride to dance. It is she who invites him. But in the midst of the dance he perceives the Sylphide, who is visible only to him and then disappears once more. He forgets everything in trying to reach her, but she always eludes him and the guests think it is high time James was married since he stands in danger of losing his reason from sheer affectionate longing.

The dancing ceases and the bride is adorned for the ceremony. Anna gives her the ring which she shall exchange for that of her bridegroom, and everyone surrounds her with congratulations and expressions of sympathy. James alone is melancholy. He stands apart from the others with the betrothal ring in his hand. The Sylphide emerges from the fireplace, snatches the ring from him, and signifies with an expression of utter despair that she must die if he marries Effy.

The bride is ready. She has given her girlhood friends a parting embrace. They summon the bridegroom, but he is nowhere to be found. General astonishment. Gurn has seen him flee to the hills with a woman. Effy is plunged in grief. Anna expresses indignation; everyone, anger and disapproval.

Gurn triumphantly mentions what Madge had predicted for him. He still talks of love and now finds support among the young girls. Effy is overwhelmed with grief and despair. She is indifferent to all consolation and leans helplessly on Anna's breast. Gurn kneels at her feet and all express the liveliest sympathy.

Act Two

The forest and night. A dense fog permits only a glimpse of the foremost trees and cliffs. To the left, the entrance to a cave.

Madge prepares for a meeting with other witches. They come from all quarters, each with lamp and broomstick, each with her familiar spirit. They dance about the fire in a circle, hail Madge, and by way of welcome empty a cup of the glowing brew she has prepared for them. Madge calls them to work. Some spin, wind, and weave a rose-colored drapery, while others dance and fence with the broomsticks. The spell is complete. They drink a farewell and the flock of witches disappear into the cave.

The fog disperses. Dawn gives way to sunrise and the landscape presents a charming blend of woods and mountains. The Sylphide leads James down from a steep mountain path, which he fearfully treads while she scarcely seems to touch the cliff with her foot. This is her kingdom. Here she will live for the one she loves, hide him from the eyes of the world, and allow him to share the joys that she prizes most highly. James is enraptured with delight and admiration. The Sylphide seems to explore each one of his wishes, brings him the loveliest flowers, and refreshes him with fruits and spring water. James regards her with rapture. He forgets everything for the one he loves and lives only to possess her. But she is more retiring than usual. She will not sit with him, easily disengages herself from his arms, and eludes him every time he ardently tries to embrace her. James is on the verge of becoming annoyed, but then she hovers about him in the most delightful attitudes. Without knowing it, James's movements take on a more airy lilt. He follows the Sylphide in her easy flight, and their dancing blends together in harmony.

Despite his love for the Sylphide and the magical power that irresistibly sweeps him away with her, the memory of Effy still returns and points out to him the injustice he has inflicted upon her. He becomes melancholy once more and he feels as drained as if he had been intoxicated.

The Sylphide perceives his state of mind and by her innocent gaiety seeks to dispel his dark thoughts. She knows a way: her sisters shall help her to cheer her beloved. At a signal they all come into view through the bushes, on the boughs, and over the cliffs. The young sylphides with wings of blue and rose color soon chase away the youth's distress. Some of them swing in airy draperies which they hang between the trees, while others stand on the tip of a bough and bend it to the ground with their weight, to have it raised into the air again by a puff of wind. Their dancing and delightful groupings arouse James's enthusiasm. He is more than ever taken with the Sylphide but she eludes his embraces and, after having disappointed him several times, she disappears at the very moment he thought to grasp her. In vain he questions the remaining sylphides. They do not answer him but fly away one after another. Anxious and grief-stricken, James cannot remain alone but rushes after the enchanting creature.

James's friends come into view on the hill. Gurn is with them. They seek and question one another about the runaway, but until now their search has been fruitless. They spread out, but Gurn discovers a hat. It belongs to James. He is about to call the others, but Madge steps out of the cave, seizes the hat, and flings it away. Gurn is frightened by the witch's sudden appearance, but she calms him, orders him to be silent and clever, as she points to the hill, from whence Effy is coming with some of her friends.

Nobody has found James and Madge now tells them of his unfaithfulness. He is lost to Effy but her prophecy will be fulfilled, for Gurn, the fine, good-hearted young fellow, is destined by fate to be Effy's husband. All the others, outraged at James's behavior, support Gurn's pleas. Effy, although deeply distressed, is nevertheless moved by the slighted Gurn's affection, and she allows him to escort her home. Madge remains alone.

James returns without having overtaken the Sylphide. His heart is a prey to regret and despair. He feels how deeply he has violated his responsibilities towards his bride, but he does not have the strength to tear himself loose from this being who, like a dream-image, charms and confuses his senses and captures his thoughts. Old Madge has been watching him secretly and approaches with feigned compassion. He readily tells her everything and says that he would gladly give his life to capture the celestial maiden if only for a single moment. "But the one you love is a *sylphide*! Naught but a talisman can bind her to you." "Give it me! In return I will bestow upon you all that I possess." "But this morning you mocked me, cast me away! " Kneeling, James begs her to forgive him for his hardness and to give him life by the possession of the Sylphide. Madge suffers herself to be moved and meaningfully hands him the rose-colored scarf: "Believe in its strength and you shall succeed! Entwine her with this blossom. Then her wings will fall and she is yours forever." Beside himself with joy and gratitude, James kisses the scarf and follows the witch to her cave with a thousand expressions of thanks.

He espies the Sylphide, sitting on a bough with a bird's nest in her hand. He waves the scarf; she climbs down and offers him her catch, but James reproaches her for her hardness towards innocent creatures. Deeply moved, she regrets what she has done and hastens to replace the nest. She now pleads for the pretty scarf, which he purposely refuses her. She begs him for it and promises never more to flee from him. Greedily, she reaches for the scarf but at the same instant he twists it about her so tightly that she cannot move her arms. The Sylphide is captured and, kneeling, asks for mercy; but James does not release the scarf before her wings have fallen off. The Sylphide puts her hand to her heart as if she felt mortally wounded. James presses her to him but she pushes him away from her. He throws himself at her feet . . . the pallor of death covers the Sylphide's brow.

James, who had thought to possess her forever and in his outburst of joy gives her a thousand caresses, suddenly stops: what has he done! The unhappy creature! By taking away her freedom has he robbed her of life? "Do not weep! You, whom I have so dearly loved! I was blessed by your tenderness but I could not belong to you, could not bestow upon you the happiness you longed for. I must die! Take your betrothal ring. Make haste, return it. You can still marry her whom you loved before me . . . Farewell! I die with the hope of your future happiness." . . .

At this moment the fortune-teller enters to rejoice at James's despair, and counters his reproaches with the icy laughter of revenge. She points to the background, where Gurn is leading Effy to the altar. The Sylphide's strength is decreasing little by little. James lies at her feet. Her sisters surround her and in their arms she breathes forth her spirit. Sylphs and sylphides veil the beloved body and carry it away through the air. Overwhelmed with grief, the unfortunate James casts yet another look at his airy mistress and falls to the ground in a swoon.

Théophile Gautier (1811–1872)
Fanny Cerrito in
Jules Perrot's LALLA-ROOCK
Marie Guy-Stéphan in
Arthur Saint-Léon's
LUTIN DE LA VALLÉE
Translated from the French by Edwin Binney 3rd

Gautier, known in the annals of literature as a great poet, novelist, and journalist, and as a leader of the romantic movement in France, is the author of some of the greatest dance criticism we have as well as the librettist of a number of ballets, including the still famous **Giselle**. *Fortunately, his deep love for Carlotta Grisi did not prevent his enjoying the charms of other ballerinas, and his descriptions of their performances provide us with marvelously distinct and evocative pictures of the dancing of the mid-nineteenth century.*

To Gautier dance was "simply the art of displaying elegant and correctly proportioned shapes in various positions favorable to the development of lines." He expected the ballerina to be beautiful and had little use for the male dancer. These selections show him in his element. The first review reports from London on a star not yet seen at the Paris Opéra; the second concerns a ballerina unusually skilled in Spanish dancing, which she had actually learned in Madrid.

The ballet of *Lalla-Roock* . . . tells of a prince, fiancé of a princess who, according to custom, has never seen him. He succeeds in becoming loved by her under the name and the costume of the poet Feramorz. At the end, it appears that the prince and the poet are the same person, and everything turns out happily. This idea of a young princess whose father's court seeks to lead her to her royal fiancé, and whose love for another increases as she nears the end of her travels, is perhaps a better subject for analysis than for pantomime, and besides, traveling action is rather difficult to localize in a theatrical performance.

The first act of this ballet shows us the palace of the great Mughal with the celebrated Aurangzeb seated on his throne, the back of which is formed by a huge peacock's tail of jewels. The poet Feramorz enters to seek the princess in the name of the king, his master.

The second act . . . shows the procession of the caravan through the

SOURCES: Review of Cerrito from *La Presse*, July 30, 1846. Review of Guy-Stéphan from *La Presse*, February 1, 1853.

desert; nothing is lacking: neither the *kamsin* [wind of the Sahara] nor the spirals of uplifted sand; we even see two redoubtable camels, whose forelegs could argue with their back legs in excellent English if they became bad-tempered.

The third act contains the obligatory recognition scene, the rejoicings which occur naturally and present us with the Festival of Roses so frequently celebrated by the Persian poets.The whole thing ends with the wedding of the prince and princess, illuminated by a myriad of lamps, lanterns, candles, and candelabra.

This very legitimate canvas is embellished by Perrot with a multitude of charming dances, as he alone knows how to create.

For us, the principal attraction of this choreographic poem was Mlle Cerito [sic], whom we had not seen previously, our earlier trips to London not having coincided with seasons when she was appearing.

Mlle Cerito, and that proves the reality of her talent, has enthusiastic supporters and implacable disparagers. For the former, she is the nymph of the dance; for the others, she is a third-rate dancer whose reputation is incomprehensible. There is no middle position; she is either accepted or rejected totally.

We were curious to see the effect that she would produce on us and to discover our opinion on this reputation which Paris has not yet consecrated.

Let us begin by *le physique*, as they say in theatrical parlance, and then speak of her talent.

La Cerito is blonde; she has blue eyes which are very soft and tender, a gracious smile despite its perhaps too frequent appearance; her shoulders, her bosom do not have that scrawniness which is characteristic of female dancers, the whole of whose weight seems to have descended into their legs. Her plump, dimpled arms do not inflict tragic anatomical details upon our sight; they are used with grace and flexibility. Nothing in this pretty upper body suggests the idea of fatigue from classes or the perspiration of training. A girl taken from her family yesterday and pushed onto the stage would be no different. Her foot is small, well-arched, with a delicate ankle and a well-rounded leg; however, whether because of a belt worn too low or a torso that is actually a little too long, her waist cuts her body into two completely equal parts, which is contrary to the laws of human proportions and particularly unfavorable for a *danseuse*. All in all, she is young, fascinating, and produces a favorable impression.

The costume which Mlle Cerito wore, without being of a rigorous exactitude, was particularly becoming. Garlands of flowers embroidered in strong colors enlivened her white gauze skirts and gave her a spring-like air which was the most stylish and the prettiest imaginable.

As a dancer, Mlle Cerito has little or no *école*; that is immediately obvious. Let these words not be considered pejoratively: we are not "classic" in relation to the dance anymore than to anything else; we simply wish to say that Mlle Cerito owes more to nature than to her training. She dances by inspiration; her talents might even disappear, we believe, if she consecrated herself to study in the hope of perfecting herself. She would lose the *innate gift* and would not achieve the *acquired one*. Her qualities consist of freshness, casualness, naiveté, which cause a fault to be atoned for by a grace. At certain moments, one might say that she is improvising, such is the happy risk in her *pas*. As with certain singers, the timbre of whose voices are their principal charm and who would be wrong to change it through practice, Mlle Cerito has, to a certain extent, a silvery and young timbre to her dancing which fatigue might crack.

No comparison can be established between her and those dancers with whom her name is often linked: Taglioni, Elssler, and Carlotta Grisi. Mlle Cerito's place, for not being so elevated, is no less marked and honorable.

In an art which is severely regulated despite its apparent frivolity, she represents the flowering of natural capacities: caprice and fantasy.

We feel that Mlle Cerito would have great success in Paris, particularly if she limited herself to dancing three or four of these brilliant *pas* with such happy vivacity that she performs as though she were dancing in her bedroom for her own particular pleasure. . . .

The Théâtre-lyrique has just found a real success. *Le Lutin de la Vallée*, that is Saint-Léon and Mme Guy-Stéphan, for the work does not exist by itself and could be described in four lines; but it furnishes the dance with an auspicious frame and that is all that is necessary.

Count Ulric has lost a locket containing the portrait of his mother and has sworn to marry the woman who will return it to him. Katti, a poor, mute girl sheltered by the charity of dame Brigitte, has found the locket, but the old lady takes it from her while she is sleeping so that her own daughter may profit by the reward. . . . Thanks to an elf, who restores the stolen locket to her, Katti becomes the wife of the powerful Count Ulric. If this marriage seems unsuitable to you, remember that Katti is mute, which is better than a dowry, and besides, she speaks such pretty words with her feet.

Now that we've done away with the plot, and we must give it this credit that it is neither long nor complicated, let us immediately get to what is important—to the dance. . . .

Mme Guy-Stéphan exhibits as natural talent an extraordinary lightness; she bounds up like a rubber ball and comes down like a feather or a snowflake. Her foot strikes the floor noiselessly, like the foot of a shadow or a sylphide, and each jump is not echoed by a dull sound of the dancer landing which recalls the marble heels of the statue of the Commander [in Molière's *Don Juan*]. Study has given her a cleanness, a precision, a finish that are rare nowadays when real dancing is neglected for voluptuous attitudes and precarious poses for which the partner is the pivot or the springboard. Her *jetés-battus* are extremely clean; her *pointes*, which are rigid and clear, never waver; and she has remarkable elevation.

Fanny Cerrito is depicted in *Lalla-Roock* in a lithograph probably after Brandard. The diaphanous, knee-length tutu, with its delicate embroidery, reflects the spirit of romantic idealism. Cerrito, however, was called "the little realist" by those who contrasted her voluptuous grace to the ethereal quality of Taglioni. In addition to creating leading roles in works composed by her husband, Arthur Saint-Léon, Cerrito was a choreographer herself, with several ballets to her credit.

The *pas* that she dances in the moonlight with the elf of the valley, who skips on the silvery spray of the waterfall, is delightfully poetic. No one could imagine anything lighter, fresher, nor more nocturnally vaporous, nor more endearingly chaste. While the girl balances in a pose of innocence and love, the elf bounds about, hovers, and traces around her circles of benevolent magic. It is charming. To be able to compose such a dance and to execute it, one has to be Saint-Léon, an exquisite intelligence served by hamstrings of steel; one has to have both mind and legs, rare attributes, even when separated.

The madrilena, danced by Mme Guy-Stéphan, who wanted to present herself in the same evening under both her classical and her romantic aspects, brought out thunders of applause and obtained the honors of an encore. It is impossible to reunite more effectively the diverse talents of Dolores Serral, Pepita Diaz, Guerrero, Espert, Oliva and Petra Cámara [Spanish dancers whom Gautier has appreciated both in Paris and in Spain] and to translate Spanish into French in a more intelligent, faithful, and poetic manner all at once. What Elssler did for the cachucha, Mme Guy-Stéphan has done for the madrilena: to fire she has added correctness; to voluptuousness, decency; to physical abandon, ordered rationality. To restate this in a single word: to personal temperament, she has added art.

Certainly we are not suspect in such a subject; we love these passionate outbursts, this mad audacity, this swooning languor, this lascivious arching, these arms that seem to gather in every wanton desire like a hay-baler, this knee that lifts the pleat of her skirt when the dancer leans back as though dying of love—all this fiery, gracious, and yet enchanting Andalusian poetry of the *tambour de basque*, castanets, fan, sombrero, and cape. Who admires more than we the velvety eyebrows, the elongated eyes which are always lowered and open slightly like a black cloud that lets the flash of lightning shine through. . . .

Mme Guy-Stéphan has placed into this dance—so dissolute, fiery, and violent—a finesse, a classical purity, which cause it to lose none of its character; the local savor is kept but rectified and concentrated into a more delicate perfume. It is the cachucha that has acknowledged itself, criticized and organized itself. The poses are more surely designed, the steps are more clearly in rhythm; knowledge has purified inspiration and art has captured nature: this madrilena will make Paris run to the Théâtre-lyrique.

Section Four

NEW LIFE FROM RUSSIA

Q: In the eighteenth century Catherine the Great of Russia imported ballet masters from Western Europe to arrange festivities for her court, while provincial nobles had their serfs trained in dancing to provide entertainments for their social gatherings. The capital, in particular, continued to lure talent: Didelot, Perrot, and Saint-Léon came to choreograph; Taglioni and Elssler to perform.

In the nineteenth century the Maryinsky Theatre in St. Petersburg, like the Bolshoi in Moscow, was state owned and controlled. Most of the auditorium was reserved for the court and high officials; less than a third of the seats were available to the public. Tastes were rigidly conservative. Ballets all followed the same pattern: the story was told by means of conventional pantomime gestures with loosely relevant dances inserted at appropriate points, though a *pas d'action* in each act was intended to be vaguely expressive. Women wore pink tights, *pointe* shoes, and short tutus—no matter what the period or geographical setting. For an Egyptian ballet, hieroglyphs were painted on their ruffled skirts; for a Spanish scene, a mantilla might top a fashionably coiffed head. Music was commissioned from one of several house composers, who dutifully provided tinkling tunes.

Though the Imperial Ballet dancers were Russian, native choreographers were seldom used, the prestige of foreigners being preferred. In the romantic period most of them had been content simply to restage in Russia works that they had created elsewhere, but when the Frenchman Marius Petipa assumed the post of chief choreographer in 1862 he began to enrich the Imperial Ballet with a repertory of original works. Showing no inclination to change the standard formula, he nevertheless managed to produce many ballets of the highest artistic quality.

With a slight story to tell and five acts to fill, Petipa managed in his best works to display the rich variety of styles, the beauty and vitality of the *danse d'école*. His patterns for the corps de ballet, sometimes arranged at home on a chessboard, showed tremendous diversity within the confines of the symmetrical designs he felt obliged to follow. The solo dances, known as "variations," were always built on a motif, usually a movement theme inspired either by the music or by some special quality of the performer for whom they were created; all exhibited meticulous structure and beauty of line, but each also had its own kinetic flavor and texture. For the standard *pas de deux*—always consisting of a canonical adagio for both dancers, a variation for each, and a technically brilliant, allegro coda—Petipa frequently endowed his combinations of academic steps with a distinctive character; if seldom overtly dramatic, these duets were often poetically expressive.

In the 1880's Petipa's gifts were stimulated by the importation of a number of fine artists from Italy. The first was the dramatic dancer Virginia Zucchi; it was said that there was more poetry in her back than in all the Italian poets put together. Next came the remarkable Enrico Cecchetti and—more to Petipa's taste, since he preferred choreographing for women—two splendid technicians, Carlotta Brianza and Pierrina Legnani. The last was famous for her mastery of the whipped turns known as *fouettés*, an achievement that fired the Russian artists with such zealous patriotism that soon Mathilde Kshesinskaya was also able to perform the thirty-two *fouettés* on *pointe*.

Petipa was fortunate again in his two ballets graced by the music of Tchaikovsky: *The Sleeping Beauty* (1890) and *Swan Lake* (1895). For the latter he assigned two acts to his assistant, Lev Ivanov, and it is one of these—the poetic lake scene in which the enchanted Swan Queen meets her prince—that is performed most often today. Ivanov's choreography was less conventional than his master's. The elegiac *pas de deux* in the second act of *Swan Lake* does not follow the traditional pattern; it is all adagio, all expressive movement. But it was Petipa, more classically restrained in feeling, more brilliant in technical invention, who dominated the contemporary ballet.

Before he died, Petipa wrote a note of encouragement to the young choreographer Michel Fokine, whose work he had just seen. Unlike the aging master, however, Fokine felt inhibited by balletic conventions —by the separation of pantomime and dancing, the attention to virtuosity that submerged expression, the monotony of style that allowed works set in ancient Greece or medieval France to be danced in tutus and *pointe* shoes.

In contrast to Ivanov, who did not press his beliefs, Fokine challenged the entrenched hierarchy of the Imperial Theatre to forego some of their outmoded rules, but he found them hard to convince. Failing to get permission for his dancers to appear appropriately barefooted in a Greek ballet, Fokine finally compromised by having them paint toes on the feet of their tights. But clearly he was not going to put up with this kind of despotism indefinitely.

In 1909 another young man whose independence had gotten him into trouble with the authorities of the Imperial Theatre formed a company of Russian dancers, including Fokine, to play a season of ballet in Paris. Serge Diaghilev—a connoisseur of the arts, bold, imaginative, with impeccable taste and remarkable vision—intended to overwhelm the cultural world of Western Europe. He did. Paris was thrilled, but less by Fokine's poetically evocative *Les Sylphides*, than by the exotic décors that Leon Bakst had designed for *Cleopatra* and the glamor of Alexandre Benois' setting for *Le Pavillon d'Armide*. They were stunned by the dancers—the delicate Anna Pavlova, the beautiful and sensitive Tamara Karsavina, the virile Adolphe Bolm. Most of all they cheered the phenomenal Vaslav Nijinsky, who appeared to be possessed by the characters he played and who seemed able to sustain himself in the air as long as he wished.

Diaghilev had a genius for selecting the right collaborators. In 1910 his choice fell on Fokine and Igor Stravinsky to create *The Firebird*, based on Russian legend. The following year, Benois joined them to produce *Petrouchka*, inspired by the puppets of Russian fairs. If the chic Paris audience was delighted with the picturesque crowds of peasants, merchants, and gypsies, they were also deeply moved by the tragedy of the characters. Unafraid to reverse the balletic turnout to depict the painfully introverted Petrouchka or to parody it for the movements of the stupid, egocentric Moor, Fokine converted the classical vocabulary to his dramatic purpose.

Nijinsky, when his turn came, took the dancers even further from their balletic base. In *Afternoon of a Faun* (1912) they moved with feet placed parallel and with their bodies in stiff profile to the audience as if they had been sculpted by an archaic Greek. In *Le Sacre du Printemps* (1913) their angular movements were violently distorted from the classic norm as they enacted their primitive ritual; the sacrificial dance of the Chosen Maiden was convulsively fragmented, completely breaking with the balletic concept of flow. Diaghilev had brought Marie Rambert from the Dalcroze School to help Nijinsky cope with the shifting rhythms of Stravinsky's dissonant score, but the indignant uproar of the audience made the music practically inaudible. Some critics felt that Nijinsky had scored a breakthrough greater than Fokine's, but since his works cannot be precisely reconstructed and he did not continue to choreograph, we will never really know.

Diaghilev next chose Leonide Massine, who excelled in character ballets: the eighteenth-century Italian comedy of *The Good-Humored Ladies* (1917) and the Spanish genre of *The Three-Cornered Hat* (1919). During the war years Diaghilev could not turn to Russia for fresh talent but sought new collaborators among the avant-guard artists working in Paris:

Matisse, Picasso, Satie, and Cocteau. The Ballets Russes became a cosmopolitan company, almost more renowned for its innovative music and décors than for its dancing. Then, completely reversing his direction, Diaghilev revived *The Sleeping Beauty* in 1921. Though it provided a brilliant showcase for the dancers, trained to perfection by Cecchetti, the production was a crushing fiasco. Attuned to expecting novelty from the Ballets Russes, the audience rejected this attempt to reinstate the values of classicism.

Diaghilev then promoted Bronislava Nijinska, who created the stark Russian peasant wedding of *Les Noces* (1923) with Stravinsky and the sophisticated *Les Biches* (1924) with Poulenc. The next year George Balanchine, who had managed to get out of Russia, joined the Ballets Russes. Starting with the modish type of choreography that Diaghilev then favored, he found his most congenial inspiration in the composer who had already given so much to the company—Stravinsky. Their *Apollo* (1928) had none of the obviously avant-garde tendencies that had marked other current productions; both the music and the choreography were firmly grounded in classical forms, with occasional witty deviations only accentuating the basic purity of line and sustained flow of movement. It was with *Apollo*, Balanchine claimed, that he first learned not to use all his ideas, to eliminate the unnecessary, to pare down to essentials; it became the touchstone of his style.

In 1929 Diaghilev died; an era had ended. But many of the artists he had discovered and developed were to continue to make ballet history: Karsavina and Rambert, along with two English dancers who had taken the names of Alicia Markova and Anton Dolin, and a young Irish girl who called herself Ninette de Valois, established ballet in England; Diaghilev's last male star, Serge Lifar, took over the Paris Opéra; Massine headed the Ballet Russes de Monte Carlo that toured Europe and America; Fokine and Balanchine contributed to the founding of the first two major ballet companies in the United States. It was an extraordinarily rich harvest.

Marius Petipa (1819–1910)
THE SLEEPING BEAUTY
Translated from the Russian by Joan Lawson

Born in Marseilles, Petipa came from a family of dancers. His brother Lucien partnered Carlotta Grisi in the premier of Giselle, *but Marius only got jobs in the provinces. In 1847 he was offered a one-year contract in St. Petersburg. In 1862 he was made chief choreographer, replacing Jules Perrot. In the course of his tenure he created sixty full-evening works, most of the distinguished repertory of the Imperial Ballet. He retired in 1903, bitterly disappointed by the failure of his last production,* The Magic Mirror.

The Sleeping Beauty *was proposed to Tchaikovsky by I. A. Vsevolojsky, the Director of the Imperial Theatre, and the scenario that Petipa prepared for the composer is dated 1889, the ballet receiving its premiere the following year. The plan carefully delineates the dramatic action, which was to be enacted with gestures of conventional pantomime, and specifies not only the character but often the timing and rhythm of the dances as well. There have been some arguments as to how peacefully the collaboration proceeded, since Tchaikovsky, unlike the regular ballet composers, was unaccustomed to such restricting dictation. Nevertheless, the Russian historian Vera Krasovskaya believes that the composer would have been completely sympathetic to Petipa's ideas.* The Sleeping Beauty, *she believes, is closer in form to symphony than to drama: "It is precisely the maximum coincidence of the musical and choreographic high points that determines the artistic perfection of the production."*

Prologue

SCENE I

The Christening of the Princess Aurora. A Ceremonial Hall in the Castle of King Florestan XIV. To the right, a platform for the King, Queen and the Fairies—the godmothers of Princess Aurora. Centre stage back, the door to an anteroom. Courtiers, standing in groups, wait the entrance of the King and Queen.

(1) The Masters of Ceremony place everyone in their place, so that they may take part in the customary offering of congratulations and good wishes to the King, Queen and powerful Fairies, who have been invited to be godmothers at Princess Aurora'a christening.

SOURCE: First published in *The Dancing Times* (December, 1942, and February, 1943).

(1) (During the raising of the curtain a drawing-room march for the entrance of the lords and ladies.)

(2) Catalabutte, surrounded by court servants, verifies the list of Fairies, to whom invitations have been sent. Everything has been accomplished, according to the King's command. Everything is ready for the ceremony—the Court is assembled—the arrival of the Fairies is expected at any moment.

(2) (For Catalabutte's little scene, the march is made a little more serious, yet half-comic.)

(3) Fanfare. Entrance of the King and Queen, preceded by pages and attended by the governesses and nurses of Princess Aurora; these carry the Royal Baby's cradle.

(3) (Fanfare. Broad and very festive music. The King and Queen only just reach the platform and the cradle is set down as Catalabutte announces the arrival of the Fairies.)

(4) Entrance of the Fairies. The Fairies, Candide, Fleur de Farine, Violante, Canary and Breadcrumbs enter the hall first.

(4) (Graceful music ¾. The King and Queen go to meet them and invite them to mount the platform.)

(5) Entrance of the Lilac Fairy—Aurora's principal godmother. She is surrounded by her own retinue of Fairies, who carry large fans, perfumes and hold the train of their Queen. At a sign from Catalabutte the pages run off and—

(5) (¾ broadly.)

(6) Young girls enter with brocade cushions on which are lying presents intended by the Queen of the Fairies for her godchild. The arrivals form pretty groups as they present each gift to Her, for whom they are intended.

(6) (¾ rather animated and danceable.) The pages and young girls appear dancing.

(7) The Fairies descend from the platform. Each in turn, they go to bless the child.

(7) (A little introduction for a Pas de Six.)

Pas de Six

A Sweet Adagio. A little Allegro.

Variations—

Candide.

Fleur de Farine. (Flowing.)

Kroshka (Breadcrumb). (Which interweaves and twines?)

Canary. (Who sings.)

Violante. (²/₄ animated.) (Plucked strings.)

The Lilac Fairy. (A sweetly happy variation.)

Coda. (¾, fast and stirring.)

(8) The Lilac Fairy, in her turn, wishes to go up to the cradle to give her gift to Aurora.

(8) (From 8–16 bars, when the Lilac Fairy wishes to go up to the cradle.)

(9) But at this moment, a loud roar is heard in the ante-room. A page runs in and tells Catalabutte that a new Fairy is arriving at the gate of the castle, one whom they had forgotten to invite to the ceremony. It is the Fairy Carabosse—the most powerful and wicked Fairy in the whole land. Catalabutte is horrified. How could he forget her; he is always so careful! Trembling he goes up to the King, to explain his shortcomings, his mistake! The King and Queen are upset. This forgetfulness of the First Lord Chamberlain will cause great unhappiness and affect the future of their dear child. Even the Fairies seem uncertain.

(9) When the noise is heard*—very animated movement.

(*Petipa repeats the words from the preceding paragraph in order to point out the position of the music more clearly. He marks these places throughout the entire programme in the same manner.)

(10) Carabosse appears in a wheel-barrow, drawn by six rats. After her come some absurd pages—cripples. The King and Queen implore her to forgive Catalabutte's forgetfulness. They will punish him in whichever way the Fairy wishes. Catalabutte, breathless with fear, throws himself at the feet of the wicked Fairy, imploring her to have mercy on him, in return for his faithful service to the end of his days. [Here and throughout the "speeches" would be rendered by pantomime gesture. Ed.]

(10) (Fantastic music.)

(11) Carabosse laughs and amuses herself by tearing out handfuls of his hair and throwing it to the rats, who eat it up. Presently Catalabutte becomes completely bald.

(11) (She laughs and amuses herself by tearing out his hair—the music must fit the situation. The pages laugh spitefully.)

(12) "I am not Aurora's godmother," says Carabosse, "but nevertheless, I wish to bring her my gift."

(12) ("I am not her godmother," the music changes and becomes cajoling.)

(13) The good Fairies implore her not to spoil the happiness of the kind Queen and persuade her to pardon the Chamberlain's unintentional forgetfulness.

(13) (The music becomes tender when the Fairies persuade her to forgive the Chamberlain.)

(14) Carabosse only laughs at them—her mirth is echoed by her crippled pages and even by her rats. The good Fairies turn away from their sister with abhorrence.

(14) (Carabosse only laughs—a slight whistling.)

(15) "Aurora, thanks to the gifts of her godmothers," says Carabosse, "will be the most beautiful, the most charming, the wisest Princess in the world. I have not the power to take these qualities away from her. But so that her happiness will never be disturbed—see how kind I am—know that if ever she pricks her finger or hand, she will fall asleep and her sleep will be eternal." (The King, Queen and entire Court are aghast.)

(15) (For this short speech—satirical, diabolic music.)

(16) Carabosse raises her wand over the cradle and pronounces her spell, then, overjoyed by her evil-doing and her triumph over her sisters, bursts out laughing. The raucous merriment of the monster is reflected by her retinue.

(16) (Pronounces her spell—a short, fantastic, grotesque dance for the crippled pages.)

(17) But the Lilac Fairy, who has still not given her gift to the child and who is hiding behind Aurora's cradle, appears from her hiding place.

Carabosse looks at her with mistrust and anger. The good Fairy bows before the cradle. "Yes, you will fall asleep, my little Aurora, as your sister Carabosse has willed," says the Lilac Fairy, "but not for ever. A day will come when a Prince will appear who, enraptured by your beauty, will plant a kiss on your forehead and you will wake from your long dream in order to become the beloved wife of this Prince and live in happiness and prosperity."

(17) (The Lilac Fairy, who has still not given her gift—music tender and a little mocking.)

(18) The infuriated Carabosse sits down in her wheel-barrow and vanishes. The good Fairies group themselves round the cradle, as if protecting their godchild from their evil sister. (Picture.)

(18) (The infuriated Carabosse—energetic, satanical music. Group around the cradle.) (Picture.)

End of Prologue

[In Act I, while a party celebrates her twentieth birthday, Aurora does prick her finger. She and the entire court fall into a deep sleep, awaiting the arrival of Prince Desiré.]

Act II

SCENE III OF THE BALLET

Prince Desiré's Hunt. (1). A woody glade, at the back of the stage, a broad river. The entire horizon is covered with thick trees. To the right of the audience is a rock, covered with plants. The sun's rays light up the landscape.

At the rise of the curtain the stage is empty. The hunters' horns are heard. It is Prince Desiré's huntsmen, hunting wolves and lynx among the pine trees. The hunters and their ladies enter the scene, intending to rest and eat on the green grass. The Prince appears almost immediately with his tutor Gallifron and some noblemen from his father's Court. The Prince and his companions are served with food.

(1) The hunting horns are heard. The music of the hunt, which changes into the motif of rest—must be very short.

(2-3) In order to amuse the young Prince, the hunters and their ladies dance a round dance, throw javelins, practice archery and invent various amusements.

(2-3) (The nobles of the King's court propose to play "Blind Man's Buff" and other games. A quick ²/₄ from 48-60 bars.)

During the games Gallifron urges his pupil to join in with his companions and particularly to become acquainted with the ladies, because he must select a bride from amongst the courtiers of his kingdom. All the kings, whose kingdoms are neighbouring to his own—only possess sons. There is no Princess of Royal blood whom he could select as his bride.

(4) Gallifron, seizing the opportunity, compels the girls—the Royal courtiers—to pass before them.

(4) (Gallifron, seizing the opportunity, another motif. 16 bars before the dance begins.)

About 24 bars for each dance of these ladies.

(5) 24 bars. Dance of the Duchesses. Noble and proud.

(6) 24 bars. Dance of the Baronesses. Haughty and finicky.

(7) 24 bars. Dance of the Countesses. Coquettish and amusing.

(8) 24 bars. Dance of the playful Marquesses. They carry little darts, with which they tease the other ladies and their cavaliers.

(9) One of the marquesses proposes to dance a Farandole, because some of the local peasants can dance it. Farandole for Coda, from 48-64 bars, the heavy tempo of a mazurka.

(Note for myself.—Groups for "Blind Man's Buff." They play with the tutor. They push him with little arrows or darts. They can finish Pas de Bourrée, or a farandole step with the peasants, who have come to present fruits to the Prince.)

All these girls try to fascinate the Prince, but Desiré, with a goblet in his hand, chuckles to himself over the fruitless efforts of these numerous beauties. His heart is still whole—he still has not met the girl of his dreams and he will never marry until he has found her.

All this is spoken during the dance.

(10) Huntsmen enter to tell the company that they have surrounded a bear in his den. If the Prince wishes to kill it, it needs a very accurate

shot. But the Prince feels tired. "Hunt without me," he says to the noblemen. "I wish to rest awhile in this very pleasant place." The nobles and courtiers go off, but Gallifron, who has drunk more than one bottle of wine, falls asleep by the Prince's side.

(10) (Huntsmen enter to tell the company they have surrounded a bear. Quick 2/4, which stops quietly as they go out. 48 bars.)

(11) Only as the hunt dies away, on the river appears a mother-of-pearl boat, adorned with gold and precious jewels. In it stands the Lilac Fairy, who is also Prince Desiré's godmother. The Prince bows before the good Fairy, who graciously tells him to rise and asks him with whom he is in love.

"You are not in love with anyone?" she asks him.

"No," answers the Prince. "The noble ladies of my country cannot capture my heart and I prefer to remain single than marry a suitable Court lady."

"If this is so," answers the Fairy, "I will show you your future bride, the most beautiful, the most charming and the wisest Princess in the whole world."

"But where can I see her?"

"I will call her vision. See if she captivates your heart and if you will love her."

(11) (Only as the hunt dies away, on the river appears the mother-of-pearl boat. Fantastic poetical music. Grand music from 48-64 bars.)

(12) The Lilac Fairy waves her wand over the rock, which opens and discloses Aurora, with her sleeping friends. At a new wave of the Fairy's wand Aurora awakens and runs on the stage with her friends. The rays of the setting sun bathe her in a rose-coloured light.

(12) (At a new wave of the Fairy's wand, Aurora awakens and runs on to the stage. A tender and happy adagio. A little coquettish adagio. Variation for Aurora and a small Coda. For the Coda the music must be muted 2/4, like in "A Midsummer Night's Dream.")

(12b) All this occurs during Aurora's dance with her friends.

The enraptured Desiré follows behind this vision, which always eludes him. Her dance, now languid, now animated, entrances him more and more. He tries to catch her, but she escapes from his arms and appears again where he never expected to find her, amongst the swaying branches of the trees.

Finally he sees her in the opening of the rock, where she finally disappears. Overcome by his love, Desiré throws himself at his godmother's feet.

(13) "Where can I find this divine goddess that you have shown me? Lead me to her—I wish to see her, to press her to my heart."

(13) (Where can I find this divine goddess that you have shown me? Very animated, passionate music—48 bars, which must last until the Panorama.)

(14) "Come," says the Fairy, and places the Prince in the boat, which begins to move down the river as Gallifron continues to sleep.

(Panorama.)

(14) (The boat moves quickly. The horizon becomes more and more

Carlotta Brianza danced Princess Aurora in the original production of *The Sleeping Beauty* in 1890, the Italian ballerina lending her virtuosic talents to the French choreographer Petipa to create one of the most remarkable of Russian ballets. In 1921 Brianza made her last appearance as a dancer in the Diaghilev production of *The Sleeping Beauty*—this time as the wicked fairy Carabosse.

austere. The sun is setting. Night comes quickly. The path of the boat is starred with silver. A castle appears in the distance, which again disappears as the river twists and turns. But now, at last, here is the castle, the end of the journey.

[Act III is the wedding of Princess Aurora and Prince Desiré.]

Michel Fokine (1880–1942)
THE NEW BALLET

Trained at the St. Petersburg school of the Imperial Russian Ballet, Fokine was inspired to rebel against the conventions of his time, first by visits to museums that showed him the beauty of the human body in nonballetic poses, and second by the performances of Isadora Duncan, who presented her natural form of dancing to Russia in 1905. His opportunity to choreograph according to his convictions came in 1909, when he joined the Diaghilev Ballets Russes for its seasons in Western Europe. After coming to the United States in 1923, Fokine restaged a number of his Diaghilev ballets for the touring Ballet Russe de Monte Carlo and for the American Ballet Theatre.

Fokine could not accept the prevailing customs of ballet production, nor could he follow the now emerging exponents of the free forms of dance that completely rejected the danse d'école. *In "The New Ballet," written in 1916 for the Russian periodical* Argus, *Fokine urges reform within the tradition. Yet he goes well beyond the position of Noverre, who claimed that ballet should unite pantomime and dance. Fokine advocated a complete unity of expression; the whole body of the dancer should portray character and feeling and this may demand the elimination, not only of virtuosity, but of standard forms which are essentially inappropriate to the theme of the particular ballet. This does not, however, imply that they are never appropriate. Here Fokine's insistence on "beauty" and the "ideal" separates him from the next step in choreographic development.*

I. On Ballet Routine

Before I discuss the traditions which hinder the natural development of the art of ballet, I wish to state that I shall consider what in my

SOURCE: From Cyril W. Beaumont, *Michel Fokine and His Ballets* (London: Beaumont, 1935).

opinion is wrong. But I shall deal with laws and traditions, and not with the talents of the artistes. It must be admitted that the creators of the old ballet possessed genius which, however, was restricted by unnecessary rules. The traditional ballet forgot man's natural beauty. It essayed to express a psychological feeling by a fixed movement, or series of movements, which could neither describe nor symbolise anything.

Not only did the spectators fail to understand the expressions of the artistes, but one artiste did not know what another was supposed to convey to him. The audience witness a number of movements but never trouble to question whether they are expressive. Some of these are familiar to them from long acquaintance. For example, it is understood that when a dancer points one finger upwards and then touches his lips with it, he is entreating a kiss; it is curious that in all ballets only one kiss is requested. If the girl to whom he makes this sign runs away from him, proudly raises her arms, points to herself, lowers her arms in front of her and then sweeps them to one side, it is intended to intimate that her would-be lover is rich while she is poor, and consequently he would soon cast her away. This incident is repeated in *Paquita, Esmeralda,* and *La Bayadère*. But this series of gestures cannot even pretend to be expressive. It is hardly likely that a man desirous of obtaining a kiss would point with his finger; but that is the traditional method of making love in a ballet. The expressiveness of the action is relatively unimportant, it is the beauty of the poses and movements, the graceful action of pointing one finger to Heaven that is all important. . . .

II. The Development of Signs

I have mentioned the above details because, in my opinion, a dance is the development and ideal of the sign. The ballet renounced expression and consequently dancing became acrobatic, mechanical, and empty. In order to restore dancing its soul we must abandon fixed signs and devise others based on the laws of natural expression. "But," it may be asked, "how can a dance be built on a sign?" Consider the *arabesque* of the good old times. "But," it may be argued, "you employed *arabesques* in *Les Sylphides*." Certainly, an *arabesque* is sensible when it idealises the sign, because it suggests the body's straining to soar upward, the whole body is expressive. If there be no expression, no sign, but merely a foot raised in the position termed *en arabesque*, it looks foolish. That is the difference between the good old, and the merely old.

Examine the prints of Cerrito, Grisi, Ellsler, and Taglioni, it will be found that their poses have a certain expressiveness. Now look through

Vaslav Nijinsky created the title role of Petrouchka in 1911. Already famous for his technical virtuosity, the dancer here proved his tremendous gifts as a dramatic artist. For this puppet-protagonist, Fokine employed turned-in positions, significant of Petrouchka's introverted character. The constricted movements contradicted the very base of the conventional classical vocabulary.

a history of dancing, on the concluding pages of which will be found the dancers of the end of the last century. Their poses are quite different. There is no sign. What does their pose express? Simply a leg extended backwards. It is neither the beginning nor end of the sign, nor its development. Instead of expressing something, the body seeks balance to avoid falling on account of the raised leg.

There is a vast difference between the dancers of the beginning of the nineteenth century, when the ballet reached its height in beauty, and those at the end of the century, when beauty was forced to give place to acrobatics. There is a complete difference in principle. Taglioni raises herself *sur les pointes* in order to be so light as to seem hardly to touch the ground. The dancer of the period when ballet was in decline uses her *pointes* in order to astonish the audience with their strength and endurance. She fills up the toe of her satin shoe and jumps on it so that the shoe hits the ground with all the strength of her muscular feet. The "steel" toe is a horrible invention of the ballet in decline. In its days of greatness, supernatural lightness was the ideal. Now, the steel toe, hard legs, and precision in execution, are the ideals.

III. The Old and the New in Ballet. The Creative Power in Ballet

I ask for the careful preservation of the beauty of the dance as Taglioni knew it. That world of fragile dreams could not support the rude acrobatic ballet and has fled from us. It will never return if we do not exert all our strength to save this highest form of the dance. But, having preserved it, this style must be employed only when it is applicable. No single form of dancing should be adopted once and for all. The best form is that which most fully expresses the meaning desired, and the most natural one that which most closely corresponds with the idea to be conveyed. For example, ballet steps executed *sur la pointe* cannot be used in a Greek Bacchic dance, on the other hand it would be unnatural to dance a Spanish dance in a Greek *chiton*. . . .

Man has always changed his plastic language. He has expressed in the most varied forms his sorrows, his joys, and all the emotions he experienced, hence his mode of expression cannot be fixed according to any one rule. The old method of production consisted in creating dances from fixed movements and poses, the mimed scenes were always expressed by a fixed manner of gesticulation, and thus the audience had to understand the theme. The most prominent creators of ballet were bound hand and foot by those laws and traditions. We must denounce this. Work of this kind is very easy for the producer and the artistes, and lightens the work of the critic. It is easy to judge whether a dancer has executed correctly the steps which he or she has performed a hundred times in other ballets. But there is one drawback to this method, a ready-made pattern does not always fit.

IV. Confusion

Creators of ballets should always endeavour to seek out that form of dancing which best expresses the particular theme, for this principle leads to great beauty. However varied the rule of ballet might become, life would always be more varied still; while ballet having no relation to reality and circumscribed by tradition naturally becomes ludicrous. The old ballet has confused periods and styles. It uses Russian top-boots and the French school of dancing in one ballet, the short ballet-skirt and historically correct Egyptian costume in another, and so forth. Is not that confusion? The style of the dance is always inharmonious with that of the costumes, theme, and period. Moreover, there is one style for classical dances, another for character dances; and all these appear in one ballet and at the same time. Such is tradition. And to give one homogeneous, harmonious thing is to sin against it, because in order to comply with ballet aesthetics it is imperative to reproduce dual styles.

V. Ballet Rules

The classical ballet came into being as a pleasure of the aristocracy and part of court ceremony. The bowing before the public, the addressing of hand movements to them, and so on, are the foundations on which the rules of ballet were built. Examine the photographs of academic dancers in, for instance, a *pas de deux*; the *danseur* always stands behind the *danseuse*. He holds her waist and looks at her back, while she faces the audience. He displays her. If I do not agree with this style of dancing, it does not mean that I ignore the school. On the contrary, I think that in order to create anything of value one must study and pass through a proper school which, however, should not be confined to the study of fixed poses and steps.

First, one must study oneself, conquer one's own body, and try to learn to feel and develop an ability to perform various movements. Ballet gymnastics are limited, they do not develop the whole body nor instil a feeling for pose and movement in all their variety. The ballet at the end of the last century was limited to several rules handed down without explanation as dogmas. It was of no avail to inquire the why and the wherefore because no one could answer such questions, they were too old. One had to accept the creed that the feet should keep to the five positions and that all movements consisted in combinations of these positions; that the arms should be rounded, the elbows held sideways facing the audience, the back straight, and the feet turned outwards with the heels well to the front. It is difficult to lose faith in these five positions in order to realise that beauty of movement cannot be limited by them.

The practice of turning the legs outward certainly develops the flexibility of the lower limbs, but exercises *en dehors* develop the feet to one side only. In order to make sure it is sufficient to look at a dancer with turned out feet in a dance requiring the feet to be in a natural position. It is obvious that she is ill at ease. Her feet are not under control. I appreciate the "turning out" of the feet in preliminary exercises, but as soon as the exercises are finished the "turning out" should cease, except in Siamese, Hindu, and exotic dances, when the feet should harmonise with the angular positions of the arms. But a barefoot dance with the feet turned out is absurd.

Another failing of ballet technique is that it is concentrated in the dancing of the lower limbs, whereas the whole body should dance. The whole body to the smallest muscle should be expressive, but ballet schools concentrate on exercises for the feet. The arms are limited to a few movements and the hands to one fixed position. What variety would not be possible if the dancer renounced the mannerism of rounded arms. And the movement of the upper part of the body, to what does that lead? A straight back, that is the ideal. One must be deaf not to become furious when the teacher continually repeats for eight or nine years one and the same rule—hold up your back. What store of beauty have painters not taken from the different positions of the body? The academic dancer, however, always faces the audience in a straight line.

The conservative critics were furious because the dancers in certain of my ballets wore sandals and Eastern shoes, and only used the traditional ballet-shoe in some ballets. The admirers of academic dancing could not understand the view that *pointes* should be used as a means and not as the sole aim of ballet. *Pointes* should be employed where they are suitable and renounced without regret where they would not serve any artistic purpose. For instance, in Eastern ballets, the bare foot or a soft shoe is more pleasing than a ballet-shoe, but the dancer in *Le Cygne* does not offend when she uses her *pointes* to suggest a soaring movement. It is right if all her body express the same feeling, but wrong if she uses her *pointes* to display her "steel" toe. She degrades herself before the audience which is watching for the strength of her toes. It is a complete misunderstanding of this beautiful mode of progression.

Forgetful of its artistic aims, ballet began to use *pointes* for quite opposite means, in fact merely to display the endurance and strength of the toes. The shoe was filled up with leather, cotton wool, and cork. But this did not make any difference to anyone, because a competition began as to who could make the most turns *sur la pointe*. The dancer's toes became ugly and it became impossible for her to show her foot without the shoe. That also did not matter. If we admit that ballet should develop mime for most styles of dancing, the basis of the school should be the teaching of natural movement. One should be able to move naturally and control the body to this end. The natural dance should follow and then one could advance to the dance of artificial movement. Ballet however begins at the end. It renounces natural movement, but surely the ballet has no right to discard what it did not possess. Vrubel had the right to paint a mutilated demon because he could draw a beautiful human body. . . .

VII. Delightful Nonsense

The step from the senseless to the expressive dance does not lead to cheap drama, to the narrow dramatisation of the dance; it expresses everything that is in the human soul. "Why," it is argued, "should ballet contain expression and drama when it should be unreal and irrational?" Someone has styled ballet "delightful nonsense." I am glad that ballet is considered "delightful," but if it were not nonsense it would have gained. Expression is as necessary to ballet as any other art, even more so. If colours and sounds do not speak they are tolerable, but an expressionless human body resembles a doll or a corpse. In pictures we look for the painter's soul. We do not accept a picture which expresses nothing; how then can we tolerate a man without expression?

Léonide Massine (1896–)
THE CREATION OF "PARADE"

A graduate of the Moscow school of the Imperial Russian Ballet, Massine choreographed his first ballet for Diaghilev in 1915; his last in 1928. As artistic director of the Ballet Russe de Monte Carlo in the 1930's, he revived some of his early works but also created a controversial series of ballets to the great symphonies—which horrified some musical purists. Later Massine choreographed more of his typical period pieces for Ballet Theatre in the United States and for numerous other companies in America and abroad.

Parade (1917) came out of Diaghilev's chic, modernist period, but its innovative contributions stemmed more from the visual concepts of Picasso and the music of Satie than from the movement invention of Massine, though his characterizations were much admired. The total effect, smart and streamlined, was

SOURCE: From *My Life in Ballet* (New York: St. Martin's Press, 1968). Reprinted by permission.

brilliant. Nevertheless, the vogue of the likes of **Parade** *did not last. As Lincoln Kirstein commented, "it was one of the first victims of the very school it launched—the cult of the contemporaneous." Notably, however,* **Parade** *was successfully revived in 1973 by the (New York) City Center Joffrey Ballet.*

During that winter of 1916–17 our studio in the Piazza Venezia was the meeting-place of an ever-widening circle of artists, which now included Pablo Picasso, whom Diaghilev had invited to Rome to collaborate on a new ballet. When he first arrived I was so busy that I had little opportunity of getting to know him, but I was intensely aware of the young Spaniard who came to watch our rehearsals, sketching the dancers and helping Bakst to paint some of the props used in the ballet. It was during the rehearsals of *Les Femmes de Bonne Humeur* that he met his future wife, Olga Kokhlova, who was dancing the part of Felicita, one of Constanza's friends.

Another member of our circle was a lean, witty, young Frenchman named Jean Cocteau, whose outrageous suggestions amused and sometimes irritated Diaghilev. But he was usually ready to listen to them, for he felt that Cocteau brought to the company a breath of *avant-garde* Paris. Now that I had finished *Les Femmes de Bonne Humeur* and *Contes Russes* I had more time to spend with them all, and soon we were seriously considering one of Cocteau's suggestions for a ballet incorporating elements of the circus and music-hall. We decided to set the scene in front of a circus tent, bringing on such characters as acrobats, tightrope walkers and conjurers, and incorporating jazz and cinematograph techniques in balletic form. Picasso was delighted by the whole concept, and suggested that the costumes should be executed in cubist style—cubism being then at its height—and he quickly produced some rough sketches, the most striking being those for the French and American managers, whom Picasso visualized as animated billboards suggesting the vulgarity of certain types of show-business promoters. For the American he devised a montage of a skyscraper with fragmentary faces and a gaudy sign reading "PARADE," which eventually became the name of the ballet.

As soon as Erik Satie, who had been commissioned to write the music for the ballet, had produced his witty, satirical score, I was able to begin work on the choreography. I found that the music, with its subtle synthesis of jazz and ragtime, offered me excellent material on which to base a number of new dance patterns. During one of our early rehearsals Cocteau told Diaghilev that he wanted to incorporate into the ballet every possible form of popular entertainment. Diaghilev agreed until the moment came when Cocteau suggested that the managers should be given lines which they would deliver through megaphones. This was going too far, even for Diaghilev, who pointed out that the spoken word was entirely out of place in a ballet. Cocteau, however, insisted that in this case the use of megaphones was perfectly valid and in tune with the cubist conception of the production. Although he lost the argument, he eventually persuaded Satie to introduce into the score a number of realistic sound effects, such as the clicking of a typewriter, the wail of a ship's siren, and the droning of an aeroplane engine. All these, Cocteau explained, were in the spirit of cubism, and helped to portray the feverish insanity of contemporary life.

We began the ballet with the entrance of the French manager, danced by Woidzikowsky, who moved in a jerky, staccato manner to match Satie's opening phrases, stamping his feet and banging his walking-stick on the floor to attract the attention of the crowd. Then came the "parade"—the name given to the efforts of fairground performers to lure the audience into their booths. A curtain was drawn, and in music-hall fashion a placard appeared announcing "Number One." This was the cue for my entrance as the Chinese conjurer, whom I envisaged as a parody of the usual pseudo-oriental entertainer with endless tricks up his sleeve. Dressed in a mandarin jacket and floppy trousers, I marched stiffly round the stage jerking my head at each step. Then going to the centre I bowed to the audience and began my act. I was at first unable to decide what sort of tricks this type of performer would do, but when I had demonstrated the opening phases of my dance to Cocteau, he suggested that I should go through the motions of swallowing an egg. The idea appealed to me. With an elaborate flourish I pretended to produce an egg from my sleeve and put it in my mouth. When I had mimed the action of swallowing it, I stretched out my arms, slid my left leg sideways till I was almost sitting down, and with my left hand pretended to pull the egg from the toe of my shoe. The whole thing took only a few minutes, but it had to be done with the most clearly defined movements and broad mime. When I had retrieved the egg I leaped round the stage again, then paused, puckered up my lips and pretended to breathe out fire. One last march round the stage, a final deep bow, and I disappeared. My entire performance, with its exaggerated movements, broad miming, and oriental mask-like make-up, was designed to present an enigmatic figure who would intrigue the fairground public and make them want to see more of him.

The American girl who followed the entry of the second manager was intended to be a more credible character. Wearing a blazer and a short white skirt, she bounced on to the stage, crossing it in a succession of convulsive leaps, her arms swinging widely. She then did an imitation of the shuffling walk of Charlie Chaplin, followed by a sequence of

Picasso designed the costume for the Manager from New York in *Parade*. A close look at the dancer's legs provides an idea of the actual scale of the structure. The accoutrements, including such "American" symbols as the megaphone and the skyscraper, impeded the dancer no less than did the similarly identifying props of the *ballet de cour*. But three centuries made a difference in the concept of "chic."

mimed actions reminiscent of *The Perils of Pauline*—jumping on to a moving train, swimming across a river, having a running fight at pistol-point, and finally finding herself lost at sea in the tragic sinking of the *Titanic*. All this was ingeniously danced and mimed by Maria Chabel-ska, who interpreted Satie's syncopated ragtime music with great charm and gusto, and brought the dance to a poignant conclusion when, thinking herself a child at the seaside, she ended up playing in the sand.

The American girl was followed by a third manager on horseback, and once again we were faced with the problem of how to convey the illusion of a horse on stage. I felt that rather than attempt a realistic presentation, it would be more in the spirit of the production to use the old music-hall device of two men wearing a horse's head with a cloth draped over them. The manager was a Negro dummy in evening dress who was bounced about by the capriciously prancing horse, jumping alternately on its front and hind legs and even sitting down. The horse was followed by two acrobats—Nemchinova and Zverev—who advanced in a series of pirouettes and arabesques, and to give the illusion of a performer delicately poised on a tightrope I made Lopokova balance herself for several seconds on Zverev's bent knee. This was followed by another flurry of pirouettes, after which Zverev lifted his partner and carried her off stage.

For the finale I devised a rapid, ragtime dance in which the whole cast made a last desperate attempt to lure the audience in to see their show. The managers shouted through their megaphones, the horse clumped round the stage, the acrobats performed amazing leaps, the American girl cavorted, the conjurer smiled and bowed. But the public remained indifferent, and when it became evident that the whole "parade" had been a failure, the horse collapsed on the ground, the acrobats stood trembling with exhaustion, the girl and the managers drooped. Only the conjurer retained his oriental calm.

Parade was not so much a satire on popular art as an attempt to translate it into a totally new form. It is true that we utilized certain elements of contemporary show-business—ragtime music, jazz, the cinema, billboard advertising, circus and music-hall techniques—but we took only their salient features, adapting them to our own ends. Some critics have seen in *Parade* a foretaste of the artistic upheaval of the immediate post-war period. It may be that it was instrumental in bringing cubism firmly before the public, and that its repercussions can be traced in certain choreographic and cinematic developments of the next thirty years, and even in such recent manifestations as pop art. These are questions which are best left to the historians of art. For my part, all I can say is that in 1917 we were mainly concerned with creating something new and representative of our own age.

André Levinson (1887–1933)
THE SPIRIT OF THE
CLASSIC DANCE

Born in Russia, Levinson moved shortly after the Revolution to Paris, where he wrote dance criticism for French newspapers and magazines. He published several collections of his reviews as well as some notable biographies of dancers.

Levinson believed in the supremacy of pure dance, opposing Fokine, whom he accused of sacrificing beauty of movement to expression, and to Diaghilev, whom he derided for subordinating choreography to music and décor. This essay provides a most precise and illuminating definition of the principles of dance classicism. Incidentally, it serves us as a convenient summation of the development of ballet technique up to this point in its history.

The great Noverre, called the "Shakespeare of the dance" by Garrick and "Prometheus" by Voltaire—who is still the most vital and thorough theoretician who has written on the subject, desired above everything to incorporate the dance into the group of "imitative arts." Carlo Blasis—the same incidentally who established the theory of classic instruction—struggled manfully to evolve some plausible connection between the spectacle of the dance and the poetry of the spoken drama. Others have conceived the dance as strictly limited to the expression of definite ideas—thereby sacrificing it to and confusing it with pantomime. It seems as though everyone had piled upon this art mistaken attributes or supplementary burdens in his efforts to redeem—even if only in a small way—the actual movements of the dance.

I can not think of anyone who has devoted himself to those characterstics which belong exclusively to dancing, or who has endeavored to formulate specifically the laws of this art on its own ground. . . . But no one has ever tried to portray the intrinsic beauty of a dance step, its innate quality, its esthetic reason for being . . . it is the desire of the dancer to create beauty which causes him to make use of his knowledge of mechanics and that finally dominates this knowledge. He subjects his muscles to a rigid discipline; through arduous practice he bends and adapts his body to the exigencies of an abstract and perfect form. In the end he brings the physiological factors—muscle contraction and

SOURCE: Reprinted with the permission of the publisher, Theatre Arts Books, New York, from *Theatre Arts Anthology*, Copyright 1925 by Theatre Arts, Inc. Copyright 1950 by Theatre Arts Books.

relaxation—completely under the domination of the sovereign rhythm of the dance. This is what makes it so difficult to separate the gymnastic elements of the dance from its ideal essence. The technique of a dancer is not like the mechanical workings of a jointed doll; it is physical effort constantly informed by beauty. This technique is no supplementary reënforcement to his art, nor is it a mere device, designed to gain easy applause, like (according to Stendhal) the art of the versifier. It is the very soul of the dance, it *is* the dance itself.

Of all the various techniques it is that of the so-called classic dance—a term designating the style of dancing that is based on the traditional ballet technique—which has prevailed in the Western world. It seems to be in complete accord not only with the anatomical structure of the European but with his intellectual aspirations as well. We find this technique in all those countries where man is fashioned like us and where he thinks in our way. The little definite knowledge we have concerning the system of gymnastics of the ancient Greeks warrants our identifying certain of their "modes" with those of the contemporary dance. Today the universality of the classic style is disputed only by the oriental dance, that finds in the Cambodgian ballet its highest and most complete expression. The superb efflorescence of the dance in Spain is in itself a vestige of an oriental civilization, repelled but not annihilated.

Opponents of the classic dance technique pretend to consider it an academic code, imposed on the dance arbitrarily by pedants and long since obsolete. It is true that it does recapitulate the experience of centuries, for we find that certain of its fundamental ideas were accepted by the dancing masters of the Italian Renaissance. It was they who first broke away from the so-called "horizontal" conception of the dance, based on outlines and figures marked by the feet of the dancer on the floor—what you might call his itinerary. The outlines of the choreographs of the seventeenth century, reproducing on paper the curving path drawn on the ground by the feet of the dancer, are the last vestiges of this "horizontal" idea, which was gradually displaced by the vertical conception of dancing—the configuration of motion in space.

. . . The five fundamental positions, which are the ABC of the dance, may seem to be the same for Feuillet, the choreographer of the "grand Siècle" and for Mademoiselle Zambelli—to mention one of the fairest flowers of contemporary classic dance. But this is not actually so. In the outlines of Feuillet that have come down to us, the feet in the first position, make an obtuse angle. In the modern they are in the same straight line in the first position, and in the other positions in parallel lines. This may seem to be a trifling detail of growth and change, when one thinks of Isadora Duncan dancing a Beethoven symphony.

But this almost imperceptible difference, this slight shift of the geometrical line, these feet pivoting at an angle of so many degrees, represents an enormously important acquisition, capable of infinite combinations and variety. This trifling detail is actually a realization of that essential principle and point of departure of classic choreography which took two centuries to prevail—that of turning the body—and more particularly the legs of the dancer—outward from its centre.

I find myself at times looking at the history of the modern dance as though it were some charming but infinitely obscure romance, that needed a key to unlock its mysteries. This key is an understanding of what a dancer means when he speaks of turning out the body. The movement of the oriental dance is concentric. The knees almost instinctively come together and bend, the curved arms embrace the body. Everything is pulled together. Everything converges. The movement of the classic dance, on the other hand, is ex-centric—the arms and the legs stretch out, freeing themselves from the torso, expanding the chest. The whole region of the dancer's being, body and soul, is dilated. The actual manifestation of this can be readily seen or even better felt in the trained body of a classical ballet dancer. The dancer spreads the hips and rotates both legs, in their entire length from the waist down, away from each other, outward from the body's centre, so that they are both in profile to the audience although turned in opposite directions. The so-called five fundamental positions are merely derivations or variations of this outward turning posture, differentiated by the manner in which the two feet fit in, cross or by the distance that separates them. In the fifth position, where the two feet are completely crossed, toes to heels, you have the very incarnation of this principle of turning outward—that is to say, of the spirit of classic dancing. The fifth position is Taglioni; the third was Camargo. A whole century of experimentation and of slow, arduous assimilation lies between the two. The orthopedic machines, true instruments of torture, that were used to turn pupils out in the days of Noverre would not be tolerated today. But it does take several years of daily exercise, beginning at the ages of eight or nine years to give a dancer the ability to perform this mechanical feat easily.

At this point, the reader may demand precisely what is gained by this hard won victory over nature. Just this—the body of the dancer is freed from the usual limitations upon human motion. Instead of being restricted to a simple backward and forward motion—the only directions in which the human body, operating normally, can move with ease and grace, this turning outward of the legs permits free motion in any direction without loss of equilibrium; forward, backwards, sideways, obliquely or rotating. The actual extent of motion possible is considerably augmented, and since the feet are thus made to move on lines parallel to each other there is no interference and many motions otherwise impossible are thereby facilitated. As a good example of this, I might cite the *entrechat*—that exhilarating movement where the dancer leaps high in the air and crosses his legs several times while off the ground. This effective "braiding" movement necessitates the turning outward of the body—otherwise the dancer's legs would block each other.

What a tiresome recital, you may be saying and all of this in trying to talk about so elusive and illusive a thing as the dance! But I assure you it is justified, for the very illusion of this enchanting art—which seems to ignore all natural laws—depends on an intelligent ordering of physical effort. The dancer then is a body moving in space according to any desired rhythm. We have seen how the turning outward of the body increases this space to an extraordinary degree, pushing back the invisible walls of that cylinder of air in the centre of which the dancer moves, giving him that extraordinary extension of body which is totally lacking in oriental dancing and multiplying to an infinite degree the direction of the movement as well as its various conformations. It surrounds the vertical of the body's equilibrium by a vortex of curves, segments of circles, arcs; it projects the body of the dancer into magnificent parabolas, curves it into a living spiral; it creates a whole world of animated forms that awake in us a throng of active sensations, that our usual mode of life has atrophied.

I have not tried to explain clearly more than one of the salient and decisive characteristics of the classic technique. The rich development of the dance that increases its sway from generation to generation corresponds to the gradual elaboration of this principle of turning outward.

If at the beginning of the classic period the dance served merely to give law and style to the carriage and deportment of the perfect courtier, or if at the time of the *"fêtes galantes"* it was still skipping and mincing, it has gradually became exalted and transfigured until it is now called upon to express the loftiest emotions of the human soul.

When once the enthusiasm of the romantic period had created the idea of the dance of elevation, it was only one step further to make the dancer rise up on his toes. It would be interesting to know at exactly what moment this second decisive factor entered in. The historians of the dance, unfortunately, are not concerned with telling us. It is however evident that this reform was at least a half century in preparation. The heel of the shoe raised up, the instep arched, the toe reached down—the plant no longer was rooted to the soil. What happened was that the foot simply refused to remain flat any longer. It strove to lengthen out the vertical lines of its structure. It gave up its natural method of functioning to further an esthetic end. And thus it is that when a dancer rises on her points, she breaks away from the exigencies of everyday life, and enters into an enchanted country—that she may thereby lose herself in the ideal.

To discipline the body to this ideal function, to make a dancer of a graceful child, it is necessary to begin by dehumanizing him, or rather by overcoming the habits of ordinary life. His muscles learn to bend, his legs are trained to turn outward from the waist, in order to increase the resources of his equilibrium. His torso becomes a completely plastic body. His limbs stir only as a part of an ensemble movement. His entire outline takes on an abstract and symmetrical quality. The accomplished dancer is an artificial being, an instrument of precision and he is forced to undergo rigorous daily exercise to avoid lapsing into his original purely human state.

His whole being becomes imbued with that same unity, that same conformity with its ultimate aim that constitutes the arresting beauty of a finished airplane, where every detail, as well as the general effect, expresses one supreme object—that of speed. But where the airplane is conceived in a utilitarian sense—the idea of beauty happening to superimpose itself upon it, the constant transfiguration, as you might call it, of the classic dancer from the ordinary to the ideal is the result of a disinterested will for perfection, an unquenchable thirst to surpass himself. Thus it is that an exalted aim transforms his mechanical efforts into an esthetic phenomenon. You may ask whether I am suggesting that the dancer is a machine? But most certainly!—a machine for manufacturing beauty—if it is in any way possible to conceive a machine that in itself is a living, breathing thing, susceptible of the most exquisite emotions.

Section Five
THE MODERN DANCE: MOVING FROM THE INSIDE OUT

O: Despite the vitality of its frontier life, its belief in rugged individualism, and its concern with a national identity, the United States long looked to Europe for its culture. Throughout the nineteenth century most of its choreographers and dance soloists came from abroad.

After the demise of the romantic ballet, touring groups carried spectacles like *The Bower of Beauty* and *The Oriental Dream* from coast to coast. Native themes were either ignored or glossed over with fantasy; when a ballet with a local setting was performed in San Francisco in 1854, the leading role was that of Fairy Minerali, Queen of the Gold Mines.

Ballet technique was considered appropriate to any subject, but by the latter part of the century it had become corrupted. Since the popular productions relied more on scenic effects than on actual dancing, members of the corps de ballet did not need much skill; most of the time they just marched in various formations, more or less in time with the music. *Barre* work was abandoned. Albert W. Newman, wearing silk hose and satin knickers, taught his pupils meanings for the five positions: first, attention; second, assurance; third, modesty; fourth, pride; fifth, artistic finish. The idea could have been influenced by the theories of François Delsarte, whose American disciples were teaching that each bodily gesture had an emotional significance. The system, originally designed for opera singers, had no real impact on ballet, but it was to have repercussions on freer forms of dance.

For other forms were emerging. The time had come for America to assert its independence. Some of the first stirrings were isolated experiments, but they served to dent the sterile pattern and to open the eyes of audiences to fresh ideas. Others, more concerted, were to change the nature of theatre dance throughout the Western world.

In the early 1890's Loïe Fuller was a minor and not very successful actress who happened one night to wear an Indian silk skirt on the stage. Fascinated by its shimmering, she started to devise solo numbers in whch she manipulated gauzy fabrics to produce amazing shapes of color and light. Though Fuller soon settled in Paris, she returned to tour America, where observers saw her extraordinary experiments with electric lighting, which seemed to turn her figure into "a golden drinking cup, a magnificent lily, a huge glistening moth." As a dancer, Fuller had no particular technical equipment, but she created a novel form of movement and revealed a tremendous potential for dance in the imaginative uses of lighting.

From Canada came Maud Allan, who wanted to revive the forms of ancient Greece. When she danced in New York in 1910, the critic Carl Van Vechten described her floating "from one pose to the next, emphasizing the plastic transitions with waving arms and raised legs and sundry poses of the head." This sounds rather like balletic flow, but Allan was bare-legged, clothed in a soft tunic, and had no virtuosity to offer. Yet this was dancing; the range of the art was expanding.

Also inspired by Greece but a more zealous missionary was Isadora Duncan. Completely opposed to the ballet—which she denounced as unnatural and harmful in its system of training, empty and unworthy in its theatrical form—she conceived of a dance that would come from the intuitions of the spirit rather than from formal structures. Duncan was adamant in her belief that movement must spring from within; that the dancer, inspired by nature or by music, would naturally respond with beautiful gestures if her soul was not inhibited by technical codes and social taboos. Duncan's own movements were ingenuous: in the early dances they were leaps and runs of spontaneous joy; later there were portraits of grief, drawn from personal tragedies, as well as noble images of humanity's struggles and conquests. One witness recalled an entire dance built simply on rising from the floor; it seemed as if the repressed of the world had shed their chains and triumphed over all tyranny. Since Duncan's art was so dependent on individual sensitivity, she founded no lasting school. In her technique, there were no seeds for development. Yet the impact of her performing was enormous. Even more important in its influence was her concept of dance as an expression of personal emotion: not a representation of the feeling of a dramatic character, but a lyric outpouring of passion.

Meanwhile Ruth St. Denis was channeling her personal emotions into a different kind of dance. Where Duncan expressed her feelings directly and immediately, St. Denis objectified hers in dramas of Eastern ritual; where Duncan danced chiefly as a soloist with simple blue curtains as her only background, St. Denis required a company and all the devices of spectacle: elaborate costumes, models of shrines and pagodas, and arrays of colored lights. Though audiences were undoubtedly attracted by the visual splendors of the productions, these were to St. Denis only the means of embodying her spiritual vision. She relied on them more than on her movement, which was minimal: an evocative walk, a subtle turn of the head, marvelous undulations of the arms. Though these Oriental works were the mainstay of the repertory of the Denishawn company, led by herself and her husband Ted Shawn, other genres were eventually added. Shawn created pieces based on American folk material. His wife ventured into abstractions designed to follow the rhythms and melodic structures of the musical scores that inspired them; for her this was another form of emotional objectification. When she turned to more specifically religious works, this time outside the Oriental context, Shawn developed a group of men dancers to show America that the male performer merited attention equal to the female.

The Denishawn company took dance seriously; they challenged the view that dance was a mere superficial form of entertainment, providing exhibitions of its power to depict, in St. Denis' phrase, "the most noble thoughts of man." But in its way the company was as escapist in concept as the romantic ballet had been; its ideas were realized under guises of ancient legends of exotic lands; its forms were borrowed from distant rituals, from folk tales of the past, from the universal abstractions of music. Even while Denishawn was cheered, fresh forces were visible in other areas of American art: painters and writers were coping with new ways of viewing the contemporary world; musicians were destroying long-respected foundations of tonality; the insights of Freud were changing man's way of regarding himself and his creativity. The philosophy of Denishawn could not last, but before it died it had helped to release dance from its previous confinement to the role of an innocuous amusement.

The next generation, bred within Denishawn, began again with the need to express personal experience. But the experience they had to express was more realistic, closer to the actualities of the society in which they lived, tougher because of its commitment to deal with the sometimes disagreeable facts of the present. To present such experience, these dancers dispensed with the ornate costumes of Denishawn, as Denishawn had dispensed with the pretty prancings of the decadent ballet. In its "black woolens" period, American dance was austere, using sharp, angular, but telling movement to speak its message.

When she left Denishawn, Martha Graham stated: "Life today is nervous, sharp, and zigzag. This is what I aim for in my dances." Spurred by her musical director Louis Horst, she listened to the new music, visited the avant-garde art galleries, and observed the Indian ceremonials of the Southwest. Like the painters who were studying primitive art, Graham was looking for a movement style at once basic to man's nature and attuned to the rhythms of contemporary life. In the beginning her style was unrelentingly strong, earthbound, percussive. There were ritual dances like *Primitive Mysteries* (1931) and dances rooted in her American heritage like *Letter to the World* (1940), which probed the life of Emily Dickinson. There were studies of Greek myth—prototypes of universal experiences of passion, guilt, and redemption; the cycle was climaxed by *Clytemnestra* (1958). Then there were some lyrical works like *Diversion of Angels* (1948), and in time the technique too became somewhat softened with rounded arms, a spiraling torso, and a lighter attack. But a tension, like animal alertness, was always present—the dancer always poised on the brink of danger and discovery.

Where Graham looked inward, to the individual's relation to his own feelings and experiences, her former colleague in Denishawn Doris Humphrey looked out at the individual's relation to the world around him. Humphrey found an arena of conflict, of striving competition, in which the person longs at once for the risk of adventure and the security of the hearth. Optimistically, though, she envisioned a potentially harmonious society, a conquest of opposing forces. Because Humphrey was intensely musical, she realized her dramatic concept in rhythmic as well as spatial forms—a fall forced by the pull of gravity, a mustering of energy to recover balance, a resolution on an exultant breath of triumph. She saw the design in the forces of nature in such works as *Water Study* (1928) and *Life of the Bee* (1929). She found material in religious sects like *The Shakers* (1931) and in the life of a bullfighter, as in *Lament for Ignacio Sánchez Mejías* (1946). But she could also dispense with specific content, creating works like *Passacaglia* (1938) that simply made visible the majestic measures of Bach.

Humphrey's partner, Charles Weidman, showed with autobiographical sketches like *And Daddy Was a Fireman* (1943) that the concern for expressing personal experiences could have its lighter side. Yet his powerful *Lynchtown* (1936) was also drawn from a childhood experience. A skilled mime, Weidman's best choreography was dramatic and shone especially in his witty sketches based on James Thurber's *Fables for Our Time* (1948). Together, Humphrey and Weidman created a rich repertory of wide-ranging styles, unusually diversified in these days of asceticism but always loyal to the principle of starting with the emotion to be portrayed, then finding the movements that would best portray it.

Working along lines similar to the self-exiles from Denishawn was a renegade from the Metropolitan Opera Ballet, Helen Tamiris. She too felt that dance had to be revitalized, had to find fresh movement to express contemporary life. But she was especially involved with the specific social issues of her time, showing her sympathy for the American Negro in *How Long Brethren?* (1937) and for the Spanish Loyalists in *Adelante* (1939). Tamiris stated her beliefs: "We must not forget the age we live in. . . . Each work of art creates its own code. . . . The dance of today must have a dynamic tempo and be valid, precise, spontaneous, free, normal, natural, and human."

These were the leaders of the American modern dance—a most unsatisfactory name, but the one that has been accepted. John Martin, dance critic of *The New York Times*, called it "expressional dance," and this is more accurate. What gave these choreographers their identity was a method: Humphrey called it "moving from the inside out," starting not with traditional steps but with an emotional concept; then seeking the way through the body to communicate that concept. Of the previous rebels, only Fokine had sought to expand the existing vocabulary to accommodate dramatic needs. The modern dance was not satisfied with this degree of change; its exponents had first to eliminate all previous forms, then start—as from the beginning—with the body and its natural impulse to express its feelings in movement. Because the choreographers differed from one another in temperament, in areas of concern, in approach to movement stylization, the modern dance was essentially heterogeneous. Only the motivation was constant.

Though the American modern dance was a largely independent phenomenon, a similar—though distinct—form had risen in Central Europe. In Switzerland in the years following World War I, Rudolf von Laban had started experimenting with the range of movements the body could enact in space and time. Codifying the possible degrees of shape, direction, and energy involved, he went on to explore the principles that determine the expressiveness of human movement. A scientist by nature, Laban began with motion rather than emotion. His own choreographic efforts were limited; his students adapted his ideas for the stage.

The most significant dancer to study with Laban was Mary Wigman. She viewed Laban's theories dramatically: space became her environment, friendly or hostile, to be indulged in or conquered. From the confrontation with space sprang both the spatial design and the rhythms of the dance. Wigman wrote of the dancer who "disturbs the unseen body of space"; "a movement of the arm changes and forms it." From such encounters came dance themes: the celebration of *Festive Rhythm*; the rebellious struggle of *Song of Fate* with its "long strides into the dark and empty space."

Wigman was primarily a solo dancer. Kurt Jooss, on the other hand, who also studied with Laban, worked with a company because he chose to express his ideas through choreographed dramas. Not inclined to deal abstractly with rhythm or design, Jooss used his master's theories to portray specific characters and conflicts. Most famous of his works is *The Green Table* (1932), a bitter denunciation of peacemakers whose hypocritical diplomacy leads only to war, where the only victor is Death—personified by a figure who relentlessly stalks his victims until all have succumbed.

The promise of the German modern dance was cut off by World War II. But in 1931 Hanya Holm had arrived in New York, sent by Wigman to open a school of German modern dance technique. Through the 1930's Holm did some notable choreography for her own concert group, though the greater part of her present reputation rests on her brilliant contribution to the Broadway musical stage. She also continued to teach and in time her students were to bring the influence of their Wigman-rooted ideas to bear on the development of the American modern dance.

Isadora Duncan (1878–1927)
THE DANCE
OF THE
FUTURE

Born in San Francisco, Duncan learned happily from her music-teacher mother, but quit her ballet classes after a few lessons because she found the movements ugly and unnatural. Dancing in sandals and a simple tunic, she made little impression in the United States, but quickly found admirers in Europe. In 1905 Duncan appeared in Russia, where Fokine was impressed although he could not agree with her rejection of classical technique. Though she danced occasionally with the pupils of the school she had established in Berlin, Duncan performed most often alone, with a single piano to accompany her with the music of Bach or Schubert. Many derided her simplicity, but Karl Federn described the reaction of many more: "Her entrance, her walk, her simple gesture of greeting are movements of beauty. She wears no tights, no frilled ballet skirts, her slender limbs gleam through the veils and her dance is religion."

"The Dancer of the Future," written about 1902, is typical of Duncan's statements about her art. What Levinson called "idealization" was deformation to her, but Fokine agreed with her about the beauty of Greek sculptures. The question of ballet versus modern dance is far from a simple one.

If we seek the real source of the dance, if we go to nature, we find that the dance of the future is the dance of the past, the dance of eternity, and has been and will always be the same.

SOURCE: Reprinted with the permission of the publisher, Theatre Arts Books, New York. Copyright 1928 by Helen Hackett, Inc. Renewed. Copyright © 1969 by Theatre Arts Books.

The movement of waves, of winds, of the earth is ever in the same lasting harmony. We do not stand on the beach and inquire of the ocean what was its movement in the past and what will be its movement in the future. We realize that the movement peculiar to its nature is eternal to its nature. The movement of the free animals and birds remains always in correspondence to their nature, the necessities and wants of that nature, and its correspondence to the earth nature. It is only when you put free animals under false restrictions that they lose the power of moving in harmony with nature, and adopt a movement expressive of the restrictions placed about them.

So it has been with civilized man. The movements of the savage, who lived in freedom in constant touch with Nature, were unrestricted, natural and beautiful. Only the movements of the naked body can be perfectly natural. Man, arrived at the end of civilization, will have to return to nakedness, not to the unconscious nakedness of the savage, but to the conscious and acknowledged nakedness of the mature Man, whose body will be the harmonious expression of his spiritual being.

And the movements of this Man will be natural and beautiful like those of the free animals.

The movement of the universe concentrating in an individual becomes what is termed the will; for example, the movement of the earth, being the concentration of surrounding forces, gives to the earth its individuality, its will of movement. So creatures of the earth, receiving in turn these concentrating forces in their different relations, as transmitted to them through their ancestors and to those by the earth, in themselves evolve the movement of individuals which is termed the will.

The dance should simply be, then, the natural gravitation of this will of the individual, which in the end is no more nor less than a human translation of the gravitation of the universe.

The school of the ballet of today, vainly striving against the natural laws of gravitation or the natural will of the individual, and working in discord in its form and movement with the form and movement of nature, produces a sterile movement which gives no birth to future movements, but dies as it is made.

The expression of the modern school of ballet, wherein each action is an end, and no movement, pose or rhythm is successive or can be made to evolve succeeding action, is an expression of degeneration, of living death. All the movements of our modern ballet school are sterile movements because they are unnatural: their purpose is to create the delusion that the law of gravitation does not exist for them.

The primary or fundamental movements of the new school of the dance must have within them the seeds from which will evolve all other movements, each in turn to give birth to others in unending sequence of still higher and greater expression, thoughts and ideas.

To those who nevertheless still enjoy the movements, for historical or choreographic or whatever other reasons, to those I answer: They see no farther than the skirts and tricots. But look—under the skirts, under the tricots are dancing deformed muscles. Look still farther—underneath the muscles are deformed bones. A deformed skeleton is dancing before you. This deformation through incorrect dress and incorrect movement is the result of the training necessary to the ballet.

The ballet condemns itself by enforcing the deformation of the beautiful woman's body! No historical, no choreographic reasons can prevail against that!

It is the mission of all art to express the highest and most beautiful ideals of man. What ideal does the ballet express?

No, the dance was once the most noble of all arts; and it shall be again. From the great depth to which it has fallen, it shall be raised. The dancer of the future shall attain so great a height that all other arts shall be helped thereby.

To express what is the most moral, healthful and beautiful in art—this is the mission of the dancer, and to this I dedicate my life.

These flowers before me contain the dream of a dance, it could be named "The light falling on white flowers." A dance that would be a subtle translation of the light and the whiteness. So pure, so strong, that people would say: it is a soul we see moving, a soul that has reached the light and found the whiteness. We are glad it should move so. Through its human medium we have a satisfying sense of movement, of light and glad things. Through this human medium, the movement of all nature runs also through us, is transmitted to us from the dancer. We feel the movement of light intermingled with the thought of whiteness. It is a prayer, this dance; each movement reaches in long undulations to the heavens and becomes a part of the eternal rhythm of the spheres.

To find those primary movements for the human body from which shall evolve the movements of the future dance in ever-varying, natural, unending sequences, that is the duty of the new dancer of today.

As an example of this, we might take the pose of the Hermes of the Greeks. He is represented as flying on the wind. If the artist had pleased to pose his foot in a vertical position, he might have done so, as the God, flying on the wind, is not touching the earth; but realizing that no movement is true unless suggesting sequence of movements, the sculptor placed the Hermes with the ball of his foot resting on the wind, giving the movement an eternal quality.

Few observers of Isadora Duncan have been able to explain the magic effect that her dancing had on audiences, and most photographers tended to snap her in poses rather than in movement. The artists tell us more. In these drawings by José Clará we seem to see Isadora as she wanted to be, as the essence of woman: "Let her dance be born of joyousness and strength and courage."

In the same way I might make an example of each pose and gesture in the thousands of figures we have left to us on the Greek vases and bas-reliefs; there is not one which in its movement does not presuppose another movement.

This is because the Greeks were the greatest students of the laws of nature, wherein all is the expression of unending, ever-increasing evolution, wherein are no ends and no stops.

Such movements will always have to depend on and correspond to the form that is moving. The movements of a beetle correspond to its form. So do those of the horse. Even so the movements of the human body must correspond to its form. The dances of no two persons should be alike.

People have thought that so long as one danced in rhythm, the form and design did not matter; but no, one must perfectly correspond to the other. The Greeks understood this very well. There is a statuette that shows a dancing cupid. It is a child's dance. The movements of the plump little feet and arms are perfectly suited to its form. The sole of the foot rests flat on the ground, a position which might be ugly in a more developed person, but is natural in a child trying to keep its balance. One of the legs is half raised; if it were outstretched it would irritate us, because the movement would be unnatural. There is also a statue of a satyr in a dance that is quite different from that of the cupid. His movements are those of a ripe and muscular man. They are in perfect harmony with the structure of his body.

The Greeks in all their painting, sculpture, architecture, literature, dance and tragedy evolved their movements from the movement of nature, as we plainly see expressed in all representations of the Greek gods, who, being no other than the representatives of natural forces, are always designed in a pose expressing the concentration and evolution of these forces. This is why the art of the Greeks is not a national or characteristic art but has been and will be the art of all humanity for all time.

Therefore dancing naked upon the earth I naturally fall into Greek positions, for Greek positions are only earth positions.

The noblest in art is the nude. This truth is recognized by all, and followed by painters, sculptors and poets; only the dancer has forgotten it, who should most remember it, as the instrument of her art is the human body itself.

Man's first conception of beauty is gained from the form and symmetry of the human body. The new school of the dance should begin with that movement which is in harmony with and will develop the highest form of the human body.

I intend to work for this dance of the future. I do not know whether I have the necessary qualities: I may have neither genius nor talent nor temperament. But I know that I have a Will; and will and energy sometimes prove greater than either genius or talent or temperament. . . .

My intention is, in due time, to found a school, to build a theatre where a hundred little girls shall be trained in my art, which they, in their turn, will better. In this school I shall not teach the children to imitate my movements, but to make their own. I shall not force them to study certain definite movements; I shall help them to develop those movements which are natural to them. Whosoever sees the movements of an untaught little child cannot deny that its movements are beautiful. They are beautiful because they are natural to the child. Even so the movements of the human body may be beautiful in every stage of development so long as they are in harmony with that stage and degree of maturity which the body has attained. There will always be movements which are the perfect expression of that individual body and that individual soul; so we must not force it to make movements which are not natural to it but which belong to a school. An intelligent child must be astonished to find that in the ballet school it is taught movements contrary to all those movements which it would make of its own accord.

This may seem a question of little importance, a question of differing opinions on the ballet and the new dance. But it is a great question. It is not only a question of true art, it is a question of race, of the development of the female sex to beauty and health, of the return to the original strength and to natural movements of woman's body. It is a question of the development of perfect mothers and the birth of healthy and beautiful children. The dancing school of the future is to develop and to show the ideal form of woman. It will be, as it were, a museum of the living beauty of the period.

Travellers coming into a country and seeing the dancers should find in them that country's ideal of the beauty of form and movement. But strangers who today come to any country, and there see the dancers of the ballet school, would get a strange notion indeed of the ideal of beauty in that country. More than this, dancing like any art of any time should reflect the highest point the spirit of mankind has reached in that special period. Does anybody think that the present day ballet school expresses this?

Why are its positions in such contrast to the beautiful positions of the antique sculptures which we preserve in our museums and which are constantly presented to us as perfect models of ideal beauty? Or have our museums been founded only out of historical and archaeological interest, and not for the sake of the beauty of the objects which they contain?

The ideal of beauty of the human body cannot change with fashion but only with evolution. Remember the story of the beautiful sculpture of a Roman girl which was discovered under the reign of Pope Innocent VIII, and which by its beauty created such a sensation that the men thronged to see it and made pilgrimages to it as to a holy shrine, so that the Pope, troubled by the movement which it originated, finally had it buried again.

And here I want to avoid a misunderstanding that might easily arise. From what I have said you might conclude that my intention is to return to the dances of the old Greeks, or that I think that the dance of the future will be a revival of the antique dances or even of those of the primitive tribes. No, the dance of the future will be a new movement, a consequence of the entire evolution which mankind has passed through. To return to the dances of the Greeks would be as impossible as it is unnecessary. We are not Greeks and therefore cannot dance Greek dances.

But the dance of the future will have to become again a high religious art as it was with the Greeks. For art which is not religious is not art, is mere merchandise.

The dancer of the future will be one whose body and soul have grown so harmoniously together that the natural language of that soul will have become the movement of the body. The dancer will not belong to a nation but to all humanity. She will dance not in the form of nymph, nor fairy, nor coquette, but in the form of woman in her greatest and purest expression. She will realize the mission of woman's body and the holiness of all its parts. She will dance the changing life of nature, showing how each part is transformed into the other. From all parts of her body shall shine radiant intelligence, bringing to the world the message of the thoughts and aspirations of thousands of women. She shall dance the freedom of woman. . . .

Ruth St. Denis (c. 1877–1968)
MUSIC VISUALIZATION

Ruth St. Denis' serious interest in dance began when she saw a poster advertising Egyptian Deities cigarettes with a picture of the goddess Isis. Though she started at once to work on an Egyptian saga, her first completed theatre piece, Radha *(1906), was set in India. Later she added Isis, the Japanese Kwannon, and the Babylonian Ishtar to her galaxy of goddesses. They became well known to many parts of America through the tours she made with her husband Ted Shawn and their Denishawn company. For the Oriental tour of 1925–26, however, the pieces based on Eastern religions were left at home, replaced by works like the newly devised music visualizations.*

The chatty, personal style of this article is characteristic of Ruth St. Denis' quite extensive literary efforts. Louis Horst was with the company at this time as musical director, a post he assumed the following year for Martha Graham. Though not mentioned here, Doris Humphrey assisted Miss St. Denis with the development of the music visualizations.

SOURCE: From *The Denishawn Magazine,* I, No. 3 (Spring, 1925).

Let me first define what I mean by the words "Music Visualization:" Music Visualization in its purest form is the scientific translation into bodily action of the rhythmic, melodic and harmonic structure of a musical composition, without intention to in any way "interpret" or reveal any hidden meaning apprehended by the dancer. There is a secondary form of music visualization, which naturally has not our keenest interest, wherein we definitely superimpose dramatic ideas or arbitrary dance forms which seem to relate themselves closely to the composition in emotional coloring, structural outline, rhythmic pattern, and general meaning. . . .

One experience which led me to this resolve to analyze and to arrive at fundamental truths about the relation of dance and music, was the performance of one of our music dancers purporting to interpret a symphony. I heard a large symphony orchestra playing one of the well-known symphonic works. I saw a woman moving about the stage in, at times, a rhythmic, and at other times a dramatic manner, which had in it much depth of feeling, much nobility of movement and much pure beauty of bodily line, but which had almost no connection with the musical composition to which she was dancing. That this dancer was trying to express through her movements the spirit of the work was quite evident, but in actual fact she could give but a few gestures, a few pregnant pauses, that in any way visualized, much less interpreted, the great symphonic work whose harmonies and dynamics were floating about her.

I went home from this performance very thoughtful, for the motives of her performance found a most profound agreement with my own. That is, I too asserted that only the greatest music was fit accompaniment for the deep and eternal things which I wanted to express through the dance. But her methods were obviously wrong. It could not be done that way. The result of my mediations was the conception of my Synchoric Orchestra, and, from the principles involved therein, the whole series of our music visualizations, from the *Bach Inventions* (which Mr. Shawn visualized) and which the Concert Dancers used, for two seasons, down to the *Schutt Suite for Violin and Piano,* which is new on this season's program.

In the case of the Bach Fugues and Inventions, we have the pure mathematics of the dance. In these there is no emotional coloring or intent, and therefore the music visualization of them should be without emotional coloring in movement. In a two-part Invention, two separate groups dance, each group moving to the notes of its own part only, and remaining still on the rests in that part. Dancing at the same time, the two groups imprint upon the eye a correlative image to the one given to the ear by the playing of this two-part Invention on the piano—that of two themes, each distinct in itself harmoniously mingling to produce a charming and perfect structural whole. This same principle is simply enlarged by using three groups for a three-part Invention and four groups for a four-voice Fugue, and so on, keeping always in view the relation of the groups so as to present a harmonious composition to the eye, as well as the exact beating out of the actual notes of each part by its group.

Collection Christena L. Schlundt

Ruth St. Denis portrays an Oriental goddess. In her dances she wanted to depict a mystical experience, particularly as she found it conceived in Oriental religions. She found it also through music. "My final use of art is impersonal," she wrote in her autobiography, "for when I dance I am really an abstraction, a creature set apart from time and space, unrelated to human things in the ordinary sense."

In other compositions, such as Beethoven's Sonata called the *Pathetique* there is obviously an emotional coloring. Some scholastic musicians argue that no emotional intent was in the composer's mind, but that sheer structural writing produced the result. However, emotional music resulted, and that must be considered in the visualization. After the abstract emotional coloring is decided upon, it must be kept in mind as influencing the quality of the gesture used throughout by the dancers.

Then, in the visualization of such a composition, these simple and obvious facts of the relation of music to movement must be obeyed:

Time value underlies all. The time in which the music is written must be recognized, and the rhythmic pattern apprehended. Then each note must have its correlative translation—an eighth note has a definite length, and its visualization must be a movement exactly as long; a quarter note is twice as long, and should be visualized by a movement twice as long.

Simple melody and simple accompaniment, obviously, would be adequately visualized as a solo dance; whereas complicated and contrapuntal writing, involving many simultaneous voices, parts or themes, should be visualized by a group of three or more dancers.

Just as there is staccato and legato in playing, so is there staccato and legato quality in bodily movement.

Dynamics must be considered. A softly struck note should be moved softly and with economy of force, while a crashing chord must be visualized with more physical energy.

The rise and fall of the melody should have some answer in the rise and fall of the body above the plane of the stage, the positions of the notes on the printed staff being in some degree analogous to the range of posture the body can control from lying flat on the stage to the highest leap above the floor.

There is sometimes a wide variety of movements that can be used equally well to visualize certain elements in the music, and here is where the selective quality of the artist comes into play. A trill in the music may be visualized as a whirl, or a vibration throughout the body accented in the arms and hands, or a *ballet emboit*, for instance. But here the quality of the movement of the visualization as a whole must govern the choice of the particular gesture. If one is visualizing an abstract composition, sonata, concerto, or etude, obviously the quality of the gesture should be kept abstract, should avoid a definite school, national or racial style—it should be universal gesture.

All of these rules are used as bases to start from. Often we depart from them ourselves for many reasons. In designing dances for entertainment purposes, the fact is borne in upon the creator that the public will stand for abstract movement only in small doses. And so, upon a sound base of rendering the value of the notes of the music into a corresponding value of movement, there is superimposed a surface idea to trick the eye of those beholders who have neither the interest nor the training to apprehend the actual visualization principles which are being applied and actually worked out in the dance which he sees. Thus in Mr. Shawn's visualization of the *Revolutionary Etude* of Chopin, he has superimposed a dramatic narrative, while at the same time the composition is visualized on rigid principles. His gesture enacting the story of the crazed revolutionist exactly parallels the melodic theme, while the whirling figures behind him symbolizing flame and fury, visualize the accompaniment. And in the *Soaring* of Schumann, the great square of silk is manipulated to give the surge of the music and to give amusement to the audience in watching its multiple forms, while the notes are just as carefully rendered by the movements of the dancers as if there were no veil. . . .

The Synchoric Orchestra, when dancing in connection with a Symphony Orchestra to visualize a symphony, would be composed of as many dancers as there were musical instruments. Each dancer would be definitely related to one certain instrument. Some arrangement of human values is desirable—such as the heavier and older dancers paralleling the heavier instruments—strong men for percussion and brass, slender youths for the wood-winds, young girls for violins, and more mature girls and women for 'cellos and basses. Each dancer would move exactly what was played by his instrument and when his instrument was silent he would be still. When all the violins played in unison, all the violin dancers would dance in a unified group, in unison of movement. A solo theme by a flute, against an accompaniment of 'cellos and basses would be seen as a solo dance movement by the flute dancer, with subordinated mass movement in the background upon the part of the dancers representing the 'cellos and basses. The whole would always maintain an architectural sense of mass composition, so that at all times the grouping was based on a sound undertaking of form.

About six years ago I visualized the two movements of the *Unfinished Symphony* of Schubert. For months I worked with more than sixty dancers who were all pupils of Denishawn, well-trained and responsive human instruments in my Synchoric Orchestra. For the obvious reason of expense, I was unable to have a symphony orchestra, but with the conductor's score, and the invaluable help of Mr. Louis Horst, our pianist-director, each instrument's scoring was studied, and the movements of that dancer worked out first separately, then in relation to the other instruments of his class, and then in relation to the form of the whole. When this was complete, we gave three performances for invited audiences in Los Angeles, and met with an extraordinary response. It is my dream to be able to give this, and other compositions of its kind, with a great orchestra. But that is a dream which must wait for someone who believes that dancing of the highest calibre is as worthy of support, and of as much benefit to mankind, as the music of a Symphony Orchestra itself.

The music of the future will have to be divided into two groups, so far as dancers and the dance public are concerned—that which is to be listened to, and that which is to be danced to. But one might say that this is true today. We have supporting music as accompaniment to singing in opera, and we have ballet music; and then we have orchestral music, symphonies, overtures, and such. Yes, but it is all the same kind of music, and the music of the dance of the future must be a different music than any we have yet heard. It must be composed for the dancers by composers who understand the fundamentals of the dance, and who have the utmost reverence for the dance as the greatest of the arts; a condition which I need not remind you does not exist today.

Beautiful, natural and noble movement can never be trained and fixed in art forms and expressed in supreme works of the dance until the music compositions are a sympathetic parallel to the capacities of the human body. At present the dancer is made to do grotesque, unnatural and futile gestures in order to meet the exigencies of an almost alien art. But until the ideal music of the future is composed upon ideal principles, we have a right to claim the use of the best, the highest and noblest works of music with which to give audible accompaniment to our noblest, best and highest thoughts as expressed through beautiful, rhythmic bodily movement. . . .

To conclude the whole matter—Visualization of Music is not the mere putting into gesture form the mechanical elements of a musical composition. But because the Creative Dancer is always striving to give expression to Divine Intelligence, and because the art of music has gone so far ahead of us in these last centuries while the dance remained the Cinderella among the arts, we have chosen the great music to aid us in making this revelation, since lesser music was not worthy of the things we have to say. We will respect and study the great music of today in order to give it adequate visualization because it says partially the same lofty things—but we believe that in order to follow the wings of the dance, music will have to soar even higher than any of its known forms.

Martha Graham (1894–)
A MODERN DANCER'S PRIMER FOR ACTION

After serving an apprenticeship with Denishawn, Martha Graham left the company in 1923, giving her first independent concert three years later. Some called her "that arty, angular woman who moves in spasms and jerks"; others considered her a new messiah; today the almost universal verdict is "genius." In the course of her long career, Graham broke new ground in many areas of theatre dance: she commissioned scores from American composers who wrote some of their finest music for her; she had Noguchi design sculptured settings that marked a new trend in stage décor. She made works that were layered with meanings, both specific and symbolic; experimented with stream-of-consciousness structures; drove dance to cope with areas of human awareness that it had never dared to touch before.

For Graham, the simplified vocabularies of Duncan and St. Denis were no more adequate than that of the ballet. She created for dance a completely new language, the one she needed "to make visible the interior landscape." The aim of technical training, as she describes it here, is still the control of the dancer's instrument. But where the ballet class was planned to increase the independent mobility of the limbs and to develop the vertical extension of the body, the Graham exercises stress the inner core that motivates movement from the center of the torso and recognize the force that must be expended to raise the body from the floor. The turnout is either eliminated or used to only a moderate degree; control emanates from the back. The effect desired is neither courtly elegance nor ethereal lightness nor yet pedestrian naturalism, but rather a reflection of "the miracle that is a human being."

I. Certain Basic Principles

I am a dancer. My experience has been with dance as an art.

Each art has an instrument and a medium. The instrument of the dance is the human body; the medium is movement. The body has always been to me a thrilling wonder, a dynamo of energy, exciting, courageous, powerful; a delicately balanced logic and proportion. It has not been my aim to evolve or discover a new method of dance training,

SOURCE: From Frederick R. Rogers, ed., *Dance: A Basic Educational Technique* (New York: Macmillan, 1941). Copyright 1941 by Macmillan Publishing Co., Inc.; renewed 1969 by Frederick R. Rogers. Reprinted by permission.

but rather to dance significantly. To dance significantly means "through the medium of discipline and by means of a sensitive, strong instrument, to bring into focus unhackneyed movement: a human being."

I did not want to be a tree, a flower, or a wave. In a dancer's body, we as audience must see *ourselves*, not the imitated behavior of everyday actions, not the phenomena of nature, not exotic creatures from another planet, but something of the miracle that is a human being, motivated, disciplined, concentrated.

The part a modern art plays in the world, each time such a movement manifests itself, is to make apparent once again the inner hidden realities behind the accepted symbols. Out of this need a new plasticity, emotional and physical, was demanded of the dance. This meant experiment in movement. The body must not only be strong, be facile, be brilliant, but must also be significant and simple. To be simple takes the greatest measure of experience and discipline known to the artist.

It may be possible for an individual dancer to proceed instinctively along these lines, but when dance involves more than the solo figure, some uniform training is necessary. Several of us, working separately, found methods of training, evolving as we worked.

The method, however, was secondary. Training, technique, is important; but it is always in the artist's mind only the means to an end. Its importance is that it frees the body to become its ultimate self.

Technique and training have never been a substitute for that condition of awareness which is talent, for that complete miracle of balance which is genius, but it can give plasticity and tension, freedom and discipline, balancing one against the other. It can awaken memory of the race through muscular memory of the body. Training and technique are means to strength, to freedom, to spontaneity.

Contrary to popular belief, spontaneity as one sees it in dance or in theatre, is not wholly dependent on emotion at that instant. It is the condition of emotion objectified. It plays the part in theater that light plays in life. It illumines. It excites. Spontaneity is essentially dependent on energy, upon the strength necessary to perfect timing. It is the result of perfect timing to the Now. It is not essentially intellectual or emotional, but is nerve reaction. That is why art is not to be *understood*, as we use the term, but is to be *experienced*.

To experience means that our minds and emotions are involved. For primarily it is the nervous system that is the instrument of experience. This is the reason music, with its sound and rhythm, is universally the great moving force of the world. It affects animals as well as human beings.

A program of physical activity which involves only, first, exercises for strength, and second, a means of emotional catharsis through so-called "self-expression dancing," will never produce a complete human being. It is a dangerous program, for it does not fit a child or an adolescent for the virtue of living.

Living is an adventure, a form of evolvement which demands the greatest sensitivity to accomplish it with grace, dignity, efficiency. The puritanical concept of life has always ignored the fact that the nervous system and the body as well as the mind are involved in experience, and art cannot be experienced except by one's entire being.

In life, heightened nerve sensitivity produces that concentration on the instant which is true living. In dance, this sensitivity produces action timed to the present moment. It is the result of a technique for revelation of experience.

To me, this acquirement of nervous, physical, and emotional concentration is the one element possessed to the highest degree by the truly great dancers of the world. Its acquirement is the result of discipline, of energy in the deep sense. That is why there are so few great dancers.

A great dancer is not made by technique alone any more than a great statesman is made by knowledge alone. Both possess true spontaneity. Spontaneity in behavior, in life, is due largely to complete health; on the stage to a technical use—often so ingrained by proper training as to seem instinctive—of nervous energy. Perhaps what we have always called intuition is merely a nervous system organized by training to perceive.

Dance had its origin in ritual, the eternal urge toward immortality. Basically, ritual was the formalized desire to achieve union with those beings who could bestow immortality upon man. Today we practice a different ritual, and this despite the shadow over the world, for we seek immortality of another order—the potential greatness of man.

In its essentials, dance is the same over the entire world. These essentials are its function, which is communication; its instrument, which is the body; and its medium, which is movement. The style or manner of dance is different in each country in which it manifests itself. The reason for this is threefold—climate, religion, and social system. These things affect our thinking and hence our movement expression.

Although its concept was the product of Isadora Duncan and Ruth St. Denis, modern dance in its present manifestation has evolved since the World War. At that time a different attitude towards life emerged.

As a result of twentieth-century thinking, a new or more related movement language was inevitable. If that made necessary a complete departure from the dance form known as ballet, the classical dance, it did not mean that ballet training itself was wrong. It was simply found not to be complete enough, not adequate to the time, with its change of thinking and physical attitude.

Photo, Barbara Morgan

In *Deaths and Entrances* (1945) the dancers are (left to right): Erick Hawkins, Martha Graham, Merce Cunningham. The "Dark Beloved" and the "Poetic Beloved" appear to the heroine, but only in her remembered vision. The dance deals with the "interior landscape" of the Brontë sisters, recalling the days of their youth from a present beset with rivalries and hatreds.

A break from a certain rigidity, a certain glibness, a certain accent on overprivilege was needed. There was need of an intensification, a simplification. For a time, this need manifested itself in an extreme of movement asceticism; there has now come a swing back from that extreme. All facilities of body are again being used fearlessly, but during that time of asceticism, so-called, much glibness was dropped, much of the purely decorative cast aside.

No art ignores human values, for therein lie its roots. Directed by the authentic or perverted magnificence, which is man's spirit, movement is the most powerful and dangerous art medium known. This is because it is the speech of the basic instrument, the body, which is an instinctive, intuitive, inevitable mirror revealing man as he is.

Art does not create change; it registers change. The change takes place in the man himself. The change from nineteenth- to twentieth-century thinking and attitude toward life has produced a difference in inspiration for action. As a result, there is a difference in form and technical expression in the arts.

2. Posture, Movement, Balance

One of the first indications of change, because it is the total of being—physical, emotional, mental, and nervous—is posture.

Posture is dynamic, not static. It is a self-portrait of being. It is psychological as well as physiological.

I use the word "posture" to mean *that instant of seeming stillness when the body is poised for most intense, most subtle action, the body at its moment of greatest potential efficiency.*

People often say that the posture of this dancer or that dancer or of all dancers is not natural. I ask, "Not natural to what?—natural to joy, sorrow, pain, relaxation, exaltation, elevation, fall?"

Each condition of sensitivity has a corresponding condition of posture. Posture is correct when it is relative to the need of the instant.

There is only one law of posture I have been able to discover—the perpendicular line connecting heaven and earth. But the problem is how to relate the various parts of the body. The nearest to the norm, as it has been observed and practiced over centuries, has been the ear in line perpendicularly with the shoulder, the shoulder with the pelvic bone, the pelvic bone in line with the arch of the foot.

The criticism that the posture of some dancers is bad because they appear to have a "sway back" is usually not justified, for a "sway back" is a weak back. Often the development of the muscles for jumping, leaping, and elevation, all of which concentrate in the hips and buttocks, is so pronounced as to give the appearance, to the uninformed critic, of "sway back."

Through all times the acquiring of technique in dance has been for one purpose—so to train the body as to make possible any demand made upon it by that inner self which has the vision of what needs to be said.

No one invents movement; movement is discovered. What is possible and necessary to the body under the impulse of the emotional self is the result of this discovery; and the formalization of it into a progressive series of exercises is technique.

It is possible and wise to teach these exercises even to the person who has no desire to dance professionally. It must, however, be emphasized that performance of these exercises is not a mere matter of "having a good time," but of achieving a center of body and mind which will eventually, but not immediately, result in a singing freedom. Throughout the performance of these technical exercises, a woman remains a woman, and a man a man, because power means to become what one *is*, to the highest degree of realization.

As in any other architectural edifice, the body is kept erect by balance. Balance is a nicety of relationship preserved throughout the various sections of the body. There are points of tension which preserve us in the air, hold us erect when standing, and hold us safely when we seem to drop to the floor at incredible speed. We would possess these naturally if they had not been destroyed in us by wrong training, either physical, intellectual, or emotional.

Contrary to opinion, the dancer's body is nearer to the norm of what the body should be than any other. It has been brought to this possible norm by discipline, for the dancer is, of necessity, a realist. Pavlova, Argentina, and Ruth St. Denis all practiced their art past the age of fifty.

3. The Aim of Method

There is no common terminology for describing the technique of modern dance. Furthermore, to describe two or three exercises would give an accent to these few beyond their importance. Therefore, rather than being a description here of actual specific practice of exercises, this is intended as an exposition of the theory behind the practice of the technical training I employ.

The aim of the method is coordination. In dance, that means unity of body produced by emotional physical balance. In technique, it means so to train all elements of body—legs, arms, torso, etc.—as to make them all equally important and equally efficient. It means a state of relativity of members in use that results in flow of movement. I have discovered whatever it is that I have discovered through practice and out of need. My theory, if it can be called such, had its origin and has its justification in practical experience.

What I say is based on one premise—dance is an art, one of the arts of the theatre. True theatricality is not a vain or egotistic or unpleasant attribute. Neither does it depend on cheap tricks either of movement, costume, or audience appeal. Primarily, it is a means employed to bring the idea of one person into focus for the many. First there is the concept; then there is a dramatization of that concept which makes it apparent to others. This process is what is known as theatricality.

I believe dancing can bring liberation to many because it brings organized activity. I believe that the exercises I use are as right for a lay person as for a professional dancer, because they do no violence anatomically or emotionally. The difference in their use for the lay person and for the professional dancer is not in their basic approach but in the degree and intensity of their application. I have always thought first of the dancer as a human being. These exercises, though their original intention was the training of professionals, have been taught to children and adolescents as well.

What follows might be termed a "Primer for Action."

4. Primer for Action

A. An Attitude Toward Dance.
   1. There must be something that needs to be danced. Dance demands a dedication, but it is not a substitute for living. It is the expression of a fully aware person dancing that which can be expressed only by means of dance. It is not an emotional catharsis for the hysterical, frustrated, fearful, or morbid. It is an act of affirmation, not of escape. The affirmation may take many forms—tragedy, comedy, satire, lyric or dramatic.
   2. There must be a disciplined way of dancing. This means learning a craft, not by intellection, but by hard physical work.
B. A Dancer's Attitude Toward the Body.
   The body must be sustained, honored, understood, disciplined. There should be no violation of the body. All exercises are but the extensions of physical capabilities. This is the reason it takes years of daily work to develop a dancer's body. It can only be done just so fast. It is subject to the natural timing of physical growth.
C. An Attitude Toward Technique.
   Technique is a means to an end. It is the means to becoming a dancer.
   1. All exercises should be based on bodily structure. They should be written for the instrument, a body, male *or* female.
   2. As the province of dance is motion, all exercises should be based upon the body in motion as its natural state. This is true even of exercises on the floor.
D. Technique Has a Three-Fold Purpose.
   1. Strength of body.
   2. Freedom of body and spirit.
   3. Spontaneity of action.

E. Specific Procedure in Technique.

All exercises are in the form of theme and variations. There is a basic principle of movement employed which deals specifically with a certain region of body—torso, back, pelvis, legs, feet, etc. The theme of the exercise deals directly with its function for body control. It is stripped of all extraneous movement or embellishments. The variations become increasingly wider in scope, moving from the specific to the general movement which embraces the use of the entire body. Variation still keeps, however, no matter how involved it becomes, its relationship to the theme.

F. Four Main Classes into Which Technique Is Divided.

1. Exercises on the floor.

All exercises on the floor are direct preparations for standing and elevation later. The first principle taught is body center. The first movement is based upon the body in two acts of breathing —inhaling and exhaling—developing it from actual breathing experience to the muscular activity independent of the actual act of breathing. These two acts, when performed muscularly only, are called "release," which corresponds to the body in inhalation, and "contraction" which corresponds to exhalation. The word "relaxation" is not used because it has come to mean a devitalized body.

In the professional class, the floor exercises take approximately twenty minutes. They comprise: a. stretching; b. back exercise; c. leg extensions.

N.B. No stretch is made by pushing the back of the student to the floor. The down movement is never helped. The spine is never touched. The leg is never stretched suddenly or forcibly by pressure. The hand never tries to straighten the knee by pressure. The leg is straightened only by slow and gradual extension.

2. Exercises standing in one place.

a. All exercises for the legs—bends, lifts, extensions, front, side, and back.

b. Hip swings.

c. Feet exercises.

d. Turns in place.

N.B. In all lifts and *pliés*, the relationship of knee to foot is closely observed. There must be no strain on knees or arches at any time. In all exercises on contraction, the shoulders and pelvic bone have a definite relationship in order to avoid all abdominal strain.

3. Exercises for elevation.
   a. Jumps in place.
   b. Open space work.
      Walks in rhythms.
      Runs.
      Turns across the floor.
      Turns in the air.
      Leaps.
      Skips.
      N.B. No elevation is attempted until at least one half hour of preliminary work is done to permit the body to become fluid. All elevation is without strain. The legs and back are strong and the body centered from the exercises which have gone before.
4. Exercise for falls.
   This exercise is a series of falls forward, side, and back in various rhythms and at various speeds. The body never strikes the floor by landing on the knees, on the spine, on a shoulder, or on an elbow or head. The joints must not be jarred or any vital part struck. Falls are used primarily as preliminary to and therefore as a means of "affirmation." In no fall does the body remain on the floor, but assumes an upright position as part of the exercise. My dancers fall *so they may rise*.

Doris Humphrey (1895–1958)
NEW DANCE

In 1928 Doris Humphrey left the Denishawn company, feeling that she had learned to dance in the styles of nearly all kinds of people—except twentieth-century Americans. The group that she formed with Charles Weidman was dedicated to the contemporary idiom, although they conceived that idiom with less violent intensity than Graham. The tours of the Humphrey-Weidman company, mostly to college campuses that became known as the "gymnasium circuit," took their work to young people throughout the country. After her retirement as a dancer in 1944, Humphrey became artistic director of the José Limón company, creating some of her finest works for her Mexican protégé.

The plan of New Dance *(1935) is representative of one vein of her work, a piece in which the drama was inherent in the movement, needing no overlay of literary subject matter; and it reveals the meticulous care with which Humphrey worked out expressive spatial patterns. Unfortunately, it does not show the equally perceptive attention she paid to rhythmic design, design made to reflect the intricate manner in which the individual weaves his personal paths in counterpoint to the group, yet always in harmony with it.*

There is a great difference between the modern dance as it is presented today and as it was presented as little as five or six years ago. When I gave my first recital in New York apart from the Denishawn company, the stage was bare, there was only one pianist for the music, and costuming was at a minimum. Now, however, the modern dance leaves this period of barrenness and comes forward as a new theatrical form.

In the past two seasons, Charles Weidman and I have developed our forms away from the recital stage, where each dance was about five minutes long, and have composed long ballets, consecutive in idea. More significant than this is the fact that these new dances are the comment of two American dancers on contemporary life. This comment naturally brings them close to the theatre, but this is a theatre of movement rather than of words.

It might be interesting to describe one of them in some detail, since the manner of building will show how a large, complex theme may be presented entirely through movement, and, I believe, more forcibly than could be done through words.

SOURCE: From Selma Jeanne Cohen, *Doris Humphrey: An Artist First* (Middletown, Conn.: Wesleyan University Press, 1972).

I have composed a trilogy of which the general theme is the relationship of man to man. There are three long works which would take an evening and a half for presentation. One is in symphonic form and two are in dramatic form. The first, *New Dance*, represents the world as it should be, where each person has a clear and harmonious relationship to his fellow beings. The second, *Theatre Piece*, shows life as it is today—a grim business of survival by competition. Much of this is done in satire. The third, *With My Red Fires*, deals with love between man and woman, and between two women.

Let me describe *New Dance* for you. It was to be a dance of affirmation from disorganization to organization. It begins with two dancers with the group standing on the blocks in the corners as audience. For this Introduction, since I wished at first to convey a sense of incompletion, I chose the Broken Form, by which I mean an unfolding continual change, with contrast but very little repetition. This is the same form that Mr. Weidman and I used in *Rudepoema*, where a movement was done several times and then discarded, giving way to new ones.

By this means I was able to present the main themes of the whole composition, which were elaborated in the remaining sections of the dance: First Theme, Second Theme, Third Theme, Processional, Celebration, and Variations and Conclusion. I used lateral lines, perpendiculars —in fact, as many varieties as possible to convey the sense of a jetting forth of movement as yet disorganized.

The movements used in this Introduction were by no means spontaneous. I had a very clear reason for them. They were mainly feet and leg themes; I consciously eliminated any free use of the hands, arms, head, and torso. My main theme was to move from the simple to the complex, from an individual integration to a group integration, and therefore I thought it best at first to confine myself to movement which was in a way primitive. The primitive urge for movement—in fact, all early dancing made use of steps and leg gestures but scarcely ever used the rest of the body with any emphasis. Therefore, until the group integration had been achieved, the feet and leg themes seemed more expressive.

There are two essential movements of the body: the change of weight and the breath-rhythm. After the various themes had been stated in the Introduction, I used this essential changing of weight as the basis for the First Theme. The Second Theme used the breath-rhythm.

The Third Theme, which was composed by Mr. Weidman, used both of these in a single section. My only function in this was to explain the general idea: that it must be a loose form, broken, unbalanced, not symmetrical, and it must have an inconclusive ending. Each of these themes was in this sense inconclusive, because each was only a part

Photo, Edward Moeller, Collection Charles H. Woodford

The sculptural molding of the dancers in the second theme of Doris Humphrey's *New Dance* clearly shows in this grouping where the central figure relates the opposing forces by letting her own body strike a balance between the contrary pulls of the two spatial directions. The dancers are (left to right): Edith Orcutt, Katherine Litz, Letitia Ide, Doris Humphrey, Ada Korwin, Beatrice Seckler, Miriam Krakovsky, Joan Levy.

of a whole. I would never perform any of these sections as separate pieces, except the Variations and Conclusion which is a summation of them all, because there is a dramatic idea behind them of which each theme expresses only a fraction.

This dramatic idea played a large part in determining what movements and what forms were necessary. After Mr. Weidman and I, as leaders and integrators, had stated our themes together and alone, it was necessary to bring the women under my orbit and the men under Mr. Weidman's before they could be finally fused.

The Broken Form would do no longer. Those themes which were stated had to be conveyed to a group, and a group never accepts immediately en masse. For the First Theme, then, I used the Cumulative Form. The leader molds the group; the women are gradually drawn into the movement. One dancer may cross the stage and return; when she crosses again, two or three more follow her until finally the whole group is doing that particular movement-phrase. This section ends inconclusively.

In Second Theme, the leader again tries to unify the group. The dance ends in a revolving pulsation, but is again not cohesive enough to make a compact whole. It is inconclusive because there are only women. In Third Theme, the men take the stage and are compelled and molded by Mr. Weidman as leader. Now all themes have been stated for the groups and to finish them the two groups must be brought together.

Processional uses the Cumulative Form once more and in movement brings the themes to a head; in dramatic idea brings the whole group to an integrated whole. I chose a slow tempo for this because that gives a sense of greater control and, theatrically, is obviously in sharp contrast to the preceding sections. The men never deviate from a perpendicular but the women are fluid and make a wavering line. It was here that I used symmetry for the first time as the best way to express cohesion and completion.

The groups have now fused and break into a Celebration, which is built in fugue form, joyous in character. The fugue was eminently suitable to express a harmonious chorus wherein no member was more important than another. It is a short theme and goes directly into a square dance, which is again consciously symmetrical. I could have used several symmetrical forms here, but chose the square dance because at a moment of climax forward movement is the most powerful. Other forms do not have that direct impact. The ballet, incidentally, has used the square a great deal but rarely uses all four sides. It confines itself to the side from the back of the stage to the front and then weakens that impact by almost walking around the other three to get back to its starting point.

Having thus unified the men's group and the women's group, one more section was necessary in order to express the individual in relation to that group. Too many people seem content to achieve a mass-movement and then stop. I wished to insist that there is also an individual life within that group life.

All previous action had taken place within an arena marked by masses of blocks along the side of the stage. Mr. Weidman and I had stated our themes in this arena before the watching crowd and had finally brought that crowd down into our field of activity. It was obvious, now that all were working in unison, that the arena was useless since there was no longer any conflict between those who do and those who watch. In order to focus the dance and fully convey that sense of unity, the curtain was lowered momentarily while the blocks were moved into a pyramid in center stage. The whirling star pattern was used around this pyramid to avoid monotony. I could have allowed the two lines of dancers to remain in one place to form a path for the new dancers who now came in and performed briefly their own personal themes. However, by having this line whirl and by having the new dancers enter from different directions, a deadness was avoided and a greater space and excitement was achieved. In this section, Variations and Conclusion, I used the Repetitional Form where the group performs the same movement. The brief solos are in Broken Form against the *basso sustenuto* of the group.

It is this method of work, which I have described for *New Dance*, that broadens the field of the modern dance, gives it a new life and a new potency. Solo dances flow out of the group and back into it again without break and the most important part is the group. Except for an occasional brilliant individual, the day of the solo dance is over. It is only through this large use of groups of men and women that the modern dance can completely do what it has always said it would do. It has not done it before mainly because a new technique and new forms had to be evolved. We were forced to work from the ground up.

Now we have reached sufficiently firm ground to be able to add those embellishments which we had been forced to discard in our search for a new technique of movement. *New Dance* and the other two works which I have not described are no longer a series of episodes strung along in a row, as too many attempts at large forms have been. They are a cohesive form in the way that symphony is and need neither music nor story as crutches to support them.

Mary Wigman (1886–1973)
THE PHILOSOPHY OF
MODERN DANCE

Wigman first studied eurhythmics with Dalcroze, then worked in movement with Laban. As if in revolt against her first teacher, her early compositions were executed in silence—her way of asserting the independence of the art of dance. Her choreographic career, which began with the **Witch Dance** *of 1914, extended into the 1960's. Centered in Germany, where she maintained her own school, Wigman also toured in Europe and the United States. Though the American modern dancers were intrigued by her work, the two nationalities actually developed their forms quite independently.*

The critic Margaret Lloyd described Wigman's dance as "largely an ecstasy of gloom, stressing the demonic and macabre, as if to exorcise through movement the secret evils in man's nature." Though this description succeeds in characterizing a majority of her pieces, it does not recognize the lighter, lyrical side of her repertory seen in dances like **Shifting Landscape** *(1930). The emphasis on the somber is confirmed, however, in this article with its references to Wigman's concern with man and his fate, and with its contrast of ballet and modern dance, the latter admitting the dark and earthbound qualities of the dancer's movement.*

The dance is one of many human experiences which cannot be suppressed. Dancing has existed at all times, and among all people and races. The dance is a form of expression given to man just as speech, philosophy, painting or music. Like music, the dance is a language which all human beings understand without the use of speech. Granted, the dance is as little an everyday expression as music: the man who begins to dance because of an inner urge does so perhaps from a feeling of joyousness, or a spiritual ecstasy which transforms his normal steps into dance steps, although he himself may not be conscious of this change.

In short, the dance, like every other artistic expression, presupposes a heightened, increased life response. Moreover, the heightened response does not always have to have a happy background. Sorrow, pain, even horror and fear may also tend to release a welling-up of feeling, and therefore of the dancer's whole being.

SOURCE: From *Europa*, I, No. 1 (May-July, 1933).

There is something alive in every individual which makes him capable of giving outward manifestation, (through the medium of bodily movement) to his feelings, or rather, to that which inwardly stirs him. . . .

I feel that the dance is a language which is inherent, but slumbering in every one of us. It is possible for every human to experience the dance as an expression in his own body, and in his own way.

What we expect from the professional dancer is the creative dance in its most intense representation. We never insist upon such an intense representation from the lay-dancer. The professional dancer is distinguished for his particular qualifications, and for his artistic contribution to the dance. He must have the divine capacity to portray the difficult language of the dance: to recreate and objectify what he feels inside of himself.

The same desire for artistic liberation, for exaltation, for personal ecstasy, for bodily movement, in short, for activating his own imagination is also present in the non-professional dancer, and therefore gives him the right to seek for himself the intense expression of the dance.

We all know that the body is an end in itself. The dancer must learn, however, when and how to control his body. He ought not to regard his body simply for itself. He must transform and cultivate it as an instrument of the dance. The dance begins where gymnastics leave off. There are subtle differences between these two forms, and it is somewhat difficult to demarcate between them. Suffice it to say, the differences are neither in the kind or in the style of bearing, but rather in those unexplainable disparities which cannot be easily put into words. The single gestures, isolated in themselves, do not make the dance, but rather the manner in which the gestures are connected in and by movement: the way in which one form of movement is organically developed from its preceding movement, and the manner in which it leads as organically into the next movement. That which is no longer apparent or obvious, which may be said to "lie between the lines" of dancing, is what transforms the gymnastic movement into that of the dance.

To recapitulate: dancing is a simple rhythmic swinging, or ebb and flow, in which even the minutest gesture is part of this flow, and which is carried along the unending tide of movement.

The dance always remains bound by the human body, which is, after all, the dancer's instrument. However, with the emotion which stirs him, and the spirituality which uplifts him, the dance becomes more than mere physical movement in space, and the dancer more than its mobile agent. From then on, it represents the internal experiences of the dancer. To put it another way: we dance the mutation or change of our spiritual and emotional conditions as they are alive in our own body, in a rhythmic to and fro.

Charlotte Rupolph in Mary Wigman's
The Language of Dance, Wesleyan University Press

Mary Wigman has described her experience of creation: " . . . the hand seizing the mantle which clung to the body, stretching high, rearing up, then with three long strides into the dark and empty space, a rhythm compelling the arm to reach up—the movement theme for *Song of Fate* was born. I could hear the cry of despair within me. Behind it was the proud and defiant: 'Nevertheless!' " (*The Language of Dance*)

The idealistic substance of the dance, and of the dance creation, are the same as that of other creative and interpretative arts. In any event, it treats of man and his fate,—not necessarily the fate of men of today, nor of yesterday, nor even of tomorrow. But the fate of man caught in his eternal and perpetual web forms the old and yet ever new theme of the dance-creation. From the crudest reality to the sublimest abstraction, man is personified in the dance. All his struggles, griefs, joys are thus represented. Man himself forms the general theme for a limitless and ever significant congeries of variations.

"What idea do you think of when you dance?" A question which is often asked me, and which is difficult to answer. For the process which we call thinking has really nothing to do with the dance. The idea for a dance may come to a creative artist in his sleep, or at any moment of the day; that is to say, it is suddenly there. The idea finds root in one's consciousness without the conjuration of thought. Just as a melodic theme comes to a composer without his knowing why or where, so an idea of movement, a dance-theme, occurs just as spontaneously to the dancer. It often happens that the dancer carries the germ of the dance-theme inside of himself for a long time before it is released. It gives him no peace until it begins to take shape and form as movement. Once this theme, which is the eventual starting point of the entire dance, is at hand, the real work on the dance-creation begins; its composition and its interpretation. This formative period keeps the dancer in a constant state of excitement until the idea of the dance has reached its final point, until it has matured into a work of art. When this moment has arrived, the dance-creator becomes the dance-interpreter. It is absolutely necessary then that the dancer portray the dance in a way that will convey the meaning and force of the inner experiences which have inspired him to conceive this dance.

The primary concern of the creative dancer should be that his audience not think of the dance objectively, or look at it from an aloof and intellectual point of view,—in other words, separate itself from the very life of the dancer's experiences;—the audience should allow the dance to affect it emotionally and without reserve. It should allow the rhythm, the music, the very movement of the dancer's body to stimulate the same feeling and emotional mood within itself, as this mood and emotional condition has stimulated the dancer. It is only then that the audience will feel a strong emotional kinship with the dancer: and will live through the vital experiences behind the dance-creation. Shock, ecstasy, joy, melancholy, grief, gayety, the dance can express all of these emotions through movement. But the expression without the inner experience in the dance is valueless.

A definite change in dancing, particularly in Germany, has been taking place these past twenty years. The revised mode of terpsichorean expression we designate as the "modern dance" in contrast to the "classic dance" or the ballet.

The ballet had reached such a state of perfection that it could be developed no further. Its forms had become so refined, so sublimated to the ideal of purity, that the artistic content was too often lost or obscured. The great "ballet dancer" was no longer a representative of a great inner emotion, (like the musician or poet) but had become defined as a great virtuoso. The ballet-dancer developed an ideal of agility and lightness. He sought to conquer and annihilate gravitation. He banned the dark, the heavy, the earthbound, not only because it conflicted with his ideal of supple, airy, graceful technique, but because it also conflicted with his pretty aesthetic principles.

Times, however, became bad. War had changed life. Revolution and suffering tended to destroy and shatter all the ideals of prettiness. Traditions, aged and cherished, were left behind. How could these old and broken-down traditions remain firm throughout this awful period of destruction? Youth seeking for some spiritual relief could no longer turn to these anile panaceas. And so youth destroyed whatever appeared static, superfluous and moribund; and in its stead set up its own spiritual demands, its own material challenges.

What this new youth demanded of life and mankind, it also demanded from the artistic expression of its time, namely, the honest reflection of its own emotional experiences in symbols of artistic creation and interpretation. It demanded this positive reflection from its literature, drama, poetry, painting, architecture, music and the dance. All of these new things were direct outgrowths from its spiritual restiveness, its material challenges.

It is therefore easy to understand why this new youth should be attracted to the modern dance, the latter being one of the things which grew out of the youth's new world. The modern dance is the expression of youth and of today, and it is as positive in its expression as all the other modern arts. . . .

Section Six

THE EXTENSION
OF THE CLASSICAL
TRADITION

Q: The Diaghilev Ballets Russes left few traces of its impact in Soviet Russia, which for some time after the Revolution was isolated from the stream of Western developments in the dance. Contemporary with Fokine, however, and advocating some of the same principles, was Alexander Gorsky, who led the ballet in Moscow from 1900 to 1924. Influenced by Stanislavsky, he produced narrative ballets marked by realism and historical accuracy. Early in the new regime, authorities encouraged the ballet to abandon its tzarist repertory in favor of works depicting the industry and happiness of the workers. Choreographers reserved classical technique, like *pointe* work, for decadent characters; the heroic protagonists were given movements drawn from folk dance styles. Such works, however, did not prove popular, and the Russians soon found that they could preserve their heritage, both in repertory and technique, and still create ballets that were attuned to Soviet thought. Following the ideas of Gorsky, the Kirov Ballet in Leningrad and the Bolshoi in Moscow developed choreography that was vigorously dramatic, whether it retold ancient legends or dealt with contemporary themes.

In the state-supported schools the legacy of the *danse d'école* was maintained but extended; jumps reached breathtaking heights; the body became incredibly flexible; a partner supported his ballerina with a single hand and held her high above his head. The Bolshoi did all this with athletic exuberance; the Kirov was softer but no less spectacular. Many dancers of extraordinary technical accomplishment came from these schools, but the most famous was the expressive ballerina Galina Ulanova. She was a beautiful and touching Giselle, but her most remarkable creation was the poetic heroine of Leonid Lavrovsky's *Romeo and Juliet* (1940), a role later taken by her flamboyant and virtuosic successor at the Bolshoi, Maya Plisetskaya.

The graduates of the two major ballet schools have served many companies, for in the Soviet Union numerous provincial cities have their own groups led by dancers trained in Moscow or Leningrad, while folk ensembles, like the brilliant one directed by Igor Moiseyev, get their personnel from these same sources. The tradition remains respected and productive.

In Western Europe, the same tradition spread from the scattering of the Diaghilev company. The first country to profit substantially from the dispersal was England, where Marie Rambert established a school and a small company in the early 1920's and Ninette de Valois soon followed. Rambert had an uncanny way of spotting choreographic talent and grooming it; de Valois chose the right people—including some prepared by Rambert—and structured a formidable organization that eventually emerged as Britain's Royal Ballet.

Of the two choreographers that Rambert was nurturing in the early 1930's, de Valois picked Frederick Ashton to lead her company. His work was clean, precise, and concentrated on design—a fine foil to her own style, which was strongly dramatic. Before long she let his growing list of contributions overshadow her own ballets like *The Rake's Progress* (1935), in which Hogarth's drawings of rowdy eighteenth-century London had provided her theme. Ashton's inspirations came less often from stories or characters (though he did use them) than from dancers, chief among them England's great lyrical ballerina Margot Fonteyn. Her musicality, her lovely classical line, and her intuitive ability to infuse the purest movements with overtones of feeling illuminated such Ashton ballets as *Daphnis and Chloë* (1951) and *Ondine* (1958). The taste of de Valois and Ashton, supported by the elegance of Fonteyn, prompted revivals of *Sleeping Beauty* and *Swan Lake*, which no longer impressed the British public as old-fashioned as they had in Diaghilev's time. Unlike the Ballets Russes, the English company was not innovative. De Valois concentrated, instead, on meticulous execution and production; evolving a distinctive style, gracious and refined, that suited the British temperament and won admirers abroad as well.

De Valois did not bid for Rambert's second choreographer, whose mettle was very different. From the beginning, Antony Tudor was dramatically oriented but not in terms of the conventional story ballet. In *Jardin aux Lilas* (1936) his Victorian characters expressed nothing directly; their movements intimated their feelings but never broke through the bounds of social constraint or classical technique. Still more modern in concept were the bleak dances of mourning in *Dark Elegies* (1937). But Tudor did not remain in England; he went to America.

In the United States interest in classical ballet, rather than ballet spectacle, had begun to revive after the tours of Anna Pavlova. In 1933 the Ballet Russe de Monte Carlo, with Massine as its chief choreographer, paid the first of a series of successful visits. The country was enchanted with the glamorous aura of the company and with its dancers, headed by the chic Alexandra Danilova and a set of teenage ballerinas, all émigrées from Russia. The few Americans who managed to get into the company were given Slavic stage names so as not to disturb the image. Massine, however, made a gesture: he tried his hand at a bit of Americana with *Union Pacific* (1935); his earlier ballets were much more successful.

Meanwhile a few Americans were trying to establish the art on a more indigenous base. Catherine Littlefield created *Barn Dance* (1937) for her Philadelphia Ballet; in Chicago, Ruth Page composed *Frankie and Johnny* (1938) on an American ballad theme; Lew Christensen from Utah did *Filling Station* (1938). But the progress was slow. In the end, it was a Russian who led the first American company to attain international stature.

In 1933 Lincoln Kirstein had invited George Balanchine to the United States, providing him with a small group of native dancers. Apart from a bow in their direction with *Alma Mater* (1935), Balanchine's repertory for the American Ballet consisted of works in his neoclassical style—soundly grounded on traditional technique, musically based, without specific story or character content, designed simply to reveal the beauty of the *danse d'école*. At one point a small touring segment, the Ballet Caravan, let young choreographers try other approaches, notably with Eugene Loring's *Billy the Kid* (1938), which was probably the first major ballet using American material. But on the whole the Balanchine style dominated. Lacking the spectacular productions of the Ballet Russe, Kirstein's company attracted comparatively small audiences and its activities were suspended in 1941.

Meanwhile, from a small group directed by Mikhail Mordkin grew the idea of an ambitious scheme: a gallery of the masterpieces of the past and the classics of the future. In 1940 Ballet Theatre made an auspicious debut with productions of such established works as *Giselle* and *Les Sylphides*, the previously unknown ballets of Tudor, and premieres by Eugene Loring and Agnes de Mille besides. But the epoch-making works were yet to come. In 1942 the eventful ballet was Tudor's *Pillar of Fire*, portraying sexual frustration without romantic glosses; then his *Romeo and Juliet*, perceived in the imagery of a quattrocento painter. In 1944 it was Jerome Robbins' *Fancy Free*, with three sailors cavorting to the jazz rhythms of Leonard Bernstein; then his *Interplay* (1945), sophisticated children's games on *pointe*. Where Tudor used classical technique but manipulated it to serve his dramatic needs, Robbins drew on the traditional language when it suited his purpose but ignored it when tap dancing or stylized natural gesture suited him better. In 1946, when Ballet Theatre was known for its innovative repertory and for its stars —Alicia Alonso, Anton Dolin, André Eglevsky, Nora Kaye, Alicia Markova, Igor Youskevitch—Balanchine and Kirstein founded Ballet Society, which two years later became the New York City Ballet.

Ballet Theatre, now directed by Lucia Chase and Oliver Smith, still found important works to present; there were de Mille's *Fall River Legend* (1947) and Herbert Ross's *Caprichos* (1949), for example. These were compelling, dramatic ballets, but they did not break new ground. In 1949 Robbins left to join the New York City Ballet, and in 1950 Tudor dropped out also. In later years the company was less fortunate in its search for new choreographers—until 1967, when it took on Eliot Feld, a young protégé of Robbins. The emphasis of Ballet Theatre turned to revivals; a new production of the complete *Swan Lake*, the Danish *La Sylphide*—and to foreign stars: Erik Bruhn from Denmark, Carla Fracci from Italy, Natalia Makarova from Russia.

Meanwhile Balanchine developed the New York City Ballet. Some concluded, and he did not deny, that economics influenced his choice of presenting ballets without décor—just a skillfully lit cyclorama; and without elaborate costumes—usually just leotards or tunics for the women, black tights and white shirts for the men. But he had aesthetic reasons as well: the conviction that nothing should interfere or distract from the purpose of ballet—the vision of the body dancing. Balanchine chose the kind of bodies he wanted; "like toothpick," he said of women. He was inspired by his ballerinas: Diana Adams, Melissa Hayden, Tanaquil LeClerq, Maria Tallchief, then Allegra Kent, Patricia McBride, Violette Verdy, Suzanne Farrell, Kay Mazzo. He was less attentive to the men, although some—Arthur Mitchell, Jacques d'Amboise, Edward Villella, Helgi Tommasson, Peter Martins—were too good to ignore. He trained all his dancers to fleetness and precision; the British called them "athletic" while the French spoke of "le style frigidaire."

Balanchine enriched the New York City Ballet's repertory annually. Apart from a few deviations into extended dramatic works like *The Nutcracker* (1954)—which set a nation-wide fashion for Christmas ballet seasons—and *Don Quixote* (1965), he kept most often to his abstract, neoclassical style, choosing music that suited his taste. He described his favorite music as "pure and heartless"; to match it he used "purified gesture—gesture with all the bugs taken out." He turned frequently to Stravinsky, continuing the line of collaboration begun with *Apollo* —*Orpheus* (1948), *Agon* (1957), and the trio of 1972 triumphs: *Duo Concertant*, *Symphony in Three Movements*, *Violin Concerto*. The musical titles were indicative of his desire to present ballet as the art of dancing in time, needing no extraneous references to dramatic action. A theoretical descendent of Gautier and Levinson, rather than of Noverre and Fokine, Balanchine declared adamantly that there could be no mothers-in-law in ballet; movement was its own self-sufficient reason for being.

Though Balanchine has created most of the New York City Ballet's repertory, Jerome Robbins has contributed some of his finest compositions to it. His later works, including *Dances at a Gathering* (1969) and *Goldberg Variations* (1971), were pure dance, classically based, yet suggestive of human relationships—a touch of teasing, of rivalry, of nostalgia. But only a transitory glimpse. "Keep it cool, very cool," he told the dancers. But the effect was nothing like Balanchine's; the Robbins ballets, despite his apparently contrary assertions, were infused with warmth. Using the full range of the dancers' technical skills, they brought a new kind of drama—subtle and understated—to the *danse d'école*.

The third major force on the American ballet scene began in 1954 with a small group led by Robert Joffrey and became the official City Center Joffrey Ballet twelve years later. Though he had been a most promising choreographer, Joffrey created fewer ballets as the company grew, though *Astarte* (1967) caught national attention for its effective use of live dance combined with film for the presentation of an erotic *pas de deux*. Joffrey's assistant, Gerald Arpino, has attracted less critical acclaim but considerable popular enthusiasm, especially for his timely pieces set to rock music. Of special importance have been Joffrey's commissions of a number of significant revivals including Jooss's *The Green Table* and Massine's *Le Beau Danube* and *Parade*.

In Europe also the picture has changed rapidly. In France, where for many years Serge Lifar ruled the Paris Opéra, rebels broke away. One of the first was Roland Petit, who created a chic version of *Carmen* (1949) and other popular works for his own company; in the 1960's Maurice Béjart, hailed as a guru by the younger generation, staged enormous arena productions with his Brussels-based Ballet of the Twentieth Century. The Royal Danish Ballet, long the isolated custodian of Bournonville, began to modernize its training and repertory in the 1950's, striving to keep its traditions alive at the same time. The Royal Swedish Ballet also brought in foreign teachers and choreographers, while Jooss-trained Birgit Cullberg formed her own company along less classical lines. Germany, where ballet had never taken a strong hold, turned from its native modern dance pioneers to import ballet choreographers for its opera houses, the Englishman John Cranko bringing the Stuttgart Ballet to a place of international prominence. Not to be outdone, England took the Russian Rudolf Nureyev into its Royal Ballet, which, under his dynamic influence, acquired a new pungency that revitalized the company's by now sedate image. The English style spread abroad when Celia Franca left de Valois to head the National Ballet of Canada in 1951.

Agrippina Vaganova (1879–1951)
THE CONSTRUCTION OF
THE LESSON
Translated from the Russian by Anatole Chujoy

Considered the founder of the Soviet system of ballet education, Vaganova was trained in the school of the Maryinsky Theatre. She retired as a performer in 1916 and began teaching shortly thereafter. Her Basic Principles of Classical Ballet, *first published in 1934, has been translated into many languages.*

Since Adice the ballet lesson has become more complicated, involving a greater variety of exercises, but still following the same general pattern. The développés *at the* barre *are a significant addition, for the twentieth century has placed more emphasis on the control and height of the extended leg. The stress on allegro is also an important change. Coordination and flow of movement seem now to have replaced Adice's accent on brute endurance.*

. . . In adagio the pupil masters the basic poses, turns of the body and the head.

Adagio begins with the easiest movements. With time it gets more and more complicated and varied. In the last grades, difficulties are introduced one after another. Pupils must be well prepared in the preceding grades to perform these complicated combinations,—they must master the firmness of the body and its stability,—so that when they meet still greater difficulties they do not lose their self-control.

A complicated adagio develops agility and mobility of the body. When, later in allegro, we face big leaps, we will not have to waste time on mastery of the body.

I want to dwell on allegro and stress its particular importance. Allegro is the foundation of the science of the dance, its intricacy and the bond of future perfection. The dance as a whole is built on allegro. . . .

When the legs of the pupil are placed right, when they have acquired the turnout, when the ball of the foot has been developed and strengthened, when the foot has gained elasticity and the muscles have toughened,—then may we approach the study of allegro.

We begin with jumps which are done by a rebound of both feet off the floor, changement de pieds and echappé. To make them easier they

SOURCE: From *Basic Principles of Classical Ballet* (New York: Dover, 1953). Reprinted by permission of Dover Publications, Inc.

are done in the beginning at the bar, facing it and holding on with both hands.

The next jump to be done is the assemblé, rather complicated in structure. This sequence has deep and important reasons.

Assemblé forces the dancer to employ all muscles from the very start. It is not easy for the beginner to master it. Every moment of the movement has to be controlled in performing this pas. This eliminates every possibility of muscular looseness.

The pupil who learns to do assemblé properly not only masters this step but also acquires a foundation for the performance of other allegro steps. . . .

In the higher grades, when it becomes necessary to make the lessons more and more complicated, all steps may be done en tournant. Beginning with simple battement tendu and ending with the most intricate adagio and allegro steps, everything is done en tournant, affording the developed and strong muscles harder work. . . .

There is nothing bad about the exercises being tedious in their monotony, although this monotony can be broken by doing the movements in different time, four-four and two-four, so that the pupils do not do them mechanically but follow the music.

In these classes a foundation is laid for the development of the muscles, the elasticity of the ligaments; a basis is instilled for the elementary movements.

All this is accomplished by systematic repetitions of the same movement a great number of times in succession. For example, it is better to do a step eight times in succession than two or four combinations in eight measures. Few, scattered movements will not achieve the aim. The teacher must be absolutely certain that the pupil has mastered the movement, that it becomes part of her and that it will be done correctly in any combination, before he may complicate the lesson without harm to the pupil. . . .

Sample Lesson

The following is a sample lesson suitable for advanced classes. The entire lesson is given on half-toe.

EXERCISE AT THE BAR

1. *Plié* in five positions. (Two measures in $^4/_4$.) One slow in $^4/_4$; one fast in $^2/_4$, on the other $^2/_4$ rise on half-toe.

2. *Battements tendus.*
Front: in $1/4$—two with *plié*, two without *plié*; three in $1/8$ (on the fourth $1/8$—rest); seven in $1/16$ (on the eighth $1/16$—rest).
To the side: the same.
Back: the same.
Again to the side: the same.
Repeat these eight measures.
The same exercise from the other foot (*).

3. *Battements fondus* and *frappés* (combination). Eight measures $4/4$.
Front: one *fondu* slow in $2/4$, two fast one in $1/4$.
To the side: the same.
Back: the same
Again to the side: the same.
Two *frappés* slow in $1/4$, three fast ones in $1/8$ (rest on the fourth $1/8$).
Do it four times.
Repeat the whole combination beginning to the back.
The same exercise from the other foot.

4. *Ronds de jambe*. Two measures in $4/4$.
Three fast *ronds de jambe par terre en dehors* in $3/8$; on the fourth $1/8$ rise on half-toe, open leg in 2nd position. Three *ronds de jambe en l'air en dehors* in $3/8$; rest on the fourth $1/8$; four *ronds de jambe en l'air en dehors* in $4/8$. *Plié sur le cou-de-pied* and *tour en dehors* in $4/8$.
Repeat entire figure *en dedans.*
The same exercise from the other foot.

5. *Battements battus* and *petits battements.* Eight measures in $4/4$.
Four times in $4/4$ double *battement battu* with a rest in pose *effacé* front in *plié* after each $1/4$. During the next measure, *battements battus* are done successively with a rest on the fourth $1/4$ in pose *effacé* front in *plié*.
Four times in $4/4$ one *petit battement* with a rest in 2nd position after each $1/4$. One measure successive *petits battements* with a rest in 2nd position in *plié* on the fourth $1/4$.
Four times in $4/4$ one *petit battement* with a rest in pose *effacé* back in *plié* after each $1/4$. One measure successive *petits battements* with a rest on the fourth $1/4$ in pose *effacé* back in *plié*. Repeat the described two measures of *petits battements* with a rest in 2nd position.
The same exercise from the other foot.

6. *Developpé*. Two measures in $4/4$.
Carry out right leg front with point to the floor, doing *demi-plié* with left leg (first $1/4$), raise right leg to 90°, straightening the knee of the left leg (second $1/4$), small, short *balancé* with the raised leg (third $1/4$),

(*) Each movement of every exercise at the bar is always done from one foot and then from the other.

carry the leg to 2nd position (fourth ¼). Bend leg in knee (first ¼), open in 2nd *arabesque* (second ¼), raise on half-toe, fall on raised leg back in *demi-plié* extending the toes of the left leg front (third ¼), rise on it quickly on half-toe, raising right leg in *attitude croisée* (fourth ¼). Do the entire combination in reverse order, from the back.

Third figure—in 2nd position, all poses to the side. The concluding pose will be in the first case *écarté* back, in the second case—*écarté* front. The same exercise from the other foot.

This exercise may also be done in ½.

7. *Grands battements jetés balancés*. One measure in ⁴/₄.

We begin by pointing the toes and carrying left leg back. Through 1st position the leg is thrust front, then back (first and second ¼), and twice through 1st position into 2nd (third and fourth ¼).

The next time: throw the leg back, front, and into position.

The same exercise from the other foot.

The body must balance as described in *battement balancé*.

EXERCISE IN THE MIDDLE

Realizing the shortness of the lesson I recommend the following order of exercises in the middle:

1. *Petit adagio*. Combine *plié* with various *developpés* and *battements tendus*.

2. In the second *petit adagio* bring in combinations with *battements fondus* and *frappés*, and *ronds de jambe en l'air*.

3. *Grand adagio*, which contains the most difficult adagio movements for the given class.

4. For the beginning of *allegro* I try to give small jumps, i.e. low and simple ones.

5. *Allegro* with big steps.

6. For the first steps on *pointes* I select those which are done on both feet: *échappé* in 2nd position and then in 4th. This precaution is necessary because, although the students are warmed up, the new movements bring into play new muscles, and these should be prepared for the work.

7. In order to balance out all muscles and tendons which have been stimulated by the work, the lesson ends with small *changements de pieds*. To develop the flexibility of the body we do *port de bras*. . . .

GRAND ADAGIO

Pose *croisé* back with left leg, *plié, coupé* on left foot and *ballonné* in *écarté* front with a stop in *effacé*, right leg bent behind knee, extend it in the same direction *effacé* back, do on it two *tours en dedans sur le cou-de-pied*, stop in *écarté* back with left leg, both arms in 3rd position, turn slowly and carry the opened leg into 1st *arabesque*, the body facing [upstage]; the arms, opened in 2nd position through preparatory position are carried front with the wrists crossed. *Coupé* on left foot and *pas ciseaux* (stop on right foot), turn to *effacé* front with the left leg, *chassé* in *effacé*, fall on left leg in *plié*, after which shift to the right leg, taking the pose *croisé* in *attitude*, turn quickly *en dehors*, stand on the left foot in 4th *arabesque*, *renversé* in *écarté* back, *pas de bourrée en dehors*, two *tours en dehors* from 4th position *sur le cou-de-pied*, *pas de bourrée en dehors* and *entrechat-six de volée* with the right leg.

ALLEGRO

1. Big *sissonne* forward in *croisé en tournant en dehors*, *assemblé* forward and *sissonne-soubresaut* in *attitude effacée* on right foot, carry left leg on the floor front, *glissade* with the right foot to the side, and *cabriole fermée* with the right leg in *effacé*.

2. (a) *Saut de basque* and *renversé sauté en dehors*; repeat; *sissonne tombée* forward in *effacé*, *cabriole* in 1st *arabesque*, *pas de bourrée*, *cabriole* in 4th *arabesque*, *sissonne tombée en tournant (en dehors)* in *croisé* front on right foot, *coupé* on left foot and *jeté fermé fondu* on right foot to the side in 2nd position.

(b) Four *sauts de basque* diagonally with arms in 3rd position, four *chaînés* diagonally [backward], preparation in 4th position *croisé* and two *tours en dehors sur le cou-de-pied*; finish in 4th position.

3. Preparation *croisé* front with the left leg, *grande cabriole fermée* in *effacé* with the right leg and turn *en dedans* on *pointes* in 5th position. Repeat. *Sissonne tombée*: back in *croisé* from right leg, in *effacé* from left leg, with right leg *jeté en tournant en dehors* forward in *croisé*, *cabriole* into 4th *arabesque* and *pas de bourrée*. This combination may also be done in waltz-time.

Yuri Slonimsky (1902–)
OUR POINT OF VIEW

Slonimsky began to write ballet criticism at the age of seventeen and soon after started to publish a series of monographs on historical dance subjects. His first book, Masters of the Ballet of the Nineteenth Century, *appeared in 1937. Soviet choreographers have created a number of ballets based on Slonimsky's librettos.*

Here he states the basic ideology of the Soviet ballet, showing that all the glorious technique, all the moving portrayals of character, should be only means to the end of communicating "a message, ennobling and purifying." Here again the ballet art is made to serve the purposes of the state, as it was in the days of the Ballet Comique. *The Soviet ballet's use of lavish mechanical equipment (not mentioned by Slonimsky) also links it to the Renaissance genre, though now the productions are intended for all the people rather than for the select elite. Yet, like Noverre, Slonimsky wants ballet to reach the heart.*

. . . When after the Revolution of 1917 the theatres were filled with new audiences representing the widest strata of society—workers, peasants, soldiers, and office employees, the question naturally arose what attitude to adopt towards an art, existing until then on the Imperial stage. Should it be cast away as something belonging altogether to the old world, or was it in need of reform?. . . .

For several years the doors of the theatres were open to the public free of charge. People were shown the ballets of the past: both the best of our classical heritage and ballets of the type mentioned above.

The new spectators passed their own judgement. Unconditionally they favoured the best ballets of the classical legacy. The most brilliant execution of such Petipa ballets as *La Fille du Pharaon, The Talisman, Le Roi Candaule* and so forth left them completely indifferent. At the same time they came to love not only *Swan Lake, The Sleeping Beauty* and *Giselle*, but also *La Fille Mal Gardée, Esmeralda* and *Don Quixote*, and this in spite of the fact that the form of expression was often quite old-fashioned, the productions outdated and the heroes themselves—fairies, princes, magicians and kings—completely alien to them.

SOURCE: From 2nd revised edition of *The Bolshoi Ballet*, published 1960 by the Foreign Language Publishing House, Moscow, U.S.S.R. Used by permission of the Am-Rus Literary Agency.

Was this conservatism, was it backwardness? No, not at all! We ourselves did not quite understand at first that by making this selection the audiences were taking a healthy point of view on the culture of the past. . . . "Anti-Imperial" views upon ballet could not, quite naturally, prevail in an art dependent on the Imperial household. But they found expression—sometimes more and sometimes less obviously—almost everywhere, practically in all noteworthy productions. All that has ever been produced for the entertainment of an empty-headed crowd is obsolete in our new ballet and should be discarded and forgotten. Such is the judgement prompted by experience. Soviet spectators have helped us to arrive at this judgement by demanding a critical approach to what we have inherited.

It became obvious that the calling of ballet, as of all arts, was to help the spectator to better understand himself and the world about him, to enrich his spiritual wealth and shape his ethical notions. Together with literature, drama and opera, ballet is a vehicle of education. . . .

Truly beautiful musical and choreographic creations boldly raise urgent problems of human existence, they always carry a message, ennobling and purifying. That is what gives them the right to immortality. Anything that fails to reach the public's mind and heart, that merely pleases the eye for a short moment, is doomed to early oblivion. These are not our words: they belong to the great Didelot. . . .

A striving to reflect the inner substance of life has become part and parcel of Soviet choreography. Soviet art cannot isolate itself from its people. This is what constitutes its novelty of principle, its entirely new mission.

It is hardly necessary to emphasise that this alone makes Soviet ballet radically different to the Imperial theatre. In those days ballet kept to the side of the road taken by literature and other arts, coming in contact with them only occasionally, whereas now it takes part in the assertion of our artistic ideals openly and directly as an equal of other arts.

Progressive art was always drawn to great literature. Literature is a wise mother that can endow its offsprings with a wealth of ideas and imagery. Its ability to penetrate beyond the surface of life cannot be equalled. Soviet ballet sees a life-giving source for further development in joining forces with literature—both classical and contemporary. . . .

The best choreographers of the past used to dream of a union of author, musician, choreographer and designer. However, in Soviet ballet alone this alliance became a necessity and therefore a law. It is immaterial by whom the book is conceived—by the choreographer, composer or professional writer. What matters is that the dramaturgical outline of the production is sketched long before the composer conceives the first bar of the music and the choreographer—the first step of the ballet. This outline is not a framework on which music and dance are simply stretched. It finds expression in terms of musical and dance imagery. The general underlying idea of the story and, therefore, of the future production, is of primary importance in Soviet ballet. The substance of this idea is embedded in the book. And this also makes Soviet ballet an antipode of the Imperial ballet. . . .

It is well known, however, that in works of art ethics is inseparable from aesthetics. Only that is beautiful which is beautiful in thought, feeling and deed. Such is the secret of true poetry.

In championing these principles, Soviet ballet breaks with the so-called "Imperial traditions" of Russian ballet in this respect as well. The Revolution gave birth to poetry all about us, on the earth that is being transformed with our own hands, and there was no need any more to look for it in the realm of beautiful fantasy. Poetry, truth, beauty is to be found not in exaggerated praise of the past, in romantic illusions, or in escape from reality, but in fighting for its ideals. Life offers us prototypes of a positive hero at every step. He is the rank-and-file but in no way run-of-the-mill toiler, he is the creator of mankind's new history. In 1919, Maxim Gorky was dreaming of a "hero nobly self-forgetting, passionately in love with his ideal, a hero in the true, broad sense of the word."

The hero of Soviet ballet is moved by love for humanity and an infinite faith in man's moral strength, he is moved by hatred of anything that prevents a full flowering of spiritual forces, that stifles man and takes away his right to peaceful labour and personal happiness.

Our theatre asserts an inseparable bond between social and private destiny and interests. For the first time the theme of the Revolution took possession of the ballet stage. The dancers were faced with a new task: more passion and energy had to be introduced into their acting. Events of popular life lent an atmosphere of heroism and pathos to the productions. The People as the leading hero came to the foreground.

Any theme—be it fairy-tale, or historical, has to be interpreted with a contemporary vision. Otherwise there will be no authenticity, no artistic merit, no chance of "immortality" for that work of art.

The powerful current of life brought new heroes to the Soviet ballet, such as had not been known for too long a time. These heroes are compatriots and contemporaries of the spectators. No matter how much we criticised these new characters sometimes, they did invariably introduce something new into art—they endowed the heroes with great generosity, with a feeling of solidarity and fraternity, with a burning concern for the fate of the people in all the parts of the world.

Our spectator always sides with those fighting for a just cause. He shows lively interest in events taking place in any part of the universe at any period. . . .

The method of socialist realism, which is the method of Soviet art, took form gradually. Life has proved that it enables us better than any other method to depict themes from reality and to create psychologically complex and truthful characters of contemporary heroes. Realism is in no way a monopoly of Soviet ballet. It is accessible to any artist of the dance, who looks for beauty in life and for a way to the hearts of his audience.

Many foreign critics do not discriminate between two trends in art—realism and naturalism. Naturalism, in actual fact, is a bitter enemy of realism. Whereas realism selects from life that which is most important, what moves man and humanity, naturalism shows up everything that falls within its vision and so turns art into something worse than a photograph—a dreary, dull record registering facts, but incapable of conveying their inner significance. Realism catches the very heartbeat of the times. It penetrates the very core of human existence and discovers its hidden springs. It generalises events, revealing the general through the particular, finding something essential for all and for everyone in separately taken phenomena. . . .

In the course of at least a century, ballet revolved round the theme of romantic love. Now *any* great love—love for one's family, friends, children, work, creations, motherland—all this becomes part of ballet. Therefore the very scope of this art has become considerably expanded.

In pre-revolutionary ballets the characters, as a rule, were static. They did not change as the plot developed. Realism armed Soviet ballet with a versatility of characters, such as had been characteristic of drama or opera. From the beginning to the end of the performance the character grows and develops: struggle makes his love nobler and purer and his hatred stronger; new feelings, new attitudes are born in him. Thus grows the tension of passions and the tension of ideas, clashing in conflict.

Realism has made *life in dance* an absolute law of scenic behaviour. The dancer lives, breathes, thinks—all in terms of dance. That is why the dramatic narrative in a ballet is not counterposed to dance. One follows from the other, forming a single whole. . . .

We wish to live through the development of the poetic plot together with the authors and the dancers. Step by step we want to take part in their struggle for the ideal, to share with them the joy of victory or the sorrow of defeat. When the heroes' destiny is linked with that of his nation, his story can't be reduced to so many short episodes. The art of *performance* (such was the Imperial ballet) becomes an art of *living the role*. The psychological development of characters and situations which, as a rule, was absent in the old days, becomes a necessity in every production. . . .

At one time, attempts were made to tie down the system of the classical dance to a definite country or a definite class, and to treat it as a product of that given epoch. It was declared that it was as changeable as the times and styles that had engendered it, and should therefore be replaced by something else.

The past few decades have proved the fallacy of such views.

Classical dancing is the quintessence of artistically generalised human movements. It is immortal when regarded as a foundation on which choreographers, musicians, ballerinas and *danseurs* build their images. Without the classical dance as the artistic language of ballet, there is no ballet. True, once the classical dance is regarded as a set of pretty gestures and steps, it loses its meaning. The use of conventional school exercises for any situation and any image inevitably leads to formalism and naturalism. Even the most cunning pattern-creating pleasing for the moment is sterile and doomed to oblivion if it is conceived outside of content.

Contrariwise, the deeper the choreographer's perception of life, the more eloquent becomes the classical dance idiom of the characters created by his inspiration.

There are no limits to the flexibility of the classical dance, provided the choreographers know how to use it. Classical dance should, indeed, be enriched and modernised—but according to its laws and purpose (that of creating an image), rather than the choreographers' whims. Classical dancing, more readily than any other kind, blends with the music, comprising a "choreographic melody." If the very nature of classical dancing is ignored, this "melody" disappears, beauty goes too, and the ugly and deformed takes possession of the stage.

However, content must be given priority if art is to attain the maximum of expression. New content is what suggests and engenders new form. New form in itself can never give birth to corresponding content. Form-making is always sterile.

The system of classical dance is an evergreen tree of scenic expression. Anything may be grafted to it. Taking this system as a basis, the choreographer should enrich and expand it. Folk dances, grotesque acrobatics, ballroom dancing, eurythmics—all this should be made into a new alloy by force of the choreographer's imagination, an alloy best suited to the images he has in mind. It is of paramount importance to remember that stage dancing has several aspects, and the preference of one to the detriment of the rest invariably ends in disaster. Only a blend of technical virtuosity, plastic expressiveness and poetic content is capable of sustaining realism in ballet.

In ballets based on new material taken directly from life the expressiveness of dance form sometimes falls short of the content. Though quite logical at the beginning, this cannot be long tolerated. Not all Soviet choreographers display enough daring and inventiveness in their use of accepted ballet forms. However, our faith in the chosen means and methods is none the weaker for it. They are correct—therefore the imperfections will be overcome.

Frederick Ashton (1906–)
A CONVERSATION

Ashton began choreographing for Marie Rambert in London in 1926, shifting to Ninette de Valois' company nine years later. The remainder of his career has been closely associated with this company, which became Britain's Royal Ballet. Ashton was largely responsible for its repertory and style, creating for it such diversified fare as the sophisticated, witty Façade *(1931); the serenely lyrical* Symphonic Variations *(1946); the delightful frolic that was his version of* La Fille Mal Gardée *(1960); the refined and very English elegance of* Enigma Variations *(1968). He was artistic director of the company from 1963 until his retirement in 1971.*

In this interview with Clement Crisp, Ashton outlines the convictions underlying the various forms of choreography he has undertaken. His insistence on the essential comprehensiveness of classical technique is reiterated by most of the choreographers represented in this section.

CRISP: *Marguerite and Armand* has just had a tremendous success. How do you view it as part of your own output?

ASHTON: I never really think about that. The thing I feel is immense relief that it's worked, but for me every ballet that I do is a job. It's my work. That's what I have to do. I'm like somebody who sets out with his implements to go and mend frozen pipes. And you know, there's too much talk about inspiration and all that kind of thing. I mean, all very well if the muse looks in . . .

SOURCE: From *Covent Garden Book, No. 15* (London: A. & C. Black, 1964). Reprinted by permission of Clement Crisp.

CRISP: But the muse must be there at ten o'clock in the morning in the rehearsal room.

ASHTON: Exactly. If she deigns to look in all the better, but you have to get down and do the job—that's really what it amounts to.

CRISP: But I suppose there are certain ballets which are your particular favourites among your own works.

ASHTON: Yes, I think the ones I like best are the ones that I feel that have furthered my development and outlook. For instance, *Symphonic Variations*. At the time that I did that there seemed to be a clutter of ballets with heavy stories and I felt that the whole idiom needed purifying. And so I made *Symphonic Variations*, and it was a kind of testament.

CRISP: It was a breath of fresh air—re-established classical dancing as the supreme function of ballet.

ASHTON: Yes. But it's difficult to say whether I have any actual favourite. One's favourite is apt to be the last one that one does, really. But looking back on it all I'm very fond of some of my very early works. I'm very fond of *Façade*, because I think it seems to me to be a complete entity in itself. It's successful in what I set out to do—which was a parody of dances of that time. And also I think that one thing one must always guard against is that if one has to do a comic ballet, one can never say "Well now, I'm going to do a comic ballet and I'm going to be funny." That must never be so. The structure of the dance must be very solid and then you superimpose the humour if it comes naturally. And I think that in *Façade* the humour seems to come quite naturally out of the actual dances. But it must be a good dance first, and then the humour comes out of that.

CRISP: Do you feel this holds good also with *Wedding Bouquet*?

ASHTON: Yes, I think the same thing. With *Wedding Bouquet*, although it is a humorous ballet, it's rather Chaplinesque in the sense that it has an underlying sadness. And there again I think all the characters are very well rounded, and what humour there is is almost a tragic humour in a way.

CRISP: What about *Scènes de Ballet*, which has always been one of my favourites of yours; I think it says a great deal about classical ballet itself; about the formulas of classical ballet. Do you agree?

ASHTON: Yes, I do. When I was doing this ballet I immersed myself in geometry and Euclid and all those things, which was very funny, because at school I could never even understand them. And also the fact that you could make the front anywhere, not necessarily as it were where the public sit and see. So that *Scènes de Ballet*, if you were to actually sit in the wings, would still have the same effect as it has from being viewed from the auditorium. You would get a different, but logical, pattern. And this was a fascinating problem to me. I used to place the dancers in theorems and then make them move along geometric lines and then at the end I used to say "Well, Q.E.D." when it worked out. Sometimes we got into the most terrible muddles, but it was a very interesting problem for me to unravel them.

CRISP: Obviously at the time you felt very strongly about the importance of classical dancing, of the academic dance, and obviously you still do.

ASHTON: Well of course I do. I think that it's the only language really. All these other "isms" that there are, and all the modern dance, are all tributaries of the mainstream. They can be used very effectively, should be used, and one should perhaps go through periods of them in order to incorporate them. You see, the classical ballet is so rich that it can take in anything, and absorb all outside influences into itself.

CRISP: Your artistic career is now 30 years old, and more, and you still go on creating new and exciting and beautiful things. This is really because you are a classical choreographer, and you live in the classical tradition.

ASHTON: Well absolutely. I couldn't possibly live in any other and I don't think there's any hope for anybody who doesn't in the long run.

CRISP: Something that Ingres once said, that the task is not to invent, but to continue.

ASHTON: I think that as regards invention one should never consciously say "Well, now I'm going to be inventive." Of course you must search for new things, but as you're doing so you must search for new modes of expression and new movements. Naturally that is very important, because otherwise the ballet becomes a sort of cliché of classical dancing. You must have a personal idiom. Your work should be recognised. People should be able to come and say "this is a Balanchine ballet. This is an Ashton ballet. Or this is a ballet by Kenneth MacMillan." If you can say that then you know that the choreographer is good, and has something personal to offer, and a language in which he expresses himself.

CRISP: Do you feel that you've ever tried to consciously give a direction to ballet? Obviously from what you've said about *Symphonic Variations* you have. You wanted to clear away a lot of dross at the end of the war. Since then do you think you have?

ASHTON: No, not really, I've tried to give a direction to myself, I think, really more than to the actual ballet. I used the medium to express what I feel in my own ideas at the time. When I do one sort of ballet I think the way to keep oneself alive is never to follow that line up with saying "this kind of ballet has been successful. I will now do a series of this sort." I do the very contrary thing. After I

Photo, Roger Wood. Dance Collection,
The New York Public Library at Lincoln Center

In Frederick Ashton's *Symphonic Variations* the dancers are (left to right): Pirmin Trecu, Rosemary Lindsay, Michael Somes, Anya Linden, Annette Page, and Brian Shaw. The beautiful décor of Sophie Fedorovitch focussed the eye on the clean, classical lines of the choreographic design—a "testament" to the self-sufficiency of ballet technique at a time when "story" ballets were abounding.

did, say, *Symphonic Variations*, I immediately take something that is completely different, and in that way you develop yourself, I think, and increase your horizon.

CRISP: But are there certain things that ballet can't do?

ASHTON: Yes, I think there are, certainly, because ballet can't get too involved in a story, in trying to express things that can only be said by words. I think the great asset of ballet is that it can heighten beyond words certain situations and give a kind of poetic evocation, so that it becomes . . . you almost can't say what the sensation that it's given you is.

CRISP: Balanchine once said that a ballet is a shape in time and space and nothing more. I think I'm misquoting slightly. But you would agree with the basic idea?

ASHTON: Yes, I would.

CRISP: This question of big ballets. They present, I suppose, the most appalling difficulties for you.

ASHTON: In one way, they're difficult to do. On the other hand, if you have a three-act ballet, you have plenty of time to develop everything. It's a very contrary thing to *Marguerite and Armand*, which is like a pill, the whole thing is digested down to a pill. The length of a three-act ballet makes it more difficult because it will have to be more inventive and you have to keep the whole thing going and keep the interest up the whole time.

CRISP: The great disadvantage for three-act ballets is quite simply the lack of scores.

ASHTON: That is the great thing, and also the lack of stories; it's very difficult to find a story which carries right through from the first act to the last. Otherwise you tend to get a story which fizzles out by the end of the second act and the third act simply becomes a series of divertissements or dances which keep the action going to the last minute. I tend to think that really the two-act ballets are almost the best, because you get the whole thing a little bit more concise and more suited to the modern taste.

CRISP: Do you have any feelings about contemporary themes for ballets, do you think these can work?

ASHTON: Yes, I think they can work. I'm sure they can work, but they are difficult to find, and the difficulty is in dressing them I think. If you keep them on point with modern dress and mackintoshes on top I think it's apt to look ridiculous. Then on the other hand if you put them into flat shoes then the thing becomes a bit pedestrian, but I'm not at all against it, if only one could find a kind of poetic expression of modern life with brilliant and inventive collaborations, then I think of course it would be perfect but the cinema does it better. It must not be forgotten, as Mallarmé said about poetry— that it was about words and *not* ideas—the same applies to choreography. It is about movement and steps and not ideas.

Antony Tudor (1909–)
TALK ABOUT NEW BALLETS
An Interview with Jack Anderson

Though he was already nineteen when he decided to dance, Tudor won the interest of Marie Rambert because of his "poetic eyes," and he choreographed his first ballet for her in 1931. Joining Ballet Theatre in 1940, he contributed major works to its repertory for the next decade. Thereafter he mounted many of them for other companies throughout the world. Tudor speaks here after the success of Echoing of Trumpets *had broken a spell of ballets that seemed to lack creative fire.*

Especially significant here is Tudor's stress on the idea that "feeling must be expressed through movement." His manipulations of the classic vocabulary negated the conventional elegance and flow of its steps with rigid arms, a contracted torso, abrupt phrasing—whatever he needed to convey the fears, griefs, or frustrations of his characters. Like Fokine, he felt no need to create a completely new language, but he stretched the technique much further than Fokine to portray the crueler aspects of contemporary feeling.

The March 27 performance of the Metropolitan Opera Ballet was an important event, not only because it was one of the company's few opportunities to display itself outside the dance interludes of the standard operatic repertoire, but because the program contained the premieres of two ballets by Antony Tudor—the world premiere of *Concerning Oracles* and the American premiere of *Echoing of Trumpets*, created three years ago for the Royal Swedish Ballet and Tudor's most important ballet in many seasons.

Ask him how he came to choreograph this powerful indictment of war, then Tudor shrugs and says, "I have no idea. I have a dreadful memory about things like that." Then he pauses and starts to remember: "I suppose it began when I heard the Martinu music. I've always liked Czech composers—Dvorak, Smetana, Janacek, Martinu, and so on. You know, I often buy armloads of records and take them home and play them. If I don't like them, I give them away. If I do happen to like a particular piece of music, it may support a ballet."

Concerning Oracles was the partial result of one of these record hunts. Tudor heard a disc containing three charming compositions of Jacques

SOURCE: From *Dance Magazine* (May, 1966). Reprinted by permission.

Ibert and decided to use them for a ballet. *Echoing of Trumpets* came about several years ago when he discovered Martinu's "Symphonic Fantasies (Symphony No. 6.)"

"One passage sounded like gunshots. Another passage reminded me of a plague of locusts," Tudor says. "Now what can one do with a plague of locusts in a ballet?" Tudor turned to the Book of Revelations in the Bible and thought of choreographing a ballet about the Four Horsemen of the Apocalypse. Literal horsemen soon disappeared from the projected work. "Yet, in a way, they're still there," Tudor points out. "Once you even begin to consider the Four Horsemen as subjects for ballet, you can be very sure that whatever ballet results will deal with unpleasant things—hunger, war, things like that."

Gradually, but firmly, the ballet took its own shape. Tudor envisioned a setting enclosed by barbed wire and dominated by a ruined bridge. He says, "I suppose it symbolizes that there's no way out (I didn't realize until I actually started staging the work that the setting I had conceived closed me in as a choreographer, giving me only one place for entrances and exits)." Tudor remembered hearing of how a Nazi soldier once crushed a Greek peasant's hand into the ground to prevent him from reaching out for a crust of bread. That incident found its way into the ballet. So did Tudor's own memories of how, as a child during World War I, the family house was shelled and he was evacuated to a shelter near the Aldershot firing range. He says, "From those days I learned a lot about soldiers and how the military mind operates. I suppose it was then that I began to associate trumpets with soldiers and war and victory. In the ballet I ask: what happens *after* the echoing of trumpets? what happens when the conquering hordes have conquered? what happens to those whose wish is more and more power?"

While the Swedish title, *Ekon av Trumpeter*, can be translated as either *Echoes* or *Echoing of Trumpets*, Tudor prefers *Echoing*: "The word has a more resonant quality about it, suggesting an on-going, rather than a finished, action."

Many members of the audience have attempted to find parallels between *Echoing of Trumpets* and Tudor's earlier ballet of grief and loss, *Dark Elegies*, choreographed in 1937. The choreographer attempts to minimize these parallels: "I dearly love to steal bits from my old ballets when I choreograph a new one. But there's nothing of *Elegies* in *Echoing*." Yet he will admit that, as a composer, Martinu was influenced by Mahler (whose "Kindertotenlieder" is the score for *Elegies*) and that scores of similar moods may prompt a choreographer to create passages similar in movement quality.

Tudor also disparages another oft-repeated view of *Echoing*. Most audiences associate the ballet with World War II and there are resemblances between the plot and the historical event of the destruction of Lidice by the Nazis. Tudor denies that this is the theme of his work: "Perhaps it's more about how people always seem to want to dominate other people. Everyone knows that's a stupid thing to do. *Yet they keep on doing it.* They never stop torturing each other with a kind of mild viciousness."

Is there a *mild* viciousness?

"Oh yes. It exists. I've known some specialists in it . . . even in ballet studios." (A wicked glint appears in Tudor's eyes, then he quickly returns to discussing the psychology of war as it applies to nations, rather than dancers.) "Take the soldiers in my ballet. They don't really rape

A complex web of human relationships reveals itself in Antony Tudor's *Pillar of Fire*: the freely flirtatious younger sister taunts her polite elders, while Hagar, (right) fearing she cannot win the man she really loves, accepts the man who offers himself to her. Months of discussions about the psychology of the characters preceded the actual choreographing of the ballet. Left to right, the original cast: Annabelle Lyon, Antony Tudor, Lucia Chase, Nora Kaye, and Hugh Laing.

the women in the village. They just torment them until they make the women feel degraded and, in so doing, they degrade themselves. It's this mutual degradation which, I think, prevails when people are under the conqueror's heel."

When a new work was commissioned by the Royal Swedish Ballet, Tudor arrived in Stockholm with ideas for two ballets: one to a Tchaikovsky score; the other, the ballet to the Martinu score. The Tchaikovsky idea evaporated, while "the Martinu took hold of me." He worked on the ballet for a month with the dancers, then kept it in the back of his head while he staged a work in Berlin and vacationed in Rome. In retrospect, he finds both cities were appropriate places in which to mull over a work about invasions and conquests. When he returned to Sweden he completed the ballet in five weeks. Work on the American production of *Echoing of Trumpets* was begun this past January with the assistance of Anna Marie Lagerborg, ballet mistress of the Royal Swedish Ballet.

Concerning Oracles grew out of the Ibert record with the tantalizing pieces of music on it and the sheer necessity of having to do a ballet to fill out the Met program with *Echoing of Trumpets* and Bournonville's *La Ventana*. One day Sallie Wilson, the American Ballet Theatre principal who has starred in many Tudor productions, casually suggested that he revive *Les Mains Gauches*, a little ballet about palmistry he had once staged at Jacob's Pillow. Tudor thought this would be too slight for the huge Metropolitan Opera House. Then he decided to include it as one section of a larger work about such varied forms of fortune telling as crystal gazing and card reading.

"People tell me the ballet is obscure," Tudor says. "I don't know why that should be. It's simply about fortune telling and there's nothing obscure about that. Everybody knows what fortune telling is like and what its problems are. It's inconclusive. When you have your fortune told, do you believe it? Does what you are told will happen to you really happen? . . . No, I've never been to a fortune teller myself. I never thought it necessary."

Tudor follows such a barrage of deliberately cryptic remarks with more immediately practical considerations: "The ballet is full of rough edges. One section falls apart completely. I haven't had time to study it, but I want to re-work it."

Tudor is, by reputation, one of the slowest and most painstaking of living choreographers. Tudor himself thinks this reputation is somewhat exaggerated: "Everyone remembers that my *Romeo and Juliet* was still unfinished on the night of its premiere. But who remembers that the reason why it was unfinished is that I didn't get all the rehearsal time I'd been promised? And absolutely no one remembers that I put *Dim Lustre* together in eleven days or something like that."

Regarding teaching one of his ballets to dancers, Tudor says, "I don't like to give explanations. I don't like to communicate anything to a dancer through the mind, especially—" (and here that malicious glint returns) "— especially considering what some dancers' minds are like." Sometimes Tudor will not even tell the details of his plot to the dancers.

He says, "I want my dancers to grow into their roles through the movements of those roles. Understanding, development, and growth must always come through movement. Otherwise, it's only veneer. I remember seeing a young dancer with tears in her eyes as she rehearsed *Dark Elegies*. I stopped her at once—feelings must be expressed through movement.

"If I've given you a role and you do the movements for that role *exactly* the way I tell you to do them, you will master that characterization. You can't fail." Tudor is emphatic—and almost perversely optimistic—on this point: "Yes, I mean that. If the dancers do the movement as I want it, they can't fail. But they must do it *exactly* as I want it. Yes, they may find it hard to do. But it's there inside them. Only with some people you have to dig for it harder."

In addition to conveying the emotional intensity of the choreography, Tudor wishes his dancers to convey the quality of the music in their performances. In the United States, where companies have only a minimum of orchestra rehearsals, the early performances of a ballet are usually still unsatisfactory because the dancers "still don't really *hear* the music." In Stockholm there were five rehearsals with the orchestra, at the Met only one.

All the same, "Everybody seems to want to do *Echoing of Trumpets*. The Met has exclusive American performing rights for a year. After that—well, we'll wait and see."

Jerome Robbins (1918–)
FANCY FREE

Trained in both classical and modern techniques, Robbins joined Ballet Theatre in 1940 and the New York City Ballet in 1949. Along with creating works for these companies, he choreographed and later completely directed a number of Broadway musicals, most notably **West Side Story** *(1957) and* **Fiddler on the Roof** *(1964). Probably the most wide-ranging of contemporary ballet makers, he has done psychological dramas and comedies; ballets set to symphonies, to jazz, and to no music at all; he has filled the stage with vibrant configurations of classical movements; and with* **Watermill** *(1972) he set a work distinguished by its oriental sparseness and containing not a single step from the ballet vocabulary.*

Fancy Free (1944) was Robbins' first ballet, an immediate hit, and an enduring favorite in the Ballet Theatre repertory. Characteristically, he never did another work quite like it. Americana had been used previously by classical companies, but the choreographers had chosen period settings. **Fancy Free** *was contemporary in subject, colloquial in idiom, while it drew on the full resources of the ballet-trained dancer. Robbins' directions to composer Leonard Bernstein are less stringent with regard to rhythms than were Petipa's instructions to Tchaikovsky, but the moods of the music are defined here with much greater precision.*

A one-act ballet based on an incident concerning three sailors on a shore leave

Characters:

THREE SAILORS	Jerome Robbins, Harold Lang, John Kriza
THE BRUNETTE	Muriel Bentley
THE RED-HEAD	Janet Reed
THE BLONDE	Shirley Eckl
(BARTENDER	Rex Cooper)

Time: The present; a hot summer night.

Place: New York.

This is the story of three sailors who are out on the town on a Shore Leave. It is a jazz ballet, light in mood, running about 15 minutes. The costumes for the sailors should be the regular dark sailors' uniforms.

SOURCE: From George Amberg, *Ballet in America* (New York: Duell, Sloan & Pearce, 1949). ©1949 by Jerome Robbins. Reprinted by permission of Jerome Robbins.

The girls should wear actual street dresses which permit free movement. The bartender should wear the usual white apron-jacket combination. The set, imaginatively designed, should represent a city street, a bar at center stage so that its interior is visible, and a lamppost stage left. The action takes place at night.

(Perhaps a subway entrance stage right—No.)

Music and Mood	*Action*
	Three sailors explode onto the stage. They are out on shore leave, looking for excitement, women, drink, any kind of fun they can stir up. Right now they are fresh, full of animal exuberance and boisterous spirits, searching for something to do, something to happen. Meanwhile they dance down the street with typical sailor movements—the brassy walk, the inoffensive vulgarity, the quality of being all steamed up and ready to go. They boldly strut, swagger and kid each other along. This section should serve as an introductory dance as well; bright, fast, gay, happy. One should feel immediately that the three are good friends, used to bumming around together, used to each other's guff . . . that they are in the habit of spending their time as a trio, and that, under all their rough and tumble exterior, there is a real affection for each other, a kind of "my buddy" feeling.
Fast, explosive, jolly, rollicking. A bang-away start.	
Transition period to slower mood.	They finally arrive at the lamppost around which they gradually settle as the first impetus and excitement of being on shore dies down. One, with his arm crooked around the pole, swings slowly back and forth; another rocks on his heels; the third leans: and the more seriously they become involved with what to do next, the quieter they become. Finally they decide that a drink is what they need. They saunter toward the bar, enter, and each approaches the bar and places his foot on the rail. They order up three beers which the bartender serves. They pick up their glasses and clink them together in a mutual toast. Simultaneously they lift, drain,
Slow, relaxed . . . music should have literal meanings as far as specific action is concerned.	

and plunk their glasses back on the bar. A moment of satisfaction; a pause of relaxation. They turn front and, as part of their habits, choose to see who pays. Two of them secretly agree on the same amount of fingers, and consequently the odd man pays. He shakes his head (as if this happens all the time, which it does), and pays. The three hitch their pants and move to the door, where they stand looking out at the night and street. One yawns, another stretches, and the third produces a slice of gum, breaks it in three parts and hands a piece to each. Each unwraps it, rolls up the paper, puts the gum in his mouth, and then with a neat kick, deftly flips the wrapper away. They stand in the doorway chewing. A pause of satisfaction, a sigh of "Now what should we do?".

Dreamy . . .
waiting . . .

Sudden, loud, change of tempo and mood. Hot boogie-woogie-influence, which quiets down to being insistent with sudden hot loud licks.

The tempo changes and the Brunette enters from the left. (She's a nice girl who doesn't mind the horseplay about to happen. In fact, she knows it's coming the minute she sees them and anticipates the fun of it.) Her quality and movements should be in the style of the music. There should be an influence of the Negro fluidity and suppleness, the under-excitement and sexuality in her walk and dancing. She has to cross the stage in front of the sailors. They are motionless except for their heads which follow her closely, their eyes sizing her up, their mouths still chewing. As she passes them, all three impudently tip their hats. She goes on smiling but ignoring them. Then they really get into action, an "Aha, a female—here we go" routine. They spruce themselves up. They pick up her walk and rhythms and try to insinuate themselves with her. They tease and heckle her, trying to get her to break down. They attempt various approaches and techniques, the "Hi, sister," etc. They snatch her bag and toss it from one to the other. She pretends to be angry with them, and annoyed, but both she and they know she isn't. She actually enjoys the attention very much, and with subtlety leads them a merry chase. Of

Transition of music and mood to next quality. As they leave, slowly, music dies

and alters.

Slow . . . torchy, somewhat low-down, but pleasant. Not sentimental or romantic at all. Blues. . . .

Sudden break in mood at reentrance of three figures . . . same in music . . . transition to theme of completion, and constant rise in music as each incident provokes further antago-

course, three sailors are too many for one girl and the competition seems too much for one of them: he tires of the horseplay and shuffling; his enthusiasm ebbs; and he allows the other two to go off trailing her. As they go off, the sailors are still persistent, and she still has her reserve about her, but it looks as if it's breaking down.

The remaining sailor watches after them a while. At the same time the Redhead enters from the opposite side. He turns to go back into the bar and they come face to face, almost bumping. He gives her the once-over quickly, and then excuses himself for bumping into her as a means of introducing himself and picking her up. She realizes it but likes it and him. He looks back to be sure the others have gone off, then turns and suggests a drink—to which she agrees, and they enter the bar. They order up a drink, finally leading into a dance. This *pas de deux* should be different in timbre than the preceding section. The dance has more depth to it. There is more open attraction between them, there being only the two of them. There are moments of casualness mixed with sudden moments of heat and intensity. On the surface, their flirtation is carried on in nice terms, but there is a sure feeling of lust underneath. The boy is very happy to have a girl all to himself—a piece of good luck—and the girl is quite content with him. He makes no rude or vulgar movements, and she is drawn to him. They make a good-looking pair. Finally he pays for her drink, and, arm in arm, they start out the door.

At this very moment, the Brunette and the two sailors reappear. Evidently she has broken down before their charm and persistence, and the three are returning for a drink together, in a happy joking mood. They spy the one sailor who is trying to make his escape with the girl "all his own." They nab him in time, whereupon he returns and introduces his girl to his two friends. They are very happy to have another

nism between the three sailors until it breaks off at the three variations

girl to share among them. The two girls know each other and go down stage for a huddle full of giggles and mischievousness. They realize that they have the advantage because there are only two of them to three men . . . that if they play their cards right they can rule the evening. Meanwhile the three men are standing apart, kind of sizing each other up again, inwardly preparing for the competition there will be for the girls. This competition underplays the whole of this next climaxing section, building constantly to a higher note each moment. The men from here on seize every opportunity to show off, not only for the girls but for their buddies as well. The girls encourage this rivalry by playing one against the other and by playing with all three.

Dance Collection, The New York Public Library at Lincoln Center

In *Fancy Free*, one of the sailors shows off his dancing skills for a dramatic purpose—he wants to win a girl. The costumes of the performers are practically identical with the clothes worn by their audience; the scene could be a neighborhood bar. Left to right, the original cast: Muriel Bentley, Jerome Robbins, Janet Reed, John Kriza, Harold Lang, Rex Cooper.

Starts here . . .

grows . . .

grows . . .

higher . . .

breaks off.

The five reenter the bar. There is a scuffle to determine who is to escort which girl, a scramble for seats, and a conflict over who is to sit next to whom. There is a frantic effort on the part of each to pay for the girls' drinks. There is a mad scramble to light their cigarettes. When they dance, there is continual cutting in, and reshuffling of partners. Finally, each sailor alone tries to show off how well he can dance. Each wants the attention; they vie for the center of the floor. The action grows more and more rough until it reaches a point at which they are on the verge of fighting. The girls intercede, and, after a moment's consideration, back two of them off the floor to allow the remaining one to show his stuff first. He gives the other two a look of triumph: they return sneers and smirks (this occurs between and after each solo dance). He starts his dance.

These three solo dances form the highlight of the ballet. Each sailor is given a chance to dance for the girls. Each dance is brilliant, flashy, and technical enough to be showy, imaginative enough to project three distinct personalities. Each should be different musically and in quality. None of them is long, but each is full enough to be a complete variation in itself, practically a *tour-de-force* dance. They cannot be described; they must be danced. Each sailor, however, has his own personal style and type of movement, which can be presented. The first is the most bawdy, rowdy, boisterous of the three. He exploits the extrovert vulgarity of sailors, the impudence, the loudness, the get-me-how-good-I-am. When he finishes, instead of the other two fighting to go next, each wants the other to go first. Finally, the second yields and dances. His dance is very different in quality . . . the music is lighter, gayer, more happy-go-lucky, come-what-may. His movements are more naive, lovable; there is more warmth, humor, and almost wistfulness about him. At last, the third dances. His keynote is his intensity. There is a feeling of the Spanish or Latin about him. There are swift, sudden movements, a strong passion and violence, an attractive flashiness and smoldering quality.

When they are finished, there is a moment's pause. The girls really get to work on them. Now comes a fast kind of finale-coda dance. It picks up from where the excitement broke off, resumption of competitive theme on higher scale . . .

building . . .

building to this climax where it breaks; wild and loose and whooping.

and before the three dances. The vitality and concentration of the excitement grows. The dance becomes hotter, almost a furious lindy hop. The girls are whirled from one man to the next, are snatched from one to the other. The boys become more violent in their contact with one another; they push, and shove and nudge until finally it happens—one shoves another too hard and a fight breaks out. Before the girls can stop it, it is a real knock-down, rough-and-tumble, bang-away fight. They jump at each other, they swing and duck, they dive and tackle and heave and throw each other. The two girls stand near-by, frightened (the situation has gone further than they intended). The boys are in a heap on the floor, arms, legs, heads, bodies entangled and weaving; grunts, groans, heaves and swings, kicks and jerks—they struggle and pant and pull and push. Suddenly one gets flung off the pile, and he rolls fast across the floor, hitting the two girls in the shins and knocking them flat. Ignoring them completely, he

bang . . . crash, etc.

dives back into the mêlée. The girls help each other to their feet, shocked and furious. They rub their sore spots and stamp their feet for attention, to no avail: the men are too busy fighting. They both spy one free head, and together, they smack it with their bags. Then they

quickly slowing up . . .

turn and exit, walking haughtily, angrily down the street. The smacked head turns in time to see them exit. After many futile attempts, he finally gets the others to stop struggling. They

slow . . .

look around. No girls. They slowly disentangle themselves and get to their feet. They walk to the door and look off one way. No one in sight. The other way. Nothing. Then they look at each

empty . . .
after-the-storm feeling

other, take in their messed clothes, cock-eyed hats, dirty and bruised faces, hurt disappointed expressions. Then they smile, increasingly as

Recovery, and.

they realize the humor, ridiculousness, and irony of the whole situation . . . their knocking themselves out so hard that the girls escape them. They laugh and smack each other on the back.

.

.

.

Return to same theme
as in opening . . .
slow . . .
relaxed . . .

They pull themselves together and decide that what they need is a drink. They go back into the bar and order up three beers. They pick up their glasses and clink them in a mutual toast. They lift, drain, and plunk them back on the bar simultaneously. A moment of relaxation . . . a pause of tired satisfaction. . . .

tired . . .

They choose to see who will pay, with the same intrigue and the same results. The "sucker" shakes his head but pays. The other two shake hands on swindling him again. Then the three

dreamy . . .

saunter to the door to stand looking out at the night and the empty streets. One yawns, another stretches, and the third produces a stick of gum which he tears in three pieces, giving a part to each. Same routine of unwrapping and flipping the paper away, etc. Then they stand there, waiting, relaxed, chewing.

Same break as in entrance of first girl . . .
perhaps a little more nasty.

The Blonde enters from the left. She is very much like the Brunette in movement and shrewdness. The sailors stand motionless, their heads following her, their eyes sizing her up. She crosses the stage and just as she gets past

It dies away . . .
quiets down . . .

them there is a general sudden movement of "Let's get into action," swiftly cut and held by a movement of "Hey, wait a minute—remember

slower . . .

what just happened." They look at each other and relax. They watch her go off stage. Then, for each other's benefit, they shrug kind of bored, and start off in the direction opposite to that the girl took. There is a strong tendency to lag, and many looks off toward the girl. They

slower . . .
suspended . . .
Crash . . .
loud . . .
finis.

get slower and slower, until finally they stop completely, watching each other, waiting for the first to make a move—one does, and bang—they are off down the street after the girl, boisterous, excited, swaggering, loud, and happy.

George Balanchine (1904–)
WORK IN PROGRESS

After graduating from the Soviet State School of Ballet in 1921, Balanchine presented some of his choreography to unimpressed audiences in Petrograd. Managing to leave Russia, he worked with Diaghilev from 1925 to 1929, coming to the United States at the invitation of Lincoln Kirstein in 1934. Since then, Balanchine's work has been linked with the group that became the New York City Ballet. In addition to creating its extensive and distinguished repertory, he has restaged many of his works for companies abroad and is probably the most influential ballet maker in the world today.

Balanchine's choreography has been consistently based on music and classical technique. When the music was Bach or Mozart, the movement was clear, balanced, elegant; when it was Ives, Webern, or Stravinsky, the classic steps were not only extended but inverted, turned inside out or upside down, stripped of their usually smooth transitions, executed with unexpected shifts of accent or strangely distorting tempos. But the point was always the music, for unlike Tudor, Balanchine is unconcerned with expressive movement. Ballet is like a rose, he has said; it's beautiful and you admire it, but you don't ask what it means.

[Balanchine has told his interviewer, Louis Botto, that he plans to choreograph fifteen ballets for the Stravinsky Festival to be produced by the New York City Ballet in June, 1972:]

Q: Have you started work on them yet?

BALANCHINE: No. I never start until I'm in the rehearsal hall. You can't plan steps ahead of time, just as you cannot plan words when you are going to write something. It's part of your ability. You have enough vocabulary and grammar in your head when you need them—everything that's required to start writing when the moment comes. That's the same as choreographing a ballet. When that moment comes—on union time—you have all the necessary equipment and ballet grammar in your head to do your work.

Q: Some of the ballets you're doing are new versions of ballets you did in the past. Will the choreography be different?

BALANCHINE: *Le Baiser de la Fée*, which I've done before, will be completely

SOURCE: From *Intellectual Digest* (June, 1972). Copyright © 1972 by Communications Research Machines, Inc. Excerpted and printed by permission.

One of the great successes of the 1973 Stravinsky festival was Balanchine's *Violin Concerto* which showed the master at his neo-classical abstract best. Unencumbered by romantic costumes or dramatic ideas, the choreographer happily set movements to music. Left to right: Nolan T'sani, Tracy Bennett, Kay Mazzo, David Richardson, Michael Steel.

different. And the *Violin Concerto* will have nothing to do with the original version, *Balustrade*. You see, when I first did it in 1941, it had scenery and costumes by Tchelitchev, and I had to make people dance in his costumes. There were pussycats and birds, and the scenery was a big leopard. But now, it will be nothing but pure music. The other ballets I'm redoing—I don't know yet what they will be.

Q: Will most of them be plotless?

BALANCHINE: Yes—most have no plot.

Q: Do you prefer a plotless ballet?

BALANCHINE: No. It depends—if it's a good plot, fine. But a plot is a very difficult thing for the dance. You cannot dance a story. You can only do very light ideas. A very simple situation. A love story, you can do. You know—two people are in love and they dance together. A *pas de deux*. But you couldn't do a complicated story to dance. You see, if you go to see a ballet with a story, and there's nothing about it in the program, you would never understand it.

Q: Yet, your ballet of *A Midsummer Night's Dream*, despite a very complex plot, was clear. Was that because we're familiar with the play?

BALANCHINE: Well—there was nothing there. It was just entrances of two couples—who are very famous—and I made it clear that they were mixed up in Shakespeare's mind. One person runs away from another, one finds somebody else—and all of a sudden they aren't in love anymore. The ballet was a very simple thing—just a little sylph dancing and Bottom turning into a donkey. But if you didn't know the Shakespeare story, you would probably ask why? Even in Shakespeare—people probably don't know why he changed into a donkey.

Q: You and Jerome Robbins are collaborating on the choreography of *Pulcinella* for the festival. Isn't it unusual for two choreographers to work together on the same ballet?

BALANCHINE: Yes, it's unusual, but when we have so much to do—over 30 ballets—we have to help each other. Robbins and I did *Firebird* together. Sometimes when we work together, he says to me, "Would you finish this section if I can't?" And I say, "Okay." When we work on *Pulcinella*, I may say to him, "I'm busy tomorrow—will you finish it?" And he will. We have the same conception, so it doesn't matter. If my knees are okay and his back is okay, we may even dance in it—on stilts.

Q: Will most of these ballets have sets?

BALANCHINE: No.

Q: Who makes the decision on that, the choreographer?

BALANCHINE: No. Money. It depends on how much you have to spend. And the company still says "Couldn't you have done without it?" In ballet, it's really better to do without expensive sets and costumes until you know if the work is a success. If you throw away lots of money on sets and costumes and it bombs, there's nothing you can do with them.

Q: Do critics make or break a ballet as they do a play?

BALANCHINE: I don't read the critics. Even if they don't like a ballet, it doesn't make any difference. We still do it and we have a full house—whether the critics like it or not. It's the public who decides. They see it and say, I like this or I don't. On Broadway, it's different. It's *so* commercial. And the tickets are *so* expensive. The producers don't give a damn about art—only money. If the public doesn't go, they close the show.

Q: You revolutionized musical comedy in the 1930s—especially in *On Your Toes*—by making ballet an integral part of the plot. Do you think you'll ever do another Broadway musical?

BALANCHINE: No. There are young people who should do that. I'm already passé. I don't like the music or the type of theater that is popular today. You have to be young to put up with the commercialism. Let them have the ulcer. I hardly ever go to the theater anymore. I know what they're doing in musicals and it's the same thing that used to be. Nobody can do anything new.

Q: With so many new ballets to create for the festival, is it difficult to come up with something original?

BALANCHINE: I never think I'm going to do something original. You don't think that way. You just do what you want to do. That's our language. Our movements have to be performed in the composer's time. That's what makes ballet so exciting—this movement of bodies in time. That's why I call Stravinsky "an architect of time." His music provides the dancer's floor. It's the reason for us to move. Without the music we don't want to move.

Q: Does the complexity of Stravinsky's music make it difficult to choreograph?

BALANCHINE: No. It just takes longer. Nothing is difficult, really, when you know it. But it takes longer to make so many people move to certain strange divisions of time. When you're working with straight music that's divided into four bars, it's simpler.

Q: Did you prefer him to write music specifically for your ballets?

BALANCHINE: No—but if he had free time, I would ask him to write something. Once he said, "Yes—I have time. What would you like?" I said, "Just start with something—a variation—anything" and he said, "Fine." So he wrote *Danses Concertantes*, which I'm choreographing for the festival. But some of his music he didn't want people to dance to.

Q: Do you do much revising?

BALANCHINE: I revise, but not as much as a playwright in the theater. He has much more time than we have. He only uses paper and pencil. He can throw away as much of that as he wants. But we have to be very fast. You see, we're on union time. I have to invent the dance, the dancers have to learn it, and the next day we do it. You don't even have the chance to go out of town to try it out. Sometimes people ask me how long it takes to create a ballet. It's impossible to say. You have to do it in whatever time—a few days or a month—that you have with the dancers.

Q: Is ballet more of a visual than an intellectual art?

BALANCHINE: Naturally. That's all there is to it. You perceive it through the eyes. A blind person could never know what ballet is, just as a deaf person can't perceive what music is. Unless he's a musician who reads music. But if you can't read music and you're deaf, there's only silence.

Q: Does ballet reflect life?

BALANCHINE: No. It's a fantasy. It has nothing to do with life. We are not real people. We are trained to dance and perform for the idea of beautiful things, but we are not people who are playing some part of life. We're like flowers. A flower doesn't tell you a story. It's in itself a beautiful thing. We have nothing to do with people on the street. I mean offstage, yes. But onstage, we train dancers that it's all artificial. We make the body perform things that the body's not supposed to do.

Q: Then, the ballet is not an emotional art, unless it moves you by the beauty of the dancing?

BALANCHINE: Naturally. A lot of people go to the theater to see their own life, their own experience. We don't give them that in the ballet. We give them something less. When you see flowers, do you have any emotion? You're moved by the color and the beauty—but what does it mean to be moved? Some people think that you have to cry to have emotions. Suppose you don't—then people believe you're cold and have no heart. Some people are hot, some cold. Which is better? I prefer cold. I have never cried at a ballet. I never cry anytime. I don't have that type of reaction. Actually, when people cry they are only thinking of themselves. They think, I'm poor, I'm unhappy, I'm lonely, why did my girl friend leave me? And so, beautiful music that is sad or a stage situation that is ethereal suddenly attaches itself to your personal life and makes you cry.

Q: Then you never put anything from your life into your ballets?

BALANCHINE: Never. Mozart never put his miserable life into his beautiful, gay music. He didn't want to portray his life. He had a beautiful idea of music—of the sound of it.

Q: Is it true that Diaghilev was more interested in scenery than dancing?

BALANCHINE: It was a different approach. Diaghilev said there were no choreographers at that time. Fokine had left—nobody could do anything—so he saved his ballet by commissioning people like Picasso and Ravel to camouflage the fact that there was no choreography. The dancers were bad—the corps de ballet was *terrible*. When I came in, I started to do more dancing, and Diaghilev was happy to see it. He had to save himself. You see, the public in France really didn't *like* dancing. All over Europe, they *don't like* dancing. They like spectacle, scenery, costumes and association with the great Picasso, the great Derain, the great this, the great that. They just want to see one performance, then everybody goes to Maxim's. The dance is forgotten. When I did my first ballet for Diaghilev, *Le Chant Du Rossignol*, which we're reviving in the festival, he told me Matisse was designing the décor and costumes. I shrugged my shoulders. Matisse? I had never heard of him.

Q: Has ballet dancing improved since those days?

BALANCHINE: It's a different type of dancing today. We are trained now to cover more space—faster. Our ears and our eyes are better. We memorize much faster. Ensembles are more complicated. They're like a Swiss watch. If Nijinsky were alive today, he would have to start all over again as a boy to be trained in the new technique. He would learn and he would be considered a great dancer today.

Q: You are doing fifteen ballets for the festival. Will the choreography be written down?

BALANCHINE: No. I never use choreographic notation. We teach it at Lincoln Center, but I never use it.

Q: Suppose another ballet company wants to do one of these ballets?

BALANCHINE: Then, I would have to go there—or someone from my company who knows the choreography—and teach it to them.

Q: Won't these ballets be preserved?

BALANCHINE: They don't have to be preserved. Why should they be? I think ballet is NOW. It's about people who are NOW. Not about what will be. Because as soon as you don't have these bodies to work with, it's already finished. This is not a question of what the story is, or what the costumes are, or preserving the ballet of 1972 for future generations. I'm staging ballets for today's bodies. For people who are here now. And you admire the way he or she looks and how they move. It's this person today—not just *anybody*. So, I'm not interested at all that there will be some dancers who could do something of mine in the future. It wouldn't be right because I would have to do it myself.

Q: Have any of your ballets ever been lost because of this lack of notation?

BALANCHINE: Oh, yes. *Caracole* was one of my lost ballets. I redid it as *Divertimento No. 15*.

Q: Then you're really not concerned that a century from now your ballets will be extinct?

BALANCHINE: Absolutely not concerned. Besides, there will be different people then. The art of dancing will disappear—or maybe it will be done with acrobats. Who knows what they're going to do? But I don't want my ballets preserved as museum pieces for people to go and laugh at what used to be. *Absolutely not.*

Section Seven

RECENT REBELS

The impact of the early modern dance had been violent—people either hated it or dedicated themselves to the cult of the revolution. But, as with all revolutions, the fervor was transitory; the excitement had to wear off as the artists got down to the business of consolidating their gains and exploring the ramifications of what had been accomplished. Unlike the ballet, in which few dancers wanted to do anything other than perform, the modern dance was geared to stimulate creativity; if choreography was a representation of personal experience, an expression of individual feeling, then each was entitled to depict his own.

From the companies of Graham and Humphrey-Weidman came young choreographers, most of them destined to develop the newly established tradition—though some were to break it.

Humphrey guided the first efforts of José Limón and remained his mentor throughout her life. His magnificent body brought special nobility to her movements; his own dances reflected her belief in the fundamental dignity of man. His first works drew on his Mexican heritage, but his themes grew in universality from the intimate tragedy of his four-character version of Othello, *The Moor's Pavane* (1949), to the baroque grandeur of *Missa Brevis* (1958). "I reach," he once wrote, "for demons, saints, martyrs, apostates, fools, and other impassioned visions." His models were the noble measures of Bach, the heroic figures of Michelangelo.

Also dramatic, but of tougher fibre than Limón, was Anna Sokolow, who had come from the Graham company. Rejecting narrative structures, she built dances on types of characters: the lonely and isolated who live in fantasy worlds, in *Rooms* (1955); the beatnik generation, in *Opus 65* (1965). Sokolow kept her stages bare, her costumes drab, so that attention was focused on telling forms of movement that derived from natural expressions of emotion. Differing from the Humphrey-Limón school of thought, she did not provide her works with optimistic endings; it was enough for her that they were provocative.

These were, in a sense, typical of the generation that followed the pioneers; but there were others—equally dissimilar—who worked deftly within the tradition which had no single style, only that consistent method of moving from the inside out.

Modern dance had broken with the established vocabulary of classical ballet, finding it inadequate to the expression of contemporary life, and had discovered other forms of movement better adapted to the portrayal of modern concerns. The change had been incited by dramatic needs, but in the process new languages had evolved, suggesting the possibility of movement provinces beyond those already explored. At mid-century the need for expressive motivation was questioned: wasn't the movement aspect of dance sufficiently interesting to make further dramatic content unnecessary? And wasn't the insistence on expressiveness limiting movement invention unnecessarily?

Leading the revolt was Merce Cunningham, who had danced with Graham. Denying himself the stimulation of plot or character portrayal, he looked for objective ways of combining and ordering movements, trying devices of chance or arbitrary systems. While musician John Cage worked independently, Cunningham arranged his dances without reference to accompanying sound patterns. The choreography was autonomous; free of drama, free of music. Nor was it bound by the conventional concept of structure. Cunningham's dances were open-ended: a number of sections were composed, but the toss of a coin could establish which sections were actually seen and in what order. Or indeterminacy was used: in *Field Dances* (1963) each participant had his own set of movements but in performance he did as few or as many as he wished and at any time that he wished. The result, Cunningham liked to say, was "beyond imagination"; he wanted to stretch the range of choreography further than the deliberate human mind could take it.

In addition to opening the field of movement and its manner of occupying time, Cunningham changed the dance's orientation in space. Asserting that any position in space was important, he upset the traditional soloist-ensemble dichotomy that had persisted from classical ballet through the days of early modern dance. With Cunningham the focus of the audience was no longer directed to the center of the stage; it was not directed at all but could wander to whatever group or individual seemed attractive at the moment. The meaning of the dance was left equally open. True, qualities seemed to emerge, and that was fine as long as the choreographer did not predetermine them. If a dance turned out to be sunny in feeling, it could be called *Summerspace* (1960); if it looked darkly ominous, it became *Winterbranch* (1965). But the choreographer's intention was simply to compose human movements in space and time.

While Cunningham made no attempt either to communicate feeling or to withhold it, Alwin Nikolais deliberately sought to wipe out vestiges of personal emotion. Believing that the dancer was limited by his pedestrian personality, Nikolais induced him to assume another identity by clothing him in fantastic garb or having him attached to a prop—a hoop, a pole, a cape—which seemed to become a part of his body. The equipment not only depersonalized the dancer but led to fresh movement ideas: How many ways can you move while holding a hoop? In dances like *Imago* (1963) and *Somniloquy* (1967), the movement of props, of fabrics, of lights, of colors, of slide projections, of electronic sounds, was an essential part of the choreography. The works were allowed to project their own kind of drama for, without explicit role playing, generic characters seemed to appear—proud, pathetic, coy, witty. Though the intention was to portray what Nikolais called the "primary qualities" of movement —feelings of heavy, light, thick, thin, fast, slow—the audience tended to make personal associations, to which Nikolais had no objection. The important thing was not to limit movement design by insisting that it represent emotions.

While both Cunningham and Nikolais used technically skilled dancers, other choreographers chose to eliminate this restriction as well. In the 1960's Ann Halprin arranged pieces that were structured by tasks: participants were assigned jobs to be done (carrying a load of objects or wading through mounds of wrapping paper), and the dance consisted of whatever movements were needed to accomplish the task. The group known as the Judson Dance Theatre resorted to nondancers in experiments that used ordinary movement, the kind any person in the street could do. But taking the movement out of its usual context gave it another look, focused attention on details or shape that would have gone unnoticed in its customary surroundings. Yvonne Rainer challenged herself to make movement as minimal as possible and discovered that, after a period of sparseness, an elbow wiggle looked positively virtuosic.

By using people who had no particular dance skills, these choreographers set up a new kind of relationship between the performer and his audience: they became peers. By erasing the distance between the skilled and unskilled, they led the audience to identify with the dancers, not as the kind of people they would like to be, but as the kind they really were.

Another limitation to be removed was the frame of the proscenium stage. Again Cunningham was the pioneer, taking his dances into art galleries to find new ways to defocus movements in space. Others tried city squares and parks, some of them devising pieces for such specific environments that they could be done nowhere else. Twyla Tharp did *Medley* (1969) on a college campus, where she used a tremendous expanse of lawn to make her audience see, now a few dancers at a great distance, then half a hundred dancers only a few feet away. Rudy Perez choreographed a ballet for automobiles (with drivers) performed in a parking lot, a modern counterpart of the horse ballets of the seventeenth century. James Cunningham's dancers finished a gymnasium presentation by running up to the bleachers and inviting the audience to join them in social dancing. It was considerably less formal than Beaujoyeulx' conclusion to the *Ballet Comique*, and everyone was wearing sneakers and jeans—but the ideas were similar.

Though many groups continued to be led by a single choreographer, some disdained this kind of dictatorship and chose a more democratic format. In some cases, individuals took turns composing; in others, they worked with improvisation, agreeing on certain rules to be observed by all but letting each player fill in the framework at will. Still others employed strict structures but worked as collaborative units that gave nearly equal authority to a core of creators. Some groups took names indicative of the cooperative nature of their venture—The House, The Collective, The Grand Union.

Then, just when it seemed that plots and skills and even the stage had been banished from contemporary choreography, they started creeping back; often one at a time, to be sure, and often in strange guises. One of the most conspicuous reversals was engineered by Paul Taylor, who had originally tested his audience's endurance by standing still and looking at them for what seemed interminable minutes. He gave in to skilled movement with *Aureole* (1962), which had an exultant wave of dancers filling the stage with swirling and leaping. Then, in *Big Bertha* (1970) he restored explicit content in a psychological study of the deterioration of a middle-class family mesmerized by a fairground automaton.

Meredith Monk's *Needle-brain Lloyd and the Systems Kid* (1970) was an outdoor pageant with multiple levels of imagery. The audience walked considerable distances to observe travelers—a couple in a boat, pioneers, horseback riders, motorcyclists—all involved in the journey of life. Kei Takei's *Diary of the Field* (1973) was a ritual of spring, a myth of creation, and a disclosure of the birth pains of making a dance.

Social consciousness, which had received little thought since the 1930's, became a significant factor, especially, though not exclusively, in the work of black choreographers. Earlier they had concentrated on theatricalizing ethnic forms. In the 1940's two dancers trained in anthropology put their research to practical use: Katherine Dunham translated ritual dances of the West Indies into presentations for both Broadway musicals and the concert stage; Pearl Primus drew on forms she had learned in Africa. A young member of Lester Horton's integrated Los Angeles company, Alvin Ailey, began his independent career along the lines of his mentor, using ritual and ethnic themes but adding to them elements from his own heritage, most notably in the suite based on traditional Negro folk music *Revelations* (1960). More recent choreographers have created ethnic works in more specifically contemporary veins, dealing with the violence and piteousness of life in the black ghettos of America, sometimes symbolically but more often with near literal realism. At the same time Arthur Mitchell, formerly a soloist with the New York City Ballet, formed the Dance Theatre of Harlem to perform works from the classical repertory as well as original choreography based on the balletic idiom.

In spite of the fact that Laban's efficient system of dance notation was not invented until after World War I and was not widely used until long after that, the ballet did have a sense of repertory. Works were passed down from one generation to the next by means of personal coaching, an older dancer teaching his role to a younger one who would teach it again when his turn came. Of course, changes were made along the way, but at least some identity persisted. Such a concept of continuity was alien to the nature of the original modern dance, where choreography was expected to represent a personal comment on contemporary life. As masterworks appeared, however, this attitude began to change; the public wanted to see not only the newest creations, but also the outstanding repertory of the past. While modern dance companies began to produce revivals, ballet companies got the idea of diversifying their repertories with works from modern choreographers. In the 1930's this would have been practically impossible; the techniques were so distinct that a dancer trained in one idiom would have had great difficulty adjusting to the demands of the other. But the modern dance had gradually broadened its base, assimilating more flowing and more virtuosic movement; meanwhile ballet choreographers were incorporating modern elements, especially those involving the use of the upper body, as dramatic situations seemed to warrant them.

In the late 1960's John Butler and Glen Tetley, both originally with Graham, received invitations to stage their works for ballet companies in Europe. Then the Royal Danish Ballet asked Paul Taylor for *Aureole* and the Royal Swedish Ballet took several pieces from José Limón. Soon after, American Ballet Theatre acquired *The Moor's Pavane*. The trend toward assimilation was climaxed (to date) when Robert Joffrey commissioned *Deuce Coupe* (1973) from Twyla Tharp. She made a witty, sophisticated commentary on styles, using the classical technique of the Joffrey company as well as the apparently casual (but highly calculated) jazz idiom of her own group, and producing the hit of the season.

Some observers have predicted an eventual merging of ballet and modern dance styles. Whether this will come about remains to be seen.

But the historical difference remains in the works of the past, and it is not so simple as just ballet versus modern. The Bournonville style distinguishes one kind of ballet; Balanchine another; Tudor still another. Graham choreography demands a particular kind of gut attack, where the Humphrey style requires a lyrical breath impulse and the Cunningham approach has a cool detachment. To reduce all of these (and more) to a mere dichotomy is to misrepresent an art that flourishes in its diversity. Our dance heritage has been enriched by numerous unique contributions. Preserving them while continuing to support innovative creativity is one of the great challenges of the present.

Merce Cunningham (1919–)
TWO QUESTIONS AND
FIVE DANCES

Merce Cunningham studied tap dancing and ballet before encountering modern dance with Lester Horton and joining the company of Martha Graham. He began to choreograph in 1943, forming his own company nine years later. His sustained collaborations with John Cage, along with associations with other avant-garde composers and designers, produced theatre pieces that were, for many years, as widely condemned as they were praised. A series of European tours, beginning in 1958, spread the influence of his ideas.

As evidenced by the following statements, Cunningham's creative methods are precisely designed; the operations of chance and indeterminacy deliberately prepared. Previously each choreographer had determined exactly what and when his observers would see and hear. With Cunningham, the structure of dance has been opened, letting in a whole new range of possibilities.

How do you go about composing a particular dance?

In a direct way. I start with a step. Using the word "step" is a hangover from my adolescent vaudeville days. I "step" with my feet, legs, hands, body, head—that is what prompts me, and out of that other movements grow, and different elements (theatre) may be involved.

SOURCE: From *Dance Perspective, 34 (Summer, 1968).* © 1968 by Merce Cunningham.

This is not beginning with an idea that concerns character or story, a *fait accompli* around which the actions are grouped for reference purposes. I start with the movement, even something moving rather than someone (pillows in the air).* And I ordinarily start with myself; not always, it may be with one or two of the dancers. But then out of this the action begins to assume its own proportions, and other possibilities appear as the dance proceeds. New situations present themselves—between the dancers, the dancers and the space, the space and the time. It is not subject to a prearranged idea as to how it should go any more than a conversation you might have with a friend while out walking. It can take a momentum of its own, that is. That leaves open the possibility of surprise (chance), and that is essential.

Would you comment on the extraordinary intensity that is said to be the most marked characteristic of the dancers in your company?

The appearance of intensity may come from their devotion to what they are doing. It can give the look of being highly involved in the moment, that urgency that doing something precisely in the largest possible way can provoke. They also seem to me to sometimes have a sense of pleasure amongst each other, which isn't intensity, but has to do with individual relationships. My company has grown with the feeling that each dancer is a separate identity; that there is not a chorus along with which there are soloists, but rather that each in the company is a soloist, and in a given dance we may act sometimes separately and sometimes together. I would like to allow each dancer to appear in his way as a dancer, and that implies a good deal of trust between us—all of us.

I train them and then I give them the movements and actions to do in the dances, but I don't expect them to do those actions exactly in the way I do them. What I look for is a way to have the dancer move in the way he would move with the best amplification of that.

This relationship of good will (sometimes it is at stake) includes not only the dancers. It also includes the musicians, Mr. John Cage, Mr. David Tudor and Mr. Gordon Mumma, and the lighting designer, Miss Beverly Emmons, who work with us and act in their separate ways. It is an anarchic process of working, a number of people dealing in their separate ways with a common situation, and out of it can come a whole: an evening of dance; a museum event; a program of music; a lecture-demonstration with movement, sound and light; a seminar; a sudden change of program (given the immediate illness of a dancer) from three works to a dance event lasting two hours, a process where

*Andy Warhol's inflated silver ones—the source of *Rainforest* (ed.).

Photo, James Klosty

Merce Cunningham dances with his company in *Canfield* (1969). A performance of the complete work could occupy an entire evening, but segments of it could be presented independently, and the parts were interchangeable in their order. With all this freedom, however, the individual movements were strictly designed within a limited range, giving the dance its distinctive atmosphere.

the incapacity of one does not impoverish the whole, although his addition would have enriched it. Out of this comes a whole not dependent upon one thing; each person and the work he does is independent, and he acts with the others, not competitively, but complementarily. It is an interdependence that brings about what you speak of as intensity. Each person, observant of the others, is allowed to act freely.

The order of the dances discussed is as tossed for by Merce Cunningham, June 14,1968.

1960: The dance *Crises* (music, Conlon Nancarrow; costumes, Robert Rauschenberg), made in the summer at the Connecticut College School of Dance, was an adventure in partnering. I decided to allow for the dancers (there were five—four girls and one man) contacting each other, but not just through holding or being held, but through being attached by outside means. I used elastic bands around a wrist, an arm, a waist or a leg, and by one dancer inserting a hand under the band on another's wrist. They were attached but also, at the same instant, free.

But where these contacts came in the continuity or where they were broken was left to chance in the composition, and not to personal psychology or physical pressure.

The gamuts of movement were individualized to some degree for the five dancers, and I worked out the particular timing of each of them.

The music (Rhythm Studies #1, #2, #4, #5, #7 and #6 for Player Piano) was added after the dance was choreographed.

Facts like this—attaching people together by outward means, in this case elastic bands—always look as though they mean something. Well, they do. Or rather they are. Here two persons are held together, not only by the invisible bonds that can tie them, but visibly, and without being the instruments of the holding.

1951: It was in a dance called *16 Dances for Soloist and Company of Three* (music, John Cage; costumes and properties, Remy Charlip) that the first use of chance in my work appeared. This dance was a series of solos, duets, trios and quartets with an over-all rhythmic structure relating the small parts to the large in both the dance and the music. The form of the dances was not thematic (it never has been), but the objects in space relating in time; in this situation the relationship being pointed out by the dance joining with the music at structure points.

The entire dance dealt with the nine permanent emotions of the Indian classical theatre tradition. The sequence of the dances was arranged expressively, with a light emotion following a dark emotion (anger followed by mirth, the odious followed by wonder). But I could find no reason why a specific light should follow a specific dark, and threw a coin and let that decide. So the order became: anger, the humorous, sorrow, the heroic, the odious, the wondrous, fear, the erotic and finally tranquility. These were all solos with the exception of the erotic, which was a duet, and tranquility, which was a dance for the four of us. The solos were concerned with specific emotional qualities, but they were in image form and not personal—a yelling warrior for the odious, a man in a chair for the humorous, a bird-masked figure for the wondrous.

There were postludes to a number of the solos. Following fear was a quartet with a small gamut of movements, which was different for each dancer, and this was choreographed by chance means. That is, the individual sequences, and the length of time, and the directions in space of each were discovered by tossing coins. It was the first such experience for me and felt like "chaos has come again" when I worked on it.

1953: *Untitled Solo* (music, Christian Wolff, For Piano I) was the first in a trilogy of solos with music by Wolff, all concerned with the possibility of containment and explosion being instantaneous. A large gamut of movements was devised for this solo, movements for the arms, the legs, the head and the torso, which were separate and essentially tensile in character, and off the normal or tranquil body-balance. These separate movements were arranged in continuity by random means, allowing for the superimposition of one or more, each having its own rhythm and time-length.

The two solos that completed the trilogy (*Lavish Escapade*, 1956, and *Changeling*, 1958) also used chance procedures in the choreography, sometimes in the smallest of fragments and at others in large ways only. But all three succeeded in becoming continuous if I could wear them long enough, like a suit of clothes.

Learning how to wear one was another thing. *Untitled Solo* was first presented at Black Mountain College in the summer. I was trying to learn it on one of those hot, muggy days, rehearsing in the steamy dining-hall atmosphere with David Tudor at the piano, and I had stopped in fatigue and despair. He said: "This is clearly impossible, but we're going right ahead and do it anyway."

1953-59: Excerpt from lecture-demonstration: The dance *Suite for Five* (music, John Cage, Music for Piano 4-84; costumes, Robert Rauschenberg), which my company and I will present this evening, is a continuation of *Solo Suite in Space and Time*, a dance in five parts that I first presented in 1953.

The trio, the duet and the quintet were made in 1956, and the solo for Carolyn Brown was added in 1958.

The action of the seven dances that now comprise the suite is deliberate; that is, the movements are short or long, often surrounded by stillness and allowed to take place without strict regard for musical cues.

The movements may strike or not with the sounds, and although the dancers know the sequences of sound, the sounds do not necessarily happen in the same rhythm or time-lengths from performance to performance. The total length of a given dance, however, is identical each time.

The special plan for the dance, which was the beginning procedure, was found by numbering the imperfections on a piece of paper (one for each of the dances), and by random procedure finding the order of the numbers. The time-lengths were also found by numbering spots on paper; the movement by working it out and tossing coins.

Sometimes a simple movement came with a long stretch of time. So we could have stillness before it and/or after it.

The dances, despite the interval of years between the compositions, were all designed to be presented with the audience on four sides, and are so given when situations allow for this.

1963: *Story* (music, Toshi Ichiyanagi, Sapporo; costumes and décor, Robert Rauschenberg) was first presented in Royce Hall at the University of California, Los Angeles. It is a dance for x-number of people and had seven dancers in it at its first performance. Since that time it has been given nineteen times in the United States, with the number of performers ranging from five to eight. The structure is indeterminate, and the length is made to be varied. It has been as short as fifteen minutes and as long as forty.

We have presented it, among other places, on a huge stage in Augusta, Georgia—actually a double stage that was situated between two auditoriums. In this case both halls were open and visible to each other with all curtains lifted, and one hall being populated, the other empty. We have presented it on the thrust stage of the Tyrone Guthrie Theatre in Minneapolis, Minnesota, with exits through the tunnels under the seats; and on a miniscule stage in Duluth, Minnesota, where—to have more flexibility and space—we employed the floor of the auditorium in front of the stage, and the stairs and doors leading to it.

The dance was choreographed in a series of sections, and these were given names for reasons of identification—"Object," "Triangle," "Floor," "Tag," "Space," "Entrance" and others. "Object," for example, refers to an actual object constructed fresh for each performance, which is moved or carried around the stage by the dancers. "Floor" indicates a duet for two of the girls, Carolyn Brown and Viola Farber, which starts at any point in the space, on or off the stage. The two dancers move in a pronounced, slow tempo across the area, possibly separated, but more often together. There is a "Five-Part Trio," which is as it says, three people who have five phrases each to contend with, the movement in this section being swift. The entire number of possibilities consists of eighteen parts, all or any group of which may be done in a given performance.

The music by Mr. Ichiyanagi is a composition, in the composer's words, for "sustained sound(s), without attack and continuous." Into this atmosphere also may come sharp, vibrant sounds. The composer has left the players free as to choice of instruments.

My original idea for the costumes was that they be picked up or found in the particular playing situation we were in, and that the set, or the way the stage looked, would also be devised from the existing circumstances and environment at the time of the performance.

The variables in the structure, which are changed at each performance, are: the length of the whole, and the length of the separate sections, and the placement of the sections in the continuity. The relationship of the sound is constantly varied, as the only agreement between the dance and the music is the length decided upon for that performance. Although the dancers listen to the sounds and are sometimes engaged by them, this is not a support and certainly cannot be counted upon to happen again.

The title does not refer to any implicit or explicit narrative, but to the fact that each spectator may interpret the events in his own way.

Alwin Nikolais (1912–)
PLAN FOR A TELEVISION PRODUCTION OF "TENT"

First a musician and puppeteer, Nikolais worked with Hanya Holm, beginning to choreograph in 1939 and establishing his own company in 1948. A completely versatile man of the theatre, he experimented with new forms of lighting (he was the first dancer since Loïe Fuller to be so intrigued by it), with slide projections, and electronic scores. His productions featured movements, lights, colors, sounds—all by Nikolais.

Naturally, he has been fascinated by the medium of television, and his scientific mind is applied to it here. **Tent** *was first choreographed for the stage in 1968; these notes, which have been edited by Marcia B. Siegel, were made for a Munich production the following year. Nikolais' exacting specifications amply demonstrate his difference from Cunningham: the master magician pulls all the strings himself, leaving not the minutest detail to chance—or anyone else for that matter. How the seventeenth century would have enjoyed these chrome-key transformations, which allow the choreographer to place his dancers (apparently) on sand or flowers or simply in mid-air, as a technical process blanks out their real, studio environment.*

SOURCE: From *Dance Perspectives* 48 (Winter, 1971).

1. Entrance and Ground Ritual

The dancers enter in single file carrying the tent. They should appear to be coming from a timeless space and into an area suggesting a primitive ceremonial ground. Yet they (the dancers) are contemporary. They unfold the tent on the ground then proceed into a suggestion of a ritual dance. This continues first with a central solo figure then into duets, trios, etc. until one point of silence when all freeze. Silver balls descend. When the balls reach the floor the dancers suddenly break and fasten the tent ends to the balls. They then walk to a large hole in the middle of the tent, whereupon it begins to rise. At this moment the slide designs color the tent and it becomes an amorphous thing which engulfs or swallows the dancers. This tent shape remains but slide changes alter its color design. Then the outer ends of the tent lift—then the whole tent rises revealing the dancers underneath to commence scene II.

TECHNICAL SUGGESTIONS & POSSIBILITIES

A. A chrome-key blue floor and cyc might give the best flexibility here. Photo stills of desert or painted abstract landscape or small model could be inserted into the chrome-blue area. The chrome blue environment could also give possibility of keying out the dancers and allowing effective use of this device in later scenes.

B. Another possibility is to shoot the procession and ritual through a small model. This however poses the problem of control of the environmental look of the floor and cyc of the actual studio area in which the dancers perform. We do have strong slides for the stage but I'm not sure how effective these would be in the necessary illumination video-wise of the dancers themselves.

C. Without model and just the use of our projections we could try to create the environment. This depends upon how effective the slide projections register on camera. Perhaps the use of fog machine might make interesting designs in space as the projections hit fog areas.

D. About the silver balls: these should give the illusion of fantasy. Although 10 are practical in that they actually control the tent, the illusion would be preferably one of design rather than mechanical function. One suggestion is that numerous other silver balls of different sizes be suspended and manipulated in various movements of ascending as well as descending, and these be superimposed upon the actual scene. An illusion that would be very effective would be that of having faces or full figures reflected in these balls. I don't know how this could be done except by previous taping in which perhaps chrome-key device could accomplish the insertion of dancers' figures or faces in the balls and this taping in turn used as superimposition on the actual scene.

The marvels of technology shape and color and envelop the bodies of the dancers in Alwin Nikolais' *Tent*. By the time of this production (1968) the choreographer had made his point about dispensing with emotional motivation to concentrate on the "drama of motion," and he could even relent a bit as he allowed his dancers to react to the variously tender and threatening manifestations of the tent.

In any case, the actual mechanics of tent lifting should not seem to be too obviously related to the balls. As a matter of fact the tent could be suspended directly without the silver balls if this would make matters easier.

E. After the tent is spread the dancers stand on the tent and begin the ritual. There is a dominant central figure. The camera can come to close-up on him and also move to full scene—at the discretion of the director.

F. The fastening of the lines to the tent should not be made too important. The dancers do this nonchalantly. This should lead to somewhat of a visual shock as the tent rises and engulfs them.

INTERLUDE 1. The problem of the interlude is that on stage the dancers require this time to change costumes. Obviously this is not essential on T.V. However, the preferable implication is that something is happening under the tent. I believe this interlude, as well as the others, depends upon the visual interest we can get out of the projections.

II. Genesis (Primitive section under tent)

The tent raises slowly revealing the dancers who should now look nude. They are first menacingly still. They are like primitive creatures. They move in sharp gestures on hands & knees, occasionally spinning. They should look somewhat like an ant heap disturbed. They do wild actions then fling themselves upward toward the tent as if to strike off the overhead barrier. Finally they fall and jump up & dart forward & back as the tent descends—covering them.

It is difficult to describe the content of this scene except to say it should give the impression of the atavistic side of man in which he reflects primal behaviorism and generic or genetic suggestions. For a few brief moments at the end they reflect a curious tenderness only to be disturbed out of it and to fall back into the enclosure of the tent.

TECHNICAL SUGGESTIONS & POSSIBILITIES

A. If the chrome-key environment is used then we can use the same technical process as at first. The inserted scene should then be that of an abstract tall grass land. It could also occasionally suggest a stonehenge. It could interchange between the two. For example it could open with the grass-lands effect. The circle which follows could appear to happen on a high rock pinnacle. For the most part the dancers should look lilliputian —as if they were microbes. Of course occasional close-ups would be effective. Also in the double insect forms—alternate effects of lighted and shadow figures would prove effective. Strong color would also be acceptable. For example the hugging section could start in full pink then gradually change to deep red until the fall when it should go back to pink suddenly, then fade into the slide pattern.

B. As in the B suggestion of the previous scene this one too could be shot through a model.

C. Straight shooting here would in my mind be least effective and in the long run more difficult. I believe it would only be possible if we could fill the environment with strong projected design. Otherwise we will be left with an obvious studio or stage-like environment which would destroy the dimensional suggestion of the piece.

INTERLUDE 2. Although the tent shape is different in this interlude the problem here is still the same. My vision here for T.V. possibility is the superimposition of motion picture on the tent of live crawling things,—such as ants, beetles, snakes, etc.

III. The Cave (Eroticism)

This section is one of innocent eroticism and needs no further explanation. It opens with the tent suspended in such a way that the central hole becomes a cave. The hole is lit up and the arms and legs of a man seen rolling. At the same time 2 female figures roll out of the side periphery of the tent onto the tent itself and are caught only in the projected design. The central male figure comes out and away from the tent. Other figures fill the hole.

This is also the scene in which I would like to use the store dummies or mannikins painted black. They would be seen first as a group opposite the male soloist after he comes out of the cave.

The two separate female figures now join the male soloist—in front of the black mannikins—with the figures in the cave as a secondary vision. This trio should dominate.

This is followed by the group coming forward and dancing in and around the mannikins which are now painted the same flesh tones as the dancers. The male dancers now lift the females like dolls. They should also lift the mannikins. The illusion should be that one cannot distinguish the mannikins from the real. The mannikins are then left in a heap on the floor as all the dancers run into the cave. The tent is lifted and the dancers disappear.

TECHNICAL SUGGESTIONS & POSSIBILITIES

A possibility here would be inserting into the exposed chrome-blue areas photos or actual previously taken tape of real nude bodies in close-up & undulating slowly. It would appear then that the dancers coming forward of the tent would be dancing on the nude bodies.

IV. The Garden

The garden should be one of fantasy and prettiness. The dancers wear silver stripes that glitter in the projected light. Whereas the 1st scene is primitive—the second erotic—this third is one of beauty & prettiness. It is an indulgence in the orgy of color and glitter. It is impressionistic in design rather than specific as in the previous ones. It is man's joy of effulgent nature—and he identifies himself with it and becomes a part of its blossoming. He walks in the garden of light and color—he runs outside of it—falls in it and plays in it. He throws it and lets it engulf him. Finally it—as all other scenes—swallows him.

TECHNICAL SUGGESTIONS & POSSIBILITIES

A. Here again the chrome-key would be effective. Insertion of delicate flowers and occasional large outrageous ones. Also glass flowers—if they could be found. The scene would also be effective fragmented by prisms, glass rods, etc. One part might be effective as if seen in a crystal ball.

B. Without chrome-key this could be shot through miniature flower garden.

C. Straight shooting is also possible here because the scene does rely strongly upon the projections as does the previous scene.

Meredith Monk
"VESSEL": AN OPERA EPIC

Graduating in 1964 from Sarah Lawrence College, where she studied both dance and music, Meredith Monk began to present concerts of her own work in the same year. She calls her productions, not dances, but "composite theatre" or "nonverbal opera," blendings of movement, voice, costumes, lights, film, objects, and environment. Nevertheless, the basic concept is choreographic. The music is usually her own composition, and she directs the entire production, though individual contributions may be made by members of her company, The House.

In this interview with Brooks McNamara, Monk discusses the structure of Vessel. *Like the work of Nikolais, it is a multimedia theatre piece, but like that of Cunningham, it is concerned with manipulations of time and space. Unlike either, it is highly emotional. The drama is conveyed obliquely, by contrast and juxtaposition that gradually define the previously obscure images. This is a journey—but Prince Charming would never have found his way. Like the works of the early modern dance, its intention is not to entertain but to provoke.*

THE DRAMA REVIEW: First, let's talk about the loft on Great Jones Street, which you used for the first part of *Vessel*.

MONK: It's about 100 feet long and 25 feet wide. It has a very low ceiling. . . .

It suggests a tunnel, or a long, narrow space in Renaissance perspective, with the floor boards going toward a vanishing point. . . .

TDR: Why did you decide to use your own house for the first part of *Vessel*?

MONK: Since the nature of my work has a lot to do with unconscious imagery and fantasy, I'm very interested in grounding it in what I call "reality space." Constructing a realistic set doesn't interest me; what

SOURCE: First published in *The Drama Review*, 16, No. 1, T-53 (March 1972). ©1972 by *The Drama Review*. Reprinted by permission. All rights reserved.

I'm interested in much more is using a reality situation and putting unusual images in that setting as counterpoint. The piece here in the loft is grounded in reality, but the images and the figures are strange. Because of that grounding in reality, the effect is surreal. When the performance moves later to the Performing Garage, it's almost totally in another world. Then, when we move to the parking lot for the third section, the performance goes back to reality set against fantasy.

TDR: When I saw the first part of *Vessel*, people were concentrated at one end of the room and there was a space which, at least during the first part of the performance, wasn't used, a space maybe 20 feet deep that created a kind of gulf between the actors and the audience at the other end.

MONK: Yes. Like a moat. The irony of the situation is that this section of the performance, which could be the most personal since it's my own house, was actually the most remote. Instead of becoming the most intimate part of the piece, it's the least intimate because I'm putting a bracket around my living situation by making it so that you are actually looking into a real room, but from a great distance away . . . what I was trying to do here, by lighting different areas at different times, was to see if I could continually transform the space and keep the audience from ever seeing what the whole space was like. When we got to the Garage, the attempt was just the opposite. There, the whole space was exposed, all at once. We saw everything at once. And all shifts of focus were done by the performers and their placement, but in the house, focus was shifted because we lit up a certain area of the room. That was a physiological shift of focus, whereas in the Garage the performers themselves shifted the focus of your eyes.

TDR: Can you give me an example of how you used lights in the first part?

MONK: Yes. There's a section where performers introduce themselves as they change into different costumes. We call that our flash forward section; what I wanted to do, since you go to the Garage later, was to present a glimpse, just a glimpse, of the characters that will appear there as if it were a coming attraction in a film. Then of course the audience goes to the Garage and actually sees them.

Each character—there are five of them sitting in the living room—is dressed in a very grotesque black costume. They're just sitting there; the image that we have, you know, is of people who have been in the loft for centuries, eons—as though they were in a castle waiting. And each person, one by one, leaves the room and goes into the kitchen and changes into a costume that has a much more specific character, a king, or a wizard—but they're very personal, very specific. And they come out and stand under a 200 watt bulb. They pull on the light cord, it's an overhead light, and they perform a scene. It's a small indication of what they're going to do in the Garage, a kind of introduction. Then they turn the light off and go back into the kitchen, change into their black clothes, and sit down again in the living room.

The house section was very much a black and white tapestry—not quite black and white because there was a bit of color, but it had a dull tone, almost the idea of black and white film. Then, when you get to the Garage, it's technicolor. For example, the madwoman who comes out and starts laughing in the loft had a greenish-grayish wig on, but then when she's in the Garage, she's got a bright red wig. The same image, except that it's color. And that's the way all of the images are.

TDR: How did you choose the properties? . . .

MONK: Well, actually I used objects in this piece which interested me a lot, and I used them like notes in a musical score. There's a repetition of certain objects that later serve different functions in different parts of *Vessel*. There's a woman with a rake in the loft; then when you go into the Garage the king's scepter is a rake, and when you go into the parking lot, the soldiers' weapons are rakes. It's like using the rake almost as you would use a note in a piece of music. Or it's like using it as an overlay, a transparency that gradually discloses levels of the object itself. . . . In the first section at the loft, objects are not of primary importance because I'm simply using objects already in my house. But later in the Garage there are many more things, more objects because the space is more abstract. For example, in the Garage, the madwoman, Lanny Harrison, has a kettle she puts herbs into. There is the cutting up of the vegetables; Monica Mosley doing calligraphy on a board; Danny Sverdlik mixing the blue mixture; Mark Monstermaker reading a book. Those are objects and activities. And all of them are almost like everyday activities, but there is a twist to them, a kind of irony. . . .

I always want to have a grounding in reality; I always need to have something that grounds because some images I use are so far away from reality, and I am trying to deal with simultaneous realities. So I try to make as much contrast as possible.

TDR: At the end of the first section, what happens?

MONK: The cast rented a bus and we get into the bus and go down to the Performing Garage, and the audience stays and has wine. Instead of keeping their distance, the audience can enter my house. Then the bus comes back for them and they go down to the Performing Garage. The bus is painted blue and has red and yellow stripes. Inside it has rugs all the way through, seats along the side, a few seats in the back of the bus, and a lot of space to sit on the floor. It's very warm and cosy. I was happy about it.

TDR: What were you trying to do with the bus in terms of the whole performance?

MONK: I called *Vessel* an epic because of the sense of journeying in the whole piece. Not only did I want the content of *Vessel* to be a journey, but the point of having the audience move from one place to another in one evening is that the audience is also on an epic, you know, they are literally going through the motions of traveling. . . .

TDR: How do you use sound in the first part at the loft?

MONK: Well, I am dealing with silence as a base and then working mostly in terms of contrasts—sometimes silence and then cutting to a very sharp sound; sometimes silence and then gradations of sound like somebody lighting a cigarette. In other words, you become more and more aware, but sometimes you become more aware by gradations or increments of sound, and sometimes the sound is just cut into very sharply. *Vessel* is structured like a piece of music; you *hear* how the piece is structured as much as you see it. That's the way I'm working now; not only am I working with music in terms of my own music, but in terms of everything I do in performance. There's lots of repetition of sound motifs like the three knockings, and the bell ringing. And all of the singing that I do with the organ has the same kind of texture even though there are different emotions and very different kinds of sound in it. But it all has the same texture, so it's like a repetition. And because of the stillness in the house all the incidental sounds become magnified. When someone's walking across the room, it's magnified; if you hear a floorboard squeak, you know, it's gigantic, because the basis is silence. If I don't teach people to hear in this piece, then I feel that I've failed, because I believe that hearing—the absolute expansion of auditory perception—is what this piece is about.

TDR: When you get to the Garage . . .

MONK: We connected the scaffolding and made an over-all Gestalt, a mountain of sorts, by hanging and draping white muslin. It's a mountain but it also looks like a clipper ship, a birthday cake. And it's very primitive. The second section of the piece is called Handmade Mountain, and we wanted very much that quality for the whole Garage, that's why we did it ourselves. I much prefer to show what I am doing. No one *designed* that mountain. We did it ourselves. In my group are weavers, and calligraphers, and people who dye fabrics—that is our group's sensibility. . . . I really like a certain kind of theatricality; I don't want to have people in blue jeans.

There's a kind of wryness to the whole Garage piece. It's not childish, it's child-like, and I think that's what we're trying for, not to lose those things. . . . A Sunday School play could use the things we do. But they wouldn't do it the same way, because they wouldn't be conscious

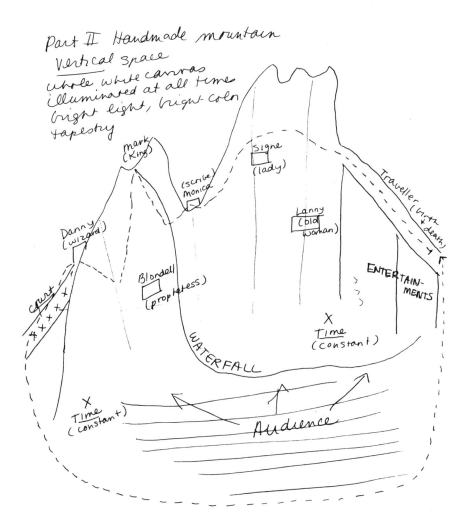

Vessel

Part II Handmade mountain
Vertical space
whole white canvas
illuminated at all time
bright light, bright color
tapestry

mark (King)

Signe (lady)

(scribe) monica

Danny (wizard)

Lanny (old woman)

Blondell (prophetess)

court

Traveller (birth + death)

ENTERTAIN-MENTS

X
Time (constant)

WATERFALL

X
Time (constant)

Audience

Meredith Monk's plan for Part II of *Vessel* shows the cubicles allotted to each performer and the path of the traveler. The room was covered with white muslin. From out of the whiteness, members of the audience let their eyes settle on whatever performing area they wanted to watch at the moment.

of what they were doing, and we're very conscious of what we're doing when we use paper bags or pieces of fabric with a hole cut in the middle for costumes.

The reason I chose the Performing Garage in the first place was that I had had an idea for a long time of doing a living tapestry piece, related to a medieval two-dimensional kind of visual perception. . . . In the first section, you're looking down a corridor at an event beyond a wall, beyond a moat; in the Performing Garage, things happen up and down; and in the third part, in the parking lot, you're looking from right to left. It's like a map, or like a cinemascope screen, or a scene photographed with a wide-angle lens.

TDR: What were you trying to do with light at the Garage?

MONK: Stage lights were available and it seemed that I should use them. But it is the most simple and direct use of them, and it is obvious that that's what it is. There's no attempt to create illusionistic lighting. Strangely, even though all the lights I used in the loft were ordinary household lamps, I would say the effect there was more illusionistic than at the Garage. In the loft, because of the darkness, the audience never sees the reality of the space, so it's as though I'm creating an illusion in a way.

TDR: Why not just use work lights in the Garage?

MONK: I don't like that kind of "scientific" look. I just wanted whiteness. . . . The tapestry keeps changing as the Gestalt of figures on that whiteness keeps changing, so I didn't have to do it with light; I just wanted to leave the light more or less constant.

I think it has to be clear how the figures work against each other. Each of the people has a cubicle. There's one person, Ping Chong, who's the traveler, who takes a path from one side of the scaffolding all the way through the mountain, around to the other side of the scaffolding, and then around the back of the audience. You don't see him for a while, and then he starts coming around again. We call that "rounds." So you get the feeling in the Garage of a kind of cyclical time situation, whereas in the house you get the feeling of time stopping, being absolutely suspended. There are a number of people on the mountain, spread out all over it, and they do different activities at the same time. It's orchestrated in such a way that perhaps two people will be doing the same activity in unison, and the others will be doing other activities; then everybody will be doing a different activity; and then, say, two more people will be doing the same activity. So that when you're in the audience, your eye keeps shifting. You are picking out what you want to see. Then other scenes are added, so that you might have two scenes simultaneously. But since the whole thing is vertical, you're seeing one on top of the other. One becomes figure, and the other becomes ground; then the first becomes ground, and the second becomes figure. It's like a tapestry that's continually changing.

During the first "round," for example, each character has five activities that he can choose from; and in the second "round" three more are added. I don't set it; I don't tell a certain person to wave at a certain point, for instance. So what you get are combinations like a slot machine. You'll have three people doing the same thing at the same time, and all of a sudden your eye starts lining things up. At other times you shift your focus, depending on which person draws your attention. It is similar with sound. Each of the performer's activities involves some kind of sound and your attention is drawn by it. So the madwoman is throwing herbs into a bowl, but she really has marbles in her hand, and you hear them clink.

TDR: Could you describe what happens when you go out of the Garage at the end of the second part?

MONK: You walk half a block away to a parking lot. The way we use the parking lot, it is a wide and not a deep space. It is probably a block wide and a third of a block deep. The audience sits on bleachers at one end. On one side, across the street, is the Canal Lumber Company and on the other side, across another street, is a church, St. Alphonsus, and you can see the tops of both buildings over the brick walls that enclose the parking lot. Straight ahead of the audience is a candy factory, an old building with a faded sign on it and a few straggly trees at its base. The ground is all asphalt, and there are eight trucks lined up facing the audience. . . . I was trying to find an outdoor space that had a specific New York ambience . . . one level of *Vessel* has to do with people opening up their eyes to New York. The park just doesn't have anything to do with the New York ambience, at least on our level. Our economic level, our life style, has most to do with complex interior spaces, and bleak outdoor spaces. This particular parking lot was the best of the large spaces I had seen. I knew I was going to be using many people and I wanted a pageant-like quality to the third part.

TDR: Can you explain how you use light in the third part?

MONK: I was trying to use every kind of light source that I could think of that was portable. So, there are five camp-fires, there's a lamp, there are two sun guns, which are power packed—in other words, these are power belts to which lighting instruments are attached so that people can carry them and run around with them. They are usually used for filming movies at night. There is a welder, and a red traffic flare. There is a kerosene torch, and lights from across the street in the church. And there are the lights from the micro-bus and motorcycles that are driven through the parking lot.

At the beginning of the piece there is cumulative lighting of different areas, so that finally you get all the realities simultaneously. For example, there is a light that represents the house from the first part—the room from the loft is now outdoors in the parking lot. That light is turned on, and goes out, and then five camp-fires are lit. Then the first sun gun is focused on a group of children, and the second sun gun is focused on people in a tree. So the effect is cumulative. That's one use of the lights. Then later there's a scene where everyone is moving at the same time. They're dancing and holding up corn cobs. My direction to the people with the sun guns was just to continue moving and lighting up different areas, because basically the whole canvas is in unison at that point. Each time a new light comes on it's lighting a different area, but the people are still performing the same activity, so it's like seeing another angle of the same thing each time.

TDR: What about the lights from the church across the street? . . .

MONK: It's like expanding the environment until you're aware of more and more and more in that parking lot. When you think you've got to the limits of the parking lot, the two brick walls, your eye moves across the street, expanding even more. I'm working like a filmmaker. I don't know why. That seems to be the way I think; the flash forward section of the first part is an example. I'm doing live movies.

SELECTIVE
BIBLIOGRAPHY

Only books and major monographs are listed here. The reader should be aware, however, that they form only a part of the historian's resources. The serious researcher also works with more ephemeral material—playbills, librettos, reviews in newspapers and periodicals, unpublished letters and diaries, records in theatre and local archives, along with vast amounts of general background information on the social and cultural history of the period he is investigating. Some of the works cited here contain extensive listings of such materials.

Citations are limited to the best books in any given area—when a choice was available. English translations of foreign language books are given wherever they exist. Paperback editions are identified with an asterisk; "R" indicates a reprint. When several reprints are available, preference is given to paperbacks and/or American publishers.

The following abbreviations are used:

Publishers:

DH: Dance Horizons, Brooklyn, N. Y.
UM: University Microfilms, Ltd., High Wycombe, Buckinghamshire (England)
WUP: Wesleyan University Press, Middletown, Conn.

Monograph Series:

DI: *Dance Index*, 1942–1948 (R: New York, Arno Press, 1971)
DP: *Dance Perspectives* (New York, Dance Perspectives Foundation, 1959–)

Introduction: The Evolution of Theatre Dance

For bibliographies: an outdated but still useful list of holdings in the British Museum is contained in Cyril W. Beaumont's *A Bibliography of Dancing* (London, 1929; R: New York, Blom) and a list of holdings in several major libraries to date in Paul Magriel's *A Bibliography of Dancing* (New York, 1936; R: London, Dance Books). The book catalogue of the Dance Collection of The New York Public Library, due for publication this year, will be indispensable. The only reference work in the field, a meagre one volume and not completely accurate, is *The Dance Encyclopedia* by Anatole Chujoy and P. W. Manchester (New York, Simon and Schuster, 1968). Briefer but more dependable is the third edition of

G. B. L. Wilson's *Dictionary of Ballet* (New York, Theatre Arts Books, 1974). More useful are the nine volumes with supplements of the broader *Enciclopedia dello Spettacolo* (Florence and Rome, Casa Editrice le Maschere, 1954–62). Peter Brinson's *Backgrounds to European Ballet* (Leyden, A. W. Sijthoff, 1966*) cites fascinating source materials in European libraries.

Of the historical surveys the best is still Lincoln Kirstein's erudite *Dance: A Short History of Classical Theatrical Dancing* (New York, 1935; R: DH*); his *Movement and Metaphor* (New York, Praeger, 1970) discusses selected ballets in a broad cultural context with lavish illustrations. *The Dancer's Heritage* by Ivor Guest (London, The Dancing Times, 1973*) is an excellent brief history of ballet. *Images of the Dance* by Lillian Moore (New York, The New York Public Library, 1966) covers the period 1581–1861, has a short but informative text, and a wealth of pictures. Also containing lavish displays of pictures and with a dependable commentary that brings the story up to date is *Ballet: An Illustrated History* by Mary Clarke and Clement Crisp (New York, Universe Books, 1973). History as revealed through technical manuals from the fourteenth century through the 19th is the subject of Ferdinando Reyna's provocative *Des Origines du ballet* (Paris, A. Tallone, 1955). Alan Story analyzes choreographic theories from Noverre to Tudor in *Arabesques* (London, Newman, Wolsey, Ltd., 1948).

More specialized works that span our chronological divisions are Cyril Beaumont's volumes devoted to the backgrounds and plots of the classical repertory: *Complete Book of Ballets* (Garden City, N.Y., Garden City Publishing Co., 1941), *Supplement to Complete Book of Ballets* (London, Putnam, 1942), *Ballets of Today* (London, Putnam, 1954), *Ballets Past and Present* (London, Putnam, 1955). *Balanchine's New Complete Stories of the Great Ballets* (Garden City, New York, Doubleday, 1968) gives more attention to choreographic design. Lillian Moore's *Artists of the Dance* (New York, 1938; R: DH*) provides brief but accurate biographies of artists from Camargo to Jooss.

Two books deal, though just adequately, with ideas about music and the dance: Paul Nettl's *The Story of Dance Music* (New York, Philosophical Library, 1947) and Humphrey Searle's *Ballet Music* (London, Cassell, 1958). More illuminating are Minna Lederman's symposium on "Stravinsky in the Theatre" (DI, Oct.–Dec., 1947) and the statements prepared by writers of commissioned scores for "Composer/Choreographer" (DP 16 1963*). Ballet design is well represented by *Art in Modern Ballet* by George Amberg (New York, Pantheon, 1946), *Ballet Design, Past and Present* by Beaumont (London, The Studio, 1946), *Modern Ballet Design* by Richard Buckle (New York, Macmillan, 1955), and *Ballet Design and Illustrations* by Brian Reade (London, Her Majesty's Stationery Office, 1967). All, naturally, are beautifully illustrated. *Dance Index* produced some notable monographs on important artists: "Pavel Tchelitchew" by Donald Windham (Jan., Feb., 1944); "Marc Chagall" (Nov., 1945); "The Stage and Ballet Designs of Eugene Berman" by Allison Delarue (Jan., 1946); and "Picasso and the Ballet" by William S. Lieberman (Nov., Dec., 1946).

Section One: The Court Ballet

Several excellent studies have been made of the court ballet. Henry Prunières, *Le Ballet de cour en France* (Paris, 1914; R: New York, Johnson Reprint Corp.) and

Margaret M. MacGowan, *L'Art du Ballet de cour* (Paris, E.C.N.R.S., 1936) trace the history from Beaujoyeulx to the mid-seventeenth century. The later decades are covered by Marie-Françoise Christout, *Le Balet de cour de Louis XIV* (Paris, A. et J. Picard, 1967) and Charles Silin, *Benserade and His Ballets de Cour* (Baltimore, Johns Hopkins Press, 1940). The *Ballet Comique de la Royne* of Balthasar de Beaujoyeulx (Paris, 1582; R: UM*) is available in the original French, while Paul Lacroix collected six volumes of librettos in *Ballets et mascarades de cour* (Geneva, J. Gayet, 1868–70). The English scene is covered by Enid Welsford in her definitive work *The Court Masque* (London, 1927; R: New York, Russell & Russell*). The splendors of Sweden's royal entertainments are depicted in "Ballet under the Three Crowns" by Mary Skeaping (DP 32, 1968*); Portugal's noble diversions are in "Feasts and Folias" by José Sasportes (DP 42, 1970*)—both unique.

Technical materials for this period include: *A Jewish Dancing Master of the Renaissance: Guglielmo Ebreo* by Otto Kinkeldey (New York, 1929; R: DH*); Fabritio Caroso's *Il Ballarino* (Venice, 1581) and *Nobilità di Dame* (Venice, 1600; both R: UM*); Cesare Negri's *Le Gratie d'Amore* (Milan, 1602; R: New York, Broude); Thoinot Arbeau, *Orchésographie* (Paris, 1589), tr. Mary Stewart Evans (New York, 1948; R: New York, Dover*); F. de Lauze, *Apologie de la danse* (1623), tr. Joan Wildeblood (London, Frederick Muller, 1952).

An interesting theoretical discussion is Guillaume Dumanoir's *Le Marriage de la musique avec la danse* (Paris, 1664; R: New York, Burt Franklin). *Des Ballets anciens et modernes* of Claude Ménestrier (Paris, 1682; R: UM*) provides a systematic and detailed analysis of contemporary choreography.

Section Two: Dance for the Eye and the Heart: The Eighteenth Century

The only publication to cover the period in England is *Famed for Dance: Essays on the Theory and Practice of Theatrical Dance in England, 1660–1740* by Ifan Kyrle Fletcher, Selma Jeanne Cohen, and Roger Lonsdale (New York: The New York Public Library, 1960*). Several of John Weaver's most important works, originally published in London, are available, among them *An Essay Towards an History of Dancing* (1712), and *Anatomical and Mechanical Lectures upon Dancing* (1721; both R: UM*). Jean Georges Noverre's *Lettres sur la danse et les ballets* (Stuttgart, 1760) may be had in the Beaumont translation (London, 1930; R: DH*), and there is Deryck Lynham's fine biography *The Chevalier Noverre* (London, 1950; R: London, Dance Books*), though Arthur Michel has demonstrated that the acknowledged master was only one, and not the first of a line of defenders of dramatic dance: "The Ballet d'Action before Noverre" (DI, March, 1947). The theory of dramatic ballet also gets brilliant support from Louis de Cahusac in *La Danse ancienne et moderne* (Paris, 1754), while an excellent later version of the theory may be found in August Baron's *Lettres à Sophie sur la danse* (Paris, 1825; R: UM*).

Marie Sallé is the only ballerina of the period to have merited an extensive, though not thorough, biography, Émile Dacier's *Une Danseuse de l' Opéra* (Paris, 1909; R: Geneva, Minkoff). There is a better one of the Vestris family, Gaston Capon's *Les Vestris* (Paris, Société du Mercure de France, 1908). Lillian Moore's pioneering study of little known performers "The Duport Mystery" (DP 7, 1960*) reveals a wealth of dance activity in the eighteenth-century United States.

Feuillet's *Chorégraphie* (Paris, 1701; R: UM*) is the key to the dance technique of the eighteenth century. Gregorio Lambranzi's *New and Curious School of Theatrical Dancing* (Nuremburg, 1716) is available in Derra de Moroda's translation (London, 1928; R: DH*), giving instructions for various character and comedy dances. For the minuet, *Le Maître à danser* of P. Rameau (Paris, 1725) is the standard text, tr. Cyril W. Beaumont (London, 1931; R: DH*). Gottfried Taubert's *Der Rechtschaffener Tantzmeister* (Leipzig, 1717), not yet translated, represents the German version, and Kellom Tomlison's *The Art of Dancing* (London, 1735; R: UM*) tells the story from England. Giovanni Gallini published two works that reflect contemporary trends in technique and theory: *A Treatise on the Art of Dancing* (London, 1762) and *Critical Observations on the Art of Dancing* (London, 1770; both R: UM*). Ballet terminology, eighteenth-century style, may be found in Charles Compan's *Dictionnaire de danse* (Paris, 1787; R: UM*). To close the era, there is Ivor Guest's first-rate edition of essays on the history of *La Fille Mal Gardée* (London, The Dancing Times, 1960*).

Section Three: The Invasion of the Air: The Romantic Era

To see why the romantic period has fascinated historians more than any other in dance history, start with Cyril W.Beaumont and Sacheverell Sitwell, *The Romantic Ballet in Lithographs of the Time* (London, Faber and Faber, 1938). Then get the facts, fully and accurately, from Ivor Guest: *The Romantic Ballet in England* (WUP, 1972); and *The Romantic Ballet in Paris* (Ibid., 1966). The prints have also been subjected to scholarly cataloging and discussion by George Chaffee for *Dance Index*: "American Lithographs of the Romantic Ballet" (Feb., 1942), "American Music Prints of the Romantic Ballet" (Dec., 1942), "The Romantic Ballet in London" (Nov., Dec., 1943), "Three or Four Graces" (Sept.–Nov., 1944). Lillian Moore performed a similar service for Currier and Ives in "Prints on Pushcarts" (DP 15, 1962*), while Edwin Binney 3rd has finished off the major collections with "A Century of German Dance Prints, 1790–1890" (DP 47, 1971*) and "Sixty Years of Italian Dance Prints, 1815–1875" (DP 53, 1973*). A tantalizing sampling of contemporary reviews is contained in Cyril W. Beaumont's *The Romantic Ballet as Seen by Théophile Gautier* (London, 1932 R: DH*). The history of Gautier's most famous libretto has been told by Beaumont in *The Ballet Called Giselle* (London, 1948; R: DH*), and all the librettos have been thoroughly examined by Edwin Binney 3rd in *Les Ballets de Théophile Gautier* (Paris, Nizet, 1966).

Naturally the ballerinas have reaped their tributes. Beaumont has translated André Levinson's biography *Taglioni* (London, Beaumont, 1930) and Doris Langley Moore has done Serge Lifar's *Carlotta Grisi* (London, Lehman, 1947). Most comprehensive are two by Guest: *Fanny Cerrito* (London, Phoenix House, 1956) and *Fanny Elssler* (WUP, 1970). Two male dancers have rated excellent biographies: "Jules Perrot," by the Soviet historian Yury Slonimsky is translated by Anatole Chujoy (DI, Dec., 1945) while Charles Didelot has received his due in Mary Grace Swift's *A Loftier Flight* (WUP, 1974). Wesleyan will also publish August Bournonville's monumental autobiography, *Mit Teaterliv* (Copenhagen, 1848), which has been translated by Patricia McAndrew. The Danish master is also the subject of a fine collection of scholarly essays, *Theatre Research Studies II* (Copenhagen, University of Copenhagen, 1972*). *Dance Index* published exemplary research on several American dancers: "John Durang" (Aug., Sept., 1942),

"Mary Ann Lee" (May, 1943), and "George Washington Smith" (Aug., 1945), all by Lillian Moore, as well as "Augusta Maywood" (Jan., Feb., 1943) by Marian Hannah Winter.

Standard and accessible on technique is Carlo Blasis' *Theory and Practice of the Art of Dancing* (London, 1820; R: New York, Dover*), but his *Code of Terpsichore* (London, 1830) contains much additional historical and theoretical material. G. Léopold Adice comments on technique and other matters in *Théorie de la Gymnastique de la danse théâtrale* (Paris, Chaix, 1859). *Bournonville and Ballet Technique* by Erik Bruhn and Lillian Moore (London, 1961; R: London, Dance Books) is a brilliant analysis of the values of the Danish school of training.

The era draws to its sad close: Ivor Guest, *The Ballet of the Second Empire* (London, A. and C. Black, 1953), "The Alhambra Ballet" (DP 4, 1959*), and *The Empire Ballet* (London, Society for Theatre Research, 1962)

Section Four: New Life from Russia

Natalia Roslavleva, *Era of the Russian Ballet* (New York, Dutton, 1966) is a comprehensive survey of the scene from the eighteenth century to the present. Two of the great ballets of Imperial Russia have been studied in scholarly detail: *The Ballet Called Swan Lake* by Cyril Beaumont (London, Beaumont, 1952) and "Marius Petipa and The Sleeping Beauty" by Vera Krasovskaya (DP 49, 1972*). The story of the Diaghilev Ballet has been told by two of the men who were associated with it: Alexandre Benois in *Reminiscences of the Russian Ballet* (London, Putnam, 1947) and Serge Grigoriev in *The Diaghilev Ballet* (London, Constable, 1953; R: London, Dance Books). John Percival's *The World of Diaghilev* (New York, Dutton, 1971*) is a readable survey of the period. Lillian Moore edited the rather bland memoirs of Marius Petipa, *Russian Ballet Master* (London, 1958; R: London, Dance Books), while Yury Slonimsky's comprehensive biography was translated by Anatole Chujoy, "Marius Petipa" (DI, May, June, 1947). Other valuable autobiographies are: Tamara Karsavina, *Theatre Street* (New York, 1931; R: DH*); Michel Fokine, *Fokine: Memoirs of a Ballet Master* (Boston, Little, Brown, 1961); Lydia Sokolova, *Dancing for Diaghilev* (New York, Macmillan, 1960); Massine, *My Life in Ballet* (New York, St. Martin's Press, 1968). Fokine's memoirs should be supplemented by Beaumont's *Michel Fokine and His Ballets* (London, Beaumont, 1935), which contains translations of Fokine's important statements about the rationale of his ballet reforms. *Diaghilev* by Arnold L. Haskell and Walter Nouvel (New York, Simon and Schuster, 1935) is not definitive, but it is the best biography we have. A better portrait of the complex personality comes from Richard Buckle's *Nijinsky* (New York, Simon and Schuster, 1972). Romola Nijinsky's life of her husband *Nijinsky* (New York, Simon and Schuster, 1935) should also be read. Two pleasant books of essays concern the era's most famous ballerina: Paul Magriel's *Pavlova* (New York, Henry Holt, 1947) and Arthur Franks' *Pavlova* (New York, Macmillan, 1956).

The reviews of two contemporary critics are outstanding: André Levinson, *La Danse d'aujourd'hui* (Paris, Editions Duchartre, 1929) and Valerian Svetloff, *Le Ballet contemporain* (Paris, R. Golick and A. Willborg, 1912).

The teaching methods of Enrico Cecchetti have been documented by Cyril Beaumont with Stanislas Idzikowski in *A Manual of the Theory and Practice of Classical Theatrical Dancing* (London, Beaumont, 1947) and with Margaret Craske in *The Theory and Practice of Allegro in Classical Ballet* (London, Beaumont, 1946). Miss Craske collaborated with Derra de Moroda on *The Theory and Practice of Advanced Allegro in Classical Ballet* (London, Beaumont, 1956).

Section Five: The Modern Dance: Moving from the Inside Out

John Martin has written the definitive books on the theory of the contemporary expressive dance: *The Modern Dance* (New York, 1933; R: DH*) and, the most comprehensive statement, *Introduction to the Dance* (New York, 1939; R: DH*). Margaret Lloyd made the only survey of the period, *The Borzoi Book of Modern Dance* (New York, 1949; R: DH*). A number of choreographers spoke for themselves in Frederick R. Rogers' collection of essays *Dance: A Basic Educational Technique* (New York, Macmillan, 1941).

Since the modern dance was so much a product of individual creativities, there are many books about single choreographers. Maud Allan wrote her own story in *My Life and Dancing* (London, Everett, 1908) and so did Loïe Fuller in *Fifteen Years of a Dancer's Life* (London, Herbert Jenkins, 1913), though the latter lady receives more objective treatment in "Loïe Fuller: The Fairy of Light" by Clare de Morinni (DI, March, 1942). Isadora Duncan's *My Life* (New York, 1927; R: New York, Liveright*) is factually untrustworthy but revealing nevertheless. More important are the ideas expressed in her *The Art of the Dance* (New York, 1928; R: New York, Theatre Arts Books). Of the many books about Duncan, the best are Irma Duncan's *Duncan Dancer* (WUP, 1966) and Victor Seroff's *The Real Isadora* (New York, Dial, 1971). Ruth St. Denis told *An Unfinished Life* (New York, 1939; R: DH*), while Christena Schlundt has meticulously chronicled the career of Denishawn in *The Professional Appearances of Ruth St. Denis and Ted Shawn* (New York, The New York Public Library, 1962*). Mrs. Schlundt has also covered *The Professional Appearances of Ted Shawn & His Men Dancers* (Ibid., 1967*), discussed the Denishawn phenomenon in the light of American values in "Into the Mystic with Miss Ruth" (DP 46, 1971*), and provided another valuable documentary in *Tamiris: A Chronicle of Her Dance Career* (New York, The New York Public Library, 1972*). The early career of a great innovator has been documented in essays collected by Merle Armitage, *Martha Graham* (New York, 1937; R: DH*) and in the telling photographs of Barbara Morgan, *Martha Graham* (New York, Duell, Sloan and Pearce, 1941). *The Notebooks of Martha Graham* (New York, Harcourt, Brace, Jovanovitch, 1973) provide remarkable insights into the workings of an extraordinary mind in the process of dance creation. Don McDonagh's *Martha Graham* (New York, Praeger, 1973) adds many facts but little insight. A choreographer's unfinished autobiography and her personal letters are the basis of Selma Jeanne Cohen's *Doris Humphrey: An Artist First* (WUP, 1972). Colleagues of an interesting California choreographer assess his contribution in "The Dance Theater of Lester Horton" (DP 31, 1967*). Rudolf von Laban's autobiography *Ein Leben für dem Tanz* (Dresden, Carl Reissner, 1935) remains the only work on this master inventor, but fortunately we have Walter Sorell's translation of Mary Wigman's illuminating discussions of her own choreography, *The Language of Dance* (WUP, 1966). A. V. Coton's *The New Ballet* (London, Dobson, 1946) is an excellent analysis of the work of Kurt Jooss. And there is Walter Sorell's rather sanguine biography *Hanya Holm* (WUP, 1969).

Lacking the established vocabulary of ballet, the modern damcers have pub-lished little on their craft. Irma Duncan has described her teacher's method in *The Technique of Isadora Duncan* (New York, Kamin, n.d.), while Gertrude Shurr and Rachael Yocum have analyzed their version of the Graham system in *Modern Dance: Techniques and Teaching* (New York, Barnes, 1949). The modern approach to choreography is, however, another matter. Louis Horst summarized the contents of his famous composition classes in *Pre-Classic Dance Forms* (New York, 1950; R: DH*) and, with Carroll Russell, in *Modern Dance Forms* (San Francisco, 1961; R: DH*). Doris Humphrey's systematic approach is lucidly analyzed in her *The Art of Making Dances* (Philadelphia, 1959; R: New York, Grove Press, 1962*).

Section Six: The Extension of the Classical Tradition

Mary Grace Swift's *The Art of the Dance in the USSR* (University of Notre Dame [Indiana] Press, 1968) covers contemporary Russia with detailed documentation; Yuri Slonimsky describes it from another point of view in *The Bolshoi Ballet* (Moscow, Foreign Languages Publishing House [1960]). Natalia Roslavleva has discussed the Russian contribution to ballet dramaturgy in "Stanislavsky and the Ballet" (DP 23, 1965). Albert E. Kahn has contributed his own marvelous photo-graphs as well as a perceptive text to *Days with Ulanova* (New York, Simon and Schuster, 1962). The British situation is reviewed by Fernau Hall in *Modern English Ballet* (London, Melrose, 1950) and by John Percival, who also includes the American picture, in *Modern Ballet* (New York, Dutton, 1970). George Amberg's *Ballet in America* (New York, Duell, Sloan and Pearce, 1949) covers the United States briefly but perceptively. The New York Public Library, however, has collected the thoroughly researched articles of Lillian Moore in "Studies in Ameri-can Dance History" which can be consulted in the Dance Collection.

The English have taken justifiable pride in their companies. Mary Clarke has traced the history of two of them: *The Sadler's Wells Ballet* (later the Royal) (Lon-don, A. and C. Black, 1955) and Ballet Rambert, *Dancers of Mercury* (Ibid., 1962). Each director has told her own story as well: de Valois in *Come Dance with Me* (London, H. Hamilton, 1957) and Rambert in *Quicksilver* (London, Macmillan, 1972). Of the several books on Britain's prima ballerina, James Monahan's *Fonteyn* (London, A. & C. Black, 1957) is the best. The development of contemporary ballet in America is traced from its beginnings in Lincoln Kirstein's "Entries from an Early Diary" (DP 54, 1973*) and followed through to its brilliant fulfillment in Anatole Chujoy's *The New York City Ballet* (New York, Knopf, 1953) and Kirstein's production with the same title (New York, Knopf, 1973). Selma Jeanne Cohen and A. J. Pischl have chronicled twenty years of performances in "The American Ballet Theatre, 1940–1960" (DP 6, 1960*). Bernard Taper's biography *Balanchine* (New York, Harper & Row, 1963) is an excellent account of the choreographer's life though it does little toward defining his artistic contribution. There are also Agnes de Mille's fine autobiographies: *Dance to the Piper* (Boston, Little, Brown, 1952), *And Promenade Home* (Ibid., 1958), and *Speak to Me, Dance with Me* (Ibid. 1972).

Contemporary technique is succinctly outlined in Agrippina Vaganova's *Basic Principles of Classical Ballet*, translated by Anatole Chujoy (New York, 1946; R: Dover*). Muriel Stuart describes the training in the school that prepares the dancers of the New York City Ballet in *The Classical Ballet* (New York, Knopf,

1952). Tamara Karsavina brings her heritage of technical knowledge to bear on *Ballet Technique* (New York, Theatre Arts Books, 1969). The extent of the present vocabulary is seen in Gail Grant's *The Technical Manual and Dictionary of Classical Ballet* (New York, 1950; R: Dover*), which distinguishes divergent usages in the various systems of teaching. The work remaining after the vocabulary has been mastered, the art of interpretation, is sensitively analyzed by one of the greatest contemporary performers: Erik Bruhn: "Beyond Technique" (DP 36, 1968*).

Two fine Englishmen have applied their perceptive minds to the theory of modern ballet: Adrian Stokes in *Tonight the Ballet* (London, Faber and Faber, 1934) and Rayner Heppenstall in *Apology for Dancing* (Ibid., 1936). Edwin Denby, America's most sensitive ballet critic, has published two volumes of essays and reviews: *Looking at Dance* (New York, 1949) and *Dancers, Buildings and People in the Streets* (New York, 1965; both R: Curtis Books*).

Section Seven: Recent Rebels

The contemporary rebels are not yet well represented in book form. The generation of consolidators define their own approaches in Selma Jeanne Cohen's collection *The Modern Dance: Seven Statements of Belief* (WUP, 1966*). The next generation is sympathetically but superficially portrayed in Don McDonagh's *The Rise and Fall and Rise of Modern Dance* (New York, 1970; R: Curtis Books*). Marcia B. Siegel examines the avant-garde in perceptive reviews in *At the Vanishing Point: A Critic Looks at Dance* (New York, Saturday Review Press, 1972*). Merce Cunningham has done his own book in characteristically experimental format: *Changes: Notes on Choreography* (New York, Something Else Press, 1968), while his colleague Carolyn Brown and others discuss his work in "Time to Walk in Space" (DP 34, 1968*). Letters and journals of Alwin Nikolais form the basis of Marcia B. Siegel's "Nik: A Documentary" (DP 48, 1971*).

One facet of black performers is well surveyed in Marshall and Jean Stearns' *Jazz Dance* (New York, Macmillan, 1968) and the full range of their activities is included in Lynne Emery's especially well-researched *Black Dance in the United States from 1619 to 1970* (Palo Alto, National Press Books, 1972).

For a solution to the problems of the preservation of choreography, see Ann Hutchinson, *Labanotation*, 2nd edition, (New York, Theatre Arts Books, 1970*). Some of the best dance on film is perceptively analyzed by Arlene Croce in *The Fred Astaire & Ginger Rogers Book* (New York, Outerbridge and Lazard, 1972), while experiments involving the film-maker as co-choreographer are provocatively considered in "Cine-Dance" (DP 30, 1967*).